Royal Air Force
BOMBER COMI
LOSSES
of the Second World

Volume 6
Aircraft and Crew Losses
1945

Royal Air Force
BOMBER COMMAND
LOSSES
of the Second World War

Volume 6
Aircraft and Crew Losses
1945

W R CHORLEY

Contents

Acknowledgements

It gives me considerable pleasure to thank those who have assisted me throughout the time it has taken to bring this series of books to fruition. Without your help, the entire project would have been immeasurably more difficult to accomplish. Such generous guidance has come from all manner of sources both official and private. It is impossible for me to name every contributor, but it would be negligence on my part if I did not acknowledge the steadfast support from the Ministry of Defence (Air Historical Branch); the staff entrusted with the research facilities at the Public Record Office, Kew and at Salisbury Library. The Commonwealth War Graves Commission, too, has from time to time aided me by answering questions that I was unable to resolve, despite frequent consultations of their invaluable cemetery and memorial registers.

But it has been the measure of assistance from so many private sources that has encouraged me to complete the daunting task of recording so much data in respect of aircraft losses (and I look forward to your continuing support as I prepare to research the casualties sustained by the Operational Training Units and Heavy Conversion Units). From the Commonwealth, Europe and every corner of the United Kingdom, correspondents have furnished me with details pertaining to bomber losses. Some letters have dealt with a single incident but more often that not I have been provided with information concerning entire units and it is patently obvious that many have shared with me the results of many years of careful research into one particular aspect of the air war. Therefore, I must apologise that a good deal of what has been submitted has, for one reason or the other, had to be shelved or truncated in order for it to blend in with the general layout of the summaries.

Thus, I now freely thank my good friends Jacques De Vos and Hans de Haan who from the outset have devoted many hours of labour in sending me valued comment. No less important has been the input from Bill Baguley and Bob Collis, while Betty Clements and her many friends have been generous in channelling details of the Polish Air Force squadrons in my direction.

Doug Cuthbertson and Harry Holmes have pai due care and attention to my many question regarding the Lancaster.

I also acknowledge everyone who has kindl provided me with details in respect of in dividual squadrons, especially those wh have sent me squadron news letters. To th fore has been Frank Haslam, Bryce Gomersall Larry Motiuk (whose account of 426 Squadro is eagerly awaited), Raymond Glynne-Owen Robert Owen, Steve Smith, Roy Walker, Joc Whitehouse, Douglas Wood and Keith Wood.

The late Keith Ford is remembered for hi decades of work in producing histories base on 51 Squadron and airfields associated wit this premier RAF squadron. Jill Rutter, too has been instrumental in helping me wit this unit as well as supplying me wit answers to general aviation questions.

I am extremely grateful to Oliver Clutton Brock and Kevin Mahoney for help in matter concerning prisoners of war and the Unite States Army Air Force respectively.

Aspects of Luftwaffe involvement have bee provided by Michael Balss, Claudio-Michae Becker, Uwe Benkel, Friedrich Braun, Thoma Hampel, Edwin Hess, Hans Hörsch, Rainer Klu Harmut Küper, Peter Menges, Herman-Jose Stolz, Olaf Timmermann and Horst Weber whil from France has come much useful informatio supplied by Roger Anthoine, Michel Francoi Ayerbe, Pierre Babin, John Paul Basset, Ren Chambareau, Andre Coilliot (via Jacques D Vos), Marcel Feisthauer, Claude Helias, Joe Huard, Yves Morieult and Laurent Viton.

Wim Govaerts, Achille Rely, Chris Van He of Belgium; F M W Auwerda, Gerrie Franken P Pouwels, Joop Siepermann, H A C van Aste of Holland; Soren Flensted of Denmark; Jua Carlos Salgado, Victor Turon from Spain an Michael Schoeman of South Africa have eac made their worthy mark.

Likewise, submissions from Stephen King Peter Walker, Deuwe Drijver, Graham Sharpe Ken Carter, Brian Walker, Jim Habberfield Don Bruce, Ray Sturtivant, David Thompson James Halley, Freddie Clark, Ron Low, Fran Harper, Stuart Tait, Michael LeBlanc, The Boiten and Gerrie Zwanenburg are noted.

Finally, to my family and to my publisher I say a special "thank you" for your suppor throughout these last seven years of labour

Bill Chorley, July 1998

Introduction

On the 6th of August 1945, a B-29 Superfortress flew high above the Japanese city of Hiroshima and released a single bomb. A short while later a searing flash followed by an awesome detonation wiped the heart of Hiroshima from the face of the earth. Three days later the exercise was repeated, this time over the port of Nagasaki. The atomic age had arrived and with it the effective end of the war in the Far East.

On the 2nd of September the Instruments of Surrender were signed by the defeated Japanese aboard the USS Missouri, moored in Tokyo Bay, thereby officially ending a world war that had lasted for six years, almost to the day.

Germany, of course, had unconditionally surrendered on 7 May, brought to her knees by the combined might of the air, sea and land forces of the Western Allies and their Soviet counterparts, which since D-Day had inexorably pushed the enemy back on two fronts until both armies met on the Elbe.

The dramatic ending to the war in the Far East, however, had been curtailed with Japan still controlling vast swathes of the Pacific and Indo-China and there is little doubt that the decision by President Harry Truman to use this weapon of mass destruction saved thousands of American lives, as the Japanese would have defended every island and acre of ground as they fell back across the Pacific towards their homeland. Thus, all the hopes that had eluded Sir Arthur Harris throughout his hard pressed bombing campaign in Europe had, on the far side of the globe, been brought to fruition in just two totally devastating raids delivered in early August 1945. Appropriately, when the end came, Harris was still in charge at High Wycombe and it is likely he felt partially vindicated that his continued championing of what might be achieved by aerial bombardment had, eventually, been realised.

But the general perception of any influence exerted by Bomber Command in bringing about victory in Europe has been largely eroded by memories of the invasion of France in June 1944 and the triumphal breakout from the beachheads in the late summer of that year. However, as has been shown in Volume 5, the Main Force squadrons played a significant part in helping to create near perfect circumstances for the invading armies to exploit the Normandy landings and for several months afterwards had continued to support the ground forces in a most effective manner. The cost, both in aircrew lives and

aircraft was high, as the statistics reported in the previous volume clearly show.

Not so well known is that Bomber Command continued to bear quite terrible casualties well into 1945 and in the last three effective months of bombing, which reduced most of what remained of Germany's major towns and cities to heaps of fire blackened rubble, in excess of 800 bombers were either lost directly to enemy action or were written off in operational circumstances. And this was at a time when the Luftwaffe was regarded as a spent force! Tragically, it was also a period when aircrews brought down over Germany appear to have been at their most vulnerable and there are many well documented instances of atrocities being carried out against captured airmen, not in the heat of battle but in cold, calculated acts mainly perpetrated by fanatical elements of the military.

Thus, the final months of the bombing campaign were played out against a backdrop of continuing successes on the ground with the Allies crossing the Rhine in late March and then advancing through central Germany until they were obliged to halt, by order of their political masters, on the Elbe and there to await the arrival of the Russian armies.

This will be expanded upon in the general text for the time has arrived to explain how the losses are to be summarised. In the last volume, these were shown under their respective raid or support headings, with training accidents and ground incidents being shown last. This slight change in procedure was felt necessary in view of the multiplicity of operations, especially in the summer of 1944 when the Main Force was frequently split into relatively small forces in order to attack obscure targets such as pilotless bomb sites, storage depots and the like. In this book, however, I am reverting to the style of the first four volumes where all losses were reported in chronological order of date with the lowest numbered squadron or unit appearing first in any sequence of casualties. This key data will be followed by the aircraft type and Mark, serial, squadron or unit code combination and, where known, the aircraft's individual letter followed by the target identity or an appropriate term describing a non-operational loss. Beneath this entry appears the names of the crew, details of their fate and a brief description explaining the circumstances that led to their loss.

Where possible I have included the time of

take off and purpose of the operation. In the majority of cases where deaths followed, I have included cemetery or memorial details that pertain to the crew as a whole, or to individuals as appropriate. During the last months of the war, the loss cards that survive occasionally omit certain facts that are helpful in determining the fates of each crew. For example, the term "safe" is frequently entered against the names of survivors and subsequent investigation of these cases leads me believe that "safe" can, in the majority of instances, be interpreted to mean prisoner of war while at other times it indicates that the person concerned returned to his unit within a few days of being reported missing. Very few cards exist for aircraft that were brought down behind the Allied lines, either through direct enemy action or otherwise. Unfortunately, squadron records are not always forthcoming in naming survivors from such aircraft and where I have not been able to accord their fate, a footnote has been appended to the summary. This lack of information is particularly noticeable in the Canadian squadron ORBs where operational flying, entered in the Form 541, is limited to the name of the captain followed by the blanket expression "and crew". Order of Battle notices, showing full crew particulars, have been attached in most of the ORBs but, unfortunately, these lists have not always proven to be accurate. In defence of the Canadians, from an historical prospective, it is acknowledged that their records are amongst the best in Bomber Command, especially in respect of day to day events and in reporting the number of points accumulated and hours flown by each member of crew during his tour of operations.

As has been my practice throughout the series, all times are quoted using the 24-hour clock system, though I am not able to say with absolute certainty if these reflect Greenwich Mean Time or local time. It is worth bearing in mind that units frequently used block times in their records, thus it is not uncommon to see two or more aircraft entered as sharing the same departure time. Furthermore, a rounding up or down to the nearest five minutes was also a common practice and this is readily apparent when cross referring data on the accident record cards against any information that may have found its way into unit documentation.

In compiling the summaries, I have referred to a myriad of sources, principal of which has been the loss cards, squadron Operational Record Books (ORBs), accident record cards and the cemetery registers published by Commonwealth War Graves Commission (CWGC). The importance of these registers cannot be overemphasised for without them it would have been nigh impossible to verify the spelling of names or establish initials and, in some cases, awards held by deceased personnel. The Allied air forces prisoner of war file (AIR20/2336) and the numerous reports filed under WO208 for escapers and

evaders have been equally useful, though data in both sets of records (held at Kew) for 1945 is extremely limited. I am also pleased to acknowledge the contributions made by fellow researchers and by survivors from the gruelling campaign that exercised the minds of all who served in Bomber Command throughout the turbulent war years.

By this time, the crew matrix should be familiar to readers and, therefore, it is suffice to say that all Lancaster and Halifax crews are shown in the order of pilot, flight engineer, navigator, air bomber, wireless operator and two air gunners. Where eight names appear, a note of explanation has been added to the majority of summaries and in those few cases where no details are given, then it will be safe to assume the aircraft was operating with two pilots, the second named being taken along for operational experience prior to being placed in charge of his own crew.

It is interesting to note that in the spring of 1945, 6(RCAF) Group headquarters issued an instruction that pilots would be required to fly 30 operational sorties, while the other members of crew would be limited to twenty-eight; thus, it can be taken that two trips in the guise of second pilot were deemed to be the norm, as far as the Canadian authorities were concerned.

The crew order in respect of 100 Group aircraft is less easy to determine, especially where 214 Squadron and 227 Squadron crews are concerned. Certainly, the Liberators of 227 Squadron were often flown without the services of an air bomber, while both squadrons employed additional wireless operators and air gunners and, as will be seen in the summaries, a complement of ten seems to have been the standard crew requirement. Mosquito crews may be regarded as pilot and navigator, though the latter was often skilled in radar and wireless procedures.

Similar to previous volumes, I have tried to amplify known crash locations with as much information as possible. For example, summaries for aircraft lost over France, Belgium and Holland include details of the Department or Province, while county titles are added to most United Kingdom crash reports, though where county towns or major cities are mentioned, the need to publish such data is considered unnecessary. Likewise, the names of European countries are omitted, unless it is thought confusion will arise.

Losses attributed to night-fighters in the final stages of the war are not so well detailed. Nonetheless, some information has been forthcoming, especially in respect of "Unternehmen Gisela" mounted by the Luftwaffe on 3-4 March.

The identity of enemy aircraft remains standard, that is to say the contemporary wartime Me is used in preference to Bf when reporting Messerschmitt types. Where such abbreviations occur, readers are advised to refer to the Glossary of Terms.

I am aware that not every aspect of the losses sustained have been reported, either through oversight on my part or due to total ignorance of the circumstances that prevailed at the time of the loss. This being said, I am confident that the bulk of Bomber Command's terrible losses at squadron level have now been recorded, while casualties incurred by the training establishments that supported bomber operations, will be revealed in the companion books that I am preparing in respect of the Operational Training Units (OTUs) and Heavy Conversion Units (HCUs). Their considerable sacrifice, too, will not go unnoticed.

Sources & Bibliography

Air Historical Branch:
Accident Record Cards
Aircraft Movement Cards
Bomber Command Loss Cards

Commonwealth War Graves Commission:
Cemetery & Memorial Registers

Public Record Office Kew:
Allied Air Forces Prisoner of War File
Bomber Command Intelligence Narrative of Operations Reports
Escape & Evasion Reports
Squadron Operational Record Books

Air-Britain (Historians) Ltd:
Royal Air Force Aircraft L1000 to N9999, James J Halley
Royal Air Force Aircraft P1000 to P9999, James J Halley
Royal Air Force Aircraft R1000 to R9999, James J Halley
Royal Air Force Aircraft T1000 to T9999, James J Halley
Royal Air Force Aircraft V1000 to W9999, James J Halley
Royal Air Force Aircraft X1000 to Z9999, James J Halley
Royal Air Force Aircraft BA100 to BZ999, James J Halley
Royal Air Force Aircraft DA100 to DZ999, James J Halley
Royal Air Force Aircraft HA100 to HZ999, James J Halley
Royal Air Force Aircraft JA100 to JA999, James J Halley
Royal Air Force Aircraft KA100 to KZ999, James J Halley
Royal Air Force Aircraft LA100 to LZ999, James J Halley
Royal Air Force Aircraft MA100 to MZ999, James J Halley
Royal Air Force Aircraft NA100 to NZ999, James J Halley
Royal Air Force Aircraft PA100 to RZ999, James J Halley
Royal Air Force Aircraft SA100 to VZ999, James J Halley
Royal Air Force Flying Training and Support Units, Ray Sturtivant, John Hamlin and
  James J Halley
The Battle File, Sidney Shail
The Halifax File, R N Roberts
The Lancaster File, James J Halley
The Squadrons of the Royal Air Force & Commonwealth 1918-1988, James J Halley
The Stirling File (Revised Edition), Bryce B Gomersall

Air Force Memorials of Lincolnshire, Mike Ingham, Midland Publishing, 1995
At First Sight, A Factual & Anecdotal Account of 627 Squadron, Alan B Webb, 1992
Based at Burn, Airmen Recall their Experiences, Hugh Cawdron, 578 Association, 1995
Beware, Of The Dog At War, An Operational Diary of 49 Squadron Spanning Forty-nine
  Years 1916-1965, John Ward, Jote Publications, 1997
Bomber Offensive, Sir Arthur Harris, Greenhill Books, 1990
Bomber Squadron of the RAF and their Aircraft, Philip Moyes, Macdonald, 1964
Confound and Destroy, 100 Group and The Bomber Support Campaign,
  Martin Streetly, Macdonald & Jane's, 1978
Confounding The Reich, The Operational History of 100 Group (Bomber Support) RAF,
  Martin W Bowman and Tom Cushing, PSL, 1996
De Havilland Mosquito Crash Log, David J Smith, Midland Counties Publications, 1980
Deutsche Nachtjagd, Personalverluste in Ausbildung und Einsatz - fliegendes Personal,
  Michael Balss, Balss, 1997
Dresden 1945 The Devil's Tinderbox, Alexander McKee, Souvenir Press, 1982
Flights of the Forgotten, Special Duties Operations in World War Two,
  A Merrick, Arms & Armour, 1989
Flying Through Fire - The Fogbuster of World War Two, Geoffrey Williams,
  Alan Sutton Publishing, 1995

Forever Strong, Story of 75 Squadron RNZAF 1916-1990, Norman Franks, Random Century, 1991
For Valour, The Air VCs, Chaz Bowyer, William Kimber, 1978
From Hull, Hell and Halifax An Illustrated History of No.4 Group 1937-1948,
   Chris Blanchett, Midland Counties Publications, 1992
Halifax At War, Brian J Rapier, Ian Allan, 1987
Halifax Crew, The Story of a Wartime Bomber Crew, Arthur C Smith, YAMP, 1987
In Brave Company, 158 Squadron Operations, W R Chorley, Chorley 1990
It's Suicide But It's Fun, The Story of 102 (Ceylon) Squadron 1917 to 1956,
   Chris Goss, Crecy Books, 1995
Ksiega Lotnikow Polskich, Poleglych Zmarlych Izaginionych 1939-1946,
   Olgierd Cumft & Hubert Kazimierz Kujawa, Wydawnictwo Ministerstwa Obrony Narodowej, 1989
Lancaster at War 2, Mike Garbutt & Brian Goulding, Ian Allan, 1979
Lancaster at War 3, Mike Garbutt & Brian Goulding, Ian Allan, 1984
Lincolnshire Air War 1939-1945, S Finn, Aero Litho Company, 1973
Making For Sweden, Part 1 - The RAF 1939 to 1945, Rolph Wegmann and Bo Widfeldt,
   Air Research Publications, 1997
Mosquito, C Martin Sharp & Michael J F Bowyer, Faber, 1967
No Flight from the Cage, Calton Younger, Sentinel Publishing, 1995
Norfolk Military Airfields, An Operational Record 1913 to 1997, Peter M Walker, Walker, 1997
On Wings of War, A History of 166 Squadron, Jim W Wright, 166 Squadron Association, 1996
Pathfinder Force, A History of 8 Group, Gordon Musgrove, Macdonald & Jane's, 1976
Pilgrimages of Grace, A History of Croft Aerodrome, A A B Todd, Alan Todd Associates, 1993
Reap The Whirlwind, The Untold Story of 6 Group, Canada's Bomber Force of World War II,
   Spencer Dunmore & William Carter, Crecy Books, 1992
Roll of Honour 115 Squadron Royal Air Force 1939-1945, D Bruce, W R Chorley, J G J de Hann,
   115 Squadron Archive, Bruce, 1996
Royal Air Force Fighter Command Losses of the Second World War, Volume 1, Norman L R Franks,
   Midland Publishing Limited, 1997
Silksheen, The History of East Kirkby Airfield, Geoff D Copeman,
   Midland Counties Publications, 1989
Some of the Many, 77 Squadron 1939-1945, Roy Walker, Hollies Publications, 1995
Straight & True, A History of Royal Air Force Leeming, Peter Coupland, Leo Cooper, 1997
The Bomber Command War Diaries, Martin Middlebrook & Chris Everitt, Midland Publishing, 1996
The Children's Encyclopedia, Edited by Arthur Mees, The Educational Book Company, 1940
The Distinguished Flying Medal, I T Tavender, Hayward, 1990
The Eighth Passenger, Miles Tripp, Corgi Books, 1971
The Lancaster at War, Mike Garbett & Brian Goulding, Ian Allan, 1971
The Right of the Line, John Terraine, Hodder & Stoughton, 1985
The Struggle for Europe, Chester Wilmot, Collins, 1952
They Led The Way, The Story of Pathfinder Squadron 156, Michael P Wadsworth, Highgate, 1992
They Shall Not Grow Old, A Book of Remembrance, Allison & Hayward, CATP Museum, 1992
To See The Dawn Breaking, 76 Squadron Operations, W R Chorley, Chorley, 1981
Two Brothers at War, Harry Ball, Janus, 1992
White Rose Base, Brian J Rapier, Aero Litho Company, 1972
Winston Churchill, Elizabeth Longford, Sidgwick & Jackson, 1974
44(Rhodesia) Squadron RAF, A N White, White, 1972
83 Squadron 1917-1969, Ronald G Low & Frank Harper, Low, 1992
467 and 463 Squadrons RAAF Roll of Honour, Frank Slack & Raymond Glynne-Owen,
   467/463 Lancaster Squadrons Association (UK), 1995

Glossary of Terms

AA	Anti-aircraft (fire)	F/L	Flight Lieutenant
ABC	Airborne Cigar	Flt	Flight
AC1	Aircraftman First Class	F/O	Flight Officer/Flying Officer
AC2	Aircraftman Second Class	FS	Fighter Squadron
Adc	Adjudant Chef (FFAF)	F/S	Flight Sergeant
Adj	Adjudant (FFAF)	Fus	Fusilier
AFC	Air Force Cross	Fw	Feldwebel/Focke Wulfe
AM	Air Ministry		
AMICE	Associate Member of the	GBE	Grand Cross of the British Empire
	Institution of Civil Engineers	G/C	Group Captain
AP	Aiming Point	Gdsm	Guardsman
ASI	Air Speed Indicator	Gefr	Gefreiter (Luftwaffe)
Asp	Aspirant (FFAF)	G-H	Blind bombing device
ASR	Air Sea Rescue	GM	George Medal
ATC	Air Training Corps	Gnr	Gunner
Aus	Australia	Grnd	Ground
BALBO	A large formation (after the	HMS	His Majesty's Ship
	name of the Italian General	Hptm	Hauptmann (Luftwaffe)
	who led large formations of	HQ	Headquarters
	flying boats on long-distance	H/T	High Tension
	flights between the wars)		
BBC	British Broadcasting Corporation	Inj	Injured
Bdr	Bombardier	Int	Interned
BS	Bomber Support		
BSc	Bachelor of Science	JG	Jaggeschwader
Bty	Battery	JP	Justice of the Peace
		Ju	Junkers
Capt	Captain		
CBE	Commander of the Order of the	Km	Kilometre
	British Empire		
CGM	Conspicuous Gallantry Medal	LAC	Leading Aircraftman
Cmdr	Commander	LCpl	Lance Corporal
CMG	Companion of (the Order of)	LNSF	Light Night Striking Force
	St. Michael and St. George	Lt	Leutnant/Lieutenant
Cne	Capitaine (FFAF)	Lt-Col	Lieutenant Colonel
CO	Commanding Officer	Ltn	Lieutenant (FFAF)
Co.	County	LSgt	Lance Sergeant
Cpl	Corporal		
CSU	Constant Speed Unit	MA	Master of Arts
CU	Conversion Unit	Maj	Major
CWGC	Commonwealth War Graves Commission	MC	Military Cross
		MCU	Mosquito Conversion Unit
DBR	Damaged Beyond Repair	MD	Doctor of Medicine
DFC	Distinguished Flying Cross	Me	Messerschmitt
DFM	Distinguished Flying Medal	MID	Mentioned in Despatches
Div	Division	Mk	Mark
Dr.	Doctor	MM	Military Medal
DSM	Distinguished Service Medal	MT	Motor Transport
DSO	Distinguished Service Order	MU	Maintenance Unit
Evd	Evaded	NCO	Non-commissioned Officer
		NF	Night Fighter
FD	Field	NJG	Nachtjagdgeschwader
FFAF	Free French Air Force	Non-op	Non-operational
Fhr	Fähnrich (Luftwaffe)	NTU	Night Training Unit
FIDO	Fog Investigation Dispersal		
	Organisation	Oblt	Oberleutnant (Luftwaffe)

OC	Officer Commanding	SAA	South African Artillery
Ofw	Oberfeldwebel (Luftwaffe)	SAAF	South African Air Force
Ogefr	Obergefreiter (Luftwaffe)	SBA	Standard Beam Approach
Op:	Operation	Scot	Scottish
ORB	Operational Record Book	SD	Special Duty
OTU	Operational Training Unit	Sgc	Sergeant Chef (FFAF)
		Sgt	Sergeant
PAF	Polish Air Force	SIS	Special Intelligence Service
PAL	Polish Army of Liberation	S/L	Squadron Leader
PFF	Pathfinder Force	Slt	Sous Leutenant (FFAF)
Pnr	Pioneer	SOE	Special Operations Executive
P/O	Pilot Officer	Sqn	Squadron
Pte	Private	SS	Schutz-Staffel
		S/S	Staff Sergeant
QC	Queen's Counsel	SSQ	Station Sick Quarters
QMS	Quartermaster Sergeant		
		TI	Target Indicator
RA	Royal Artillery	T/o	Take off
RAAF	Royal Australian Air Force	T/S	Technical Sergeant
RAF	Royal Air Force		
RAF(VR)	Royal Air Force	Uffz	Unteroffizier (Luftwaffe)
	(Volunteer Reserve)	UK	United Kingdom
RAN	Royal Australian Navy	US	United States
RCAF	Royal Canadian Air Force	USAAF	United States Army Air Force
RCM	Radio Countermeasures		
Regt	Regiment	VC	Victoria Cross
Revd	Reverend	VHF	Very High Frequency
RF	Royal Fusiliers		
Rfn	Rifleman	WAAF	Women's Auxiliary Air Force
RK	Ritterkreuz	W/C	Wing Commander
RN	Royal Navy	W/O	Warrant Officer
RNAF	Royal Norwegian Air Force	WO1	Warrant Officer First Class
RNZAF	Royal New Zealand Air Force	WO2	Warrant Officer Second Class
ROC	Royal Observer Corps	W/T	Wireless Telegraphy
RSigs	Royal Signals		
R/T	Radio Telephony	2Lt	Second Lieutenant
SA	South African	+	Fatal Casualty

Chapter 1

Victory in Europe

1 January to 8 May 1945

At the dawn of what was to be the year of victory, the Allied armies on the Western Front were still heavily engaged in reversing the successes gained by the surprise German offensive in the Ardennes. Throughout the second half of a bleak December, Allied ground forces had been put to their sternest test since D-Day and it was not until the end of the month that the crisis was finally averted.

Inclement flying weather had severely hampered reaction from the air but it will be recalled that Bomber Command had struck at centres of communications, while on Boxing Day a combined force of Halifaxes and Lancasters, aided by a dozen Mosquitoes, had carried out a good attack against enemy armour and troop concentrations established in snow covered fields near St-Vith. This support was carried over into 1945 and on New Year's Day, a small force of Mosquitoes, supplied by 8 Group, bombed rail tunnels in the Eifel region between the River Rhine and eastern Belgium. In total, fourteen tunnels were attacked for the loss of a 692 Squadron crew whose aircraft was hit by flak as it flew over high ground southeast of Schuld towards Adenau. Blazing furiously the bomber plunged into the ground, neither airman standing any chance whatsoever of getting clear from such low altitude.

Meanwhile, 5 Group had been tasked to bomb the Dortmund-Ems Kanal near Ladbergen and though the raid proved to be a success overall, for 9 Squadron it was a bitter sweet occasion with four Lancasters destroyed and with one of their wireless operators, Flight Sergeant George Thompson, winning the penultimate Bomber Command air VC of the war.

From the outset 9 Squadron were dogged with ill-fortune. Two Lancasters crashed within minutes of each other, one coming down almost as soon as it became airborne and the second as it sped along Bardney's main runway. Amazingly, one airman, Pilot Officer R C Flynn RCAF, survived from the first crash, while, happily, all walked away from the second with no more than cuts and bruises to show for their terrifying ordeal.

Flight Sergeant Thompson was already airborne as these dramas were unfolding, his New Zealand skipper, Flying Officer R F H Denton, heading towards a convergence point over northern France before continuing in loose formation towards their objective.

Everything proceeded to plan and in due course Denton, now flying at 10,000 feet, entered the target area. Visibility was generally good and in the absence of any serious amounts of cloud the attack was seen to be going well, though the ground defences were putting up a stiff and accurate barrage of flak.

Within seconds of bombing, Denton's Lancaster received a direct hit from an 88mm shell which tore through the soft skinned undersurfaces and wreaked havoc in the central fuselage. Fluid from ruptured hydraulic lines spurted forth in all directions creating a violent fireball that engulfed both gun turrets. Almost simultaneous with the first explosion came a second, this being slightly ahead and on the starboard side. Shards of red hot shrapnel ripped into the nose compartment and removed most of the Perspex from the cockpit. Another swathe of splinters cut into the starboard inner motor which was soon streaming smoke and flame. Automatically, a stunned Flying Officer Denton activated the extinguisher button and to his relief the flames soon died away.

Meanwhile, George Thompson had gone to the aid of the two gunners who were trapped in their burning turrets. With total disregard for his own safety, Thompson managed to extricate the unconscious mid-upper gunner, Sergeant E J Potts, and carried him forward to a relatively safe position where he continued to beat with his bare hands at Potts' still smouldering clothing. Satisfied he had done all that was possible for this airman, Flight Sergeant Thompson went back through the inferno and by banging hard on the clamshell doors attracted the attention of the rear gunner, Sergeant J T Price. Price had already suffered serious burns to his head but despite being in a state of shock he summoned up his strength and in considerable pain followed the gallant wireless operator through the choking smoke to where the still unconscious mid-upper gunner lay.

George Thompson was now in a pitiful state, having sustained dreadful burns to the exposed parts of his body, but with an iron will he reported to his pilot and explained the situation concerning his two companions.

Denton, relatively unscathed, was struggling manfully with the controls, edging all the while towards the Rhine but unable to prevent the Lancaster from losing valuable height, or to steer clear of a fresh concentration of ground fire, which found its mark amongst the workings of the inner starboard engine. Dredging up the last reserves of his flying skill, the young New Zealander at last crossed the battle lines and minutes later force landed in a field near the hamlet of Grolder in Holland.

Their arrival had not gone unnoticed and soon the local inhabitants were doing everything in their power to assist those badly injured. Flying Officer Goebel, whose hands were severely frostbitten, soon found himself back in England but his six companions were rushed to Eindhoven and admitted to a Catholic hospital. Throughout the journey Sergeant Potts was quite delirious from the terrible burns that he had received but, mercifully, he lapsed into a coma and remained unconscious until his death the next day.

Flight Sergeant Thompson was transferred to Brussels where for the next three weeks he clung tenaciously to life, but, cruelly, pneumonia set in and he died on 23 January, two days after Group Captain C C McMullen, the Station Commander at Bardney, had submitted his recommendation that Thompson be awarded the Victoria Cross. This was duly approved and details of the supreme gallantry shown by this unassuming son of a Scottish ploughman from Trinity Gask in Perthshire were published in the London Gazette on 16 February.

Flying Officer Denton's fine qualities of airmanship did not pass unrecognised and, subsequently, he received an immediate DFC.

Returning to the events of New Year's Day, three separate raids were launched during the evening against targets in the Ruhr and on another inland waterway, namely the Mittelland Kanal near Gravenhorst. Two of the raids produced reasonable results, but an attempt to destroy a benzol plant at Dortmund was a total failure. Target marking was late and scattered, and even the defences seemed disorganised. Flying Officer R J Hampshire of 158 Squadron reported seeing fires several miles apart on bearings west and south of the aiming point. Officially, no aircraft were lost from this attack but in reality two Halifaxes were destroyed in serious crashes over Yorkshire. Likewise, only one Lancaster was reported missing from the strike on railway yards at Vohwinkel but two Lancasters crashed in Belgium after running into American anti-aircraft fire near Namur while a third aircraft managed to limp away and crash-land in France at Juvincourt airfield. At least twenty-nine aircrew died that night, including the Commanding Officer of 75 Squadron, Wing Commander R J Newton DFC RNZAF, whose Lancaster crashed near the Dutch town of Maastricht.

The weather at the beginning of January was miserable; penetratingly cold with snow and brisk winds that cut to the marrow those responsible for servicing the bombers on the bleak airfields that now stretched throughout the length of eastern Britain. Despite these awful conditions, Bomber Command kept up its pressure on targets in central and southern Germany, while the night of 4-5 January was mainly devoted to an assault on one of the last remaining enemy garrisons in France. Sited at the mouth of the Gironde lies the town of Royan where the Wehrmacht continued to deny the Allies access to the port facilities of Bordeaux. With the bulk of American forces long since departed from the region, the task of securing Royan had been handed to the French Resistance but, it seems, little progress was made and, thus, came about the involvement of High Wycombe.

Three bomber groups were alerted and at around midnight Lancasters from stations controlled by 1, 5 and 8 Groups commenced taking off for what, I suspect, was generally regarded as a welcome diversion from the recent run of operations.

In the event, the visit to this previously untroubled town resulted in heavy damage and very serious loss of life, not to the enemy, but to the inhabitants that had remained.

Bomber Command lost seven Lancasters, two in a mid-air collision as the force headed homewards, while earlier a 57 Squadron crew had taken to their parachutes after icing caused a total loss of power from both starboard engines. Not surprisingly, recriminations followed, though as Martin Middlebrook makes clear in his admirable assessments of Bomber Command's War Diaries, no blame was attached to High Wycombe.

Twenty-four hours later, Hannover was approached from the north-west and subjected to its heaviest air raid since October 1943. Substantial damage was caused, but a significant night-fighter presence cost the Command dearly. The flak, too, was vicious and accurate and it is likely Flying Officer S H McFadden's 415 Squadron Halifax, inbound at the time, fell victim to batteries sited north of Twistringen. Four managed to get out, though Flying Officer N Conner RCAF, the navigator, tumbled through the arc of one of the propellers, losing his left leg in the process. Showing remarkable clarity of mind, Conner pulled the ripcord and then proceeded to wrap what remained of the torn trouser cloth across his wounds. He was still conscious when he fell into a forest clearing and despite the excruciating pain he forced himself to apply a tourniquet in order to staunch the flow of blood. Throughout the rest of the night and well into the next day he lay in his perilous state until a farmer came his way and took him to a local hospital. Here, a German surgeon cleaned up his terrible injuries and within three months Flying Officer Conner was repatriated, visiting his Squadron in late April before returning to Canada.

Raids on Hanau, Neuss and München followed and it is believed quite appreciable damage was caused at all three targets. Weather conditions then deteriorated and major operations were confined to daylight attacks on railway yards at Krefeld and Saarbrücken, though sandwiched between these events was a strike by thirty-two Lancasters and a single Mosquito on the U-boat pens at Bergen in Norway. Considerable destruction was caused when at least three Tallboys sliced through the protective concrete covers and blasted away valuable support facilities. Two submarines were slightly damaged and at least one surface vessel was sent to the bottom of the harbour.

As the bombers withdrew, day-fighters in the shape of Fw 190s were sighted and it was not long before the air was thick with tracer. One burst caught the rear turret of Flight Lieutenant R J Harris's Lancaster, wrecking the mechanism but leaving Flight Lieutenant W T G Gabriel unscathed. For the next seventeen minutes Gabriel calmly kept up a running commentary, clearly interpreting the fighters intentions and enabling his skipper to thwart no less than fifteen attacks. Flight Lieutenant L E Marsh RCAF was also in considerable difficulties. A cannon shell had badly damaged one engine and when at last he threw off his pursuers the altimeter was reading a mere 900 feet and the air speed indicator was showing 360 miles per hour! Subsequently, Marsh and his fellow 9 Squadron compatriot, Gabriel, were awarded immediate DFCs.

Three Lancasters were shot down, one from 9 Squadron, bringing their losses in the first half of an eventful January to five, and two from 617 Squadron.

Night raiding by Main Force units resumed on 13-14 January, when nearly 300 aircraft carried out a second attack on Saarbrücken. Again, much damage was inflicted on the rail yards, while at Pölitz, near Stettin on the Baltic coast, 5 Group reduced much of the local oil producing plant to a shambles of smouldering ruins. More success was gained the following night when oil production from the Merseburg-Leuna facility was severely disrupted and the momentum was maintained on 16-17 January when on what was to be the busiest night of the month, Main Force squadrons concentrated their efforts on three synthetic oil centres as well as carrying out an area attack on Magdeburg. Including support from 100 Group, 1,238 sorties were despatched, from which over thirty bombers failed to return, Magdeburg accounting for around half of this number.

Of the three oil targets visited, Zeitz, near Leipzig, cost the Command ten Lancaster bombers, principally from the 1 Group units.

The return of inclement weather reduced operations throughout the second half of January, and a split raid on Stuttgart late in the month proved to be an extremely lack lustre affair which in no way justified the loss of a dozen aircraft.

Spirits, nonetheless, were high as news from the eastern front continued to report the successes gained by the Soviet armies in their mid-January offensive. Such news led the 415 Squadron diarist to report that bets were being placed at East Moor that Hitler would ask for an armistice on or by 3 February! This extremely over optimistic view quickly evaporated and the same diarist was to note a very close call involving Warrant Officer J S McKenzie RCAF, whose Halifax was

one of the 323 aircraft sent to Wanne Eickel on 2-3 February. His gunners had already beaten off two night-fighter attacks prior to reaching the aiming point and then, thirteen minutes after bombing, flak punched a hole through the port mainplane opening up a six to eight inch diameter hole behind the inner engine.

Shrapnel from the same burst carried away a large portion of the Perspex from the mid-upper turret and badly wounded the occupant, Flying Officer W C Broad RCAF. Skilfully, McKenzie retained control and over the next quarter of an hour evaded a further three approaches from enemy fighters. It is not known if Warrant Officer McKenzie had placed a wager on the outcome of the war but had he done so no doubt a rueful reflection crossed his mind as he headed towards Woodbridge and an emergency landing.

In truth, the Wehrmacht was continuing to offer stiff resistance, especially in the area of the Reichswald. It will be recalled that as long ago as early October 1944, Bomber Command had heavily bombed the towns of Kleve and Emerich in order to frustrate enemy intentions towards the exposed Allied right flank near Nijmegen. Now, with XXX British Corps gearing up for a major assault through the Reichswald, Main Force crews were briefed on 7 February for two swingeing night raids on Goch and Kleve. A shade over 460 bombers were earmarked for the attack on Goch, while an already badly blitzed Kleve was allocated 295 Lancasters supported by ten Mosquitoes. Weather conditions, especially in the region of Goch, were far from promising and a number of crews report hearing the Master Bomber mulling over how best to get the attack under way. Eventually, he broadcast "Basement 5", thus ordering crews to bomb from below the cloud base, now estimated to be around 5,000 feet.

At first the bombing was extremely effective but with less than half of the force completing their attack the entire area became enveloped in dense smoke and the raid was promptly aborted. It was at this stage in the proceedings that life for the bomber crews became extremely hazardous. Withdrawing towards the battle lines the raiders came under intensive light flak and then having reached Belgium they ran into anti-aircraft fire from Allied batteries established to protect the port facilities of Antwerpen from the menace of flying-bombs.

Several Halifaxes, and a Lancaster returning from the Kleve operation, were brought down over a narrow corridor between southern Holland and northern Belgium. Night-fighters are believed to have claimed two Halifaxes, while at least four bombers went down after colliding in the air and it is from a survivor from one of these aircraft that gives a clear account of what happened. "We were turning on a course for home when there was a violent explosion. I turned to help the skipper, Jack Beeson (Flying Officer J L Beeson RAAF), who was struggling to maintain control. The nose section forward of the cockpit was completely missing. Jack ordered us to bale out and I asked if I could help him, but he waved me off. I picked up my parachute and made my way to the rear hatch, where I could see Pat (Flight Sergeant P A Murphy) preparing to jump. I clipped on my 'chute and followed him out. As I descended there was another explosion, which I assumed to be the aircraft crashing."

Three airmen survived; the flight engineer and author of this brief account, Sergeant Alex McQuilkin, Flight Sergeant Murphy and his fellow air gunner, Flight Sergeant L A E Papworth. The rest perished as their 158 Squadron Halifax plunged into a forest twixt Lüllingen and Geldern. From the other Halifax, a 77 Squadron machine, no one was able to get out before it crashed some five kilometres southwest of Winnekendonk.

While the aircrews rested, XXX Corps began their advance but at Kleve this soon ground to a halt amidst flooded roads and rubble strewn streets. Much bitter fighting was to follow before this area of Germany would be secured.

The following night, Pölitz was re-visited and such was the scale of damage inflicted by this second attack that no further supplies of synthetic oil were forthcoming from this plant for the remainder of the war. Not so successful was the raid on Wanne-Eickel which for the fourth time since mid-January had escaped any major inconvenience. Meanwhile, plans were afoot for a series of operations aimed at cities in eastern Germany. For three weeks past, the Soviet armies had been making spectacular progress, driving hard through central Poland and by early February their infantry, with armour and artillery support, were engaging the Wehrmacht in fierce fighting along Germany's eastern borders. Four targets were under active review; Berlin, Chemnitz, Dresden and Leipzig, the former already being subjected to near nightly attack from the Mosquitoes of the Light Night Striking Force (LNSF).

The directives for Operation Thunderclap reached High Wycombe from the Air Ministry in late January. Because of the consequences that were to follow and the general castigation of Bomber Command, and in particular the vilification of Sir Arthur Harris, it is important to stress that Operation Thunderclap (which had originally been conceived as long ago as August 1944) had the full support of the War Cabinet and in particular that of Winston Churchill. Churchill, along with the President of the United States, an ailing Franklin D Roosevelt and Joseph Stalin, Russia's all powerful dictator, were due to meet at Yalta at the beginning of February 1945. Understandably, amongst the wide range of complex issues discussed was the present conduct of the war and in light of his backing for Thunderclap, Winston had no hesitation in agreeing to Stalin's request for active air operations behind the German lines, particularly on communications

and railway choke points. Thus, the four cities mentioned dovetailed neatly into the requirements of the Soviet leader, though the emphasis on Berlin was not so marked as had been the case in August 1944 when both the RAF and American bomber forces were being considered for a massive daylight raid on the German capital.

Roosevelt, too, agreed that American participation in these attacks would be forthcoming and within days of the conference ending the scene was set for what was to be one of the most devastating bomber raids of the Second World War.

Dresden was the target chosen and but for the weather the Americans would have led the way with a daylight strike on the 13th. As it was, it fell to Bomber Command to carry out the first raid, this being mounted in two stages during the night of 13-14 February with 5 Group leading and employing their own low-level marking techniques.

This proved to be a moderately effective attack, though there were no spectacular fires 'and only one Lancaster failed to return. Three hours later, Pathfinders flew in the van of the second phase and their marking was so accurate and the bombing that followed was so concentrated, Dresden literally reeled beneath a carpet of bombs.

Long before the arrival of the final waves flames had engulfed most of the city and such was the intensity of the inferno that a firestorm developed, the like of which had not been witnessed since the raids on Hamburg in July 1943.

At the time the city was thronged with refugees fleeing ahead of the advancing Soviet armies and in the general confusion abounding it is unlikely that a true casuality figure will ever be established, but contemporary historians believe somewhere in the order of 50,000 perished, mainly civilians. In the eyes of the planners, Dresden had been an unqualified success, especially as the weather improved to allow the USAAF to bomb the railway yards to good effect on the 14th, with a second raid aimed at continuing the dislocation of communications twenty-four hours later.

However, within days of these punishing attacks the Americans became alarmed at how their public at home might perceive these operations and various policy statements were given out at press briefings held at Supreme Headquarters of the Allied Expeditionary Forces, emphasising the continuing pursuance of the USAAF towards bombing military objectives. Scapegoats were being actively sought and to his discredit, though this was not to come about until late March, Churchill, too, took steps to distance himself from any responsibility for what had happened. Inextricably, the seeds of disinformation were effectively sown into the minds of many and for close now on fifty years the critics of Bomber Command have used Dresden as the stick to berate the actions of Harris and to sully the achievements of thousands of aircrew who did so much to ensure that victory over a despotic regime would be accomplished, whatever the cost.

While the Lancasters had been busy over Dresden, over 300 Halifaxes with PFF support bombed an oil plant at Böhlen, south of Leipzig, but complete cloud cover led to a surfeit of scattered bombing and little, if any damage was caused. Likewise, Chemnitz escaped relatively unbruised when over 700 aircraft struck on 14-15 February.

The second half of February was extremely active with raids on oil producing centres being maintained, while devastating area attacks were delivered on industrial targets at Dortmund, Duisburg, Worms, Essen, Pforzheim and Mainz. In the same period, several close support operations were flown against Wesel, a smallish town not far distant from forward positions of the Allied armies inching towards the Rhine. On four successive days between the 16th and 19th medium sized raids were directed against this strategically placed centre. On the 16th, under clear skies, the bombing was well concentrated and by the end of the attack the railway yards and nearby town were covered by thick plumes of smoke. The next visit was inconclusive, due to the Master Bomber halting proceedings after just eight from the 247 Halifaxes despatched had bombed. But on the 18th and 19th Lancasters from 3 Group, employing G-H techniques, caused very heavy damage to the station and surrounding areas.

The night bombing of Dortmund, Duisburg and Worms also resulted in much destruction with the response from the enemy defences being particularly viscous. Fourteen Lancasters failed to return from Dortmund, visited on 20-21 February, while six Halifaxes and a 156 Squadron Lancaster were lost from the raid on Düsseldorf where the Rhenania Ossag oil refinery was the principal objective. Amongst the missing Halifaxes was a veteran from 158 Squadron named Git Up Dem Stairs, whose nose section was adorned with Donald Duck characters, each carrying a flag emblazoned with the target name. When lost, a total of ninety-three symbols had been applied along with various decorations and crew scrolls.

Twenty-four hours later, equally heavy blows were aimed at Duisburg and Worms, with 5 Group using its low level marking to good effect on the Mittelland Kanal near Gravenhorst. Interference from night-fighters was felt at all three locations and this account from Flying Officer D R McLean, an air bomber with 578 Squadron, vividly illustrates how quickly a seemingly normal situation could be turned into one of acute danger within moments of such an attack commencing. "I had just gone into the nose, after leaving my Gee position alongside the navigator, to set up for bombing when the mid-upper gunner, Doc Watson (Flight Sergeant Watson), called out that he had seen a Ju 88 on our starboard side flying straight and level,

obviously in the process of checking our air speed or acting as a decoy. The skipper (F/O R J Ingham) immediately ordered "open fire" and a few seconds later came the shout, "a hit, he's going down". Our elation was promptly dampened when the flight engineer announced over the intercom, "port engines on fire", to be followed shortly after by the dreaded words from the skipper, "jump, jump", for we were about to go out of control. Whilst the navigator was in the act of pulling up the escape hatch behind me and I was kneeling on my 'chute next to the bomb sight looking out for fighters, the aircraft was struck by a hail of tracer bullets from head on and at an angle of about sixty degrees, which seemed to be coming straight for my eyes.

The next thing I knew, I was tipping head over heels on top of the bomb sight, with a brief glimpse of seeing the nose splitting open a few inches behind me. As I gathered my senses, I found myself in the detached and inverted nose cone of the aircraft, my head just above the edge with a 360 degrees view all round and looking up at a lovely starlit sky."

Flying Officer McLean thinks he fell at least a couple of thousand feet, still in the shattered nose section before fully realising the seriousness of his situation. In his dazed state he only managed to fit one clip of the parachute harness before being ejected into space and minutes later, minus his flying boots, he crashed awkwardly through the branches of a pine tree. His left arm was dislocated from its socket and he sustained numerous cuts and abrasions before finally arriving on the ground.

He remained at liberty for the remainder of the night but was picked up the next day by a forestry worker and taken by tractor to a nearby army unit. No one else from his crew survived and all had died in the second 578 Squadron Halifax reported missing, that captained by Flight Lieutenant P Brown.

Altogether, Bomber Command lost, or reported as written off, forty-five aircraft that night, nineteen of this number being concerned with the Worms operation. Of the rest, most were shared out between Duisburg and the Mittelland Kanal raids, but a clandestine operation to Germany flown by 161 Squadron resulted in the loss of a Hudson piloted by Flight Lieutenant D T Oliver, while the continuing raids on Berlin by the LNSF claimed a 571 Squadron Mosquito damaged beyond repair following an emergency landing at Brussels-Melsbroek.

Forty-eight hours later, the relatively untouched town of Pforzheim, situated east-southeast from the more familiar centre of Karlsruhe, came under sustained attack from the air. For the second time in February, a combination of accurate PFF marking followed by well concentrated bombing from the Main Force, saturated a city centre. In a little over twenty minutes, approximately 370 heavy bombers passed over the aiming point, delivering a shade over 1,800 tons of high explosives and incendiaries. Huge fires sprang up and within seconds these had merged into a raging inferno that burnt out over eighty per cent of the built up area. Over 17,000 of the population died in the conflagration, a figure that brought Pforzheim into an unenviable third place in the league tables of deaths caused in a single night by aerial bombardment on towns in Germany. Only Dresden and Hamburg could lay claim to even worse suffering.

Ten Lancasters were brought down near the target and two others were abandoned over France. These included a 582 Squadron aircraft flown by a South African, Captain E Swales who, since August 1943, had been seconded to the Royal Air Force for operational duties. His involvement with PFF had begun the previous July and when assigned to the Pforzheim operation his expertise was such that he was given the responsibilities of Master Bomber, a role that he had been familiar with since the turn of the year.

On reaching the target area, his Lancaster was fired upon by a night-fighter but instead of taking evasive action, Swales held his course and succeeded in releasing the target indicators over the aiming point. By this time the starboard inner engine had been wrecked, along with the rear turret and fuel was streaming from wing tanks damaged in the first few seconds of the attack. Undeterred, Captain Swales began to orbit the town, broadcasting instructions to the leading wave of bombers, now fast bearing down on Pforzheim. Perhaps not surprisingly, a second engagement commenced, this time the stream of cannon fire lacing in from the port side and hosing along the entire length of the fuselage and into one of the engines, which had to be shut down.

Displaying a stubbornly gritty streak, the South African continued to control the raid until he was satisfied his presence was no longer required before giving attention to the matter of getting his badly crippled Lancaster back to base. Their situation was bleak; most of the instrument panel had been shot away and with full power available from only two engines, Swales was finding it extremely difficult to maintain any semblance of control. Consequently, it was decided to try to make for Manston in Kent, but with each passing mile the bomber became less and less manageable and all the while height was being lost at an alarming rate.

Eventually, the battle lines were crossed, by which time the bomber had descended into the tops of thick cumulus cloud. In his heart, Captain Swales now knew that their chances of reaching the Channel, let alone crossing the broad strip of sea, were minimal. Then, as his aircraft continued to buck and wallow in the turbulence an ominous crack sounded through the fuselage, the Lancaster yawing violently. A control rod connecting the rudder pedals to the rudders had snapped and the end was fast approaching. In

the next few terrifying seconds, seven crew members responded to their skipper's urgent calls to bale out, but for Captain E Swales SAAF there was no chance whatsoever for him to leave and his body was found the next morning, still strapped to his seat, hands firmly locked to the controls.

Thirty-two air VCs were won during World War II, including two awarded to members of the Fleet Air Arm. From this gallant band, nineteen had flown in Bomber Command and two had belonged to the Advanced Air Striking Force, whose exploits were reported in the first volume of bomber losses. Captain Swales was the thirty-first recipient and details of his heroism were Gazetted on 24 April 1945, the citation ending with the words, "giving his life that his comrades might live." This epitaph, sadly, could be applied to numerous Bomber Command pilots who, but for the myriad of official reasons, never qualified for their country's most prestigious gallantry award.

In addition to the losses sustained from the Pforzheim raid, 97 Squadron reported one of their Lancasters missing from an accurate attack on the submarine pens at Horten in Oslo Fjord and 100 Group signalled the disappearance of a Radio Countermeasures (RCM) Halifax fielded by 192 Squadron. Both aircraft had fallen victims to night-fighters, the former crashing near Asjardstrand while the latter went down near Stuttgart. There were no survivors from either aircraft. Despite the extremely hazardous tasks undertaken by the squadrons of 100 Group, their casualties were slightly less than those reported from the Main Force units. However, twenty-four hours after the Pforzheim raid, Bomber Command ordered a diversionary sweep over northern France with the intent of drawing the Luftwaffe into the air and expending much valuable aviation fuel for, it was envisaged, little gain. The bulk of the diversionary force was made up by aircraft from the training establishments, with 100 Group weighing in with over thirty RCM sorties as useful support. The results were tragic; four Halifaxes from 462 Squadron based at Foulsham failed to return and a 214 Squadron Fortress, out from Oulton, crashed near Ittenbach, a town east of the Rhine and roughly 12 kilometres southeast from the centre of Bonn. Eight of its ten-man crew died instantly, while Flight Lieutenant L G Fowler died from his injuries leaving as the sole survivor Flight Sergeant G J E Jennings who was flying as an air gunner.

From the four Halifaxes missing from 462 Squadron, twenty-six aircrew died leaving four survivors from one aircraft and Flight Sergeant R A Gould as the sole fortunate airman from Flight Lieutenant A J Rate's aircraft. Burning fiercely after being hit by flak, Rate's bomber went down at Boisheim and, as later reported by Flight Sergeant Gould, within sight of the gun flashes from Allied artillery positions less than ten kilometres away.

Meanwhile, all the training aircraft withdrew safely, but one Halifax from 1663 CU at Rufforth developed engine trouble and while dealing with the problem control was lost and the bomber dived into the Leicestershire countryside, killing all seven members of crew who belonged to the Free French Air Force.

The momentum that had built up in the second half of February continued throughout March. Such was the overwhelming strength of Bomber Command, raids were flown practically around the clock and the weight of bomb tonnage delivered rose to record levels. In Germany, five long weary years of war were having its effect on the administrative system necessary for the survival of a modern industrial power and by March 1945, this system was close to breaking point. Across the land chaos threatened as the day to day order of life broke down. As mentioned in my introduction, the last few months of the war were the most hazardous for Allied airmen unfortunate enough to find themselves in the hands of those who still adhered to the Nazi party dictates and the fanatical outpourings from their leader, Adolf Hitler.

The more fortunate who finished up in the hands of the regular armed forces appear to have received reasonable treatment, but mob rule was rife in certain areas and it was where these situations existed that most of the atrocities took place. Even the military and civil powers, such as the police, seemed reluctant to intervene and in some cases actively participated in the crimes being committed.

March began with an area assault, by day, on the city of Mannheim with PFF using skymarking techniques due to total cloud cover over the target area The following day, two blistering attacks were launched against the cathedral city of Köln, already badly devastated from numerous visits made since May 1942, and now within sight of Lieutenant-General Courtney H Hodges First US Army. No official reports are available from either city, but there can be little doubt that further misery was brought to bear on those less fortunate inhabitants who remained.

Without pause, the Command organised two night raids, one towards the still functioning Dortmund-Ems Kanal and the other against the Bergkamen synthetic oil-plant at Kamen on the eastern fringes of the Ruhr. Both operations were eminently successful with no further stocks of oil emerging from Kamen, while two massive breaches in the banks of the Kanel near Ladbergen signalled the end of this key waterway. No aircraft were lost over Kamen, but seven Lancasters were shot down in the course of the Dortmund-Ems raid. However, as the two bomber streams returned across the North Sea, so the Luftwaffe were in the process of despatching large numbers of night-fighters with orders to intercept the bombers as they prepared to land. Twixt the flat expanses of East Anglia and the bleak north Yorkshire moors the intruders

struck, inflicting very severe losses and causing considerable alarm amongst ground personnel who, like their aircrew counterparts, had been caught by no little surprise. Within little more than an hour of intense combat, the Luftwaffe shot down at least twenty-four bombers, including several from the Heavy Conversion Units engaged on night flying exercises.

Several salutary accounts were entered in squadron diaries and two examples, both taken from Canadian units, will suffice. At East Moor, home to 415 Squadron, the diarist wrote, "The tranquillity of the night was disturbed by the presence of enemy raiders, who paid a special call but did no damage. A total blackout was imposed through the medium of the Master Switch. The physiological effect of the raid will be beneficial and should help to defeat the air of complacency displayed by some personnel."

The Station Commander at Skipton-on-Swale took a prosaic stance and promptly imposed a news blackout, this being duly noted in the records for 424 Squadron, "A security silence has been imposed on all experiences, opinions and rumours of last night's enemy intrusion."

It was, however, far too late in the day for the Luftwaffe to turn the tables as it had come close to doing twelve months previous. Nonetheless, it had been a sharp reminder that vigilance was necessary at all times; for that alone, "Unternehmen Gisela", as the operation is known, had served a purpose.

While the casualties sustained on 3-4 March had been due to the intervention of man, a substantial number of the losses incurred on 5-6 March were a direct result of inclement weather. The occasion was the last attack by the Main Force on Chemnitz, one of the targets selected for Operation Thunderclap. As the bombers took off, a cold front made its presence felt, especially over the Vale of York. Worst affected were the RCAF squadrons based at Tholthorpe and Linton-on-Ouse. No less than seven Halifaxes crashed shortly after becoming airborne, mainly due to icing. Throughout the entire operation, crews had to battle continuously against the elements, using up far more petrol than had been envisaged. Consequently, having completed their mission, many were obliged to seek diversionary airfields as they made the long flight home. One such case involved Pilot Officer J H Menary RCAF, out from Tholthorpe and in very serious trouble as he tried to reach Juvincourt in France. At approximately 0130 hours, his Halifax broke through the cloud cover only to find visibility severely impaired by layers of thin white mist. Moments later, the crew felt a violent impact as their bomber crash-landed on soft ground some eight kilometres north of their intended destination. Menary had unwittingly flown into an obstruction. Two members of crew were injured, but the rest emerged relatively unscathed from the wreck.

Not so lucky were the crew of a 419 Squadron Lancaster which spun in over Buckinghamshire killing everyone on board. Altogether, it had been a sorry night all round. Statistics show fifty-one bombers written off, one of these being a 426 Squadron Halifax that had fallen onto a secondary school in York. In addition to six crew members killed, five civilians lost their lives and eighteen were injured, some seriously. The sole survivor from the Halifax, Pilot Officer J Low RCAF, was himself quite badly hurt and it is reported that he later married the nurse who cared for him during his recovery.

Heavy losses, too, followed in the wake of operations to Dessau and Harburg on 7-8 March; nineteen Lancasters either failed to return or crashed during the course of the Dessau raid, this total including a century making aircraft from 550 Squadron that bore the chilling name, The Vulture Strikes. Captained by Flying Officer C J Jones RCAF, three members of its crew died while four sat out the remaining weeks of the war as prisoners. Harburg, where the focus of attention had been an oil producing plant, claimed another thirteen Lancasters, all from 5 Group units, while attacks on other targets cost the Command a further eight aircraft. Anyone who may have believed the remaining months of the bombing campaign to have been a "piece of cake" should, perhaps, revise their thoughts on the subject.

Despite being practically starved of fuel, the Luftwaffe continued to infiltrate the bomber streams, causing quite serious losses until almost the final hours. On the other side of the coin, Bomber Command maintained its unyielding pressure on the towns and cities across what remained of Germany. Two examples of this awesome strength were witnessed on consecutive days in mid-March when first Essen and then Dortmund were the recipients of crushing blows. On the 11th, a record number of 1,079 heavy bombers and Mosquitoes released 4,661 tons of bombs over Essen with such accuracy that the city was to all intents and purposes paralysed. This "record" lasted a mere twenty-four hours, for Dortmund was to receive the attention of 1,108 aircraft and a swinging 4,851 tons of high explosives and incendiaries. I have mentioned that Essen was left paralysed; at Dortmund a similar picture emerges with the few factories still capable of maintaining war production smashed beyond recognition. The two raids, both delivered in daylight, cost Bomber Command a mere eight aircraft.

Attacks on oil producing centres followed, with reasonable results being achieved while on 16-17 March, Harris sent his airmen deep into southern Germany to bomb Nürnberg and Würzburg. Few need reminding of what happened on Nürnberg a year previous and by a cruel quirk of fate, history came close to being repeated when from a force of less than 300 Lancasters, supported by sixteen Mosquitoes, no less than twenty-four of the four-engined bombers were shot down, most by night-fighters that had penetrated the bomber stream ahead of the attack. Twelve months ago, the percentage rate of losses had been 11.9 percent; this time the figure was 8.7 but for 1 Group, whose squadrons made up the bulk of the force, the return was 10.4 percent of the 231 Lancasters mustered. Several squadrons lost two or more aircraft, while from 12 Squadron four crews were reported missing. Meanwhile, 5 Group had been assigned to Würzburg lying northwest of Nürnberg and until now a relatively untroubled town. All this was to alter in a raid which practically wiped out the central parts of the city and leaving an estimated 4,000 to 5,000 fatal casualties in its wake. Seven Lancasters were lost, including a 44 Squadron machine which crashed, with total loss of life, into the sea off Skegness. This tragedy occurred within eighteen minutes of leaving Spilsby and only two bodies were subsequently recovered. Nürnberg, too, suffered considerable damage with many essential services, such as gas supplies and transport, badly disrupted.

March was now entering its final weeks and on the ground the Allied armies were preparing for one last big push. Away to the east, the Wehrmacht were fighting a dogged withdrawl towards Berlin, while in the west their sorely depleted divisions were about to be driven back from the natural defensive barrier of the Rhine. Numerous bridges had already been destroyed in order to deny the Allies an easy crossing and though American troops now controlled large areas of land along the west bank, including most of Köln which had been entered on the 5th, three days after the "blistering attacks" referred to earlier, the grey waters of the river still denied them access to the heart of Germany.

But, as the German High Command knew only too well, it was a foregone conclusion that a crossing would be made and though the resolve of their army commanders remained firm the ability of their soldiers to withstand any such assault was diminishing by the day. Consequently, when the blow fell, during the night of 23-24 March, resistance quickly crumbled. It should be noted, however, that elements of the 9th US Armoured Division had as early as 7 March made a surprise crossing of the Rhine at Remagen, a small town lying northwest of Koblenz and this small bridgehead was duly held while awaiting the principal battle under the direction of Field-Marshal Montgomery's 21st Army Group.

With the Allied armies across the Rhine, in strength, the encirclement of the Ruhr was put in train. Bomber Command's involvement in this last set piece battle included the bombing of Wesel on 23-24 March, this luckless town being immediately opposite the projected line of advance. In fact, a British commando brigade managed to steal across the river ahead of the bombing and, thus, as the dust cleared, were able to rush the dazed defenders and secure the first footholds on the eastern bank and northwest of the Ruhr. Many kilometres downstream and in the region of Oppenheim, a small town on the west bank south of Mainz, General George S Patton's US Third Army had managed to get six battalions of the 5th US Infantry Division across the river, virtually unopposed. Patton was jubilant that this had been achieved the night before Montgomery's main thrust at Wesel.

During the 24th, with amphibious operations in full swing and with airborne landings about to begin, the Command struck at communications and synthetic-oil producing plant in the Ruhr. Losses were minimal, from the night attack on Wesel, an outbound 50 Squadron Lancaster, flown by Flying Officer M L C Lillies RAAF, developed serious engine trouble and diverted to Florennes airfield in Belgium. The subsequent emergency landing went well until the bomber ran into a crater and wiped off its undercarriage. No one was hurt, but the aircraft was abandoned as beyond worthwhile salvage. Likewise, from the raids flown during the 24th, a 158 Squadron Halifax was hit by flak over Gladbeck and was last sighted going down, flames streaming from burning wings tanks, and with several parachutes deploying before it ploughed into the ground. From the operations against the benzol plants, two Lancasters were lost, one of these being from 150 Squadron and from which all seven members of crew parachuted safely. Three, at least, and maybe four, were taken into custody, only to be handed over to a mob who first beat them and then shot them out of hand. A fifth also died and of the two survivors, one, Flight Sergeant J H Gillies RAAF, owes his life to a member of the Todt Organisation who at considerable risk to himself, rescued the Australian and spirited him to safety.

Although there can be no excuse whatsoever for such barbarism, Hitler had within the last few days issued an edict declaring that no consideration should be afforded to anyone, foe or friend alike; everything that might be of future use to the enemy should be destroyed, regardless of the misery that this would bring to the German people. In his now demoniacal state of mind, Germany as a nation should collectively fall upon its sword and perish.

Main Force operations for what remained of March were daylight affairs, aimed at targets mainly located in central Germany, with night operations principally the prerogative of the LNSF, though 100 Group were active on most nights. Berlin, now bracing itself for the inevitable onslaught from the Soviets, and from whom no quarter could be expected, was bombed time and time again by Mosquitoes and, consequently, casualties amongst their ranks were frequent. A high proportion, however, occurred as the crews came into land, or soon after recrossing the East Anglia coastline. Many involved experienced airmen and, certainly, the work rate of the LNSF squadrons was much higher than those of the Main Force. Sorties in excess of fifty were common place and when the Dutchman, Flight Lieutenant A A J Van Amsterdam of 139 Squadron was shot down north of Brandenburg on 27-28 March by a Messerschmitt Me 262 jet propelled fighter, flown by Oberfeldwebel Karl-Heinz Becker, he had exceeded 100 operational flights, a remarkable achievement by any standards. Van Amsterdam died, but his navigator, Squadron Leader A J Forbes RCAF, managed to bale out and was duly made a prisoner. Jet propelled fighters also made their presence felt during a medium sized raid on the Blohm and Voss shipyards at Hamburg on the last day of a hectic month.

Ripping through the bomber formations, cannons blazing, the jets accounted for most of the eleven bombers lost, the Canadians suffering the worst with three Halifaxes and five Lancasters shot from the sky. Friends who escaped this withering intrusion claim some of the fighters were loosing off rocket projectiles, these finding their mark on at least one Lancaster, that flown by Flying Officer G P Haliburton RCAF of 419 Squadron, still operating out of Middleton St. George.

In the context of world events, April 1945 was a month of significant importance. At its beginning all four major political players, Churchill, Roosevelt, Stalin and Hitler, were alive; even the hapless Benito Mussolini had yet to meet his fate. Within the next thirty days, three were to die, the first being the American President, Franklin D Roosevelt. The serious deterioration in the President's health had been plainly evident for all to see at Yalta and on the 12th, during a sitting for his portrait, he collapsed and died later that same day.

Churchill, it is reported, was totally stunned when given the news the following day. Next to go was the unlamented Mussolini summarily executed, along with his mistress, on the 28th after being caught by Italian partisans. And then, on the last day of the month, the chief architect responsible for the terrible suffering and abject misery inflicted across the breadth of Europe, Adolf Hitler, died by his own hand.

For the millions of Jewish people, and others, exterminated in the concentration camps that besmirched the very ground on which they stood, it was of little comfort that the tyrant was dead but the world had not long to wait before the stark horror of this evil regime would be laid bare for all to witness.

April was also the last full month of the bombing campaign, though in truth with the Allied armies across the Rhine and advancing swiftly into central Germany, there was little left for the Command to do and, in fact, before the month was out many squadrons were busy with the heart warming task of ferrying home liberated prisoners of war. However, there was still some work remaining and following a quiet start, 247 Lancasters from 1 Group squadrons, headed by eight PFF Mosquitoes, set out on the 3rd to attack a military barracks at Nordhausen. The aiming point was accurately marked and the bombing that followed was well concentrated. Tragically, and possibly unbeknown to the planning staff at High Wycombe, large numbers of forced labour workers were billeted at Nordhausen where, in the aftermath of the August 1943 raid on Peenemünde, they had been set to work hollowing out an underground complex of tunnels and workshops necessary for the continuance of Germany's rocket research programme. There are no details as to how many died but it is believed the total was considerable, especially as what remained of the barracks were bombed to good effect the following day, this time by 5 Group. Two Lancasters failed to return from the first attack and a single aircraft never made the return trip on the 4th.

What principal bombing now remained was aimed at ship building and port facilities at Hamburg and Kiel, though oil producing centres and communications choke points were not neglected. The results of these operations sounded Germany's death knell; U-boat production was all but brought to a halt, while the long battle to deny the enemy oil finally ended on 20 April, when 3 Group sent 100 Lancasters to destroy a storage depot at Regensburg. One bomber was hit by flak and fell at Burgweinting, some five kilometres southeast from the centre of Regensburg. One airman survived, Flight Sergeant E Parker, the tail gunner. Five now rest in the CWGC War Cemetery at Dürnbach, while their Royal Norwegian Air Force navigator, Second Lieutenant G Dietrishon, is presumed to have been taken back to his native Norway. Later in the day, Mosquitoes from the LNSF visited Berlin for the last time and by dawn of the 21st, no less than six separate attacks had taken place. By day, on 22 April, over 750 heavy bombers and sixteen Mosquitoes went to Bremen to soften up the defences ahead of XXX Corps. Not all were able to bomb, cloud, plus a good deal of smoke which rose in the wake of the first wave's attack, led to the Master Bomber cancelling the operation.

Two Lancasters were hit by flak over the target area, one being a 622 Squadron aircraft piloted by Flight Lieutenant E G Cook. Approaching the aiming point, his Lancaster received a direct hit which blew the port outer engine from its frame and removed six feet from outboard section of the wing. On Cook's orders, six members of the crew baled out, but then he managed to bring his crippled bomber under control and decided to try and make for the Allied lines. Uncertain of his precise position, Flight Lieutenant Cook eventually found himself over that part of Holland still occupied by the Wehrmacht and having sustained further damage from light flak, was obliged to make his exit and sit out the last few weeks of war as a guest of the enemy. The second Lancaster, from 153 Squadron based at Scampton, crashed not far from Jade, killing everyone on board.

These were not the only casualties on this bright spring day. A 218 Squadron crew got into difficulties while returning from Bremen and, subsequently, crashed as they approached to land at Chedburgh. Earlier, a 49 Squadron machine had come down in tragic circumstances at Fulbeck. Six aircrew perished and fifteen ground staff, who were on parade near the station's motor transport section, died as the Lancaster smashed into their midst.

And thus the drama, the toil and pain of the bombing campaign drew to a close. On the 25th, coastal batteries on the island of Wangerooge were heavily bombed (the island of Heligoland and its military installations had suffered similarly seven days previous), while other squadrons made the long haul to Berchtesgaden, practically straddling Germany's border with Austria, to attack the mountainous Eagle's Nest chalet and nearby barracks, much favoured by Hitler and his Nazi party hierarchy. Seven crews failed to return from Wangerooge, at least six falling as a result of mid-air collisions, while two Lancasters, one from 460 Squadron and the other from 619 Squadron, were lost on Berchtesgaden.

As mentioned earlier, the welcome task of flying home liberated prisoners of war began on 26 April, while the next day Bomber Command became involved in another humanitarian operation, the air dropping of vital supplies to the near starving Dutch trapped in an area of western Holland, still very much under the heel of the Wehrmacht. By negotiation with the commanders at the scene the Allies were able to ensure safe passage for their aircraft and before the surrender came into effect on 8 May, well in excess of 2,800 Lancaster sorties had been flown with excellent ground marking support from 8 Group and its versatile Mosquitoes. Known respectively, and appropriately, as Operations Exodus and Manna, the vast majority of these flights passed off without incident, but on 9 May, the first day of peace in Europe, a 514 Squadron Lancaster, captained by Flying Officer D Beaton, got into trouble soon after leaving the French staging airfield at Juvincourt. Beaton tried desperately to regain the departure aerodrome but crashed near Roye-Amy, killing all six aircrew and twenty-four passengers, a cruel fate for them all but particularly so for the passengers, many of whom having endured long years of captivity. And, in respect of the bombing campaign, which ended on 2-3 May with 8 Group and 100 Group attacking targets in the Kiel area and over the port itself, three aircraft, all from 100 Group units, were lost. First to go was a Mosquito from 169 Squadron, crewed by Flying Officer R Catterall and Flight Sergeant D J Beadle, hit by flak as it ran in to drop napalm on Jagel airfield, while not long afterwards, two RCM Halifaxes out from North Creake collided in the air over Meimsdorf, a village east of the Eider and about five kilometres south-southwest from the centre of Kiel. Thirteen airmen died, though miraculously there were survivors from both aircraft.

Within forty-eight hours of their deaths, German officers came to the Tactical Headquarters of General Bernard Law Montgomery's 21st Army Group on Lüneburg Heath and under the watchful eye of the Allied staff, signed a surrender paper for all enemy forces remaining in northwest Germany, Denmark and Holland. Effectively, the war in Europe was over, though it was not until midnight on 8 May, that the unconditional surrender of Germany came into full effect. As recounted, Adolf Hitler was already dead; soon the majority of his contemporaries would be behind bars and awaiting trial for their heinous war crimes. It is not within the remit of this book to dwell overlong on this subject, but suffice to say that Nurnberg was destined to play host to their trials and this city will forever be associated with the rise and fall of National Socialism.

For other reasons, well covered by these books, Nurnberg will occupy a special place in Bomber Command's illustrious history as marking the lowest point in Harris's unfulfilled resolve to bring Germany to the surrender table ahead of any invasion of the Continent. Paradoxically, though he failed to achieve this aim, Nurnberg can be cited as the starting point of that great resurgence of effort that, ultimately, was to restore peace to a war ravaged Europe.

1 Jan 1945	**9 Sqn**	**Lancaster I**	NG223 WS-D	**Op: Ladbergen**
	F/O P W Reaks	+		T/o 0810 Bardney to bomb the Dortmund-Ems Kanal
	Sgt T Scott	+		near Ladbergen. Those who perished rest in the
	F/S F Alton	pow		Reichswald Forest War Cemetery. W/O Bates,
	W/O E P Bates	+		whose commission was awaiting promulgation, was
	F/S S W G Currigan	+		the son of Sir Percy Elly Bates GBE 4th Baronet
	F/S V S Peace	pow		and Lady Bates of Neston, Cheshire.
	F/S W G Bamforth	pow		

	9 Sqn	**Lancaster I**	NG252 WS-R	**Op: Ladbergen**
	F/O C S Newton RCAF	+		T/o 0747 Bardney similarly tasked but dived into
	Sgt C Booth	+		the ground shortly after becoming airborne, due
	F/S P Grant	+		to loss of power on one or both port engines. Of
	P/O R C Flynn RCAF	inj		those who died, three are buried in Harrogate
	Sgt L G Kelly	+		(Stonefall) Cemetery. F/O Newton RCAF hailed
	F/S E H Cooper RCAF	+		from Rockwood, Michigan, while P/O Stevens RCAF
	P/O R S Stevens RCAF	+		had married Margaret Jean Slade Stevens from
				Batford, Hertfordshire. It is further advised

that the crew's regular flight engineer, Sgt N Gregory, was destined to team up with F/O E I Waters RNZAF, whose regular engineer, Sgt Booth, had perished in this tragedy.

	9 Sqn	**Lancaster I**	PD368 WS-A	**Op: Ladbergen**
	F/O J W Buckley RAAF			T/o 0750 Bardney similarly tasked and crashed
	Sgt K E Dawes	inj		almost immediately. Sgt Dawes is not thought
	F/O W C Shutler			to have been seriously hurt.
	F/O A Nolan			
	F/S I L Moore RAAF			
	Sgt R G Round			
	Sgt R A C Copperwaite			

	9 Sqn	**Lancaster I**	PD377 WS-U	**Op: Ladbergen**
	F/O R F H Denton RNZAF			T/o 0744 Bardney similarly tasked. Hit by flak
	Sgt W N Hartshorn	inj		over the target area and later further damaged by
	F/S E Kneebone			ground fire as it neared the battle lines. Sub-
	F/O E R Goebel	inj		sequently, crash-landed in a field near the
	F/S G Thompson	inj		Vosbergstraat at Grolder (Noord-Brabant), 3 km
	Sgt E J Potts	inj		SW of Heesch. Six were admitted to Eindhoven
	Sgt J T Price	inj		Catholic Hospital, where Sgt Potts died from
				his burns. F/S Thompson was transferred to

50 Military Field Hospital where he succumbed to his wounds on 23 January. He is buried in Brussels Town Cemetery; details of his posthumous Victoria Cross were published in the London Gazette on 16 February 1945.

	128 Sqn	**Mosquito XVI**	PF411 M5-B	**Op: Railway Tunnels**
	F/L L C R Wellstead DFC DFM	+		T/o 0641 Wyton but crashed due to engine failure. F/L Wellstead, whose DFM had been Gazetted on 13
	F/L G P Mullan DFC	+		February 1942, following a Wellington tour with 99 Squadron, is buried in Bournemouth North Cem-

etery; F/L Mullan rests in Scotland at Tillicoultry Cemetery, Clackmannanshire.

1 Jan 1945	**467 Sqn**	**Lancaster I**	**PA169 PO-S**	**Op: Ladbergen**

F/O M G Bache DSO RAAF
Sgt E Wilson   inj
F/S S H Nelson RAAF
F/O L E Patison RAAF
F/S C J Dreger RAAF
F/S L G Court RAAF
F/S J M Jay RAAF

T/o 0734 Waddington to bomb the Dortmund-Ems Kanel near Ladbergen. Hit by flak nearing the AP but continued with the attack and bombed at 1117 from 11,700 feet. Turning away, hit for a second time, this time in No.1 port petrol tank. Despite his skills in cross-feeding fuel supplies, Sgt Wilson was unable to prevent both port engines from failing. A valiant effort by all members of crew ensured the Lancaster regained the Allied lines, where it was abandoned and crashed near the hamlet of Hansenberg (Limburg), 3 km NW of Venray. The two injured airmen were taken to a hospital at Eindhoven.

	692 Sqn	**Mosquito XVI**	**PF414 P3-P**	**Op: Railway Tunnels**

F/L G D T Nairn   +
Sgt D Lunn   +

T/o 0651 Graveley. Hit by flak and crashed 0833, with both engines blazing, into hilly country SE of Schuld and towards Adenau. Both now rest in Rheinberg War Cemetery. On 16-17 October 1944 (see Volume 5 page 455), this crew had crashed heavily on return from Köln, but made a quick recovery from their injuries and at the time of their death, they had completed forty operational sorties.

1-2 Jan 1945	**10 Sqn**	**Halifax III**	**LV785 ZA-C**	**Op: Dortmund**

F/O C Winter
F/S I W King   inj
P/O L E Cunningham   inj
F/S A C Smith   inj
F/S W A Waite   +
P/O D C Bishop RCAF
F/S H J Newling   +

T/o 1635 Melbourne to bomb a coking plant. Outbound, at 2,000 feet, the starboard outer began to misfire and after jettisoning the bomb load over the North Sea, the crew returned to base. On approach, F/O Winter realised he was too high but while trying to go round again the Halifax collided with a tree, killing F/S Newling and crashed into a field at Laytham Grange Farm, just to the S of the airfield and burst into flames. The navigator, P/O Cunningham, was severely injured and was helped by the farmer, Mr William Bennett and other members of the crew. Of the two who died, F/S Waite from Chelsea was buried in nearby Pocklington Burial Ground, while F/S Newling lies in Cambridgeshire at Granchester (SS Andrew and Mary) Churchyard.

Note. Flight Sergeant Smith was later to write a detailed account of this crash and this, along with his other experiences, was later published under the title Halifax Crew, The Story of a Wartime Bomber Crew.

	15 Sqn	**Lancaster I**	**ME850 LS-D**	**Op: Vohwinkel**

F/O H Whittingham
Sgt A McNish
Sgt S Merrifield
F/S J Graham
F/S G Dodd
Sgt J Hasler
F/S T Hayday

T/o 1600 Mildenhall to attack the railway yards. Damaged by American AA fire over Belgium and later crash-landed 2050 in France on Juvincourt airfield. No injuries reported.

	50 Sqn	**Lancaster I**	**NF984 VN-**	**Op: Gravenhorst**

F/O H H Skilling RNZAF
Sgt F C Clark
F/O L H E Redford
F/S D J Cruickshank RNZAF
F/S J W Booth
Sgt J A Meadows
Sgt E A McDonald

T/o 1651 Skellingthorpe to bomb the Mittelland Kanal near Gravenhorst. Hit by flak and, later, the crew were ordered to bale out. F/S Cruickshank RNZAF complied, but then control improved and a forced landing was made at 2112 on Juvincourt airfield from where six were ferried home by air the next day. On 6 January, they were joined at Skellingthorpe by F/S Cruickshank who was none the worse for his adventures.

	50 Sqn	**Lancaster I**	**NG127 VN-D**	**Op: Gravenhorst**

F/O V G Sagar

T/o Skellingthorpe similarly tasked but swung out of control, whereupon the undercarriage gave way. No injuries reported, but the Lancaster was deemed beyond economical repair.

Note. Crew details are omitted from 50 Squadron records and details of the incident have been obtained from the Accident Record Card. Such practices of ignoring take off accidents were not unusual at this stage of the war.

1-2 Jan 1945	**75 Sqn**	**Lancaster III**	**ME321 AA-N**	**Op: Vohwinkel**

W/C R J Newton DFC MID RNZAF	+	T/o 1548 Mepal to attack the railway yards. Crashed near the Dutch town of Maastricht.
P/O R J Aitchison RNZAF	+	Seven are commemorated on the Runnymede Memorial
F/S J S Hoskins	+	while Sgt Brennan lies in Jonkerbos War Cemetery
Sgt H Sansome	+	It is believed W/C Newton RNZAF was engaged on
F/S A Lee	+	his 50th operational sortie.
Sgt V J Clark	+	
Sgt M Brennan	+	
Sgt L J Cooke	+	

102 Sqn	**Halifax III**	**LW158 DY-P** **Op: Dortmund**
P/O M O Laugham RAAF	inj	T/o 1645 Pocklington to attack a coking plant.
Sgt E Davies	inj	Crash-landed 2226 on return to base, having
F/S K Knight	inj	undershot the runway and collided with a build-
F/S J H Sheridan	+	ing. F/S Sheridan is buried in Galashiels
Sgt S Westwood	inj	(Eastlands) Cemetery. At 35, he was above
Sgt J Bettney	inj	the average age of Bomber Command aircrew.
Sgt J Coleman		

115 Sqn	**Lancaster I**	**NG332 IL-D** **Op: Vohwinkel**
S/L A A F Mills	+	T/o 1610 Witchford to bomb the railway yards.
F/S J D K Sterling RNZAF	+	Believed homebound when caught in a barrage of
Sgt C D Bassett	+	American AA fire near Namur. Out of control,
P/O G D Long RAAF	+	the Lancaster fell at 2010 onto farmland at
F/O J D Booth	+	Emines (Namur), 11 km SE of Gembloux. Later,
F/S J E W Fenwick	+	21st Army Group signalled that burials had taken
F/S E D Mathison RCAF	+	place at Fosse US Temporary Military Cemetery,
F/S J W McLeod RCAF	+	though all now lie in Leopoldsburg War Cemetery.

At 19, P/O Long RAAF was one of the youngest
Australian navigators killed on bomber operations in the Second World War.
By way of contrast, F/O Booth was thirty-five.

218 Sqn	**Lancaster I**	**PB768 XH-B** **Op: Vohwinkel**
F/O R G Grivell RAAF	+	T/o 1606 Chedburgh similarly tasked. Hit by
Sgt L Peckett	+	flak over the target at 21,000 feet, sustaining
F/S H Clements RCAF	+	damage to the fuel supply feeding the port inner
F/O G Ingram RCAF	inj	engine. This engine was stopped. Over Namur,
Sgt K Bennett	+	homebound, the Lancaster was hit twice, in quick
Sgt E P Buttrum-Gardiner	+	succession, by American AA fire and the entire
Sgt R E Keel	+	port side caught fire. As the order to bale out

was given, the Lancaster spun and fell at Emines
in the Belgian Province of Namur, 11 km SE of Gembloux. Those who died were
buried in the Fosse US Temporary Military Cemetery, since when their remains
have been taken to Leopoldsburg War Cemetery.

Note. On page 69 of The Eighth Passenger by Miles Tripp (Corgi Books, 1971),
the author describes visiting George Ingram in SSQ Chedburgh, following a local
operation to remove a piece of shrapnel lodged in the air bomber's back.

239 Sqn	**Mosquito VI**	**PZ340 HB-** **Op: BS**
F/O I G Walker	+	T/o 1637 West Raynham tasked for a low level
F/O J R Watkins	+	intruder sortie. On return, called base on R/T

at 2016 but crashed four minutes later near
Narborough Hall, situated on the N side of Marham airfield, Norfolk. F/O
Walker was taken back to his home at Dumfries, but F/O Watkins, who hailed
from Wanstead in Essex, was buried at Little Massingham (St. Andrew) Churchyard.

Note. The Squadron ORB reports that F/O Walker was recalled from a gunnery
course at nearby Massingham and crewed up with F/O Watkins, attached from
141 Squadron, in order to meet a maximum effort ordered by 100 Group HQ.

571 Sqn	**Mosquito XVI**	**MM124 8K-U** **Op: Hanau**
F/O H Ross	+	T/o 1619 Oakington. Homebound, broke from
Sgt H Cook	+	cloud and crashed 2130 into trees at Stetch-

worth, 10 miles E of Cambridge and totally
wrecked. F/O Ross is buried in Aberdeen (Springbank) Cemetery, Peterculter
while Sgt Cook is the sole service burial in Summerseat (Rowlands) Methodist
Churchyard at Ramsbottom in Lancashire.

| 2 Jan
1945 | 100 Sqn | Lancaster I | LL898 HW-L | Training |

F/L V Weatherley RNZAF +
Sgt J Dubois +
F/O W S Cameron +
F/O R Warwick +
Sgt P Share +
Sgt G H Thirkettle +

Dived into the sea at 1003 from 5,500 feet while carrying out bombing practice. All six members of crew are commemorated on the Runnymede Memorial.

| 2-3 Jan
1945 | 77 Sqn | Halifax III | MZ335 KN-R | Op: Ludwigshafen |

F/S D W Muggeridge
Sgt W B Keal
Sgt A H Croll
Sgt H Wright
Sgt W Forbes
F/S C E Foster
Sgt M E Taylor

T/o 1504 Full Sutton but lost power and crashed out of control, finishing up in a field just beyond the airfield boundary. There are no reports to suggest anyone was seriously hurt.

| 100 Sqn | Lancaster III | PB518 HW-P | Op: Nurnberg |

F/O P M Bunn pow
Sgt D J J Timms +
F/O L J Holford pow
F/O R E Marsh pow
Sgt J E Benton +
Sgt W C Muir +
Sgt R Poulsom +

T/o 1510 Grimsby. Those who died are buried in Dürnbach War Cemetery.

| 102 Sqn | Halifax III | NR186 DY-U | Op: Ludwigshafen |

F/L J Marvin RCAF

T/o 1506 Pocklington. On return to base at 2210 the Halifax overshot the runway and lost its main undercarriage as it ran over a ditch, identified in Civil Defence records as being in Canal Lane.

Note. The quality of the microfilm is so poor that the names of the crew, none of whom were hurt, defy all attempts at identification.

| 105 Sqn | Mosquito XVI | PF431 GB-K | Op: Bremen |

F/L G Donald pow
F/O F T Watson DFM +

T/o 1739 Bourn. Crashed at Wilsum, Germany, some 11 km E from the Dutch frontier, and on the main road leading northwards from Neuenhaus to Emlichheim. F/O Watson, who had flown his previous tour with 9 Squadron, is buried in the Reichswald Forest War Cemetery. His DFM had been Gazetted on 10 December 1943.

| 139 Sqn | Mosquito XX | KB222 XD-R | Op: Berlin |

F/L J P O Howard DFC RCAF +
F/L D G Williams DFC +

T/o 1640 Upwood. Crashed at Natho, 10 km ESE of Zerbst. Both officers now rest in Berlin 1939-1945 War Cemetery, having been brought here from Natho Friedhof.

| 149 Sqn | Lancaster I | NG362 OJ-S | Op: Nurnberg |

F/O H H Jones
Sgt S Kirkpatrick
Sgt F A Biggs
F/O J H Woodward
Sgt W L Mumford
Sgt J F McNicol
Sgt G C Graham

T/o 1532 Methwold. On return to base the crew were unable to lower the flaps and F/O Jones elected to make a flat approach. While doing so, the main wheels caught a hedge on the airfield boundary and seconds later the Lancaster struck one of the local defence gun pits. This caused the bomber to swing into nearby trees, whereupon the port wing dug into the ground and the Lancaster crashed 2227, bursting into flames. Fortunately, the crew were able to scramble clear before flames engulfed the wreckage.

| 150 Sqn | Lancaster I | NG421 IQ-M | Op: Nurnberg |

F/O G L Russell +
Sgt G Hargreaves +
F/S P H Rodwell +
F/S F Jones +
Sgt J G Hammond +
Sgt J T Frampton +
Sgt G E W Redmile +

T/o 1510 Hemswell. Collided 2310 in the air with a 153 Squadron aircraft, both Lancasters coming down at Sudbrooke, 3 miles NNE of Lincoln. All are buried in United Kingdom cemeteries.

2-3 Jan
1945

153 Sqn   **Lancaster III**   **PB515 P4-N**   **Op: Nurnberg**

F/O D C Reid RCAF	+
Sgt R C Richards	+
F/S C H Pogson RCAF	+
F/S M V Durling RCAF	+
Sgt R Taylor	+
F/S D D Hoskins RCAF	+
F/S A J Eberle RCAF	+

T/o 1455 Scampton. Lost in the manner described at the foot of the previous page. The five RCAF members of crew rest in Harrogate (Stonefall) Cemetery. Sgt Richards is buried at St. Pancras Cemetery, Finchley, while his fellow countryman, Sgt Taylor, was taken back to Yorkshire for burial in Sheffield (Shiregreen) Cemetery.

166 Sqn   **Lancaster III**   **LM687 AS-N**   **Op: Nurnberg**

P/O S J Buck	
Sgt A J Mackenzie	
F/S J Bennett RCAF	
F/O A W Brown RCAF	
Sgt J D Bendall	
Sgt J P Tasker RCAF	
Sgt N Baker RCAF	+

T/o 1450 Kirmington. At 2057 hit by AA fire near the battle lines, position and height being given as 4855N 0645E at 10,000 feet, sustaining severe damage. Approximately five minutes later, the crew baled out over France. Sgt Baker RCAF is believed to have struck the tail-plane as he left his turret; he now rests in Choloy War Cemetery, having been brought here from a temporary US Military Cemetery at Grand Failly. Apart from F/O Brown RCAF, the survivors were home in England by 5 January.

166 Sqn   **Lancaster III**   **ND635 AS-M**   **Op: Nurnberg**

P/O R H Chittim RCAF	+
Sgt J Perry	+
Sgt J D J L Tarlton	+
F/S G H Pearson	+
F/S R S Brown DFM	+
Sgt W J Morgan RCAF	+
Sgt J C Lillis RCAF	pow

T/o 1455 Kirmington. Those who perished rest in Dürnbach War Cemetery. F/S Brown had flown previously with 101 Squadron, his award being published in the London Gazette on 6 June 1944. Sgt Tarlton's parents lived in Brussels, his English father having married Nelly Fievez of Belgium.

Note. This Lancaster bore the name "Frandson's Frolics".

166 Sqn   **Lancaster III**   **PB635 AS-G**   **Op: Nurnberg**

F/O H Burgoyne GM	+
Sgt W E Lane	+
F/S J H Gilbert	+
F/S M Leyland	+
WO1 R V Weston RCAF	+
Sgt T F Stewart	+
Sgt L E Riggs RCAF	+

T/o 1510 Kirmington. Hit by AA fire N of Poitiers, France. All are buried in Choloy War Cemetery. It is possible WO1 Weston's second Christian name, Verdun, was chosen in memory of the French soldiers who died in the battles of the First World War. It is known that his body, along with that of F/S Gilbert, was brought to Choloy from a temporary US Military Cemetery at Grand Failly.

300 Sqn   **Lancaster I**   **PB823 BH-T**   **Op: Nurnberg**

S/L B B Janas PAF	+
Sgt M Wrus PAF	+
Sgt W Omiotek PAF	+
W/O J Banys PAF	+
Sgt S Zielinski PAF	+
F/S W M Heine PAF	+
Sgt R Drozdowicz PAF	+

T/o 1516 Faldingworth. Exploded in the vicinity of Laix (Meurthe-et-Moselle), Baslieux and Ville-au-Montois, three villages some 12 km E to SE of Longuyon. All are buried in Pierrepont French National Cemetery, about 9 km SE of Longuyon, having been brought here from the temporary US Military Cemetery at Grand Failly.

347 Sqn   **Halifax III**   **MZ984 L8-G**   **Op: Ludwigshafen**

Sgt J P Leclercq FFAF	+
Sgt Dufaure FFAF	
Ltn D F Cottard FFAF	
Adj F Adauist FFAF	
Sgc A Morel FFAF	
Sgc H Aubiet FFAF	
Sgt E Usai FFAF	inj

T/o 1509 Elvington. Hit by American AA fire while flying at 9,000 feet and is thought to have come down at Courcelles-sur-Nied (Moselle), some 10 km SE from the centre of Metz. Six baled out, as ordered, but Sgt Leclercq FFAF was unable to clear the aircraft in time to save his life. It is assumed he is buried in France.

Note. It is not possible to report the burial details for Sgt Leclercq FFAF as I am informed by one of my contacts in France that the French do not have an organisation comparable to CWGC and, therefore, it is extremely difficult to report on such matters. Thus, the verification of names and initials of those who died is near impossible, due to this lack of official records. I have, however, received a list of deceased FFAF personnel that served with Bomber Command and though initials are omitted from some of the names, I have tried to reconcile all reported deaths against this paper.

2-3 Jan 1945	**405 Sqn** **Lancaster III**	**PB477 LQ-B**	**Op: Nurnberg**

2-3 Jan 1945

405 Sqn   **Lancaster III**   **PB477 LQ-B**   **Op: Nurnberg**

W/C K J Lawson   +   T/o 1554 Gransden Lodge. Crashed at Rohrau,
DSO & Bar DFC   3 km ENE from the small town of Nufringen.
Sgt S Rhodes   pow   Those who died rest in Dürnbach War Cemetery.
P/O S H Fitzhenry RAAF   +   W/C Lawson had participated in at least 92 op-
S/L N Crawford DFC RCAF   +   erational sorties, while F/L Duke had served
F/L E C Duke DFM   +   in India with 31 Squadron, details of his DFM
F/O G E Geeves DFC RCAF   +   having been published on 21 November 1941. At
WO1 D G Plyley RCAF   pow   35, S/L Crawford RCAF was senior in years to
                            the majority of operational aircrew.

419 Sqn   **Lancaster X**   **KB700 VR-Z**   **Op: Nurnberg**

F/L A G R Warner RCAF   T/o 1426 Middleton St. George. Returned safely
                           but with suspected hydraulic problems. Bounced
heavily on landing at 2338 and the Lancaster ran some fifty yards off the end
of the runway. While attempting to regain the perimeter track, the starboard
outer propeller clipped a mechanical digger and moments later a fire broke out
and though the crew were able to get clear, the Lancaster was destroyed.

Note. Named "Ruhr Express", this had been the first Canadian built Lancaster
and upon its untimely end had completed forty-nine operational sorties.

3 Jan 1945

467 Sqn   **Lancaster I**   **NF908 PO-C**   **Training**

F/O W V W Allamby RAAF   +   T/o 1430 Waddington for fighter affiliation
Sgt N Lees   +   training. At approximately 1600, the bomber
F/L J I Pritchard RAAF   +   flew into high ground that was shrouded in
F/S G J Dunbar RAAF   +   cloud some 4 miles NNE of Leek, Staffordshire.
F/S R Emonson RAAF   +   All were buried in Chester (Blacon) Cemetery.
F/S T E H Wright RAAF   +
F/S C C Watson RAAF   +

622 Sqn   **Lancaster I**   **NF964 GI-L**   **Op: Dortmund**

F/L W E M Dean   +   T/o 1245 Mildenhall for a G-H raid on the Hansa
Sgt H R Willicombe   +   benzol plant. Exploded 1534, scattering debris
F/O L G Mead   +   over the target area. All were buried in the
P/O V C Bullock RCAF   +   Hauptfriedhof at Dortmund, since when their
F/S J MacFarlane   +   remains have been taken to the Reichswald
F/S R Harland   +   Forest War Cemetery.
Sgt G W Brown   +

4 Jan 1945

103 Sqn   **Lancaster III**   **ND861 PM-H**   **Training**

P/O C J Weight   +   T/o 1424 Elsham Wolds. The weather deteriorated
P/O G E Widdicombe   +   during the course of the sortie and as the crew
F/O M D Pickersgill   +   tried to regain their base, they encountered a
Sgt H G Backway   +   blizzard and crashed 1440 into the River Humber
Sgt C F Hillier   +   near the fishing and commercial port of Hull.
Sgt C Lloyd   +   All are commemorated on the Runnymede Memorial.

4-5 Jan 1945

50 Sqn   **Lancaster I**   **PD292 VN-H**   **Op: Royan**

F/O V G Sagar   +   T/o 0059 Skellingthorpe to attack the German
Sgt A Jones   +   garrison dominating the mouth of the Gironde.
F/S D Jackson   +   Lost without trace. All are commemorated on
F/S J C McFee RCAF   +   the Runnymede Memorial. F/O Sagar, and likely
F/S W R Dawes   +   most of those here mentioned, had been involved
F/S J H Peill   +   in a take off accident a few days previous.
F/S J H Goddard   +

57 Sqn   **Lancaster III**   **PB348 DX-T**   **Op: Royan**

F/O A R Curran RAAF   T/o 0045 East Kirkby similarly tasked. Soon
Sgt D Howells   after becoming airborne, the crew encountered
Sgt R Denholm   very severe icing and within a few minutes
Sgt E Starmer   both starboard engines ceased to function.
Sgt N Ward   Attempts to feather the two units were un-
Sgt H Terry   successful and their plight worsened as the
Sgt F Gregan   ASI became effected by the icing. Bombs were
                            jettisoned but after forty-five minutes of
flying, the crew were obliged to abandon the aircraft. Subsequently, the
wreckage of their Lancaster was found on the beach twixt the Lincolnshire
resort of Mablethorpe and nearby Theddlethorpe St. Helen. No one was hurt.

4-5 Jan 1945	106 Sqn	Lancaster III	PB617 ZN-B	Op: Royan

106 Sqn   **Lancaster III**   **PB617 ZN-B**   **Op: Royan**

4-5 Jan 1945

```
106 Sqn          Lancaster III   PB617 ZN-B                Op: Royan
F/O A H Scott RAAF        +      T/o 0025 Metheringham to bomb a German garrison
Sgt P A Lane             +       dominating the entrance to the Gironde river.
F/O B T Roberts RAAF     +       Crashed at St-Palais-sur-Mer (Charente-Maritime)
F/O V D Powell RAAF      +       where all rest in the local communal cemetery
F/O C A Cassidy RAAF     +       alongside AC1 F Parton, who lost his life when
F/S C R Mangnall RAAF    +       the Lancastria was bombed on 17 June 1940.  The
F/S P W K Walter RAAF    +       village is located some 5 km W of Royan.

189 Sqn          Lancaster III   ME300 CA-P                Op: Royan
F/O J I Coad             +       T/o 0040 Fulbeck similarly tasked.  Homebound,
Sgt G A T Boyson         +       collided with a 467 Squadron Lancaster, both
Sgt J C Dunville         +       machines coming down at 0422 over Allied held
F/S H B Hodder           +       territory near Cognac in the Department of
F/S M Browne RAAF        +       Charente.  Those who died are buried in Cognac
Sgt T R Dunne            +       (Crouin) Communal Cemetery.  Sgt Dunne hailed
Sgt R Powell             +       from Dublin in the Irish Republic.
```

Note. Also resting in this cemetery are two officers from 23 Squadron whose Mosquito crashed in the area on 28 November 1942.

```
463 Sqn          Lancaster I     PB695 JO-R                Op: Royan
F/O J Milne RAAF         +       T/o 0041 Waddington similarly tasked.  Came
Sgt E A Freeman          +       down in the target area.  Four are buried,
F/S S A Brown RAAF       +       alongside two airmen from 214 Squadron (see
F/S C L Fincham RAAF     +       Volume 4 page 103), in Royan Roman Catholic
F/S W A Simpson RAAF     +       Cemetery, while three are commemorated on
F/S J F Prince RAAF      +       the Runnymede Memorial.  Their average age
F/S C F Walters RAAF     +       was twenty-one.

467 Sqn          Lancaster III   ND473 PO-N                Op: Royan
F/O R B Eggins RAAF              T/o 0109 Waddington similarly tasked.  Lost
Sgt S F Baker                    in the circumstances as described in the
F/S J J B Grady RAAF             summary for 189 Squadron.  All baled out
F/S P J Madden RAAF              and there are no reports of injury.
F/S C McC Cahill RAAF
F/S A B Walker RAAF
F/S R V Richardson RAAF

619 Sqn          Lancaster III   ND728 PG-N                Op: Royan
F/O D Gray RAAF          +       T/o 0122 Strubby similarly tasked.  It is
Sgt A Johnson            +       believed Sgt Bartholomew survived the crash
F/S E A Morley           +       as his date of death is shown as 8 January.
F/S H Insley             +       He is buried in Soulac-sur-Mer (Olives)
W/O L J Symonds RAAF     +       Communal Cemetery near two soldiers who
Sgt R Brown              +       died on 17 June 1940. The other members
Sgt W B Bartholomew    inj       of crew have no known graves.
```

5 Jan 1945

```
15 Sqn           Lancaster I     LL923 LS-O                Op: Ludwigshafen
F/S D H Williams         +       T/o 1129 Mildenhall to bomb railway yards.
Sgt S J Dolan            +       Those who died are buried in Rheinberg War
F/O W Young              +       Cemetery.
F/S A B Nicklin          +
F/S G I Rugless RAAF     +
Sgt E E Parkhouse        +
Sgt D T Darby          pow

85 Sqn           Mosquito NF.30  MV558 VY-                 Air Test
F/L J Lomas                      T/o 1407 Swannington but the port engine boost
                                 control failed and the undercarriage was raised
in order to stop. The crew escaped injury, but the Mosquito was damaged beyond
economical repair.
```

Note. The Mosquito NF.30 first appeared off the production lines in April 1944, but problems with the exhaust shrouds delayed their operational use until much later in the year. The aircraft reported in the above summary was built by the parent company and arrived at 218 MU on 1 November 1944, passing to 85 Squadron at Swannington eight days later. A record of its flying hours has not been noted.

5 Jan 1945	90 Sqn	Lancaster I	HK603 WP-D	Op: Ludwigshafen

F/O C E Wakeham RAAF	pow	
Sgt R C Boyle	pow	
F/S H E Worsnop	pow	
F/O R A Kirkland	pow	
F/O F H R Kemp RAAF	+	
Sgt J Healy	pow	
Sgt J M Bilton	pow	
Sgt V I Michael	+	

T/o 1132 Tuddenham to bomb railway yards. Hit by flak and crashed 1510 at Mutterstadt, some 5 km WSW from the centre of Ludwigshafen. The two airmen who died are buried in Rheinberg War Cemetery. Sgt Bilton was flying in the mid-under gun position.

5-6 Jan 1945	7 Sqn	Lancaster III	PB526 MG-N	Op: Hannover

F/O L T Friedrich RNZAF	+
Sgt H C Johnston	+
Sgt A H Grant	+
F/S R G Moore RNZAF	+
F/S B D Jenkins RNZAF	+
Sgt N R Howell	+
Sgt C F Bates	+

T/o 1628 Oakington. Shot down by a night-fighter and crashed 1850, roughly 12 km SSW from Bad Zwischenahn, where all were buried in the local Friedhof on 9 January. Their graves are now located in Sage War Cemetery.

10 Sqn	Halifax III	NA114 ZA-K	Op: Hannover

F/O C R Sifton	+
Sgt W Bainbridge	+
P/O W E Bransgrove	+
F/S W A Daniel	+
F/S D A Bullock	+
Sgt B Jackson	+
F/S L D I Coates	+
F/S N E Freshwater	+

T/o 1649 Melbourne. Shot down by a night-fighter and crashed near Lemgo, a large town some 10 km N of Detmold. On impact the bomber caught fire. All are buried in Hannover War Cemetery. F/S Coates was occupying the mid-under gun position.

35 Sqn	Lancaster III	PB343 TL-M	Op: Hannover

F/O K Potts DFC	+
F/S M B Sharp	+
F/O M A Mills RCAF	+
F/O A J Reeder RCAF	+
F/S G A Pope	+
F/S R W Bentley	+
Sgt V M B Halls	+

T/o 1627 Graveley. Hit by flak and believed to have crashed 1904 between Reide and Thedinghausen, two small towns 12 km SSE and 14 km SE respectively from the centre of Bremen. Four are buried in Sage War Cemetery, but F/O Potts and both Canadians are commemorated on the Runnymede Memorial. At 19, F/O Mills RCAF was one of the youngest navigators to lose his life on Bomber Command operations.

51 Sqn	Halifax III	LV952 MH-F	Op: Hannover

P/O A Leach	+
Sgt P Neale	+
F/S J S Staples	+
F/S W G Bowen	+
F/O L A Wilson RAAF	+
F/S W M Burton	+
Sgt D E F Thomsett	pow

T/o 1647 Snaith. Crashed 1927 at Leinhausen. Those who died rest in Hannover War Cemetery.

51 Sqn	Halifax III	MZ767 MH-D	Op: Hannover

F/O G I Hodgson RNZAF	+
Sgt B W Duffell	pow
F/S J G Orr RAAF	pow
F/O R J Crane RAAF	pow
F/S D Keirs RAAF	pow
W/O A Allan	+
Sgt A W T Boulton	+

T/o 1637 Snaith. Claimed by a night-fighter and crashed 2005 at Brandlecht, 5 km SSE from the centre of Nordhorn. The pilot and both air gunners are buried in the Reichswald Forest War Cemetery, having been recovered from Brandlecht Evangelical Friedhof. It is reported that F/S Keirs RAAF was wounded.

51 Sqn	Halifax III	MZ918 MH-U	Op: Hannover

F/S E G Stevens	+
Sgt A R Pritchard	+
F/S W S Spratt	+
F/S J R Whitmore	+
F/S R A Gibbs	pow
Sgt J H Yearsley	+
Sgt E Timms	pow

T/o 1636 Snaith. Crashed circa 1930 roughly 3 km W of Kaltenweide, a village some 12 km N from the centre of Hannover, where those who perished lie in the local war cemetery. Sgt Pritchard was nineteen years of age and had, until recently, served with the Air Training Corps. In contrast, Sgt Yearsley was 35 and well over the average age associated with operational aircrew.

5-6 Jan
1945

61 Sqn	Lancaster I		PA165 QR-V	Op: Houffalize

F/O J E Sears   +
Sgt R W B Baldwin   +
Sgt M W Stobart   +
F/O R B Anderson MID RNZAF   +
F/S G Malcolm   +
Sgt L A Williams   +
W/O N McKay   pow

T/o 0025 Skellingthorpe to bomb a supply route in the Belgian Ardennes. Crashed in the target area. Those who died were buried, probably near the wreckage of their aircarft. Four now rest in Houffalize Communal Cemetery, while Sgt Baldwin and Sgt Williams now lie at Hotton War Cemetery, having been brought here from the temporary US Military Cemetery at Foy.

77 Sqn	Halifax III		MZ360 KN-A	Op: Hannover

F/O P A Fitzgerald   pow
Sgt S S Carter   +
F/S K J A Bicknell   +
F/S D J Parsons   +
Sgt A C Overett   +
Sgt J M Pickering   +
Sgt F Meekison   +

T/o 1648 Full Sutton. Crashed circa 1925 roughly 1 km SE from the town of Steinhude on the south-eastern side of the Steinhuder Meer. Those who lost their lives rest in Hannover War Cemetery. Sgt Pickering, who came from Lisburn in Northern Ireland, was 39 and was amongst the oldest airmen killed on bombing operations during 1945.

100 Sqn	Lancaster III		JB603 HW-E	Op: Hannover

F/O R Barker   +
Sgt A S Gordon   +
F/S F S Elliott   +
F/S A A Law   +
P/O J M C Wilson RAAF   +
Sgt E Gillen   +
Sgt B G Aldred   +

T/o 1910 Grimsby. Crashed 2300 near the hamlet of Haarbroek (Gelderland), 7 km SE of Gorssel, where all were buried in the general cemetery on 11 January.

Note. Thirty servicemen, all airmen, lie in Gorssel General Cemetery, twenty-nine of this total falling while flying with Bomber Command.

102 Sqn	Halifax III		LL597 DY-X	Op: Hannover

F/L J T Jones   pow
Sgt S J W P Franklin   +
F/S J H D Bax   pow
F/S G A Wilson   pow
Sgt W Shaw   +
Sgt J Harding   +
W/O R Jones   +
F/S R English   +

T/o 1658 Pocklington. Shot down by a night-fighter and exploded, crashing 1910 near Littel some 5 km SSW of Wardenburg. Those who died lie in Sage War Cemetery. At eighteen, Sgt Franklin was amongst the youngest airmen killed on Bomber Command operations in 1945. W/O Jones is des-cribed as a pilot, though he was operating the mid-under gun. F/S Wilson was admitted to RAF Hospital Cosford on 4 May 1945.

Note. Olaf Timmermann states that in September 1982, an engine from this Halifax was found on farmland about 80 to 100 metres from where the bulk of the wreckage fell.

102 Sqn	Halifax III		MZ796 DY-M	Op: Hannover

F/O J F Bergman RCAF   pow
P/O J F Shirley   +
F/O C C Smith DFC   +
F/O D W Dale RCAF   pow
F/S E L Stevens RCAF   +
Sgt C N Aune RCAF   +
F/S H A Dunphy RCAF   +

T/o 1655 Pocklington. Hit by flak and crashed 1945 about 1 km SW from Mariensee, 6 km NNE of Neustadt am Rübenberge. Those who lost their lives rest in Hannover War Cemetery.

102 Sqn	Halifax III		NA602 DY-Y	Op: Hannover

Capt R W F Heiden SAAF   +
Sgt P Morgan   +
F/S W K Quill RAAF   +
P/O E M Boorman   pow
F/S J F Valery RAAF   +
Sgt A I Johns   +
W/O M J E Tyler   +
Sgt R O Jones   +

T/o 1652 Pocklington. Believed to have come down 1925 at Frielingen, 6 km NE of Wunstorf. Capt Heiden SAAF of Cape Town and those who died are buried in Hannover War Cemetery. The last three named were all operating as air gunners, despite Sgt Johns being described in the CWGC register as an air bomber.

Note. Constructed by Fairey Aviation, this Halifax was delivered to 102 Squadron from 45 MU on 3 August 1944 and apart from a spell of local re-pairs during the October, saw continuous service until it was lost in the circumstances, here described.

5-6 Jan **1945**	**103 Sqn**	**Lancaster III**	**PB528 PM-D**	**Op: Hannover**

103 Sqn	**Lancaster III**		**PB528 PM-D**	**Op: Hannover**
F/O J R Barnes	pow			
Sgt G R Wilding	pow			
F/S J C Tear	pow			
F/S M E F Haslam	pow			
F/S D G Ireland	pow			
Sgt A C Clark	+			
Sgt S Cook	+			

T/o 1908 Elsham Wolds. Believed to have crashed 2159 some 3 km S of Springe bei Alvesrode and about 13 km NW of Elze. Both air gunners are buried in Hannover War Cemetery.

142 Sqn	**Mosquito XXV**	**KB397 4H-P**	**Op: Berlin**
F/L B Eichler	+		
Sgt G Logie	+		

T/o 1702 Gransden Lodge. Engine failure while in the circuit, lost height and hit a tree at Hatley Park near Gamlingay, 14 miles WSW from Cambridge. F/L Eichler of Czechoslovakia is buried in Cambridge City Cemetery while Sgt Logie rests at Elgin New Cemetery.

158 Sqn	**Halifax III**	**MZ395 NP-C**	**Op: Hannover**
F/O J H Robinson	pow		
Sgt R L Watkins	+		
F/S M A Belcher	pow		
F/O F A Toplis	pow		
F/S A G Scarff	+		
Sgt A J Ralph	pow		
Sgt D H Pemble	+		

T/o 1644 Lissett. Homebound, hit by cannon fire from a night-fighter and fell 1940, burning, at Heyen, 3 km N of Bodenwerder on the Wesel, some 18 km SSE of Hameln. Five managed to leave the Halifax before the port wing collapsed, but Sgt Pemble was found suspended from a tree, having died from exposure. Along with Sgt Watkins and F/S Scarff, he rests in Hannover War Cemetery.

158 Sqn	**Halifax III**	**MZ432 NP-Q**	**Op: Hannover**
F/O A G Robertson RCAF	pow		
Sgt G Dacey	+		
F/S T M Laurie	pow		
F/O G W Cross RCAF	pow		
Sgt J J Bromfield	pow		
F/S J D E Rae RCAF	pow		
WO2 G E Marion RCAF	pow		

T/o 1701 Lissett. Sgt Dacey is reported to have baled out but his body was never found and he is commemorated on panel 274 of the Runnymede Memorial. At 35, he was above the average age of Bomber Command airmen. It is reported that Sgt Bromfield managed to avoid being captured until 13 January.

158 Sqn	**Halifax III**	**NR190 NP-T**	**Op: Hannover**
F/L W McLennan			
F/S R Statham			
F/S E G Huband			
P/O P A J Carroll			
F/S M Spivey	inj		
F/S S Hibbert			
Sgt A Day			

T/o 1702 Lissett. Approaching the AP when struck by a Lancaster that was being pursued by a night-fighter. The force of the collision tore the starboard inner from its frame and badly damaged control surfaces. Following a difficult return, F/L McLellan crash-landed 2156 at Woodbridge airfield, Suffolk. F/S Spivey required treatment for his badly frost bitten fingers, amputation of the worst effected being necessary. For his devotion to duty in trying to restore communications, he was awarded an immediate DFM, while his skipper received an immediate DFC, both awards being Gazetted on 23 March 1945. Other members of crew were decorated later.

158 Sqn	**Halifax III**	**NR251 NP-B**	**Op: Hannover**
F/L A Elliott	+		
Sgt W B Morton	evd		
F/S A M H Norris	pow		
F/S I A H Croad	evd		
F/S P D Watson	evd		
Sgt D McMahon	pow		
Sgt R H Dickson	evd		

T/o 1647 Lissett. Homebound, very badly shot about by a night-fighter and partially abandoned before crashing 2015 between Haarle and Nijverdal (Overijssel), 16 km W of Almelo. F/L Elliott, who had married Gladys Letitia Elliott of New Westminster in British Colombia, rests at Hellendoorn General Cemetery.

169 Sqn	**Mosquito VI**	**NT116 VI-**	**Op: BS**
F/S R J Keller	+		
F/S J B Thorburn	+		

T/o 1700 Great Massingham to patrol SW of Duisburg in support of Main Force operations on Hannover. Both airmen, who had joined the Squadron on New Year's Day, are buried in Holland at Maarheeze (Sterksel Monastery) Cemetery, close to where their aircraft crashed.

Note. This cemetery is within the grounds of the Monastery which, in September 1944, was taken over by the British Army and used as a hospital. Over the next twelve months, 42 service personnel were buried here, mainly soldiers who died from their wounds or in accidents in the general area covered by the cemetery.

| 5-6 Jan 1945 | 207 Sqn | Lancaster III | | NE168 EM-F | Op: Houffalize |

5-6 Jan
1945

207 Sqn	Lancaster III		NE168 EM-F	Op: Houffalize
F/O M L Perez RAAF		+		
Sgt E Deller		+		
Sgt G E Patterson		+		
F/S W L Cleary		+		
Sgt J Kennedy		+		
Sgt J G Shepherd		+		
Sgt K A W Ottewell		pow		

T/o 0052 Spilsby to attack supply channels in the Belgian Ardennes. Presumed crashed in the target area. Those who died rest in Houffalize Communal Cemetery. At 35, Sgt Kennedy was over the age of airmen associated with Bomber Command airmen. Although described as a wireless operator air gunner, F/S Cleary was carrying out the duties of air bomber.

347 Sqn	Halifax III		LL557 L8-U	Op: Hannover
Ltn E De Lueze FFAF		pow		
Sgc R Juste FFAF		pow		
Ltn C Courvalin FFAF		pow		
Slt J Vezolle FFAF		+		
Sgt M Chabourd FFAF		pow		
Sgt H Bastian FFAF		evd		
Sgt P Meau FFAF		+		

T/o 1638 Elvington. Abandoned in the vicinity of Saerbeck, a town 13 km SSW from Ibbenbüren. Slt Vezolle's parachute failed to deploy, while Sgt Meau FFAF was shot by a member of the Feld-gendarmerie; he was buried in the Roman Catholic Friedhof at Saerbeck. Sgt Bastian FFAF found refuge in a convent and remained there until Allied forces overran the area.

408 Sqn	Halifax III		NR209 EQ-A	Op: Hannover
F/L A F Scheelar RCAF		+		
Sgt J Daly		+		
F/O D Elkin RCAF		pow		
F/O F A Winter RCAF		pow		
F/O F T Leithead RCAF		+		
P/O L J Benville RCAF		+		
F/O W A Baker RCAF		pow		

T/o 1641 Linton-on-Ouse. Crashed around 1950 at Hollenstede, 2 km SSE from Fürstenau. Those who died rest near Oldenburg at Sage War Cemetery. F/L Scheelar RCAF came from Kimball, Minnesota. His was an experienced crew, all having flown 23 to 25 sorties apiece.

Note. Principally equipped with Halifax VIIs since July 1944, 408 Squadron held around half-a-dozen Halifax IIIs, this being the first to be reported missing.

415 Sqn	Halifax III		MZ476 6U-Y	Op: Hannover
F/O S H McFadden RCAF		pow		
Sgt J J Burton		pow		
F/O N Conner RCAF		pow		
F/O E Rhind RCAF		+		
F/S J A Rinder RCAF		+		
F/S J T Clarke RCAF		+		
F/S F T Graves RCAF		pow		

T/o 1623 East Moor. Crashed 1900 into the Dehmse Wald, about 5 km N of Twistringen. Those who lost their lives rest in Sage War Cemetery. F/O Conner RCAF fell through a propeller arc and lost his left leg. Subsequently, he was repatriated and visited the Squadron on 22 April, before going home to Canada.

419 Sqn	Lancaster X		KB722 VR-A	Op: Hannover
P/O N D Mallen RCAF		inj		
Sgt P N Hall		inj		
F/O J A F Miller RCAF				
Sgt R S Dickson RCAF		inj		
WO2 R B Cameron RCAF				
Sgt N R Poole RCAF		inj		
Sgt C Drinka RCAF				

T/o 1907 Middleton St. George. Outbound at 20,000 feet when at 2117 damaged in both inner engines by fire from a Lancaster, ahead and slightly below. Course was set for Brussels but later altered for Juvincourt, which was found to be fog bound. The crew then tried to reach Manston but when the pilot saw a gap in the overcast, he crash-landed 0020 in a field near Guise (Aisne) and close to the road leading to St-Quentin. All were flown back to England, two with sprained ankles, having initially received treatment for their injuries at a US Military Hospital at St-Quentin.

420 Sqn	Halifax III		MZ471 PT-V	Op: Hannover
F/L L W Brand RCAF		+		
P/O D W Walker DFC		+		
F/O R W Landers RCAF		pow		
Sgt J W Vandenbergh RCAF		+		
F/S J H Warren RCAF		pow		
F/S D O Palmer RCAF		pow		
F/S G A Noble RCAF		pow		

T/o 1639 Tholthorpe. Reported shot down by a night-fighter. Those who died in the crash are buried in Hannover War Cemetery, while F/S Noble RCAF lies in Dürnbach War Cemetery, his death being reported on 20 January. Apparently, despite being gravely wounded, he tried to evade capture but was picked up at Osterwald and taken to Res Lazarett W at Hannover. He was then taken to Hohemark (Oberursel) where he died. P/O Walker had flown twenty-eight sorties, the others seven, except for the pilot and F/S Palmer RCAF who had each completed eight.

Note. Accepted by 420 Squadron, ex-works, on 24 October 1944, this Halifax saw a little over two months of operational service.

-6 Jan
945

425 Sqn	Halifax III	MZ860 KW-E	Op: Hannover
F/S J T R Cauely RCAF	pow		
Sgt E J Faulkner RCAF	pow		
F/O J J P Lesperance RCAF	pow		
WO2 J A F Piche RCAF	+		
Sgt R R M Cantin RCAF	pow		
Sgt J Y J C Lamarre RCAF	+		
F/S J A Cote RCAF	pow		

T/o 1623 Tholthorpe. Shot down at 1940, while approaching the AP and crashed near the town of Stolzenau, some 16 km WNW of the Steinhuder Meer. Those who died rest in Hannover War Cemetery.

425 Sqn	Halifax III	NP999 KW-W	Op: Hannover
F/O V E Brimicombe RCAF	pow		
Sgt S H Moore	+		
F/O L U Coleman RCAF	pow		
F/O M D Berry RCAF	pow		
F/S G R Delong RCAF	pow		
F/S D C MacKeigan RCAF	pow		
F/S G E Hutton RCAF	pow		

T/o 1630 Tholthorpe. Nineteen year old Sgt Moore is buried in Sage War Cemetery.

425 Sqn	Halifax III	NR178 KW-J	Op: Hannover
F/O J W A Seguin RCAF	pow		
Sgt G B Noonan	+		
F/O J A M Bilodeau RCAF	pow		
Sgt J G A B Cantin RCAF	pow		
P/O J M R Lapierre RCAF	pow		
F/S J J G Huet RCAF	pow		
Sgt B G Simonin RCAF	+		

T/o 1624 Tholthorpe. Reported shot down by a night-fighter and may have crashed 1918 some 2 km E of Schneeren, a village N of the Steinhuder Meer and 9 km WNW from Neustadt am Rübenberge. Those who died are buried in Hannover War Cemetery.

Note. Only two NCOs with the surname Cantin were reported missing this night and both were from 425 Squadron. Both had applied for commissions, which were promulgated soon after they had been reported missing.

427 Sqn	Halifax III	NR257 ZL-Y	Op: Hannover
S/L B G Crew DFC RCAF	+		
Sgt J D Smith	+		
F/L J S H Dodge RCAF	pow		
F/O H W Campbell RCAF	pow		
F/L J D Johnston DFC RCAF	pow		
F/O C Kelway RCAF	+		
F/O T Osler RCAF	+		

T/o 1625 Leeming. Hit by flak and crashed 1930 at Dudensen, 10 km N of Neustadt am Rübenberge. Those who died rest in Hannover War Cemetery. S/L Crew RCAF was OC B Flight and on his second tour of operations, while F/L Johnston RCAF was the Squadron's Signals Leader.

429 Sqn	Halifax III	LV964 AL-T	Op: Hannover
P/O G Hay RCAF	+		
P/O F J Nicholson	+		
F/O J L M R Savard RCAF	+		
WO2 J J M Tremblay RCAF	+		
P/O R H Couzens	+		
F/S F N Brown RCAF	+		
F/S T A Gabriel RCAF	+		

T/o 1633 Leeming. Crashed circa 1915 just to the SW of Wachendorf, 7 km SE of Syke. The first two named have no known graves, the others are buried in Sage War Cemetery. The crew were within sight of being screened; P/O Hay RCAF had completed 30 sorties and his crew had logged between 27 and 28 trips apiece.

432 Sqn	Halifax VII	NP759 QO-C	Op: Hannover
F/L J E Sales RCAF	+		
Sgt J Dalton	pow		
F/O J L Marcille RCAF	pow		
F/S S J Aikens RCAF	pow		
WO2 R J P Young RCAF	pow		
F/S C H McInnes RCAF	+		
F/S J F Charles RCAF	pow		

T/o 1648 East Moor. Claimed by the 8th Flak Division and believed crashed 1915 at Mehringen some 2 km N of Hoya, which straddles the Weser 15 km SSW of Verden. The two airmen who died rest in Hannover War Cemetery, having been brought here from graves discovered at Hoya.

432 Sqn	Halifax VII	NP817 QO-D	Op: Hannover
W/C J G Stephenson RCAF	pow		
Sgt B M Hodges	pow		
F/O W E Fleming RCAF	pow		
F/O R G Donaldson RCAF	pow		
F/O E B Pickthorne RCAF	pow		
WO1 W T McMahon RCAF	pow		
F/O T R Bond RCAF	pow		

T/o 1650 East Moor.

5-6 Jan 1945	**550 Sqn**	**Lancaster I**		**NG331 BQ-M**	**Op: Hannover**

```
5-6 Jan    550 Sqn           Lancaster I    NG331 BQ-M            Op: Hannover
1945       F/O J C Adams RCAF           +    T/o 1915 North Killingholme.  Believed shot down
           Sgt W P Scott               +    by flak, crashing circa 2150 into the Hindenburg
           F/S B Sterman               +    Strasse at Langenhagen in Hannover's northern
           F/O W R Elcoate RCAF        +    outskirts.  Wreckage was scattered over a radius
           F/S F Papple                +    of 800 to 1,000 metres.  Those who perished rest
           F/O F S Renton              +    in Hannover War Cemetery.
           Sgt K D Winstanley        pow


           571 Sqn          Mosquito XVI    ML942 8K-             Op: Berlin
           F/O F L Henry RNZAF              T/o 1710 Oakington.  Homebound, abandoned over
           F/S R A Stinson RAAF            France in the vicinity of Douai.  Neither air-
                                           man was hurt and both resumed operations on 22-2?
                                           January with a visit to Hannover.
```

Note. I am advised by Keith Wood, who has carried out a detailed study of 57 Squadron, that this Mosquito was amongst the first quartet of aircraft delivered to the Squadron on 12 April 1944 and is positively identified on 93 operational entries in the unit's records.

```
           578 Sqn           Halifax III    RG367 LK-O            Op: Hannover
           F/L R B Sledge                  T/o 1627 Burn.  Bombed the AP at 1922 and while
           Sgt W Atkins                    homebound was overtaken at 1940 by a 76 Squadron
           P/O J V Bouzek RCAF             Halifax MZ693 MP-F flown by F/S H L Ball RCAF. A
           F/O F W Asker                   collision occurred and F/L Sledge and crew, sub-
           F/S F G Fisher                  sequently, baled out near Sleidinge (Oost-Vlaan-
           F/S F Eplett                    deren), some 10 km NNW from the centre of Gent.
           F/S J Allen                     F/S Ball RCAF made a safe return and following
                                           repairs by 60 MU, his Halifax was put back into
           service on 17 February, just a few days before he lost his life on operations
           to Worms.


           635 Sqn           Lancaster III  PB564 F2-H            Op: Hannover
           F/L I B Hayes               pow    T/o Downham Market.  Believed crashed 1850 at
           F/L J Hendry               pow    Zuidvelde (Drenthe), 10 km NW from Assen.  It
           F/S A L Hall               pow    is believed F/L Hayes had completed 53 sorties
           F/L W M Douglas            evd    while W/O Clayton is reported to have arrived
           F/L J N Steel              pow    in the United Kingdom on 26 April.
           W/O R B Warner             pow
           F/S J W Emms               pow
           W/O A D Clayton            evd
```

Note. My grateful thanks to Hans de Haan and Olaf Timmermann for their fine work in tracing crash location details in respect of this operation. From the times of take off, it may be deduced the raid was split into two phases. For further details pertaining to the Hannover operation (and for the majority of all operations identified in this and previous volumes), readers should consult the AIR24 class records, held at the Public Record Office, which report an analysis of the bombing campaign through a numbered sequence of Bomber Command Intelligence Narrative of Operations summaries. Also, most useful is Martin Middlebrook and Chris Everitt's celebrated Bomber Command War Diaries.

```
6-7 Jan    10 Sqn            Halifax III    LV909 ZA-P            Op: Hanau
1945       F/L W D Harrow              +    T/o 1506 Melbourne.  Collided over Oberscheld
           F/S F J Walker             +    with a 415 Squadron Halifax, which fell near
           P/O R C Hollings           +    Eibach, 3 km E of Dillenburg.  F/L Harrow, an
           F/S A H Calvert            +    experienced bomber pilot with over 30 sorties
           F/S J Draper               +    to his credit, P/O Hollings and F/S Calvert lie
           Sgt M A Solomon            +    in Hannover War Cemetery.  The others have no
           F/S R W Thomas             +    known graves.


           51 Sqn            Halifax III    MZ811 MH-X            Op: Hanau
           P/O S J Bunn               +    T/o 1542 Snaith.  Of the four who died, three
           Sgt H Hardwick             +    are buried in Dürnbach War Cemetery, while
           F/S H R Smith             pow    panel 272 of the Runnymede Memorial commemorates
           F/S T W Richards           +    the name of F/S Richards.  It is reported that he
           Sgt C G Green             pow    survived after parachuting but was murdered soon
           Sgt N Wilcock             pow    after being captured.  Sgt Wilcock was very badly
           Sgt R V S Wilson           +    beaten before being taken into safe custody.
```

6-7 Jan
1945

103 Sqn	Lancaster III		PB637 PM-L	Op: Gardening

F/O C Pearton   +   T/o 1607 Elsham Wolds setting course for the
Sgt D Fell   +   Baltic. Lost without trace. All are commemorated
W/O S E Abrams   +   on the Runnymede Memorial. Sgt Fell and W/O
P/O H J Hutcheson RAAF   +   Abrams were regular airmen whose service numbers
W/O W E Burcher RAAF   +   indicate entry to the Royal Air Force circa 1938.
Sgt G Williams   +
Sgt C H Palmer   +

Note. A reliable private source in Holland offers the possibility that this
crew fell victim to Major Werner Huseman of I./NJG3.

158 Sqn	Halifax III		MZ366 NP-M	Op: Hanau

F/S K M Anderson RAAF   inj   T/o 1544 Lissett. On return to base, overshot
Sgt R D C Munday   inj   and crashed 2215 behind the Blue Post Inn at
Sgt H Lomas   inj   North Frodingham, 10 miles SSW of Bridlington,
Sgt K W T Sutton   inj   Yorkshire. Sgt Sutton died from his injuries
Sgt L Lamb   inj   and he is buried in Southport (St. Cuthbert)
Sgt S D Till   inj   Churchyard.
Sgt G O Tuohy   inj

Note. The crew had arrived at Lissett on 3 December 1944 and were engaged in
their sixth sortie; their Halifax was named "Lili Marlene". When written off
this bomber had taken part in sixty-two operational sorties.

158 Sqn	Halifax III		NR195 NP-I	Op: Hanau

F/O J J Krefter RAAF   +   T/o 1544 Lissett. Crashed 1850 at Grossauheim
Sgt A T Clyde   +   some 4 km SSE from the centre of Hanau and on
F/S L G Morgan   +   the E bank of the River Main. All are buried
Sgt J Gore   +   in Dürnbach War Cemetery.
F/O K R Nerney RAAF   +
Sgt E H M Barr   +
Sgt P S Cotterell   +

171 Sqn	Halifax III		NA687 6Y-A	Op: BS

F/L G Cox   +   T/o North Creake. Crashed near Ambly (Namur)
Sgt S R Fenwick   +   roughly 8 km ESE from Rochefort. All rest in
F/O R Maden   +   Ambly Communal Cemetery. W/O Davy was the
W/O A C Cheese   +   specialist equipment operator.
F/S A E Meekings   +
W/O F E T Davy   +
WO2 C D Mison RCAF   +
F/S C D C Farlie   +

218 Sqn	Lancaster I		LM187 XH-H	Op: Neuss

F/O D Banton   T/o 1557 Chedburgh. Thrown out of control at
Sgt W E Sims   +   19,000 feet in the target area and bombs were
F/O R Lillis   inj   jettisoned due to over speeding of the port
F/O J Griffin   outer engine. Height was lost and soon the
Sgt R P Longley   inj   Lancaster became near impossible to control.
Sgt S Brown   Abandoned and crashed 1936 at Nethen (Brabant)
Sgt S H Laity   some 10 km SSW from the centre of Leuven. Sgt
                                     Sims left the aircraft clinging to Sgt Longley
but fell to his death when Longley's parachute opened. In recognition of his
gallant attempt to save the life of a friend, Sgt Longley was awarded the CGM,
details being Gazetted on 13 April 1945. Badly injured after landing in a tree
and falling over twenty feet to the ground, Longley was to spend the next six
months in various hospitals. F/O Lillis was treated at 8 General Hospital
in Brussels for severe facial injuries. Nineteen year old Sgt Sims rests in
Heverlee War Cemetery.

415 Sqn	Halifax III		MZ456 6U-P	Op: Hanau

F/O L R Belcher RCAF   +   T/o 1542 East Moor. Lost in the circumstances
Sgt L D A Mawson   +   described in the summary reported for 10 Squadron.
F/O H P Breir RCAF   +   F/O Strosberg RCAF rests in Hannover War Cemetery
F/O M Strosberg RCAF   +   but his six companions have no known graves. F/O
F/O H C Irvine RCAF   +   Elgie RCAF was flying the fourth sortie of his
F/O S W Elgie RCAF   +   second tour of operations.
F/S N A Butler RCAF   +

6-7 Jan 1945	**431 Sqn**	**Lancaster X**	**KB821 SE-P**	**Op: Hanau**

431 Sqn   **Lancaster X**

F/L B M Adilman RCAF	+
F/O L K James RCAF	+
F/O G R Pool DFC RCAF	+
F/O F J Nickerson RCAF	+
F/O T McQuitty RCAF	+
F/O A W Staves RCAF	+
P/O W G Gillissie RCAF	+

KB821 SE-P   **Op: Hanau**

T/o 1504 Croft. Three rest in Dürnbach War Cemetery and four are perpetuated on the panels of the Runnymede Memorial. F/O Pool RCAF had initially trained as an air bomber and flew his first tour of duty in that capacity. He then re-mustered as a navigator and when killed was engaged on his second operational tour.

462 Sqn   **Halifax III**

P/O M W Rohrlach RAAF	+
Sgt J D Beardmore	+
Sgt J S Sanderson	+
F/S N S Scott	+
F/S D H Laurence RAAF	pow
F/S L G M Mannell RAAF	+
Sgt V C Topham	+
Sgt E G Baker	+

MZ469 Z5-N   **Op: BS**

T/o 1619 Foulsham. Those who died rest in Belgium at Hotton War Cemetery. F/S Mannell RAAF was the specialist equipment operator. Both air gunners were aged nineteen.

622 Sqn   **Lancaster I**

F/O E S Francis RAAF	+
Sgt R C Soanes	+
F/S A D Steeden	+
F/S G R Traylen	+
F/S W Kelly	+
F/S W McRae	+
F/S P A Christie	+

NF939 GI-D   **Op: Gardening**

T/o 1608 Mildenhall and set course for Danzig Bay. Lost without trace. All are commemorated on the Runnymede Memorial.

635 Sqn   **Lancaster III**

F/L J A Rowland RAAF	pow
F/S W R Hill	+
P/O C D Mackenzie	+
F/L H R Sindall	+
F/L I T Yanovich RNZAF	+
F/O J R Donald RAAF	+
F/O C F Jelley DFC	+
Sgt R Whybrow	+

PB228 F2-N   **Op: Hanau**

T/o 1550 Downham Market. Those who perished rest in Dürnbach War Cemetery. F/L Yanovich RNZAF was flying as a second air bomber. It is likely this aircraft exploded in flight, throwing clear F/L Rowland RAAF.

7-8 Jan 1945	**12 Sqn**	**Lancaster I**		

12 Sqn   **Lancaster I**

F/O R D K Hanbidge RCAF	+
Sgt R Rickeard	+
F/S G Flaxman	+
F/S H Croucher	+
F/S N G Prescott	+
F/S J Gynane RCAF	+
Sgt G Durnan RCAF	+

PB851 PH-S   **Op: Munchen**

T/o 1833 Wickenby. Lost without trace. All are commemorated on the Runnymede Memorial. F/O Hanbidge RCAF was the son of Robert Leith Hanbidge QC of Kerrobert, Saskatchewan. F/S Flaxman was 36, well above the average age of operational aircrew.

49 Sqn   **Lancaster III**

F/O A J Bolter	+
Sgt J Court	+
Sgt T E Walker	+
Sgt J T Sanderson	+
W/O F C Miller RAAF	+
Sgt A F Butcher	+
Sgt C L Atkins	+

PB586 EA-V   **Op: Munchen**

T/o 1650 Fulbeck. All are buried in France at Villeneuve-St-Georges Old Communal Cemetery. Two members of crew, Sgt Butcher and his fellow air gunner Sgt Atkins were, at 36 and 35 respectively, well over the age associated with Bomber Command aircrew.

103 Sqn   **Lancaster I**

F/O M A Mathieson RAAF	+
Sgt E W Evans	+
F/S H F Stephens	+
F/S J W Bickerton	+
F/S C T Pollard RAAF	+
Sgt D Sleep	+
Sgt R A Marett	+

NF999 PM-T   **Op: Munchen**

T/o 1821 Elsham Wolds. All are buried in Dürnbach War Cemetery. Sgt Sleep, aged 19, was an ex-ATC cadet, while his companion, Sgt Marett, had been called up under the provisions of the RAFVR Military Training Act of July 1939.

Note. Initially received on 1 September 1944 by 576 Squadron, this Armstrong Whitworth built Lancaster was transferred the next day to 103 Squadron. Between 24 September and 21 October it underwent local repairs for damage received on operations, continuing in use until reported missing from München.

7-8 Jan 1945	103 Sqn	Lancaster I	NN766 PM-R	Op: Munchen

P/O W J McArthur RCAF	+	T/o 1823 Elsham Wolds. Outbound, crashed onto
Sgt R P Candy	+	high ground near Hohrodberg (Haut-Rhin), 4 km
F/O R J Lougheed RCAF	+	N from the small town of Munster. Initially,
F/S M Greenstein RCAF	+	the crew were buried by local Nuns some 25 metres
WO2 M H Horne RCAF	+	from the point of impact, but since then their
F/S D J McAulay RCAF	+	bodies have been brought to the communal cemetery
F/S D F Campbell RCAF	+	at Munster. A memorial, however, has been placed
		at the crash site. F/O Lougheed RCAF was the son
		of Dr. M S Lougheed of Winnipeg.

Note. Nineteen airmen are buried in the French Department of Haut-Rhin; all gave their lives in the service of Bomber Command.

	106 Sqn	Lancaster I	PB724 ZN-N	Op: Munchen

F/O J N Scott	+	T/o 1650 Metheringham. It is believed that while
Sgt L D Knapman	+	over the target, an escape hatch was accidentally
F/O K C Darke	+	jettisoned. Homebound, the crew encountered snow
F/O R D Dunlop	+	showers, accompanied by very severe icing, and
Sgt H J Stunnel	inj	were obliged to descend. Thus, while flying low
Sgt J F Elson	+	the Lancaster flew into trees near the village
Sgt R D Needle	inj	of Meligny-le-Grand (Meuse), 10 km WSW of Void-
		Vacon. Those who died lie in Choloy War Cemetery.

	162 Sqn	Mosquito XXV	KB407 CR-R	Op: Hannover

W/O W J H Henley		T/o 2045 Bourn. During the operation, the main
Sgt J Clark		tank feed to the engines failed and the pilot of
		another Squadron Mosquito, F/L A J Marshall,

heard the crew on R/T saying they were about to bale out. Both did so and landed, unscathed, in safe hands near Venray, Holland.

	166 Sqn	Lancaster I	NG290 AS-B	Op: Munchen

F/O W Y J Soper RCAF	+	T/o 1820 Kirmington. Believed to have come down
Sgt J K Walker	+	near the town of Münsingen, about 50 km SE from
F/O G A Humberstone RCAF	+	Stuttgart. All now lie in Dürnbach War Cemetery.
F/O J K McLean RCAF	+	
F/S V D Elliott RCAF	+	
F/S J G MacKay RCAF	+	
F/S A E Wells RCAF	+	

	169 Sqn	Mosquito VI	PZ351 VI-	Op: BS

F/L B D Bonakis	+	T/o 2012 Great Massingham and headed for the
Sgt R S Garland	+	Mannheim area. Shot down by a night-fighter
		and fell 700 metres N of Aufstettin (Röttingen)

and about 6 km NE from Weikersheim. Both are buried in Dürnbach War Cemetery. Sgt Garland had been attached from 85 Squadron.

	170 Sqn	Lancaster III	PB397 TC-X	Op: Munchen

F/O N K Dunlop RAAF	+	T/o 1826 Hemswell. All are buried in Dürnbach
Sgt J H Pinsent	+	War Cemetery. Sgt Miller was a member of the
Sgt T Miller	+	Auxiliary Air Force and is likely to have begun
F/S R S Bennett	+	his service in the mid-1930s. F/S Bennett,
F/S J Mace	+	described in the CWGC register as a navigator,
Sgt P Day	+	was nineteen, as was Sgt Pinsent.
F/S C A Robinson	+	

	405 Sqn	Lancaster III	PB229 LQ-X	Op: Munchen

F/O L G Sparling RCAF	+	T/o 1950 Gransden Lodge. Believed to have
F/S R A Quinn RCAF	+	collided in the air with a 635 Squadron aircraft
F/O J Allan RCAF	+	crashing at Unterpfallenhofen, 19 km SSE from the
F/O L W Splatt RCAF	+	centre of Nürnberg. F/O Sparling RCAF, his flight
P/O N L W Scott RCAF	+	engineer and both air gunners rest in Dürnbach War
F/S D H Brown RCAF	+	Cemetery. The others have no known graves.
F/S D Veri RCAF	+	

Note. This Lancaster bore the unusual name of "Honk Tonk". Its career was some-what chequered with at least two spells of inactivity while undergoing repairs on site, the last being completed on 25 November 1944. The number of hours flown are not recorded.

7-8 Jan
1945

467 Sqn   **Lancaster III**   **JB286 PO-L**   **Op: Munchen**

F/O W A McNamee RAAF	+	
Sgt H W Kirsh	+	
F/S H J Williams RAAF	+	
F/S J D Gloury RAAF	+	
F/S S Servos RAAF	+	
F/S L J Saulwick RAAF	+	
F/S M B Bruckner RAAF	+	

T/o 1707 Waddington. After ten hours in the air this Lancaster crashed 0415 and exploded near the village of Eye, 3 miles NE from the centre of Peterborough. No bodies were found and it is thought likely the crew abandoned the aircraft while over the sea. All are commemorated on the Runnymede Memorial. F/S Gloury RAAF was the son of Cmdr John Arthur Gloury RAN. Their average age was twenty-one.

550 Sqn   **Lancaster I**   **NG363 BQ-P**   **Op: Munchen**

F/O C J Clarke RCAF	+	
Sgt J T Tunstall	+	
F/S H E Miell RCAF	+	
F/O A L Coldwell RCAF	pow	
Sgt L O Precieux	+	
F/S F W Bradley RCAF	+	
F/S L A J Gauthier RCAF	+	

T/o 1815 North Killingholme. Those who died rest in Dürnbach War Cemetery. Nineteen year old Sgt Precieux was the son of Jules Henri and Marie Alicia Fanellie Precieux of Phoenix on the island of Mauritius.

576 Sqn   **Lancaster I**   **PA173 UL-Q2**   **Op: Munchen**

F/O E L Saslove RCAF	+	
Sgt R Hoyle	pow	
F/O M Chisick RCAF	pow	
F/O G Davies	pow	
Sgt R F Hood RCAF	pow	
Sgt A S B Campton RCAF	+	
Sgt W G McClelland RCAF	+	

T/o 1815 Fiskerton. F/O Saslove RCAF and both air gunners are commemorated on the Runnymede Memorial.

619 Sqn   **Lancaster III**   **ND957 PG-M**   **Op: Munchen**

F/O C K Flockhart RAAF	+	
Sgt P S Graves	+	
Sgt R W Price	+	
F/S R W Keightley	+	
F/S E A Smith RAAF	+	
Sgt T L Letchford	+	
F/S A F Murdoch	+	

T/o 1654 Strubby. Homebound, disintegrated over St-Pierre. All now rest in Villeneuve-St-Georges Old Communal Cemetery. Their average age was twenty-one.

626 Sqn   **Lancaster I**   **LL961 UM-S2**   **Op: Munchen**

F/O R M Smith RCAF	+	
Sgt C J Lane		
F/O J K Yeaman RCAF		
F/O D Rymer RCAF		
F/S G M Magee RAAF		
F/S D F Crowe RCAF		
Sgt W McLean	+	

T/o 1844 Wickenby. Outbound, collided with a 150 Squadron Lancaster and abandoned just to the S of Laon in the Department of Aisne. F/O Smith RCAF now rests in the Canadian War Cemetery at Dieppe, while Sgt McLean is buried in Clichy New Communal Cemetery. The other Lancaster PB781, flown by F/L R J Rose RCAF, returned to Hemswell and was little damaged.

626 Sqn   **Lancaster III**   **JB661 UM-C2**   **Op: Munchen**

F/O K A Stroh RCAF	+	
Sgt E Leather	+	
WO2 D R Hutchins RCAF	+	
F/O J H Clark RCAF	+	
F/O J P H Terreau RCAF	+	
F/S W J Rahkola RCAF	+	
F/S K R Joslin RCAF	+	

T/o 1847 Wickenby. All are buried in Dürnbach War Cemetery. All were older than the average bomber crew with two in their 30s and the rest with the exception of 23 year old WO2 Hutchins RCAF, in their middle to late 20s.

630 Sqn   **Lancaster I**   **PD317 LE-G**   **Op: Munchen**

F/O G E Billings	inj	
Sgt S Harris	inj	
F/S A Hobson	+	
F/O L Knowles	inj	
Sgt J Duncan	inj	
Sgt D A Holloway	+	
F/S D Todd RAAF	inj	

T/o 1645 East Kirkby but the port inner engine failed soon after becoming airborne. Bombs were jettisoned and the crew returned to base but on touch down at 1759 the Lancaster bounced and the pilot opened the throttles in an attempt to go round again. However, the port wing dropped and the Lancaster cartwheeled across the airfield, F/O Billings sustaining injuries that necessitated the amputation of an arm. The two airmen who died are buried in their home towns. The remainder of the crew, it was subsequently reported, made a good recovery.

7-8 Jan 1945	635 Sqn	Lancaster III	PB173 F2-C	Op: München

F/L R M Clarke RAAF	+	T/o 1902 Downham Market. Believed lost in the
F/S T Robertshaw	+	manner as described in the 405 Squadron summary.
P/O W T Pethard	+	Five are commemorated on the Runnymede Memorial
P/O G K Hendy RAAF	+	but both air gunners are buried in Dürnbach War
F/S C D Mountain	+	Cemetery. It will be recalled that F/L Clarke
P/O A A Wiggins	+	RAAF had crashed, without injury to himself or
F/S J H Watson	+	to his crew, on 14 September 1944 (see Volume 5

page 423). The summary for this incident drew attention to his brother, P/O John Yorks Clarke RAAF who lost his life while flying with 158 Squadron the previous year (see Volume 4 page 292).

10-11 Jan 1945	128 Sqn	Mosquito XVI	PF403 M5-T	Op: Hannover

S/L R F L Tong	+	T/o 1707 Wyton. Banking steeply, control was
DFC Twice MID		lost and the Mosquito crashed into Cambridge
F/L M J M Lagesse DFC	+	Road, Godmanchester, Huntingdonshire. S/L Tong

is buried in Gravesend Cemetery; F/L Lagesse of Curepipe, Mauritius, who was a Barrister at Law, lies in Cambridge City Cemetery.

12 Jan 1945	9 Sqn	Lancaster I	NG257 WS-N	Op: Bergen

F/O E C Redfern DFC	+	T/o 0848 Bardney with a Tallboy and set course
F/S J W Williams	+	for the U-boat pens. Shot down over the target
Sgt R W R Cooper	+	area. All are commemorated on the Runnymede
F/O O P Hull	+	Memorial. F/O Redfern is believed to have
Sgt L G Roberts	+	participated in at least 39 operational sorties.
Sgt W Brand	+	
Sgt D Winch	+	

	105 Sqn	Mosquito XVI	MM226 GB-	Op: Bochum

F/O J L De Beer		T/o 1645 Bourn but swung to port and the left
F/L L Tierney		main wheel dug into a pile of hard frozen snow

causing the undercarriage to collapse.

	617 Sqn	Lancaster I	NF992 KC-B	Op: Bergen

F/O I S Ross RAAF	+	T/o 0846 Woodhall Spa armed with a Tallboy and
F/S W Walter	+	briefed to attack the U-boat pens. Came down
W/O S R Anderson DFM	+	in the sea circa 1315 off the Norwegian coast,
P/O E G Tilby	+	this being witnessed by other Squadron crews
F/O M Ellwood DFM MID	+	and, subsequently, an ASR Warwick dropped a
F/S L D Griffiths	+	lifeboat. Sadly, six are commemorated on the
F/S A F McKellar	+	Runnymede Memorial, while F/O Ellwood is now

buried in Trondheim (Stavne) Cemetery having been washed ashore on 13 March 1945 and laid to rest in Nesna Cemetery. His DFM, gained during service with 97 Squadron, had been Gazetted on 29 December 1942, while that awarded to W/O Anderson had been published on 14 September 1943 following service with 467 Squadron. Apart from the two DFM holders, all had forced-landed in Russia on 11 September 1944 (see Volume 5 page 416).

Note. Robert Owen, to whom I am indebted for notes pertaining to 617 Squadron, writes that F/O Ellwood had participated in the fateful daylight raid on Augsburg in April 1942 (see Volume 3 pages 71 and 72 for details). His posting to 617 Squadron had been effective on 18 January 1944, and between then and his date of death, he had taken part in 29 sorties, bringing his overall score to sixty-three.

	617 Sqn	Lancaster I	PD233 KC-G	Op: Bergen

F/L H J Pryor DFC	pow	T/o 0840 Woodhall Spa similarly armed and tasked.
W/O A L Winston	pow	Crashed at Lille Landon on Austrheim, an area of
F/O H Ellis DFC	pow	Norway NW of Bergen. F/L Kendrick is believed to
F/L G A Kendrick	inj	have died from his wounds on 15 January, though
P/O A Hepworth	pow	his entry in the Bergen (Mollendal) Church
F/L E N Armstrong DFC	pow	Cemetery register shows 12 January. W/O Temple's
W/O E C Temple DFM	pow	DFM had been Gazetted on 12 November 1943. Both

had been involved in serious crashes with 617 Squadron (see Volume 5 page 36 and Volume 4 page 259 respectively). Flying with the crew on this sortie was the Squadron's Gunnery Leader, F/L Armstrong.

Note. Flight Lieutenant Kendrick is reported to have baled out but likely struck his head as he did not deploy his parachute. He was found, lying in deep snow, with severe scalp wounds and back injuries.

12-13 Jan 1945	77 Sqn	Halifax III	MZ812 KN-X	Op: Gardening

F/L M P Braund	+	T/o 1745 Full Sutton. Lost without trace. All
Sgt G F Rutherford	+	are commemorated on the Runnymede Memorial. F/L
F/O A T Hewett	+	Braund's twin brother, F/L John Prower Braund,
F/O J A Masheder	+	died a month later while engaged on mine laying
Sgt L F Connell	+	duties. He, too, served with 77 Squadron and
Sgt J Donaldson	+	the service numbers of the twins indicate they
Sgt D Atkinson	+	were commissioned on the same day.

424 Sqn	Halifax III	LV998 QB-Y	Op: Gardening

F/O M C Grant RCAF	+	T/o 1724 Skipton-on-Swale for mine laying duties
Sgt J Pollard	+	off Flensburg. Of those who perished, three were
F/O J G Agnew RCAF	pow	laid to rest in Denmark on 20 January in Abenra
F/O M G Fife RCAF	+	Cemetery; F/S Archer RCAF has no known grave,
F/S C T Reilly RCAF	+	while Sgt Pollard and F/O Fife RCAF are buried
F/S W E Archer RCAF	+	in Kiel War Cemetery.
F/S R C Carnegie RCAF	+	

Note. Abenra Cemetery contains the graves of 154 service personnel. Of this total, at least 141 died in the service of Bomber Command. The crew summarised above and that appearing below were the last reported missing from 424 Squadron as a Halifax equipped squadron.

424 Sqn	Halifax III	MZ805 QB-X	Op: Gardening

F/O A M Mackie DFC RCAF	+	T/o 1722 Skipton-on-Swale similarly tasked. Lost
Sgt J J Farquhar	+	without trace. The Memorial at Runnymede perpet
F/S J S Netzke RCAF	+	uates their names.
F/O H D Christie RCAF	+	
WO1 H A Carruthers RCAF	+	
F/S F W Dobbs RCAF	+	
F/S C H Hudson RCAF	+	

429 Sqn	Halifax III	NR173 AL-D	Op: Gardening

F/L A R Milner RCAF	pow	T/o 1718 Leeming similarly tasked. Two W/T
Sgt K Turner	pow	messages were intercepted from this aircraft,
F/O H K Frair RCAF	pow	the first at 2131 indicating the crew were
F/O R H Barnes RCAF	pow	preparing to bale out. Four minutes later,
WO1 H L Johnson RCAF	pow	a second message gave their position as 5520N
F/S O H Sulek RCAF	pow	0858E.
F/S J G Small RCAF	pow	

13 Jan 1945	195 Sqn	Lancaster I	HK686 A4-E	Op: Saarbrucken

F/O E J Cotter	T/o 1144 Wratting Common to bomb railway yards.
Sgt J A Edey	While over France an oil leak developed in the
Sgt R Holmes	starboard inner engine, resulting in the motor
F/S V W Martin	catching fire. The flames spread rapidly and
F/O D C Roberts	the order to bale out was given, the Lancaster
Sgt W T Coxon	crashing 1515 near Epernay in the Department of
Sgt A Cassley	the Marne. It is thought five members of crew
	were injured, three seriously.

428 Sqn	Lancaster X	KB793 NA-E	Training

P/O W S McMullen RCAF	+	T/o 1749 Middleton St. George with its crew
F/S Dykes RCAF	inj	of six briefed for a cross-country exercise.

Late in the flight, the port inner engine caught fire and the order to abandon was given. Fearful that his aircraft might crash on Darlington, P/O McMullen RCAF remained at the controls until he was certain the bomber was clear of the built up area. By this time it was too late for him to bale out and he died in the ensuing crash at 2049 at Lingfield Farm. His grave is in Harrogate (Stonefall) Cemetery. In recognition of this selfless act, Darlington City Council has since named a road in his memory and placed a cairn at the crash site. Apart from F/S Dykes RCAF, the mid-upper air gunner, no other names are mentioned in the Squadron ORB.

Note. I am extremely grateful to Bill Baguley for sending much of the detail used in this summary and, in addition, I acknowledge his unstinting labours in perusing the information reported in They Shall Grow Not Old, that wonderful tribute to those who lost their lives in the service of the Royal Canadian Air Force.

13-14 Jan 1945	**77 Sqn**	**Halifax III**	**MZ321 KN-Q**	**Op: Saarbrucken**

W/C J D R Forbes AFC
Sgt A G Evans
F/O N Laidler
F/O J W Beale
F/O A P Pemberton
F/O B E Holmes
F/O J A Kennedy

T/o 1532 Full Sutton but the starboard outer caught fire and the Halifax was forced-landed circa 1545 on farmland 1 mile NE of Stamford Bridge, 7 miles ENE from the centre of York. The crew escaped with only superficial injuries. Some debris is reported to have finished up in the River Derwent.

Note. I have pleasure in acknowledging the help given by Roy Walker, who has been instrumental in publishing a Roll of Honour for 77 Squadron, titled Some Of The Many.

347 Sqn　　　　　　**Halifax III**　　**LL590 L8-L**　　　　　　**Op: Saarbrucken**

Adj E Jouzier FFAF　　　　　+
Adj M Humbert FFAF
Cne R Brachet FFAF　　　　　+
Ltn C Habez FFAF
Sgt R Rigade FFAF
Sgt R Memin FFAF
Sgc R Malterre FFAF　　　　　+

T/o 1510 Elvington. At approximately 2010 French time, struck from behind by a Halifax from 51 Squadron and was partially abandoned before crashing at Guerny (Eure), 10 km SW of Gisors in the neighbouring Department of Oise. The other Halifax, MZ465 MH-Y piloted by F/O A L Wilson, lost nine feet from nose, taking with it the navigator and air bomber (F/S T S H Whitehouse and F/S D Hauber) but was subsequently landed at Ford airfield in Sussex. F/S Whitehouse is buried in Berthenonville Churchyard; F/S Hauber lies at Rouen in the extension to St-Sever Cemetery.

515 Sqn　　　　　　**Mosquito VI**　　**PZ465 3P-**　　　　　　**Op: BS**

S/L C V Bennett DFC　　　　　+
F/L R A Smith　　　　　　　　+

T/o 1648 Little Snoring to patrol the Husum-Jagel region of NW Germany. Lost without trace. Both are commemorated on the Runnymede Memorial. S/L Bennett was aged 33, his navigator was thirty-seven.

619 Sqn　　　　　　**Lancaster I**　　**PB842 PG-Y**　　　　　　**Op: Politz**

F/O B P Curran RAAF　　　int
Sgt D H Drew　　　　　　　int
F/S R I Wilson　　　　　int
F/S M P B Quigley　　　int
Sgt J Haigh　　　　　　　int
F/S F A M Blakeley　　　int
F/S F W Roots　　　　　　int

T/o 1652 Strubby to attack an oil plant. Bombed successfully, but while clearing the target area came under attack from a Me 410, which in turn was claimed destroyed by return fire from F/S Roots. With its No.1 port fuel tank ruptured, the Lancaster was flown to Sweden, landing at Rinkaby. In due course, repairs were carried out and the crew, with a Swedish officer escorting, ferried their aircraft to Linköping, where it was stored until being broken down for scrap in 1946. Most of the crew left Stockholm, by Dakota, for home on 10 March.

630 Sqn　　　　　　**Lancaster I**　　**PB880 LE-B**　　　　　　**Op: Politz**

F/O J W Langley　　　　　int
Sgt J R Thomas　　　　　int
F/S G B Gaughan　　　　　int
F/S I J Penglase RAAF　int
W/O S H Potter RNZAF　　int
W/O E J Edwards　　　　　inj
F/S T W Panting RCAF　　int

T/o 1628 East Kirkby similarly tasked. Outbound, the starboard outer gave cause for concern and while passing over Denmark the unit caught fire. All attempts to quell the flames and feather the propeller failed and after gaining the coast of Sweden, the crew began to bale out from 8,000 feet in the vicinity of Bastad. Sadly, W/O Edwards struck the tailplane and sustained head injuries of such severity that he died the following day. He is buried in the municipal cemetery at Hälsingborg (Pälsjö). All had returned to the UK by 19 April. Although not unique, it was unusual to have three Commonwealth air forces represented in one crew.

Note. An excellent account of the two incidents, here referred too, appear in Making For Sweden, Part 1 - The RAF 1939 to 1945, written by Rolph Wegmann and Bo Widfeldt and published in the UK by Air Research Publications.

14 Jan 1945	**105 Sqn**	**Mosquito IX**	**ML902 GB-**	**Transit**

F/L T C Walmsey
F/O E Povey DFM

T/o 1217 Manston but the port engine faltered causing a swing and loss of the undercarriage. The crew, neither of whom were hurt, had landed at Manston following operations to Saarbrücken on 13-14 January. F/O Povey had served with 207 Squadron and details of his award had appeared in the London Gazette on 14 May 1943.

| 14 Jan 1945 | 105 Sqn | Mosquito IX | ML922 GB- | Op: Saarbrucken |

F/L D Tidy
F/L G H Barr DFC

T/o 1246 Bourn. Unable to attack following loss of power from the starboard engine, thus necess-itated an emergency landing at Brussels-Evere. Repairs were not put in hand and the Mosquito was struck off charge on 7 June.

| | 408 Sqn | Halifax VII | NP798 EQ-J | Ground |

Caught fire at 1245 while being made ready for operations to Grevenbroich and exploded. There are no reports of injuries.

| | 425 Sqn | Halifax III | MZ466 KW-P | Training |

F/O J W R Walsh RCAF	+
Sgt K M Hillis RCAF	+
F/O J J R Gingrass RCAF	+
F/O R J Dubeau RCAF	+
WO2 J J M Simard RCAF	+
F/S R O Custeau RCAF	inj
F/S J L A Chauvin RCAF	+

T/o 1851 Tholthorpe for a cross-country flight. At 2145 the Halifax flew into the ground near Whitestone Cliff, moments after breaking from cloud, roughly 1 mile NE of Dialstone Farm, near Thirsk, Yorkshire. Those who died were buried in Harrogate (Stonefall) Cemetery. The sole survivor was pulled from the wreckage by a local inhabitant, who was later honoured for his brave actions, and taken to RAF Hospital Northallerton with multiple fractures.

| 14-15 Jan 1945 | 9 Sqn | Lancaster I | NN722 WS-Z | Op: Leuna |

F/O K A Cook RAAF	+
Sgt H Taylor	+
F/S R Watt	+
F/S B C MacKnight RAAF	+
F/S M J McNamara RAAF	+
F/S J E B MacLean RAAF	+
F/S M J Kerrigan RAAF	pow

T/o 1621 Bardney to bomb a synthetic oil plant. Almost certain to have crashed in Germany and likely that the graves of those who died in the crash were found by US authorities as they now rest in France at Choloy War Cemetery. The tail gunner, F/S Kerrigan RAAF, died in captivity on 22 March and he is buried in Berlin 1939-1945 War Cemetery.

Note. Harry Holmes imparts the useful information that this Lancaster was badly damaged on 17-18 December 1944, while attacking München. A repair team was sent from AV Roe, arriving on site on 21 December, and following 566.25 man hours of labour, NN722 was declared ready for use on 2 January. Total costs in labour and materials amounted to £107 6s 5d.

| | 12 Sqn | Lancaster III | LM714 PH-L | Op: Leuna |

F/O J B Murray RCAF	pow
Sgt E J Burke	pow
F/O K G Gutensohn RCAF	+
F/O E W Rech RCAF	+
F/S K MacDonald RAAF	pow
Sgt F T White	+
Sgt J Robertson	+

T/o 1922 Wickenby similarly tasked. Shot down by Ofw Schmidt, II./NJG6 flying a Me 110 out from Mainz-Finthen, crashing 2310 near Steindorf some 3 km SW from the centre of Wetzlar. Those who died were buried at Steindorf Friedhof and were subsequently handed over from the local Bürgermeister to the Officer Commanding No.3 Section of 85 Graves Concentration Unit (British) in April 1947, and on the 24th of that same month taken to Hannover War Cemetery.

Note. I am grateful to Claudio Michael Becker for this very precise information.

| | 50 Sqn | Lancaster I | LM234 VN-K | Op: Leuna |

F/O A H Nicol RAAF	+
Sgt D F Kirby	+
F/O A M Young	+
F/S W E Boutcher RAAF	+
F/S H L Wilson RAAF	+
Sgt L P Duffy	pow
Sgt W S McClelland	pow

T/o 1555 Skellingthorpe similarly tasked. Hit by flak and crashed near Reichmannsdorf, in the heart of the Forst Reichmannsdorf, 14 km SW from Saalfeld. Those who died are buried in Berlin 1939-1945 War Cemetery.

| | 61 Sqn | Lancaster III | LM720 QR- | Op: Leuna |

F/O W G Corewyn	+
Sgt P R Earl	+
F/S R C Battersby	+
F/S E J Boakes	+
F/S S J James	+
Sgt J Douglas	+
Sgt R Richardson	+

T/o 1630 Skellingthorpe similarly tasked. On return flew into a radar mast on Bord Hill and crashed 0121 near Langham airfield, Norfolk. Poor weather conditions and the possibility that the crew may have received a garbled W/T message advising the destination of a diversionary air-field are thought to have been contributory factors in this accident. All rest in various United Kingdom cemeteries.

14-15 Jan **85 Sqn**   **Mosquito NF.30**   **MV565 VY-**   **Op: BS**
1945
F/L C B Bryan   +   T/o Swannington for high level support of both
F/L H Wood   +   the Leuna raid and operations over the Ruhr.
                                     Towards the end of the patrol, the crew called
to say they were low on fuel and a vector to Woodbridge was given. A second
R/T message indicated the crew were coming in to land, but nothing further was
heard. However, a local ROC post logged an aircraft going into the sea roughly
1 mile off the Suffolk port of Felixstowe and the timings of this report and
the second R/T call practically coincide. Both are commemorated on the
Runnymede Memorial. F/L Wood came from Salisbury in Southern Rhodesia.

106 Sqn   **Lancaster III**   **PB122 ZN-Y**   **Op: Leuna**
F/O D R McIntosh RAAF   +   T/o 1610 Metheringham to bomb a synthetic oil
Sgt F A Kendall   +   plant. Homebound, when at 2359 the Lancaster
F/S R A Quiney   +   flew into the ground at an acute angle near
F/S R H Thompson   +   Vignacourt (Somme), 16 km NW of Amiens. All lie
F/S W H Butt RAAF   +   in the extension to St-Sever cemetery at Rouen.
Sgt G Fletcher   +   Their average age was 22, with their skipper
Sgt D S Ford   +   being the oldest at thirty-one. F/S Thompson
                                     came from Livingstone in Northern Rhodesia.

128 Sqn   **Mosquito XVI**   **MM194 M5-K**   **Op: Berlin**
F/O A W Heitmann RAAF   +   T/o 2100 Wyton.. Partially abandoned, after
P/O A N Gould   running out of fuel, before crashing 0234 near
                                     Chatteris, Cambridgeshire. F/O Heitmann RAAF
is buried in Cambridge City Cemetery; his navigator landed unharmed.

128 Sqn   **Mosquito XVI**   **PF401 M5-G**   **Op: Berlin**
F/O D H Swain   T/o 2102 Wyton. Overshot 0202 on return to
P/O M E Bayon   base and crash-landed. No injuries reported.

128 Sqn   **Mosquito XVI**   **PF404 M5-H**   **Op: Berlin**
F/O T J S Adam   +   T/o 2101 Wyton but the starboard engine failed
F/S A J Casey RAAF   +   and the crew died while trying to force-land
                                     three minutes later at Woodhurst, 5 miles NE
of Huntingdon. Both are buried in Cambridge City Cemetery.

128 Sqn   **Mosquito XVI**   **PF437 M5-**   **Op: Berlin**
F/O H E Boulter   T/o 2106 Wyton. Homebound, abandoned 0216 out
Sgt C Hart   of fuel, both airmen landing near the airfield.

139 Sqn   **Mosquito XVI**   **MM132 XD-**   **Op: Berlin**
S/L R J G Green DFC & Bar   +   T/o 2105 Upwood. While making a beam guided
F/L J H Robson DFC   +   approach to Little Staughton airfield, Hunt-
                                     ingdonshire, the Mosquito flew into a tree and
crashed 0200 roughly 1 mile short of the runway. Visibility at the time was
extremely poor. Both officers were taken for burial in their native Yorkshire.

139 Sqn   **Mosquito XX**   **KB263 XD-P**   **Op: Berlin**
F/L P J Drane DFC   +   T/o 2105 Upwood. While trying to get into
F/O K Swale DFC   +   Thurleigh aerodrome, Bedfordshire, in weather
                                     conditions described as appalling, the Mosquito
clipped a hedge and crashed 0215 in the airfield circuit. Both are buried in
their home towns.

223 Sqn   **Liberator IV**   **TT336 6G-R 44-10597**   **Op: BS**
F/L G Noseworthy RCAF   T/o 1606 Oulton for Jostle duties in support of
Sgt A L Evens RCAF   +   the Grevenbroich raid. Either hit by Allied AA
F/O G R Palmer RAAF   inj   fire (as suggested in Squadron records) or des-
Sgt R Hartop   +   patched by a night-fighter, at 6,000 feet near
F/S W A Gray RCAF   +   Meerhout (Antwerpen), a small town some 8 km SE
W/O J G Galley DFM   +   of Geel. Those who died, including F/O Palmer
W/O R E Ralph   +   RAAF who lived long enough to be admitted to
F/O F A Mason   +   hospital, rest in Leopoldsburg War Cemetery.
F/L G Trail   +   W/O Galley had served with 15 Squadron, his DFM
F/S D K Clark RCAF   +   being Gazetted on 22 August 1941.
Sgt J Mellers

Note. This was the first Liberator reported lost from 223 Squadron.

14-15 Jan	300 Sqn	Lancaster I	PA160 BH-E		Op: Leuna
1945	F/O M Kozubski PAF				

14-15 Jan 1945

300 Sqn **Lancaster I** PA160 BH-E Op: Leuna
F/O M Kozubski PAF
Sgt A Jackowski PAF
P/O A Kosciukiewicz PAF
Sgt E Micko PAF
Sgt M Perlak PAF
Sgt G Sigall PAF
Sgt T Niemiec PAF

T/o 1916 Faldingworth to bomb an oil refinery. Returned to base and was flying downwind when it hit the ground at 0325 near Goltho Hall in the airfield circuit. Four of the crew were injured, one seriously, though none are named in the Squadron records.

415 Sqn **Halifax III** NA611 6U-T Op: Grevenbroich
F/S E F Sirtonald RCAF inj
Sgt D L Broughton inj
F/S M Campbell RCAF inj
F/O G T Abel RCAF
F/S F Fasang RCAF inj
F/S E H Engman RCAF inj
Sgt W Dekur RCAF inj
F/S E L Gates RCAF

T/o 1553 East Moor but swung out of control and finished up in woods bordering the airfield. The Halifax caught fire, but all escaped serious injury, though most needed treatment for minor burns. Apart from Sgt Dekur RCAF, the mid-under air gunner, the crew had arrived at East Moor from 76(RCAF) Base on 30 December 1944.

419 Sqn **Lancaster X** KB769 VR-I Op: Leuna
F/L G O Tedford RCAF +
Sgt R J Williams +
F/O J Q Eddy RCAF pow
F/O G D Spencer RCAF +
P/O C S Thomson RCAF +
F/S H M Rumball RCAF +
F/S A G McKay RCAF +

T/o 1842 Middleton St. George to bomb synthetic oil production plant. Homebound, intercepted by a night-fighter and set on fire. F/O Eddy RCAF parachuted, landing amongst trees and escaping serious injury. Those who died lie in Hannover War Cemetery, having been brought here from graves discovered at Bad Neustadt an der Saale. At 37, Sgt Williams was well over the age normally associated with operational airmen. F/S Rumball RCAF is described in the CWGC register as a navigator.

419 Sqn **Lancaster X** KB799 VR-W Op: Leuna
F/O N R Vatne RCAF +
Sgt B C Mitchell RCAF pow
F/O H R Eager RCAF pow
F/O N V Hoas RCAF pow
F/S E Chatwin RCAF pow
F/S R C Woods RCAF pow
P/O G C Woods RCAF pow

T/o 1847 Middleton St. George similarly tasked. Hit by flak while leaving the target area, both main fuel tanks being holed. Course set for the Allied lines but the engines failed and the order to abandon was given. Six did so, but F/O Vatne RCAF failed to get clear; he is buried in Rheinberg War Cemetery.

431 Sqn **Lancaster X** KB806 SE-X Op: Leuna
F/O M A MacLeod RCAF +
Sgt J Mann +
F/O C Gurevitch RCAF +
F/O G R R H Craib RCAF +
F/S C B Macdonell RCAF +
WO2 O J Rau RCAF +
F/S D C Cockwell RCAF pow

T/o 1848 Croft similarly tasked. Collided with a Me 109 over the target area and exploded, throwing clear F/S Cockwell RCAF. Those who perished are buried in Berlin 1939-1945 War Cemetery.

432 Sqn **Halifax VII** NP691 QO-V Op: Grevenbroich
F/L A R A Bews RCAF

T/o 1530 East Moor tasked to destroy railway yards. Bombed the AP at 1938 from 18,500 feet but eleven minutes later, having descended to 14,000 feet, came under attack from a night-fighter whose fire shot away the tail wheel and punched several holes through the starboard wing. Landed 2143, without injury to the crew, and subsequently written off as beyond economical repair.

460 Sqn **Lancaster III** ND822 AR-N Op: Leuna
P/O G D Walker RAAF +
Sgt J G Forrest +
F/S R W Hamilton RAAF +
F/S K Hutchings RAAF +
F/S E R Winton RAAF +
F/S L R Barnden RAAF +
F/S B B Peterson RAAF inj

T/o 1903 Binbrook to attack synthetic oil producing plant. Heard, faintly, on R/T at 2148 and landing instructions were passed. Nothing further was heard and at 2214 the Lancaster crashed near Ludford Magna airfield in Lincolnshire. F/S Peterson RAAF died from his burns on 20 January; with the other RAAF members of crew he rests in Cambridge City Cemetery. Sgt Forrest is buried at Hebburn Cemetery on the south bank of the River Tyne and well known to sailors who survived the torpedoing of HMS Kelly in the North Sea on 9 May 1940.

14-15 Jan	462 Sqn	Halifax III	LL598 Z5-A	Op: BS

1945

F/O A E Astill RAAF   +
Sgt G A Sandy   inj
F/S P Swarbrick RAAF   +
W/O S J Minett RAAF   +
W/O S R Fuller RAAF   +
Sgt L E Miles   +
F/S M G Isaac RAAF   +
F/S N O Reed RAAF   inj

T/o 1633 Foulsham but having climbed to around 4,000 feet, the starboard outer caught fire. Feathering action was initiated, but soon afterwards the propeller began to windmill. Orders to bale out were given, but only two got away (both being badly injured on landing) before the starboard wing came off, causing the Halifax to crash 1703 some 2 miles W of Shipdham airfield, Norfolk. Those who died rest in Cambridge City Cemetery.

463 Sqn	Lancaster I	NG193 JO-D	Op: Leuna

F/O R A Leonard RAAF   pow
Sgt R C Kimber   pow
F/S K M Vaughan RAAF   pow
F/L D L Dickson RAAF   pow
F/S V G Dingey RAAF   pow
F/S E E Evans RAAF   pow
F/S G F Chomley RAAF   pow

T/o 1631 Waddington to attack synthetic oil producing plant.

571 Sqn	Mosquito XVI	ML976 8K-A	Op: Berlin

F/O J Maddocks   +
F/S J Phillips   +

T/o 1746 Oakington. Attempted to land at Brussels-Melsbroek but the weather was very foggy and while trying to locate the runway, the Mosquito flew into a tree and crashed. Both rest in Brussels Town Cemetery.

578 Sqn	Halifax III	MZ583 LK-S	Op: Dulmen

F/O D Connop RNZAF   +
Sgt A G Briggs   +
P/O W J R Williams   +
P/O J W J Pringle   +
P/O E A Steele   +
F/O J Whitter DFM   +
F/S D W Andrews   +
F/O E H Rhodes   +

T/o 1852 Burn to attack a Luftwaffe fuel storage depot. All are buried in the Reichswald Forest War Cemetery. F/O Whitter flew with 76 Squadron during 1943, sharing in the destruction of at least two enemy aircraft. His DFM was published on 29 February 1944. F/S Andrews was manning the mid-under gun position.

625 Sqn	Lancaster I	PD388 CF-Z	Op: Leuna

F/O H W Hazell DFC   +
Sgt O J Pulford   +
P/O S Sellers   +
F/O M J Shenton   +
F/S J E Hughes   pow
Sgt A W Hall   +
Sgt W J Harrison   pow

T/o 1914 Kelstern to a bomb a synthetic oil plant. Of those who died, four are commemorated on the Runnymede Memorial, but Sgt Pulford's body was discovered in the Eifel region of Germany on 8 March, near Dümpelfeld, some 6 km N of Adenau. It is likely he was found by American forces as he was taken to Belgium and interred at Henri-Chapelle. His grave is now in Hotton War Cemetery. At 40, Sgt Hall was well above the age associated with operational aircrew.

626 Sqn	Lancaster I	LL959 UM-A2	Op: Leuna

F/L D S Nelson RCAF   pow
Sgt O Old   +
F/O T R Murray DFC RCAF   +
F/O V H Halstead RCAF   +
F/O R J Lacey   +
F/S A M O Walker RCAF   +
F/S C C Merriman RCAF   +

T/o 1905 Wickenby similarly tasked. Exploded S of the target area, ejecting F/L Nelson RCAF. Of the six who perished, three rest in Berlin 1939-1945 War Cemetery and three are commemorated on the Runnymede Memorial.

692 Sqn	Mosquito XVI	MM128 P3-	Op: Berlin

F/O G R P Chaundy DFM   +
F/S G F Ayre RAAF   +

T/o 2106 Graveley. Both are buried at Antwerpen in the city's Schoonselhof Cemetery. F/O Chaundy had served in the Middle East with 148 Squadron, details of his DFM having appeared in the London Gazette on 23 March 1943.

692 Sqn	Mosquito XVI	MM150 P3-	Op: Berlin

F/O J P Morgan RNZAF   +
Sgt J A McK Sturrock   +

T/o 2109 Graveley. Ran low on fuel and at 0240 the crew baled out near Greenham Common airfield in Berkshire. F/O Morgan RNZAF struck the fin and failed to open his parachute, while 19 year old Sgt Sturrock for unknown reasons released his 'chute before reaching the ground. He rests in Great Northern London Cemetery, East Barnet; his pilot is in Cambridge City Cemetery.

| 14-15 Jan | 1666 CU | Lancaster I | HK756 ND- | Op: Sweepstake |

14-15 Jan 1945   1666 CU   Lancaster I   HK756 ND-   Op: Sweepstake

F/O V R Adams RCAF +   T/o Wombleton as part of a diversionary sweep
Sgt L F B Goodwin RCAF +   by aircraft drawn from training establishments
F/O J Klatman RCAF +   Lost without trace. The Memorial at Runnymede
F/O W A Booth RCAF +   perpetuates their names. F/O Adams RCAF was
F/S W A Wegenast RCAF +   aged nineteen and as such was amongst the
Sgt M La V Long RCAF +   youngest Canadian pilots to lose his life
Sgt W H G Field RCAF +   in operational circumstances.

16-17 Jan 1945   10 Sqn   Halifax III   LW167 ZA-O   Op: Magdeburg

F/O W E L Whitbread +   T/o 1836 Melbourne. Lost without trace. All
Sgt E H Giles +   are commemorated on the Runnymede Memorial.
F/S E W S Tomkins +
F/S R S Must +
F/S H E Derrington +
Sgt H L Watkins +
F/S A G Hopkins +

10 Sqn   Halifax III   NA237 ZA-C   Op: Magdeburg

F/O A J Marshall +   T/o 1831 Melbourne. Shot down by a night-
Sgt A H Griffiths +   fighter and crashed 2230 at Hörsum, 20 km SSW
Sgt W F Paxton pow   from the centre of Hildesheim. Those who died
F/S K D Lawrence pow   rest in Hannover War Cemetery.
F/S D H Elsome pow
Sgt J Thornley +
Sgt R C Tuck pow

12 Sqn   Lancaster I   LM213 PH-G   Op: Zeitz

F/O W Kerluk RCAF +   T/o 1730 Wickenby to bomb the Braunkohle-Benzin
Sgt F J Tate +   synthetic oil plant. Those who perished now lie
F/O D J Bailey RCAF +   in the Reichswald Forest War Cemetery. Sgt Tate
Sgt W J Glass RCAF +   was an ex-ATC cadet from Douglas on the Isle of
Sgt G J Harris +   Man.
Sgt D E Linington RCAF +
Sgt A F Hymers RCAF pow

12 Sqn   Lancaster I   NN712 PH-A   Op: Zeitz

F/O S P Whyte RCAF +   T/o 1729 Wickenby similarly tasked. Crashed
Sgt J D Griffin +   between the small town of Büdingen and the
Sgt R Redmond +   village of Dudenrod, some 4 km to the north.
F/O L W Ferguson RCAF +   Those who died are buried in Dürnbach War
Sgt H J Smalley +   Cemetery.
F/O A L Staley RCAF pow
F/L J H Marsh +

23 Sqn   Mosquito VI   RS507 YP-C   Op: BS

F/L T Anderson-Smith pow   T/o 1739 Little Snoring for intruder duties
F/O A C Cockayne +   over Stendal. Crashed 2130 at Beckedorf, 3 km
SW from the centre of Hermannsburg, where 35
year old F/O Cockayne was buried in the local Friedhof. Since 1945, his body
has been exhumed and taken to Becklingen War Cemetery. Prior to volunteering
for war service, he had been a schoolmaster. On his release from captivity,
F/L Anderson-Smith was admitted to RAF Hospital Wroughton.

Note. This crew were within two operational sorties of completing their tour.
Their aircraft was from a batch of 109 Mosquitoes, manufactured at the parent
company's plant at Hatfield, and delivered to service between October 1944
and January 1945.

51 Sqn   Halifax III   LW461 MH-Y   Op: Magdeburg

F/O E M Popplewell +   T/o 1848 Snaith. Those who lost their lives lie
F/S J J Atkinson +   in Becklingen War Cemetery. WO2 Hisette RCAF of
F/S D L Johns +   Cornwallis, Nova Scotia, held a Bachelor of Arts
WO2 A J J Hisette RCAF +   degree, while F/S Muddiman's service number
F/S A A Muddiman +   indicates he had been accepted for pilot training
Sgt R A Boydell pow   with the pre-war Royal Air Force (Volunteer
Sgt L Annis +   Reserve), though as will be realised, he was
to subsequently qualify as a wireless operator.

16–17 Jan	75 Sqn	Lancaster I		PB761 AA-Y	Op: Wanne-Eickel

16–17 Jan
1945

75 Sqn   **Lancaster I**   **PB761 AA-Y**   **Op: Wanne-Eickel**

F/L T D Blewett RNZAF	+
Sgt R H Hunswicks	inj
F/S B T Cornell	inj
F/O J S Wilson RNZAF	+
W/O J Smyrk	inj
Sgt W H Pridmore	inj
Sgt K Hollins	inj

T/o 2330 Mepal to attack a benzol plant. Crashed 0420 while returning to base, coming down near Woodditton, 13 miles E of Cambridge. Both New Zealanders are buried in Cambridge City Cemetery. F/S Cornell was critically injured and he died on 18 January; his grave is in Southgate Cemetery.

100 Sqn   **Lancaster I**   **PA189 HW-P**   **Op: Zeitz**

F/L F T Quigley RCAF	+
F/O H O Berger DFM	+
F/S R C Roller RCAF	+
F/O W M Chapman RCAF	+
Sgt J H Guy	+
F/S M S McMaster RCAF	+
F/S J D Gibbons RCAF	+

T/o 1731 Grimsby to bomb the Braunkohle-Benzin synthetic-oil complex. Crashed at Questenberg some 4 km NE of Rossla on the Nordhausen to Sangerhausen road. All rest in the 1939–1945 War Cemetery at Berlin, having been brought here from Questenberg. F/O Berger's previous tour had been with 101 Squadron and details of his DFM appeared in the London Gazette on 21 April 1944. F/O Chapman's brother, Kenneth Louis Chapman, died while on service.

101 Sqn   **Lancaster III**   **LM472 SR-V2**   **Op: Brux**

F/O F D McGonigle	+
Sgt J R McDowell	+
F/S J E Knight RAAF	pow
F/S R W L Hart RAAF	+
F/S L Collins RAAF	+
P/O J K Armour RCAF	+
Sgt R J Beckett	+
Sgt D Conroy	+

T/o 1748 Ludford Magna with two navigators to bomb a synthetic-oil plant in western Czecho-slovakia. Those who died are buried in Berlin 1939–1945 War Cemetery. P/O Armour RCAF was the specialist equipment operator.

102 Sqn   **Halifax III**   **LW179 DY-Y**   **Op: Magdeburg**

S/L A H Jarand	+
Sgt E E Pope	+
W/O D Galbraith	+
P/O E L Davis RCAF	+
P/O J M Carter RAAF	+
Sgt G C Telfer	+
Sgt J Wilson	+

T/o 1838 Pocklington. Crashed between the towns of Langelsheim and Wolfshagen. S/L Jarand was a pre-wear regular officer who hailed from St. Marks on the Isle of Man. Initially, he was buried on 13 February at Wolfshagen, but since then he has been exhumed and his grave, along with those of the crew, is now in Hannover War Cemetery. At 37, Sgt Pope was well over the average age of operational aircrew.

153 Sqn   **Lancaster I**   **NG335 P4-V**   **Op: Zeitz**

F/O C W Byers RCAF	+
Sgt J B M Kelleher	+
F/S E C McLenaghan	+
F/S F C Irving RCAF	+
WO1 R K Crow RCAF	+
F/S R C Shilliday RCAF	+
F/S M Frank RCAF	+

T/o 1730 Scampton to bomb the Braunkohle-Benzin synthetic-oil plant. Lost without trace. All are commemorated on the Runnymede Memorial.

158 Sqn   **Halifax III**   **MZ927 NP-Y**   **Op: Magdeburg**

F/O J A S Stewart	+
Sgt V E Washer	pow
F/S H G Hall RCAF	pow
F/O H F Parkes	pow
Sgt R J Knight	+
F/O A Cox	+
F/O G V R Yeulett	+

T/o 1916 Lissett. Came down near Hordorf, a village on the W bank of the Bode, 4 km SSW of Oschersleben. F/O Yeulett, at 35 above the average age of operational aircrew, was buried at Hordorf but his grave is now with the others who died in Berlin 1939–1945 War Cemetery. As a crew, they were on their fourteenth sortie, having started in mid-November 1944 when Jülich had been the target.

166 Sqn   **Lancaster III**   **ME296 AS-V**   **Op: Zeitz**

F/O E P Burke RAAF	+
Sgt T E Carr	+
F/S G K E John	pow
P/O J M Meggitt RAAF	pow
F/S G W Kirk	pow
F/S G Anson	pow
F/S T R Wood	pow

T/o 1725 Kirmington to attack the Braunkohle-Benzin synthetic-oil plant. The two airmen who died are buried in Rheinberg War Cemetery.

16-17 Jan	186 Sqn	Lancaster I		NG147 AP-C	Op: **Wanne-Eickel**

1945	F/L R R Tait	+

186 Sqn — Lancaster I — NG147 AP-C — Op: **Wanne-Eickel**

F/L R R Tait	+
Sgt P A Sumpter	+
F/S T B Darney	+
F/O H C Dutfield	+
F/S W S Gamble	+
P/O G S Haslam	+
Sgt T L Lenton	+

T/o 2315 Stradishall for a raid on synthetic-oil producing plant but crashed three minutes later, exploding on impact, at Kedington, a little over a mile ENE from Haverhill, Suffolk. Three rest in Haverhill Cemetery; the others are buried in their home towns.

214 Sqn — Fortress III — KJ103 BU-M — Op: BS

F/O N T Scott	
Sgt R J Willing	
F/O R V Houston RCAF	inj
F/O T V McKee RCAF	+
Sgt D V Lewis	
F/O E T Hardman RAAF	
F/S R Smith	
Sgt B J Lunn	
Sgt C Brown	
F/S R J Knickle RCAF	

T/o 1800 Oulton for Jostle duties. Hit a tree on return to base, crashing 0240 near the air-field. F/O McKee RCAF is buried in Brookwood Military Cemetery. Six unnamed members of crew were injured, but one has been subsequently identified as F/O Houston RCAF.

Note. Jock Whitehouse, to whom I am most grateful for notes relating to 214 Squadron, states that this Fortress had a reputation as a poor performer with an above average thirst for petrol and a marked reluctance to climb.

300 Sqn — Lancaster I — PD257 BH-O — Op: Zeitz

W/O R Bakinowski PAF	pow
Sgt K T Tomasik PAF	pow
Sgt S Seidengart PAF	pow
P/O F Matuszewski PAF	+
Sgt M Piotrowski PAF	+
Sgt M Sasin PAF	pow
Sgt A Smoczkiewicz PAF	+

T/o 1748 Faldingworth to bomb the Braunkohle-Benzin synthetic-oil plant. Crashed at Kleinfurra some 10 km SSW from the centre of Nordhausen. Those who died were buried in Kleinfurra Friedhof but since the cessation of hostilities, their remains have been taken to Berlin 1939-1945 War Cemetery.

Note. Although Betty Clements, who has kindly dealt with my table of 300 Squadron casualties, believes the above interpretation of names to be correct, one source reports the air bomber's surname as Matuszkiewicz.

347 Sqn — Halifax III — MZ986 L8-B — Op: Magdeburg

Cne X Marin FFAF	+
Adj A Villeneuve FFAF	+
Ltn R Frangolacci FFAF	pow
Ltn J Minvielle FFAF	pow
Adc L Vuillemont FFAF	+
Sgc P Dargenton FFAF	+
Sgc R Meunier FFAF	pow

T/o 1918 Elvington. Cne Marin FFAF is believed to have flown 25 operational sorties.

347 Sqn — Halifax III — NA572 L8-L — Op: Magdeburg

Cne J Bresson FFAF	+
Sgt Kannengiesser FFAF	pow
Cne G de Sauvebeuf FFAF	pow
Ltn A Ronat FFAF	pow
Adj R Rabier FFAF	+
Sgt R Poilbout FFAF	+
Sgt L Martin FFAF	pow

T/o 1855 Elvington. Crashed between the villages of Wölfingen and Poppenburg, 3 km SW from the small town of Nordstemmen, itself some 10 km WNW from the centre of Hildesheim. It is thought Cne Bresson FFAF had completed twenty-three operational missions.

405 Sqn — Lancaster III — PB402 LQ-M — Op: Zeitz

F/L H L Payne RCAF	+
Sgt H A Marshall	+
F/O H E Novak RCAF	+
F/O D G McKay RCAF	+
P/O A B Miller RCAF	+
F/S J A Bruggeman RCAF	+
F/S B R Cunliffe RCAF	+
F/S N L L Smith RCAF	+

T/o 1813 Gransden Lodge to assist in the marking of the Braunkohle-Benzin synthetic-oil plant. Crashed at Pfaffenhausen. All are buried in Dürnbach War Cemetery. P/O Miller RCAF was flying in the capacity of visual air bomber.

Note. There are least four locations in Germany named Pfaffenhausen but in respect of this aircraft, it is believed the place so named is on the road between Krumbach and Mindelheim.

16-17 Jan
1945

415 Sqn		Halifax III
F/L W F Borrett RCAF	+
Sgt G A V Binne RCAF	pow
F/O D M Sloan RCAF	pow
F/O T K Daniel RCAF	pow
F/S R A Collins RCAF	pow
F/S K W Bradley RCAF	pow
F/S P R Mogridge RCAF	+

NR253 6U-L   **Op: Magdeburg**
T/o 1825 East Moor. Crashed at Borne, 19 km SSW from the centre of Magdeburg. The two airmen who died rest in Berlin at the city's 1939-1945 War Cemetery, having been brought here from graves traced to the town of Langenweddingen.

420 Sqn		Halifax III
F/L E B McCutcheon DFC RCAF	+
F/O T C Jones	+
F/O D W Ritchie RCAF	pow
F/O J G Welk RCAF	+
P/O J G Skidmore RCAF	pow
P/O G A Haacke RCAF	pow
P/O D O Mackey RCAF	pow

NA183 PT-M   **Op: Magdeburg**
T/o 1834 Tholthorpe. Claimed by a night-fighter and crashed 2145 at Bokensdorf, 9 km NW from the centre of Wolfsburg. Those who perished rest in Hannover War Cemetery.

420 Sqn		Halifax III
F/O R A Ireland RCAF	+
Sgt R Hutchinson	+
F/O W L Dennis RCAF	+
F/O W Webb RCAF	+
F/S L J Penny RCAF	+
F/S F W Poole RCAF	pow
F/S S Cameron RCAF	pow

NA188 PT-E   **Op: Magdeburg**
T/o 1839 Tholthorpe. Believed to have fallen victim to a night-fighter, crashing 2230 in the vicinity of Alfeld (Leine), a town on the Leine some 20 km SSW from the centre of Hildesheim. Those who died rest in Hannover War Cemetery.

420 Sqn		Halifax III
F/L E W Watson RCAF	+
Sgt A K Parker	+
P/O C W Way DFC	+
F/O Q J Louie RCAF	+
P/O W J D Partridge RCAF	+
F/S D J Jacobi RCAF	pow
F/S T Lynch RCAF	pow

NA192 PT-Q   **Op: Magdeburg**
T/o 1846 Tholthorpe. Those who died are buried in Berlin 1939-1945 War Cemetery. F/O Louie RCAF, for whom no details of his next-of-kin are known, had the unusual Christian names of Quan Jil. P/O Partridge RCAF was the son of the Revd A M Partridge of Napanee, Ontario.

420 Sqn		Halifax III
F/S R E Harvey RCAF	+
Sgt J F McCormick RCAF	+
Sgt P E Morissette RCAF	pow
F/O C F Bryce RCAF	pow
Sgt R J Wilson RCAF	pow
F/S K D Reid RCAF	pow
F/S A J Little RCAF	pow

NR205 PT-L   **Op: Magdeburg**
T/o 1840 Tholthorpe. The two airmen who died rest in Becklingen War Cemetery.

426 Sqn		Halifax III
F/L R H Galbraith RCAF	+
Sgt J McI Davidson	+
F/O R R Broadfoot RCAF	pow
F/O J W Shirey RCAF	+
F/S J M MacDonald RCAF	pow
F/S A M Lacchia RCAF	pow
F/S B W McNicol RCAF	pow

RG350 OW-K   **Op: Magdeburg**
T/o 1916 Linton-on-Ouse. Shot down by a night-fighter, crashing 2230, it is believed at Börry some 10 km SE of Hameln. Debris was scattered over 100 metres from the point of impact. Those who died are buried in Hannover War Cemetery.

Note. One of a handful of Halifax IIIs held by 426 Squadron, this example had been accepted from 425 Squadron on 6 December 1944, who in turn had taken delivery two days previous from the English Electric works. Its flying hours are not recorded.

426 Sqn		Halifax VII
F/O R N Swift RCAF	
Sgt R Watson	
F/O C E Sowerby RCAF	
F/O D J Andrews RCAF	
F/S J H Tapp RCAF	
F/S G L McCallum RCAF	
F/S R S Martin RCAF	

NP795 OW-T   **Op: Magdeburg**
T/o 1835 Linton-on-Ouse but the starboard tyre burst, causing the Halifax to swing off the runway. Moments later, the undercarriage gave way thus seriously damaging the aircraft. On 9 February the airframe was lodged at a repair facility but on 3 March all work ceased and the airframe was struck off charge.

16-17 Jan
1945

429 Sqn   **Halifax III**   **MZ427 AL-E**   **Op: Magdeburg**

F/O F H Biddle RCAF	pow
Sgt R H V Streetfield	pow
F/O C E Chapman RCAF	pow
F/S R A Deck RCAF	pow
P/O R H S Bourne RCAF	pow
F/S F G Peters RCAF	pow
F/S J R Phillips RCAF	pow

T/o 1859 Leeming. F/O Biddle RCAF was engaged on his 32nd sortie; his crew were flying their thirtieth.

434 Sqn   **Lancaster X**   **KB850 WL-O**   **Op: Zeitz**

F/L A Kiehl Bauch RCAF	+
F/S D Turner RCAF	+
F/O G G Shaw RCAF	+
F/O N G Fadden RCAF	+
P/O W T Wilson RCAF	+
P/O A G Carolan RCAF	+
P/O W D Martin RCAF	+

T/o 1719 Croft to attack the Braunkohle-Benzin synthetic-oil plant. All are buried in Dürnbach War Cemetery. It is possible F/S Turner RCAF was an Englishman serving with the RCAF; certainly, he had married Margaret Kathleen Turner of Church Stretton and it seems likely from evidence in the CWGC cemetery register that his parents, too, lived in the same area.

Note. This was the first Lancaster X reported missing from 434 Squadron since converting to the type in December 1944.

466 Sqn   **Halifax III**   **NP969 HD-Q**   **Op: Magdeburg**

F/O L F B Barrett RAAF	+
Sgt W E C Mount	+
F/S C F White	pow
F/S H F King	+
F/S W T Simpson RAAF	+
Sgt J Powell	+
F/S F W Lee	+

T/o 1847 Driffield. The six airmen who died are buried in Berlin 1939-1945 War Cemetery. At 35, F/S Lee may be considered old as far as operational aircrew were concerned.

514 Sqn   **Lancaster I**   **PB906 JI-B2**   **Op: Wanne-Eickel**

F/O G D Orr	+
F/O M L Matkin RCAF	+
Sgt R Werrill	+
F/S J Bryson	+
F/S T F Wilson	+
F/S A McGlone	+
F/S H E Bishop	+
F/S G Spencer	+

T/o 2312 Waterbeach to attack a benzol plant. Lost without trace. All are commemorated on the Runnymede Memorial.

576 Sqn   **Lancaster I**   **PD309 UL-W2**   **Op: Zeitz**

F/O C R Pegg RAAF	
Sgt R Pearson	
F/O B Fitzpatrick RAAF	
F/O A R A Crameri RAAF	
F/S R Taylor RAAF	
Sgt R Ainzstein	inj
F/S A A Shearer RAAF	

T/o 1745 Fiskerton to bomb the Braunkohle-Benzin synthetic-oil plant. Called on W/T at 0120, advising the Lancaster was over Belgium and about to be abandoned. All were later reported safe; Sgt Ainzstein requiring treatment for a broken ankle. It was further reported the crew had fought an engagement with two jet propelled aircraft and may have destroyed one.

578 Sqn   **Halifax III**   **NA603 LK-T**   **Op: Magdeburg**

F/O R L Maloney RAAF	pow
Sgt C G Atkins	pow
P/O P H Clews	pow
F/O I G Owen	+
F/S C T Moore RAAF	pow
Sgt H G Skeats	pow
P/O F J Fitzgerald RCAF	pow
Sgt T W Spencer	pow

T/o 1823 Burn. Last heard on W/T at 1951, by Riccall, broadcasting wind speed and direction. Believed to have been shot down by a fighter at 2110, crashing 600 metres S of Gross Vahlberg, 5 km WSW of Schöppenstedt. F/O Owen is buried in Hannover War Cemetery. The mid-under gun position had been manned by P/O Fitzgerald RCAF.

582 Sqn   **Lancaster III**   **NE130 60-T**   **Op: Zeitz**

F/O P J McVerry RNZAF	
Sgt G Fallon	
F/O W B Thorby	
F/S J A Denton	
F/S J Carroll RAAF	
Sgt T Myatt	
Sgt W McNamara	+

T/o 1835 Little Staughton to assist in the marking of the Braunkohle-Benzin synthetic-oil plant. Presumed abandoned over Allied held territory, while homebound. Sgt McNamara of the Irish Republic is buried in Clichy New Communal Cemetery.

16-17 Jan 1945	640 Sqn	Halifax III	NR204 C8-C	Op: Magdeburg

F/L S S Jenkins MID   +
Sgt T Featherstone   +
F/S J L McCallum   +
F/S D Davey   +
F/S D S Mitchell   +
Sgt H Richardson   +
Sgt W F Merrick   +

T/o 1836 Leconfield. Lost without trace. All are commemorated on the Runnymede Memorial. Sgt Featherstone came from Birr, Co. Offaly in the Republic of Ireland.

17 Jan 1945	15 Sqn	Lancaster I	PB802 LS-F	Training

F/O J H Crone RAAF   +
Sgt R Devlin   +
Sgt G R Lake   +
F/S L R Wilkins   +
P/O L M Riordan RAAF   +
F/O W E Fuller   +
F/O H H Freedman   +

T/o 1603 Mildenhall on a cross country and bombing exercise. Dived into the ground 2130 at Harling, about 8 miles ENE from Thetford, Norfolk. The first five named are buried in Cambridge City Cemetery. Both air gunners were claimed by their next-of-kin.

	157 Sqn	Mosquito XIX	TA446 RS-Q	Air Test

F/O B Gale
F/O G T Lang

Landed with its wheels retracted, on grass, at Shipdham airfield, Norfolk. No injuries.

18-19 Jan 1945	128 Sqn	Mosquito XVI	MM220 M5-K	Op: Sterkrade

F/L J W G Smith
Sgt C C Hill

T/o 2322 Wyton. Landed 0130 Brussels-Melsbroek, with its port engine unserviceable, whereupon the undercarriage collapsed. No one was hurt.

Note. Some publications incorrectly assign this Mosquito to 169 Squadron which, as a Bomber Support unit, was not equipped with the Mk.XVI.

	142 Sqn	Mosquito XXV	KB446 4H-X	Op: Sterkrade

F/L F C Young
S/L T M Jones RCAF

T/o 2323 Gransden Lodge to bomb an oil refining facility. Crash-landed 0209, in Belgium, while on the home leg. No reports of injury.

	142 Sqn	Mosquito XXV	KB447 4H-S	Op: Sterkrade

F/O T Disson
F/S R D Johnston

undercarriage in the process.

T/o 2327 Gransden Lodge similarly tasked. On return to base at 0221, the Mosquito touched down only to swing off the runway, losing its undercarriage in the process. Neither member of crew was hurt.

20 Jan 1945	582 Sqn	Lancaster III	PB182 60-D	Training

F/O A J Keely RAAF

Overshot and crash-landed 1550 while trying to land at Oakington airfield, Cambridgeshire. No injuries reported.

21-22 Jan 1945	142 Sqn	Mosquito XXV	KB463 4H-W	Op: Kassel

S/L R S Don DFC   +
F/O G I Allan DFC RCAF   +

T/o 1845 Gransden Lodge. Lost without trace. Both officers are commemorated on the Runnymede Memorial. At 43, F/O Allan RCAF was amongst the oldest Canadians killed on Bomber Command operations during the war.

Note. Since reforming at Gransden Lodge on 25 October 1944, as part of Bomber Command's LNSF, 142 Squadron had written off ten of their Canadian built Mosquitoes. However, the above crew were the first to be reported missing from operations.

22-23 Jan 1945	153 Sqn	Lancaster I	NG185 P4-A	Op: Duisburg

F/O K W Winder   +
Sgt D B George   +
Sgt A J Rabin   +
F/O M A Smith RCAF   +
Sgt R Evans   +
Sgt G B Hamilton RCAF   +
Sgt T O'Gorman   +

T/o 1640 Scampton. Likely to have crashed in Germany, where the bodies of the crew were either discovered by an American graves inspection team, or found almost immediately by US forces, as all were taken into Holland and interred at Margraten. Since then, their remains have been transferred to Venrary War Cemetery. At 18, Sgt Hamilton RCAF was one of the youngest Canadians killed on bombing duties during 1945.

22-23 Jan 1945	153 Sqn	Lancaster III	PB636 P4-D	Op: Duisburg

F/L A E Jones DFC   +
Sgt S S James   +
F/S J J L McDonell RAAF   +
F/S C L Cullen   +
W/O J E Bateup RAAF   +
Sgt R V Trafford   +
Sgt A Simpson   +

T/o 1645 Scampton. Lost without trace. All are commemorated on the Runnymede Memorial. At 39, Sgt James, whose second Christian name was Strettle, was well over the age for airmen employed on operational duties with Bomber Command.

	346 Sqn	Halifax III	LW438 H7-K	Op: Gelsenkirchen

Cne R Martin FFAF

T/o 1900 Elvington but swung violently and lost its undercarriage as it ran through a hedge bordering the airfield. No injuries, but the Halifax was damaged beyond repair.

	347 Sqn	Halifax III	LL587 L8-	Op: Gelsenkirchen

Ltn C M Petus FFAF   inj
Sgt Tribert FFAF   +
Ltn C Desessard FFAF
Ltn J Mignon FFAF
Adj J Coqueron FFAF   inj
Sgc A Lindebert FFAF
Adj F Riviere FFAF

T/o 1908 Elvington. Homebound at 7,000 feet, with the port outer feathered, when a fire broke out in the port inner engine. Apart from the flight engineer, all baled out before the aircraft crashed 0200 at Woodford, 6 miles ESE of Kettering, Northamptonshire. Ltn Petus FFAF died from a combination of his injuries and exposure.

26 Jan 1945	431 Sqn	Lancaster X	KB803 SE-N	Training

F/O J F Morton RCAF

Lost engine power during a feathering exercise and crash-landed 1636 in a snow covered field at Yafforth, a village less than a mile WNW from the centre of Northallerton in Yorkshire. No injuries reported.

	578 Sqn	Halifax III	NA574 LK-D	Training

F/L N Garforth   +
F/S J Sweet   +
P/O J B Curtis
F/S I L Johns RCAF   +
F/S R D Walker
Sgt R J Horton   +
Sgt T C House   +

While at 5,000 feet NW of York and returning to base from a fighter affiliation exercise, the port outer failed. Attempts to feather the unit were unsuccessful and moments later flames were seen spreading along the outer part of the wing. Without warning, part of the wing then sheered off and only two members of crew were able to escape by parachute before the bomber plunged into the ground at 1502 near West Haddlesey, 5 miles SW of Selby, Yorkshire. Those who died are buried in various cemeteries.

26-27 Jan 1945	85 Sqn	Mosquito NF.30	MV546 VY-P	Training

F/L T W Redfern   +
F/O A F Witt   +

T/o Swannington for night training, but a sudden deterioration in the weather necessitated a recall, the crew being instructed to use the Mother procedure for homing. However, the pilot called on R/T and said, "There is no future in this" and moments later there was an explosion as the Mosquito dived into the ground near Oulton airfield, Norfolk. Both officers were taken to their home towns for burial.

28 Jan 1945	15 Sqn	Lancaster I	HK618 LS-G	Op: Koln

F/O S H Bignell RAAF   pow
Sgt F Keable-Buckle   pow
F/S J W Lacey RAAF   pow
F/S D G Jones   pow
F/S C A Russell RAAF   pow
F/S T M Thoroughgood RAAF   pow
W/O J V Higgins   pow
F/S W A Wilkie RAAF   pow

T/o 1015 Mildenhall to attack the railway yards in the Gremberg district. Shot down before reaching the target area. W/O Higgins was manning the mid-under gun position.

	218 Sqn	Lancaster I	LM281 HA-E	Op: Koln

F/L V W Hodnett   pow
Sgt J N Sherry   pow
F/S D I Humphrey   pow
F/S F T Reynolds   pow
Sgt T F Morgan   pow
Sgt J Gough   pow
Sgt A Allman   pow

T/o 1049 Chedburgh similarly tasked. Hit by flak and last seen at 1410 in the target area losing height with both port engines stopped.

28 Jan	218 Sqn	Lancaster I	PD296 HA-B	Op: Koln
1945				

218 Sqn   **Lancaster I**   **PD296 HA-B**   **Op: Koln**

28 Jan 1945

W/O G D Evers	+
Sgt E N J Francis	+
F/O F J Norton	pow
F/S A Morris	+
F/S D C Allen	+
F/S E Holland	+
Sgt E B Barradell	+
W/O J Towns DFC	+

T/o 1046 Chedburgh as Squadron lead aircraft for the raid on Gremberg marshalling yards. Hit by flak and crashed 1400 at Bergisch-Gladbach, 14 km ENE from the centre of Köln. F/O Norton sustained shrapnel wounds to an arm; his seven companions rest in the Reichswald Forest War Cemetery. Sgt Francis was 40, well over the age for operational airmen. Had W/O Evers returned, he would have been screened from further operations.

428 Sqn   **Lancaster X**   **KB763 NA-S**   **Training**

P/O H L Clark RCAF	+
Sgt P H Morris	+
F/S B Crabb RCAF	inj
F/S J H Carter RCAF	+
Sgt S Filipchuk RCAF	+
F/S J W Ross RCAF	+

T/o 1429 Middleton St. George with six crew aboard. At 1740, the Lancaster broke clear of the overcast and hit the ground, bursting into flames, at Elton Hall, probably on the SW outskirts of Stockton-on-Tees, Durham. The RCAF members of crew who died are buried in Harrogate (Stonefall) Cemetery, while Sgt Morris has been interred in Bromley (Plaistow) Cemetery.

28-29 Jan 1945

51 Sqn   **Halifax III**   **MZ794 MH-T**   **Op: Stuttgart**

F/O J D Brayshaw	
Sgt A J Woods	
F/S J A Green	inj
F/O S E Mount	
Sgt A J Holland	
Sgt D Earlham	
Sgt R C Fenner	+

T/o 2016 Snaith. Bombed the AP at 2336 from 19,500 feet, encountering heavy flak. Soon afterwards, attacked twice by a Me 109 whose fire killed Sgt Fenner. Badly damaged, the Halifax landed on an American airstrip, A58 in France. Nineteen year old Sgt Fenner, an ex-ATC cadet from Bury St. Edmunds, lies in the old communal cemetery at Villeneuve-St-Georges.

105 Sqn   **Mosquito IX**   **ML923 GB-Z**   **Op: Stuttgart**

F/L G L S McHardy DFC	+
F/O G R P Duncan	+

T/o 1838 Bourn. Both rest in France at Choloy War Cemetery, brought here from an American cemetery at Grand Failly, where they had first been buried on 30 January.

153 Sqn   **Lancaster III**   **PB638 P4-O**   **Op: Stuttgart**

F/O O M C Jones DFC	+
Sgt P R Jenkinson DFM	+
F/S J F Dormer	+
F/S E W Fletcher	+
F/S J W Milburn	+
F/S J Coles	+
F/S H Ferguson	+

T/o 1925 Scampton. All are buried in Dürnbach War Cemetery. The London Gazette, issued on 11 December 1945, carried news of Sgt Jenkinson's award. His skipper was an Oxford University graduate.

156 Sqn   **Lancaster III**   **PB186 GT-A**   **Op: Stuttgart**

F/L J H Freeman RCAF	+
Sgt R Breaks	+
F/O D Watson RCAF	+
F/O N P Hibbert DFC	+
F/S J G Shaw	+
F/S J R Wood	+
F/S J F Kaviza RCAF	+

T/o 2020 Upwood. Came down at Vaihingen in the SW suburbs of Stuttgart. All were buried in the local Friedhof, since when their bodies have been removed to Dürnbach War Cemetery. F/O Hibbert was the son of Maj John Percy Magull Hibbert MC.

300 Sqn   **Lancaster I**   **PB846 BH-K**   **Op: Stuttgart**

F/L Z E Zarebski PAF	+
F/S J N Gerwatowski PAF	pow
P/O R A Paszkowski PAF	+
P/O Z Wesolowski PAF	pow
Sgt P Barzdo PAF	pow
Sgt K Cymbala PAF	+
Sgt R Mankowski PAF	pow

T/o 1958 Faldingworth. Crashed at Berneck on the SE side of the Schwarzwald and about 2 km N from the small town of Altensteig. Those who died are buried in Dürnbach War Cemetery. F/L Zarebski PAF had made his way to England via Romania and France, going on to fly fighters with 308, 303 and 306 Squadrons before converting to twins and a spell at 18 OTU. Ironically, his transfer to Bomber Command was for health reasons! He was born on 11 May 1914.

28–29 Jan	**405 Sqn**	**Lancaster III**	**PB650 LQ-U**	**Op: Stuttgart**

1945

405 Sqn	Lancaster III	PB650 LQ-U	Op: Stuttgart
F/O F H Cummer RCAF	+	
Sgt W McCabrey	+	
F/S E R Savage RCAF	+	
F/O W B Turner RCAF	+	
F/S G A Smith RCAF	+	
F/S J MacC Rae RCAF	+	
F/S D A MacDougall RCAF	pow	

T/o 2035 Gransden Lodge. Believed to have come down at Deufringen, 2 km W from the small town of Aidlingen. Those who lost their lives rest in Dürnbach War Cemetery, alongside seventeen other airmen from their Squadron who died in the January round of operations. F/O Cummer RCAF came from Seattle in Washington State.

408 Sqn	Halifax VII	NP743 EQ-K	Op: Stuttgart
P/O C L Johnston RCAF	+	
Sgt T H Chandler	+	
F/O N G Baily RCAF	+	
F/O J A O'Brien RCAF	+	
P/O J C Mortley RCAF	+	
F/S F Henry RCAF	+	
F/S B E House RCAF	+	

T/o 1953 Linton-on-Ouse. All are buried in Dürnbach War Cemetery. F/O Baily RCAF was an accountant from Georgetown, Ontario. This was a scratch crew with a wide variety of operational experience ranging from none in the case of P/O Mortley RCAF to 27 sorties apiece in respect of F/O Baily RCAF and F/O O'Brien RCAF.

408 Sqn	Halifax VII	NP746 EQ-E	Op: Stuttgart
F/O R M Wallis RCAF	+	
Sgt L J Collinson RCAF	+	
F/O T B Little RCAF	+	
F/O H T McGovern RCAF	pow	
F/S P Myerson RCAF	+	
F/S T P Quinn RCAF	+	
F/S R L Stewart RCAF	+	

T/o 1943 Linton-on-Ouse. Those who perished lie in Dürnbach War Cemetery. F/O Little RCAF held a Bachelor of Arts degree.

424 Sqn	Halifax III	LW164 QB-C	Op: Stuttgart
W/C E M Williams AFC RCAF	+	
Sgt L Tongue	+	
WO2 R J Nicolls RCAF	+	
F/S R E Chatfield RCAF	+	
WO2 G J Doyle RCAF	+	
F/O W Fleming RCAF	+	
F/O J E H B Tremblay RCAF	inj	

T/o 1921 Skipton-on-Swale but swung out of control, crashed and exploded, the blast throwing F/O Tremblay RCAF clear of the flames. Critically injured, he was rushed to RAF Hospital Northallerton. Those who died are buried in Harrogate (Stonefall) Cemetery. W/C Williams RCAF was a regular officer; along with his two air gunners he was engaged on his second tour of operations.

Note. This was the last Halifax III written off by 424 Squadron, now about to convert to Lancasters. It had completed sixty-seven operational sorties and had been the favourite Halifax for Flying Officer M R Tidy RCAF during the summer of 1944.

426 Sqn	Halifax VII	NP768 OW-Q	Op: Stuttgart
W/C F C Carling-Kelly RCAF	pow	
Sgt J A Bromley	pow	
Sgt S G Rundle RCAF	+	
F/O D J Bird RCAF	pow	
F/O H J Dales RCAF	pow	
F/O A L Evans RCAF	+	
F/O P Hyde RCAF	+	

T/o 1906 Linton-on-Ouse. Shot down by a night-fighter. Those who lost their lives are buried in Dürnbach War Cemetery.

428 Sqn	Lancaster X	KB770 NA-D	Op: Stuttgart
S/L H L Kay RCAF	+	
Sgt R W Gullick	+	
F/O R L Stapleford RCAF	pow	
F/O G J Liney RCAF	+	
F/O J W Blades RCAF	+	
F/S F L Jolicoeur RCAF	+	
F/S E F Ossington RCAF	pow	

T/o 1638 Middleton St. George on his first sortie as a flight commander. Those who died are buried in Dürnbach War Cemetery. S/L Kay RCAF was the son of Dr. Amos Frank Kay MD of Pittsburgh, Pennsylvania. It is believed he was a regular Canadian air force officer.

460 Sqn	Lancaster III	ND970 AR-S	Op: Stuttgart
F/O P N Birt RAAF	+	
Sgt A Field	pow	
F/S E S Symes RAAF	pow	
F/S E G Truman RAAF	pow	
F/S D R Benbow RAAF	pow	
F/S D G O'Hara RAAF	+	
F/S S G Wilson RAAF	+	

T/o 1948 Binbrook. Those who died rest in Dürnbach War Cemetery. F/O Birt RAAF was the son of Lt-Col Charles William Howard Birt DSO and Two Bars. F/S Wilson RAAF came from Nowra in New South Wales, a place familiar to those who served in the Pacific with the Fleet Air Arm.

31 Jan– 1 Feb 1945	109 Sqn	Mosquito IX	ML915 HS–	Op: Duisburg

W/O H M Smith
F/S W R Wade

T/o 0359 Little Staughton and headed for the Hamborn district of Duisburg. Attempted to land at 0654 on one engine at Knocke-Le-Zoute airfield in Belgium but overshot and finished up in a ditch. No injuries reported.

1 Feb 1945	622 Sqn	Lancaster I	HK617 GI–Q	Op: Monchengladbach

F/O R G A Conacher RCAF
Sgt F J Hogan
Sgt E O Thompson
Sgt J Green
F/S H A Edwards
Sgt A D Falconer
Sgt E Baxter   +
Sgt J Marlborough

T/o 1329 Mildenhall to participate in a G-H raid. Outbound, the port inner failed and caught fire, the flames spreading rapidly to engulf most of the airframe. The order to bale out was given and all did so but, tragically, Sgt Baxter's parachute canopy began to burn and the mid-under gunner fell to his death. He is buried in Lille Southern Cemetery. The Lancaster crashed in the vicinity of Arras.

Note. The Squadron ORB shows the crash location as between Tilloy and le Preux Monchy, but I am not able to find either location on my maps of the Arras area.

	692 Sqn	Mosquito XVI	MM183 P3–	Transit

F/L Boothright

T/o 1655 Manston but the port engine lost power and the crew put back to the airfield, crash-landing 1715, wheels retracted. No injuries reported.

1–2 Feb 1945	50 Sqn	Lancaster I	PD346 VN–V	Op: Siegen

F/O C R Fairbairn DFC RAAF   +
Sgt J Pannett   +
F/O J S E Locock   +
W/O B S Smith RAAF   +
F/O A B Fitzhardinge RAAF   +
F/S N G Jones   pow
Sgt C E Atkins   pow

T/o 1638 Skellingthorpe. Those who died are buried in Rheinberg War Cemetery.

	61 Sqn	Lancaster I	NF912 QR–	Op: Siegen

S/L H W Horsley AFC   +
W/O H J Pyke   +
F/S S Fleet   +
F/S V D Merrow   +
F/S L Chapman CGM   +
F/S A A Sherriff DFM   +
Sgt R T Hoskisson   inj

T/o 1542 Skellingthorpe but the port outer cut as the Lancaster became airborne. Exercising considerable skill, S/L Horsley succeeded in flying a very tight circuit and one minute later he force-landed on the airfield. As he touched down, there was an explosion, followed by fire. Those who died are buried in various cemeteries. F/S Chapman won the CGM, Gazetted 9 May 1944, for steadfastly remaining at his post, despite being severely wounded, while on operations to Nürnberg on 30-31 March 1944. F/S Sherriff's DFM was published on 25 May 1945. He was a regular airman whose service number suggests entry to the service in the late 1920s or early '30s.

Note. Please refer to Volume 5 page 432 for details pertaining to S/L Horsley's evasion following operations over the Dortmund-Ems Kanal on 23-24 September 1945.

	76 Sqn	Halifax III	MZ516 MP–V	Op: Mainz

F/S P J McBrinn RCAF   +
F/O H R Mock   +
F/S F A Farley
F/O R W Wheatley
F/S K Rogers
P/O R J Cowie RCAF   +
F/O K W Oddy   +
Sgt J P Ellingson RCAF   +

T/o 1603 Holme-on-Spalding Moor. Homebound, and flying at 7,000 feet over East Anglia, when the starboard outer commenced vibrating. Attempts to feather the motor were unsuccessful and with the situation deteriorating rapidly the order to abandon was given. Three complied before the Halifax plunged into the ground at 2145 at Jones Farm, Heath Road, Banham, 6 miles NW of Diss in Norfolk. The RCAF members of crew were taken to Brookwood Military Cemetery. F/O Oddy, the mid-under air gunner, was on his second operational tour. It is observed P/O Cowie RCAF came from Los Angeles.

Note. This Halifax was named "Vera The Virgin" and had flown 77 sorties. Photographs displaying the nose art show that bottles were used in lieu of the more conventional bomb symbol to indicate sorties flown, while Vera is depicted with her left hand on hip and with two fingers raised on her right hand, but not quite in the style popularised by Churchill!

1-2 Feb
1945

100 Sqn   **Lancaster III**   **PB572 HW-F**   **Op: Ludwigshafen**

F/L F L Conn DFC RAAF	+
F/O R B A Dukelow	+
Sgt J A Wilson	+
F/S J R Hartshorn	+
F/O P G Hughesdon	+
F/O G R P Blackbourn	+
F/S J Brady RAAF	+
Sgt E C Hemmant	+
Sgt W F Hart	+

T/o 1555 Grimsby. All are buried near Bad Tolz in Dürnbach War Cemetery. The unusual crew combination of nine included two pilots and two navigators.

101 Sqn   **Lancaster I**   **ME863 SR-K**   **Op: Ludwigshafen**

F/L R D Boyd RAAF	+
Sgt J McA Johnston	+
Sgt K R Moore	+
Sgt D H Widdows	+
F/S E T Summerson RAAF	+
P/O K G Fenske RCAF	+
Sgt J O'Donnell	+
Sgt J W Hodder	+

T/o 1557 Ludford Magna. Collided in the air with another Lancaster, both aircraft falling at 1906 near Sorneville (Meurthe-et-Moselle), 18 km ENE of Nancy. F/S Summerson RAAF lies in Sorneville Communal Cemetery, but his seven companions rest at Choloy War Cemetery. It is reported their burials were handled by the 7th US Army, funeral being held at Epinal, prior to their subsequent removal to Choloy. P/O Fenske RCAF was the specialist equipment operator.

101 Sqn   **Lancaster III**   **JA715 SR-C**   **Op: Ludwigshafen**

F/L R A W Harrison	
Sgt J B Breare	+
F/S R J F Swain	+
F/S G H Hillman	+
Sgt F Smith	+
Sgt R Whiteford	
F/S D J Mackay	+
Sgt J Squire	+

T/o 1544 Ludford Magna and lost in the manner described above. It is thought that those who perished were taken by the Americans to Epinal since when their remains have been exhumed and interred in Choloy War Cemetery. Sgt Squire had recently served in the Air Training Corps. The specialist equipment was operated by Sgt Whiteford.

101 Sqn   **Lancaster III**   **PB256 SR-P**   **Op: Ludwigshafen**

F/O R J Clark RNZAF	+
Sgt G W Higginson	+
F/S K R Hendren RAAF	+
F/S J M M McGinn RNZAF	+
F/S L R Ironmonger	+
P/O J Kenny RCAF	+
Sgt N C Gordon	+
Sgt R R Etherton	+

T/o 1550 Ludford Magna on ABC duties. Crashed in the target area. All are buried in Dürnbach War Cemetery. Although by no means unique, it was unusual to find all three Commonwealth air forces represented in one crew and, perhaps, especially so as P/O Kenny RCAF, the specialist equipment operator, was an American from New York. F/S McGinn RNZAF had been born in London but had moved to Christchurch, New Zealand, on the remarriage of his mother to William George Longney.

106 Sqn   **Lancaster I**   **LM215 ZN-F**   **Op: Siegen**

F/O R F Gray
Sgt B A W Hewitt
F/S R C Adams
F/O K D Aitken
Sgt E W Winter
Sgt H Pickersgill
Sgt W E Sharman

T/o 1615 Metheringham. Hit by flak and later obliged to crash-land 2115 in France at Juvincourt airfield. No injuries reported.

139 Sqn   **Mosquito XXV**   **KB498 XD-**   **Op: Berlin**

F/L M H Wallis
F/O F W Crawley DFC

T/o 0157 Upwood. On return to base at 0624 overshot the runway and crashed through a barbed wire fence. No injuries reported.

162 Sqn   **Mosquito XXV**   **KB509 CR-Z**   **Op: Berlin**

P/O B A J Way
Sgt K A P Fossitt

T/o 0203 Bourn. Bombed the AP from 26,000 feet at 0402. On return to base, touched down at 0632 but promptly swung off the runway, losing its undercarriage. Neither member of crew was injured.

Note. Having examined a number of accident record cards in respect of Mosquito crashes, it is quite apparent that the collapse of the undercarriage unit frequently led to the scrapping of the airframe, though often as not the aircraft was consigned to a repair facility.

1-2 Feb
1945

166 Sqn	Lancaster I	ME648 AS-J2	Op: Ludwigshafen
F/L E Spankie DFC RCAF	+		
Sgt R Stennett	+		
F/L J E Shannon DFC	+		
F/S H H Teggart	+		
F/S A McIvor	+		
F/S J P Brown RCAF	+		
P/O F A Coombs RCAF	+		

T/o 1525 Kirmington. Crashed at Niederlustadt, where all were buried in the local Friedhof, some 4 km W of the small town of Lingenfeld. Since the cessation of hostilities, their remains have been removed to Rheinberg War Cemetery.

166 Sqn	Lancaster I	NG391 AS-M	Op: Ludwigshafen
P/O D M Smithers	pow		
Sgt E A Bradshaw	pow		
Sgt B C Long	+		
F/S R D Story	pow		
Sgt J Allman	+		
F/S S Willis	+		
Sgt J D Craig	+		

T/o 1530 Kirmington. Those who lost their lives are buried in Dürnbach War Cemetery.

166 Sqn	Lancaster I	PD385 AS-W	Op: Ludwigshafen
F/L E A Pollock	+		
Sgt R G Coles	+		
Sgt A S Scott	+		
F/S J Hall	+		
Sgt E Luke	+		
F/O R C Flutter	+		
F/O T D Brown	+		

T/o 1555 Kirmington. All are buried in Dürnbach War Cemetery. F/L Pollock came from Vina del Mar in Chile; F/S Hall and Sgt Luke both hailed from Northumberland, the former from Willington Quay and the latter from Willington. At 38, F/O Brown was well over the age normally associated with operational aircrew. By way of contrast, ex-Halton apprentice, Sgt Coles, was nineteen.

170 Sqn	Lancaster III	ME302 TC-U	Op: Ludwigshafen
F/O D Jeavons			

T/o 1529 Hemswell but swung off the runway and ran through a ditch, whereupon the undercarriage collapsed, wrecking the Lancaster. No injuries reported.

Note. 170 Squadron ORB omits the names of the crew involved in this incident.

433 Sqn	Lancaster I	NG460 BM-A	Op: Ludwigshafen
S/L H K Stinson DFC RCAF	+		
P/O E H Thompson	+		
F/O D J McMillan RCAF	+		
F/O A W Belles RCAF			
P/O J T McShane RCAF	+		
P/O R Pierson RCAF	+		
P/O R J Thompson RCAF			

T/o 1523 Skipton-on-Swale. Bombed the AP at 1928 from 17,000 feet and was hit by flak. On return the Lancaster entered turbulent weather while in cloud and control was lost, two of the crew managing to bale out from 2,000 feet before their aircraft crashed near Low House, roughly 1,000 yards NW from the town of Driffield, Yorkshire. The four RCAF officers are buried in Harrogate (Stonefall) Cemetery; P/O Thompson rests in Hampstead Cemetery, Cricklewood.

Note. These were the first casualties sustained by 433 Squadron in 1945 and it was also their first Lancaster write off. Three more would be lost before the end of the war, from which not one man survived.

463 Sqn	Lancaster I	NG275 JO-K	Op: Siegen
F/O F H Smith RAAF	pow		
Sgt E Moss	pow		
P/O R O Bailey RAAF	+		
P/O B A Donaghue RAAF	pow		
F/S R T Simonson RAAF	pow		
P/O E J Earl RAAF	pow		
F/S E R Cameron RAAF	pow		

T/o 1629 Waddington. P/O Bailey RAAF is buried in the Reichswald Forest War Cemetery. With 28 sorties to his credit, F/O Smith RAAF would likely have been screened by the end of February.

467 Sqn	Lancaster I	NG197 PO-G	Op: Siegen
F/L J K Livingstone DFC	+		
F/L R W G Eagle RAAF	pow		
F/O E G Parsons	pow		
S/L D O Sands	pow		
F/O W D McMahon RAAF	pow		
F/O J Pendergast	pow		
F/O R H Browne	pow		
F/O E C Ellis RAAF	pow		

T/o 1557 Waddington. F/L Livingstone is buried in Rheinberg War Cemetery. Although it was not unique to find an all officer crew, it was unusual to say the least. It is much suspected all had completed one tour.

| 1-2 Feb | 550 Sqn | Lancaster I | RA502 BQ-Z | Op: Ludwigshafen |

1-2 Feb 1945 — **550 Sqn** — **Lancaster I** — **RA502 BQ-Z** — **Op: Ludwigshafen**

F/O A W L Lohrey RNZAF
Sgt V B Cassapi
F/S E C Wethorpe
Sgt W G Anderson
Sgt N Tinsley +
Sgt A James +
Sgt A Jarnell

T/o 1556 North Killingholme. Homebound, involved in a midair collision, possibly with a Lancaster from 170 Squadron piloted by F/O Dixie DFC RCAF, and abandoned near Chateau Salins before crashing 2002 at Fleville-devent-Nancy (Meurthe-et-Moselle) some 5 km SSE from the centre of Nancy. The two airmen who died are commemorated on the Runnymede Memorial; both were 20 years of age. The other aircraft returned safely, though the tail gunner, P/O V J Fernquist RCAF, had sustained mortal injuries; he lies in Harrogate (Stonefall) Cemetery.

627 Sqn — **Mosquito IV** — **DZ627 AZ-X** — **Op: Siegen**

F/L R Baker +
Sgt D G Betts +

T/o 1714 Woodhall Spa. Believed hit by flak and reported to have crashed onto a road. Both are resting in the Reichswald Forest War Cemetery. F/L Baker came from Vancouver in British Columbia.

692 Sqn — **Mosquito XVI** — **MM224 P3-** — **Op: Berlin**

F/O P J Q Back
F/O D T N Smith DFC

T/o 1840 Graveley. On return, attempted to land at Rougham airfield near Bury St. Edmunds in Suffolk, but overshot the runway and crashed 2330, hitting a car and injuring the four civilian occupants. The Mosquito crew escaped with little more than shock and minor abrasions.

2 Feb 1945 — **109 Sqn** — **Mosquito XVI** — **MM155 HS-** — **Training**

F/L L A Bolin RCAF inj

T/o 1900 Little Staughton and on return to base, floated well beyond the threshold. Realising he was not going to get down, F/L Bolan RCAF attempted to overshoot but the port engine cut and the Mosquito crash-landed, clipping Lancaster NG443 belonging to the resident 582 Squadron. It is not thought the injuries were serious.

239 Sqn — **Mosquito VI** — **PZ245 HB-** — **Air Test**

P/O P Falconer
P/O W G Armour

Forced-landed, due to failure of the starboard engine, in a field at Lords Farm, Deeping St. Nicholas, 5 miles SSW of Spalding, Lincolnshire. Neither crew member was hurt.

Note. This was the last Mosquito VI written off by 239 Squadron, now in the process of receiving Mosquito NF.30s.

2-3 Feb 1945 — **10 Sqn** — **Halifax III** — **RG443 ZA-Q** — **Op: Wanne-Eickel**

F/O R A Gibbs MID +
Sgt J Ashton +
F/S L H Chell +
F/O P Cook pow
F/O W P Parham +
Sgt T C Smith +
Sgt W H Seabridge +

T/o 2032 Melbourne to bomb an oil refinery. Came down W of the Maas twixt the villages of Haelen in the Province of Limburg and Nunhem, 17 km E of Weert. Three rest in Jonkerbos War Cemetery and three are buried at Venray War Cemetery.

44 Sqn — **Lancaster I** — **PA195 KM-V** — **Op: Karlsruhe**

F/O C Worrall +
Sgt W J Wilson +
Sgt J R Fuller +
F/S J A Clements +
F/S J Watt +
Sgt J E Judd +
F/S G E Maidment +

T/o 2005 Spilsby. All are buried in Dürnbach War Cemetery. F/O Worrall came from Salisbury in Southern Rhodesia, while Sgt Wilson, his flight engineer, hailed from Banbridge, Co. Down in Northern Ireland. At 31, F/S Maidment was the oldest member of the crew, the others being aged between twenty and twenty-two.

44 Sqn — **Lancaster I** — **SW251 KM-X** — **Op: Karlsruhe**

F/L T E Gallivan RCAF +
Sgt A Balloch +
F/O O W Armstrong RCAF +
F/S L H Beaumont RCAF +
Sgt S J Bowden +
F/S E C Dufresne RCAF +
F/S D W Johnson RCAF +

T/o 1948 Spilsby. All are buried in Dürnbach War Cemetery. Sgt Balloch came from Broken Hill in Northern Rhodesia, while at 18 F/S Dufresne RCAF was amongst the youngest Canadians to die on Bomber Command operations in the remaining months of the war. His name, along with those of F/S Beaumont RCAF and Sgt Bowden, is also inscribed on the Runnymede Memorial.

2-3 Feb	**50 Sqn**	**Lancaster I**	**NG381 VN-A**	**Op: Karlsruhe**
1945	F/O T S A Tarrant RNZAF	+	T/o 2035 Skellingthorpe. All are buried in
	Sgt D A Dorey	+	Dürnbach War Cemetery.
	Sgt A T A Marden	+	
	Sgt J R Hassan	+	
	Sgt H Whiteley	+	
	Sgt J E Look	+	
	Sgt W W Hammond	+	

50 Sqn	**Lancaster I**	**PA223 VN-D**	**Op: Karlsruhe**
F/O E Harrop	+	T/o 1940 Skellingthorpe. Exploded and crashed
Sgt R MacGowan	+	approximately 4 km SW of Hochfelden (Bas-Rhin)
F/S R D Heppenstall	+	a small town some 25 km NNW from the centre of
WO2 F C Wrynn RCAF	+	Strasbourg. It is assumed F/S Tolson RCAF was
F/S J L Russell	+	either blown clear or managed to parachute. He
F/S J Leeming RCAF	+	duly returned to Skellingthorpe. The others
F/S J E Tolson RCAF		are buried in France at Choloy War Cemetery.

51 Sqn	**Halifax III**	**MZ487 MH-Z**	**Op: Wanne-Eickel**
F/L W R Arnold RNZAF	+	T/o 2014 Snaith to bomb an oil refinery. Those
Sgt D W Farrar	+	who died are buried in Rheinberg War Cemetery.
P/O F D K Balflour RNZAF	pow	F/O Bell is described in the CWGC register as
F/O K T Bell	+	a wireless operator/air gunner, but it is
W/O W Poston	+	believed he was carrying out the duties of an
Sgt J S Kewell	+	air bomber.
Sgt W Osmond	+	

61 Sqn	**Lancaster I**	**NG241 QR-Y**	**Op: Karlsruhe**
F/L J Lipton		T/o 1953 Skellingthorpe. Outbound, an oil pipe
W/O J G Robertson		fractured in the outer starboard engine causing
W/O A Westwell DFM		a serious fire. Abandoned and crashed near
F/O J Gregory		Hannonville-Suzemont (Moselle), some 25 km WSW
P/O W F Holland		of Metz. W/O Westwell had flown with 97 Squadron
W/O A Barfoot DFM		while W/O Barfoot had served with 207 Squadron,
W/O I F Bowden		their awards having been Gazetted on 14 May and
		10 December 1943 respectively.

78 Sqn	**Halifax III**	**NA167 EY-F**	**Op: Wanne-Eickel**
F/O J L Gutzewitz RNZAF	+	T/o 2026 Breighton to bomb an oil refining plant.
F/S W J Paterson	pow	Of those who died, three are buried in the Reich-
P/O L B Stuart RNZAF	pow	swald Forest War Cemetery, while F/S Fletcher is
P/O L P O'Brien RNZAF	pow	commemorated on panel 268 of the Runnymede
F/S F V Robinson	+	Memorial. Until recently, Sgt Cowell had been
Sgt E H Fletcher	+	a member of the Air Training Corps.
Sgt F Cowell	+	

90 Sqn	**Lancaster I**	**HK610 WP-Z**	**Op: Wiesbaden**
W/C W G Bannister	+	T/o 2052 Tuddenham but just 33 minutes into the
Sgt R Swan	+	operation, a midair collision occurred involving
F/L H A W Williams	+	another Squadron Lancaster. Out of control, W/C
Sgt A Moore	+	Bannister's aircraft crashed and exploded at
Sgt J J Chidwick	+	Hengrave, 3 miles NW from Bury St. Edmunds in
Sgt G L Webb	+	Suffolk. Three are buried in Beck Row (St. John)
WO2 J Train RCAF	+	Churchyard; the others rest in various United
Sgt D F Luxford	+	Kingdom cemeteries. W/C Bannister was a noted

athlete who had represented England in the 1936
Olympic Games held in Berlin. For much of his war service, he had specialised
in armaments, serving in the Middle East and in Canada. He had been appointed
to W/C rank as early as 1 March 1941, less than seven years from relinquishing
his commission in the Territorial Army and entering Cranwell as a Pilot Officer.
It is further noted that he had gained a Bachelor of Arts degree from Cambridge
University, where he read Anthropology.

Note. In 1987 Peter and Maureen Wilson compiled an excellent tribute to the
76 airmen buried in Beck Row and I am indebted to them for their biographical
notes concerning W/C Bannister. The second Lancaster was PD336 flown by F/O
C W R Harries and contrary to some reports, this aircraft was not written off.
Ironically, however, it came to grief a few weeks later while being captained
by W/C Bannister's successor.

2-3 Feb 1945	**149 Sqn**	**Lancaster I**	**NN708 OJ-Q**	**Op: Wiesbaden**
	F/L L E Button RAAF	+	T/o 2031 Methwold. Crashed at Niederbrechen, a
	W/C L H Kay DFC	+	town on the main road between Limburg and Bad
	Sgt J C Botting	+	Camberg. Those who lost their lives are buried
	Sgt H Ormerod	pow	in Hannover War Cemetery. It is reported that
	F/O F M G Harrison	pow	W/C Kay had only recently taken up his post of
	W/O P H Wales RAAF	+	commanding officer.
	Sgt F Bryant	pow	
	Sgt C S Bowers	+	

	158 Sqn	**Halifax III**	**MZ403 NP-G**	**Op: Wanne-Eickel**
	F/O H R H Meredith RCAF		T/o Lissett with the intention of attacking an
	Sgt D A G Boyden		oil refinery, but turned back following loss of
	P/O D H Budreau RCAF		power from the port outer. On landing at 0045,
	F/S A M Murray RCAF		the Halifax ballooned back into the air followed
	WO1 H W Harper RCAF		by a very heavy second arrival, which collapsed
	F/S G Springham RCAF		the tail oleo and caused serious structural
	F/S A A Bower RCAF		damage to the rear fuselage. No injuries are
			reported and after languishing on the airfield

for nearly four months, the Halifax was struck off charge on 15 May 1945.

	189 Sqn	**Lancaster I**	**NG307 CA-F**	**Op: Karlsruhe**
	F/O G E Locke	+	T/o 2022 Fulbeck. Homebound, the Lancaster flew
	Sgt J C Whyte	+	into dense cloud and not long afterwards fell out
	F/S W J Treadwell	+	of control and crashed 2250 in France at Jarny in
	F/S A D Blencowe		the Department of Meurthe-et-Moselle and in the
	F/S R J Young RAAF	+	SE outskirts of Conflans-en-Jarnisy. Those who
	Sgt G E Brook	+	perished were buried by the Americans at Foy,
	Sgt R Powell		in Belgium, since when their bodies have been
			exhumed and transferred to Hotton War Cemetery.

It will be recalled that Sgt Powell, a regular airman who had joined the RAF
in the 1920s, had parachuted a month previous while on operations to Royan.
F/O Locke was a qualified architect and surveyor.

	189 Sqn	**Lancaster I**	**PB743 CA-E**	**Op: Karlsruhe**
	F/O J O Davies	+	T/o 2011 Fulbeck. F/O Ellis lies in Dürnbach
	F/O J B Leslie	+	War Cemetery, but the others who died have no
	F/O G Langmead	+	known graves. F/S Cromarty had flown previously
	F/O T O E Ellis	+	with 61 Squadron and details of his award had
	Sgt E L Evans	+	been Gazetted on 2 June 1944. At 39, F/O Leslie
	F/S B Edwards	+	was amongst the oldest officers killed on bomber
	F/S L W Cromarty DFM	pow	operations in 1945.

	189 Sqn	**Lancaster I**	**PB840 CA-K**	**Op: Karlsruhe**
	F/O W D Kelly RAAF	+	T/o 2018 Fulbeck. Crashed at Unteröwisheim some
	Sgt J Howarth	+	6 km NE of Bruchsal. Those who died now rest in
	F/O R J Webb RCAF	+	Dürnbach War Cemetery. F/S James, at least, was
	F/S A L James	+	brought here from a grave in the Ulstadtfriedhof
	W/O J H Grubb	+	located about 2 km W of Unteröwisheim, having
	F/S F A Fox	+	been buried here on 9 February. Sgt Dyson is
	Sgt R F Dyson GM	pow	reported to have been found by a German civilian
			who delivered him up to Oblt Workaensfer at

Dienssteele, who in turn had him admitted to a hospital in Karlsruhe. It is
further reported that Sgt Dyson arrived home on 25 July; he was a pre-war
regular and gained his George Medal for his brave actions when Lancaster I
PB745 crashed on 26-27 November 1944 (see Volume 5 page 494).

	189 Sqn	**Lancaster I**	**PB848 CA-Q**	**Op: Karlsruhe**
	F/L N P Blain RCAF	+	T/o 2009 Fulbeck. Those who lost their lives
	F/S F T J Nicholls	+	now rest in Dürnbach War Cemetery. F/O Porter
	WO2 R E Fulcher RCAF	+	hailed from St. Peter Port on the Channel Island
	F/O K S Porter	+	of Guernsey and had been an Exhibitioner of
	Sgt K C R Alder	+	Peterhouse and Scholar for the year 1941-1942
	F/S A E Smith	+	and Wrangler in 1942.
	F/S D F Clement RCAF	pow	

Note. 189 Squadron had previously enjoyed reasonable fortune, losing only
four aircraft twixt October 1944 and the end of the year. In the last four
full months of the war, fifteen Lancasters were written off.

227 Sqn	Lancaster I		ME759 9J-D	Op: Karlsruhe
F/O D Geddes		pow	T/o 1954 Balderton.	
Sgt R Elborn		pow		
Sgt A T Mayne		pow		
Sgt S H Page		pow		
Sgt B G Lawrence		pow		
Sgt P Gaughan		pow		
Sgt B J T Cox		pow		

300 Sqn	Lancaster I		ME744 BH-P	Op: Wiesbaden
F/L Z Kapciuk PAF		+	T/o 2104 Faldingworth. Hit by flak and crashed
Sgt B Wilk PAF		+	into a wooded area near Rambach in the NE suburbs
Sgt R Reder PAF		+	of Wiesbaden. Five of those who died now rest in
F/O J Branszted PAF		+	Dürnbach War Cemetery, but Sgt Reder's grave
Sgt F Jurewicz PAF		+	could not be found.
F/O Z Modro PAF		+	
Sgt M T Masiorski PAF		pow	

408 Sqn	Halifax VII	NP757 EQ-B	Op: Wanne-Eickel
F/O J D Baird RCAF		T/o 2010 Linton-on-Ouse with the intent of bomb-
Sgt P J A O'Connell		ing an oil refinery but the crew experienced
F/O J M Black RCAF		engine problems of such severity that an hour
F/O E A Kapanauik RCAF		later they were forced to bale out, leaving the
WO2 W G Hudson RCAF		Halifax to crash at North Witham, 9 miles SSE of
F/S R G Hughes RCAF		Grantham, Lincolnshire and just to the W of the
F/S W J Baty RCAF		A1 below the village of Colsterworth. Two of

the crew sustained quite serious injuries while
a third was less badly hurt. Their names are not identified in Squadron records.

419 Sqn	Lancaster X		KB750 VR-N	Op: Wiesbaden
P/O B W Martin RCAF		+	T/o 2041 Middleton St. George. Homebound when
Sgt J McAfee		+	hit by flak. The order to bale out was given
F/O R W Hodgson RCAF		+	but only F/S McTaggart RCAF complied before the
F/O J A F McDonald RCAF		+	Lancaster crashed with great force just over a
F/S P F English RCAF		+	kilometre S of Wolf, a village on the Mosel and
F/S R A Nisbet RCAF		+	3 km NNW of Traben-Trabach. Those who died were
F/S W J McTaggart RCAF		pow	buried near the crash site, since when their

bodies have been taken to Rheinberg War Cemetery.

426 Sqn	Halifax VII		NP819 OW-B	Op: Wanne-Eickel
F/O J P Talocka RCAF		+	T/o 2044 Linton-on-Ouse to bomb an oil refinery.
Sgt G Needham		+	Very badly damaged by flak, which necessitated a
F/O J M Styles RCAF		+	diversion to Manston airfield in Kent. However,
F/O S G Arlotte RCAF		+	F/O Talocka RCAF was not satisfied with his
WO2 S E McAllister RCAF			approach and decided to go round again. While
F/S J A Chisamore RCAF		+	doing so, he lost control at 600 feet and the
F/S A G Bradley RCAF		+	Halifax dived into the ground at Castle Farm

near the aerodrome. Of the six who died, five
are buried in Brookwood Military Cemetery, while Sgt Needham was taken back to
his home and laid to rest in Scunthorpe (Brumby and Frodingham) Cemetery.

428 Sqn	Lancaster X		KB725 NA-L	Op: Wiesbaden
F/L V M Gadkin RCAF		inj	T/o 2017 Middleton St. George. Turned back
P/O R A Playter RCAF		+	with engine failure and crashed 0037 after
P/O J A Keating RCAF		+	overshooting the duty runway, coming down
			between Longnewton and Elton, 4 miles WSW

from the centre of Stockton-on-Tees, Durham. Both air gunners were buried
in Harrogate (Stonefall) Cemetery. The remaining members of crew were not
seriously injured and, thus, have not been named in the Squadron records.

428 Sqn	Lancaster X		KB792 NA-I	Op: Wiesbaden
F/L D E Berry AFC RCAF		+	T/o 2020 Middleton St. George. Exploded over
P/O J C Harris MID		+	the target area. Those who lost their lives
F/L C J Ordin RCAF		+	are buried in Dürnbach War Cemetery. P/O Harris
P/O F E Hogan RCAF		+	was the son of Maj George Arthur Harris CBE DSO
F/O C Walford RCAF		+	of Belfast. Most were operating for the 30th
P/O K M Hammond RCAF		+	time and as such were nearing the end of their
P/O C M Roche RCAF		pow	tour of duty.

| 2-3 Feb | 432 Sqn | Halifax VII | NP704 QO-L | Op: **Wanne-Eickel** |

2-3 Feb
1945

432 Sqn   **Halifax VII**   **NP704 QO-L**   Op: **Wanne-Eickel**

F/L G H Thompson RCAF	+
Sgt R G E Silver RCAF	+
F/O H Bloch RCAF	+
F/O J T Robinson RCAF	+
WO2 A M Jones RCAF	+
Sgt R R Vallier RCAF	+
Sgt W H Haryett RCAF	+

T/o 2013 East Moor to attack an oil refinery. All are buried in the Reichswald Forest War Cemetery, having, it is believed, been brought here from the Nordfriedhof at Düsseldorf.

460 Sqn   **Lancaster I**   **PB807 AR-H**   Op: **Wiesbaden**

F/O J Maguire RAAF	+
Sgt R B Newton	+
F/S N W Everett RAAF	+
F/S R H Whiticar	pow
W/O D B May RAAF	+
F/S D G Russell RCAF	+
Sgt W G Potter	+

T/o 2042 Binbrook. Crashed at Riedelbach some 17 km NW of Bad Homburg-vor-der-Höhe. Those who lost their lives rest in Dürnbach War Cemetery. F/O Maguire RAAF had married Nellie Maguire of Doncaster. Although not unique, it was unusual to find an RCAF airman flying with an Australian squadron.

460 Sqn   **Lancaster III**   **ME326 AR-P**   Op: **Wiesbaden**

G/C K R J Parsons RAAF	
Sgt W T Jeffries	+
F/S F J Flattery	+
Sgt J H Bull	+
F/S W A Cunningham RAAF	+
Sgt W A George	+
F/S F Human	inj

T/o 2045 Binbrook. Homebound when involved in a midair collision at 19,000 feet with a 626 Squadron Lancaster, both machines falling circa 2300 at St-Maxent (Somme), 8 km SW of Abbeville. Those who died, including F/S Human who is reported to have succumbed to his injuries, rest in the extension to Abbeville Communal Cemetery.

463 Sqn   **Lancaster I**   **ME298 JO-B**   Op: **Karlsruhe**

F/O R K Oliver RAAF	+
Sgt C W Gordon	pow
F/S J Willcocks RAAF	pow
W/O J Johnson RAAF	+
F/S W A Taylor RAAF	+
F/S R J Lyons RAAF	+
F/S A B Barrett RAAF	+

T/o 2007 Waddington. Those who died now lie in Dürnbach War Cemetery.

467 Sqn   **Lancaster I**   **LM100 PD-D**   Op: **Karlsruhe**

F/O A N G Robinson RAAF	+
Sgt L Ginno	+
F/S B H Elliot RAAF	+
F/S J C Jarrett RAAF	
F/S K J King RAAF	+
F/S R F Cross RAAF	+
F/S W T Paine RAAF	+

T/o 2016 Waddington. Homebound, lost power from the starboard inner engine and the order to feather the unit was given. Moments later the remaining engines failed and though the crew were told to jump, only the air bomber managed to get clear before the Lancaster fell at 2248 near Signy-l'Abbaye (Ardennes), 23 km WSW of Charleville-Mezieres. Those who lost their lives are buried in Clichy New Communal Cemetery. It is reported that F/S Jarrett RAAF made good his escape from just 700 feet.

467 Sqn   **Lancaster III**   **PB306 PO-J**   Op: **Karlsruhe**

F/L N S C Colley	+
F/O J M Inkster RAAF	+
Sgt D G Howdle	+
W/O B F Weber RAAF	+
F/S A H Pearce RAAF	+
F/S F E Everatt RAAF	+
F/S F J Bean RAAF	+
F/S P J Carter RAAF	+

T/o 1951 Waddington. All are buried in Dürnbach War Cemetery. F/L Colley was married to Frances Joan Colley of Moncton, New Brunswick. Their average age was twenty-one.

514 Sqn   **Lancaster I**   **NN772 JI-C2**   Op: **Wiesbaden**

F/O W E McLean RCAF	+
Sgt F G Maunder	+
F/S N W Nightingale	+
Sgt S W Moore	pow
Sgt A T Blackshaw	+
Sgt G H Berridge	pow
Sgt W Harvey	+

T/o 2050 Waterbeach. Hit by flak and came down at Springen, 6 km W of Bad Schwalbach. Those who perished were initially buried at Springen, but since the cessation of hostilities their bodies have been exhumed and taken to Dürnbach War Cemetery. Springen, a village, is located about 19 km NW from the centre of Wiesbaden, so it is likely that the crew were settling into their bombing run when the flak struck.

| 2-3 Feb 1945 | 576 Sqn | Lancaster I | NG119 UL-D2 | Op: **Wiesbaden** |

576 Sqn   **Lancaster I**   NG119 UL-D2   Op: **Wiesbaden**

2-3 Feb 1945

F/O R C Sowerbutts   +
P/O M D Groundwater   +
Sgt H W Porter   +
F/S H J O'Connor   +
Sgt H J Knightbridge   +
Sgt G Lester   +
Sgt R E Streatfield   +

T/o 2128 Fiskerton. Crashed at Kautenbach on the Wiltz river, 13 km NNW of Ettelbruck in the Grand Duchy of Luxembourg. All are buried in Belgium at Hotton War Cemetery, having been brought here from a temporary military cemetery at Foy. F/O Sowerbutts held a Bachelor of Science degree and was an Associate Fellow of the Royal Aeronautical Society. His two air gunners were both nineteen years of age. It is believed F/O J J Hiscocks was originally assigned as the mid-upper air gunner but was replaced by Sgt Lester.

576 Sqn   **Lancaster I**   PD312 UL-R2   Op: **Wiesbaden**

F/L S T Boullier
Sgt D Barclay
Sgt J McVey
F/O P J Smith
Sgt E Ashley
Sgt R E Laverty RCAF
Sgt F V Snanton RCAF

T/o 2047 Fiskerton. Outbound, abandoned 2250 due to an engine fire, over France and in the general vicinity of Beauvais. There are no reports to suggest anyone was badly hurt.

619 Sqn   **Lancaster III**   PB210 PG-V   Op: **Karlsruhe**

F/L E J F Smith   pow
Sgt H Bowden   +
F/S E A Rex   +
P/O D C McNie RCAF   +
F/O E J Mortis   +
F/S P Turner   +
Sgt J R A Ramsay   +

T/o 2007 Strubby. The six members of crew who lost their lives are now resting near Bad Tolz in Dürnbach War Cemetery.

626 Sqn   **Lancaster I**   PD286 UM-O2   Op: **Wiesbaden**

F/L B J Grindrod
Sgt F S Nicholl
F/S K R Collin RAAF
W/O D D Thomson RAAF
F/S W A Pierce RAAF
Sgt R H Burrows
Sgt H K Norton   +

T/o 2050 Wickenby. Lost in the manner described in the 460 Squadron summary. Sgt Norton lies in the extension at Abbeville Communal Cemetery.

640 Sqn   **Halifax III**   MZ492 C8-X   Op: **Wanne-Eickel**

P/O N H Sisley RAAF   +
Sgt P R Jeffries   +
Sgt T A Gibson   +
Sgt A Gray   +
Sgt M Delahunty   +
Sgt B W O Dockerty   +
Sgt J S Whitmee

T/o 2036 Leconfield for an attack on an oil refining plant but at 500 feet the pilot reduced power and, at the same time, commenced banking steeply to port. Moments later, the time being quoted as 2048, the Halifax crashed into Lakes Wood at Lockington, 6 miles NNW of Beverley, Yorkshire. P/O Sisley RAAF was buried in Harrogate (Stonefall) Cemetery, while the others were taken to their homes towns. It is believed Sgt Whitmee escaped practically unscathed.

Note. This had been a typical night for Bomber Command. 1,252 sorties had been despatched, the majority being concerned with the three principal targets identified in these summaries. Officially, twenty-one aircraft failed to return, but when all known losses are taken into account, as reported, the overall figure becomes thirty-four.

101 Sqn   **Lancaster III**   PB457 SR-V   **Ground**

4 Feb 1945

Destroyed by fire at 1410 while hangared at Ludford Magna and undergoing its seventy-five hour inspection.

12 Sqn   **Lancaster III**   ME316 PH-V   Op: **Bottrop**

3-4 Feb 1945

F/O J L Walters RAAF   +
Sgt J M Gibb   +
Sgt S R Harris   +
F/S W Blyth   +
F/S K O Langham RAAF   +
F/S C Butler   +
Sgt H Boulding   +

T/o 1641 Wickenby to bomb the Prosper benzol plant. All are buried in the Reichswald Forest War Cemetery.

3-4 Feb 1945	15 Sqn	Lancaster I	PD419 LS-V	Op: Dortmund

15 Sqn   **Lancaster I**   **PD419 LS-V**   **Op: Dortmund**

F/O J M Morris RNZAF   pow
Sgt G J Owen   pow
F/O J S Wilkinson RNZAF   pow
F/S J A Taylor RNZAF   pow
W/O H Campbell   pow
P/O H E Slingsby   +
F/S E C Temperton RNZAF   +

T/o 1604 Mildenhall to bomb the Hansa benzol facility. Both air gunners rest in Rheinberg War Cemetery. At 38, P/O Slingsby was well above the average age of operational aircrew.

75 Sqn   **Lancaster III**   **ND801 JN-X**   **Op: Dortmund**

F/O R B Crawford RNZAF   inj
Sgt R Allred
F/S Boulton   inj
Sgt C Bullock   inj
Sgt D Scott   inj
Sgt A Smith
Sgt J Tutty

T/o 1641 Mepal similarly tasked. On return to base at 2223 overshot the runway, crashing into a house.

90 Sqn   **Lancaster I**   **PA158 WP-S**   **Op: Dortmund**

F/L J J Buning   +
Sgt M J F P Goddard   +
P/O H S Nickless RAAF   +
F/O S B S Bishop RCAF   +
Sgt A H Edwards   +
Sgt E E Bemrose   +
Sgt J G Brown   +

T/o 1614 Tuddenham similarly tasked. All are buried in Rheinberg War Cemetery. The parents of F/L Buning lived in Holland at Den Haag; Sgt Goddard is described in the CWGC cemetery register as an air gunner.

100 Sqn   **Lancaster III**   **PB569 HW-Y**   **Op: Bottrop**

F/L R Ordell DFC RAAF   +
Sgt C Scurr   +
P/O I R Osborne RAAF   +
W/O J G T Killen RAAF   +
F/S K K Reynolds RAAF   +
F/S R K McKaskill RAAF   +
F/S J Harper   pow

T/o 1605 Grimsby to bomb the Prosper benzol works. Those who died were buried near Venray on 16 February, since when their remains have been taken to Mierlo War Cemetery.

105 Sqn   **Mosquito XVI**   **MM151 GB-**   **Op: Wurzburg**

F/L D M Smith   inj
Sgt K R Aspden   inj

T/o 1736 Bourn. Homebound, low on fuel and with the starboard engine stopped, the crew headed for Knocke-Le-Zoute airfield in Belgium. On approach the port engine cut, out of petrol, and the Mosquito crashed at 2202. Both members of crew were taken to hospital.

Note. Built by the parent company, this Mosquito had been issued to 692 Squadron on 2 July 1944, ex-works, prior to being transferred four days later to 105 Squadron. Its total flying hours are not recorded and it is worth placing on record that information pertaining to hours flown seem to be omitted from the majority, if not all, aircraft movement records that were terminated in 1945 for operational reasons or loss in flying accident.

153 Sqn   **Lancaster I**   **PD378 P4-L**   **Op: Bottrop**

F/O D B Freeborn RCAF
Sgt D A R Morley
F/O W A Brodie RCAF   +
F/S H V Constable
F/S J A Eastman
Sgt J L Stalley
Sgt T O McNamara

T/o 1600 Scampton to attack the Prosper benzol plant. Came under a sustained attack from a Ju 88, whose fire killed F/O Brodie RCAF. Soon afterwards, the Lancaster was abandoned over a part of Holland held by the Allies. F/O Brodie was taken to Eindhoven (Woensel) General Cemetery, since when his body has been exhumed and reinterred at Groesbeek Canadian War Cemetery.

156 Sqn   **Lancaster III**   **ME366 GT-H**   **Op: Bottrop**

F/L J G E Evans RAAF   pow
W/O F Parr DFM   +
F/L F C Salt   +
F/O C P Clark   +
P/O W H Preece RAAF   pow
P/O G C McKenna RAAF   +
F/O J Costigan RAAF   pow

T/o 1652 Upwood to mark the Prosper benzol plant. Those who died rest in the Reichswald Forest War Cemetery. W/O Parr, an ex-Halton apprentice, won his award while flying with 101 Squadron, details being published on 10 December 1943.

3–4 Feb 1945	156 Sqn	Lancaster III	PB505 GT-F	Op: Bottrop

156 Sqn   Lancaster III   PB505 GT-F   Op: Bottrop

F/L M Spinley DFM MID RNZAF   +
F/O L Mooney DFM   +
F/O J H Lascelles DFM   +
F/L K H French   +
W/O L J Hutson RNZAF   +
W/O A Brown DFM   +
F/S H A Holmes   +

T/o 1646 Upwood to mark the Prosper benzol works. Crashed near Hechtel (Limburg), 22 km N of Hasselt, Belgium. Those who died rest in Leopoldsburg War Cemetery. The DFM recipients had flown with 37 Squadron, 101 Squadron, 78 Squadron and 75 Squadron, their awards being published on 16 February 1943, 21 January 1944, 15 June 1943 and 13 August 1943 respectively.

170 Sqn   Lancaster I   NN739 TC-Q   Op: Bottrop

F/L G P Alexandra   +
Sgt C A Matthews   +
F/O B J O'Regan   +
F/O N P W Pedersen   +
Sgt P H Malkin   +
Sgt A McSkimming   +
Sgt R F Niles   +

T/o 1633 Hemswell to bomb the Prosper benzol plant. It is known that all were taken to the Reichswald Forest War Cemetery, but their graves could not be identified when the permanent grave markers were placed. Thus, all are commemorated by special memorials type A, numbered 1 to 7 inclusive. F/O Pedersen was of Danish extraction.

186 Sqn   Lancaster I   HK688 AP-W   Op: Dortmund

F/L E G Hunt   +
Sgt G E Lowndes   +
F/O W J Jenkins   +
F/O J Ross   +
F/S W C Webley   +
Sgt H Stainthorpe   +
Sgt J A Sparke   +

T/o 1620 Stradishall to bomb the Hansa benzol facility. Crashed 1947 at Westerfilde im Wald some 4 km E of Castrup-Rauxel. All were laid to rest on 15 February in the Hauptfriedhof at Dortmund, since when their remains have been taken to the Reichswald Forest War Cemetery.

460 Sqn   Lancaster III   PB301 AR-J   Op: Bottrop

F/L G A F Davies RAAF   pow
Sgt R F Winstanley   +
F/O V Dunn RAAF   +
F/O J D Avery RAAF   pow
F/O G S Brown RAAF   +
F/S N B Bird RAAF   +
F/S F H Wilkins RAAF   +

T/o 1627 Binbrook to attack the Prosper benzol plant. Those who lost their lives rest in the Reichswald Forest War Cemetery. F/O Brown RAAF of Gawler in South Australia held a Diploma in Agriculture (Roseworthy).

514 Sqn   Lancaster III   LM685 JI-B2   Op: Dortmund

F/O W J K Fisher RCAF   +
F/S W B Warr   +
F/O A Q Downward RCAF   +
F/O D E Stephens RCAF   +
F/S R Hardy RAAF   +
Sgt A R McWhinney RCAF   +
Sgt A H Morrison RCAF   +

T/o 1619 Waterbeach to attack the Hansa benzol works. All are buried in the Reichswald Forest War Cemetery. F/S Warr is described in the CWGC cemetery register as a pilot.

550 Sqn   Lancaster I   PD221 BQ-R   Op: Bottrop

F/O R G Nye   +
Sgt C Stuart   +
Sgt J Holding   +
Sgt J F Moyle   +
W/O W J Howson   +
Sgt W H Cook RCAF   +
Sgt L C Taerum RCAF   +

T/o 1631 North Killingholme to bomb the Prosper benzol plant. Shot down by a night-fighter and crashed near Westerbeek (Noord-Brabant), 9 km SW from the small Dutch town of Boxmeer. All rest in Oploo (Westerbeek) Roman Catholic Cemetery, their graves being near those of five soldiers who died in the autumn of 1944. At eighteen, Sgt Taerum RCAF was amongst the youngest airmen killed on bomber operations in 1945.

4 Feb 1945	619 Sqn	Lancaster III	ND792 PG-R	Training

619 Sqn   Lancaster III   ND792 PG-R   Training

F/O G M Proctor RNZAF

Overshot 1039 the Strubby runway, crashed and lost its undercarriage. No injuries reported.

4–5 Feb 1945   35 Sqn   Lancaster III   ME334 TL-Q   Op: Bonn

F/L A E Johnson MID   +
Sgt C A Butler   +
F/S G B Thomas   +
F/O H Coulton   +
F/S R M Jenkins   +
F/S R Neale   +
F/S D F Hadland   +

T/o 1831 Graveley. Crashed at Bonn-Beuel on the E bank of the Rhine, where all were first laid to rest. Since then, their remains have been removed to Rheinberg War Cemetery.

4-5 Feb 1945	128 Sqn	Mosquito XVI	MM199 M5-Q	Op: Hannover

F/L J K Wood RAAF   +   T/o 1806 Wyton. Hit by flak and, according to
F/O R Poole   +   captured enemy papers, totally destroyed after
crashing NW of Ronnenberg and towards Benthe,
9 km SW from the centre of Hannover. Both rest in Hannover War Cemetery.

Note. Details pertaining to this loss were communicated to the Commanding
Officer Notts Yeomanry by the Burgomeister of Benthe.

	419 Sqn	Lancaster X	KB787 VR-M	Op: Bonn

F/L J P Barlow RCAF   +   T/o 1723 Middleton St. George. Outbound, and
F/O L F Edmonds   +   while flying in cloud, collided with a Lancaster
F/O D W Spence RCAF   +   from 433 Squadron. Both machines crashed S of
F/L D J A Buchanan DFC   +   Vielsalm (Luxembourg) in the Belgian Ardennes.
    RCAF   Airmen from the RAF Regiment assisted in the
P/O C T Sutter RCAF   recovery of the fourteen who died and later
F/O J A Gibbs RCAF   +   marked their temporary graves with crosses.
F/L W R Kearns RCAF   +   Since then, their remains have been taken to
Hotton War Cemetery.

	433 Sqn	Lancaster I	PA219 BM-M	Op: Bonn

F/L H D Mara DFC RCAF   +   T/o 1734 Skipton-on-Swale and lost in the manner
F/O C H Howard RCAF   +   described above. Three of the five married RCAF
Sgt L J Sims   +   officers had wedded English girls, namely Ena
F/O W L Melbourne RCAF   +   Mary Mara of Bath, Ruth K Howald of York and Joan
F/O A J Tyrrell RCAF   +   Audrey Tyrrell from Dorchester-on-Thames in
P/O N A Hurst RCAF   +   Oxfordshire.
WO2 B T Sheeran RCAF   +
P/O W G Whitton RCAF   +

5 Feb 1945	128 Sqn	Mosquito XVI	PF412 M5-D	Air Test

F/L T A Empson RNZAF   Crash-landed on Wyton airfield following engine
failure. No injuries reported.

5-6 Feb 1945	571 Sqn	Mosquito XVI	MM115 8K-X	Op: Berlin

F/O K C S Legge   +   T/o 0215 Oakington. Lost without trace. Both
F/O B O Davis   +   are commemorated on the Runnymede Memorial. Mary
Elizabeth Legge, mother of F/O Legge, held the
MBE while F/O Davis was an Associate of the Institute of Chartered Accountants.

6 Feb 1945	90 Sqn	Lancaster I	LM157 WP-C	Air Test

F/L K J Sullivan RAAF   Crash-landed 1520, due to engine failure, in a
Sgt J L Mathias   +   field at Chippenham, 15 miles NE of Cambridge.
As the Lancaster skidded to a stop, it collided
with a pole and caught fire. Sgt Mathias rests in Beck Row (St. John) Cemetery.
Nine airmen were aboard and though Sgt Mathias was the only fatal casualty, five
others were injured but their names are not shown in Squadron records.

7 Feb 1945	15 Sqn	Lancaster I	ME434 LS-D	Op: Wanne-Eickel

F/L G G Hammond RAAF   pow   T/o 1146 Mildenhall to bomb oil production plant.
F/O D W Cook   pow   Hit by flak W of Krefeld and, likely, abandoned.
F/O D L Howell   pow
F/O J E Murphy   pow
P/O A T Gamble   pow
F/O W U A MacIntosh   pow
P/O L F Clarke   pow

7-8 Feb 1945	12 Sqn	Lancaster I	NF925 PH-T	Op: Kleve

F/L J H Somerville RCAF   +   T/o 1909 Wickenby. Crashed at Nistelrode (Noord-
Sgt J L Fryer   +   Brabant), a small community midway between Oss
F/O J T Collins RCAF   +   and Uden. Initially, all were laid to rest at
F/O H J MacMillan RCAF   +   Nistelrode, since when their bodies have been
F/S D H Phillips   +   taken to Groesbeek Canadian War Cemetery. Both
P/O G A Wood RCAF   +   air gunners were aged nineteen and both had been
P/O W C Wilson RCAF   +   commissioned on the same day. It is also noted
that F/O Collins RCAF had married Gladys Mary
Collins of Parkstone, while P/O Wood RCAF was an American from Hartford in the
State of Connecticut.

7-8 Feb
1945

50 Sqn	Lancaster I	PD316 VN-A	Op: Ladbergen

F/L J Boyle	+
Sgt G Ansell	+
Sgt S Hoggett	+
F/S H R Hand	pow
F/S D G Rodwell	+
Sgt R G Turner	pow
Sgt P R Jones	+

T/o 2059 Skellingthorpe and set course for the Dortmund-Ems Kanal. Those who died are buried in the Reichswald Forest War Cemetery.

77 Sqn	Halifax III	MZ689 KN-Z	Op: Goch

F/S D W Muggeridge	+
Sgt W B Keal	+
Sgt A H Croll	+
P/O H Wright	+
Sgt W Forbes	+
W/O C E Foster	+
W/O J Stewart	+
Sgt M E Taylor	+

T/o 1905 Full Sutton to bomb enemy troop and transport ensconced in and around Goch. At 2225 collided with a 158 Squadron Halifax some 20 km SSE of the target area and crashed soon afterwards 5 km SE of Winnekendonk, where all were buried. Since 1945, their bodies have been exhumed and taken to the Reichswald Forest War Cemetery. W/O Stewart, who had been accepted for pilot training with the pre-war Volunteer Reserve, was occupying the mid-under gun position. It will be recalled that apart from W/O Stewart, all had been involved in a serious take off crash in the early part of January.

83 Sqn	Lancaster III	PB181 OL-C	Op: Ladbergen

F/L A P Weber	inj
F/S G Summers	+
F/S E S Thorn	+
F/S G H Lonsdale	+
F/S J D Lauther	+
F/S L F F Scull	+
F/S R J H Jackson	+
F/S J W Stazaker	+

T/o 2058 Coningsby to attack the Dortmund-Ems Kanal near Ladbergen. Thought to have collided with a 97 Squadron Lancaster, crashing at Best (Noord-Brabant). Those who died are buried in cemeteries at Nederweert and Eindhoven. F/L Weber was thrown clear and landed by parachute. He subsequently returned to Coningsby.

97 Sqn	Lancaster III	ND961 OF-U	Op: Ladbergen

Lt C W McGregor SAAF	+
Sgt J Shield	+
F/O A J Norton	+
F/L G S Johnson DFC & Bar	+
F/L R C Smalley RCAF	+
F/S R H Cheatle RAAF	+
F/S P G Cannon	+
Sgt D S Lennie	+

T/o 2105 Coningsby similarly tasked and believed lost in the circumstances described above. All were laid to rest in Eindhoven (Woensel) General Cemetery, since when F/L Smalley RCAF has been transferred to the Canadian War Cemetery at Groesbeek. F/L Johnson was flying as the visual air bomber.

102 Sqn	Halifax III	LW142 DY-N	Op: Goch

F/O R W Smallwoods	+
Sgt J Gallagher	+
F/O W W Russell	+
F/O B R James	+
Sgt P D Hewitt	+
Sgt J M Lennon	+
Sgt W B Scott	+

T/o Pocklington to bomb transport and troop positions. Came down at Hamme Mille (Brabant) some 12 km SSE from the centre of Leuven and on the main road leading S to Namur. All rest in Heverlee War Cemetery. Sgt Gallagher was 39, well above an age associated with operational airmen.

102 Sqn	Halifax III	NA175 DY-Q	Op: Goch

W/O W R Smith	+
Sgt J G Grist	
F/S W A McPherson	
F/S A G Kingdom	inj
F/O J Crisp	
Sgt W Ollerton	
Sgt B Peckham	inj

T/o Pocklington similarly instructed. On the home leg intercepted by a night-fighter and partially abandoned over Belgium, two members of crew sustaining injuries. The Halifax came down circa 0100 some 400 metres from a zinc factory at Lommel (Limburg); W/O Smith lies in Leopoldsburg War Cemetery.

141 Sqn	Mosquito VI	PZ348 TW-J	Op: BS

S/L P A Bates DFC	+
F/O W G Cadman DFC	+

T/o 2200 Little Snoring. Shot down by a night-fighter, crashed and exploded at Hollage, 3 km W from the centre of Wallenhorst. Both officers lie in Hannover War Cemetery. F/O Cadman's father was Maj William Henry Cadman MBE. Enemy papers relating to this crash say the Mosquito was 98 percent destroyed. It is further noted that S/L Bates commanded the Squadron's A Flight.

7-8 Feb
1945

158 Sqn   **Halifax III**   **NP973 NP-P**   **Op: Goch**

F/O J L Beeson RAAF	+
Sgt A McQuilkin	pow
P/O W G Bennett	+
P/O R E Jones	+
P/O L J Nichols RAAF	+
F/S P A Murphy	pow
F/S L A E Papworth	pow

T/o 1911 Lissett to attack enemy concentrations of both troops and transport. Reached the target area but at 2222 the Master Bomber cancelled the raid. Flying at around 3,500 feet, collided head on at 2225 with a 77 Squadron Halifax, when both aircraft were roughly 20 km SSE of Goch. Two minutes later F/O Beeson RAAF ordered his crew to bale out but only three could do so before the bomber plunged into a forest between Lüllingen and Geldern. Those who died now lie in the Reichswald Forest War Cemetery. F/S Papworth evaded capture until 10 February, when he was apprehended by the Volkssturm.

169 Sqn   **Mosquito VI**   **NT176 VI-C**   **Op: BS**

F/L J B J Smith	+
F/O K R Goldthorpe	+

T/o 2226 Great Massingham and set course for Bonn. Crashed between Terlinden (Limburg) and Hoogcruts, two hamlets practically on Holland's border with Belgium and 13 km SE of Maastricht. Both are buried in Venray War Cemetery, having been brought here from the US Military Cemetery at Margraten.

207 Sqn   **Lancaster I**   **NN724 EM-X**   **Op: Ladbergen**

F/O L J Fowler RAAF	pow
Sgt E H Copley	evd
F/S S E Hanson	evd
F/O R W Young	evd
F/O J G Eaton RAAF	pow
F/S W G Cheesman	evd
Sgt N S Levick	pow

T/o 2058 Spilsby to attack the Dortmund-Ems Kanal at a point near Ladbergen.

347 Sqn   **Halifax III**   **NA197 L8-H**   **Op: Goch**

Sgt J M A Bagot FFAF	+
Adj H Moll FFAF	
Ltn B L H Pelliot FFAF	+
Ltn R Rollet FFAF	
Sgc R Brillard FFAF	
Sgt M J Lemithouard FFAF	+
Adj A Loiselot FFAF	

T/o 1859 Elvington to attack troop and transport concentrations. Crashed at the hamlet of Veluwe in the Dutch Province of Noord-Braband some 7 km SSE from Uden. Of those who died, two have no known graves while Ltn Pelliot FFAF is buried in Paris having being first interred at Eindhoven (Woensel) General Cemetery.

347 Sqn   **Halifax III**   **NA260 L8-G**   **Op: Goch**

Adc J M G Aulens FFAF	+
Sgc R G Patry FFAF	+
Cne G Stanislas FFAF	
Slt C P M Rognant FFAF	+
Sgc H A Berdeaux FFAF	+
Sgt M J A Bordier FFAF	+
Sgt R V E Bordelais FFAF	+

T/o 1857 Elvington similarly tasked. Shot down by a night-fighter and crashed at Asten (Noord-Brabant), 19 km ESE of Eindhoven. Cne Stanislas FFAF was thrown clear and landed by parachute, in Allied hands. Slt Rognant FFAF is buried in Weert (Swartbroek) Churchyard where his grave marker shows 7 March 1945 as his date of death. Sgt Bordier FFAF rests on Zeeland in the French Military Field of Honour at Kapelle. The others who died, having been buried in Eindhoven (Woensel) General Cemetery, have been returned to France.

431 Sqn   **Lancaster X**   **KB818 SE-G**   **Op: Goch**

F/O S P Sorensen RCAF	

T/o Croft similarly instructed. Lost power on two engines and later wrecked in an emergency landing at Ford airfield in Sussex. No injuries reported.

Note. In the preamble to the notes concerning this operation, reported in 431 Squadron ORB, SE-G is shown as a participating aircraft. However, in the reports that follow, no details of the Lancaster, or its crew, are given.

462 Sqn   **Halifax III**   **MZ479 Z5-B**   **Op: BS**

W/O B A Simms	
Sgt M A Hewlett	
F/S J Carr	
F/S R Nicklin	
F/S A E Morris RAAF	
F/S P W Hutton RAAF	
Sgt A N Buist	
Sgt K K Kift	

T/o 2137 Foulsham but soon after an engine burst into flames and the crew turned back. Later, as ordered, seven baled out after which W/O Simms skilfully crash-landed 2215 on Hethel airfield in Norfolk, then being used by the USAAF and home to the Liberators of the 389th Bomb Group. The special equipment operator was F/S Hutton RAAF.

7-8 Feb 1945	467 Sqn	Lancaster I		NG455 PO-H	Op: Ladbergen

	467 Sqn	**Lancaster I**	
	W/C J K Douglas DFC AFC RAAF	+	
	Sgt B H Parker	pow	
	P/O H M S Stuart RAAF	+	
	W/O J B Nanscawen RAAF	+	
	F/O L W E Baines RCAF	pow	
	F/O J A Strichland RAAF	evd	
	F/S B O Bean RAAF	pow	
	F/S M G Thompson RAAF	pow	

NG455 PO-H   **Op: Ladbergen**

T/o 2102 Waddington to bomb the Dortmund-Ems Kanal near Ladbergen. Those who died lie in the Reichswald Forest War Cemetery. The loss card indicates that 23 year old W/C Douglas RAAF of Vaucluse in New South Wales had participated in 124 operational sorties. F/O Baines RCAF was flying as an air bomber. As remarked upon in a previous summary, it was unusual to find an RCAF officer operating with an Australia dominated bomber squadron.

	692 Sqn	**Mosquito XVI**	
	F/O P B Doran	+	
	Sgt D H Beckolt	pow	

MM182 P3-Q   **Op: Mainz**

T/o 2012 Graveley. F/O Doran, a veteran of 52 operational missions, is buried in Rheinberg War Cemetery.

8-9 Feb 1945	**15 Sqn**	**Lancaster I**	
	F/L J H Cowie RCAF	+	
	F/L A N L McQueen	+	
	Sgt J Malcolm	+	
	F/O P J Day	+	
	F/S G C Dickinson	+	
	Sgt A T Dobson	+	
	Sgt J Gregory	+	
	F/S M E Hathaway	+	
	Sgt J W Hall	+	

HK620 LS-W   **Op: Krefeld**

T/o 0313 Mildenhall to bomb Hohenbudberg railway yards. Sgt Dobson is commemorated on panel 274 of the Runnymede Memorial; the others are buried in Brussels Town Cemetery. The unusual crew combination comprised of two pilots and three air gunners, F/S Hathaway occupying the mid-under gun position.

	44 Sqn	**Lancaster III**	
	F/L K Mangos RNZAF	+	
	Sgt T S FitzPatrick	pow	
	F/S D D Finlayson	+	
	F/S J N Sheehan RAAF	pow	
	F/L K R Bingham DFC	+	
	Sgt W J James	+	
	Sgt M Jones	+	

ME299 KM-E   **Op: Politz**

T/o 1650 Spilsby to take part in the first wave attack on a synthetic-oil production plant. The five who perished have no known graves.

	49 Sqn	**Lancaster III**	
	F/L S R Galloway	+	
	Sgt H W J Hardy	+	
	F/S T O Bolton	+	
	F/O G W A Kidd	+	
	F/S L Randall	+	
	F/S E Ellis	pow	
	F/O W Dron	+	

ME353 EA-Q   **Op: Politz**

T/o 1649 Fulbeck similarly tasked. Those who lost their lives are buried in Poland at Poznan Old Garrison Cemetery, where F/O Dron is shown in the cemetery register as a pilot.

	50 Sqn	**Lancaster I**	
	P/O T H Hewett	pow	
	Sgt R A Murray	pow	
	Sgt E D Mobberley	+	
	F/S J Maltby	+	
	P/O B Martin	+	
	F/S A E Whitams	+	
	F/S L B Waller	+	

NG385 VN-P   **Op: Politz**

T/o 1639 Skellingthorpe similarly tasked. Came down in shallow water near Wollin. The bodies of those who died were recovered but later only one grave was found, that of Sgt Mobberley who was taken to Poland for burial in Poznan Old Garrison Cemetery. His four companions are commemorated on the Runnymede Memorial.

	57 Sqn	**Lancaster III**	
	F/O B A Clifton RAAF	int	
	Sgt D P Aplin	+	
	F/S J K Wilson	+	
	F/S E C Slaughter	+	
	F/S P L Kirkpatrick RAAF	+	
	Sgt F V J Dunstone	+	
	Sgt C K Davey	+	

PB382 DX-N   **Op: Politz**

T/o 1703 East Kirkby similarly tasked. Hit by AA fire after entering Swedish air space and crashed on farmland at Brohult near Hjortshög. Those who died are buried in Halsingborg (Palsjö) Municipal Cemetery.

Note. A detailed account of what happened to this Lancaster during the course of its attempt to reach Pölitz is reported in Making for Sweden written by Rolph Wegmann and Bo Widfeldt.

8-9 Feb
1945

61 Sqn	Lancaster I
F/O N T Collins RAAF	pow
Sgt W T Lake	pow
Sgt S F Heaven	pow
F/O R Bloomfield	pow
W/O R W Pratt RAAF	pow
Sgt D J Everson	pow
Sgt W J R Scott	+

LL911 QR-X   **Op: Politz**
T/o 1633 Skellingthorpe in the first phase strike against a synthetic-oil production plant. Sgt Scott is buried in Poland at Poznan Old Garrison Cemetery.

61 Sqn	Lancaster I
F/L R W Bartlett	+
F/O K Middlemast	pow
F/S N T Nuttall	pow
F/S A E Hector	pow
W/O P Styles	pow
F/S T C King	pow
Sgt B Courtney	pow

PB737 QR-E   **Op: Politz**
T/o 1652 Skellingthorpe similarly tasked. F/L Bartlett is buried in Berlin at the city's 1939-1945 War Cemetery.

61 Sqn	Lancaster I
F/O B S Tasker RAAF	+
Sgt T McKnight	pow
F/O E Walker	pow
F/S W R R Boobyer	pow
F/S R M McKenzie RAAF	+
Sgt S W Herring	+
Sgt V A Edwards	+

PB759 QR-N   **Op: Politz**
T/o 1659 Skellingthorpe similarly tasked. Those who died rest in Poznan Old Garrison Cemetery.

83 Sqn	Lancaster III
F/L D G Bates	+
F/S J R Farrow	+
P/O A M B Hughes	+
F/L G O Cameron RAAF	+
F/S F W Cotton	+
F/O J Fletcher	pow
F/S D Hancock	pow

ND696 OL-O   **Op: Politz**
T/o 1707 Coningsby similarly charged. Believed shot down at Rüdersdorf, 26 km ESE from the centre of Berlin where those who died rest in the city's 1939-1945 War Cemetery.

186 Sqn	Lancaster I
F/S E Morris	+
Sgt A S Pitt	+
Sgt E M Chetwynd-Stapylton	+
F/S R Wellington	+
Sgt W Stephens	+
Sgt J Finlayson	+
Sgt D McB Crowe	+

HK650 AP-T   **Op: Krefeld**
T/o 0345 Stradishall to attack the Hohenbudberg railway yards. Hit by flak and exploded, showering debris over Schwafheim, a built up area W of the Rhine and some 4 km SE of Moers. All lie in the Reichswald Forest War Cemetery, brought here from Schwafheim.

192 Sqn	Halifax III
F/S B L Butler RNZAF	+
Sgt K G Cheshire	+
F/O D P M Finnigan	+
F/S D W Webb	+
Sgt R D Mitcheson	+
F/O N Burrows	+
Sgt E A E Tucker	+
Sgt B F Woods	+

MZ342 DT-B   **Op: BS**
T/o 1941 Foulsham for operations in the vicinity of Stettin. Homebound at 2,000 feet, involved in a midair collision with Lancaster I PD376 flown by P/O D E J Chalkley of 625 Squadron. The accident occurred circa 0120 in position 5617N 0748E and though the Lancaster escaped serious damage, the Halifax fell into the sea. Six, including F/O Burrows the specialist operator, have no known graves while F/S Webb is buried in Esbjerg (Fourfelt) Cemetery, with Sgt Woods resting next to Able Seaman Gordon Henry Smith of HMS Pintail and an unknown soldier in Husby Churchyard.

214 Sqn	Fortress III
P/O J P Robertson RNZAF	+
Sgt T W H Usher	+
F/S P G Buckland	+
F/S G S M Fowler RAAF	+
F/S F R Olds RNZAF	+
W/O L J Bennett RNZAF	+
Sgt W Bunyan	+
Sgt E Dobson	+
Sgt R J Carrott	+
Sgt W T Banner	+

HB796 BU-T   **Op: BS**
T/o 0329 Oulton tasked to dispense Window W of the Ruhr. Presumed lost over the sea as most, apart from four, are perpetuated by the Memorial at Runnymede. P/O Robertson RNZAF is buried in Brookwood Military Cemetery; Sgt Bunyan lies in Bolton (Astley Bridge) Cemetery; Sgt Dobson was cremated at Bradford Crematorium, while Sgt Banner rests in Sutton-in-Ashfield Cemetery.

8-9 Feb 1945	**405 Sqn**	**Lancaster III**		**ND912 LQ-X**	**Op: Politz**

F/O H B McIntyre RCAF	+	T/o 1914 Gransden Lodge to assist in the marking
F/S A E S Kiff	+	of the second phase attack on the synthetic-oil
F/O L H Mahler RCAF	+	plant. Lost without trace. All are commemorated
P/O A L J St. Pierre RCAF	+	on the Runnymede Memorial.
P/O T A Stone RCAF	+	
P/O M J Martin RCAF	+	
F/S A M Fostey RCAF	+	

415 Sqn	**Halifax III**		**NR249 6U-J**	**Op: Wanne-Eickel**

F/O G K Grier RCAF	+	T/o 0256 East Moor to bomb an oil refining plant.
Sgt J M Andrews		Homebound, hit by flak over the enemy garrison at
F/O P Mikalchuk RCAF	pow	Dunkerque and crashed 0750 into no mans land. All
F/S J M Marshall RCAF	pow	baled out, though F/O Grier RCAF is reported to
F/S J B Horrigan RCAF	pow	have died before reaching the ground. Five landed
F/S W G Johnston RCAF	pow	inside the enemy perimeter but Sgt Andrews found
F/S J N Aicken RCAF	pow	himself on the Allied side of the lines, near an

army unit, and was soon taken to safety. His skipper is buried in the Canadian War Cemetery at Calais.

425 Sqn	**Halifax III**		**LW394 KW-Z**	**Op: Wanne-Eickel**

F/O W M Mark RCAF		T/o 0242 Tholthorpe similarly tasked. Bombed the
Sgt J J Whyte		AP at 0616 from 18,500 feet but soon afterwards
P/O R F Daniels RCAF	inj	the starboard outer caught fire and the crew
F/O W Wotherspoon RCAF		took to their parachutes at 0726 over Belgium
F/S W H Ketcham RCAF	inj	not far from Ieper. F/O Daniels RCAF fractured
P/O A C McLean RCAF		a leg and was taken to 30 General Hospital at
F/S H A Sanderson RCAF		Lille in France, while F/S Ketcham RCAF went to
F/S A A Alger RCAF		Brussels and 8 General Hospital having torn the

cartiledge in his left knee. F/S Sanderson RCAF had been manning the mid-under gun.

426 Sqn	**Halifax VII**		**NP682 OW-R**	**Op: Wanne-Eickel**

F/O J D Wadleigh RCAF	inj	T/o 0247 Linton-on-Ouse similarly tasked but as
Sgt J D Campbell RCAF	+	the aircraft climbed the starboard outer engine
F/S G H Fetherston RCAF	+	caught fire. Before the bombs could be jettisoned
F/O G A Cahoon RCAF	+	the Halifax lost height and crash-landed 0250 at
F/S M K Grant RCAF	inj	Cowthorpe crossroads, not far from Ruddings Farm
F/S J C Laing RCAF	+	and near Wetherby, Yorkshire. Soon afterwards an
Sgt C E Houston RCAF	+	explosion tore the bomber asunder. Those who

died rest in Harrogate (Stonefall) Cemetery.

619 Sqn	**Lancaster III**		**ME314 PG-W**	**Op: Politz**

F/O H T Hesketh RAAF	+	T/o 1709 Strubby as part of the first phase
Sgt T H Fullwood	+	attack on the oil plant. F/S Moyle RCAF is
F/O R A Hudson	+	buried in Berlin 1939-1945 War Cemetery; the
F/S J F E Moyle RCAF	+	others who died are perpetuated by the Runnymede
Sgt A C St. Leger	+	Memorial.
F/S J L MacDonald RCAF	+	
F/S L E Marsh RCAF	pow	

630 Sqn	**Lancaster III**		**ND554 LE-A**	**Op: Politz**

F/O R B Knight RNZAF	+	T/o 1656 East Kirkby similarly instructed.
Sgt A R Newby	+	Lost without trace. All are commemorated on
F/S J Montague	+	the Runnymede Memorial.
Sgt N E A Sharpe	+	
F/S J Lamont RNZAF	+	
Sgt L Young	+	
Sgt S L Cameron	+	

Note. As will be observed from the summaries, operations for the night were spread over many hours with some raids nearing completion before others had started.

Feb 1945	**83 Sqn**	**Lancaster I**		**NG453 OL-M**	**Ground**

LAC T B Graves MID	+	Destroyed 1225 by fire at Coningsby after a
AC2 R A Mures	+	bomb fell from its trolley and ignited. It

is not precisely known if the two casualties were a direct result of this incident, but rest in the local cemetery.

9 Feb 1945	83 Sqn	Lancaster III	PB478 OL-E	Ground

Destroyed in the circumstances described on the previous page. It is observed that AC2 Mures was an ex-ATC cadet.

9-10 Feb 1945	138 Sqn	Stirling IV	LK279 NF-L	Op: SOE

F/S L S Tucker RAAF +
Sgt W M Haragan +
F/O G E Mercer +
F/S G C Toes +
F/S R Y French RAAF +
W/O R J Ball +
F/S W J Carthew +

T/o Tempsford on Operation Tablejam 190 and set course for Denmark. Crashed in a blizzard over Gamborg Fjord, E of Sönderskov and S of Faeno Island. Five have no known graves, but F/S French RAAF is buried in Fredericia Northern Cemetery, while in Middelfart New Cemetery lies F/S Carthew whose body was recovered from the Baltic on 9 June 1945. The age of F/O Mercer is not known, but of the rest not one was over twenty-two.

Note. This was the first Stirling and first clandestine loss in 1945.

10 Feb 1945	139 Sqn	Mosquito XVI	MM189 XD-	Ground

S/L C G Killpack

At 1200, during engine running, at Upwood, the undercarriage collapsed. No injuries reported.

	420 Sqn	Halifax III	MZ375 PT-X	Ground

Wrecked at Tholthorpe in circumstances similar to those described above. Again, there are no reports of anyone being hurt.

	460 Sqn	Lancaster I	PB812 AR-	Training

F/S R A G Miller RAAF +
F/S F A C Nesbit-Bell +
F/S R L Pope RAAF +
F/O J J Downing RAAF +
F/S G M Dockery RAAF +
F/S A G Robinson RAAF +

Dived into the ground 1550 at Caythorpe, some 8 miles NNE of Grantham and on the main road leading northwards towards Lincoln. All are buried in Cambridge City Cemetery.

10-11 Feb 1945	462 Sqn	Halifax III	MZ402 Z5-V	Op: BS

F/L F H James RAAF
Sgt S G Rother
W/O T H McFarlane RAAF
F/S N E Teede RAAF
F/S J D Fraser RAAF
F/S R Blundell RAAF
F/S T P Ledwith RAAF
F/S H W Colman RAAF

T/o 0126 Foulsham for Window duties, which were duly carried out. On return to base at 0440 the Halifax swung off the runway and lost its undercarriage. No one was hurt, but the bomber was damaged beyond repair. The special equipment had been manned by F/S Blundell RAAF.

12 Feb 1945	192 Sqn	Halifax III	MZ852 DT-A	Training

P/O D K Worrard RAAF

T/o 1847 Foulsham for a navigation exercise during which two engines failed. The crew headed for an emergency landing at Greenham Common in Berkshire, touching down at 2017 but, unfortunately, on the wrong runway and practically in the overshoot area. In the ensuing crash, the Halifax collided with three gliders and a radar hut. Two crew members were badly hurt and an American airman on the ground, Sgt Robert B Craven USAAF of the 438 Troop Carrier Group, 88th Squadron, was killed. He is buried in US Military Cemetery, Cambridge.

13-14 Feb 1945	76 Sqn	Halifax III	NA163 MP-K	Op: Bohlen

F/L W T MacFarlane
Sgt W Farquhar
F/S J B Portwood
F/S G C Gallagher
F/S C G Shepherd
Sgt G S Taylorson
W/O N C Davidson

T/o 1804 Holme-on-Spalding Moor to attack the Braunkohle-Benzin oil works. Bombed the AP at 2202 from 18,000 feet but on return was diverted to Chedburgh airfield in Suffolk. Directed to a dispersal pan, F/L MacFarlane taxied along the perimeter track but when he applied the brakes the Halifax ran on and at 0203 the port wing struck a tree damaging the bomber beyond repair. No one was injured.

Note. Transferred from 78 Squadron to 76 Squadron, this Halifax participated in twenty-three operational sorties between 16 November 1944, when the target was Jülich, and the raid referred to above. Flight Lieutenant MacFarlane was soon back on operational duties, continuing to operate throughout March and into April, when his crew attacked Bayreuth in the afternoon of the 11th.

13-14 Feb 1945	**77 Sqn**	**Halifax III**	**MZ803 KN-G**	**Op: Bohlen**

F/S A G Simmons	+	
Sgt B Robinson	+	
F/S J C R Bignell	+	
F/S R E Nicholas	+	
Sgt J Swain	+	
Sgt G A Hubbard	+	
Sgt H J Vidamour	+	

T/o 1845 Full Sutton to bomb the Braunkohle-Benzin plant. All are buried in Berlin 1939-1945 War Cemetery. Sgt Robinson had, until recently, served with the Air Training Corps.

---

103 Sqn   **Lancaster III**   **LM682 PM-O**   **Op: Dresden**

P/O D G Rimmington RAAF	+
Sgt G Turner	+
Sgt G R Gilfillan	+
F/S E V Staples	+
Sgt A H Pettman	+
Sgt W H Swan	+
Sgt F A Rushworth	+

T/o 2140 Elsham Wolds on Operation Thunderclap. Crashed at Winterkasten, 12 km ENE of Bensheim. All are buried in Dürnbach War Cemetery. Sgt Turner and both air gunners were only nineteen years of age; their Australian skipper was 21.

---

115 Sqn   **Lancaster I**   **PB686 KO-D**   **Op: Dresden**

F/O A H Dick	
Sgt C D Rickard	
F/S D R Copland	
F/O L Willson RCAF	
F/O S W Berwick	
Sgt R Whittle	
Sgt G Preston	+

T/o 2150 Witchford similarly tasked. Homebound when forced to abandon due to an engine fire, the Lancaster crashing at Joncourt (Nord), 12 km N of St-Quentin. Sgt Preston is buried at nearby Cambrai in the city's Route de Solesmes Communal Cemetery.

---

186 Sqn   **Lancaster I**   **NG353 AP-X**   **Op: Dresden**

P/O W C James RAAF	+
Sgt J D Hall	+
F/S D Wood	+
F/S A L Bragg	+
Sgt E M Holliday	+
Sgt H C Whaites	+
Sgt J Murphy	+

T/o 2203 Stradishall similarly tasked. All are buried in Berlin 1939-1945 War Cemetery.

---

300 Sqn   **Lancaster I**   **PA185 BH-W**   **Op: Dresden**

W/O M Mykietyn PAF	+
Sgt A Jameliniec PAF	+
W/O J Placzek PAF	+
F/S M F Ogorzal PAF	+
Sgt A Kaczmarz PAF	+
F/S B Nizinski PAF	+
Sgt L S Goldowski PAF	+

T/o 2147 Faldingworth similar tasked. Twelve minutes later and while still gaining height, collided with a 550 Squadron Lancaster. Both aircraft exploded and fell at Stotts Farm, Apley, 3 miles SW of Wragby, Lincolnshire. Only three bodies could be identified and taken to Newark for burial in the Polish Plot. As with all PAF casualties, their names appear on the Polish Air Force Memorial at Northolt.

---

405 Sqn   **Lancaster III**   **PB183 LQ-C**   **Op: Dresden**

F/L M O Frederick RCAF	pow
F/O J A Kaucharik RCAF	+
F/L J K Knights DFC RCAF	+
F/O D B Olson RCAF	+
F/O E W Connolly RCAF	+
F/O J Armitt RCAF	+
P/O R A French RCAF	+
P/O F M Gordon RCAF	+

T/o 2214 Gransden Lodge similarly tasked. Of those who perished, four are buried in Dürnbach War Cemetery and three are commemorated on the Runnymede Memorial. F/O Connolly RCAF, who was flying as a second air bomber, had married Iris Louisa Connolly of Winson Green in Birmingham.

---

463 Sqn   **Lancaster III**   **NG234 JO-E**   **Op: Dresden**

F/O N C Fernley-Stott RAAF	+
Sgt R Marriott	+
F/S T B McManus RAAF	+
F/S B T T Wilson RAAF	+
F/S M J Coleman RAAF	+
Sgt J Johnson	+
F/S A M White RAAF	pow

T/o 1733 Waddington similarly tasked. Of the six who lost their lives, five are buried in the 1939-1945 War Cemetery at Berlin, while panel 275 of the Runnymede Memorial perpetuates the name of Sgt Johnson. All four Australians came from the State of New South Wales; two were 21 and two were twenty, as was Sgt Johnson.

Note. Although part of a batch of Mk.I Lancasters, built by Armstrong Whitworth at their Coventry factory, the movement card for this particular aircraft has been annotated Mkk.III. No flying hours totals recorded.

13-14 Feb 1945	550 Sqn	Lancaster I	NF932 BQ-B2	Op: **Dresden**

550 Sqn   **Lancaster I**   **NF932 BQ-B2**   **Op: Dresden**

F/L E S Allen	+	T/o 2139 North Killingholme on Operation
Sgt E T Smith	+	Thunderclap but twenty minutes into the flight
F/S A B Dennison	+	collided with a 300 Squadron Lancaster and
F/S G A Maginley	+	crashed in the manner described previously.
P/O J R Byrne	+	The bodies of the two air gunners were found
Sgt R G Crump	+	but of the rest none could be identified and
F/O J E Murray-Shirreff	+	their names are commemorated on the Runnymede

Memorial. At 42, Sgt Smith was not only well above the average age of operational aircrew, but he was one the oldest airmen killed on Bomber Command operations in World War II.

576 Sqn   **Lancaster I**   **PD232 UL-O2**   **Op: Dresden**

F/O R R J Young	+	T/o 2125 Fiskerton similarly tasked. All are
Sgt K G Greathead	+	buried in Dürnbach War Cemetery. The two air
Sgt G R James	+	gunners were aged nineteen.
F/O H N Cheeseman	+	
Sgt D P Bannister	+	
Sgt H E Ward	+	
Sgt E W Webb	+	

14 Feb 1945   9 Sqn   **Lancaster I**   **NF937 WS-E**   **Op: Altenbeken**

F/L J J Dunne DFC RAAF	+	T/o 0747 Bardney armed with a Tallboy and headed
Sgt H J Ockerby	+	for a railway viaduct E of Paderborn. Crashed at
P/O M J Thain	+	Sasserath, 11 km SSE of Bad Münstereifel. All
F/O C L Philpott	+	are lying in Rheinberg War Cemetery. F/L Dunne
F/S J W Knight	+	RAAF is reported to have flown 26 operational
P/O J T Rose RCAF	+	sorties.
F/S J F Jordan	+	

161 Sqn   **Stirling IV**   **LK236 MA-Y**   **Training**

F/O E Timperley	+	While flying in poor visibility, hit by a
Sgt D H Mayers	+	Mustang of the 383rd FS flown by F/O T W Kiley
F/S P N Carr	+	USAAF and crashed at Potton, 3 miles E from
F/O G C Wiggins RAAF	+	Sandy, Bedfordshire. Four rest in Cambridge
F/S C W Saunders RAAF	+	City Cemetery; F/O Timperley was cremated at
Sgt P N Ellis	+	Stockport Crematorium, while at nearby Stock-
Sgt W G Cornish	+	port (Willow Grove) Cemetery lies Sgt Mayers.

Sgt Cornish was taken to nearby Wooburn Cemetery, while F/O Kiley USAAF is buried in US Military Cemetery, Cambridge.

14-15 Feb 1945   10 Sqn   **Halifax III**   **MZ793 ZA-X**   **Op: Gardening**

P/O J Grayshan	+	T/o 1807 Melbourne and headed for the Baltic
Sgt R Maddock-Lyon	evd	and the Kadet Channel. Crashed at Asmindrup
F/S A J Berry	+	some 7 km S of Holbaek, Denmark, having been
P/O S Chaderton	pow	picked up by a night-fighter. P/O Grayshan
F/S P Andrews	pow	and F/S Berry are buried on Zealand in Holbaek
F/S H L Mills	evd	East Churchyard. Aided by the Danish resistance
F/S J Petre	evd	three members of crew reached neutral Sweden.

75 Sqn   **Lancaster I**   **NG113 AA-D**   **Op: Chemnitz**

F/L G S Davies RNZAF	pow	T/o 2025 Mepal. F/S Chalmers died in captivity
Sgt I R H Evans	pow	on 2 March and he is now buried in Dürnbach War
F/S C C Greenhough RNZAF	pow	Cemetery.
F/S H E Chalmers	pow	
F/S T M White	pow	
F/S R Muir	pow	
Sgt J J Maher	pow	

77 Sqn   **Halifax III**   **MZ924 KN-D**   **Op: Gardening**

F/L J P Braund	+	T/o 1805 Full Sutton and headed for the Kadet
Sgt R L Leforte	+	Channel. Came down in the Smalandsfarvandet,
F/O J Ritchie	+	S of Zealand. All were recovered from the sea
F/O A Wood	+	and now rest in various Danish cemeteries. It
F/S M C Eddleston	+	will be recalled that a month previous, F/L
Sgt D S Watson	+	Braund's brother, F/L Marwood Paul Braund of
Sgt R E Russell	+	77 Squadron, disappeared without trace while

engaged on a similar mission.

14-15 Feb 1945	**78 Sqn**	**Halifax III**	**MZ791 EY-T**	**Op: Chemnitz**

78 Sqn	Halifax III	MZ791 EY-T	Op: Chemnitz

14-15 Feb 1945

78 Sqn   **Halifax III**   **MZ791 EY-T**   **Op: Chemnitz**

F/L J Davidson
Sgt W Robertson
P/O E Tidman
F/S K C Cutting
Sgt W C Black RAAF
Sgt S McGladdary
Sgt W J Gall

T/o 1723 Breighton. Outbound, the navigation aids failed and at 2121 from 13,000 feet an alternative target was bombed. On return, the crew arrived 0042 at Manston airfield in Kent and though there are no reports of injuries, the Halifax was deemed beyond repair and was eventually struck off charge on 5 July.

78 Sqn   **Halifax III**   **MZ799 EY-X**   **Op: Gardening**

F/L R S Cumming   +
P/O J S Rice   +
P/O J S Thompson   +
P/O S A W Tressider   +
F/S E P Yates   +
F/S I Williams   +
P/O M Schwartz RCAF   +

T/o 1802 Breighton and headed for the Kadet Channel. Lost without trace. All are commemorated on the Runnymede Memorial. It is believed all had flown in excess of thirty sorties. P/O Rice was an ex-Halton apprentice.

100 Sqn   **Lancaster III**   **LM623 HW-S**   **Op: Chemnitz**

P/O T F Townley   pow
Sgt L L Foster   pow
Sgt J C Cape   pow
Sgt K F Day   pow
Sgt G F Longley   pow
Sgt E G Emery   pow
Sgt P Garner   pow

T/o 2015 Grimsby possibly on the first sortie of their operational tour.

115 Sqn   **Lancaster III**   **LM725 KO-X**   **Op: Chemnitz**

F/O E A Slogrove   +
Sgt R S R Booker   +
F/S K Freakes   +
F/O F J Hegan   +
Sgt G Sanderson   +
Sgt L Davies   +
Sgt R I P Eckford   +

T/o 2037 Witchford. Crashed near Haveluy in the Department of Nord, 9 km WSW of Valenciennes. All are buried in Haveluy Communal Cemetery.

153 Sqn   **Lancaster I**   **NN803 P4-O**   **Op: Chemnitz**

F/L C R Mills RCAF   +
Sgt J J O'B Heady   +
F/O L A MacDonald RCAF   +
F/O R S Stanzel RCAF   +
Sgt W H Wicks   +
F/S J H Wilson RCAF   +
F/S C J A Caryi RCAF   +

T/o 2005 Scampton. Both air gunners and nineteen year old F/O MacDonald RCAF, one of the youngest serving Canadian navigators, are buried in Berlin 1939-1945 War Cemetery. The others have no known graves.

158 Sqn   **Halifax III**   **MZ350 NP-R**   **Op: Chemnitz**

F/O J D Gapes RNZAF
Sgt E V Payne
F/S N A S Marsh
P/O J M Scott
F/S N R Grant RAAF
Sgt L Powick
Sgt C T Bird

T/o 1708 Lissett. Outbound, both port engines began to misfire and soon after turning for home the starboard outer lost power. Abandoned and crashed 2000 into woods near Vireux-Molhain and Vireux-Wallerand (Ardennes), some 10 km SW from Givet, a small town near the French-Belgian border. All were soon reunited and returned unscathed to Lissett via Paris.

Note. This Halifax may be classed as a veteran having taken part in sixty-nine operational sorties. Delivered to Lissett on 6 July 1944, its first operation had been to Calais on 18 July with Flight Sergeant R E Johnson RCAF at the controls. On this occasion it displayed the code NP-P but was painted as NP-R in time for its second sortie, Stuttgart on 24-25 July.

166 Sqn   **Lancaster I**   **PD394 AS-P**   **Op: Chemnitz**

F/O D S Kemp RCAF   +
F/S J McCreadie   +
F/O E C Hill   +
F/O M A O'Callaghan   +
W/O A G Flack   +
Sgt H W Oates   +
Sgt F W Wakefield   +

T/o 2050 Kirmington. All are buried in Berlin 1939-1945 War Cemetery.

14-15 Feb	189 Sqn	Lancaster I	RA517 CA-B	Op: Rositz

14-15 Feb
1945

189 Sqn   Lancaster I   RA517 CA-B   Op: Rositz

F/O A C Strachan	+	T/o 1704 Fulbeck to bomb an oil refinery.
Sgt J L Fallows	+	Reported to have crashed near another four-
Sgt W R Powell	+	engined aircraft, some 5 km W of Wittenberg
F/S A J McKay	+	and in the vicinity of a large oil plant.
Sgt V E Filaratoff	+	Five are commemorated on the Runnymede Memorial
Sgt F E Wright	+	and two, Sgt Fallows and F/S McKay, are buried
Sgt J Davies	+	in Berlin 1939-1945 War Cemetery.

Note. Previous to this loss, 189 Squadron had reported five crews missing and in each case the tail gunner had survived.

420 Sqn   Halifax III   NA179 PT-B   Op: Chemnitz

F/O W S Anderson RCAF	+	T/o 1701 Tholthorpe. Called to say the crew
Sgt H Evans	+	were returning to base with the starboard outer
F/O J C Sinden RCAF	+	unserviceable. Eye witnesses saw the Halifax
F/O L I Jones RCAF	+	in the circuit, but while turning finals it spun
F/O S A Hay RCAF	+	out of control from 600 feet and crashed 2008
F/S W H Giles RCAF	inj	about 1 mile N of the airfield and near Alne,
F/S E A H Sills RCAF	+	a village just W of the York to Darlington rail
		line. The RCAF members of crew were buried in

Harrogate (Stonefall) Cemetery; Sgt Evans was claimed by his next-of-kin.

424 Sqn   Lancaster I   PB899 QB-A   Op: Gardening

F/L F C Aldworth RCAF	+	T/o 1758 Skipton-on-Swale for operations over
Sgt L F Davis	+	Pomerania Bay (code named Willows). Lost without
F/O E E Reaney RCAF	+	trace. All are commemorated on the Runnymede
F/S K A Miller RCAF	+	Memorial.
F/S G S Guthrie RCAF	+	
F/S V B Smith RCAF	+	
F/S K C McMurchy RCAF	+	

Note. This was the first Lancaster reported missing from 424 Squadron.

427 Sqn   Halifax III   MZ355 ZL-W   Op: Gardening

S/L W B Brittain RCAF	pow	T/o 1801 Leeming for mine laying duties over the
Sgt P De Metz	pow	Kadet Channel. Shot down at Knaplund, 4 km NNE
F/O C J Driscoll RCAF	pow	from the small town of Hoven in western Jutland
F/O H McKay RCAF	pow	where both air gunners rest in Hoven (Brande)
F/O R V Dallin RCAF	pow	Cemetery. S/L Brittain RCAF had recently taken
P/O E M Ford RCAF	+	up the duties of OC B Flight following the loss
P/O J F Peak RCAF	+	of S/L Crew DFC RCAF the previous month.

427 Sqn   Halifax III   ML422 ZL-N   Op: Chemnitz

F/O V S Roy RCAF	+	T/o 1649 Leeming. Those who lost their lives
Sgt H L C Mayer RCAF	pow	are buried in Berlin 1939-1945 War Cemetery.
F/S A R Williams RCAF	pow	An unconfirmed report states that F/S Scorah
Sgt A L Morrison RCAF	pow	RCAF survived the crash but died a few hours
F/S A N Scorah RCAF	+	later while being treated for his terrible
Sgt A J Cybulskie RCAF	+	burns in a local hospital. The crew were on
Sgt H Gallagher RCAF	+	their first operational sortie.

429 Sqn   Halifax III   MZ865 AL-V   Op: Gardening

F/L R C Charlton RCAF	+	T/o 1803 Leeming for mining duties over the
Sgt W Fedorchuk RCAF	+	Kadet Channel. Violated Swedish airspace and
F/O R A Thorne RCAF	+	was shot down by AA fire, crashing 2058 into
P/O R J McCallum RCAF	+	the sea roughly 8 km off Falsterbo lighthouse.
F/O K W Rainford RCAF	+	Six bodies were eventually recovered and buried
F/S G J L Barnes RCAF	+	in cemeteries both in neutral Sweden and occupied
F/S S E Bostwick RCAF	+	Denmark. P/O McCallum RCAF is perpetuated on
		Runnymede on panel 280 of the memorial. The

aircraft's tail gunner, F/S Bostwick RCAF, was an American from Washington.

Note. Three of the crew are buried in Halsingborg (Palsjö) Municipal Cemetery, Sweden, where all forty-seven graves are those of airmen who fell in the service of Bomber Command. Their dates of death range from 26 September 1940 (see Volume 1 page 113) to 15 February 1945.

| 14–15 Feb | 432 Sqn | Halifax VII | RG449 QO–S | Op: Chemnitz |

14–15 Feb 1945

432 Sqn   Halifax VII   RG449 QO–S   Op: Chemnitz

S/L J H Thompson RCAF	pow
Sgt G L Sorrell	+
F/O J J Serne RCAF	pow
F/O A R A Borland RCAF	pow
F/O S A Harrison RCAF	pow
F/S R J Stringer RCAF	pow
P/O R J Thomson RCAF	pow

T/o 1649 East Moor. Sgt Sorrell, who at 36 was well over the average age of airmen associated with Bomber Command, is buried in Hannover War Cemetery.

434 Sqn   Lancaster X   KB741 WL–C2   Op: Chemnitz

F/O D A Magrath RCAF	+
Sgt B Granka RCAF	+
F/O G M B Barlow RCAF	+
F/O J J McElhone RCAF	+
F/O L Medynski RCAF	+
F/S G E Robertson RCAF	+
Sgt G A McLarty RCAF	pow

T/o 1652 Croft borrowed by 431 Squadron. Those who lost their lives now rest in Berlin at the city's 1939–1945 War Cemetery. F/O McElhone RCAF was an American from Detroit in the State of Michigan.

463 Sqn   Lancaster I   NN721 JO–T   Op: Rositz

F/L J G Padgham	pow
Sgt R Lister	+
F/S D Lewis RAAF	pow
W/O A E W Knight RAAF	+
F/S D C Hannaford RAAF	pow
Sgt W J Bilton	pow
Sgt R L Gard	pow

T/o 1707 Waddington to bomb an oil refinery. Sgt Lister and W/O Knight RAAF are buried in Berlin 1939–1945 War Cemetery.

625 Sqn   Lancaster I   NF996 CF–J2   Op: Chemnitz

F/L R Cunliffe	+
Sgt D W Hayes	+
F/O A G Slocum RCAF	+
F/O E J Lowther	+
Sgt D Williams	+
Sgt W P Pass	+
Sgt T H Hatton	+

T/o 2009 Kelstern. Five rest in the 1939–1945 War Cemetery at Berlin, while F/O Slocum RCAF and Sgt Williams are commemorated on panels 280 and 277 respectively of the Runnymede Memorial.

630 Sqn   Lancaster I   LL966 LE–P   Op: Rositz

Lt G R Lacey SAAF	+
Sgt D K W Mayes	+
F/O R E Proudley	+
F/O A Wallwork RAAF	+
F/S K G Fogarty RAAF	+
Sgt A Carson	+
Sgt H G Davies	+

T/o 1651 East Kirkby. Lt Lacey SAAF is buried in Belgium at Heverlee War Cemetery; the next five named are commemorated on the Runnymede Memorial, while Sgt Davies rests in the 1939–1945 War Cemetery at Berlin. It seems likely that an American graves inspection team came across the remains of Lt Lacey SAAF.

635 Sqn   Lancaster III   PB287 F2–T   Op: Chemnitz

F/L J D F Cowden DFC	+
F/O W Gabbott DFM	+
F/O J R C Donohue DFC	+
S/L R A Boddington DFC & Bar	+
F/L J F Craik DFC	+
F/S H Botterill DFM	+
F/L J S Davidson	+
F/S J T McQuillan DFM	pow

T/o 1727 Downham Market. Those who died are buried in Berlin 1939–1945 War Cemetery. The recipients of the DFM had their awards published on 15 June 1943, 12 February 1946 and 30 June 1944 respectively. F/O Gabbott had served with 10 Squadron, while F/S McQuillan's tour had been with 61 Squadron. F/L Davidson, the only member of crew undecorated, was 43 years old, way above the average for operational aircrew, and hailed from Belfast. It is further reported that S/L Boddington's identity disk was eventually returned via a French farmer. F/O Cowden's previous tour had been with 158 Squadron; his air bomber then had been the late F/S James Campbell who in 1957 wrote Maximum Effort followed in 1973 by The Bombing of Nuremberg; he was also a Lobby Correspondent for the Daily Mirror.

640 Sqn   Halifax III   MZ856 C8–S   Op: Chemnitz

P/O H M De Bij	+
Sgt S W Ede	+
F/S F H Riches	+
F/S B Longworth	+
Sgt B Whitfield	+
Sgt T E Teanby	+
Sgt J R Ridsdale	+

T/o 1704 Leconfield. All are buried in Dürnbach War Cemetery. There are no next-of-kin details in the CWGC register for P/O De Bij, but his Christian names Henri Mari strongly suggest he hailed from Belgium. The same register shows Sgt Ridsdale as a flight engineer.

14-15 Feb 1945	640 Sqn	Halifax III	NP953 C8-G	Op: Chemnitz

F/O K Weber RAAF +   T/o 1702 Leconfield. Those who perished rest in

F/S W S H Strong DFM +   Berlin 1939-1945 War Cemetery. F/S Strong, who

F/S R S Hall   pow   joined the regular air force in the late 1920s,

F/S G D Stean +   or early '30s, gained his award during a tour

F/S R H Lock RAAF +   with 158 Squadron, details being Gazetted on 15

F/S N R Lamphear RCAF +   February 1944. F/S Lamphear RCAF was an American

Sgt S J Price +   from Seattle in Washington State.

15-16 Feb 1945	157 Sqn	Mosquito XIX	TA402 RS-F	Op: BS

F/L L W Basan +   T/o 2200 Swannington and made for the Stuttgart

F/S R D Keefe   area. Eventually, ran out of fuel and abandoned

over France in the vicinity of Cherbourg. F/S
Keefe landed safely but the body of his skipper was found nearly 3 km from the
wreckage of their aircraft. He is buried in Bayeux War Cemetery.

17 Feb 1945	51 Sqn	Halifax III	MZ765 MH-E	Op: Wesel

F/L T N G Winning +   T/o 1159 Snaith. Outbound, the starboard inner

Sgt V C Gilbert   inj   caught fire and the Halifax crashed 1325 at

F/L A S Russell   Manning's Heath, 2 miles SE of Horsham, Sussex.

Sgt J Webb +   F/L Winning succeeded in getting out of the air-

F/O P Haselton   craft but slipped through his harness and fell

F/S R S Heseltine   inj   to his death. He is buried on the east boundary

W/O A Hughes   inj   of Elmdon (St. Nicholas) Churchyard, Solihull,

while Sgt Webb rests in the extension to Abram
(St. John) Churchyard in Lancashire.

	76 Sqn	Halifax III	RG444 MP-U	Op: Wesel

S/L W H R Whitty   inj   T/o 1138 Holme-on-Spalding Moor. On return, and

Sgt J Opde   inj   while trying to join the circuit, flew into

Sgt B Emerson   inj   high ground on Brantingham Wold, 1 mile N from

F/O C R Bobby +   Elloughton on the N side of the Humber and about

Sgt M J Rattue   inj   10 miles W from the centre of Kingston upon Hull.

Sgt C W Boyers   inj   F/O Bobby, recently of 10 Squadron, was cremated

Sgt V Hudson   inj   at Coventry (Canley) Crematorium.

	347 Sqn	Halifax III	LL573 L8-B	Op: Wesel

Adc A Vidal FFAF   T/o 1131 Elvington. Crash-landed 1402 at Carnaby

Adj L Portesseau FFAF   airfield, Yorkshire, following an in-flight fire

Ltn L Guenois FFAF   in the outer port engine. At first it was thought

Slt G Piccot FFAF   the damage was repairable, but on 25 July the

Sgc J Chanson FFAF   aircraft was struck off charge. However, the

Adj A Bruno FFAF   airframe remained reasonably intact and was still

Sgt R Pizel FFAF   extant at the time of the March 1946 census.

	420 Sqn	Halifax III	NR126 PT-X	Op: Wesel

F/O M B Stock RCAF +   T/o 1126 Tholthorpe. At approximately 1745, the

Sgt B C Crollie +   Halifax flew into a hillside at 1,600 feet above

F/O R B Trout RCAF +   sea level near a spot known as Shillmoor in the

F/O R A O Floripe RCAF +   Cheviot Hills some 14 miles SW of Wooler, North-

P/O T L O'Kane RCAF +   umberland. Of the six killed, all five RCAF

F/O D L Neil RCAF +   officers rest in Harrogate (Stonefall) Cemetery,

F/S J A Beasom RCAF   inj   while Sgt Crollie was claimed by his next of kin.

F/O Floripe RCAF came from Toledo, Ohio.

Note. The 420 Squadron ORB contains several confusing statements pertaining
to this loss. The Wesel operation is correctly identified as taking place on
17 February, by day, but the entry for the above crew indicates they crashed
on 18 February, thus suggesting the crew had landed away and were in transit
at the time of their death.

18-19 Feb 1945	626 Sqn	Lancaster I	NF907 UM-K2	Op: Gardening

F/O K G Hollaway RAAF +   T/o 1753 Wickenby for operations over the German

Sgt R F Edwards +   Bight. Lost without trace. All are commemorated

Sgt T W Gascoigne +   on the Runnymede Memorial. Their average age was

Sgt J T Jones +   twenty-one.

W/O R D Gill RAAF +

Sgt E Harrison +

Sgt D W Hughes +

| 18-19 Feb 1945 | 626 Sqn | Lancaster I | PA216 UM-C2 | Op: Gardening |

626 Sqn   Lancaster I   PA216 UM-C2   Op: Gardening

18-19 Feb
1945

F/O H L Lucas +
Sgt A M Watson +
F/S G P Holmes +
F/S R L Lewis +
F/S E E Jenkins +
Sgt F W Underhill +
F/S J Webber +

T/o 1754 Wickenby for operations over the German Bight. Lost without trace. All are commemorated on the Runnymede Memorial.

---

90 Sqn   Lancaster I   PD336 WP-P   Op: Wesel

19 Feb
1945

W/C P F Dunham DFC +
Sgt J E Bennett +
F/O T Metcalfe RCAF +
F/O H F J Carlton +
Sgt L A Page +
Sgt J E Bozeat +
P/O F A Cresswell +

T/o 1324 Tuddenham. Came down in the Rhine near Xanten. Bodies were also recovered at nearby Bislicher and since their initial burial at both locations, two have been taken to the Reichswald Forest War Cemetery and two to Rheinberg War Cemetery. Three are commemorated on the Runnymede Memorial. W/C Dunham had recently taken command of the Squadron following the death earlier in the month of W/C Bannister and the events leading to his loss are associated with the Lancaster here summarised.

---

627 Sqn   Mosquito XXV   KB401 AZ-E   Op: Bohlen

19-20 Feb
1945

W/C E A Benjamin DFC & Bar +
F/O J E Heath DFM +

T/o Coningsby borrowed by 54 Base and flown by the Master Bomber assigned to the Böhlen raid. Hit by flak and crashed in the target area.
W/C Benjamin is buried in Berlin 1939-1945 War Cemetery; F/O Heath, whose DFM was Gazetted on 18 January 1944, following a tour with 50 Squadron, is commemorated on panel 267 of the Runnymede Memorial. His second Christian name was Ettock.

---

428 Sqn   Lancaster X   KB855 NA-F   Training

20 Feb
1945

W/C M W Gall RCAF

Lost power at 2,000 feet from both port engines and forced-landed 1509 at Middleton St. George, skidding beyond the runway and ending up amongst some trees. All escaped with no more than a bad shaking.

---

76 Sqn   Halifax III   NA164 MP-U   Op: Dusseldorf

20-21 Feb
1945

F/O R Roupe
F/L P M M Smith
F/S S Correlli
F/S B Maylin
F/S A Duncombe
Sgt R Doel
Sgt J Coul

T/o 2210 Holme-on-Spalding Moor to attack the Rhenania Ossag oil refinery in the Reisholz district. Landed 0209 on an airstrip in France with both starboard engines feathered. On touch down the Halifax veered off the strip and came into contact with some tar barrels. The tail wheel was ripped off and the port main tyre burst, damaging the bomber beyond repair. No one was hurt and the crew were soon returned to Holme-on-Spalding Moor.

---

101 Sqn   Lancaster I   PB671 SR-M   Op: Dortmund

S/L T J Warner pow
F/O G L Halsall RCAF +
Sgt W Hartell pow
F/O A Jeffcoat pow
W/O J A M Bird pow
F/O D W Weston DFC +
Sgt E C Roberts pow
Sgt S J Stephens +

T/o 2125 Ludford Magna. Those who lost their lives are buried in the Reichswald Forest War Cemetery.

---

102 Sqn   Halifax III   NP950 DY-Q   Op: Dusseldorf

F/L W R McEvoy

T/o 2159 Pocklington to bomb the Rhenania Ossag oil refinery in the Reisholz district. Returned to base with the starboard inner engine unserviceable, touched down at 0431 but overran the runway and ended up in a ditch. No injuries reported.

Note. The quality of the microfilm is so poor that it is impossible to read the names of the crew with any degree of accuracy. Details of the pilot and the circumstances concerning the write off of this Halifax have been taken from the accident record card.

20-21 Feb	150 Sqn	Lancaster I	PD421 IQ-F	Op: Dortmund
1945	F/O F Moresby RNZAF			
	Sgt F J Howell	+		
	Sgt E R Edwards	+		
	Sgt T W Heron	+		
	Sgt W Hastings	+		

T/o Hemswell. Crashed at Hagen (Westfalen), where those who died were initially buried. Two, Sgt Howell and Sgt Edwards, now lie in the Reichswald Forest War Cemetery and two are commemorated on panel 275 of the Runnymede Memorial. It is assumed that F/O Moresby RNZAF and two others, their aircrew positions cannot be ascertained, survived.

Note. With effect from February 1945, 150 Squadron adopted a system of restricted crew details to the name of the pilot.

153 Sqn	Lancaster I	NN785 P4-D	Op: Dortmund
F/L W Holman RCAF	pow		
P/O P Thorne	+		
Sgt A Martin	+		
F/O R C Taylor RCAF	pow		
WO2 V S Reynolds RCAF	pow		
F/S H J Burton	+		
F/S E S Neil RCAF	+		
F/S A D Kall RCAF	pow		

T/o 2125 Scampton. Crashed at Hasslinghausen. Those who died were taken to the Hauptfriedhof at Dortmund, since when their bodies have been brought to the Reichswald Forest War Cemetery.

156 Sqn	Lancaster III	PB701 GT-Q	Op: Dusseldorf
F/L A D Pelly	pow		
F/S R Morgan	pow		
F/O D F Sinfield DFC	+		
F/O A J MacLeod RCAF	pow		
Sgt J D Routledge	pow		
W/O W G Pearce RAAF	pow		
F/S E C Bangs	+		
F/S T S Carr	+		

T/o 2242 Upwood to mark the Rhenania Ossag oil refinery in the Reisholz district. F/O Sinfield, an Exhibitioner at Bedford Modern School and at 19 one of the youngest decorated navigators to lose his life on bombing operations, and both air gunners, rest in Rheinberg War Cemetery. Sgt Routledge was the visual air bomber.

158 Sqn	Halifax III	LV920 NP-D	Op: Dusseldorf
F/O C J P Ramsey RCAF	+		
Sgt W M Philpotts	pow		
P/O G Pond	pow		
P/O A M Lang RCAF	pow		
F/S F W Grant	+		
F/S H J Bailey RCAF	pow		
F/S H F Tyler RCAF	pow		

T/o 2141 Lissett to attack the Rhenania Ossag oil refinery in the Reisholz district. Reported crashed at Drecke Bauernhof, Fuerde. The two who died rest in the Reichswald Forest War Cemetery. F/O Ramsey RCAF was the son of Col Colin Worthington Pope Ramsey CMG.

Note. This Halifax was named "Git Up Dem Stairs" and had been delivered to 158 Squadron on 7 March 1944. It was engaged on its 94th operational sortie.

158 Sqn	Halifax III	RG436 NP-M	Op: Dusseldorf
F/S J Grills RAAF	inj		
Sgt W J Jones	inj		
Sgt K G Kemp	+		
Sgt S Richardson	+		
Sgt J Duncan	inj		
Sgt A McSporran	inj		
Sgt W L Colquhoun	+		

T/o 2150 Lissett similarly tasked. Shot down by a night-fighter in the vicinity of Jülich and crashed in territory controlled by the Ninth US Army. Three of the four injured were taken to Brussels and later Sgt Jones was transferred to a rehabilitation centre at Hoylake near Liverpool, where he was reunited with F/S Grills RAAF. The three who died were taken to Holland and laid to rest in the US Military Cemetery at Margraten. Their graves are now in Venray War Cemetery.

Note. A personal account from Sergeant W J Jones describing his escape from the Halifax, summarised above, appears in the history of 158 Squadron, written by the author of these volumes, under the title In Brave Company.

166 Sqn	Lancaster I	NG183 AS-D	Op: Dortmund
F/L D W Hill RCAF	+		
Sgt E Haines	+		
F/O S A Tafler RCAF	+		
F/S H A Neal RCAF	+		
F/S F H J Harris	+		
Sgt R E Kearney RCAF	+		
Sgt W J Doherty RCAF	+		

T/o 2135 Kirmington. Crashed near the Hansa Bergwerk in the Huckarde district of Dortmund. All were buried in the Hauptfriedhof, but since the establishment of the permanent Allied war cemeteries, their remains have been brought to the Reichswald Forest.

| 20-21 Feb | 166 Sqn | Lancaster I | PA179 AS-A | Op: Dortmund |

20-21 Feb
1945

166 Sqn   **Lancaster I**   **PA179 AS-A**   **Op: Dortmund**

S/L K L Collinson DFC +	T/o 2145 Kirmington. All lie in Rheinberg War
P/O A J Adams DFC +	Cemetery. At least three were in their 30s, P/O
F/S C E Miller +	Adams at 36 being the senior. F/S Miller had been
F/O J M Sinclair DFC +	a scholar at St. Dunstan's College.
F/S A C Harrison +	
F/L J Barritt DFC +	
Sgt C R Anderson +	

166 Sqn   **Lancaster I**   **RA501 AS-N**   **Op: Dortmund**

S/L R Walters DFC	T/o 2135 Kirmington. Very severely damaged by
Sgt P Bates	flak which wounded F/S Vinall and, subsequently,
Sgt F L S Sharp	diverted to Manston airfield in Kent. Here, a
F/S M J Vinall inj	crash-landing was made at 0400, the Lancaster
Sgt E J Johnson	being damaged beyond all reasonable repair.
F/S B R Calvin RAAF	
Sgt A C Manktelow	

223 Sqn   **Liberator VI**   **TS520 6G-J**   **Op: BS**

F/O J W Thompson RCAF +	T/o 2236 Oulton on Window duties. Shot down
F/S J H Kendall +	by a night-fighter and crashed SE of Dortmund.
F/S R Wynn +	It is assumed that those who died were recovered
F/O R W Johnson pow	by an American graves investigation unit as they
W/O W F Baker pow	were next buried at Margraten in a US Military
W/O R A Palmer pow	Cemetery. Their graves are now at Venray War
F/S D Bryant +	Cemetery.
F/S B Maxwell RCAF pow	
F/S R M Wood RCAF +	
Sgt E E Whittaker +	
F/S G R Graham pow	

300 Sqn   **Lancaster I**   **PB722 BH-J**   **Op: Dortmund**

F/L J Konarzewski PAF +	T/o 2142 Faldingworth. Hit by flak and blew
F/S W Jakimowicz PAF pow	up over Bergisch-Gladbach. F/L Konarzewski PAF
Sgt S Modrany PAF +	and Sgt Modrany PAF are buried in the Reichswald
Sgt R Burkacki PAF pow	Forest War Cemetery. On arriving in the United
Sgt T R Picho PAF pow	Kingdom from captivity, Sgt Picho PAF was taken
Sgt A Gorczycki PAF pow	to RAF Hospital Wroughton.
Sgt Z Raczynski PAF pow	

405 Sqn   **Lancaster III**   **PB530 LQ-Q**   **Op: Dortmund**

S/L H F Marcou AFC RCAF pow	T/o 2220 Gransden Lodge. F/S Bolland, whose
F/S G E Bolland DFM +	award was not published until 1 March 1946, left
F/O T W Downey pow	the aircraft by parachute but did not survive the
F/O R O Norse RNZAF pow	descent. He is buried in the Reichswald Forest
F/O B G Smoker pow	War Cemetery, having been brought here from the
F/O J A Lewis pow	Hauptfriedhof at Dortmund.
F/O J T Ross RCAF pow	
T/S J W Verner USAAF pow	

419 Sqn   **Lancaster X**   **KB804 VR-E**   **Op: Dortmund**

F/O L A Blaney RCAF +	T/o 2126 Middleton St. George. Hit by flak,
Sgt T S Instone pow	twice, while approaching the AP. With flames
WO2 D Hanna RCAF +	streaming from the starboard wing and from the
F/O P H Owen RCAF pow	bomb bay, the crew were ordered to bale out.
P/O A Kindret RCAF pow	Six complied, but WO2 Hanna's parachute failed
F/S L J Nozzolillo RCAF pow	to deploy. Along with his skipper, he rests in
P/O R Althan RCAF pow	the Reichswald Forest War Cemetery.

424 Sqn   **Lancaster I**   **ME456 QB-K**   **Op: Dortmund**

F/S W J G Cozens RCAF	T/o 2136 Skipton-on-Swale. Hit by flak while
Sgt J R Kubin RCAF +	running towards the AP and not long afterwards
F/O G D Ree RCAF	a night-fighter struck. As a result, the two
F/O H Rubenstein RCAF	starboard engines failed as did the hydraulics.
Sgt J Butler RCAF pow	The Allied lines were regained where five crew
Sgt A T Skett RCAF pow	managed to bale out, but two drifted back into
Sgt E J Rhodes RCAF	enemy territory. A brilliant forced-landing was
	executed, for which F/S Cozens RCAF was duly

awarded the DFM, Gazetted 18 May 1945. Sgt Kubin RCAF has no known grave.

20-21 Feb 1945	427 Sqn	Halifax III	NP942 ZL-T	Op: Monheim

```
20-21 Feb    427 Sqn          Halifax III   NP942 ZL-T              Op: Monheim
1945         F/L J M Murphy RCAF     pow      T/o 2147 Leeming to attack the Rhenania Ossag
             Sgt G B Tate            pow      oil refining plant. The two officers who died
             F/O G F Mann RCAF       pow      were found in the wreckage of their aircraft.
             F/O E Essenburg RCAF     +       Both now rest in Rheinberg War Cemetery.  WO2
             WO2 E A Perdue RCAF     pow      Perdue RCAF was on the first sortie of his
             F/O A J Breault RCAF    pow      second tour of operations.
             P/O J M Wallace RCAF     +

             431 Sqn          Lancaster X   KB809 SE-Q              Op: Dortmund
             P/O J W Kopp RCAF        +       T/o 2125 Croft.  Crashed 0120 at Hohensyburg
             Sgt W S Dickson RCAF     +       on the N side of the River Ruhr and 9 km SSE
             F/O I C MacCugan RCAF   pow      from the centre of Dortmund.  Those who died
             WO2 F E Lehman RCAF     pow      were taken to the Hauptfriedhof at Dortmund,
             F/S L E Hoffman RCAF     +       but since 1945 their bodies have been removed
             F/S H R Dailey RCAF     pow      to their present resting place in the Reich-
             F/S F E Newman RCAF      +       swald Forest War Cemetery. F/S Newman RCAF was
                                              35 and, thus, was older than most aircrew.

             432 Sqn          Halifax VII   RG455 QO-X              Op: Monheim
             F/O E F Patzer RCAF      +       T/o 2213 East Moor to bomb the town's Rhenania
             Sgt C I Grant           +       Ossag oil works.  Those who died are buried in
             F/O G B Henson RCAF     pow      Rheinberg War Cemetery.
             F/O A H May RCAF        pow
             P/O F S Daley RCAF      pow
             F/S J W B McIntosh RCAF pow
             F/S W G Mendenhall RCAF  +

             460 Sqn          Lancaster III   PB471 AR-F2            Op: Dortmund
             F/L A E Jenkins RAAF    inj      T/o 2137 Binbrook. Crashed at Linkhout in the
             P/O F S Stone           +       Belgian Province of Limburg, 6 km E of Diest,
             F/O S C Swift RAAF      +       the aircraft falling into a wooded area known
             F/O H T Campbell RAAF   +       locally as Mierenberg.  Those who died lie in
             F/O B M Clegg RAAF      +       Hasselt (Kruisveld) Communal Cemetery.  Badly
             F/S B Braddock RAAF     +       injured after landing in a tree, F/L Jenkins
             Sgt A Graham            +       RAAF was taken to a hospital at Diest.
```

Note. Jacques De Vos writes that local historian, Rudy Kenis, traced Flight Lieutenant Jenkins RAAF in Australia and was instrumental in arranging for him to return to Linkhout where a small monument and plaque exists in memory of his crew, parts of the monument being made from wreckage recovered.

```
             576 Sqn          Lancaster I   NF975 UL-J2             Op: Dortmund
             F/O R S Bastick         +       T/o 2141 Fiskerton.  Lost without trace.  All
             Sgt F G J Martin        +       are commemorated on the Runnymede Memorial.
             F/S W G Frost RAAF      +
             F/S W V Bibby           +
             F/S J Coates            +
             Sgt H A Sargent         +
             Sgt R L Swaffer         +

             578 Sqn          Halifax III   NA618 LK-N              Op: Dusseldorf
             F/O I Denley RAAF       pow      T/o 2154 Burn to bomb the Rhenania Ossag oil
             Sgt W Bean              +       refinery in the Reisholz district.  Attacked
             F/S F E Mayer           pow      by a Ju 88 and exploded soon after.  The two
             F/S C G Jerram          +       airmen who died lie in the Reichswald Forest
             F/S D J Ford RAAF       pow      War Cemetery.  W/O Mason was flying as the
             F/S J A Cahill RCAF     pow      mid-under air gunner and is reported to have
             W/O J Mason             pow      been badly injured. Apart from this NCO, the
             Sgt J F Maguire         pow      others had arrived on 24 November 1944.

             578 Sqn          Halifax III   NR191 LK-K              Op: Dusseldorf
             F/O R Carabine          pow      T/o 2147 Burn similarly tasked and lost in a
             Sgt J Benson            pow      manner very similar to that described above.
             F/O H E J Perry         +       Those who perished now lie in the Reichswald
             F/O J R M Mills         +       Forest War Cemetery.  All had arrived, ex-44
             F/S N Earnshaw          pow      Base, on 3 October 1944 and, thus, had become
             Sgt P Blake             +       well established in their tour of operations.
             Sgt G D Gibb            pow
```

20-21 Feb 1945

625 Sqn	Lancaster I	NG267 CF-Y	Op: Dortmund
F/O W P Maloney DFC RCAF	+		
P/O W G Pearce	+		
F/O G H P Shephard RCAF	+		
F/O H R Dart RCAF	+		
WO2 J A Dickson RCAF	+		
F/S B S Thompson RCAF	+		
Sgt O Harding RCAF	+		

T/o 2122 Kelstern. Crashed 0130 at Hagen after exploding in the air. F/O Maloney RCAF, his flight engineer and both air gunners rest in the Reichswald Forest War Cemetery; the others have no known graves but it is known that F/O Dart RCAF was buried in the Hauptfriedhof at Dortmund.

626 Sqn	Lancaster III	LM726 UM-P2	Op: Dortmund
F/O W N Patterson RCAF	+		
Sgt A T Dixon	+		
F/O A J Beck RCAF	+		
F/O J Crawford	+		
Sgt K J Etherington	+		
Sgt T Whitby	pow		
Sgt H D Rutt	+		

T/o 2128 Wickenby. Crashed circa 0130 into a wood near Hagen-Haspe. Those who died were laid to rest in the Hauptfriedhof at Dortmund, since when four have been reinterred in the Reichswald Forest War Cemetery. Panels 279 and 266 respectively of the Runnymede Memorial perpetuate F/O Patterson RCAF and F/O Crawford.

21-22 Feb 1945

7 Sqn	Lancaster III	PA978 MG-O	Op: Worms
F/L J B M Liddell	pow		
Sgt W E Pickering	+		
F/S G F Sage	+		
F/S J R Mears	+		
F/S H M Watson	+		
F/O G A Robertson	+		
Sgt N H Clydesdale	pow		
Sgt P L W Scott	+		

T/o 1718 Oakington. Those who died are buried in Dürnbach War Cemetery. On being liberated, Sgt Clydesdale was admitted to RAF Hospital Wroughton. F/S Watson was flying as the visual air bomber. At 19, F/O Robertson was one of the youngest officers killed on Bomber Command operations in 1945.

10 Sqn	Halifax III	NR189 ZA-Z	Op: Worms
F/S R L Parsons	pow		
Sgt R Palmer	pow		
F/S J Oakes	pow		
F/S N W Longstaff	pow		
Sgt H T S Jones	evd		
Sgt A Colville	pow		
Sgt R W Jarvis	pow		

T/o 1649 Melbourne.

10 Sqn	Halifax III	RG426 ZA-X	Op: Worms
F/L H G Hurrell	+		
Sgt R Stokes	pow		
P/O A F H Nickels	pow		
F/S E J Summerfield	pow		
Sgt H J Webb	pow		
Sgt R G Hyslop	pow		
Sgt H E Whyles	+		

T/o 1700 Melbourne. F/L Hurrell, who came from Newport on the Isle of Wight, and Sgt Whyles are buried in Rheinberg War Cemetery.

35 Sqn	Lancaster III	ME335 TL-O	Op: Duisburg
F/O J J Osmond RAAF	pow		
F/S J K Spedding DFM	pow		
F/O W Wolk RAAF	pow		
Sgt B J B Carr	pow		
W/O A E Aston	pow		
F/O B W Golden DFC	+		
W/O G A Perry DFM RAAF	pow		

T/o 2026 Graveley. F/O Golden is buried in the Reichswald Forest War Cemetery. F/S Spedding and W/O Perry RAAF had their awards published in the London Gazette on 24 July and 19 January 1945 respectively. It is believed F/L Osmond RAAF had flown in the region of seventy operational sorties.

Note. Flight Lieutenant Osmond RAAF commenced operational flying in July 1943 with 466 Squadron before being posted for PFF duties with 35 Squadron. Sadly, he died in a motorcycle crash in January 1946, soon after returning to Western Australia. I am indebted to Flying Officer Robert M Hilliard DFC RAAF, who had crewed with Flight Osmond twixt July 1943 and October 1944, for these details.

35 Sqn	Lancaster III	ME367 TL-R	Op: Duisburg
F/L F W G Tropman DFC RAAF	+		
P/O R M Hallett	pow		
F/O R T Johns	pow		
F/L H D Mitchell	pow		
P/O N W Curtis RAAF	pow		
P/O M H McVey	pow		
P/O G J North	pow		

T/o 2023 Graveley. F/L Tropman RAAF, a veteran PFF pilot with at least 62 operational sorties to his credit, rests in the Reichswald Forest War Cemetery.

21-22 Feb
1945

49 Sqn	Lancaster I	NG327 EA-K	Op: Gravenhorst

F/O E P Smith RNZAF +
Sgt J Corbett pow
F/S J Newby +
F/O E F Hook pow
Sgt E J F McCarthy +
Sgt C F P Burridge +
F/S R J Simpson RCAF +

T/o 1717 Fulbeck to attack the Mittelland Kanal near Gravenhorst. Shot down at Mehr, 12 km NW from Wesel. Five are now buried in the Reichswald Forest War Cemetery having been recovered from graves found at Mehr. Tragically, F/O Hook was killed during a strafing attack by Allied aircraft near Feucht on 4 April. His grave is in Dürnbach War Cemetery.

Note. The death of Flying Officer Hook was not the only case of prisoners of war losing their lives in these circumstances (as has been noted in previous published volumes) and the worst incident occurred near Gresse on 19 April, when Typhoons carried out several firing passes over a column of prisoners that were being forced-marched towards the west. Further details of this sorry incident are reported in the prisoner of war appendix to this volume but readers may wish to avail themselves of No Flight from the Cage by Calton Younger and Two Brothers At War by Harry Ball for additional information.

49 Sqn	Lancaster III	PB568 EA-Y	Op: Gravenhorst

F/O R Mallinson pow
Sgt E Stansill pow
P/O H Eberley RCAF evd
F/S J F Le Marquand pow
F/S M H Makofski evd
P/O F E Grimsdale pow
F/S J P Gascoyne +

T/o 1718 Fulbeck similarly tasked. F/S Gascoyne is buried in the Reichswald Forest War Cemetery. Across the nearby Dutch frontier, in Jonkerbos War Cemetery near Nijmegen, is the grave of his brother, Pilot Officer George Gascoyne DFM, who died while flying with 23 OTU against Essen on 1-2 June 1942 (see Volume 3 page 110). It is believed all were making their 35th sortie.

50 Sqn	Lancaster I	LL741 VN-X	Op: Gravenhorst

F/O P G Anderson RCAF +
Sgt D W Laws
F/S R Campbell RCAF +
F/S D A McCauley +
F/S W R Southcott RCAF +
F/S D A McFayden RCAF +
Sgt F S Langton +

T/o 1702 Skellingthorpe similarly instructed. Partially abandoned, and it is reported that F/S McCauley fell to his death with the canopy of his parachute on fire, before crashing near Helenaveen (Noord-Brabant), 12 km ESE of Asten. The four RCAF members of crew are buried in the Canadian War Cemetery at Groesbeek while F/S McCauley and Sgt Langton, whose body was found in the wreckage, rest at Overloon War Cemetery.

50 Sqn	Lancaster I	RF138 VN-D	Op: Gravenhorst

F/O P H Hatcher +
Sgt W Dolan +
F/S K Parkin +
F/S W E Dalby +
F/S J Woodhouse +
Sgt J Shearer +
Sgt J O'Brien pow

T/o 1704 Skellingthorpe similarly instructed. Those who died rest in the Reichswald Forest War Cemetery.

76 Sqn	Halifax III	NR121 MP-E	Op: Worms

P/O H L Ball RCAF +
Sgt J Faulkner +
F/O W B Mallen RCAF +
P/O W J Phillips RCAF +
W/O E Boydell +
F/S J Pennington RCAF +
F/S J J McNeil RCAF +

T/o 1649 Holme-on-Spalding Moor. Crashed at Hohen-Sülzen, 10 km WSW from the centre of Worms. All rest in Rheinberg War Cemetery. It will be recalled that P/O Ball RCAF had a close shave when his aircraft collided with a 578 Squadron Halifax while returning from Hannover earlier in the year. On that occasion he reached base and landed safely, his aircraft being little damaged.

77 Sqn	Halifax III	NP967 KN-Z	Op: Worms

F/O W T Brennan RCAF pow
Sgt J W Talbot pow
F/O M N Firth RCAF +
F/O K W Joy RCAF pow
Sgt W Haile pow
F/S K C McKeown RCAF +
Sgt A Robinson pow

T/o 1645 Full Sutton. Believed to have come down at Horchheim in the SW outskirts of Worms. F/O Firth RCAF lies in Rheinberg War Cemetery, but fellow Canadian, F/S McKeown RCAF has no known grave and he is commemorated on panel 280 of the Runnymede Memorial. At 38, he was amongst the oldest airmen killed on active service.

21-22 Feb 1945	83 Sqn	Lancaster III	NE165 OL-Y	Op: Gravenhorst
	G/C A C Evans-Evans DFC	+		
	F/O S Marsh	+		
	S/L W G Wishart	+		
	DSO DFC & Bar			
	F/L W C Fitch DFC GM	+		
	F/O D A J W Ball DFM	+		
	F/S R J Takle	+		
	F/O C Coombes	+		
	P/O E H Hansen RAAF	+		

T/o 1707 Coningsby to mark the Mittelland Kanal near Gravenhorst. Shot down by a night-fighter and crashed in a liberated part of Holland at Gertruda Farm, owned by the Ypna family, at Rips (Noord-Brabant), 12 km NE of Helmond. Those who died lie in Mierlo War Cemetery. G/C Evans-Evans was the Station Commander at Coningsby and at 43 was one of the oldest senior officers killed on bomber operations during the entire war. In way of contrast, his highly decorated navigator, S/L Wishart, was 22 and thus ranks amongst the youngest squadron leaders killed in action. F/O Ball had gained his DFM, Gazetted 12 November 1943, while flying with 207 Squadron.

Note. See Volume 2 page 21 for details of a 115 Squadron Wellington crash involving Group Captain Evans-Evans. It is further noted that his younger brother Flight Lieutenant Gwynne Evans-Evans of 2804 Squadron RAF Regiment was killed on 2 October 1944. He is buried in Belgium at Leopoldsburg War Cemetery.

	158 Sqn	Halifax III	MZ351 NP-X	Op: Worms
	F/S A C Widdowson	+		
	Sgt F J Fox	pow		
	P/O T Dillon	pow		
	P/O J M Scott	pow		
	F/S M E Jordan RAAF	pow		
	Sgt C W Sibley	+		
	Sgt F L C Mewis	pow		

T/o 1727 Lissett. Crashed at Dirmstein, 11 km SW of Worms. The two airmen who died rest in Rheinberg War Cemetery, having been brought here from Dirmstein.

	158 Sqn	Halifax III	MZ813 NP-Y	Op: Worms
	F/O R J Hampshire	inj		
	Sgt K D Baracatt	inj		
	P/O T F Morrison	+		
	F/S D R C Glossop	inj		
	Sgt E Dixon	+		
	Sgt J W Kenny	+		
	Sgt A Ainsley	+		

T/o 1726 Lissett. Outbound, crashed 1945 into trees at Belford Hall Farm, Knodishall, 1 mile WSW of Leiston, Suffolk and caught fire. Those who died were taken to their home towns for burial.

	158 Sqn	Halifax III	NR177 NP-W	Op: Worms
	F/O J L Hackman RCAF	pow		
	Sgt J Crane	pow		
	F/O S A Hearst RCAF	pow		
	F/O J F Coghlan RCAF	pow		
	F/S J D Edgar RCAF	pow		
	W/O G W Culham	pow		
	F/O R R Anweiler RCAF	pow		

T/o 1706 Lissett. Crashed at Odenbach, 27 km NNW of Kaiserslautern. F/O Hearst RCAF and and F/O Anweiler RCAF were repatriated, the former being admitted to RAF Hospital Uxbridge on or by 1 April. F/O Anweiler RCAF attempted to evade capture and managed to walk 34 km, despite suffering from a broken ankle, before being apprehended near Birkenfeld.

	161 Sqn	Hudson III	T9405 MA-K	Op: SIS
	F/L D T Oliver	pow		
	W/C G Watson DFM	+		
	F/L O M Morgan RCAF	pow		
	F/L F M Jarman RAAF	pow		
	F/O J M Hartman	+		

T/o 2110 Tempsford on Operation Croc and set course for Germany. Hit by flak and probably came down 0024 between Bokeloh and Lammersfelde some 3 km E and 6 km SE respectively from the centre of Meppen. W/C Watson, whose DFM had been Gazetted on 29 December 1942, following service with 149 Squadron, is buried in Rheinberg War Cemetery, while F/O Hartman lies in the Reichswald Forest War Cemetery, having been recovered from a grave found at Bokeloh. The advance in rank from F/S in December 1942 to W/C by February 1945 was remarkable, even by war time standards. On his release from captivity, F/L Oliver was admitted to RAF Hospital Wroughton.

Note. This was the last Hudson to be lost on a sortie authorised by Bomber Command. However, 161 Squadron which was soon to leave the ranks of Bomber Command, continued to use the Hudson on clandestine missions until the end of the war. As ever, I acknowledge the generous assistance of Freddie Clark and Bryce Gomersall in matters pertaining to 161 Squadron. For a further insight concerning some of the operations flown by this Squadron, readers should consult Hugh Verity's We Landed By Moonlight (Ian Allan).

| 21-22 Feb 1945 | 170 Sqn | Lancaster I | NN744 TC-V | Op: Duisburg |

170 Sqn   **Lancaster I**   **NN744 TC-V**   **Op: Duisburg**

F/L T C B Smith	+
F/S L R Willis	inj
F/S J C Hartley RAAF	pow
W/O A C M Bates	pow
F/S W F E Moss	pow
F/S J Downing	pow
F/S R E Price	pow

T/o 1909 Hemswell. Crashed at Aijen (Limburg) where F/L Smith was first buried. His grave is now in Jonkerbos War Cemetery. F/S Willis is reported to have died from his wounds while being treated in a German staffed hospital on 6 April. He is buried in Holland at Steen-wijkerwold (Kallenkote) General Cemetery in the Province of Overijssel.

170 Sqn   **Lancaster III**   **PB573 TC-H**   **Op: Duisburg**

F/L M A Coderre RCAF	
Sgt H P Morrison	
F/O R W Cooper RCAF	
F/O K A Flanigan RCAF	
F/S A V Lewis	
F/S F R MacInnis RCAF	
F/S F H Paterson RCAF	+

T/o 1907 Hemswell. Hit by predicted flak at 2320 while flying at 16,000 feet. The port inner caught fire and the order to bale out was given, five complying. Meanwhile, F/S Paterson RCAF had made his way forward and as he prepared to jump, along with his skipper, so a night-fighter struck, scoring hits along the starboard wing. This caused the Lancaster to dive and F/S Paterson was knocked unconscious and moments later he fell through the open hatch. He is commemorated on panel 282 of the Runnymede Memorial.

189 Sqn   **Lancaster I**   **NG321 CA-V**   **Op: Gravenhorst**

F/O P Glenville	+
Sgt F Pallister	+
F/S L S Harper	+
F/S T J Perry	+
W/O C J Gallagher RNZAF	+
F/S J L Nolan	pow
Sgt L Moore	+

T/o 1727 Fulbeck to attack the Mittelland Kanal near Gravenhorst. Those who died are buried in the Reischswald Forest War Cemetery.

207 Sqn   **Lancaster I**   **PB814 EM-T**   **Op: Gravenhorst**

F/O T B Phelan RCAF	+
Sgt H Winning	+
P/O E Grundy	+
F/S A A Oak	+
Sgt F C J O'Shea	+
F/S J B Davey RCAF	+
Sgt J A Holmes	pow

T/o 1653 Spilsby similarly tasked. Those who died are buried in the Reichswald Forest War Cemetery. F/O Phelan RCAF of Toronto had married Brenda Mary Phelan of Chick, Denbigshire.

207 Sqn   **Lancaster III**   **PB295 EM-I**   **Op: Gravenhorst**

WO1 C O Huntley RCAF	evd
Sgt J T Lupton	+
Sgt J Gardiner RCAF	+
F/S A A Swihura RCAF	+
F/S M E Granbois RCAF	+
Sgt J W Spence RCAF	pow
F/S R C MacNicoll RCAF	+

T/o 1657 Spilsby similarly tasked. Crashed at Bocholt. Those who lost their lives are buried in the Reichswald Forest War Cemetery, having been found in graves at Bocholt. Sgt Gardiner RCAF was the foster-son of Capt Stuart and Ella Cork, while F/S Swihura RCAF, an American from Babylon on Long Island, New York, was the stepson of Joseph A Kiernan.

227 Sqn   **Lancaster I**   **PB690 9J-V**   **Op: Gravenhorst**

F/L J B Osborne	evd
Sgt R A Scutt	pow
F/S T O Kydd	evd
F/S J G Redman	pow
P/O B H Lee RAAF	pow
F/S S A F Diplock	pow
F/S R W Sheen	pow

T/o 1729 Balderton similarly tasked. It is noted that Sgt Diplock returned to the United Kingdom on or around 7 April, thus suggesting his time in captivity was spent close to where he was captured.

227 Sqn   **Lancaster III**   **PB666 9J-J**   **Op: Gravenhorst**

F/O P I Green	+
Sgt H R Piper	+
WO1 A F Dales RCAF	pow
WO1 D E Cassidy RCAF	pow
Sgt H Roberts	pow
Sgt F G Edwards	+
Sgt W Lancaster	pow

T/o 1721 Balderton similarly tasked. Crashed circa 2200 on land owned by Mr Damkot of Het Woold K21 (Gelderland), Wintersijk. Those who died are buried in the local general cemetery where 38 of the fifty service graves are the resting places for airmen of Bomber Command.

21-22 Feb 1945	346 Sqn	Halifax III		NA547 H7-V	Op: Worms

346 Sqn   Halifax III   **NA547 H7-V**   **Op: Worms**

Slt P Bayle FFAF	+
Sgt E Bardes FFAF	+
Ltn E Joumas FFAF	+
Sgc G Dugnat FFAF	+
Sgt G Bourreau FFAF	+
Sgt L Martrou FFAF	+
Sgt A Esquilat FFAF	+

T/o 1635 Elvington. Crashed at Löllbach, 5 km N of Lauterbecken on the River Glan. Apart from Slt Bayle FFAF, all now rest in Cronenbourg National Cemetery (Bas-Rhin), France.

346 Sqn   Halifax III   **PN179 H7-M**   **Op: Worms**

Adj P Soucille FFAF	+
Adj J Aquaviva FFAF	+
Cdt R Breard FFAF	+
Slt J Fauvet FFAF	+
Sgc J Lemaire FFAF	+
Sgt L Zavaterro FFAF	+
Sgc P Chiericci FFAF	+

T/o 1702 Elvington. Crashed at Klein Bockenheim some 13 km WSW from the centre of Worms. Burials took place at Klein Bockenheim Friedhof, but it is assumed all have since been taken to their homes in France. It is believed Cdt Breard FFAF had flown in the region of thirty operational sorties.

408 Sqn   Halifax VII   **NP711 EQ-O**   **Op: Worms**

F/L D McW Sanderson RCAF	+
Sgt J Wilson	+
F/O R B Smith RCAF	+
F/O W J Gilmore RCAF	+
F/S W W Wagner RCAF	+
F/S N P H Anderson RCAF	+
F/S D E Sherman RCAF	+

T/o 1714 Linton-on-Ouse. All are buried in Rheinberg War Cemetery. Similar to F/O Baily RCAF who had lost his life the previous month, F/O Smith RCAF had been an accountant.

408 Sqn   Halifax VII   **RG477 EQ-N**   **Op: Worms**

F/L R H Fleming RCAF	pow
Sgt S A Powell	pow
F/O H O Hinson RCAF	pow
F/O G M Keech RCAF	pow
F/S J Gazo RCAF	pow
F/S A R Olson RCAF	pow
F/S D Steele RCAF	pow

T/o 1621 Linton-on-Ouse.

427 Sqn   Halifax III   **NR288 ZL-F**   **Op: Worms**

P/O W R Wilson RCAF	pow
Sgt J F W Taylor	+
F/O L Webster RCAF	+
WO2 R R Stuart RCAF	+
F/S D A Henderson RCAF	+
F/S L O Foisy RCAF	+
F/S A J McLeod RCAF	+

T/o 1623 Leeming. Those who lost their lives are buried in Rheinberg War Cemetery.

Note. These were the last casualties sustained by 427 Squadron, now about to convert to Lancasters. However, the Squadron lost two more Halifaxes after loaning them to 429 Squadron. It is pleasing to report that after a trouble free conversion programme, 427 Squadron operated without loss for the remaining weeks of the war.

432 Sqn   Halifax VII   **NP803 QO-I**   **Op: Worms**

F/O R I Bradley RCAF	pow
Sgt J W Reid RCAF	pow
F/O J A Fraser RCAF	pow
F/O R H Mueller RCAF	pow
P/O J G Stephen RCAF	pow
Sgt V L Shulz RCAF	pow
Sgt D C Duffy RCAF	pow

T/o 1630 East Moor. It is believed Sgt Schulz RCAF normally flew using the surname "Smith".

432 Sqn   Halifax VII   **RG451 QO-D**   **Op: Worms**

F/L E S Maguire RCAF	+
Sgt A A McDonald	+
F/L J G Maguire RCAF	+
F/O C W McMillan RCAF	+
F/L C S Moir RCAF	+
F/S F T McLachlan RCAF	pow
F/S E J McClarty RCAF	+

T/o 1644 East Moor. Those who died are buried in Rheinberg War Cemetery. It must surely have been unique to find a crew whose surnames began with a common letter. F/L E S Maguire RCAF came from Winnipeg while F/L J G Maguire RCAF hailed from Jasper in Alberta. It is not known if they were in any way related.

21-22 Feb 1945	432 Sqn	Halifax VII	RG476 QO-T	Op: Worms

F/O F D Baxter RCAF	pow	T/o 1617 East Moor. Believed to have crashed,
Sgt A C Hobbs	+	according to HQ 3rd Army sources, on the E bank
F/O J A Bleich RCAF	+	of the Nahe and S of Bad Münster am Stein-
F/O G E Creswell RCAF	+	Ebernburg, a small town just below Bad Kreuznach.
F/O G E Armstrong RCAF	pow	At least one body, that of F/O Creswell RCAF, was
F/S A J Hunter RCAF	+	identified and taken for burial at a US Military
F/S S E Waterbury RCAF	pow	cemetery in Strasbourg, France. Since then, his

body has been exhumed and, surprisingly, taken
back to Germany for interment with the others who died in Dürnbach War Cemetery.

460 Sqn	Lancaster I	NG468 AR-J2	Op: Duisburg

F/O B Hepper RAAF	pow
Sgt G F Rudge	pow
F/S A R Main RAAF	pow
F/O A Flynn RAAF	pow
F/S C G Cooper RAAF	pow
F/S R C Styles RAAF	pow
F/S F J Sheridan RAAF	pow

T/o 1927 Binbrook.

463 Sqn	Lancaster I	NG329 JO-Z	Op: Gravenhorst

F/O G H Farrow RAAF		T/o 1706 Waddington to attack the Mittelland
Sgt S B Bridgman	inj	Kanal near Gravenhorst. Homebound, shot down
F/O P Harris		by a night-fighter flown by Maj Heinz-Wolfgang
W/O E D Bermingham RAAF		Schnaüfer of NJG4, out from Gutersloh, and
F/S J B Wiltshire RAAF		abandoned 2111 in the vicinity of Helmond. All
Sgt F Bone		landed in Allied held territory and were taken
Sgt F T Clay		to Eindhoven. Three days later they were flown

back to base in a Squadron Lancaster. Following
a spell in RAF Hospital Wroughton, Sgt Bridgman rejoined his crew in May 1945.

Note. A full account of what happened to this crew is published in Lancaster
at War 3, by Mike Garbett and Brian Goulding, published in 1984 by Ian Allan.

463 Sqn	Lancaster I	PB804 JO-A	Op: Gravenhorst

W/C W A Forbes DSO DFC RAAF	+	T/o 1719 Waddington similarly tasked. Those who died lie in the Reichswald Forest War Cemetery.
F/L J H Dean	pow	F/O Costello had served with 49 Squadron and
F/O J A Costello DFM	pow	details of his award had appeared in the London
F/L W J O Grime	pow	Gazette on 15 October 1943. The last three
F/O W McLeod	+	named were all flying as air gunners.
W/O A J Norman	+	
P/O W L Worden	pow	
F/L J A Loftus	pow	

463 Sqn	Lancaster III	LM548 JO-P	Op: Gravenhorst

F/O L R Pedersen RAAF	+	T/o 1708 Waddington similarly tasked. Hit by
Sgt T P Freeman	pow	flak and fell near Weert in the Dutch Province
F/S F E Gould RAAF	+	of Limburg. Those who lost their lives now lie
W/O R K Dixon RAAF	evd	in Eindhoven (Woensel) General Cemetery.
F/S E T Sumner RAAF	+	
F/S R Heel	+	
Sgt L Harkness	+	

550 Sqn	Lancaster I	NN715 BQ-A	Op: Duisburg

W/C B Ball	pow	T/o 1916 North Killingholme. Crashed near
F/L D E A Luger	pow	Westhofen, 4 km SW of Schwerte. The two airmen
Sgt R L Gibbs	pow	who died are buried in Rheinberg War Cemetery.
Sgt G Hancock	+	F/L Luger is reported to have arrived home on
F/O S R Angill	pow	8 May but had to be admitted soon afterwards
Sgt R Gray	pow	to Manchester's Christie Hospital, where he
Sgt F G Jones	+	died on 29 May. His grave is in Bandon Hill
Sgt D B Boyce	pow	Cemetery, Beddington.

571 Sqn	Mosquito XVI	PF398 8K-	Op: Berlin

F/O F L Henry RNZAF	T/o 2204 Oakington but attacked Breman as an
F/S R A Stinson RAAF	alternative. Diverted to Brussels and crash-

landed 0140. Neither airmen was injured. It
will be recalled that in January both had baled out over France.

21-22 Feb 1945	576 Sqn	Lancaster I	ME735 UL-B2	Op: Duisburg

576 Sqn   **Lancaster I**   **ME735 UL-B2**   **Op: Duisburg**

F/L C H Living RCAF +
Sgt J F A Mooney +
F/O R C Hill +
F/O J A Russell RCAF +
F/S G L V Tabor +
Sgt H Burrows +
Sgt H Peach +

T/o 2013 Fiskerton. Crashed with great force, and exploded, between 4 and 5 km S of Kevelaer. All were buried on site, but their bodies have since been recovered and brought to the Reichswald Forest War Cemetery.

576 Sqn   **Lancaster I**   **NG464 UL-O2**   **Op: Duisburg**

F/L K Halnan RCAF
Sgt W G Young
F/O E N Weldon RCAF
F/O G T Shepherd RCAF
Sgt F R Lait
F/S H G C Farey
Sgt R M Gray

T/o 1940 Fiskerton. Hit by flak which caused a fire to break out in the bomb bay and rendered the hydraulic system unserviceable. Course was set for Juvincourt but the crew were obliged to bale out in the vicinity of Reims. No injuries reported.

576 Sqn   **Lancaster I**   **RA516 UL-Q2**   **Op: Duisburg**

F/L C D Thieme
Sgt K Wallis
F/S H W Vine +
W/O J H Lowing RAAF
F/S C B Robinson RAAF +
Sgt C N Crouch
Sgt L Hull +

T/o 1939 Fiskerton. Believed to have crashed in the vicinity of Roermond (Limburg). The funeral services for the three who died were held on 23 February at Eindhoven (Woensel) General Cemetery.

578 Sqn   **Halifax III**   **NA670 LK-L**   **Op: Worms**

F/O R J Ingham +
F/S D G Baxter +
F/S J R Shepley RAAF +
F/O D R McLean pow
Sgt S A Wellstead +
F/S N Watson +
Sgt D G Weaver +

T/o 1643 Burn. While approaching the AP came under attack from a Ju 88, which is believed to have been damaged in the exchange of fire. Both port engines, however, were set ablaze and the order to bale out was given. Before the crew could react, a second attack developed which resulted in the Halifax breaking up, the bulk of the wreckage falling onto the banks of the Isenach at Hardenburg, 3 km WNW from Bad Dürkheim. Those who died rest in Rheinberg War Cemetery having been brought here from Hardenburg Friedhof.

Note. I am indebted to Flying Officer Danny McClean for his description of events that led up to the loss of this Halifax. Much of what he was able to report appears in the narrative section of this chapter.

578 Sqn   **Halifax III**   **RG353 LK-E**   **Op: Worms**

F/L P Brown +
Sgt J Grindlay +
F/S G T McCauley RCAF +
F/O A J Combaz RCAF +
F/S W J Hunter +
F/S H Mann +
F/S C J T Watt +

T/o 1630 Burn. Hit by flak and crashed at Obersülzen, 3 km ENE from the small town of Grünstadt. F/L Brown, a regular officer, and F/S Mann are buried in Rheinberg War Cemetery. The others are commemorated on the Runnymede Memorial.

582 Sqn   **Lancaster III**   **PB652 60-L**   **Op: Duisburg**

F/O J Gale
Sgt J Buxton
F/S A MacDougall
F/S N P Smith
WO2 C M Hutton RCAF
Sgt G T Everett
Sgt C A H Dixon

T/o 2032 Little Staughton. Bombed from 17,000 feet at 2300 and returned to base at 0028. No indication of anything untoward has been noted in the Squadron records, but the movement card for this Lancaster shows it was damaged beyond repair, through battle damage, on this date and was struck off charge on 12 March 1945.

626 Sqn   **Lancaster I**   **LM105 UM-T2**   **Op: Duisburg**

F/O D Rodger +
Sgt H B King +
F/O R W Donner +
F/O T J O'Neill RCAF +
F/S C R Badger +
Sgt R Thomson +
WO1 R S Pyatt RCAF +

T/o 1929 Wickenby. The first six named are buried in the Reichswald Forest War Cemetery but WO1 Pyatt RCAF lies in Holland at Nederweert War Cemetery. This suggests his body was found by an American graves inspection team.

| 21-22 Feb | 635 Sqn | Lancaster III | PB668 F2-M | Op: Worms |
| 1945 | | | | |

F/L R W Toothill
F/S J A Davies
F/O J N Luard
F/S W W Colvin
Sgt F W Stone
Sgt F W Coombes
Sgt S H Fortune

T/o 1722 Downham Market. Five minutes prior to reaching the AP, the starboard inner failed. The attack continued, during which flak wrecked the port inner and bombs had to be jettisoned. It was then discovered that the bomb doors were jammed in the open position and, later, as the crew tried to reach Juvincourt, the electrics began to fail. The battle lines were crossed at 5,000 feet and with the starboard outer misfiring, a forced-landing was made at 2120 in a field near Thiercelet in the Grand Duchy of Luxembourg. No one was hurt.

| 22 Feb | 218 Sqn | Lancaster I | NG450 HA-B | Op: Gelsenkirchen |
| 1945 | | | | |

F/O J E G Muschamp +
Sgt J Simpson pow
Sgt E Porter pow
Sgt J Halsall pow
Sgt D R White pow
Sgt G Hogg +
Sgt T F Darragh +

T/o 1308 Chedburgh to attack an oil production plant. Hit by flak at 18,000 feet and partially abandoned over the target area, Sgt Simpson arriving near a flak battery and sustaining a broken ankle and rib fractures. All four survivors were badly beaten by a member of the Gestapo. Their liberation came at midday on 29 April 1945, when units of the Third US Army, commanded by General George S Patton, reached their camp. F/O Muschamp, son of G/C George Allen Rodolphe Muschamp, and both air gunners are buried in the Reichswald Forest War Cemetery. Sadly, Sgt Halsall never fully recovered from the terrible injuries that he received and he died in 1950.

| 22-23 Feb | 105 Sqn | Mosquito XVI | RV298 GB- | Op: Erfurt |
| 1945 | | | | |

S/L I L T Ackroyd
F/O E F Casey

T/o 1740 Bourn. Abandoned 2140 SE of Bruges after running out of fuel at 32,000 feet.

| 23 Feb | 158 Sqn | Halifax III | PN380 NP-M | Op: Essen |
| 1945 | | | | |

F/O C W Hall RCAF +
Sgt W A Frost +
F/O G A Hoggard RCAF +
F/O D W Bateman RCAF +
Sgt M Sills +
F/S W R Cookson RCAF +
F/S W G Roberts RCAF +

T/o 1200 Lissett. Lost without trace. All are commemorated on the Runnymede Memorial.

| | 192 Sqn | Halifax III | LW172 DT-H | Ground |

Damaged beyond repair on No. 8 dispersal pan at Foulsham after being hit by a 239 Squadron Mosquito (see 23-24 February) that had landed in poor visibility and as FIDO was being put into operation.

| | 429 Sqn | Halifax III | LW139 AL-P | Training |

F/L P F Robb RCAF +
Sgt A E Lowthwaite inj
F/L D S MacNabb RCAF inj
F/O F E Casher RCAF inj
F/O D M McMurchy RCAF inj
F/S H H Hockley RCAF inj
F/S C S Hopf RCAF inj

T/o 1539 Leeming. Called base on R/T at 1735 advising that the port outer had failed and requesting immediate landing instructions. Eye witnesses saw the Halifax make an approach but then climb away for a second circuit. While doing so, the port inner cut and the aircraft banked steeply, still climbing to port, before plunging into the ground at 1739 between the villages of Exelby and Londonderry, bursting into flames. Six gravely injured airmen were pulled from the flames and taken to SSQ Leeming. Here, F/S Hockley RCAF died at 2300, while F/L MacNabb RCAF and F/O Casher RCAF passed away the next morning at RAF Hospital Northallerton, where they had been transferred with the other survivors. Their graves, and that of F/L Robb RCAF, are in Harrogate (Stonefall) Cemetery. Contrary to what is reported in other sources, the crew were engaged on training and not on operations to Essen.

| 23-24 Feb | 97 Sqn | Lancaster III | PB588 OF-E | Op: Horten |
| 1945 | | | | |

F/L B J Hines +
Sgt J McD Sinclair +
F/L M R McQuillan RCAF +
F/S A J Marrable +
Sgt D Moroney +
F/L J Ray +
F/S C W Palmer +

T/o 1650 Coningsby to attack U-boat facilities in Oslo Fjord. Shot down during an exchange of fire with a Ju 88, crashing at Asjardstrand. Six lie in Tonsberg Old Cemetery, but panel 272 of the Runnymede Memorial perpetuates the name of Sgt Moroney. F/L Ray was 38, well over the age associated with operational aircrew.

101 Sqn	Lancaster I		PA237 SR-V	Op: Pforzheim

101 Sqn	Lancaster I	
F/L W W Watt	+
Sgt R E A Winstone	+
F/S S R Allen	+
F/O A W Stuart	+
Sgt G A Stephens	+
Sgt J A Slater	+
Sgt D Mortimer	+

PA237 SR-V   Op: Pforzheim

T/o 1613 Ludford Magna. All are buried in Dürnbach War Cemetery. The CWGC cemetery register describes F/L Watt as being an air bomber.

101 Sqn	Lancaster I	
F/L W A McLenaghan RCAF	pow
F/S W R Searle RAAF	pow
Sgt C G Vicary DFM	pow
F/O J K Balcombe RCAF	pow
F/O N W Ingeberg RCAF	pow
WO1 L F Kennedy RCAF	pow
F/S F R Boyd RCAF	pow
F/S F R Fletcher RCAF	pow

RA523 SR-I   Op: Pforzheim

T/o 1547 Ludford Magna. Shot down over the target area. Details of Sgt Vicary's award appeared in the London Gazette on 30 October 1945.

103 Sqn	Lancaster I	
F/O C S Hart RAAF	+
Sgt M C Godfrey	pow
F/S K O Williams	pow
F/S K F Lord	pow
F/S A A McGrath RAAF	+
Sgt W D Rich	pow
Sgt R Jones	pow

NF909 PM-J   Op: Pforzheim

T/o 1606 Elsham Wolds. F/O Hart RAAF and his wireless operator and fellow countryman, F/S McGrath RAAF are commemorated on panel 283 of the Runnymede Memorial. Both came from New South Wales, the former from Curl Curl, the latter from The Rock.

103 Sqn	Lancaster I	
F/L R F Dobson	+
W/O E E Standing	+
Sgt A K Parker	+
P/O L P Curtin RAAF	+
W/O A N Fletcher RAAF	+
P/O W J M Bailie RAAF	pow
Sgt R Nolan	+
Sgt D J Reeves	+

RA515 PM-N   Op: Pforzheim

T/o 1546 Elsham Wolds. Those who died rest in Dürnbach War Cemetery. F/L Dobson is believed to have flown somewhere in the order of thirty-one operational sorties.

138 Sqn	Stirling IV	
F/S E W Sinkinson	+
Sgt G A Letts	+
Sgt F W Webster	+
Sgt B R Haslar	+
Sgt G Cole	+
Sgt H T Batten	+
P/O A Sharman	+

LK149 NF-D   Op: SOE

T/o Tempsford on Operation Tablejam 181 and headed for Denmark. Presumed lost while over the sea. Sgt Letts and P/O Sharman are buried in Sondre Nissum Cemetery, while Sgt Webster lies at Haurvig Cemetery, both burial places being on Denmark's western coast. The other members of crew have no known graves.

150 Sqn	Lancaster I	
F/O P A G Ythier	+
Sgt J A Clark	pow
F/S L B Horrox	pow
F/O A W Delieu	+
F/S R S Lewis	+
Sgt R H Conning	+
Sgt W E Buckley	pow

PB780 IQ-T   Op: Pforzheim

T/o Hemswell. Crashed at Neuhausen. Those who died are buried in Dürnbach War Cemetery. F/O Ythier was the son of Dr. Pierre Rene Ythier of Rose Hill, Mauritius. Sgt Clark was subsequently admitted to RAF Hospital Wroughton. F/O Delieu is reported to have parachuted but was killed as he tried to get away from the scene.

Note. Oliver Clutton-Brock, editor of the Bomber Command Association newletter, writes that the case of Flying Officer Delieu's death was investigated but in February 1948 the War Crimes Group (NW Europe) closed the file.

166 Sqn	Lancaster III	
F/O E L Ellis	+
Sgt R C Finlayson	pow
F/O J W Rae	pow
F/S D Taylor	+
F/S D W Eastcott	+
Sgt A G Chapman	+
Sgt R Richards	+

ND506 AS-L2   Op: Pforzheim

T/o 1540 Kirmington. Those who lost their lives are buried in Dürnbach War Cemetery.

23-24 Feb 1945	170 Sqn	Lancaster III	PB595 TC-J		Op: Pforzheim

F/L W M Constable RCAF	+	
Sgt L Ashton	pow	
F/O R R Sommers RCAF	pow	
F/S D Peletz RCAF	pow	
WO2 S Hart RCAF	pow	
F/S D E Le Liever RCAF	+	
F/S R J H Johnstone RCAF	+	

T/o 1519 Hemswell. Crashed some distance N of the small town of Mühlacker, located 12 km NE from Pforzheim. Those who died are now buried in Dürnbach War Cemetery. It is reported F/S Peletz RCAF sustained a broken leg and that he was subsequently admitted to a French hospital.

192 Sqn   Halifax III   MZ449 DT-Y   Op: BS

F/S G A C Morgan	+
Sgt E Spencer	+
F/S A M Brunton	+
F/S J F Carvell	+
F/S D J Paterson RAAF	+
F/O G E Barking	pow
Sgt W M Wilkinson	+
Sgt L W Greaves	pow

T/o 1625 Foulsham in support of operations over Pforzheim. Shot down near Stuttgart, by a night-fighter. Those who died are buried in Dürnbach War Cemetery. F/O Barking was the specialist equipment operator. On his release from captivity, Sgt Greaves was taken to RAF Hospital Cosford.

192 Sqn   Halifax III   NA241 DT-O   Op: BS

F/L W H P Mitchell RAAF	+
Sgt F Parkins	+
Sgt A K Goodall	+
F/O A W Clark	+
F/S J L Kerr	+
P/O R Powell	pow
Sgt R N Seager	+
F/S T G Campbell RCAF	+

T/o 1610 Foulsham similarly tasked. Crashed near the town of Holzgerlingen below Boblingen. Those who died lie in Dürnbach War Cemetery. F/S Kerr´s parents lived in Brazil at Rio de Janeiro. P/O Powell was the specialist equipment operator.

239 Sqn   Mosquito NF.30   NT354 HB-   Op: BS

F/S L E Twigg	+
F/S R H Turner	inj

T/o 1752 West Raynham similarly tasked. On return, weather conditions were marginal and the crew diverted to Foulsham, landing at 2240 but well down the runway. By doing so, they were unable to stop and at high speed ran into a 192 Squadron Halifax (see 23 February) parked on its dispersal pan. A fire broke out and the Mosquito was destroyed. F/S Twigg is buried in Brinsworth (St. George) Churchyard. The accident happened just as FIDO was being ignited and it is thought the pilot may have been disorientated by the sudden rush of flames and smoke.

Note. This was the first Mosquito NF.30 written off by 239 Squadron.

300 Sqn   Lancaster I   NG266 BH-L   Op: Pforzheim

F/L A Filipek PAF	+
Sgt J Mrozek PAF	+
P/O F Magierowski PAF	+
P/O M L Ziegenhirte PAF	+
F/S C Kowalski PAF	+
Sgt S Trzepiota PAF	+
Sgt W Sadowinski PAF	+

T/o 1604 Faldingworth. Picked up by a night-fighter and sent down between Eutingen and Niefern, two sizeable areas on the NE outskirts of Pforzheim. At least two rest in Dürnbach War Cemetery. As is the case with all Polish Air Force casualties, their names will be on the Memorial at Northolt.

300 Sqn   Lancaster I   PA161 BH-X   Op: Pforzheim

F/S H E Jachacz PAF	pow
Sgt S Leja PAF	pow
F/O J Barcikowski PAF	+
P/O R Z Peisker PAF	pow
F/S R Lisak PAF	+
F/S J Stokarski PAF	+
Sgt Z Minkler PAF	pow

T/o 1616 Faldingworth. Homebound, when attacked and shot down by a night-fighter, crashing near Sindelfingen. Those who died lie in Dürnbach War Cemetery.

550 Sqn   Lancaster I   LM273 BQ-O   Op: Pforzheim

F/O D H Grundy RCAF	pow
Sgt E W King	pow
WO2 R T Sowter RCAF	+
WO2 R C McLauchlan RCAF	pow
F/S L F Figg	pow
Sgt E Mackenzie	+
Sgt E C Jarvis	+

T/o 1601 North Killingholme. WO2 Sowter RCAF is reported to have been killed as he left the stricken bomber. His grave, along with those of the two air gunners, is in Dürnbach War Cemetery. Sgt King later entered RAF Hospital Wroughton where he received treatment for a badly broken ankle.

23-24 Feb 1945	550 Sqn	Lancaster I	NF998 BQ-D	Op: Pforzheim

F/O R D Harris RCAF
Sgt K J B Smith
F/S D J Yemen RCAF
F/O G J Nicol RCAF
Sgt G P Kelleher
Sgt M T Ditson RCAF
Sgt D J Hicks RCAF

T/o 1558 North Killingholme. Bombed the AP at 2008 from 8,000 feet but was very badly damaged when struck by incendiaries from another aircraft. The crew headed for Manston airfield in Kent but crashed 0013 on arrival; no injuries reported.

582 Sqn	Lancaster III	PB538 60-M	Op: Pforzheim

Capt E Swales VC DFC SAAF +
F/S G W Bennington DFM
S/L D P D Archer DSO DFC
P/O R A Wheaton RAAF
F/L C Dodson DSO DFC
P/O A V Goodacre RAAF
F/S B Leach
P/O N Bourne RCAF

T/o 1636 Little Staughton as Master Bomber. Sustained very severe damage over the target area at the hands of night-fighters. Exercising skilful airmanship and sheer willpower Capt Swales SAAF regained the Allied lines and baled out his crew. Before he could make his own escape, the Lancaster hit H/T wires and crashed at Chappelle-aux-Bois (Nord), S of Valenciennes. Capt Swales was awarded a posthumous VC, Gazetted 24 April 1945, while F/S Bennington's DFM appeared in the 20 July 1945 edition. P/O Wheaton RAAF was flying as a second navigator. Capt Swales is not, as may be expected, buried in France but lies in Belgium at Leopoldsburg War Cemetery.

Note. Hans de Haan of Wijchen suggests that Hptm Gerhard Friedrich of II./NJG1 may have fired the shots that crippled this Lancaster. The events leading up to Captain Swales SAAF receiving the highest award that could be bestowed are described in 'For Valour', The Air VCs by Chaz Bowyer and published by William Kimber in 1978. This book not only records the heroism of those who received this accolade between 1939 and 1945, but also reports on those who gained air VCs in the First World War.

608 Sqn	Mosquito XX	KB350 6T-B	Op: Berlin

F/O R A A Doherty DFC +
F/O L Moore +

T/o 1816 Downham Market. Lost without trace. both officers are commemorated on the Runnymede Memorial. F/O Doherty had completed at least sixty-five operational sorties.

625 Sqn	Lancaster I	PB815 CF-O	Op: Pforzheim

F/O D R Paige RCAF
Sgt R B Bennett
WO2 J P Sullivan RCAF   inj
F/S J A Puttick
F/S J Bettany
F/S K E Campbell RCAF
F/S J K McRorie RCAF

T/o 1629 Kelstern. Bombed the AP at 2002 from 7,400 feet and while clearing the target area suffered the same fate that befell the 550 Squadron Lancaster that was to crash-land at Manston. Later, the crew baled out over France from where, it is reported, WO2 Sullivan RCAF landed heavily and sprained an ankle.

4 Feb 1945	61 Sqn	Lancaster I	RF137 QR-E	Ground

LAC B Burnell +
LAC C H Higgins +
LAC H G Wilson +

Exploded 1846 on its dispersal pan at Skellingthorpe airfield, Lincolnshire. Earlier in the day, this Lancaster had been involved in an abortive raid on the Dortmund-Ems Kanal and it is likely the accident occurred as the bomber was being de-armed. LAC Wilson of Plumstead in London is buried in Cambridge City Cemetery, his two colleagues were taken to their home towns. LAC Higgins was aged 41. Eleven other airmen were injured in this incident.

61 Sqn	Lancaster I	SW277 QR-	Ground

Written off by the blast from RF137 exploding.

415 Sqn	Halifax III	NP936 6U-P	Op: Kamen

WO2 L A Russell RCAF +
F/S L Trowsdale +
WO2 J Gallagher RCAF +
F/O P Pokryfka RCAF +
WO2 C C B Craigie RCAF +
F/S R C Brown RCAF +
F/S W H Jones RCAF +

T/o 1309 East Moor to destroy a synthetic-oil plant in the Bergkamen district. All are buried in the Reichswald Forest War Cemetery. The parents of WO2 Cragie RCAF lived at Ludlow in the State of Massachusetts.

24-25 Feb	214 Sqn	Fortress III	HB805 BU-C	Op: BS
1945	F/O J M Shorttle DFM	+		
	F/L F R Woodger	+		
	F/L L G Fowler DFC	inj		
	P/O R W Towell	+		
	F/O K C Allan	+		
	W/O F H Dix MID RNZAF	+		
	F/O A M Jones DFM	+		
	F/S S L Jones	+		
	F/S T W J Pollard	+		
	F/S G J E Jennings DFM	pow		

T/o 1715 Oulton for Window duties. Crashed near Ittenbach, a town E of the Rhine and about 12 km SE from the centre of Bonn. The majority of those who died are buried in Rheinberg War Cemetery, but F/L Fowler, who was gravely injured, rests alongside a Polish soldier in Zuidlaren General Cemetery, Holland, having died here on 15 March. The three DFM holders had served respectively with 199 Squadron, 115 Squadron and 76 Squadron, details of their awards being published on 14 September and 15 June 1943 and 30 June 1944. The father of W/O Dix RNZAF, Herbert George Dix, held the Military Medal. F/L Woodger had served with 214 Squadron in 1942, surviving an operational crash on 20-21 November of that year (see Volume 3 page 264).

	462 Sqn	Halifax III	MZ447 Z5-A	Op: BS
	F/L A J Rate RAAF	+		
	Sgt S J A Pegram	+		
	F/S E J Maslin	+		
	F/S R A Gould	pow		
	F/S V J Trunk RAAF	+		
	F/O D N Kehoe RAAF	+		
	Sgt J Holloway	+		
	Sgt M J Husband	+		

T/o 1658 Foulsham to mingle with a diversionary sweep heading towards northern France and consisting mainly of aircraft from the training establishments. Hit by flak and crashed circa 2130 at Boisheim, 4 km SE of Breyell, Germany and a mere 7 km or so E of the border with Holland. Those who died were buried at Breyell, since when their remains have been brought to the Reichswald Forest War Cemetery. F/O Kehoe RAAF was the specialist equipment operator.

Note. On 9 June 1995, the Lowestoft Journal reported the events that led up to the loss of this Halifax and the subsequent return to Boisheim by Reginald Gould and his friend, Steve Smith, in order to recover a part of this aircraft which has since been lodged with the Norfolk and Suffolk Aviation Museum at Flixton. Although the cause of loss is officially described as being due to flak, it is possible a Me 109 from III./NJG11 may have been involved.

	462 Sqn	Halifax III	MZ448 Z5-	Op: BS
	F/L F H Ridgewell	+		
	Sgt R G Hodgson	pow		
	F/O W J Mann RAAF	pow		
	F/O W K Watson	pow		
	F/O J R Boyce RAAF	pow		
	F/O T Pawsey	+		
	Sgt G E Rolls	+		
	Sgt J G Lynch	+		

T/o 1701 Foulsham similarly tasked. Of the four who perished, three have no known graves but Sgt Lynch is buried in Holland at Venray War Cemetery. On being released from captivity, F/O Mann RAAF and fellow Australian F/O Boyce were taken to RAF Hospital Wroughton. The specialist equipment was operated by F/O Pawsey.

	462 Sqn	Halifax III	MZ461 Z5-G	Op: BS
	F/O V C Ely RAAF	+		
	Sgt R Hetherington	+		
	F/S D J Critchley	+		
	F/O P Millhouse	+		
	F/O J H Hering RAAF	+		
	Sgt M Ogilvie	+		
	F/S G Robinson	+		

T/o 1705 Foulsham similarly tasked. Three, including the pilot, are commemorated on the Runnymede Memorial and four, including both air gunners, are buried in the Reichswald Forest War Cemetery. Unusually, this Halifax was being operated with a seven-man crew.

	462 Sqn	Halifax III	PN429 Z5-E	Op: BS
	F/L J S Tootal	+		
	Sgt T E David	+		
	F/S W F Duncan RAAF	+		
	W/O E R W Oliver RAAF	+		
	W/O N J Hall RAAF	+		
	F/S G Harrison-Broadley	+		
	F/S P J P Carlon RAAF	+		
	F/S M A Smith RAAF	+		

T/o 1703 Foulsham similarly tasked. All are buried in Rheinberg War Cemetery. F/S Harrison-Broadley was the specialist equipment operator. Their average age was twenty-two.

Note. It will be recalled that 462 Squadron had started life in the Middle East as a heavy bomber unit before disbanding at Celone in Italy on 3 March 1944. On 12 August, the Squadron was reformed at Driffield as part of 4 Group, transferring to 100 Group and moving to Foulsham on 29 December. The above losses were their heaviest in a single night as a BS Squadron.

24-25 Feb 1945	1663 CU	Halifax III	PN366	Op: Sweepstake
	Slt J Grimaud FFAF	+		
	Sgc R Arrache-Quesne FFAF	+		
	Ltn J Dedieu FFAF	+		
	Asp G Roque FFAF	+		
	Sgt F Rougier FFAF	+		
	Sgt M Laurent FFAF	+		
	Sgc R Blassiaux FFAF	+		

T/o 1720 Rufforth and set course for northern France. Homebound, the port inner caught fire and while dealing with the situation the outer port engine was feathered by mistake. From their investigation, the accident inspectors deduced the Halifax had struck the ground at around 2200 in a steeply banked turn to port and had disintegrated on impact, wreckage being spread over a wide area at Edmondthorpe, 7 miles ESE from Melton Mowbray in Leicestershire. Initially, all were buried in Cambridge City Cemetery, since when their remains have been taken to their homes in France.

25 Feb 1945	75 Sqn	Lancaster III	LM740 AA-B	Op: Kamen
	F/S L S B Klitscher RNZAF	pow		
	Sgt W H H Brewer	pow		
	F/O D W King	pow		
	F/S W C F Pilkington	pow		
	F/O J D Craven	pow		
	Sgt K A Blackbee	pow		
	Sgt D W S Amos	pow		

T/o 0948 Mepal as part of an all 3 Group G-H raid on a synthetic-oil plant. Believed hit by heavy flak NW of Wesel and observed to turn for home with its port inner engine feathered. Presumed abandoned soon afterwards.

25-26 Feb 1945	128 Sqn	Mosquito XVI	PF409 M5-Z	Op: Erfurt
	F/O D W Rhys			
	F/O F J Kennelly			

T/o 1833 Wyton. Returned to base at 2258, but subsequently written off with battle damage at the Martin Hearn repair facility on 17 May 1945.

	427 Sqn	Halifax III	MZ452 ZL-E	Op: Gardening
	F/L I B Benson RCAF	+		
	Sgt J C Baker	+		
	F/O V B Fleming RCAF	+		
	F/S J G R Buchanan RCAF	+		
	WO2 W R Field RCAF	+		
	F/S R F Piercy RCAF	+		
	F/S E R Alm RCAF	+		

T/o 1658 Leeming borrowed by 429 Squadron and set course for a mine laying operation over Oslo Fjord. Lost without trace. All are commemorated on the Runnymede Memorial.

26 Feb 1945	12 Sqn	Lancaster III	PB243 PH-D	Training
	P/O K R H Lindley	+		
	F/S R C Abbs	+		
	Sgt C B Douglas	+		
	F/S E J D Stone	+		
	Sgt S A Bragg	+		
	Sgt E G Andrews	+		

Dived into the ground at 1438 near Straiton le Vale, 5 miles NE of Market Rasen, Lincolnshire. Sgt Bragg was cremated at Stockport Crematorium while the others rest in various United Kingdom cemeteries. P/O Arthur Alan Hewson Lindley, brother of P/O Lindley, died on 1 August 1942 while flying with 107 Squadron on operations to Vlissingen (see Volume 3 page 173).

	75 Sqn	Lancaster I	ME450 AA-W	Op: Dortmund
	F/O N H Thorpe RNZAF	+		
	Sgt J L Duke	inj		
	Sgt G W McManus	+		
	F/S J McK Alfred	+		
	F/S A Francis RNZAF			
	Sgt F H Saffill	+		
	Sgt H Hark	inj		

T/o 1052 Mepal for a G-H raid, by 3 Group, on the Hoesch benzol-oil production facility. On return, crashed near Chatteris, Cambridgeshire. Sgt McManus and F/S Alfred, the latter from Port of Spain on the island of Trinidad, are buried in Cambridge City Cemetery; F/O Thorpe RNZAF was taken to Ilford (Barkingside) Cemetery. Sgt Duke died on 28 February and he was cremated at Stockport, while Sgt Saffill rests in Maldon Cemetery.

26-27 Feb 1945	138 Sqn	Stirling IV	LK272 NF-P	Op: SOE
	F/L P B Cornwallis	+		
	F/O L J Gornall DFC	+		
	P/O S A Pepworth DFM	+		
	F/O J E Stanton RAAF	+		
	W/O B D Tovey RAAF	+		
	F/S S S Hagerty RCAF	+		
	Sgt J E Cory	+		

T/o 1939 Tempsford on Operation Crupper 37 and set course for Norway with four agents aboard. Reported shot down by flak over the North Sea. The crew are commemorated on the Runnymede Memorial, but the fate of the agents is not reported. P/O Pepworth had flown a tour of operations with 106 Squadron and details of his award had been published on 15 October 1943. It was unusual for ex-5 Group personnel to return for a second tour posted to an establishment unconnected with their previous group.

27 Feb 1945	**76 Sqn**	**Halifax III**	**LL579 MP-L**	**Op: Mainz**

F/L R J P Barrell — pow
P/O H Osbourn — +
F/S L E Cannock — +
F/O R J L Boucher RCAF — +
F/S F W Heron — +
F/S H B Tennant — +
F/S G F Terry — pow

T/o 1323 Holme-on-Spalding Moor. Crashed in the target area. Those who lost their lives rest in Rheinberg War Cemetery. On release from captivity, both survivors were admitted to RAF Hospital Wroughton.

186 Sqn **Lancaster I** **NG175 AP-J** **Op: Gelsenkirchen**

F/L N C Cowley — +
Sgt N P Etheridge — +
F/S J E Peach — +
F/S J M Young — pow
F/S H G Kimber — pow
Sgt J Sneddon — +
Sgt D J G Gibb — +

T/o 1120 Stradishall for a G-H guided strike on the Alma Pluto benzol plant. Hit by flak at the moment of bombing at 1429 and seen to go down, streaming flames before disappearing into the cloud cover. Those who died are buried in the Reichswald Forest War Cemetery. F/L Cowley had flown at least 27 operational sorties.

427 Sqn **Halifax III** **RG347 ZL-G** **Op: Mainz**

F/O R McD Scott RCAF — +
F/S F G Fisher RCAF — +
F/O S T Carson RCAF — +
F/O K F Whitehouse RCAF — +
P/O A Mackie RCAF — +
F/S M J Brewer RCAF — +
F/S J H MacKachern RCAF — inj

T/o 1242 Leeming borrowed by 429 Squadron but while travelling at high speed the starboard tyre burst, sending the Halifax hurtling out of control. From the ensuing crash and explosion that followed, only the tail gunner survived and he was rushed to RAF Hospital Northallerton. His six companions were buried in Harrogate (Stonefall) Cemetery.

Note. The previous flight for this Halifax had been as ZL-G but 429 Squadron records, although acknowledging it had been borrowed from 427 Squadron, show the individual aircraft letter as P.

1409 Flt **Mosquito XVI** **NS731** **Op: SD Mainz**

S/L R D McLaren DFC — +
F/L J A L Lymburner RCAF — pow

T/o Wyton for a weather reconnaissance sortie to the Mainz area. S/L McLaren of Toronto but serving in the Royal Air Force as a Volunteer Reserve is buried in Rheinberg War Cemetery. He had married Joyce Catherine McLaren from Hildenborough in Kent.

Note. This was the only operational loss sustained by 1409 Flight in 1945. The 1980 CWGC publication for Rheinberg erroneously reports Squadron Leader McLaren as belonging to 149 Squadron.

28 Feb- 1 Mar 1945	**128 Sqn**	**Mosquito XVI**	**PF451 M5-C**	**Op: Berlin**

F/O N M McNulty RAAF — +
F/O J R A Machonachie RCAF — +

T/o 1820 Wyton. On return to base the pilot was seen to bank steeply, as if trying to line up with the runway. He then seemed to initiate overshoot procedure, only to stall and crash at Rattlesden, 4 miles W of Stowmarket, Suffolk. F/O McNulty RAAF was taken to Cambridge City Cemetery, while his Canadian navigator rests in Brookwood Military Cemetery.

Note. This Mosquito had been inspected on 25 February by a representative of the Swedish Air Force. Amongst those who witnessed its final departure had been Richard Dimbleby from the BBC.

608 Sqn **Mosquito XX** **KB273 6T-E** **Op: Berlin**

F/O H W Tyrell — evd
Sgt H J Erben — pow

T/o 1828 Downham Market.

1 Mar 1945	**103 Sqn**	**Lancaster I**	**PD272 PM-K**	**Op: Mannheim**

F/O A S Thomson — +
F/O F J Brickman — +
Sgt R C Pain — pow
F/S W H Tromp — +
P/O J M Peace — +
F/S A J Crampin — +
F/S J L Rochester RCAF — +
F/S J W Grice RAAF — +

T/o 1149 Elsham Wolds. Those who died rest in Dürnbach War Cemetery.

1 Mar	153 Sqn	Lancaster I	NG184 P4-U	Op: Mannheim
1945	F/O J Rhodes	+		
	Sgt M F Kingdom	+		
	F/O P C H Clark	+		
	F/O D G Webb	+		
	F/S J E Livick	+		
	F/S T J Bicknell	+		
	F/S H Cutherbertson RCAF	+		

T/o 1150 Scampton. Last heard on W/T at 1635 advising that the English coast was being crossed. It can only be assumed that the crew turned back over the sea as five are commemorated on the Runnymede Memorial and two, F/O Rhodes and F/S Livick, are buried in cemeteries at Great Bircham and Cambridge respectively.

	166 Sqn	Lancaster I	ME447 AS-E	Op: Mannheim
	F/O G R Phelps	+		
	Sgt R T Terry	+		
	F/S W F Webster	+		
	F/O J Johnson	+		
	F/O L J Rich	+		
	Sgt C L Milner	+		
	Sgt L J Jeffery	+		

T/o 1140 Kirmington. All rest in Dürnbach War Cemetery. At 38, Sgt Milner was well over the average age of operational airmen.

1-2 Mar	57 Sqn	Lancaster III	ND572 DX-F	Training
1945	F/O R J Anscomb	+		
	Sgt G E Dandy	+		
	Sgt D Whitefoot	+		
	F/S C J Waters	+		
	Sgt C W Watts	+		
	Sgt F D Leahy	+		
	Sgt E Davis	+		
	AC2 H M Aitken	+		

Collided in the air with a 207 Squadron Lancaster, while engaged on night fighter affiliation training, both aircraft falling at 0118 on Fen Farm, Ruskington, some 4 miles NNE of Sleaford, Lincolnshire. All are buried in separate cemeteries. AC2 Aitken had been accepted for training to be a navigator.

	207 Sqn	Lancaster III	ME473 EM-N	Training
	F/L E McM Lawson RAAF	+		
	Sgt G W Flitt	+		
	F/O W W Lord	+		
	F/S A Henderson	+		
	Sgt R Richardson	+		
	Sgt G Wilkinson	+		
	Sgt R C Banks	+		
	LAC J Morrison	+		

T/o 0021 Spilsby and lost in the circumstances described previously. Six bodies were recovered but F/S Henderson and Sgt Banks, the latter from Nakuru, Kenya, are commemorated on the Runnymede Memorial. F/L Lawson RAAF was the son of Revd Archibald Frederick Lawson of Camberwell, Victoria, while F/O Lord's father was Herbert Arthur Lord CBE and a Justice of the Peace. LAC Morrison was a batman who had joined the crew for air experience flying.

Note. The crash site was excavated by the Lincolnshire Aircraft Recovery Group in August 1996 and the remains of Sgt Banks were recovered. He was buried with full military honours on 25 October 1996. In respect of the 57 Squadron aircraft, Ad ven Zantvoort reports that it had previously seen service with 103 Squadron as PM-M and had been badly shot about by a Fw 190 while operating to Berlin on 24-25 March 1944, killing Sergeant B Thomas, the tail gunner. A crash landing was made at Dunsfold, during which the Lancaster ran into a B.17G Fortress belonging to the 452nd Bomb Group. Subsequently, five members of the crew received gallantry awards.

	692 Sqn	Mosquito XVI	ML969 P3-	Op: Erfurt
	F/L G R Green			
	F/L J A Perry			

T/o 1903 Graveley. During the sortie, the ASI failed and on return to base at 2310 the Mosquito landed heavily, causing the undercarriage to give way. Soon afterwards the wreckage caught fire, but both crew escaped unharmed.

Mar	12 Sqn	Lancaster I	NN800 PH-A	Op: Koln
945	F/O R D N Saunders	pow		
	Sgt D Lewis	pow		
	Sgt N A Clarke	pow		
	F/O J Willis	pow		
	Sgt G H Pearce	pow		
	Sgt J M Cartmell	+		
	Sgt M A Callaghan	+		

T/o 0700 Wickenby. Both air gunners are buried in Rheinberg War Cemetery. Sgt Callaghan hailed from New Ross, Co. Wexford, in the Republic of Ireland.

Note. For several weeks past and from March until the end of the war, loss cards frequently show surviving members of crew as "safe". Unfortunately, unit records are not at all clear as to what fate had befallen the survivors. Thus, future summaries will try to reflect this confusing state of affairs.

2 Mar **1945**	**51 Sqn**	**Halifax III**	**MZ451 MH-F**	**Op: Koln**

2 Mar
1945

51 Sqn　　　　　　**Halifax III**　　**MZ451 MH-F**　　　　　　　**Op: Koln**

F/O F S Eastwell　　　　　　+　　T/o 0720 Snaith. Believed to have crashed in
Sgt A Nicolson　　　　　　　　　Germany, though F/O Eastwell was taken to Belgium
F/S G A Chugg　　　　　　　　　and buried at Henri-Chapelle. However, since
F/S D P Murnane　　　　　　　　then his remains have been transferred to Hotton
F/S J S Henderson　　　　　　　War Cemetery. His crew are described as "safe"
Sgt J P Watson　　　　　　　　　but it is likely they spent a period of time in
Sgt H M Walcott　　　　　　　　captivity.

100 Sqn　　　　　　**Lancaster III**　　**LM723 HW-H**　　　　　　　**Op: Koln**

F/O W H Evans　　　　　　　　　T/o 0704 Grimsby. Hit by flak but regained the
Sgt J J Paxton　　　　　　　　　Allied lines and forced-landed 1136 some 20 km
F/S J L Pearson　　　　　　　　from the Belgian city of Gent. No injuries
F/S A W Dack　　　　　　　　　　reported.
F/S J G Sutherland
Sgt K W J Hodges
Sgt F Burdett

300 Sqn　　　　　　**Lancaster I**　　**NG501 BH-U**　　　　　　　**Op: Koln**

F/L W Wyganowski PAF　　　　+　　T/o 0714 Faldingworth. Crashed in the vicinity
Sgt J Filek PAF　　　　　　　+　　of Zulpicher Strasse and Vottfried Strasse, Köln.
Sgt E Kulikowski PAF　　　　+　　It is very much suspected their bodies were found
P/O J Babiarz PAF　　　　　　+　　at various times and by different organisations
F/S J R Horobiowski PAF　　+　　as their graves are scattered across three
F/S S Chetnicki PAF　　　　　+　　countries. Three rest in the Polish Field of
F/S B Filipiak PAF　　　　　+　　Honour at Lommel; F/L Wyganowski PAF is buried
　　　　　　　　　　　　　　　　　in Hotton War Cemetery; two were taken to Holland
while F/S Horobiowski PAF is interred at the Reichswald Forest War Cemetery.

300 Sqn　　　　　　**Lancaster I**　　**PB854 BH-I**　　　　　　　**Op: Koln**

F/L M Kirkilewicz PAF　　　+　　T/o 0710 Faldingworth. At least three were laid
Sgt N Wieckowski PAF　　　　+　　to rest at Henri-Chapelle, ahead of being buried
F/O A B Nieszkodny PAF　　　+　　in the Polish Field of Honour at Lommel, while
Sgt E H Szymanski PAF　　　　+　　F/O Nieszkodny PAF lies in the Reichswald Forest
Sgt M Kulik PAF　　　　　　　+　　War Cemetery. All, of course, are commemorated
Sgt J Mrozinski PAF　　　　　+　　on the Polish Air Force Memorial at Northolt.
Sgt S Cwenar PAF　　　　　　　+

408 Sqn　　　　　　**Halifax VII**　　**RG472 EQ-T**　　　　　　　**Op: Koln**

F/O H R Sproule RCAF　　　pow　　T/o 0721 Linton-on-Ouse. Homebound, when hit by
Sgt A D Dennis RCAF　　　　pow　　flak which killed F/S Paxton RCAF and F/S Street
F/O J E Moran RCAF　　　　　pow　　RCAF. The other members of crew baled out just
F/O V D J Mousseau RCAF　pow　　moments before their aircraft exploded and fell
F/S J G Paxton RCAF　　　　　+　　near Bad Godesberg on the W bank of the Rhine,
F/S J Street RCAF　　　　　　+　　SE of Bonn. The two airmen who died were first
F/S V T Hunt RCAF　　　　　pow　　buried at Bad Godesberg, since when their remains
　　　　　　　　　　　　　　　　　have been taken to Belgium and interred in Hotton
　　　　　　　　　　　　　　　　　War Cemetery.

460 Sqn　　　　　　**Lancaster I**　　**RA524 AR-V**　　　　　　　**Op: Koln**

F/L J H Holmes RAAF　　　　　+　　T/o 0703 Binbrook. All five Australians and
Sgt J Devlin　　　　　　　　　+　　Sgt Devlin were initially buried at Henri-
W/O H V Gordon RAAF　　　　　+　　Chapelle, though their graves are now located
F/S E Parkinson　　　　　　　+　　in Hotton War Cemetery. F/S Parkinson, however,
F/S J M Gerrard RAAF　　　　　+　　is buried in Rheinberg War Cemetery and, thus,
F/S T A Thomson RAAF　　　　　+　　it is likely the crew were found by both British
F/S G W Rankin RAAF　　　　　+　　and American graves inspection units.

622 Sqn　　　　　　**Lancaster I**　　**HK769 GI-D**　　　　　　　**Op: Koln**

F/O M E M Ray　　　　　　　　+　　T/o 1301 Mildenhall as part of the second phase
Sgt W J Ormshaw　　　　　　　+　　attack on this city, using G-H. Hit by flak and
F/O C P Boyle RCAF　　　　　　+　　presumed crashed in the target area. All lie in
F/S D G Lewis　　　　　　　　+　　Belgium at Hotton War Cemetery. F/O Ray's father
F/S G R Conley RAAF　　　　　+　　Lt William Ray MM had been killed while serving
Sgt P S Armitage　　　　　　　+　　with the Home Guard on 19 June 1944. He was 58
P/O E B Boyce RCAF　　　　　　+　　years old and rests in Lewisham (Hither Green)
Sgt W F Heywood　　　　　　　+　　Cemetery where his CWGC register entry indicates
　　　　　　　　　　　　　　　　　he was formerly QMS of the 2nd Battalion of The
Durham Light Infantry in which he served with honour between 1914 and 1918.

2 Mar 1945	625 Sqn	Lancaster III	PB158 CF-G2	Op: Koln

2 Mar 1945 — 625 Sqn — Lancaster III — PB158 CF-G2 — Op: Koln

F/O T N Downes RAAF +
P/O R Blackley
F/O L E Murray RAAF +
F/O A J Bloy RAAF
F/S K T Brown RAAF +
Sgt A J Sayers +
F/S W W Foy RAAF +

T/o 0730 Kelstern. Exploded in the air. It is likely that the bodies of those who died were recovered by American forces which entered the city a few days later. Taken in the first place to Henri-Chapelle, their graves are now located at Hotton War Cemetery. The two survivors are described as "safe".

640 Sqn — Halifax III — NP965 C8-Y — Op: Koln

F/L K Robinson DFM +
F/S D H G Tiley +
F/O F E Watkin RAAF +
F/O B F O'Neill RAAF +
F/O H H Wolfson RAAF +
F/S J H W Turner +
F/S C K Fielder +

T/o 0740 Leconfield. All are buried in Belgium at Heverlee War Cemetery. No details have been traced concerning the DFM awarded to the pilot.

Note. These were the last major raids carried out on this much battered city. Such was the extent of destruction that much visible evidence of the bombing could still be seen when the author served at nearby Butzweilerhof between 1956 and 1958. During this time, much reconstruction was achieved, particularly in those areas that were to prosper with many fine departmental stores. It was a time when the German people continued to have a deep fear of the Soviets and the consequences that would befall them if an invasion materialised from the Eastern Bloc.

2-3 Mar 1945 — 139 Sqn — Mosquito XX — KB268 XD-C — Op: Berlin

F/O G Coleman DFM
F/L R Cooper DFC

T/o 1822 Upwood. Returned safely at 2305 but had sustained flak damage of such severity that repairs were regarded as uneconomical. The DFM awarded to F/O Coleman had been Gazetted on 23 March 1943, following his time spent in the Middle East with 148 Squadron.

3 Mar 1945 — 426 Sqn — Halifax VII — PN231 OW- — Ground

Cpl C S Forrest RCAF inj

At around 1500, while undergoing engine runs at Linton-on-Ouse, the undercarriage gave way. Cpl Forrest RCAF, who was close by, sustained a broken arm and from all accounts was extremely fortunate not to have been more seriously hurt, or even killed.

3-4 Mar 1945 — 10 Sqn — Halifax III — HX332 ZA-V — Op: Kamen

F/L J G L Laffoley RCAF +
P/O K H V Palmer inj
Sgt C H Finch +
F/S S Hamilton inj
P/O L A Thorndycraft RCAF +
F/S P H Field +
P/O W Kay inj
Sgt E W Bradshaw +

T/o 1823 Melbourne. On return, and while flying between 2,500 and 3,000 feet, intercepted by a Ju 88, possibly flown by Lt Arnold Döring from 10./NJG3, and sent down circa 0145 on Spellow Hill, Staveley, 6 miles SE of Ripon, Yorkshire. All three survivors were critically injured. Those who died are buried in various United Kingdom cemeteries.

12 Sqn — Lancaster III — ME323 PH-P — Training

P/O A G Thomas +
F/S T McCaffray +
F/S R L Horstmann RAAF +
F/S W N Pridmore RAAF +
F/S G E Davis RAAF +
F/S A Cryer RAAF +
F/S A H Weston RAAF +

Shot down by an intruder and crashed circa 0110 between Stockwith and Blyton, two villages 3 miles NW and NE respectively from Gainsborough in Lincolnshire. The five Australians were taken to Cambridge City Cemetery, while P/O Thomas and Sgt McCaffray are buried in their home towns.

12 Sqn — Lancaster III — PB476 PH-Y — Training

F/O N A Ansdell +
Sgt R F D Shafer +
F/O A Hunter +
F/O A G Heath +
Sgt R O Parry +
Sgt A H Walker +
Sgt W Mellor +

Lost in similar circumstances, crashing 0029 at Weekly Cross near the small Lincolnshire town of Alford, where four were buried in the local cemetery. The average age for the crew was twenty-two.

3-4 Mar	44 Sqn	Lancaster III	ME442 KM-V	Op: Ladbergen
1945				

F/O J J F Ryan RAAF +	T/o 1842 Spilsby to raid the Dortmund-Ems Kanal
Sgt T H Jarman +	at a point near Ladbergen. Homebound, picked
F/S R R Russell +	up by an intruder and shot down circa 0100 to
F/S H J Terry +	crash amongst trees in Grannington Park on the
Sgt H Birch +	Brocklesby Estate near Grimsby, Lincolnshire.
Sgt H Payne +	F/O Ryan RAAF and Sgt Birch rest in Cambridge
Sgt W H Rogan +	City Cemetery; the others are buried in their
	home towns, the two air gunners both hailing
	from the city of Liverpool.

76 Sqn	Halifax III	MZ680 MP-R	Op: Kamen

P/O H Bertenshaw inj	T/o 1823 Holme-on-Spalding Moor. On return,
Sgt H Wood	and while banking in readiness to join the
F/S G Austin	airfield circuit, attacked from below by an
F/S G F H French	intruder whose fire set light to the starboard
F/S D Skilton	outer and fuel tanks. All baled out, circa 0115,
Sgt M Shearman inj	some getting clear from less than 600 feet and
Sgt L Sporne	landing in the vicinity of Cadney, 3 miles SSE
	of Brigg, Lincolnshire. Most sustained injuries

of a minor nature, but Sgt Shearman was very badly hurt and was destined to
spend many months undergoing hospital treatment.

76 Sqn	Halifax III	NA584 MP-E	Op: Kamen

P/O P P Oleynik RCAF	T/o 1818 Holme-on-Spalding Moor. Attacked by
Sgt H C Firmin	a Ju 88 intruder while on finals to land and,
F/S D G MacMillan	in consequence, diverted to Carnaby where a
WO2 J D Menard RCAF	crash-landing was made at 0110, the Halifax
F/S R J Freeman	finishing up amongst some parked aircraft.
F/S W T Maltby RCAF +	F/S Maltby RCAF, who was killed during the
F/S R C MacDougal	attack, lies in Harrogate (Stonefall) Cemetery.

77 Sqn	Halifax III	NR210 KN-Z	Op: Kamen

F/O J McL Gaddes RNZAF	T/o 1835 Full Sutton. On return to base came
Sgt K W Thompson	under attack circa 0045 from a Ju 88, which was
P/O J T Hobbs	successfully evaded. Ten minutes, or so, later
P/O P G Bullen	F/O Gaddes RNZAF crash-landed at Full Sutton.
W/O F N Chapman RAAF	F/S Mustoe received local treatment for his
W/O V C Protheroe	injuries.
F/S H Mustoe inj	

153 Sqn	Lancaster III	LM750 P4-R	Op: Gardening

F/O L J R Gregoire DFC +	T/o 1645 Scampton for mine laying duties over
RCAF	the Baltic in an area code named Silverthorne.
Sgt W L James +	Lost without trace. All are commemorated on the
WO2 M M Sandomirsky RCAF +	Runnymede Memorial. W/O McGregor had flown with
WO2 K L D McCoy RCAF +	61 Squadron, his DFM having been published on 26
W/O D S McGregor DFM +	May 1942. WO2 McCoy RCAF had been the sole sur-
F/S J E Sabine RCAF +	vivor from a 626 Squadron Lancaster lost during
F/S W W Webber +	a raid on Duisburg on 21-22 May 1944 (see Volume
	5 page 232). After making a successful evasion,

he had resumed operational flying only to fall with victory in sight.

157 Sqn	Mosquito XIX	TA404 RS-M	Op: BS

F/S J A Leigh +	T/o 1956 Swannington to support the Kamen raid.
F/S L R J Lucas +	Lost without trace. Both airmen are perpetuated
	on panel 271 of the Runnymede Memorial. F/S

Leigh had at least one air combat victory to his credit, having claimed a Me 1_
destroyed during operations on 17-18 December 1944.

158 Sqn	Halifax III	PN437 NP-X	Op: Kamen

F/L C A Rogers +	T/o 1830 Lissett. On return to base, ordered to
P/O C J W Muir +	disperse due to enemy air activity but at around
F/O D J Harris +	0030 was shot down by an intruder, crashing at
F/S R H Houldey +	Sledmere Grange, 7 miles NW of Great Driffield
F/S J W Middleton +	in Yorkshire. F/S Middleton lies in Harrogate
Sgt J J E Dent +	(Stonefall) Cemetery; the others were taken to
Sgt E A J Farrow +	their home towns. Until recently, both air
	gunners had served in the Air Training Corps.

3-4 Mar	169 Sqn	Mosquito XIX	MM640 VI-H		Op: BS
1945	S/L V J Fenwick		+		T/o 2050 Great Massingham. On return to base,
	F/O J W Pierce		+		told to divert to Coltishall and while doing so

fell victim to a Ju 88, crashing circa 0040 near
The Mill between Buxton and Lamas, some 5 miles N of Norwich and about a mile W
from their intended destination. S/L Fenwick was taken to his home town, while
F/O Pierce was buried at Cambridge City Cemetery.

	171 Sqn	Halifax III	NA107 6Y-T		Op: BS
	S/L P C Procter		inj		T/o 1838 North Creake tasked for Mandrel duties.
	F/S H Laking				Flying at 3,000 feet on the home leg, attacked by
	F/O B T Twinn				a Ju 88 and crippled. The crew baled out from
	F/O W Braithwaite		inj		around 1,000 feet, leaving their aircraft to fall
	F/L N G Errington				circa 0100 at Walnut Tree Farm, South Lopham, a
	F/O W G Hayden				village some 5 miles WNW of Diss, Norfolk and on
	W/O A P Richards		inj		the main road leading to Thetford. F/O Hayden was
	F/O E V Stephenson		inj		the specialist equipment operator.

	189 Sqn	Lancaster I	NG325 CA-H		Op: Ladbergen
	F/O S J Reid RCAF		+		T/o 1837 Fulbeck to bomb the Dortmund-Ems Kanal
	Sgt F N Benson		+		near Ladbergen. On return, intercepted by an
	F/O T J Nelson RCAF		+		intruder, crashing 0118 near the railway station
	F/O H G Harrison		+		at East Rudham, 6 miles WSW of Fakenham, Norfolk.
	F/S R W McCormack		+		The four RCAF members of crew are buried in
	F/S G F Caley RCAF		+		Brookwood Military Cemetery, the others rest
	F/S M R Bullock RCAF		+		in their home towns. Shortly before being shot

down, the Lancaster overflew West Raynham with
its navigation lights on, these being extinguished and the colours of the day
fired more or less as the enemy aircraft opened up with its cannons.

	189 Sqn	Lancaster I	PA197 CA-B		Op: Ladbergen
	F/O T Dykins		pow		T/o 1834 Fulbeck similarly tasked. Came down at
	Sgt W S Jones		pow		at Bevergern, a small town on the S bank of the
	F/O P E Thompson DFC		+		Kanal some 5 km SSE of Hörstel. The three air-
	F/S B Jackson		pow		men who died are buried in the Reichswald Forest
	W/O J Crawford RNZAF		+		War Cemetery. It is believed Sgt Looms had been
	F/S D F Cook		+		a member of the regular air force since the late
	Sgt D Y Looms		pow		1920s or early '30s.

	192 Sqn	Mosquito IV	DZ491 DT-N		Op: BS
	F/L A E Roach RAAF				T/o 2027 Foulsham and headed for the Kamen area.
	F/O H Cooper				Returned to base at 0007 but swung off the run-

way and finished up, wrecked, in a ditch. There
are no reports of anyone being injured.

	192 Sqn	Halifax III	LV955 DT-G		Op: BS
	F/O E D Roberts		inj		T/o 2007 Foulsham for electronic intelligence
	Sgt J C Anderson		+		operations over the North Sea. On return, caught
	F/O W Darlington RCAF		+		at 1,200 feet by a Ju 88 whose fire set light to
	F/S R G Holmes		+		the wing tanks and wrecked both inner engines.
	W/O W S Clementson		+		Only F/O Todd, the specialist operator, was able
	F/O R G Todd				to jump before the blazing Halifax was attacked
	Sgt K A Sutcliffe		inj		for a second time. Moments later, the bomber
	Sgt R T Grapes		+		crashed 0059 at Ainsley's Farm, Fulmodestone,

4 miles ENE of Fakenham, Norfolk. Two were
dragged clear before flames totally engulfed the wreckage; both were admitted to
RAF Hospital Ely. Those who died rest in various cemeteries, F/O Darlington RCAF
likely being claimed by a relative as he lies in Crewe (Coppenhall) Cemetery. It
is further reported that F/O Roberts was subsequently treated at the specialist
burns unit at East Grinstead, finally being discharged in 1947.

	207 Sqn	Lancaster I	NG204 EM-M		Op: Ladbergen
	F/O H V Miller		+		T/o 1838 Spilsby to bomb the Kanal at a point
	Sgt A C Fox		+		near Ladbergen. All now rest in the Reichswald
	P/O C M Leisk		+		Forest War Cemetery. P/O Leisk is described in
	F/O A N Lacey		+		the cemetery register as being a pilot, though
	Sgt J J Samuels		+		his duties on this, his final mission, was that
	F/S A Johnston RCAF		+		of a navigator.
	F/S G J Phillips RCAF		+		

3-4 Mar 1945	**214 Sqn**	**Fortress III**	**HB815 BU–J**	**Op: BS**

3-4 Mar 1945

214 Sqn   **Fortress III**   **HB815 BU–J**   **Op: BS**

P/O H Bennett DFC	+
Sgt L E Billington	+
F/S H Barnfield	+
W/O L J Odgers RAAF	+
F/S W Bridden	+
F/S L A Hadder	+
F/S F Hares	+
Sgt A McDirmid	inj
W/O R W Church	inj
Sgt P J Healy	+

T/o 1840 Oulton on Window duties. On return to base, fell to the guns of a Ju 88 flown by Lt Arnold Döring, 10./NJG3. On fire, the Fortress crash-landed 0051 at Lodge Farm on the airfield boundary. Those who perished rest in various cemeteries.

227 Sqn   **Lancaster I**   **NG170 9J–S**   **Op: Ladbergen**

F/O J M Johnston RAAF	+
Sgt P Mahon	pow
WO1 P D Ross-Ross RCAF	+
F/S V H Binch	+
W/O P J Buckman RAAF	+
F/S G A Jeans	pow
F/S J B Gayland	pow

T/o 1852 Balderton to bomb the Dortmund-Ems Kanal near Ladbergen. Shot down by a night-fighter and crashed at Altenberge. The four who died rest in the Reichswald Forest War Cemetery. On being released from captivity, F/S Gayland was admitted to RAF Hospital Cosford.

346 Sqn   **Halifax III**   **NR229 H7–D**   **Op: Kamen**

Cne P Notelle FFAF	inj
Ltn E Boussy FFAF	inj
Ltn C Martin FFAF	
Ltn B Flous FFAF	inj
Sgt P Santoni FFAF	
Sgt J Neri FFAF	
Sgt J Mallia FFAF	inj

T/o 1827 Elvington. Diverted on return to base and while flying at 2,500 feet in the circuit of Croft airfield, came under attack from a Ju 88 flown by Fw Günter Schmidt, IV./NJG3. Return fire was given before the Halifax crashed 0214 at Rockcliffe Farm, Hurworth, 3 miles SSE from Darlington, Durham. Some reports suggest two civilians were killed after being struck by the blazing bomber as it skidded along the ground.

347 Sqn   **Halifax III**   **NA680 L8–H**   **Op: Kamen**

Cne P Laucou FFAF	+
Sgt P Le Masson FFAF	+
Asp L Viel FFAF	
Slt H Giroud FFAF	
Sgt C Pochont FFAF	
Sgt M Hemery FFAF	
Sgt P Charriere FFAF	

T/o 1812 Elvington. Homebound, caught by an intruder and crashed at about 0105 near the airfield at Cranwell, Lincolnshire. Five, as ordered, baled out but Sgt Le Masson FFAF had been wounded and was unable to help himself. Cne Laucou FFAF, without hesitation, remained at the controls and made a desperate, but unsuccessful, attempt to forced-land.

347 Sqn   **Halifax III**   **NR235 L8–O**   **Op: Kamen**

Ltn J Terrien FFAF	+
Adj J Puthier FFAF	
Ltn R Mosnier FFAF	
Slt R Michelon FFAF	
Sgc C Dugardin FFAF	
Sgt R Delaroche FFAF	
Sgt A Dunand FFAF	

T/o 1818 Elvington. Homebound, shot down by an intruder and crashed circa 0115 at Glebe Farm, Sutton upon Derwent, 7 miles SSE of York. Six managed to leave the stricken aircraft but Ltn Terriern FFAF was found near the wreckage. He is likely buried in France, though at first he would have been taken to Harrogate (Stonefall) Cemetery.

460 Sqn   **Lancaster I**   **NG502 AR–J**   **Training**

F/O W B Warren	
Sgt A Streatfield	+
F/O S Gannon	
F/S F D Kelly	
F/S R E Davey RAAF	+
F/L R D Grinter	
Sgt R J Jackson	

At around 0130, shot down by a Ju 88 flown by Fw Heinrich Conse of 7./NJG5 and fell, burning, into fields near Barfield House, Langworth, some 7 miles NE of Lincoln. The two airmen who lost their lives rest in Cambridge City Cemetery.

Note. The circumstances of this crash are reported on pages 78 and 79 of Lincolnshire Air War 1939-1945 by S Finn. Observer Taylor, of the Royal Observer Corps, witnessed the attack and roughly fifteen minutes later, Observer J P Kelway ROC was killed when the same Ju 88 shot up his car on the nearby Welton to Spridlington road. Moments later, the enemy intruder crashed, killing its crew, after flying into telegraph wires. They were buried a few days later in Scampton (St. John The Baptist) Churchyard, while Observer Kelway ROC rests in Lincoln (Newport Road) Cemetery.

3-4 Mar				
1945	**463 Sqn**	**Lancaster I**	**NG469 JO-D**	**Op: Ladbergen**

F/O F J Howells DFC RAAF	+	T/o 1832 Waddington to attack the Kanal near
Sgt D Bates	+	Ladbergen. Those who died are buried in the
Sgt P T Barlow	+	Reichswald Forest War Cemetery. F/S Foreman
F/S E K Foreman RAAF	pow	RAAF was admitted to RAF Hospital Wroughton on
F/S O B Elliott RAAF	+	12 April, a month before Sgt Miller arrived back
Sgt C E Billard	+	in the United Kingdom.
Sgt J M H Miller	pow	

466 Sqn		**Halifax III**	**NR179 HD-C**	**Op: Kamen**

P/O A P W Shelton RAAF	+	T/o 1823 Driffield. Bombed the AP at 2203 from
Sgt W E Welsh	+	20,000 feet but on return to base was obliged to
F/S P Hogan RAAF		go round again and while doing so the airfield
F/S R R Johnson RAAF	+	lights were extinguished. Climbed to 4,000
F/S G W Dixon RAAF	+	feet and set course for an alternative air-
F/S G Lain RAAF		field only to fall to a Ju 88 at about 0110
F/S V Bullen RAAF		and crash at Fridaythorpe, 9 miles WNW from

Great Driffield, Yorkshire. The three RAAF
members of crew lie in Harrogate (Stonefall) Cemetery, while Sgt Welsh was
taken back to his home town.

466 Sqn		**Halifax III**	**NR250 HD-N**	**Op: Kamen**

P/O A E Schrank		T/o 1843 Driffield. Bombed the AP at 2205 from
Sgt J W Hodgson		20,000 feet. On return to base attacked circa
F/S J W Tobin		0040 by an intruder. All baled out safely, but
F/S J A Todd		what happened to the Halifax is something of a
F/S J A Hadlington		mystery. The Squadron records, which are very
Sgt P Stewart	inj	spartan, merely indicate it crashed at Skell-
Sgt J W Kernaghan		ingthorpe; other sources suggest it fell onto

a cottage at Friskney, 8 miles SW of Skegness
in Lincolnshire, while Thirkleby Wold near West Lutton, 10 miles NW of Great
Driffield, Yorkshire, is also quoted. Sgt Stewart's injury was not serious.

467 Sqn		**Lancaster I**	**PB806 PO-W**	**Op: Ladbergen**

W/C E Le P Langlois DFC RAAF	+	T/o 1845 Waddington to bomb the Kanal near the
F/S J Scott	+	town of Ladbergen. Those who died are commem-
F/O A F Reid DFC RAAF	+	orated on the Runnymede Memorial. W/C Langlois
F/O J H Willmott RAAF	pow	RAAF had recently taken command of the Squadron
F/O E C Patten DFC RAAF	+	following the loss of their previous CO during
F/O C J Cameron RAAF	+	a raid on this same target. F/O Patten RAAF
F/O R E Taylor RAAF	pow	had married Gladys Muriel Patten of Liverpool.

467 Sqn		**Lancaster III**	**LM677 PO-V**	**Op: Ladbergen**

F/O R B Eggins RAAF	+	T/o 1854 Waddington similarly tasked. Crashed
F/S G A R Prichard MID	+	at Havixbech, 14 km WNW from the centre of
F/S J J B Grady RAAF	pow	Münster. Those who died lie in the Reichswald
F/S P J Madden RAAF	+	Forest War Cemetery, having been brought here
F/S C McC Cahill RAAF	+	from Nottuln. Pamela Ida Prichard, sister of
F/S A B Walker RAAF	+	F/S Prichard, died on active service. Their
F/S R V Richardson RAAF	+	father was Capt Neville Arthur Prichard RN.

Apart from F/S Pritchard, all had been obliged
to bale out of their Lancaster during operations to Royan in the January.

467 Sqn		**Lancaster III**	**ME453 PO-L**	**Op: Ladbergen**

F/O R T Ward RAAF	+	T/o 1853 Waddington similarly tasked. All are
F/S M Venton	+	buried in the Reichswald Forest War Cemetery.
F/S H Callaghan	+	No age is indicated for F/S Smith, but of the
F/S R V Smith	+	rest Sgt Drennan of Cork in the Irish Republic
W/O C H Terras RAAF	+	was the senior at twenty-two. F/S Venton is
Sgt W A A Chatters	+	identified in the register as a pilot.
Sgt T E Drennan	+	

Note. 467 Squadron lost eleven aircraft on operational sorties during the
period January to May 1945, five of this number on the Dortmund-Ems Kanal.

608 Sqn		**Mosquito XXV**	**KB411 6T-M**	**Op: Berlin**

S/L E S Few DFC AFC	T/o 1819 Downham Market. Forced-landed 2313
P/O S S Campbell	at Manston in Kent. No injuries reported.

3-4 Mar	640 Sqn	Halifax III	NP931 C8-J	Op: Kamen

1945

P/O P B Manton RAAF	+
F/S C E Cox	+
Sgt K R Stocker	+
Sgt E R Knowles	+
Sgt J H Law	+
Sgt J B Pridding	inj
Sgt E J V Thompson	inj

T/o 1812 Leconfield. On return tried to land at Woodbridge in Suffolk, but while approaching the runway crashed circa 0020 into woods known as The Thicks, near Butley village located just to the NE of the airfield. It is believed an intruder was responsible. Of those who died, P/O Manton RAAF rests in Cambridge City Cemetery while the others were taken to their home towns. Sgt Pridding is reported to have died from his injuries on 6 March.

Note. On this night, the Luftwaffe mounted Unternehmen Gisela which involved large numbers of night-fighters crossing the North Sea and mingling with the bombers as they prepared to land. As will be seen from the summaries reported, considerable success was achieved, albeit at some cost to the intruders. Thus, an appendix has been prepared which identifies the majority of Luftwaffe casualties and, in addition, lists those aircraft from the training establishments that were caught up in the general mayhem.

4-5 Mar	138 Sqn	Stirling IV	LJ999 NF-Q	Op: SOE

1945

F/O L G Steven	pow
Sgt J T Breeze	pow
F/O N E Tilly	pow
F/S J F Kyle	pow
F/S G M Maude RAAF	pow
Sgt W L Clark	pow
Sgt J H Bloomer	pow

T/o 2348 Tempsford on Operation Tablejam 241 and headed for Denmark. Homebound, at 150 feet, when an explosion sent the aircraft out of control to crash in shallow water in Ringkobing Fjord.

Note. This was the last crew reported missing from 138 Squadron prior to its transfer within 3 Group to Main Force bombing duties and re-equipping with Lancasters.

161 Sqn	Stirling IV	LK312 MA-W	Op: SOE

W/C M A Brogan DFC MID	+
F/O F J Watson DFM	+
F/O N Clarke	+
F/O H T Wigley DFC	+
F/L H O Sharman DFC	+
W/O F Mahoney	+
W/O E E Gray	+

T/o 2334 Tempsford on Operation Tablejam 209 and headed for Denmark. Shot down by a flak ship and crashed into the Limfjorden off Livo Island. All are buried in various Danish cemeteries. F/O Watson, in company with Sgt D A Boards, gained an immediate DFM over Hamburg in July 1943. Details of this, along with the DFC won by their skipper F/O R Waugh, appeared in the London Gazette on 2 August 1943. At 37, F/O Clarke was above the average age of operational aircrew.

Note. On 9 March, 161 Squadron was transferred from Bomber Command to 38 Group where it continued with its SOE/SIS duties. During the remaining weeks of the war, 161 Squadron lost four Hudsons and two Stirlings, while a fifth Hudson was involved in a fatal crash at Brussels soon after the cessation of hostilities. Wing Commander Brogan, writes Bryce Gomersall, had flown at least 58 sorties his operational flying commencing in the autumn of 1941 with 149 Squadron. Tragically, the family was to lose another son, Warrant Officer J J Brogan, who was killed on 26 March 1945, when his 524 Squadron Wellington crashed while taking off for an operational sortie from Langham. A third son, Major W G St S Brogan saw active service with the Coldstream Guards and survived the war.

5 Mar	149 Sqn	Lancaster I	NF972 OJ-H	Op: Gelsenkirchen

1945

F/L B M Williams RAAF	+
Sgt E T Turner	pow
F/S H Wormall-Phillips	pow
F/S R Taylor	pow
F/S A E London RAAF	+
Sgt N E Smith	pow
Sgt W Summers	pow

T/o 1044 Methwold to attack by G-H methods the Consolidation benzol-plant. Hit and crippled by flak, possibly while over the target area, at 1404, its demise being witnessed by aircrews from 514 Squadron. Both Australians are buried in the Reichswald Forest War Cemetery.

Note. 149 Squadron was remarkably fortunate throughout its time as a Lancaster squadron, the statistics indicating 1,630 sorties were flown for the loss of only four aircraft to enemy action, while a fifth aircraft was written off at Methwold in the January. In the post-war years, a further five aircraft of the type were destroyed or damaged beyond repair and in the autumn of 1949, the Squadron converted to Lincolns.

5 Mar 1945	163 Sqn	Mosquito XXV	KB619 -T		Op: Berlin

F/L J Watson

Taxied 0100 into a ditch on Wyton airfield,
Huntingdonshire and damaged beyond repair.

	514 Sqn	Lancaster I	NN775 JI-F2		Op: Gelsenkirchen

F/O H G S Kerr	+
Sgt W Marsden	+
F/S G Smith	+
F/O F Clarke	+
F/S A Olsen RAAF	+
Sgt C G Hogg	+
Sgt H P Thomas	+

T/o 1035 Waterbeach for a G-H attack on the
Consolidation benzol plant. Crashed at Bunsbeek
in the Province of Brabant. All are buried in
Heverlee War Cemetery. Sgt Thomas had enlisted
in Canada, though he lived at Beckford Kraal,
Clarendon on Jamaica.

5-6 Mar 1945	10 Sqn	Halifax III	MZ948 ZA-E		Op: Chemnitz

F/L F D Moss	pow
Sgt H W Tasker	+
F/S R E Davenport	+
WO2 L W Webster RCAF	+
F/S R C Fowler	pow
Sgt L L Hall RAAF	+
F/S F Fearnley	+
F/S S Hodgson	pow

T/o 1708 Melbourne. Those who died rest in
Dürnbach War Cemetery. F/S Fearnley, who was
manning the mid-under gun position, was 39,
well above the age normally associated with
Bomber Command aircrew. His service number
and that of F/S Hodgson suggest both joined
the service on the same day between April and
October 1941.

Note. The two operations, now to be summarised, were part of the continuing
theme of Operation Thunderclap where the aim was to dislocate communications
ahead of the advancing Soviet armies, as well as to destroy oil supplies and
other commodities useful to the enemy. Both attacks were deemed successful.

	10 Sqn	Halifax III	NR131 ZA-N		Op: Chemnitz

F/L A D Stephen	+
Sgt T T Elliott	+
F/S K V Rees	+
F/S B Robson	+
F/O H C Maria RNZAF	+
P/O C J Roberts RCAF	+
F/O R E Heap DFM	+

T/o 1657 Melbourne. Crashed near Stalag IXC
at Mühlhausen, all bodies being recovered from
the wreckage by the prisoners of war. Two weeks
later, on 20 March, despite an order forbidding
a burial service, funeral proceedings were conducted by the Senior Chaplain, Revd J R Bamber MA.
Since 1945, their remains have been taken to
Berlin 1939-1945 War Cemetery. F/O Heap, a
regular airman, had gained his DFM on a previous tour with the Squadron, the
London Gazette publishing details on 13 July 1943. F/S Rees had joined the
service as an apprentice clerk in the late 1920s.

	35 Sqn	Lancaster III	ME333 TL-S		Op: Chemnitz

S/L F Watson DFC	+
F/S G Cross DFM	+
F/L K S Smith	+
F/S S O Scott	+
W/O L G Holland DFM	+
F/O P J Pentelow RNZAF	+
W/O V A Roe CGM DFM	+

T/o 1728 Graveley. Lost without trace. All
are commemorated on the Runnymede Memorial. The
DFM recipients, in order of crew, had their
awards Gazetted on 27 March 1945, 19 October
1943 and 13 June 1944 respectively. W/O Holland
had flown a tour with 51 Squadron, but W/O Roe
was a long serving member of 35 Squadron. F/O
Pentelow RNZAF had wed Emma Caroline Pentelow
of Calgary, Alberta, Canada.

	44 Sqn	Lancaster III	LM654 KM-L		Op: Bohlen

F/O J S Peterswald RAAF	pow
Sgt D F MacShane	pow
F/O R D Temple	pow
F/S N D Askill	pow
F/S J R Tulloch	pow
Sgt D Howells	evd
Sgt J W Horne	pow

T/o 1704 Spilsby to bomb a synthetic-oil plant.

	50 Sqn	Lancaster I	NF918 VN-N		Op: Bohlen

F/O D N King	+
Sgt K R Still	+
Sgt A R Stafford	+
F/S G J Thomas	+
Sgt D W S Bay	+
Sgt N Russell	+
Sgt J Barton	+

T/o 1721 Skellingthorpe similarly charged.
All are buried in Dürnbach War Cemetery. At
thirty-seven, Sgt Russell was well above the
average age of operational aircrew.

5–6 Mar
1945

| 57 Sqn | Lancaster I | NG410 DX-G | Op: Bohlen |

F/O R Dimond RAAF   inj
Sgt O Shorey
Sgt H Duerden
Sgt L Curtis
W/O I Wright RNZAF
F/S R Field
Sgt C Griffin

T/o 1703 East Kirkby to attack a synthetic-oil plant. On the return flight, ran short of fuel and in the ensuing forced-landing at 0333 near Nuneaton in Warwickshire, the Lancaster was damaged beyond repair. It is not thought that F/O Dimond's injuries were of a serious nature.

| 76 Sqn | Halifax III | MZ905 MP-H | Op: Chemnitz |

F/L H V Perry

While taxying towards the duty runway, F/L Perry was obliged to stop in order to allow another aircraft to pass ahead. Upon moving off at 1710, F/L Perry's Halifax was struck by F/L G E Peterson RCAF at the controls of NA219 MP-D. The latter sustained relatively minor damage, but F/L Perry's aircraft was deemed to be beyond economical repair and was scrapped. No injuries reported.

| 102 Sqn | Halifax VI | RG502 DY-Q | Op: Chemnitz |

F/O J A Hurley   +
Sgt A J E Morton   pow
F/S H H Briggs   +
F/O A V Valentine   pow
Sgt J T Smith   +
Sgt T Cooney   +
Sgt K E White   pow

T/o 1733 Pocklington. Crashed near Volyne on the Volynka, roughly 6 km SSW of Strakonice in Czechoslovakia. Those who died are buried in Praha War Cemetery.

Note. This was the first Halifax VI reported missing from a Bomber Command operation and for 102 Squadron it was their third Q for Queenie to be lost in succession.

| 103 Sqn | Lancaster III | ME392 PM-Y | Op: Chemnitz |

F/O G W Exel RCAF   +
Sgt G H Wilson   pow
F/O J H McKenna RCAF   pow
F/O M F Griffin RCAF   +
F/S F P Monaghan   pow
F/S J L Cooke RCAF   pow
W/O D King   pow

T/o 1651 Elsham Wolds. The two officers who lost their lives are commemorated on panel 279 of the Runnymede Memorial. It is affirmed that F/O Griffin RCAF made a successful exit from the Lancaster.

| 103 Sqn | Lancaster III | PB563 PM-G | Op: Chemnitz |

F/L M R Norem   +
F/O K Jackson RNZAF   +
F/O G L Taylor   +
F/S J A Green   +
F/S J A Wright   +
F/O F W Elliott DFM   +
Sgt R S Brown   +
Sgt W Seeckts   +

T/o 1716 Elsham Wolds. All are buried in Berlin 1939-1945 War Cemetery. F/O Elliott had served previously with 207 Squadron and details of his DFM had appeared in the London Gazette as long ago as 20 April 1943.

| 109 Sqn | Mosquito XVI | PF447 HS- | Op: Hallendorf |

F/L A M Payne   +
F/L J V Evans   +

T/o 1853 Little Staughton. Attacked the AP at 2142 from 32,000 feet but after advising the success of their mission, the crew headed for Brussels-Melsbroek, tragically crashing while trying to land. Both are buried in Brussels Town Cemetery. F/L Evans held a Bachelor of Arts degree (Lampeter).

| 139 Sqn | Mosquito XX | KB271 XD-T | Op: Berlin |

F/L A O'Grady RAAF
F/L L D Groome DFC

T/o 1808 Upwood. Overshot and crashed 2015 on return to base. No injuries reported.

| 153 Sqn | Lancaster I | PB872 P4-X | Op: Chemnitz |

F/O W J Bailey   +
Sgt J Howard   +
F/O R G D Adlam RNZAF   +
F/O E J S Morris   +
Sgt J Dixon   +
Sgt W B Meechan   +
Sgt W Simpson   +

T/o 1640 Scampton. All are buried in Praha War Cemetery. Their average age was 21. Both air gunners were ex-ATC cadets from Scotland, the former from Ayrshire and the latter from Lanarkshire.

5-6 Mar	**170 Sqn**	**Lancaster III**	**ME320 TC-L**	**Op: Chemnitz**
1945	F/L E R Thornton	+		
	Sgt J P Plant	+		
	F/O W E Weber RCAF	+		
	F/O W A Brydon RCAF	+		
	W/O J J McNally RAAF	+		
	Sgt D Wager	+		
	Sgt C A Ebbs	+		

T/o 1700 Hemswell. W/O McNally RAAF rests in the 1939-1945 War Cemetery at Berlin, the other members of crew are commemorated on the Runnymede Memorial. On panel 168 of this Memorial is the name of Sgt Geoffrey Herbert Wager, brother of Sgt Wager, who died on 21 May 1943 while flying Defiants with 515 Squadron. Both were aged nineteen when they met their death. Sgt Ebbs came from Dublin in the Republic of Ireland.

Note. It is believed the Defiant in which Sergeant Wager died was AA658 reported missing from a flight over the English Channel.

192 Sqn	**Halifax III**	**NR180 DT-S**	**Op: BS**
F/L N Irvine RCAF	pow		
Sgt L A Howard	pow		
F/L J E Nixon RCAF	evd		
F/O D E Banks RCAF	pow		
W/O J A Martin RAAF	pow		
W/O R F Young	evd		
F/S W J McCullough RCAF	pow		
F/S A C Searle RCAF	pow		

T/o 1716 Foulsham. Badly shot about by a fighter, reported as a Me 262, and in the ensuing chaos flew into the tail of a Lancaster which was last seen going down out of control. F/L Irvine RCAF decided to head for the Russian lines but it is believed the crew baled out over territory still held by the Wehrmacht. However, at least two were picked up by Soviet troops and passed to safety. The remainder are presumed to have become prisoners of war. W/O Young was the special equipment operator.

Note. Oliver Clutton-Brock advises that F/S McCullough RCAF spent some time in a Polish hospital, having sustained gun shot wounds from a Russian soldier. Furthermore, Gordon Thomas and Alan Wingate published an account of this loss in 1954 in their book Descent into Danger.

199 Sqn	**Stirling III**	**LJ617 EX-E**	**Op: BS**
F/L J A Thurlow RCAF	+		
Sgt A Plumtree	inj		
F/O R G Noon-Ward RCAF	inj		
F/S E A Evans	inj		
F/O A A Twaddle RNZAF	inj		
P/O T R Nichols RCAF	inj		
F/L F Fenning	inj		
F/S W J Phillips	inj		

T/o 1642 North Creake for Mandrel screening duties. While circling at 18,000 feet, over France, hit by American AA fire and crashed 1930 near Thionville. Seven members of the crew managed to abandon the stricken bomber but their skipper was not amongst them; he is commemorated on panel 278 of the Runnymede Memorial. P/O Nichols RCAF was the special equipment operator.

Note. This was the last Stirling reported missing from 199 Squadron and the type made its last operational appearance with the Squadron on 14-15 March, after which date Halifaxes equipped all flights. Since becoming a Special Duties unit in May 1944, Stirling losses had been limited to eight aircraft, a remarkably fine achievement. This particular Stirling had been from the batch LJ611-LJ653 and had operated with 171 Squadron, flying twenty sorties as 6Y-P and later 6Y-K prior to its moving to 199 Squadron where it flew a further twenty-seven missions.

207 Sqn	**Lancaster I**	**NG230 EM-F**	**Op: Bohlen**
F/O W S De Garis RAAF	+		
Sgt A S Burt	+		
F/O G Morris	+		
F/S S F Giles	+		
W/O A E Wood	+		
Sgt W Drysdale	+		
Sgt W H Edge	+		

T/o 1716 Spilsby to attack a synthetic-oil plant. Lost without trace. All are commemorated on the Runnymede Memorial.

207 Sqn	**Lancaster III**	**ME386 EM-G**	**Op: Bohlen**
F/O A H Wakeling	+		
F/S G L Dickenson	+		
Sgt D J Browne	+		
Sgt W T G Cobden	+		
Sgt T Beattie			
Sgt J E L Brett			
Sgt A J P Clark			

T/o 1734 Spilsby similarly tasked. On return, came down in the River Witham near Boston in Lincolnshire. Of the four who perished, Sgt Cobden was taken to Cambridge City Cemetery, while the others rest in their home towns.

5-6 Mar 1945	227 Sqn	Lancaster I	PB644 9J-R	Op: Bohlen

227 Sqn   **Lancaster I**   **PB644 9J-R**   **Op: Bohlen**

5-6 Mar 1945

F/L G A McQuaker RAAF	pow
F/O W N R Pearce RAAF	+
Sgt J Robb	pow
Sgt W A Senior	pow
F/S E Thompson	pow
Sgt K Pratt	pow
F/S C B Carter	pow
F/S J Connell	pow

T/o 1727 Balderton to attack a synthetic-oil plant. Abandoned, but F/O Pearce RAAF, who had accompanied the crew for operational experience, had the tragic misfortune to land in a tree. Possibly dazed, or perhaps not realising how far he was above the ground, he released his parachute harness and fell to his death. He lies in Dürnbach War Cemetery.

346 Sqn   **Halifax III**   **MZ738 H7-H**   **Op: Chemnitz**

Slt A Fonteix FFAF	+
Sgt J Leroy FFAF	+
Ltn J Rouvel FFAF	+
Sgc M Schilling FFAF	+
Sgt B Houdelot FFAF	+
Sgt J Gorias FFAF	+
Sgt R Farnier FFAF	+

T/o 1712 Elvington. It is presumed their graves are now in France.

347 Sqn   **Halifax III**   **NR226 L8-P**   **Op: Chemnitz**

Ltn J J Santi FFAF	
Sgt B Maincuerix FFAF	
Cdt M Noirot FFAF	
Ltn R Barrois FFAF	
Sgt G Cadeau FFAF	
Sgt J Descousis FFAF	
Sgt R Burel FFAF	

T/o 1704 Elvington. Crash-landed 0109 on return at Friston airfield, Sussex. There are no reports of anyone being badly hurt.

415 Sqn   **Halifax III**   **NA204 6U-J**   **Op: Chemnitz**

F/L W R Mitchell RCAF	pow
F/O R C Barteaux RCAF	pow
F/S A E Ridley RCAF	pow
F/O R D Loveridge RCAF	pow
P/O F T Mudry RCAF	pow
P/O W D Mosey RCAF	pow
F/S W B Gill RCAF	pow
P/O J R Gendron RCAF	pow

T/o 1645 East Moor. The majority of this crew had arrived at East Moor on 18 October 1944, on posting from 61 (RCAF) Base.

419 Sqn   **Lancaster X**   **KB845 VR-L**   **Op: Chemnitz**

F/O C L Reitlo RCAF	+
Sgt J A S King RCAF	+
P/O J E Hanley RCAF	+
F/O W N De Witt RCAF	+
P/O F R Leet RCAF	+
Sgt N R Poole RCAF	+
F/O G J Hollinger RCAF	+

T/o 1629 Middleton St. George. Homebound, when control was lost, probably due to severe icing, and crashed at Drayton Parsloe, 10 miles NNE of Aylesbury, Buckinghamshire. All rest in Brookwood Military Cemetery. It will be recalled that Sgt Poole RCAF had been slightly injured after his Lancaster had forced-landed in France while raiding Hannover in the January.

420 Sqn   **Halifax III**   **NA184 PT-W**   **Op: Chemnitz**

F/O E W Clark RCAF	+
Sgt J B Kirby	+
F/O D V Freed RCAF	inj
F/O W H Oakes RCAF	+
F/S R J Arnold RCAF	inj
WO1 H M O'Connor RCAF	inj
F/S J A Epoch RCAF	+

T/o 1628 Tholthorpe but iced up and crashed 1650 at Marrow Flat Farm, just over a mile NE of Dishforth aerodrome. The three RCAF airmen were taken to Harrogate (Stonefall) Cemetery, while Sgt Kirby was claimed by his next-of-kin.

420 Sqn   **Halifax III**   **NA190 PT-U**   **Op: Chemnitz**

P/O R F Sollie RCAF	+
Sgt R L Dinnen	+
F/S W Gaba RCAF	+
P/O E S Kaechele RCAF	+
F/O R G Smith RCAF	+
F/S J H Waugh DFM RCAF	
Sgt R O Battler RCAF	+

T/o 1629 Tholthorpe but iced up and crashed 1720 into Hayton Woods near Hazelwood Castle, 3 miles SW of Tadcaster, Yorkshire. F/S Waugh RCAF, who won an immediate DFM (Gazetted as recently as 9 January 1945) for the destruction of an enemy night-fighter over Oberhausen the previous November, baled out safely. His six less fortunate companions were buried in Harrogate (Stonefall) Cemetery. Sgt Dinnen came from Ballyjamesduff, Co. Cavan in the Republic of Ireland.

5-6 Mar 1945	420 Sqn	Halifax III	NP959 PT-N	Op: Chemnitz

F/L V R Glover RCAF	pow	T/o 1630 Tholthorpe. F/S Kastner RCAF is
F/O D M Mottrick RCAF	pow	reported to have died from his wounds within
Sgt H W Skipper	pow	hours of being admitted to a German hospital.
P/O J R Gordon RCAF	pow	It is likely his grave was located by the US
F/O V L McKinnon RCAF	pow	authorities as he now lies in France at Choloy
WO2 D F Broadfoot RCAF	pow	War Cemetery.
F/S J J M Kastner RCAF	inj	
F/S H E MacKenzie RCAF	pow	

420 Sqn	Halifax III	NR144 PT-H	Op: Chemnitz

P/O J H Menary RCAF		T/o 1623 Tholthorpe. Bombed the AP from 16,000
Sgt J G Johnston RCAF		feet at 2145. Homebound, ran low on petrol and
F/S A A Rich RCAF		the crew decided to head for Juvincourt. At
F/S R A Nicol RCAF	inj	approximately 0130 the Halifax emerged from
F/S R M Stirling RCAF		cloud and while flying through thin patches
F/S D H Goodwin RCAF		of mist, clipped a pole standing on high ground.
F/S D McClellan RCAF	inj	Seconds later the bomber crash-landed on soft
		earth some 8 km N of its intended destination.

F/S Nicol RCAF sustained a bruised right leg and F/S McClellan RCAF emerged
from his turret with a cut forehead; the rest escaped with a bad shaking.

424 Sqn	Lancaster I	NG458 QB-H	Op: Chemnitz

F/L D A Ross RCAF	+	T/o 1642 Skipton-on-Swale. Of the six who lost
Sgt A K Rayner	+	their lives, five have no known graves while
F/O H McE Weaver RCAF	+	F/O Seaby RCAF is buried in Berlin 1939-1945
F/O A V Cash RCAF	+	War Cemetery. All had just about reached the
F/O F E Seaby RCAF	+	halfway point of their tour of duty.
F/S J M Atchison RCAF	+	
F/S C J Antonek RCAF	pow	

425 Sqn	Halifax III	MZ454 KW-S	Op: Chemnitz

F/O A R Lowe RCAF	+	T/o 1640 Tholthorpe but iced up and partially
Sgt J L Lynch RCAF	+	abandoned before crashing 1702 some 200 yards
F/O E S Brabbins RCAF		from Little Ouseburn, 9 miles NW from Harro-
F/O J F Brownell RCAF		gate and badly damaging the church and Moat
F/S K J S McCuaig RCAF		Hall. The four who died were buried in Stone-
F/O P J Hall RCAF	+	fall Cemetery, but since 1945 F/O Lowe RCAF has
P/O J W Hyde RCAF	+	been exhumed and taken back to his native America
		where he now rests in Fairview Cemetery, Red Bank

in the State of New Jersey. At 35, P/O Hyde RCAF was above the average age of
Bomber Command aircrew.

Note. In 1995, a Memorial Porch was erected at Little Ouseburn Church,
thus perpetuating the memories of those who died fifty years previous.

425 Sqn	Halifax III	MZ845 KW-J	Op: Chemnitz

P/O M S H Anderson RCAF	+	T/o 1647 Tholthorpe but at 1658 was involved in
P/O J D F E Roy RCAF	+	a midair collision with a 426 Squadron aircraft
P/O J E R Beaudry RCAF	+	and both Halifaxes crashed some 300 yards W of
F/O R E O Charron RCAF	+	Manor House and just S of Linton-on-Ouse air-
F/S A J De Cruyenaere RCAF		field and on the S side of the Ouse. In those
F/S J L P Seguin RCAF	+	last few fateful moments, F/S De Cruyenaere RCAF
P/O J L G Pelletier RCAF	+	managed to bale out. His six friends are buried
		in Harrogate (Stonefall) Cemetery.

425 Sqn	Halifax III	PN173 KW-Q	Op: Chemnitz

F/O J J A L Desbiens RCAF	+	T/o 1651 Tholthorpe. Those who died are buried
Sgt A E Minguet RCAF	+	in Berlin 1939-1945 War Cemetery.
F/S G E J Tremblay RCAF	pow	
F/O J A Parent RCAF	pow	
F/S H J M J D´Avril RCAF	+	
F/S G L J Langeum RCAF	pow	
F/S L P Lamontagne RCAF	pow	

Note. This Halifax was manufactured by Fairey Aviation and delivered, ex-
works, to Tholthorpe on 22 November 1944 and taken over by 425 Squadron.
It seems to have operated without being damaged until its demise, as described above. No flying hours totals appended.

5-6 Mar 1945	426 Sqn	Halifax VII	LW210 OW-Y	Op: Chemnitz

```
5-6 Mar    426 Sqn          Halifax VII   LW210 OW-Y              Op: Chemnitz
1945       F/L I Emerson RCAF        +     T/o 1639 Linton-on-Ouse but soon encountered
           Sgt W T Symes             +     very severe icing and at around 1700 broke up
           F/O A M Hutchison RCAF    +     in flight, scattering wreckage onto Nunthorpe
           F/O T M Campbell RCAF     +     Avenue, York.  In addition to the six crew
           P/O J Low RCAF          inj     members killed, five civilians died and a
           F/S J N MacDougall RCAF   +     further eighteen were injured, mostly when
           Sgt R H Turner RCAF             an engine sliced through the roof of a local
                                           secondary school and demolished the kitchen
           area. Sgt Symes was taken to his home for burial; his five RCAF companions
           were interred in Harrogate (Stonefall) Cemetery. It is reported that F/S Low
           RCAF later married the nurse who tended to him as he recovered in hospital.

           426 Sqn          Halifax VII   NP793 OW-H              Op: Chemnitz
           F/O H S Watts RCAF        +     T/o 1642 Linton-on-Ouse. Iced up and crashed
           P/O W A Togwell           +     circa 1700 at Westfield Farm, Kirkbymoorside,
           F/O F M Myers RCAF        +     6 miles WNW from Pickering and on the road to
           F/S W A Way RCAF          +     Sowerby, Yorkshire.  The six RCAF airmen rest
           WO1 B J McCarthy RCAF     +     in Harrogate (Stonefall) Cemetery, F/S Bigger-
           F/S M W Coones RCAF       +     staff being eighteen years of age. P/O Togwell
           F/S R A Biggerstaff RCAF  +     is buried at Derby (Nottingham Road) Cemetery.

           426 Sqn          Halifax VII   NP799 OW-J              Op: Chemnitz
           F/L J G Kirkpatrick RCAF  +     T/o 1645 Linton-on-Ouse. Shot down by a night-
           Sgt I Giles               +     fighter. Panel 275 of the Runnymede Memorial
           F/O R E Fennell RCAF      +     perpetuates the name of Sgt Giles, while the
           F/O R E Stillinger RCAF   +     others who died rest in Berlin 1939-1945 War
           WO1 J A H Larson RCAF     +     Cemetery.
           F/S W H Denison RCAF    pow
           F/S R B Gunderson RCAF    +

           426 Sqn          Halifax VII   PN228 OW-A              Op: Chemnitz
           S/L E T Garrett RCAF      +     T/o 1648 Linton-on-Ouse but collided with a
           Sgt E S Jerome            +     425 Squadron Halifax and crashed in the manner
           F/O J L Atkinson RCAF     +     described on the previous page, though much of
           F/O K G Parker RCAF       +     the wreckage from this aircraft was found at
           WO2 W G Miller RCAF       +     Poolspring near Nun Monkton, 8 miles NW from
           WO2 J B Linstead RCAF     +     the centre of York. All six Canadians lie in
           WO2 H D McLeod RCAF       +     Harrogate (Stonefall) Cemetery; Sgt Jerome was
                                           taken for burial in his home town.

           428 Sqn          Lancaster X   KB778 NA-Y              Op: Chemnitz
           F/O W Mytruk RCAF       inj     T/o 1644 Middleton St. George.  Bombed the AP
           Sgt C R Hazelby           +     from 16,500 feet at 2154, but while returning
           F/O W R Ashdown RCAF      +     across Belgium iced up and crashed into woods
           F/O D A Wade RCAF         +     at an area known as Baraque de Fraiture (Lux-
           P/O E J Snell RCAF              embourg) and some 14 km NE of la Roche-en-
           F/S T J Chevrier RCAF           Ardenne.  Those who died are now buried in
           F/S E L Schofield RCAF          Hotton War Cemetery. F/O Mytruk RCAF was taken
                                           to a hospital at Malmedy.

           429 Sqn          Halifax III   LV996 AL-K              Op: Chemnitz
           F/L M W Sanderson RCAF    +     T/o 1652 Leeming. Homebound, crashed at Halling
           P/O W R Strand RCAF       +     some 4 miles SW of Gillingham, Kent. All were
           P/O J P Nault RCAF        +     buried in Brookwood Military Cemetery.
           P/O H N Prince RCAF       +
           P/O A S Leroux RCAF       +
           F/S A G Caldwell RCAF     +
           F/S P F Gonroski RCAF     +
```

Note. These were the last Halifax casualties sustained by 429 Squadron, now about to convert to Lancasters. As a Halifax unit, the Squadron had operated variants of the type since August 1943, sustaining a total of fifty-nine lost on operational mission, plus six destroyed in training accidents. Accidents on the ground claimed a further four airframes. The Halifax, here summarised, had been accepted by 427 Squadron on 17 April 1944, flying sixty-three sorties before being transferred to 429 Squadron and destroyed in the circumstances here described, this being its third sortie with the Squadron. During its time with 427 Squadron, it had twice been damaged on operations.

5-6 Mar 1945	**431 Sqn**	**Lancaster X**	**KB858 SE-G**	**Op: Chemnitz**

F/O S A Reid RCAF	+
Sgt W A Salisbury	+
F/O H J Feldhans RCAF	+
F/O H J Beaton RCAF	+
WO2 C B MacDonald RCAF	+
Sgt H R Harris RCAF	+
Sgt H Guttormson RCAF	+

T/o 1635 Croft. Crashed at Oberweldbach, 15 km ENE of Herbon. All are buried in Hannover War Cemetery.

432 Sqn　　　**Halifax VII**　　　**RG475 QO-L**　　　　　　**Op: Chemnitz**

S/L E A Hayes RCAF	+
F/L J G Clothier RCAF	+
P/O D E Cooke	+
F/O C M Hay DSO RCAF	+
P/O D J Ringrose RCAF	+
F/L G R Harris MID RCAF	+
F/S M B Nielsen RCAF	+
F/S G M Orser RCAF	+

T/o 1630 East Moor. Fell victim to AA fire from a coastal battery sited near Walton on the Naze, Essex. Thus, P/O Cooke died just over 30 miles NW of his home at Leigh-on-Sea. With six other members of crew, he is buried in Brookwood Military Cemetery. F/L Clothier RCAF, however, was probably claimed by relatives as his grave is in Monmouthshire at Rockfield (St. Cenhedlon) Churchyard, Llanga-ttock-vibon-Avel United. It is reported he was beginning his third tour of operations having re-mustered to a pilot from the trade of air gunner. He remained undecorated; both air gunners were nineteen years of age.

Note. Over the years, 308 Squadron ATC has salvaged parts from this Halifax.

434 Sqn　　　**Lancaster X**　　　**KB842 WL-L**　　　　　　**Op: Chemnitz**

P/O J Kitchen RCAF

T/o 1635 Croft. Bombed from 16,500 feet at 2154 and was almost immediately involved in a midair collision with a Halifax that was in the process of being shot down by a Ju 88. The night-fighter crew then turned their attention on the Lancaster, causing much damage to the hydraulic system and starboard wing. Return fire, however, succeeded in driving the enemy fighter away, possibly damaged, and P/O Kitchen RCAF succeeded in getting his badly mauled aircraft back to Carnaby in Yorkshire where it was written off in the ensuing emergency landing. No one was hurt.

460 Sqn　　　**Lancaster III**　　　**PB557 AR-A2**　　　　　　**Op: Chemnitz**

F/L J C Holmes DFC RAAF	+
F/S T T Clarke RAAF	+
Sgt J Young	+
F/O D G Hudspeth RAAF	+
F/S R E Hayward	+
F/O I S Baudinette RAAF	+
F/L T E V Morgan DFM RAAF	+
W/O E O T Mayne RAAF	+

T/o 1629 Binbrook. Outbound, hit by flak and crashed at Pfieffe, 5 km ESE of Spangenberg. All are buried in Hannover War Cemetery, brought here from graves found at Melsungen. F/L Holmes RAAF had flown at least 40 sorties, while F/L Morgan RAAF was on his second tour with the Squadron. Details of his DFM had been published on 7 December 1943. F/S Hayward came from Bonavista in Newfoundland, though he had enlisted in the UK sometime after November 1941. It is believed W/O Mayne RAAF hailed from Aberdare in Glamorgan.

463 Sqn　　　**Lancaster I**　　　**NG401 JO-G**　　　　　　**Op: Bohlen**

F/O A G Belford RAAF	
F/S H F Burchett	
F/O D L Wheeler RAAF	
F/S J P Polkinghorn RAAF	
F/S E G Jowitt RAAF	
F/S P R Shipperd	inj
F/S P Jobson RAAF	inj

T/o 1719 Waddington to attack a synthetic-oil plant. Approaching the AP, hit by flak which wounded F/S Jobson RAAF in his left eye and caused the aircraft to roll over to starboard. Fuel streamed from No.3 starboard wing tank and after regaining control, bombs were jettisoned at 2201 from 12,000 feet, about 10 km W of the target. Then followed an eventful flight to Juvincourt airfield, where a fast landing removed first the starboard wheel followed moments later by the port wheel. F/S Shipperd was injured and with F/S Jobson RAAF he was treated in a local hospital.

466 Sqn　　　**Halifax III**　　　**MZ914 HD-**　　　　　　**Op: Chemnitz**

F/L C M Halpin RAAF	
Sgt W Watt	
F/S C J McLaughlin RAAF	
F/S F Noble RAAF	
W/O C C Brooks RAAF	
F/S H C Brookershire RAAF	
F/S C W Nagle RAAF	

T/o 1654 Driffield but experienced severe control problems and returned to base, landing at 1905. The following day, the Halifax was declared beyond the capacity for local repairs but it is believed the airframe languished at Driffield until 12 April 1945, when a decision was made to strike the aircraft off charge.

5-6 Mar
1945

| 515 Sqn | Mosquito VI | NS992 3P- | Op: BS |

W/O W A Halstead
F/S C A Jones

Taxied onto the Little Snoring runway from the marshalling point, as instructed, at 2035 but while lining up was struck by Mosquito VI RS608 from 23 Squadron, captained by F/O Cooke. No one was hurt, and F/O Cooke's aircraft was repaired (and later transferred to the French Air Force). An inspection of the 515 Squadron revealed very serious damage to the mainplanes and it was duly struck off charge. Meanwhile, the crew immediately transferred to Mosquito 457 and completed an uneventful sortie.

| 576 Sqn | Lancaster I | PD403 UL-F2 | Op: Chemnitz |

F/O C J Rouse RCAF   +
Sgt R H Twin   +
Sgt J T J Magee RCAF   +
F/S K R Marston   +
F/S D H Hadlow   +
F/S W W Dewar RCAF   +
Sgt R W Abrams RCAF   +

T/o 1655 Fiskerton. Believed to have crashed in the target area, as F/O Rouse RCAF is reported to have been buried in the Reichenhainer Strasse Friedhof. His grave, however, could not be found and along with five other members of crew, he is commemorated on the Runnymede Memorial. F/S Hadlow rests in Berlin 1939-1945 War Cemetery.

| 578 Sqn | Halifax III | LL559 LK-U | Op: Chemnitz |

F/O E Dawson
Sgt H A Naris
F/S R J B Capon
F/S W F Willcox
P/O E A Calcutt
Sgt J G Marshall
Sgt N H Sellers

T/o 1709 Burn. Bombed the AP at 2156 from 16,000 feet. Low on fuel, landed 0204 at Bovingdon in Hertfordshire but swung on touch down and ran into another Squadron Halifax that had arrived twenty-six minutes previous, and was now parked on the edge of the runway. Both machines were wrecked but no one was injured.

Note. The above crew did not operate again with 578 Squadron, being posted on 15 March to 51 Squadron at Snaith.

| 578 Sqn | Halifax III | NA173 LK-K | Op: Chemnitz |

F/O J W Howard RCAF
Sgt J Watts
F/O C F Wilschke RCAF
F/O F E Smith RCAF
W/O A L Francis RAAF
F/S H R McNeal RCAF
F/S H F Jepson RCAF

T/o 1657 Burn. Bombed the AP at 2146 from 16,500 feet. Landed, low on petrol, 0138 at Bovingdon airfield, Hertfordshire and was marshalled to a parking place just off the runway. Here it was struck and damaged beyond repair in the circumstances described above.

Note. This crew continued with 578 Squadron, flying on operations to Essen on 11 March and participating in the raid against Wuppertal two days later.

| 582 Sqn | Lancaster III | PB475 60-C | Op: Chemnitz |

F/O J C Gould   +
Sgt A Denbeigh   +
F/S R F Barnett RAAF   +
W/O G Torr RAAF   +
W/O E W Hemsworth RAAF   +
Sgt G J P Ralph   +
Sgt G Hart

T/o 1733 Little Staughton. Homebound, when a TI that had failed to release exploded, sending the Lancaster hurtling into the ground at 0100 near Bellingdon, 2 miles NW from Chesham in Buckinghamshire. Those who died are buried in Oxford (Botley) Cemetery at North Hinksey. Sgt Hart managed to parachute to safety.

| 608 Sqn | Mosquito XX | KB197 6T-A | Op: Berlin |

F/L M H M Maclean DFC RAAF +
Sgt R Todd   +

T/o 1823 Downham Market. Crashed near Braine-le Comte (Hainaut), a small town on the Halle to Soignies road and about 6 km NE from the latter. Initially, both were buried in a field close to where they crashed but their graves are now in Leopoldsburg War Cemetery.

| 625 Sqn | Lancaster I | NG240 CF-F2 | Op: Chemnitz |

F/O J W Alexander RCAF   pow
Sgt O C Lear   pow
F/O W Petrashenko RCAF   pow
F/O F R Chapman RCAF   pow
F/S C W Morgan   pow
Sgt R Pyett   pow
Sgt J V Williams   pow

T/o 1639 Kelstern. Believed to have crashed on the island of Rügen at Presnitz, 11 km NW of Bergen. It is reported that Sgt Williams escaped while being marched towards Moosburg and made tracks for the Allied lines near Nürnberg. He arrived home on 22 April, roughly three weeks ahead of the rest of the crew.

5-6 Mar	625 Sqn	Lancaster I		PD375 CF-R	Op: Chemnitz

1945

625 Sqn	Lancaster I	PD375 CF-R	Op: Chemnitz
F/L A D Cook	pow		
Sgt S L Lowe	pow		
Sgt T H Scowcroft RCAF	pow		
F/S F W Brooks	pow		
Sgt W Allen	pow		
Sgt C H Bartlett	+		
Sgt J H Porter	+		

T/o 1636 Kelstern. Both air gunners are buried in the 1939-1945 War Cemetery at Berlin. It is reported that Sgt Allen was seriously wounded.

635 Sqn	Lancaster I	PB921 F2-N	Op: Chemnitz
F/L K A Beattie RNZAF	pow		
F/S G Williams DFM	+		
F/L K Usher DFC	+		
F/L D L Venning DFC	+		
F/O R S Goddard RCAF	+		
F/S G W Hatton DFM	+		
F/S D D Adam DFM	+		

T/o 1721 Downham Market. Those who died are commemorated on the Runnymede Memorial. The three members of crew decorated with the DFM had their awards Gazetted on 12 February 1946, 16 January and 13 April 1945 respectively, F/S Hatton gaining his award with 51 Squadron. F/L Venning, a navigator by trade but thought to have been flying on this occasion as an air bomber, had been a scholar at Magdalen Collage, Oxford, gaining a Bachelor of Arts degree.

Note. This was the first Lancaster I reported missing from 635 Squadron.

640 Sqn	Halifax III	NR120 C8-M	Op: Chemnitz
F/O H M Sells			
Sgt J Boyd			
W/O R Lees			
W/O J Brett			
F/O E H Melvin			
Sgt A C Nicol			
F/S M A Shaw			

T/o 1655 Leconfield. Bombed the AP at 2156 from 17,000 feet but while homebound ran low on fuel. Uncertain of their position, the crew baled out, all landing without injury, over France.

6 Mar	105 Sqn	Mosquito IX	ML924 GB-	Op: Wesel

1945

105 Sqn	Mosquito IX	ML924 GB-	Op: Wesel
W/C T W Horton DFC RNZAF			
F/L W Jones DFC			

T/o 1907 Bourn. On return, landed at 2220 with one engine stopped, bounced and damaged the Mosquito beyond repair. No injuries.

105 Sqn	Mosquito IX	MM237 GB-	Op: Wesel
S/L R Burrell	inj		
F/O J McCulloch	inj		

T/o 2120 Bourn. Shortly after crossing the East Anglia coast on return, the Mosquito was intercepted by one of our own night-fighters and shot down, out of control. The crew managed to bale out, just moments before their aircraft hit the ground S of Frayling Abbey, Norfolk.

Note. Losses to "friendly fire" had been quite prevalent in 1945, as will have been noted, particularly over Belgium and France where aircraft had fallen foul of anti-aircraft fire. Incidents of mistaken identity were less common, but was acknowledged as the cause in this case.
Note. This had been an eventful evening for Squadron Leader Burrell, whose first attempt to raid Wesel had to be aborted with engine trouble. He had then joined the second wave and was in the process of establishing contact with base for landing instructions when the above incident occurred.

109 Sqn	Mosquito XVI	PF429 HS-B	Op: Wesel
S/L G M Smith	+		
F/L W A Jones DFC	+		

T/o 1453 Little Staughton to Oboe mark MT and troop concentrations. While taking over the lead formation, comprising of six Mosquitoes, collided with MM193 and last sighted diving steeply into cloud at 15,000 feet with its tailplane damaged. Both officers are commemorated on the Runnymede Memorial. The other Mosquito made a safe return to base.

514 Sqn	Lancaster III	ME365 JI-T	Op: Salzbergen
F/O L Flack RCAF	+		
Sgt W J Watson	+		
F/O R A Young RCAF	+		
F/S F A Wall	+		
F/S P F O´Donohue RAAF	+		
Sgt A Reilly	+		
Sgt D Heeley	+		

T/o 0819 Waterbeach to bomb the Wintershall oil plant at Salzbergen, NW of Rheine, using G-H methods. Blew up 1205 over the target area All are buried in the Reichswald Forest War Cemetery.

6-7 Mar 1945	44 Sqn	Lancaster I	NG396 KM-G	Op: Sassnitz

F/O B F Boyle RCAF   +   T/o 1831 Spilsby to bomb harbour facilities.
Sgt W C Thornton   +   Presumed lost over the Baltic. The Runnymede
F/S J Pickup   +   Memorial perpetuates the names of six members
F/S W J C Turner   +   of crew, but Sgt Thornton who came from Cashel,
F/S T W Doggart   +   Co. Tipperary in the Republic of Ireland, is
F/S J C Smith   +   buried in Denmark at Svino Churchyard.
Sgt C J Hance   +

Note. All fifty-four identified airmen lying in Svino Churchyard died in Bomber Command service.

	227 Sqn	Lancaster III	PB610 9J-O	Op: Sassnitz

F/L M W Bell   T/o 1816 Balderton similarly tasked. On return
F/O L S Smith   to base at 0346, the starboard tyre burst as the
F/O E Foster   Lancaster touched down. This caused the bomber
F/O G F Orry   to swerve and leave the runway. A fire broke
F/O H A Thomas   out but the crew managed to scramble clear and
Sgt R C S Wells   there are no reports of anyone being seriously
Sgt R O H Stephen   hurt.

7-8 Mar 1945	12 Sqn	Lancaster I	NN741 PH-O	Op: Dessau

F/L D Belot DFC   +   T/o 1648 Wickenby. According to a Frenchman who
Sgt E C M Trott   +   was working in Germany, this Lancaster crashed
F/S C Daintith DFM   +   near Neckartenzlingen, a small town on the E
F/S P Cotton   +   bank of the Neckar, 7 km NNW from Metzingen.
W/O J H Tinsley RAAF   +   All are buried in Dürnbach War Cemetery. F/S
Sgt W L Burbidge   +   Daintith's DFM did not appear in the London
Sgt L H Shaiel-Gosling   +   Gazette until 12 February 1946.

	35 Sqn	Lancaster III	ME361 TL-H	Op: Hemmingstedt

S/L D B Everett   +   T/o 1853 Graveley as Master Bomber for the raid
  DFC & two Bars   on the Deutsche Erdoel oil refinery. Shot down
P/O K G Munro RAAF   +   2200 in the target area. S/L Everett, a highly
F/O J M Aylieff DFC   +   respected PFF captain with 89 sorties to his
F/L C G Mitchell DFC RCAF   +   credit, is buried with his in crew in Hamburg
F/L C O Russell DFC   +   Cemetery, Ohlsdorf. His operational service had
F/L R C Chapman   +   commenced in April 1943 with 158 Squadron based
F/O R M Weller DFC   +   at Lissett. After completing eight sorties, he
F/O A H J Pidgeon   +   was posted to 35 Squadron for PFF duties and it
   is likely he remained on continuous operational
duty until his death. F/L Russell was flying as a second air bomber.

	44 Sqn	Lancaster I	NN768 KM-K	Op: Harburg

F/O E T Jetson RAAF   +   T/o 1826 Spilsby to bomb oil facilities.
Sgt W J Florence   pow   Twenty year old F/O Jetson RAAF of Launceston
F/S B Smith   pow   in Tasmania is commemorated on panel 283 of
F/S A Stevens   pow   the Runnymede Memorial.
F/S R C Silson   pow
Sgt W P Cazaly   pow
F/S R A Bosley   pow

	44 Sqn	Lancaster III	PB417 KM-R	Op: Harburg

F/O P W B Morgans   T/o 1825 Spilsby similarly tasked. Sgt Graham
Sgt R P S Sawbutts   is described as receiving hospital treatment in
W/O C A Dayton   France, but it is not clear if this was immediate
F/O N D Nicolle   or after the cessation of hostilities. The loss
Sgt P Brooks   card merely describes the crew as "safe", but
Sgt I Graham   this could be interpreted as "safe in captivity".
Sgt E E Barnes   W/O Dayton enlisted in Rhodesia circa June 1940.

	49 Sqn	Lancaster III	PB537 EA-X	Op: Harburg

F/O R W G Stark RAAF   +   T/o 1745 Fulbeck similarly tasked. Believed down
Sgt J F Brennan   pow   2215 at Sandbostel, 9 km SSW from the centre of
W/O J C Yeoman RAAF   pow   Bremervörde. Those who died now rest in Beck-
W/O R McP Bairnsfather RAAF   +   lingen War Cemetery, having been brought here
F/S A T J Lovett RAAF   +   from Sandbostel. Sgt Gilbert came from Arklow,
Sgt R C Gilbert   +   Co. Wicklow in the Irish Republic.
Sgt J P Dixon   pow

7-8 Mar 1945	**57 Sqn**	**Lancaster I**	**PB852 DX-V**	**Op: Harburg**

57 Sqn   **Lancaster I**   **PB852 DX-V**   **Op: Harburg**

```
7-8 Mar    57 Sqn            Lancaster I    PB852 DX-V              Op: Harburg
1945       F/O C W Baush              +      T/o 1825 East Kirkby to bomb oil installations.
           Sgt T N Dunlop            +      Lost without trace. All are commemorated on the
           F/S N Cooper              +      Runnymede Memorial.
           F/S J E Thompson          +
           F/S D S Whitehouse        +
           F/S J L Stone             +
           W/O D Forbes              +
```

```
           61 Sqn            Lancaster I    NF988 QR-T              Op: Harburg
           F/L S E Miller            +      T/o 1743 Skellingthorpe similarly tasked.
           F/O H G Underwood         +      Six rest in Becklingen War Cemetery, while
           F/S G McChrystal          +      panel 268 of the Runnymede Memorial per-
           F/O H A Hunt              +      petuates the memory of F/O Underwood.
           F/S R T Galloway          +
           W/O G D Mummery RAAF      +
           F/S I A Hay               +
           Sgt J E Norcutt         pow
```

```
           61 Sqn            Lancaster I    NG182 QR-K              Op: Harburg
           F/O S P Pearce          pow      T/o 1802 Skellingthorpe similarly tasked.
           Sgt W A M Johnstone       +      Crashed at Winsen (Luhe), between the target
           Sgt W K MacCullum       pow      and Lüneburg. Those who died rest in Hamburg
           F/O T H B Kirkby          +      Cemetery, Ohlsdorf. Sgt Fitzpatrick came from
           Sgt A J Deverell          +      Dublin in the Republic of Ireland.
           Sgt K L Mowl              +
           Sgt J Fitzpatrick         +
```

```
           61 Sqn            Lancaster III  ME474 QR-V              Op: Harburg
           F/O F S Farren RAAF       +      T/o 1750 Skellingthorpe similarly tasked.
           Sgt W McMarth             +      Crashed into the sea. Two bodies, those of
           F/S T L Benson            +      F/O Farren RAAF who had married Monica Cicely
           Sgt J Sinclair            +      Farren of Kidlington and 37 year old Sgt
           F/S W S H Tandy           +      McMarth, were washed ashore. The former
           Sgt A Lockett             +      rests in Holland at Nederweert War Cemetery
           Sgt N Peckham             +      while the latter is buried in Germany at
                                            Becklingen War Cemetery. The others have
           no known graves. At 35, Sgt Lockett was above an age normally associated
           with Bomber Command airmen.
```

Note. Hans de Haan reports that Flying Officer Farren RAAF was initially taken to the US Military Cemetery at Margraten, thus suggesting his body had either been recovered by Americans, or handed over to their care. Margraten is one of nine US Military cemeteries in north-west Europe, and contains the bodies of 8,301 servicemen.

```
           101 Sqn           Lancaster I    PD268 SR-O              Op: Dessau
           S/L M V Gibbon AFC        +      T/o 1708 Ludford Magna. Lost without trace.
           W/O I H Bond              +      All are commemorated on the Runnymede Memorial.
           F/O R T Cawthorp          +      Sgt Mahr RCAF was responsible for the specialist
           Sgt W Canning             +      equipment; Sgt Canning came from Dublin. Both
           Sgt L F Tyrrell           +      air gunners were in their 30s, Sgt Matthews
           Sgt R W Mahr RCAF         +      being 32 while Sgt Preston was 39, well over
           Sgt A F Matthews          +      the average age of operational aircrew. In
           Sgt C E Preston           +      contrast, Sgt Mahr RCAF was only nineteen.
                                            S/L Gibbon had served since the late 1920s
           or early '30s. Although it is not specifically mentioned, it is possible
           the crew had been tasked for ABC duties, this being a Squadron commitment
           until May 1945.
```

```
           103 Sqn           Lancaster I    NF913 PM-H              Op: Dessau
           F/O S L Saxe RCAF         +      T/o 1702 Elsham Wolds. Those who perished
           Sgt J J Bent            pow      lie in the Reichswald Forest War Cemetery.
           F/O M Shatzky RCAF        +      Although shown here as prisoners of war, the
           F/S R L Leavers           +      loss card simply describes the three survivors
           F/S K C McGinn RCAF       +      as "safe".
           WO2 A D Cruickshank RCAF pow
           F/S R C Snell RCAF      pow
```

7-8 Mar
1945

103 Sqn   **Lancaster I**   **RA500 PM-B**   **Op: Dessau**

F/O W E Nightingale RCAF	+
Sgt H S Simpson	
F/S R B Mayahay RCAF	inj
F/S R H Almas RCAF	
Sgt D Strickland	
F/S M Hawreliak RCAF	
F/S J A Goldie RCAF	inj

T/o 1728 Elsham Wolds. While nearing the AP, came under attack from a couple of Ju 88s, the port and starboard outer engines being damaged and F/S Mayahay RCAF badly wounded. Damage was also caused to both turrets and the aircraft's electrical and hydraulic systems. Both would be assailants were beaten off and with fuel pouring from No.1 starboard tank and with most of the starboard fin and rudder shot away, the crew managed to regain the Allied lines where all baled out. Tragically, F/O Nightingale failed to open his parachute and he now rests in France at Choloy War Cemetery. Although serving with the RCAF, his home was Kingswear in Devon.

103 Sqn   **Lancaster III**   **JA857 PM-M**   **Op: Dessau**

F/O W J Havell	+
F/S J Roy	+
Sgt N G Mayo	+
Sgt J G Smith	+
Sgt G H Burch	+
Sgt A H Whyte	+
Sgt A G Fry	pow

T/o 1701 Elsham Wolds. Shot down circa 2200 at Grossneuhausen, some 3 km from the airfield at Kolleda. It is reported that Sgt Fry parachuted but was captured and shot the next day by Polizist Kohle. Buried at Vogelsberg Friedhof, his body was exhumed in August 1947 and taken to Berlin 1939-1945 War Cemetery. The rest are perpetuated by the Runnymede Memorial.

Note. I am indebted to Oliver Clutton-Brock for the information pertaining to Sergeant Fry's death.

128 Sqn   **Mosquito XVI**   **RV305 M5-U**   **Op: Berlin**

S/L J D Armstrong RCAF	+
F/O W E Whyte RCAF	+

T/o Wyton. Returning to base on one engine, the crew decided to land at Gilze-Rijen airfield in Holland. Eye witnesses state the Mosquito made a downwind approach and crashed while trying to go round again. Both are buried in the Canadian section of Bergen op Zoom War Cemetery.

170 Sqn   **Lancaster III**   **ME388 TC-H**   **Op: Dessau**

F/O J S Walker RAAF	+
Sgt W H C Fuller	+
F/S J Mahoney	+
F/S L Thomas	+
P/O K G Powell	+
F/S D C Palmer RAAF	+
F/S W D Callaghan RAAF	+

T/o 1704 Hemswell. All are buried in the Reichswald Forest War Cemetery, where the CWGC register describes Sgt Fuller as being a pilot. Their average age was 21, F/S Palmer RAAF being the eldest at twenty-five.

170 Sqn   **Lancaster III**   **ME418 TC-V**   **Op: Dessau**

F/O H W Fuller	+
Sgt W G Austen	+
Sgt D U Hart	+
F/S W S J Moore	+
F/S R Johnson	+
Sgt T Dixon	+
Sgt P Kane	+

T/o 1653 Hemswell. Crashed and burst into flames at Morsleben, 6 km ESE from the centre of Helmstedt. All were buried at Morsleben, since when their remains have been taken to Berlin 1939-1945 War Cemetery. There is no hint of any relationship between F/O Fuller of this aircraft and Sgt Fuller from the one summarised above.

171 Sqn   **Halifax III**   **NA111 6Y-Y**   **Op: BS**

F/L J M Stone	pow
F/S S Stuart	+
F/O K G Thomas RCAF	+
F/O H A Coutts RCAF	+
F/S J Wyatt	+
F/O D C Biggar	+
F/S N P Baker	+
F/S A W Ferme	+

T/o 1720 North Creake and set course for Münster armed with a mixture of bombs and clusters. Those who perished are buried in the Reichswald Forest War Cemetery. F/O Biggar was responsible for the special equipment. It is noted that F/L Stone was repatriated on 3 April 1945.

Note. In addition to its bombing role, this Halifax was equipped with Mandrel and carried a large quantity of Window. The loss card indicates a Flying Officer D C Bigges RCAF as operating with the crew, as well as identifying Flying Officer Biggar. However, the former is not included in the Squadron records and no RCAF casualty has been traced to an RCAF officer bearing this name.

7–8 Mar	189 Sqn	Lancaster I		NG308 CA–G	Op: Harburg
1945	F/L J T Ormiston		pow		
	Sgt J T Russell		pow		
	F/L A F W Polden		+		
	F/S D E Barker		pow		
	F/S B V Levesley		pow		
	Sgt W C Brown		pow		
	Sgt W Prince		pow		

T/o 1804 Fulbeck to attack oil production facilities. All baled out, but it is reported that F/L Polden died while trying to evade capture. His death, however, must have taken place very soon after he parachuted as the Becklingen War Cemetery register shows he died on 7 March. F/S Barker broke an ankle.

	189 Sqn	Lancaster I		NG416 CA–M	Op: Harburg
	F/O D A Smith		inj		
	Sgt R C Powell		pow		
	F/O G M Ward DFC		pow		
	F/S F B Walsh		pow		
	F/S A C Innes RAAF		+		
	Sgt D H Henson		inj		
	Sgt E L Preece		pow		

T/o 1805 Fulbeck similarly tasked. Shot down by a night-fighter and crashed 2225 at Ostlich Hassel, 14 km SE of Bremervörde. The two injured airmen were taken to a prisoner of war camp at Fallingbostel where both died within hours of their arrival. Along with F/S Innes RAAF, they lie in Becklingen War Cemetery.

	189 Sqn	Lancaster I		NG417 CA–P	Op: Harburg
	F/L F J Abbott		+		
	F/O H Henderson		+		
	F/S J F Charlton		+		
	F/S J P Rowan		+		
	F/S W Ashford		+		
	P/O J C Oberneck		+		
	F/S K White		+		

T/o 1815 Fulbeck similarly tasked. Crashed at Jeddingen, 5 km WSW of Visselhövede. All were buried in Becklingen War Cemetery, since when P/O Oberneck, who was born in Brussels on 9 November 1920, has been brought home to rest in the Field of Honour at Brussels Town Cemetery. At 40, F/O Henderson was one of the oldest officers killed in the last months of the war.

	189 Sqn	Lancaster III		ME452 CA–Q	Op: Harburg
	F/O A B Kennedy RNZAF		pow		
	Sgt M M Howe		+		
	F/S J Hughes		pow		
	F/S F H Heron		+		
	F/S J O S Picton		+		
	Sgt W G Gedge		+		
	Sgt B C Johnson		pow		

T/o 1807 Fulbeck similarly tasked. Crashed at around 2230 at Frelsdorf, 17 km W from Bremervörde and N of the main road leading towards Bremerhaven. Those who lost their lives are buried in Becklingen War Cemetery. Three were nineteen and F/S Heron was twenty. F/S Hughes is reported to have sustained a fractured pelvis.

Note. And so 189 Squadron's run of ill luck continued and for the second time in just over a month, four of their crews had failed to return from a single operation. Looking at their 1945 casualties as a whole, it is seen that at least seventy-seven lost their lives and twenty-six survived, most having to spend the last weeks of the war in captivity. An unusual feature in respect of 189 Squadron is that apart from a brief period in the first war as a night-flying training unit, its World War II service was limited to a Bomber Command role, continuing to 20 November 1945.

	195 Sqn	Lancaster I		NG186 A4–O	Op: Dessau
	F/L P Scott		+		
	Sgt A K Robinson		+		
	F/O R Appleyard DFM		+		
	F/O T M Draper RCAF		+		
	W/O R S Howe		inj		
	Sgt D H Sheppard		+		
	Sgt K Woodburn		+		

T/o 1706 Wratting Common. Believed to have crashed near the small town of Büttstadt, E of the main highway between Kölleda and Weimar. W/O Howe died from his wounds on 15 March, while being treated at Büttstadt Krakenhaus. With his six companions, he now lies in Berlin 1939–1945 War Cemetery. F/O Appleyard gained his DFM with 106 Squadron, details being published on 27 June 1944.

Note. 195 Squadron had a run of excellent fortune in 1945, and the above crew were the only airmen reported missing twixt January and May. Tragically, as it turns out, six baled out safely and landed unhurt, only to be brutally put to death by the SS. W/O Howe, meanwhile, was found by Herr Kurt Stiebritz and he cared for the wounded airman until 13 March, when an SS doctor from Buchenwald Concentration Camp arrived and, having diagnosed that pneumonia was present, gave the airman an injection and told Herr Stiebritz to take him to hospital. It is believed this was a genuine attempt to save W/O Howe's life. Unusually, of the thirteen Lancasters written off by the Squadron between October 1944 and March 1945, twelve had been lost on daylight operations.

7-8 Mar	214 Sqn	Fortress III	KJ106 BU-G	Op: BS

7-8 Mar 1945

214 Sqn — Fortress III — KJ106 BU-G — Op: BS

F/O G Stewart RNZAF +
Sgt W P Mulhall pow
F/S H McC McClymont +
F/O N Peters +
P/O J W Winstone RNZAF +
F/S J V Mathews RAAF pow
Sgt A J Goldson pow
F/S H L Henderson RCAF +
W/O J Henderson pow
Sgt K C Phelan pow

T/o 1814 Oulton for Jostle duties over the Hamburg area. Those who died are buried in Becklingen War Cemetery. It is noted that three Commonwealth air forces were represented in this crew. When released from captivity, Sgt Phelan was taken to RAF Hospital Cosford.

218 Sqn — Lancaster I — PD278 HA-V — Op: Dessau

F/L K J MacKenzie RNZAF +
Sgt T Slater +
F/O D V Myers +
F/O J V McShane +
F/S D D Duckworth +
Sgt N Hicks +
Sgt R Scrowther +

T/o 1723 Chedburgh. Believed to have been shot down by a night-fighter, crashing at Marisfeld, 11 km ESE from Meiningen. All are buried in the Friedhof at Marisfeld, but on 1 July 1950, their bodies were exhumed and transferred to Berlin for interment in the 1939-1945 War Cemetery. Their average age was twenty-two.

408 Sqn — Halifax VII — NP718 EQ-B — Op: Hemmingstedt

P/O G D Daughters RCAF +
Sgt J Huspeka RCAF pow
WO2 B C Patterson RCAF pow
F/O S Lasko RCAF pow
F/S A G Allen RCAF +
F/S R G McManus RCAF +
WO2 N G Baird RCAF +

T/o 1843 Linton-on-Ouse. Lost to the combined fire power of fighter and flak, crashing circa 2200 at Nordhastedt, 7 km ESE of Heide. The four who died are buried in Kiel War Cemetery. At 37, F/S McManus RCAF was amongst the oldest Canadians killed on bomber operations in 1945.

419 Sqn — Lancaster X — KB797 VR-K — Op: Dessau

F/O B T MacNeill RCAF +
Sgt R T Wilson RCAF +
F/O W E Short RCAF +
Sgt E V Beach RCAF +
F/S H O Cole RCAF pow
Sgt D C Jamieson RCAF pow
Sgt R L Mitchell RCAF +

T/o 1657 Middleton St. George. The names of the five RCAF airmen who died are perpetuated on the Runnymede Memorial.

424 Sqn — Lancaster I — NG346 QB-N — Op: Dessau

F/O D W Lighthall RCAF pow
Sgt J A Bellamy RCAF +
F/S G W Laut RCAF +
F/S P W Davies RCAF +
Sgt P Y Yanai +
F/S J W Allan RCAF +
F/S D Bellantino RCAF +

T/o 1645 Skipton-on-Swale. Those who perished are buried in Rheinberg War Cemetery. The crew had arrived with the Squadron as recently as 6 February 1945. F/O Lighthall RCAF visited Skipton-on-Swale on 10 May 1945, presumably on his way home to Canada.

424 Sqn — Lancaster I — NG457 QB-C — Op: Dessau

F/O T L Foley RCAF +
Sgt J Klem RCAF +
F/O D W B Robinson RCAF +
F/O D A Stanfield RCAF +
F/O T S Lawrence RCAF +
Sgt S Rosu RCAF +
Sgt K F Seaman RCAF pow

T/o 1646 Skipton-on-Swale. Crashed at Dabringhausen, a town E of the Rhine and some 14 km ENE of Leverkusen. F/O Lawrence RCAF is believed to have baled out safely, but he rests with the others who died in Rheinberg War cemetery. At 19, F/O Robinson RCAF was one of the youngest Canadian navigators killed on bomber operations in 1945. His skipper had flown two sorties as a second pilot and he died while taking his crew on their operational debut.

425 Sqn — Halifax III — MZ815 KW-C — Op: Hemmingstedt

P/O W D Corbett DFC RCAF +
Sgt J G Forsyth +
P/O J W Hickson RCAF +
F/O V P McAllister RCAF +
P/O G N Ware RCAF +
F/S J R Morin RCAF +
F/S L J Parent RCAF +

T/o 1819 Tholthorpe. Lost without trace. All are commemorated on the Runnymede Memorial. At eighteen, F/S Parent RCAF was amongst the youngest air gunners killed on operations in 1945.

7-8 Mar 1945	550 Sqn	Lancaster III	ME428 BQ-O		Op: Dessau

7-8 Mar 1945

550 Sqn   Lancaster III   ME428 BQ-O   Op: Dessau

F/O R D Harris RCAF	+
Sgt K J B Smith	+
F/S D J Yemen RCAF	pow
F/O G J Nicol RCAF	pow
Sgt G P Kelleher	pow
Sgt E R Robinson	+
Sgt D J Hicks RCAF	pow

T/o 1704 North Killingholme. F/O Harris RCAF is commemorated on panel 279 of the Runnymede Memorial; Sgt Smith and Sgt Robinson rest in Berlin 1939-1945 War Cemetery. All had been involved in a serious incident while raiding Pforzheim on 23-24 February.

550 Sqn   Lancaster III   ME503 BQ-R   Op: Dessau

P/O S W Nielson RAAF	+
Sgt A Finnigan	pow
F/S B M Trowbridge RAAF	+
Sgt R Kerr	+
Sgt J Stuart-Ritson	+
Sgt C A DeLaveleye	+
Sgt R F Stevens	pow

T/o 1708 North Killingholme. Those who died were buried in Berlin 1939-1945 War Cemetery but since the cessation of hostilities, Belgian born Sgt DeLaveleye has been brought to Uccle (Drieweg) Communal Cemetery in the southern outskirts of Brussels. Both survivors, noted as "safe", reached the UK on 3 April 1945.

550 Sqn   Lancaster III   PA995 BQ-V   Op: Dessau

F/O C J Jones RCAF	+
Sgt S J Webb	pow
F/O J Buckmaster RCAF	+
WO2 L W Harvey RCAF	+
Sgt F M Main	pow
Sgt S Pelham	pow
Sgt M B Smith	pow

T/o 1659 North Killingholme. Shot down by a Ju 88 circa 2130, crashing at Schauen, 2 km S of Oster-wieck, Germany. Two have no known graves, while WO2 Harvey RCAF lies in Nederweert War Cemetery, having been brought here from Margraten. Sgt Smith escaped in late March, contacting American forces. He returned to his unit on 11 April.

Note. This Lancaster was accepted by 550 Squadron on 29 May 1944, and named "The Vulture Strikes". When lost, its operational sortie tally had exceeded the century mark; no flying hours totals recorded.

576 Sqn   Lancaster I   PD363 UL-K2   Op: Dessau

F/O G H Paley	+
Sgt R Beales	+
F/S R P Belshaw	+
F/S R Potter	+
F/S G B Burns	+
Sgt R Black	+
Sgt C S Mason	+

T/o 1655 Fiskerton. Heard on W/T at 2135 broadcasting wind speed and direction. All are buried in Choloy War Cemetery. Sgt Beales was 38, and as such was well above the average age of Bomber Command aircrew.

Note. This Lancaster had been given the name "Mighty Atom".

576 Sqn   Lancaster I   RF120 UL-D2   Op: Dessau

F/O C T Dalziel	pow
Sgt P R Montgomery	+
Sgt W E May	+
F/S W E Bradbury	pow
F/S A Burns	+
Sgt G T Thorley	+
Sgt D O'Sullivan DSM	+

T/o 1706 Fiskerton. Crashed between the towns of Plettenberg and Attendorn. Of the five who died, four were buried at the former and one, thought to be Sgt O'Sullivan, at the latter. A pre-war regular, his grave is now in Rheinberg War Cemetery, while those of his four friends are at the Reichswald Forest War Cemetery.

578 Sqn   Halifax III   LL558 LK-R   Op: Hemmingstedt

F/L G O Powell	+
P/O J Thornber	+
P/O G E F Sadler	pow
P/O D A Bradbury	+
F/S J C E Toft	pow
F/S F Blunstone	inj
F/L W H Polgrean	+
F/S S A Gilbert	+

T/o 1834 Burn. Shot down through the combined fire from flak and a night-fighter, crashing at about 2215 near Averlak, 5 km N of Brunsbüttel. Five of those who died, including the mid-air gunner F/L Polgrean, rest in Hamburg Cemetery at Ohlsdorf, while F/S Blunstone who died from his wounds at Marne Holste Marine Krankenhaus on 9 March is buried in Kiel War Cemetery.

578 Sqn   Halifax III   NR150 LK-P   Op: Hemmingstedt

F/L K Shaw	+
Sgt K Relton	+
P/O P J Hargreaves	+
P/O L Carter	+
F/S H W Parker	+
F/S H T Hayes	+
F/S F R Palmer	+

T/o 1831 Burn. Last heard calling for help on W/T at 2224 and believed to have crashed in the sea soon after. F/L Shaw is buried in Kiel War Cemetery; his crew have no known graves. These were the last casualties reported from the Squadron prior to being disbanded on 15 April 1945.

7-8 Mar 1945

619 Sqn   **Lancaster I**   **NG286 PG-Y**   **Op: Harburg**

F/L G M S McMorran RCAF	+
Sgt K Phillips	pow
F/O H E Hanson RCAF	pow
F/O T Turner RCAF	pow
F/S V W Lambert	+
Sgt S J J Maton	+
F/S E Dellow	pow

T/o 1816 Strubby to bomb refining plant. Those who died are commemorated on the Runnymede Memorial. F/L Albert Elmore McMorran RCAF, younger brother of F/L McMorran RCAF, died a month later while flying with 619 Squadron on operations to Leipzig. He is buried in Berlin 1939-1945 War Cemetery.

619 Sqn   **Lancaster I**   **PB699 PG-Z**   **Op: Harburg**

F/O C P Sparkes RNZAF	+
F/S D R Lloyd	+
F/O R N Ferguson RNZAF	+
F/O C E Eyles	+
F/S P N Black RNZAF	+
F/O B W Eynon	+
Sgt J Bryce	+

T/o 1822 Strubby similarly tasked. All rest in Hamburg Cemetery, Ohlsdorf. F/O Ferguson RNZAF had married Cicely Evelyn Ferguson of Kew.

625 Sqn   **Lancaster I**   **NG324 CF-L2**   **Op: Dessau**

F/L H Chapman	+
Sgt J R Lyons	
F/S G A Lee	+
F/O T S Akenhead	+
F/S T J Crossman	+
Sgt B S F Hessey	
Sgt F Walker	

T/o 1701 Kelstern. Crashed 2045 at Verse Talsperre, 6 km ESE from Lüdenschied, though it is reported burials took place at Loh, some way from the crash site. Four now rest in the Reichswald Forest War Cemetery. "Safe" has been annotated against two names and it is assumed Sgt Hessey, too, survived.

635 Sqn   **Lancaster III**   **ND735 F2-P**   **Op: Dessau**

F/S T Kelly	+
Sgt J S Mohum	+
F/S T Ashworth	+
F/S J Levey	+
Sgt F M Harvey	+
F/S W J Goodbody	+
Sgt A J D Wares	inj

T/o 1730 Downham Market. Crashed 2100 near Friesenhagen, 5 km W of Freudenberg. The first six named now lie in the Reischswald Forest War Cemetery, having been brought here from Friesenhagen. Sgt Wares was taken to Wissen only to be killed in an air raid on 11 March. His grave is now in Rheinberg War Cemetery.

8-9 Mar 1945

163 Sqn   **Mosquito XXV**   **KB568**   **-V**   **Op: Kassel**

F/L F W Cooper	
F/S A E Gillespie RAAF	+

T/o 1845 Wyton. Nineteen year old F/S Gillespie RAAF from Chatswood in New South Wales is buried in the Reichswald Forest War Cemetery. He was amongst the youngest Australian navigators to be killed on operations during the Second World War. F/L Cooper is described as "safe".

415 Sqn   **Halifax III**   **NA186 6U-U**   **Op: Hamburg**

WO1 I A F McDiarmid RCAF	pow
Sgt W J R Gale	pow
F/S W L Mracek RCAF	pow
F/S A R Hibben RCAF	pow
F/S F E Adams RCAF	pow
F/S N Tonello RCAF	pow
F/S G M Roberts RCAF	pow

T/o 1804 East Moor for an attack aimed at U-boat assembly yards. Believed crashed at around 2135 near Fischbek, 8 km WNW from the centre of Harburg. All had been posted, ex-76 (RCAF) Base, to 415 Squadron on 28 December 1944.

Note. It was quite unusual to have an all NCO crew on a 6 Group squadron at this late stage of the war and especially so as six were Canadians.

462 Sqn   **Halifax III**   **MZ370 Z5-L**   **Op: BS**

F/L F H James RAAF	pow
Sgt S G Rother	pow
W/O T H McFarlane RAAF	pow
F/S N E Teede RAAF	pow
W/O J D Fraser RAAF	pow
F/S R W C Hutton RAAF	pow
F/S T P Ledwith RAAF	pow
W/O H W Colman RAAF	pow

T/o 1801 Foulsham and headed for the Dortmund area, F/S Hutton RAAF being responsible for the special equipment. It will be recalled this crew had crashed on return from operations a month previous.

608 Sqn   **Mosquito XXV**   **KB406 6T-K**   **Op: Berlin**

F/L L N Hobbs	
F/O R Dennis RAAF	

T/o 1820 Downham Market. Both officers are described on the loss card as "safe".

| 9 Mar 1945 | 90 Sqn | Lancaster I | PA254 WP-A | Op: Datteln |

F/L B J Aldhous MID	+
Sgt S Power	+
P/O C D Palmer	+
F/O J C Paton RAAF	+
P/O C Foy	+
F/S A Smee	+
Sgt R South	+
Sgt A F C Smith	

T/o 1037 Tuddenham carrying two navigators for a G-H raid on the Emscher Lippe benzol works. Brought down by flak. Of the seven who died, six are buried in the Reichswald Forest War Cemetery, but F/L Aldhous rests in Holland at Venray War Cemetery, having been brought here from Margraten. It is, therefore, most likely his grave was found by an American graves inspection team. Sgt Smith is described as "safe".

| | 466 Sqn | Halifax III | LV949 HD- | Training |

F/L J S Hutton RAAF

T/o 1111 Driffield for a navigation exercise but the undercarriage was raised prematurely resulting in damage to the unit. The crew were instructed to make for Carnaby where the Halifax was wrecked at 1311 in the ensuing forced-landing. No one seems to have been injured.

| 10 Mar 1945 | 420 Sqn | Halifax III | NR123 PT-F | Training |

F/O M Tederan RCAF

T/o 1858 Tholthorpe and landed 2328 at Carnaby with low brake pressure. The Halifax swung off the runway and finished up amongst trees. F/O Tederan RCAF, who had arrived from 76 (RCAF) Base on 16 February, was undergoing a Squadron check flight.

| 11 Mar 1945 | 10 Sqn | Halifax III | MZ433 ZA-X | Transit |

| W/O E Poley |
| Sgt R Spratt |
| F/S A Johnson |
| F/S H Ebden |
| W/O M Cohen |
| Sgt R Speight |
| F/S R Grayson |

Landed 1739 at Carnaby, on return from Essen, with unserviceable hydraulics. Local repairs were quickly completed and the crew set off for Melbourne, landing here at 1945. However, their arrived was on the heavy side and the Halifax ballooned back into the air before crashing back on the runway, the undercarriage promptly collapsing. A fire broke out, but the crew evacuated smartly and were unhurt.

| | 153 Sqn | Lancaster I | NG201 P4-T | Op: Essen |

F/O E W Gibbins	+
Sgt E T West	+
F/S C Cole	+
F/S W L Shield	+
F/S S Craddock	+
Sgt B T Gough	+
Sgt J Mitchell	+

T/o 1125 Scampton. Crashed in the target area and all were buried soon afterwards in the Süd West Friedhof. Five now lie in the Reichswald Forest War Cemetery, while F/S Craddock and Sgt Mitchell are commemorated on panels 270 and 276 respectively of the Runnymede Memorial.

| | 431 Sqn | Lancaster X | KB853 SE-A | Op: Essen |

W/C R F Davenport RCAF	+
Sgt A C Pettifor RCAF	+
F/O D K J Hector RCAF	+
F/O W Rink RCAF	+
WO2 C W Fraser RCAF	+
P/O H G Bishop DFC RCAF	+
F/S C R Lecky RCAF	+

T/o 1142 Croft. Crashed in the target area and all were laid to rest in the Süd-West Friedhof. Six are now buried in the Reichswald Forest War Cemetery, while F/S Lecky RCAF was exhumed by an American graves inspection team and interred on 17 May at Margraten. Since then his remains have been recovered to Venray War Cemetery. F/O Hector RCAF had graduated from Toronto University.

Note. As was usually the case, command of the Squadron passed to one of the flight commanders, in this instance Squadron Leader Smith RCAF. However, his tenure was brief and Wing Commander W McKinnon DFC arrived on 18 March and took over the helm for the remaining weeks of the war.

| | 434 Sqn | Lancaster X | KB834 WL-Y | Op: Essen |

F/L R J Fern RCAF	+
P/O W T Jones	+
F/L A G Rowe DFC RCAF	+
F/O T D Copeland RCAF	+
F/O J R Latremouille RCAF	+
F/O G Scott RCAF	+
F/O J A H B Marceau RCAF pow	

T/o 1138 Croft. Hit by flak and crashed within seconds of completing its bombing run, plunging into the target area. Six bodies were later recovered from Plot B at the Süd-West Friedhof and taken to the Reichswald Forest War Cemetery. F/O Marceau RCAF was very badly wounded and was to undergo many years of hospital treatment. Apart from 37 year old P/O Jones, who had served previously with 419 Squadron, the crew were on their second tour of operations.

| 11 Mar | 463 Sqn | Lancaster I | LM130 JO-N | Training |

11 Mar 1945 — 463 Sqn — Lancaster I — LM130 JO-N — Training

P/O N H Orchard RAAF +
F/S R F Neale +
Sgt D A Charles +
Sgt H Rollins +
Sgt W F H Elcome +
Sgt B J Patch +
Sgt H Shaw +

While participating in fighter affiliation training, collided with Hurricane IIc PZ740 of 1690 Flight, flown by F/O S F Parlato DFC RNZAF, and crashed into The Ashholt Field at Blankney village, 9 miles N of Sleaford, Lincolnshire. All are buried in various UK cemeteries, most, including the Hurricane pilot in Cambridge City Cemetery.

Note. The Lancaster had been named "Nick the Nazi Neutralizer", featuring a horned laughing devil painted on the nose with a clawed right index finger pointing at the letter "N".

619 Sqn — Lancaster I — LM207 PG-E — Op: Essen

F/O E H Hooker
Sgt G P T Pullen
F/S R K Appleton
WO2 M S Reside RCAF
Sgt J Schofield
F/S F V Verney RCAF
Sgt W H P Barnett

T/o 1211 Strubby. Outbound, got into difficulties and while trying to land 1510 on Evere aerodrome in Belgium, overshot the runway and was wrecked. The crew escaped injury.

Note. For as long as ex-Bomber Command aircrew survive, Essen will be one of the targets most firmly etched in their mind. A visit to Essen was regarded by all as a very hazardous experience with a hot reception from the defences a near certainty. As an industrial city, Essen escaped relatively lightly in the early war years, but from March 1943 onwards, Bomber Command reduced much of its heart to rubble and by the spring of 1945, vast areas were a waste land with those inhabitants remaining reduced to living in the cellars of their shattered homes.

NTU — Lancaster III — PB669 — Training

F/L A C Diemer MID +
F/O K L Pile DFM +
F/L B C Brooker DFC & Bar +
F/L A M Stewart +
F/L J Robertson DFM +
F/O C A Robson +
F/S D W Kidd +
W/O S Oldfield +

T/o Warboys borrowed by 156 Squadron and crashed 1430 at Old Weston, about 1 mile E of Molesworth airfield in Northamptonshire. All are buried in cemeteries scattered across the British Isles. F/O Pile and F/L Robertson had served previously with 166 Squadron and 97 Squadron respectively, their DFMs having been Gazetted on 19 September 1944 and 11 June 1943.

11-12 Mar 1945 — 692 Sqn — Mosquito XVI — PF450 P3- — Op: Berlin

F/L A W Waugh RAAF +
F/O L R Corrigan inj

T/o 1828 Graveley but lost power on one engine and the crew headed back towards the airfield. The approach was made at 1852, but the Mosquito overshot the runway, crashed into a hedge and caught fire. F/L Waugh RAAF is buried in Cambridge City Cemetery; his navigator received extensive burns.

12 Mar 1945 — 103 Sqn — Lancaster I — LM131 PM-V — Op: Dortmund

F/O B F Wright RCAF
Sgt F E Carter +
W/O J Coulson
F/S G R Tracey RCAF
Sgt B Heath
F/S K Coleman
F/S A J Bocinfuso RCAF

T/o 1303 Elsham Wolds. Struck by a bomb which became embedded in the mainplanes. On regaining the Lincolnshire coast, the crew baled out leaving their crippled bomber to fall near the village of Elsham, 9 miles ENE of Scunthorpe. Sgt Carter's body was found nearby, his parachute having failed to deploy. He is buried in Denton (St. Margaret) New Churchyard.

106 Sqn — Lancaster I — RA503 ZN-B — Op: Dortmund

W/O F E Baker +
Sgt D Y Carter +
F/S H G Harding +
F/S W J Cooper +
F/S G J P O'Brien RAAF +
Sgt K R Haw +
Sgt H Gillender RCAF +

T/o 1330 Metheringham. Lost without trace. All are commemorated on the Runnymede Memorial. W/O Baker had joined the Royal Air Force in the early 1930s; his flight engineer's second Christian name was Yukin.

162 Sqn — Mosquito XX — KB214 CR- — Ground

Burnt during maintenance at Bourn airfield.

2 Mar 1945	460 Sqn	Lancaster III	PB187 AR-E	Op: Dortmund

P/O G L Burgess RAAF	+	T/o 1255 Binbrook. Carried out a successful
F/S P C Sweetman	+	attack and was observed by the crew of another
Sgt D A Little	+	Squadron aircraft to be making their way in the
F/S J D Bryant RAAF	+	directions of the Allied lines. Those who died
Sgt K Grundy	+	rest in the Reichswald Forest War Cemetery. F/S
Sgt P J Brown	+	Sweetman's parents lived in California at
Sgt E D Grant	+	Westlake, Daly City. Sgt Grant is described on
		the loss card as "safe".

Note. Similar to the previous day's raid on Essen, Dortmund had now been bombed for the final time by Main Force Bomber Command and, like Essen, this important manufacturing centre was now little more than a ruin.

2-13 Mar 1945	103 Sqn	Lancaster I	ME449 PM-T	Op: Gardening

S/L S Slater	evd	T/o 1743 Elsham Wolds for operations over the
Sgt K Foster	evd	Kattegat. Shot down by a night-fighter (Maj
F/O H A S Mitchell RAAF	evd	Werner Husemann, I./NJG3) and crashed 2145 at
P/O M H Bertie RAAF	evd	Lyne, 8 km S of Tarm on Jutland's west coast.
W/O T Fairclough	evd	Both air gunners are buried in a joint grave,
F/S H J Porter RAAF	+	which is located in a plantation some 2 km SE
Sgt D Morris	+	of the town and on the road to Oddum.

	153 Sqn	Lancaster I	RA526 P4-J	Op: Gardening

F/O K A Ayres DFC	+	T/o 1735 Scampton similarly tasked. Came down
Sgt W C Taylor	+	in the seas off the Danish island of Samso.
F/S R J McMinn	+	Five of the six who died rest in Trandbjaerg
F/O R Mains	pow	Churchyard, their graves being alongside two
F/S D Head	+	airmen from 408 Squadron who died in separate
Sgt R Wilson	+	Hampden crashes on 15 May 1942 (see Volume 3
Sgt D Cox	+	page 93). Panel 272 of the Runnymede Memorial
		perpetuates the name of F/S McMinn.

	433 Sqn	Lancaster I	NG233 BM-E	Op: Gardening

F/O J P Farrell RCAF	+	T/o 1746 Skipton-on-Swale similarly tasked.
Sgt T Orr	+	Crashed in the sea. On 30 May 1945, the body
F/S J H Wilson RCAF	+	of F/O Plante RCAF was washed in by the tide
F/O A V Plante RCAF	+	and he is buried in Horsens West Church Cem-
P/O G A Kennedy RCAF	+	etery. His six companions are commemorated
F/S D W Hodge RCAF	+	on the Runnymede Memorial.
F/S T C Pierson RCAF	+	

3 Mar 1945	109 Sqn	Mosquito XVI	ML982 HS-	Training

Form AM 78 identifies this aircraft as being destroyed on this date in a flying accident. No record of this can be traced.

	627 Sqn	Mosquito XVI	NS536 AZ-B Bar	Training

F/O A McLellan RAAF		Wrecked 1128 after overshooting the airfield
		at Boscombe Down in Wiltshire. The crew had

been engaged in H2S training and neither were hurt. Four days later and F/O McLellan RAAF was involved in a second non fatal accident.

3-14 Mar 1945	23 Sqn	Mosquito VI	PZ436 YP-Z	Op: BS

Lt E Lignon FFAF	+	T/o 1858 Little Snoring for intruder duties
F/O M Callas RAAF	+	over Handorf and Münster airfields. Last
		heard on R/T at 2032 by the crew of Mosquito

YP-O (F/L Thomas and F/S Halliday) saying they were going to drop their TI, and seconds later reporting they could see a fire. Nothing further was heard. F/O Callas RAAF, whose Christian name was Manoel, rests in the Reichswald Forest War Cemetery. It is assumed Lt Lignon FFAF is buried in France.

	150 Sqn	Lancaster I	NG263 IQ-A	Op: Gelsenkirchen

F/L G M Young	inj	T/o 1722 Hemswell. Homebound, abandoned with
F/S T Willis		two engines ablaze and crashed 2244 at White
P/O J Donald		House Farm, Watlington, 15 miles SE of Oxford.
P/O K Thornley		35 year old F/S Taylor, the wireless operator,
F/S J H Taylor	+	failed to get clear. He is buried in Kent at
F/S Robertson		Gillingham (Woodlands) Cemetery. F/L Young
Sgt Driver		sustained fractures to both legs on landing.

13-14 Mar 1945	163 Sqn	Mosquito XXV	KB476 -W	Op: Berlin

F/O Harris
F/O Wynes

T/o 1838 Wyton. Reported to have crash-landed 2336 at Hulten (Noord-Brabant) and quite close to the airfield at Gilze-Rijen. No injuries.

14 Mar 1945	75 Sqn	Lancaster I	PB741 AA-E	Op: Hattingen

F/L E G Parsons +
Sgt C A Longstaff +
Sgt W Phinn +
F/S F H Ebbage +
F/S E Ramsay +
Sgt J L Beard +
Sgt J Nichol +

T/o 1348 Mepal for a G-H strike on a benzol plant at Heinrich Hutte. Sgt Longstaff and F/S Ebbage have no known graves but the rest are buried in the Reichswald Forest War Cemetery. There are indications that F/L Parsons had flown thirty operational sorties.

101 Sqn   Lancaster III   DV298 SR-J   Op: Dahlbruch

S/L I Macleod-Selkirk +
Sgt F Milton +
F/O R C Pitman +
F/O G W Hess RCAF +
Sgt A Pringle +
Sgt J Toy +
Sgt F W Hughes +
Sgt R Hurley +

T/o 1742 Ludford Magna tasked for ABC duties. Very likely to have come down in Germany as the crew were buried by the Americans at Margraten in Holland. Their graves are now located in Venray War Cemetery. Sgt Toy, a nineteen year old ex-ATC cadet, was the specialist operator. F/O Hess RCAF was an American from New York City while at 35, Sgt Hughes was above the average age of operational airmen.

14-15 Mar 1945	49 Sqn	Lancaster I	RF153 EA-K	Op: Lutzkendorf

F/L J N McPhee RCAF +
Sgt P F Ivett +
F/O G A Robinson RCAF +
F/O R F Thompson RCAF +
F/S T G W Dew +
F/S E G C Richards RCAF +
F/S G L Corrigan RCAF   evd

T/o 1647 Fulbeck to bomb the Wintershall synthetic oil plant. Those who perished are now resting in Berlin 1939-1945 War Cemetery.

50 Sqn   Lancaster I   NG177 VN-L   Op: Lutzkendorf

F/L F J Ling RCAF +
Sgt H C Lomax +
F/O B W Rutland RCAF +
F/S E L Howard +
WO2 R L Thompson RCAF +
F/S R B Millman RCAF +
F/S A W Holmes RCAF +

T/o 1634 Skellingthorpe similarly tasked. Lost without trace. All are commemorated on the Runnymede Memorial. Sgt Lomax was 36, well over the age normally associated with airmen employed on operational duties.

51 Sqn   Halifax III   NP932 MH-J   Op: Homberg

F/O S G Chopping +
P/O D J Hovell +
Sgt G Williams +
F/S G H Elliott +
F/S M S G Mumford +
F/S J S Davies +
F/S V H Andrews +
Sgt J L Bird +

T/o 1721 Snaith to block the town area and thus prevent its use as a communications route to the battle front. On return to base, made three attempts to land before crashing 2330 at the WAAF site and near Pollington village, 8 miles S of Selby, Yorkshire. All rest in various UK cemeteries.

57 Sqn   Lancaster I   NG398 DX-N   Op: Lutzkendorf

F/O C D Pauline RAAF +
Sgt J Davies +
F/S C F J Hole +
F/S G Cartwright +
Sgt R M Cocozza +
Sgt C Q Rafferty +
Sgt J F Shearron +

T/o 1700 East Kirkby to bomb the Wintershall synthetic oil plant. All are buried in Dürnbach War Cemetery.

85 Sqn   Mosquito NF.30   MV541 VY-B   Op: BS

F/L I A Dobie
P/O A R Grimstone DFM +

T/o 1910 Swannington in support of the Lützkendorf raid, course being set for Schweinfurt. Crossing the battle lines, hit by American AA fire and crashed roughly 15 km W of Koblenz. P/O Grimstone, whose DFM had been Gazetted on 1 October 1943 for service with 85 Squadron, was initially buried at Grand Failly; he now lies in Choloy War Cemetery. F/L Dobie was not hurt.

4-15 Mar
945

106 Sqn	Lancaster I		LL948 ZN-V	Op: Lutzkendorf
P/O B E Barrow RAAF		+		
Sgt H Castle		+		
F/S H Bedford		+		
W/O J B Cossart RAAF		+		
F/S R K Locke RAAF		+		
Sgt G H Armstrong		+		
Sgt J S Hussey		pow		

T/o 1705 Metheringham to bomb the Wintershall synthetic oil plant. Those who died are commemorated on the Runnymede Memorial.

157 Sqn	Mosquito XIX		MM650 RS-J	Op: BS
P/O B E Miller RAAF		+		
P/O R G Crisford RAAF		+		

T/o 1930 Swannington in support of the raid on Lützkendorf. Both are buried in Rheinberg War Cemetery, having been brought here from a US Military Cemetery at Romberg (Kierspe). Recently commissioned, the two officers had been on continuous operational duty since February 1944. Their failure to return to Swannington cast a shadow of gloom over the entire Squadron.

189 Sqn	Lancaster I		NX567 CA-Q	Op: Lutzkendorf
F/O G J Austin		+		
Sgt J McBeth		pow		
F/S T G Storey		pow		
F/S J W Purdy		pow		
F/S C T Hall		+		
F/S E Atterby		+		
F/S W R Clydesdale		pow		

T/o 1709 Fulbeck to bomb the Wintershall synthetic oil plant. Those who lost their lives are buried in Dürnbach War Cemetery.

207 Sqn	Lancaster I		LL902 EM-A	Op: Lutzkendorf
F/O M J H Cooke		+		
P/O R Fairclough		+		
P/O H B Boddy RCAF		+		
F/S J W Laing		+		
F/S R G A Breach		+		
F/S F R Stead		+		
P/O J D'Arcy		+		

T/o 1647 Spilsby similarly tasked. Encountered poor visibility while returning to base and flew into the ground near Little Rissington airfield, Gloucestershire. All are buried in cemeteries within the United Kingdom. P/O D'Arcy, who came from Athenry, Co. Galway in the Irish Republic, lies alongside his skipper in Oxford (Botley) Cemetery at North Hinksey. P/O Boddy RCAF was taken to Brookwoood Military Cemetery.

207 Sqn	Lancaster I		NG399 EM-O	Op: Lutzkendorf
F/O J E Cranston		pow		
P/O A S Fletcher		pow		
F/S T Hannaby		pow		
F/S A A V Howse		pow		
F/S H W Bishop		+		
F/S P B Kehoe		pow		
Sgt C H Watkins				

T/o 1658 Spilsby similarly tasked. F/S Bishop and Sgt Watkins rest in Berlin at the city's 1939-1945 War Cemetery.

214 Sqn	Fortress III		HB802 BU-O	Op: BS
F/L H Rix		pow		
Sgt L J Pound		pow		
P/O H T Sargeant RAAF		pow		
F/O W J Lovell-Smith RNZAF		pow		
W/O A R Irvine RAAF		pow		
Sgt A D Mackintosh		pow		
F/S J L Cuttance RNZAF		pow		
F/S R O Douglas RNZAF		pow		
Sgt R Gamble		pow		
Sgt B Burgess		pow		

T/o 1720 Oulton for Jostle duties in support of the attack on Lützkendorf. The specialist equipment operator was Sgt Mackintosh.

227 Sqn	Lancaster I		PA214 9J-P	Op: Lutzkendorf
F/L M W Bell		+		
F/L S T Rouse		+		
F/O L S Smith		+		
P/O P T Edwards		+		
F/O G F Orry		+		
F/O H A Thomas		+		
F/S R C S Wells		+		
Sgt G F C Stephenson		+		

T/o 1705 Balderton to bomb the Wintershall synthetic oil plant. All are buried in Dürnbach War Cemetery. Sgt Stephenson was the son of F/L George Stephenson, a regular service officer. Most of the crew had been involved in a serious landing accident on return from Sassnitz a week previous.

14-15 Mar 1945	227 Sqn	Lancaster I	RA546 9J-J	Op: Lutzkendorf

227 Sqn   Lancaster I   RA546 9J-J   Op: **Lutzkendorf**

F/L M L Hunt RNZAF   inj
WO1 W A Johnson RCAF   +
F/O W F Possee DFC   +
P/O A T Harvey RNZAF   pow
F/S A T Bell RAAF   pow
F/S R Nesbit   inj
F/S S H H Jobson   pow
F/S J W Harrison   pow

T/o 1703 Balderton to attack the Wintershall synthetic oil plant. May have crashed near Illesheim, 4 km SW from Bad Windsheim. The two airman who died in the crash and the two who subsequently died from their wounds on 18 March and 8 April respectively, in descending order of crew, are buried in Dürnbach War Cemetery. All three Commonwealth air forces were represented in this crew.

347 Sqn   Halifax III   MZ909 L8-A   Op: **Homberg**

Cne C Brunet FFAF   +
Sgt P Lugaro FFAF   +
Slt C Fauchet FFAF   +
Asp P Trollard FFAF   +
Sgt J Miller FFAF   +
Sgt M Delauzun FFAF   +
Sgt B Giraudon FFAF   +

T/o 1708 Elvington to block communications routes to the battle front. It is presumed all now rest in France.

347 sqn   Halifax III   NA681 L8-G   Op: **Homberg**

Adc A Vidal FFAF   inj
Adj L Portesseau FFAF   +
Ltn L Guenois FFAF
Slt G Piccot FFAF
Sgt J Chanson FFAF
Adj A Bruno FFAF
Sgt R Pizel FFAF

T/o 1714 Elvington similarly tasked. Crashed at Firenne-Florenne (Namur), a large village 22 km W of Dinant. Adj Portesseau FFAF is reported to have been buried in US Military Cemetery Neuville-en-Condroz. It will be recalled that the crew had been involved in a serious crash on 17 February.

424 Sqn   Lancaster I   NN777 QB-F   Op: **Zweibrucken**

P/O R A R McInroy RCAF
Sgt E Walker RCAF
Sgt D W Cotte RCAF
F/O R W Walker RCAF   inj
WO2 B W Pearson RCAF   inj
Sgt M J Menzie RCAF
Sgt E J Philip RCAF

T/o 1633 Skipton-on-Swale to block the town in order to deny the Wehrmacht communication to the forward areas. Attacked the target successfully at 2016 from 13,600 feet but on regaining the Yorkshire coast ran short of fuel. On entering the circuit at Dishforth, the Lancaster began to turn to port and lose height. Unable to resume level flight, P/O McInroy RCAF crash-landed 234? with two members of his crew sustaining minor injuries.

15 Mar 1945	77 Sqn	Halifax VI	RG507 KN-J	Op: Bottrop

77 Sqn   Halifax VI   RG507 KN-J   Op: **Bottrop**

F/L T S Kilpatrick   pow
Sgt J M O'Connell   pow
Sgt A G Green   pow
F/S H P Sheridan   pow
P/O L J Ward   pow
F/O A Frost   +
Sgt K Rodgers   pow

T/o 1317 Full Sutton to bomb the Mathias Stinnes benzol plant. F/O Frost rests in the Reichswald Forest War Cemetery. Upon his release from captivity, Sgt Green was taken to RAF Hospital Wroughton.

Note. This was the first Halifax VI reported missing from 77 Squadron.

102 Sqn   Halifax VI   RG498 DY-N   Op: **Bottrop**

F/L W L M Dick

T/o 1332 Pocklington similarly tasked. Bombed the AP at 1618 from 19,000 feet, but sustained very serious flak damage. Diverted to Manston, landing here at 1743. Its arrival was only semi-controlled and soon afterwards a fire broke out. It is believed the crew escaped relatively unharmed, but the microfilm quality is so poor that their names are quite unreadable.

15-16 Mar 1945	153 Sqn	Lancaster I	NG488 P4-A	Op: Misburg

153 Sqn   Lancaster I   NG488 P4-A   Op: **Misburg**

P/O E J Parker   pow
P/O J J Nevens   +
F/O G H Small RCAF   +
F/O H J Lodge   +
WO2 R Taylor RCAF   +
Sgt A W Preston RCAF   +
Sgt L Williams   +

T/o 1700 Scampton to bomb the Deurag oil plant. Those who died rest in Hannover War Cemetery.

5-16 Mar 945	214 Sqn	Fortress III	HB803 BU-L	Op: BS

F/O P J Anderson	T/o 1745 Oulton for Jostle operations in the
F/S H T Harmsworth	Misburg region. Severely damaged in a Schräge
F/O F T A Burnett	Musik attack from a Ju 88 (5030N 0740E) which
F/O J A Morton	started fires in the fuselage and port wing.
F/L J E Cryer +	The rear gunner managed to drive off the enemy
W/O M C White +	fighter and course was set for the Allied lines.
F/O L Moran	On crossing the battle lines, American AA guns
W/O J Hunter	opened up, believing they were firing at a Me
F/S G Mercer	262 jet propelled fighter! Abandoned and came
W/O L T Wheeler	down some 6 km S of Kruft, a town W of the Rhine
	and some 20 km WNW from Koblenz. The two airmen

who died now rest in France at Choloy War Cemetery.

Note. On this night, Fortress III HB779 BU-L captained by Flight Lieutenant J G Wynne (later destined to fly Valiants with 214 Squadron at the time of the 1956 Suez crisis) was engaged on operations in the course of which nine members of his crew baled out over enemy territory. Five were subsequently murdered, but Jock Whitehouse has been able to report that Mrs Majorie Frost, widow of Flying Officer Harold Frost DFM who was one of the five shot on 17 March, went to Huckenfeld in 1997 and in a most moving ceremony unveiled a plaque commemorating those who died, and the rest of the crew, and then gave her forgiveness of those responsible for this terrible crime. She also visited the grave of Herr Gustav Schmidt, who was the town's Burgermeister at the time of the atrocity and who subsequently died in prison in 1951 while serving a sentence for his part in what happened. Flight Lieutenant Wynne succeeded in flying his crippled Fortress back to Bassingbourn and following repairs, it continued in service, hence its omission from these summaries. However, in recognition of what has been reported concerning this tragic affair, the names of the crew are appended below. Those who died now rest in Dürnbach War Cemetery.

F/O J W Vinall DFM + Twice MID	Flight Engineer	DFM 14 September 1943
F/L D P Heal pow	Navigator	
F/L G Pow pow	Air Bomber	
F/L T H Tate pow	Wireless Operator	
F/S N J Bradley pow	Air Gunner	
F/O G A Hall +	Air Gunner	
F/O H Frost DFM +	Air Gunner	DFM 13 July 1943
F/L S C Matthews DFC +	Air Gunner	
F/S E A Percival DFM +	Air Gunner	DFM 19 September 1944

346 Sqn	Halifax III	MZ830 H7-V	Op: Hagen

Sgt G A Lacaze FFAF +	T/o 1700 Elvington. Crashed 2359 into high
Adj J Gribouva FFAF +	ground near Duggleby, 11 miles NW from Great
Ltn J Deplus FFAF +	Driffield, Yorkshire. At the time of the crash
Asp F Dufresnoy FFAF +	the crew were slightly off track and accident
Sgt J Charpentier FFAF +	investigators reported that the Halifax had
Sgt G Tartarin FFAF +	hit the ground, with its wheels down. All were
Sgt P Touzart FFAF +	buried in Harrogate (Stonefall) Cemetery.

346 Sqn	Halifax III	NA166 H7-G	Op: Hagen

Sgt L Lourdeaux FFAF +	T/o 1718 Elvington. Crashed 2101 near Hasselt
Sgt F Hautcoeur FFAF +	in the Belgian Province of Limburg. Those who
Ltn G Poncet FFAF	died were taken to Hasselt for burial, but it
Ltn H Lamontagne FFAF +	is likely their graves, along with those of
Sgt J Bernasconi FFAF	their comrades mentioned above, are now in
Sgt A Desplaces FFAF	France.
Sgt G Brulet FFAF +	

347 Sqn	Halifax III	NR287 L8-C	Op: Hagen

Cdt G Ostre FFAF +	T/o 1702 Elvington. On return to base, crashed
Sgc M Sciolette FFAF inj	circa 2345 at high speed into a stone wall near
Cne R Chevalier FFAF +	Scawton, 8 miles ENE of Sowerby, Yorkshire. The
Ltn A Chemin FFAF +	five who died were buried in Harrogate (Stone-
Adj H Chabres FFAF +	fall) Cemetery, since when their bodies have
Sgt R Raymond FFAF +	been returned to France. A plaque commemorating
Sgc A Tilliers FFAF inj	their sacrifice, however, has since been placed
	in Scawton Churchyard.

15-16 Mar
1945

| 405 Sqn | Lancaster III | NE119 LQ-P | Op: Misburg |

F/O L N Laing MID RCAF +
Sgt R Morris +
F/O I W Bonter RCAF pow
F/O D G Smith RCAF +
F/O R M Hyde RCAF pow
F/S F J Marsh RCAF +
F/S J R Crisp RCAF pow

T/o 1759 Gransden Lodge to mark the Deurag oil refinery. Reported crashed 2125 at Bad Grund. F/O Laing RCAF parachuted, but landed in a tree. Releasing his harness, he fell some 30 feet and was found dead with both legs fractured. He is buried with the others who died in Hannover War Cemetery. It is believed they, too, baled out safely but were put to death upon being captured

| 405 Sqn | Lancaster III | PB516 LQ-T | Op: Misburg |

F/L K E Parkhurst RCAF +
Sgt L Dovaston +
F/O H E Wort RCAF +
P/O R B Jones RCAF +
F/O C A Boulton RCAF +
P/O D I Galbraith RCAF +
P/O F J Miller RCAF +
F/S D A Holliday RCAF +

T/o 1749 Gransden Lodge similarly tasked. All are buried in Hannover War Cemetery. F/O Boulton RCAF was flying as the visual air bomber.

| 419 Sqn | Lancaster X | KB814 VR-N | Op: Hagen |

F/S C W Parish RCAF +
Sgt P V Bowman RCAF evd
F/O H R J Hennessey RCAF +
F/S C Ginter RCAF evd
F/S C H Vickery RCAF +
Sgt T J Bristow RCAF evd
F/S M W Bredin RCAF +

T/o 1627 Middleton St. George. Believed to have been claimed by a night-fighter operating over the Rhine and crashing 2045, possibly near Mönchengladbach. About a week later, funerals for those who died were held at US Military Cemetery Margraten, since when their remains have been taken to Nederweert War Cemetery.

| 419 Sqn | Lancaster X | KB870 VR-K | Op: Hagen |

F/L M W McLaughlin RCAF inj
F/S W W Lightfoot RCAF inj
F/O H L Garriock RCAF +
F/O B V Saunders RCAF inj
WO1 A Sutherland RCAF +
F/O E B Carleton DFM RCAF +
P/O J M Charbonneau RCAF inj

details of his DFM having been

T/o 1638 Middleton St. George. Shot down, over Allied held territory, by a night-fighter. Those who died were taken to Margraten, since when their remains have been transferred to Nederweer War Cemetery. The four survivors were treated a a US Military Hospital before being flown back t the UK to continue their recovery. F/O Carleton RCAF had flown his first tour with 427 Squadron, published on 14 September 1943.

| 420 Sqn | Halifax III | NR172 PT-Y | Op: Hagen |

P/O J V L A Patry RCAF +
Sgt G R Odell
F/O A M Fournier RCAF +
Sgt J J R Lanctot RCAF
WO1 J A Paiement RCAF
F/S C J Panneton RCAF
F/S J D Goupil RCAF

T/o 1725 Tholthorpe borrowed by 425 Squadron. Believed shot down over Allied held territory. P/O Patry RCAF rests in Rheinberg War Cemetery while panel 280 of the Runnymede Memorial perpetuates the name of F/S Fournier RCAF. It is believed he made a successful exit from the doomed Halifax.

| 425 Sqn | Halifax III | PN172 KW-G | Op: Hagen |

F/L J R Laporte RCAF
Sgt J J R Arcand RCAF +

nearing Charleroi in Belgium, came under attack at 2118 from a night-fighter whose fire smashed the Perspex nose cone (the air bomber, unnamed, had just vacated his position to join the navigator). Moments later, a second burst of cannon fire set light to the starboard outer and the crew were ordered to bale out. Sgt Arcand RCAF was last seen near the rear exit, having gone aft to inspect the flak damage, and his body was later discovered in the wreckage which was located NW of Gosselies. He is buried in Hotton War Cemetery.

T/o 1730 Tholthorpe. Bombed the AP from 18,700 feet at 2036 and one minute later sustained flak damage to the central fuselage. Homebound, and

| 428 Sqn | Lancaster X | KB846 NA-I | Op: Hagen |

F/L J D C Craton RCAF
P/O G T Llewellin RCAF +
F/L R W Newton RCAF +
F/S R C Hamill RCAF +
F/O D C Graham RCAF +
F/O E R Evans RCAF +
F/O B B Gray RCAF

T/o 1644 Middleton St. George. Reported shot down by a Ju 88 over the target area. Five lie in Nederweert War Cemetery, brought here from Margraten. The two survivors were back in the UK by the end of the month. All are reported to have been second tour veterans; remarkably, none appear to have been decorated.

15–16 Mar 1945	**431 Sqn**	**Lancaster X**	**KB815 SE–K**	**Op: Hagen**

431 Sqn   **Lancaster X**   **KB815 SE–K**   **Op: Hagen**

15–16 Mar
1945

F/L R R Haw RCAF +
P/O A C Harris +
F/L A G Edwards RCAF +
F/O G H Davis RCAF +
F/O J L V Morin RCAF +
P/O P P Repsys RCAF +
F/S R E Horne RCAF +

T/o 1621 Croft. Crashed at Perwez (Brabant) some 29 km SSE from the centre of Leuven. All are buried in Perwez Churchyard, their graves being near that of F/L J L Sullivan of 607 Squadron whose Hurricane P2621 was shot down on 14 May 1940. At 35, P/O Harris was above the average age of operational airmen.

432 Sqn   **Halifax VII**   **NP689 QO–M**   **Op: Hagen**

F/O S M Bonter RCAF +
Sgt D Colquhoun +
F/O H E Vachon RCAF pow
F/O A T Hinchliffe RCAF pow
WO2 E E V Anderson RCAF pow
Sgt D C Lawton RCAF +
Sgt T D Scott RCAF +

T/o 1707 East Moor. Sgt Scott RCAF baled out successfully but on 3 April he was murdered by the Gestapo and buried at Hagen (Remberg) Friedhof. With the others who died, he now lies in the Reichswald Forest War Cemetery.

434 Sqn   **Lancaster X**   **KB835 WL–J**   **Op: Hagen**

F/O J O Stewart DFC RCAF +
Sgt T C Kossatz RCAF +
F/O L W Armstrong RCAF +
F/O J D Ball RCAF +
WO2 J A Whitehead RCAF +
F/S W G White RCAF +
F/O J H Ayotte RCAF

T/o 1631 Croft. Shot down by a Ju 88 and crashed just to the S of Landen (Brabant) a large village some 12 km SE of Tienen. Five of those who died were taken for burial in the neighbouring Province of Limburg, at Hasselt (Kruisveld) Communal Cemetery. WO2 White RCAF is commemorated on panel 281 of the Runnymede Memorial. F/O Ayotte RCAF is reported to have parachuted near Liege, some distance from the crash site.

550 Sqn   **Lancaster I**   **NG287 BQ–Q**   **Op: Misburg**

F/O R F Wallace RNZAF +
Sgt W Field +
Sgt H J Brownett +
F/O R W Stephens +
Sgt G B C Capon evd
Sgt I F Tait RCAF +
Sgt R H Laney pow

T/o 1718 North Killingholme to bomb the Deurag plant. Crashed at Roth, 3 km NW of Eibelshausen. Those who died rest in Hannover War Cemetery.

582 Sqn   **Lancaster III**   **ND849 60–P**   **Op: Hagen**

F/O W H T Underwood DFC +
Sgt W J Goodwin +
F/S R W Robson +
F/O J W Lewis +
W/O R P Cantwell RAAF +
Sgt G Murray +
Sgt G O Willer +

T/o 1808 Little Staughton. Lost without trace. All are commemorated on the Runnymede Memorial. F/S Robson held a Bachelor of Arts degree, while Sgt Murray came from Lanesboro, Co. Longford in the Irish Republic.

Note. The raid on Hagen, a straightforward area attack, was particularly devastating, especially so as only 267 aircraft were tasked including the target marking element. Bombing was mainly concentrated in the central and eastern areas of the town, leaving 30,000 to 35,000 citizens homeless.

12 Sqn   **Lancaster I**   **PD207 PH–W**   **Op: Nurnberg**

16–17 Mar
1945

F/O J L Wallace
Sgt W Tracey
F/O D McL Harrison
F/O W R Brooke
F/S G Smith
F/S D E Adams
F/S R E Hardick

T/o 1706 Wickenby. Bombed the AP at 2129 from 13,000 feet, after which the crew diverted to Junvincourt airfield, France. Apparently, no one was injured and the Squadron records are devoid of explanation as to why the Lancaster was written off. However, AM Form 78 states it received irreparable battle damage.

12 Sqn   **Lancaster I**   **PD275 PH–K**   **Op: Nurnberg**

F/L K W Daymond RCAF +
Sgt A W Hathaway +
F/O B C Kerr RCAF +
F/O J H Clarke RCAF pow
P/O W J Malyon RCAF +
P/O H Woffenden +
Sgt N McNicol +

T/o 1707 Wickenby. Crashed at Asbach, 6 km WSW from Roth. Those who died rest in Dürnbach War Cemetery. At 36, P/O Woffenden was well over an age normally associated with operational airmen. F/L Daymond RCAF was drawing near to the end of his operational tour with twenty-six sorties completed.

16-17 Mar 1945	12 Sqn	Lancaster I		RF181 PH-G	Op: Nurnberg

16-17 Mar
1945

12 Sqn		Lancaster I	RF181 PH-G	Op: Nurnberg
F/O D O R Dickey	pow			
Sgt W J Charles	+			
F/S C H Irving RAAF	+			
F/S A Henry	pow			
W/O W A Neill RAAF	+			
F/S W G Brown RCAF	+			
Sgt J T Nicholls	+			

T/o 1716 Wickenby. Abandoned, possibly at a very low altitude as five are reported to have died after falling into trees near the small town of Oberrot. Their graves are now in Dürnbach War Cemetery.

12 Sqn		Lancaster I	RF188 PH-U	Op: Nurnberg
F/O K W Mabee RCAF	+			
Sgt G A Clarke	+			
Sgt L E Rae	+			
F/O A R Hovis RCAF	pow			
Sgt D W Debonnaire	+			
Sgt M M Barker RCAF	+			
F/S T K Imperious RCAF	pow			

T/o 1728 Wickenby. Crashed at Ottensoos, 7 km W of Hersbruck and N of the railway leading to Lauf an der Pegnitz. Those who lost their lives are now resting at Dürnbach War Cemetery.

12 Sqn		Lancaster III	ME526 PH-F	Op: Nurnberg
F/O I L Felgate DFC RAAF	+			
Sgt H F Nixon	pow			
F/S R F L Barber RAAF	+			
Sgt J C Devine	pow			
W/O J Hyde RAAF	+			
F/S V J Arnold RAAF	+			
F/S G S Barbeler RAAF	+			

T/o 1714 Wickenby. Crashed at Alberndorf, 4 km ESE of Ansbach. Both air gunners hailed from Queensland; along with their fellow countrymen they now lie in Dürnbach War Cemetery. F/O Felgate RAAF had flown 34 operational sorties.

Note. My narrative states 12 Squadron reported four aircraft missing, which is correct. The fifth aircraft, identified in the above summaries, was lost in France and, therefore, could be accounted for.

44 Sqn		Lancaster III	ND869 KM-M	Op: Wurzburg
F/L W H Shephard	+			
Sgt A W Beauchamp	+			
F/S J Allan	+			
F/S R B Judge	+			
Sgt D F Brown	+			
Sgt R D Snape	+			
Sgt R F G Mitchell	+			

T/o 1743 Spilsby but crashed eighteen minutes later into the sea off Skegness on the Lincolnshire coast. The bodies of F/L Shephard and Sgt Mitchell were recovered, the latter being found some 300 yards off the town's pier, and taken to Cambridge City Cemetery. The others are commemorated on the Runnymede Memorial.

49 Sqn		Lancaster I	NG352 EA-J	Op: Wurzburg
F/O J B Gibson	pow			
Sgt G P Roberts	pow			
F/O D Edwards	pow			
F/S R M Henderson	pow			
Sgt D J Hughes	+			
Sgt A Finnerty	+			
Sgt J Evan	pow			

T/o 1802 Fulbeck. Sgt Hughes had the tragic misfortune to fall into the hands of the SS and he was shot on 18 March by one Joseph Axt. With Sgt Finnerty, who came from Newry, Co. Down in Northern Ireland, he is buried in Dürnbach War Cemetery.

Note. After the war, Joseph Axt was apprehended by the Allies and brought to trial, subsequently being sentenced to death for his war crimes.

49 Sqn		Lancaster III	ME454 EA-E	Op: Wurzburg
F/O D H Whent	inj			
Sgt F R Haylock	+			
Sgt F P Anderson	inj			
Sgt E J Sullivan	inj			
Sgt R H Usher	inj			
Sgt G C Leeke	+			
Sgt H Darbyshire	+			

T/o 1803 Fulbeck. Presumed lost over Allied held territory. Sgt Haylock and Sgt Leeke are buried in France at Choloy War Cemetery, while panel 274 of the Runnymede Memorial perpetuates the name of Sgt Darbyshire.

61 Sqn		Lancaster I	RF176 QR-T	Op: Wurzburg
F/L H B Grynkiewicz	+			
Sgt W M Ratcliffe	+			
F/S J L Jones	+			
F/S E J Day	+			
F/S E W Gibbs	+			
F/S G E Gwalter	+			
F/S E W Browne	+			

T/o 1724 Skellingthorpe. All are buried in Dürnbach War Cemetery. F/L Grynkiewicz had a Bachelor of Science degree, while F/S Day had married Elizabeth Agnes Day of Regina, Saskatchewan.

| 16-17 Mar | **100 Sqn** | **Lancaster III** | **ND644 HW-N** | **Op: Nurnberg** |

16-17 Mar
1945

100 Sqn　　　　**Lancaster III**	**ND644 HW-N**　　　　　　　**Op: Nurnberg**
F/O G A O Dauphinee RCAF　　+	T/o 1756 Grimsby. Shot down near Kraftshof
F/S M R Jeffery　　　　　　+	some 8 km NNW from Nürnberg Bahnhof. Those
F/O D B Douglas RCAF　　　pow	who died rest near Bad Tolz in Dürnbach War
F/O W R Vale RCAF　　　　　+	War Cemetery, having been brought here from
P/O R S Bailey　　　　　　pow	graves found at Kraftshof. Both survivors
F/S W H Johnson RCAF　　　+	were wounded and F/O Douglas RCAF was sub-
F/S L E Bedell RCAF　　　+	sequently repatriated to Canada.

100 Sqn　　　　**Lancaster III**	**PB117 HW-D**　　　　　　　**Op: Nurnberg**
F/O C J Cooper　　　　　　+	T/o 1723 Grimsby. Those who perished, in-
F/S D C Stevens　　　　　+	cluding 18 years old F/S O'Reilly RCAF, rest
F/S C H Weicker RCAF　　　+	in Dürnbach War Cemetery.
F/S J P Edmondson　　　　+	
Sgt J Mitchell　　　　　　+	
F/S R J O'Reilly RCAF　　+	
F/S G F Hersey RCAF　　　pow	

103 Sqn　　　　**Lancaster I**	**ME848 PM-E**　　　　　　　**Op: Nurnberg**
F/O E W Armour RCAF　　　pow	T/o 1717 Elsham Wolds. Crashed at Schwäbisch
F/S E Young　　　　　　　pow	Hall. Sgt Fox is buried in Dürnbach War
F/S S H McRoberts RCAF　　pow	Cemetery. Most of the survivors were quite
F/O A R Mackenzie RCAF　　pow	badly injured, at least two sustaining bone
Sgt W H Fox　　　　　　　+	fractures.
F/S J B McCormick RCAF　　pow	
F/S J D Smith　　　　　　pow	

103 Sqn　　　　**Lancaster I**	**NG492 PM-D**　　　　　　　**Op: Nurnberg**
F/L A L Stepharnoff RCAF　+	T/o 1714 Elsham Wolds. All are buried in
Sgt J Grant　　　　　　　+	Dürnbach War Cemetery. It is believed all
P/O H K Stott　　　　　　+	were engaged on their 28th sortie.
WO2 R I Parks RCAF　　　　+	
F/S A Davies　　　　　　　+	
F/S W Whitehead　　　　　+	
F/O R Wilkinson　　　　　+	

103 Sqn　　　　**Lancaster I**	**NN758 PM-S**　　　　　　　**Op: Nurnberg**
F/O A C Watt RCAF　　　　+	T/o 1715 Elsham Wolds. Crashed near the town of
Sgt J F Jackson　　　　　+	Laichingen where, in the NW corner of the local
F/S G W Blackshaw　　　　+	Friedhof, those who died were laid to rest in a
F/S W H Fetherstone RCAF　+	common grave. Since the cessation of hostilities
F/S J S Hickey　　　　　　+	their remains have been exhumed and reinterred
F/S A C Bellisle RCAF　　pow	at Dürnbach War Cemetery.
F/S A E Wotherspoon RCAF　+	

153 Sqn　　　　**Lancaster III**	**PB642 P4-W**　　　　　　　**Op: Nurnberg**
P/O P J Parsons　　　　　+	T/o 1720 Scampton. All are buried in Dürnbach
F/S J K Finlayson　　　　+	War Cemetery. Their average age was twenty-two.
Sgt S D Wager　　　　　　+	
Sgt A R Quinton　　　　　+	
F/S M Swap　　　　　　　　+	
Sgt E Finch　　　　　　　+	
Sgt W S Keenleyside　　　+	

166 Sqn　　　　**Lancaster I**	**PA234 AS-M**　　　　　　　**Op: Nurnberg**
F/O K P Muncer DFC　　　pow	T/o 1714 Kirmington. Down near Grosshabersdorf
Sgt V Jones　　　　　　　+	some 21 km WSW from the centre of Nürnberg. Of
F/O W H Gerrard　　　　　pow	the five who died, F/O Buckland has no known
F/S J Paterson　　　　　+	grave, while four lie in Dürnbach War Cemetery.
F/O R G Buckland　　　　　+	F/O Muncer was found, minus his left arm and he
F/O J V Gardner　　　　　+	was tended to by a German farmer's wife, who
Sgt W C J Reynolds RCAF　+	arranged his admission to hospital. Meanwhile,

a French prisoner found the severed arm, removed
the inscribed watch and sent it to the Red Cross. Subsequently, it was returned
to F/O Muncer who, in 1947, was instrumental in obtaining the early release of
the German farmer's son, himself a prisoner of war in England.

Note. I am grateful to Jock Whitehouse, a relative of Flying Officer Muncer,
for the poignant details reported above.

16–17 Mar	166 Sqn	Lancaster I		RF154 AS–B	Op: Nurnberg

16–17 Mar 1945

166 Sqn   Lancaster I   RF154 AS–B   Op: Nurnberg

F/O H F Churchward RCAF	pow
Sgt E W Hull	pow
F/O L F Etherington RCAF	pow
F/O J L Goddard RCAF	pow
F/S A V White	pow
Sgt J Goldstein	+
Sgt R T Green	pow

T/o 1712 Kirmington. Sgt Goldstein is buried in Dürnbach War Cemetery. Until recently, both Sgt Hull and Sgt Green had served with the Air Training Corps.

166 Sqn   Lancaster III   PB153 AS–J2   Op: Nurnberg

Sgt W L Hilder	+
Sgt R T C Guscott	+
F/S J W Richards	+
F/S E A Roy RNZAF	+
F/S M D S Davis RNZAF	+
Sgt E C Wilkie	+
Sgt I Titmus	pow

T/o 1725 Kirmington. Possibly came down near Elsenz, 7 km NW of Eppingen. Those who died now rest in Dürnbach War Cemetery, where the register describes Sgt Guscott as a pilot.

170 Sqn   Lancaster III   LM749 TC–Y   Op: Nurnberg

F/L E G Brown	+
Sgt L W Dunn	+
F/S R W Wight	+
F/O F G Cliffe	+
F/S W F G Dawson	+
Sgt B C Ricketts	+
Sgt H P C Seignot	+

T/o 1710 Hemswell. All rest in Dürnbach War Cemetery.

170 Sqn   Lancaster III   ME307 TC–O   Op: Nurnberg

P/O A H Young DFC	evd
Sgt A R Gernon	pow
F/L R L Rogers	pow
F/O F T Rowan RCAF	pow
F/S C W Stewart RNZAF	pow
F/S B D Searson	pow
Sgt T Tomlinson	+

T/o 1733 Hemswell. Sgt Tomlinson is buried in Dürnbach War Cemetery. It is reported that P/O Young contacted Allied forces at 6 Army Group on 24 April.

170 Sqn   Lancaster III   ME496 TC–K   Op: Nurnberg

P/O A Steainstreet	+
Sgt D S Cady	pow
Sgt R Surtees	+
Sgt J Burns	pow
Sgt S W Kirk	pow
Sgt R C Rayment	+
Sgt C Edwards	+

T/o 1731 Hemswell. Hit in the rear turret by enemy fire, Sgt Edwards likely being killed as a consequence. The order to bale out quickly followed, but only three managed to get away. Sgt Cady is reported to have been slightly injured. Those who died are buried in Dürnbach War Cemetery.

460 Sqn   Lancaster I   PB816 AR–E2   Op: Nurnberg

F/O V J Hedley RAAF	+
Sgt A J Macdonald	+
F/S A W Halls RAAF	pow
F/S J W Prouse RAAF	+
F/S M J Parry RAAF	+
F/S M K Jurd RAAF	+
F/S K W Binder RAAF	+

T/o 1727 Binbrook. Those who lost their lives are buried in Dürnbach War Cemetery. The CWGC register describes Sgt Macdonald as a pilot.

467 Sqn   Lancaster I   PD231 PO–T   Op: Wurzburg

F/O E W Thomas RAAF	+
Sgt T Helstrip	+
F/O G Moses RAAF	+
F/S J L Isles RAAF	+
W/O M E Margules RAAF	+
F/S R W H Smith	+
Sgt B A Davies	pow

T/o 1746 Waddington. Crashed, when roughly five minutes flying time from the target, in a wood some 500 metres SW of Aufstetten and 4 km NE of the small town of Röttingen and 7 km NNW from Creglingen. Those who died are buried in Dürnbach War Cemetery.

Note. Their Lancaster had been built by Metro-Vickers and delivered, ex-works, to 467 Squadron at Waddington on 1 August 1944. Damaged in action on 7-8 February 1945, it was repaired on site by an AV Roe working party and returned to service on 17 February. The total number of hours flown has not been appended.

16–17 Mar 1945	550 Sqn	Lancaster I	NG336 BQ–B	Op: Nurnberg

550 Sqn — Lancaster I — NG336 BQ–B — Op: Nurnberg

F/L R J Liefooghe — pow
Sgt I Jones — +
F/S A E Higgins — +
P/O R E Hughes — +
F/S V C Davidson — +
Sgt F E Self — +
Sgt D Anthony — +

T/o 1724 North Killingholme. Crashed near Schwabisch Hall, where it is likely those who died were initially buried. Their graves are now in Dürnbach War Cemetery. F/L Liefooghe was born on 26 June 1920 at Arques in France.

576 Sqn — Lancaster I — PA265 UL–O2 — Op: Nurnberg

F/S J F Ryan RAAF — +
Sgt J E Taylor — +
Sgt A W Garnet RCAF — +
F/S K L Challis — +
Sgt D W E Swift — +
Sgt J Symonds — +
Sgt H A Hall — pow

T/o 1725 Fiskerton. Those who died rest in Dürnbach War Cemetery.

576 Sqn — Lancaster I — PB785 UL–L2 — Op: Nurnberg

F/L F E Dotten RCAF — +
Sgt J Eve — +
F/O W F Nicol RCAF — +
F/O D S Quinn RCAF — +
F/S J S M Gibb RCAF — +
F/S R J Saundercook RCAF — +
F/S E J Peverley RCAF — +

T/o 1715 Fiskerton. All are buried in Dürnbach War Cemetery. At 36, Sgt Eve was well over the age normally associated with airmen flying with Bomber Command. It is believed F/O Quinn RCAF preserved his mother's maiden or family name by taking Swallow as his second Christian name.

576 Sqn — Lancaster III — ME317 UL–C2 — Op: Nurnberg

F/S P F Sattler RAAF — pow
F/S W E A Jeffery — +
Sgt P F G A Garner — pow
F/O N Whiteley — pow
Sgt W Walker — +
Sgt K G Durston — +
Sgt D F Wood — +

T/o 1720 Fiskerton. The last three named lie in Dürnbach War Cemetery, while F/S Jeffery is perpetuated by the Runnymede Memorial, panel 271.

619 Sqn — Lancaster I — NG503 PG–W — Op: Wurzburg

F/O T E Farrow RCAF — +
F/S E K Ireland — +
F/O L Tilley RCAF — +
F/L C W McBride RCAF — +
Sgt J Macpherson — +
F/O J D Johnston RCAF — +
F/S H Mino RCAF — +

T/o 1757 Strubby. All are buried in Dürnbach War Cemetery.

625 Sqn — Lancaster I — NG169 CF–B2 — Op: Nurnberg

F/O E F Seear — +
Sgt E G Wilson — +
Sgt G J A Kenvin — +
Sgt K J Holmes — +
Sgt J F Logan — +
Sgt H Smither — +
Sgt E K Day — +

T/o 1753 Kelstern. All are buried in Dürnbach War Cemetery. At 41, Sgt Day was amongst the oldest airmen killed on Bomber Command operations in the Second World War. He was more than twice the age of his fellow air gunner, Sgt Smither. The parents of Sgt Logan lived in Canada at Windsor, Ontario. Sgt Wilson is identified in the CWGC register as a pilot.

625 Sqn — Lancaster I — RF145 CF–Z — Op: Nurnberg

F/O P M Rolls RAAF — +
Sgt D B Jones — +
F/S R C Rhodes RAAF — +
F/S T M Ryan RAAF — pow
F/S J W Teague RAAF — +
F/S C J Tarrant RAAF — +
Sgt G A Clarke — +

T/o 1746 Kelstern. Of those who lost their lives, Sgt Jones, described as a pilot, lies in Dürnbach War Cemetery, while the others are commemorated on the Runnymede Memorial. F/O Rolls RAAF was the son of Dr. C J Rolls of Kidderminster in Worcestershire.

Note. This was a late production Lancaster, manufactured by Armstrong Whitworth and initially received by 100 Squadron on 20 February 1945. Two days later, it was transferred to 625 Squadron. A record of its flying hours has not been kept.

16-17 Mar	626 Sqn	Lancaster I	PD393 UM-N2	Op: Nurnberg

1945

F/L J Cox	pow	
Sgt R Owen	+	
F/O G C Warren	+	
F/O S S Quinn RCAF	pow	
F/S J W Williams	+	
F/S D R Egan	+	
Sgt R I Noessen	pow	

T/o 1718 Wickenby. Crashed at Burgoberbach, 7 km SSE from Ansbach. Those who died were buried at Burgoberbach Friedhof, just 50 or so metres N from where their Lancaster came down. Since 1945, their remains have been borne to Dürnbach War Cemetery, where F/O Warren is commemorated by a special memorial.

630 Sqn	Lancaster I	LM260 LE-S	Op: Wurzburg

W/O D I Plumb	+
Sgt P Ackland	+
F/S A Michaels	+
F/S J H Croucher	+
Sgt R Jeffery	+
Sgt K H Greenfield	+
Sgt J D Baker	+

T/o 1744 East Kirkby. All rest in Dürnbach War Cemetery. Both air gunners were nineteen years of age.

Note. I am advised by Harry Holmes that commencing at 2125 hours on 16 March each year, the town's church bells are rung for precisely nineteen minutes in memory of the estimated 5,000 inhabitants who died.

17 Mar	550 Sqn	Lancaster I	NG132 BQ-F2	Training

1945

F/O A C Lockyer RNZAF	+
Sgt T Drawbridge	
Sgt W Berry	+
W/O H L Farmer	+
Sgt L Elliott	+
Sgt S Matthews	+
Sgt D Lucey	+

Shot down by an intruder (Fw Rudi Morenz from IV./NJG2) at 1800 and crashed on Sunk Island in the River Humber. It was the crews' first flight since joining the Squadron. Five of those who died lie in cemeteries both in England and in the Republic of Ireland, while W/O Farmer's name is perpetuated on panel 269 of the Runnymede Memorial.

627 Sqn	Mosquito IX	ML906 AZ-	Training

F/O A M McLellan RAAF

T/o 1530 Woodhall Spa for a navigation exercise but while flying at 4,000 feet the starboard CSU failed and having feathered the unit, the crew returned to base. However, on their approach to the runway, the port throttle lever jammed and the Mosquito crash-landed 1715, fortunately without injury to the crew. Less than a week previous, F/O McLellan RAAF had crash-landed at Boscombe Down.

17-18 Mar	85 Sqn	Mosquito NF.30	NT254 VY-	Op: Anti-intruder

1945

P/O S J Harrop DFC	+
W/O G C Redmond	+

T/o Swannington to patrol off the Dutch Frisian island. Lost without trace. Both airmen are commemorated on the Runnymede Memorial.

139 Sqn	Mosquito XVI	MM219 XD-	Op: Berlin

F/L G J L Oliver	inj
W/O T Tyler DFM	inj

T/o 1920 Upwood. During the sortie, a smell of burning pervaded the cockpit and in the ensuing emergency landing at 2100, the Mosquito overshot the runway and caught fire. W/O Tyler had previously flown with 49 Squadron and details of his award appeared in the London Gazette on 15 February 1944.

142 Sqn	Mosquito XXV	KB455 4H-H	Op: Berlin

F/L R M Williams
F/S I C McLeod RAAF

T/o 1911 Gransden Lodge but the starboard engine cut. Braking was applied but too late to prevent the Mosquito from running into the overshoot area. Still travelling at speed, F/L Williams had no alternative but to raise the undercarriage. No one was injured, but the aircraft was deemed to be beyond economical repair.

18-19 Mar	77 Sqn	Halifax VI	RG501 KN-K	Op: Witten

1945

F/O B E Marsh
P/O F G Gibbon
Sgt P L Kimber
F/S J Llewellyn
F/S A W Skinner
F/S D A R Davies
F/S R Duncanson

While taxying at 0056 the Halifax swung from the Full Sutton perimeter track, whereupon the undercarriage gave way. Moments later, the inner port engine burst into flames; the crew, however, managed to get clear without anyone being hurt.

18-19 Mar 1945	77 Sqn	Halifax VI	RG529 KN-C	Op: Witten
	F/L E Ward	+	T/o 0047 Full Sutton. All were buried in the	
	Sgt R A C Pearce	+	Hauptfriedhof at Dortmund, since when their	
	F/S J A Anderson	+	bodies have been exhumed and taken to Rheinberg	
	P/O T M Kerr	+	War Cemetery.	
	P/O S G de Vis RAAF	+		
	F/S J Dyke	+		
	P/O W J Edwards	+		

Note. Oliver Clutton-Brock suggests all baled out in the vicinity of Opladen only to be shot within hours of being captured. Three Germans, at least, were implicated for their part in this crime and one, Lt Karl Schaefer, received a fifteen year prison sentence. Of the other two, one escaped before being brought to trial and the other was, subsequently, executed.

	102 Sqn	Halifax VI	PP179 DY-A	Op: Witten
	F/L R D Jeff	+	T/o 0051 Pocklington. Crashed at Dortmund-	
	F/S J G Fraser	+	Brechten. All are buried in the Reichswald	
	F/S V J Sutherland	+	Forest War Cemetery.	
	F/S W N Birkett	+		
	Sgt G R Grimsdell	+		
	Sgt G E Emerson	+		
	Sgt E G Hick	+		

	103 Sqn	Lancaster I	NG491 PM-R	Op: Hanau
	F/O A W Essex RAAF	+	T/o 0043 Elsham Wolds. Lost without trace.	
	Sgt C H Gregory	+	All are commemorated on the Runnymede Memorial.	
	F/S A E Whiteing	+		
	Sgt W J Jewiss	+		
	Sgt S Armitage	+		
	Sgt J E Aldridge	+		
	Sgt L Pendleton	+		

	105 Sqn	Mosquito XVI	MM170 GB-D	Op: Witten
	F/L L F D King	+	T/o 0341 Bourn on their operational debut with	
	F/L D P Tough	+	105 Squadron. Lost without trace. Both officers	
			are commemorated on the Runnymede Memorial.	

	162 Sqn	Mosquito XX	KB191 CR-L	Op: Berlin
	F/L D W Skillman		T/o 1908 Bourn. Bombed the AP from 27,000 feet	
	F/O F J Tempest		at 2130, descending almost immediately to 16,000	
			feet for the return flight. Later, the crew	

sensed (rather than felt) an explosion, followed by an acute smell of burning. Soon after, Gee and the W/T equipment failed, and while making an emergency landing 0023 at Woodbridge, the undercarriage collapsed. No injuries reported.

	346 Sqn	Halifax III	MZ741 H7-A	Op: Witten
	Ltn A F Gonthier FFAF	+	T/o 0035 Elvington. Crashed near the hamlet of	
	Sgc G M Patris FFAF	+	Nöllenberg and in the direction of Beyenburg,	
	Slt P Capdeville FFAF	+	8 km ESE from Wuppertal. Those who died were	
	Sgc A Dussaut FFAF	+	buried in the Roman Catholic Friedhof at Bey-	
	Sgc R Reynaud FFAF		enburg, since when, it is assumed, their bodies	
	Sgt R Hellmuth FFAF	+	have been taken back to France. The loss card	
	Sgt V St-Jevin FFAF	+	describes Sgc Reynaud FFAF as being "safe".	

	405 Sqn	Lancaster III	PB451 LQ-G	Op: Witten
	F/O G E Peaker RCAF	+	T/o 0132 Gransden Lodge. All are buried in	
	Sgt A Kirkcaldy	+	Rheinberg War Cemetery. Sgt Kirkcaldy at 36	
	F/O E Hayes RCAF	+	was above the average age of operational airmen	
	F/O R S Butterworth RCAF	+	while it is further observed that F/O Butter-	
	Sgt R P Smith RCAF	+	worth RCAF was an American from Richville, New	
	WO2 R M Baker RCAF	+	York. He was a graduate of Clarkson College	
	F/S E F Perrault RCAF	+	where he had been a Member of the Phalanx	
	F/S J P H Adam RCAF	+	Honorary Fraternity. Sgt Smith RCAF was flying	
			as the visual air bomber.	

Note. This was the last crew posted missing from 405 Squadron during its tenure as a PFF squadron. In late May 1945, the Squadron moved to Linton-on-Ouse and converted to Lancaster Xs, leaving for Canada on 16 June 1945.

18-19 Mar   **415 Sqn**   **Halifax III**   **NP938 6U-T**   **Op: Witten**
1945   F/O J S McGuire RCAF   T/o 0002 East Moor. Homebound, forced-landed
        Sgt B Howard   0550, due to engine failure, near Epinoy in the
        F/O N H Dalziel RCAF   Pas-de-Calais and some 8 km NW of Cambrai in the
        WO2 T A J Barnett RCAF   neighbouring Department of Nord. No injuries are
        F/O P Donlan RCAF   reported.
        F/S J D Renaud RCAF
        F/S A Begin RCAF

Note. Only Flying Officer McGuire RCAF is positively identified as most
RCAF units at this time entered merely the name of the pilot. The six
names that follow were posted from 61 (RCAF) Base, with Flying Officer
McGuire, to East Moor on 7 November 1944.

420 Sqn   **Halifax III**   **MZ910 PT-Q**   **Op: Witten**
F/O G J Keeper RCAF   pow   T/o 0025 Tholthorpe. Believed to have been
P/O A V Padgham RCAF   pow   abandoned SE of Barmen. F/O Armstrong is re-
F/O R G Reid RCAF   pow   ported to have been killed instantly on landing
F/O D M Armstrong RCAF   +   and he was buried by members of his crew. His
Sgt A F Domke RCAF   pow   grave is now in Rheinberg War Cemetery.
F/S A H Butler RCAF   pow
F/O W G Bridgeman RCAF pow

425 Sqn   **Halifax III**   **MZ482 KW-G**   **Op: Witten**
P/O A J G Temple RCAF   +   T/o 2355 Tholthorpe. Collided over Belgium
P/O L G Hinch RCAF   +   with a Mosquito from 515 Squadron, both machines
F/O F H Irwin RCAF   +   crashing near Ciney (Namur), 14 km ENE from
P/O J S Wilson RCAF   +   Dinant. F/S Balyx RCAF was thrown clear and
F/O G N J Le Jambe RCAF +   landed by parachute. He was treated for his
F/S A Banks RCAF   +   injuries at Ciney. Those who were not so
F/S G A Balyx RCAF   +   fortunate now rest in Hotton War Cemetery.
                                      F/O Irwin RCAF was an American from Beverly
                                      Hills, California.

425 Sqn   **Halifax III**   **MZ495 KW-R**   **Op: Witten**
P/O C B Racicot RCAF   pow   T/o 2359 Tholthorpe. Abandoned and crashed
Sgt P Panasuk RCAF   +   W of the target area. Sgt Panasuk RCAF, the
F/O R Marc-Aurele RCAF pow   only fatality, rests in Rheinberg War Cemetery.
F/S J A P Demouchel RCAF pow
F/S M H Depot RCAF   pow
F/S E G Gregory RCAF   pow
F/S R S Le Boeuf RCAF pow

425 Sqn   **Halifax III**   **NP939 KM-V**   **Op: Witten**
P/O J T E P Giguere RCAF   T/o 2358 Tholthorpe. Bombed the AP at 0416 from
F/S R M Kelusky RCAF   inj   16,000 feet and was homebound when the starboard
                                     inner failed. Unable to maintain height, the
crew were obliged to make a forced-landing at 0725 at Handy Grass near High
Wycombe in Buckinghamshire. F/S Kelusky RCAF, the wireless operator, wrenched
his shoulder but did not require admittance to hospital. The remaining members
of crew are presumed to have escaped unharmed as none are mentioned by name in
the Squadron records.

460 Sqn   **Lancaster III**   **PB155 AR-K**   **Op: Hanau**
P/O G S Browne RAAF   +   T/o 0052 Binbrook. Crashed 0812 while making
Sgt J N David   +   an approach to Kelstern airfield in Lincolnshire
F/S L W Grant RAAF   +   All RAAF members of crew were taken to Cambridge
W/O G T McBryde RAAF   +   City Cemetery, while Sgt David rests in Bushbury
F/S J Stacey RAAF   +   (St. Mary) Churchyard, Wolverhampton. At the
W/O A E Moss RAAF   +   time of the accident, low cloud had reduced
F/S R C Schodde RAAF   +   visibility and Kelstern were trying to home
                                      the crew towards the runway.

515 Sqn   **Mosquito VI**   **NS957 3P-**   **Op: BS**
F/L A W Hirons DFC   +   T/o 0035 Little Snoring to patrol Kitzingen
F/S P C Williams   +   airfield. Lost in the manner described for
                                      425 Squadron. Both airmen rest at Hotton War
                                      Cemetery.

18-19 Mar 1945	550 Sqn	Lancaster III	ME548 BQ-Q		Op: Hanau

F/L N A Burrows   +
Sgt R C Smith
Sgt A Wilson
F/O W R Campbell RAAF
Sgt R F Gorman
Sgt L B Towson   +
Sgt A J Miles

T/o 0041 North Killingholme. Abandoned over no man's land. The two airmen who died rest in Rheinberg War Cemetery, The others were gathered up by units of the US XIIth Corps and spent several exciting days advancing with these forces into Germany.

	640 Sqn	Halifax III	MZ494 C8-B		Op: Witten

F/L A W Huckle DFC   +
P/O W E C Ralph   +
F/L W A Walton RCAF   +
F/O J B Willoughby RCAF   pow
F/S S McKaig   +
F/S W G Allingham   +
F/S M Barrett   +

T/o 0044 Leconfield. Of the six who died, five lie in the Reichswald Forest War Cemetery, while panel 278 of the Runnymede Memorial perpetuates the name of F/L Walton RCAF. It is reported F/O Willoughby RCAF was wounded.

	1663 CU	Halifax III	NP974		Op: Sweepstake

P/O R W Aldridge

T/o 2230 Rufforth and set course for the French city of Strasbourg. Homebound, ran low on fuel and being uncertain of their position, the crew baled out at 0620 over Scunthorpe, Lincolnshire. The Halifax then banked northwards and flew for a considerable distance before falling to earth at Duggelby, 11 miles NW of Great Driffield, Yorkshire. Two members of crew landed awkwardly and were injured.

19 Mar 1945	90 Sqn	Lancaster I	HK608 WP-P		Op: Gelsenkirchen

F/O J W Paine
F/S H J Wood   inj
Sgt T W Wickam
Sgt D S Turney   inj
Sgt W S Blackett
Sgt T M Potter
Sgt Yardley-Latham   inj

T/o 1244 Tuddenham to attack the Consolidation benzol works. Hit by flak while approaching the AP and again, twice, within seconds of completing the bombing run. Then, over Düsseldorf, sustained further flak damage and soon afterwards fires broke out in three engines. Subsequently, a forced-landing was made at 1644 in position 5015N 0625E, which places the Lancaster about 7 km S from the centre of Mönchengladbach.

	218 Sqn	Lancaster I	RA532 XH-L		Op: Gelsenkirchen

P/O I Johnson
Sgt D Moore
Sgt H Christian
Sgt G James
Sgt N Robinson
Sgt A Spence
Sgt J Makiw

T/o 1307 Chedburgh similarly tasked. Hit by flak which rendered both outer engines unserviceable. Course was set for Brussels-Evere, where an emergency landing was made at 1730, the Lancaster being damaged beyond repair. No injuries reported.

	571 Sqn	Mosquito XVI	PF387 8K-J		Air Test

P/O A F Ceeley   +
F/O W E H O'Bryan RCAF   +

T/o 1109 Oakington but the port engine failed and the crew turned back, only to overshoot and crash 1121 at Burgess Field, Second Cuckoo Grove near Cottenham, 6 miles N of Cambridge. Both were taken to Brookwood Military Cemetery; they had arrived on the Squadron five days previous on posting from 16 OTU.

Note. Keith Wood advises this Mosquito was allotted to 571 Squadron on 12 July 1944 and is believed to have completed 74 operational sorties.

20 Mar 1945	7 Sqn	Lancaster III	PB667 MG-Q		Op: Recklinghausen

F/O L P Bacon RAAF   +
Sgt H McClements   +
F/S R R Evans   +
F/O G H Huttlestone   +
W/O P A Tennant RNZAF   +
Sgt J A Cornwall   +
Sgt J E Taylor   +

T/o 1031 Oakington to mark the railway yards. On return, came down near the Schelde estuary on land owned by Mr Remijn at Nieudorp (Zeeland) on Zuid Beveland. All bodies were recovered and their graves are now in Bergen op Zoom War Cemetery. F/S Evans of Port Talbot was a Member of the Pharmaceutical Society.

	85 Sqn	Mosquito VI	NS998 VY-		Training

F/L G H Ellis   +
Sgt W P Reidy   +

Turned tightly to line up with the drogue aircraft, stalled and spun in over The Wash. Both are commemorated on the Runnymede Memorial.

20-21 Mar 1945	50 Sqn	Lancaster III	ME441 VN-W	Op: Bohlen

50 Sqn   Lancaster III

P/O A N Levy RAAF	+
Sgt L Henshaw	+
Sgt E G Friend	
F/S D Swingler	+
F/S S Chapman	+
Sgt T L Hill	+
Sgt P C Hopper	+

ME441 VN-W   Op: Bohlen

T/o 2353 Skellingthorpe to bomb a synthetic-oil plant. Six are known to have perished; five lie in Germany at the Reichswald Forest War Cemetery but F/S Swingler is buried in Belgium at Hotton War Cemetery, thus strongly suggesting his body was recovered by American authorities. It is further supposed that Sgt Friend survived. At 35, Sgt Henshaw was above the average age of operational airmen.

57 Sqn   Lancaster I

F/O C A Cobern RAAF	+
Sgt K C Ashun	+
F/O W F Calderbank	+
F/S W S Searby	inj
Sgt R Bates	inj
Sgt E Lawrence	inj
Sgt A Ramsbottom	+

RA530 DX-Y   Op: Bohlen

T/o 2345 East Kirkby similarly tasked but within the next few minutes the Lancaster ploughed into a house near Stickney, some 7 miles NNE of Boston and on the main road leading to the Lincolnshire town of Spilsby. F/O Cobern RAAF is buried in Cambridge City Cemetery, the others who died were taken to their home towns. F/S Searby died from his injuries on 1 April. The house was lived in by a family, surnamed Chapman.

57 Sqn   Lancaster III

F/L A R Palling RAAF	+
F/S G W Ackerman	+
P/O V R Campbell RAAF	+
P/O G O H Lind RAAF	+
W/O C Jardine RAAF	+
F/S J Henderson	+
F/S M O'Loughlin	+

LM653 DX-Q   Op: Halle

T/o 2342 East Kirkby on a diversionary raid to Halle. All are buried in Hannover War Cemetery. This was an experienced crew with over 30 sorties to their credit. Of the four Australians, three hailed from Western Australia while F/S Palling RAAF came from the State of Victoria.

61 Sqn   Lancaster I

F/O K W Ainsworth	+
Sgt L D Mills	+
F/O R Breakwell	+
F/O P Hawkins	+
F/S A W Snelling	+
Sgt P Kitching	+
Sgt F M Lancaster	+

NG386 QR-P   Op: Bohlen

T/o 2345 Skellingthorpe to bomb a synthetic-oil plant. Lost without trace, though it is said an identity card bearing F/S Snelling's name was found near Espenhain, 6 km ESE of Böhlen. All are commemorated on the Runnymede Memorial.

61 Sqn   Lancaster I

F/O J F Swales RAAF	+
Sgt A J M Davies	+
F/O C H Saunders	+
F/S R Taylor	+
F/S D M Easton RAAF	+
Sgt W Lane	+
Sgt T Torney	+

RA560 DX-K   Op: Bohlen

T/o 2334 Skellingthorpe similarly tasked. All are buried in Dürnbach War Cemetery.

97 Sqn   Lancaster III

F/O J D Cottman RAAF	+
Sgt J W Cross	+
P/O A G Murray RAAF	+
F/S J S Coster RAAF	+
W/O H J Arney RAAF	+
F/S V E Petschel RAAF	+
F/S L J Bull RAAF	+

PA973 OF-C   Op: Bohlen

T/o 2353 Coningsby similarly tasked. Lost without trace. All are commemorated on the Runnymede Memorial. Five of the six Australians came from the State of Victoria, while their navigator, P/O Murray RAAF, hailed from Lismore in New South Wales.

189 Sqn   Lancaster I

F/L R Miller DFM	+
F/S K A Horne	+
W/O N Stott DFM	+
F/O R F Moneypenny	+
F/L C G Hall	+
F/O J S Holmes	+
P/O J M Navin	+

RF132 CA-K   Op: Bohlen

T/o 2350 Fulbeck similarly tasked. Lost without trace. All are commemorated on the Runnymede Memorial. Most were on their second tours; F/L Miller's DFM had been gained while flying Wellingtons with 150 Squadron, while W/O Stott had completed his first tour with 50 Squadron. Details of their awards had been published in the London Gazette on 22 September 1942 and 10 December 1943 respectively.

20-21 Mar 1945	**207 Sqn**	**Lancaster I**		**PA196 EM-D**	**Op: Bohlen**

```
20-21 Mar    207 Sqn          Lancaster I    PA196 EM-D                 Op: Bohlen
1945         F/O R A Lewis RAAF          +   T/o 2343 Spilsby to bomb a synthetic-oil
             Sgt C J Dewdney             +   plant. Lost without trace. All are commemorated
             F/O J D Smith              +   on the Runnymede Memorial. Their average age
             F/S G Matsumoto             +   was twenty-two.
             W/O W B Judd RAAF           +
             Sgt H O Collin              +
             Sgt T A Lawton              +

             214 Sqn          Fortress III   HB785 BU-A                 Op: BS
             F/O R V Kingdon RCAF        +   T/o 2340 Oulton on Jostle duties in support of
             Sgt W D Dale               +   the Böhlen operation. All rest in Dürnbach War
             WO2 W A Routley RCAF        +   Cemetery. F/O Donald RCAF, the specialist
             WO2 J W Pellant RCAF        +   operator, was an American from Indianapolis.
             F/S D F Miller             +   F/O Kingdon's second Christian name was Verdun,
             F/O D N Donald RCAF         +   likely given to commemorate the sacrifice of the
             F/S H M Carter RCAF         +   French army in the First World War.
             Sgt W Perkins              +
             WO2 R G Wilson RCAF         +
             Sgt D Parker               +

             223 Sqn          Liberator VI   TS526 6G-T                 Op: BS
             F/S N S Ayres              +   T/o 2322 Oulton on Jostle duties. The nine
             Sgt D Marsden              +   airmen who died rest in Hannover War Cemetery.
             W/O A E Redford            +   On being released from captivity, W/O Cole was
             F/O H B Hale               +   admitted to RAF Hospital Wroughton.
             W/O J E Bellamy            +
             W/O A C Cole             pow
             Sgt E D T Brockhurst       +
             F/S J D Cairns             +
             Sgt L J Vowler             +
             W/O S E Silvey             +
```

Note. As a Bomber Support squadron, 223 Squadron operated for less than a year, during which time its total losses amounted to just three Liberators. Considering the nature of their duties, this was a remarkably good record.

```
             227 Sqn          Lancaster I    PA259 9J-Z                 Op: Bohlen
             F/L R D King RAAF        pow   T/o 2339 Balderton to attack a synthetic-oil
             F/O W H Pitts RAAF         +   plant, after first making a feint run over Halle.
             Sgt R W Fytton             +   Nearing the turning point to Halle, and flying at
             F/O W T Neilson          pow   15,000 feet, came under attack from a night-
             F/S W A Roots            pow   fighter. Disintegrated and fell near Eschwege.
             F/S B T Long RAAF        pow   Those who died are buried in Berlin 1939-1945 War
             Sgt L E Baxter RCAF        +   Cemetery.
             Sgt L Marshall             +
```

Note. F/L King RAAF wrote an account of his capture, this being published in 1990 in a booklet titled, "We Flew, We Fell, We Survived" and issued by the Western Australia Branch of Members of the Royal Air Force ex-Prisoner of War Association.

```
             419 Sqn          Lancaster X    KB786 VR-P                 Op: Heide
             F/O R W Millar RCAF        +   T/o 0151 Middleton St. George to bomb an oil
             Sgt S D Booth             +   plant. Shot down by a night-fighter and likely
             F/L H B Rubin DFC RCAF     +   crashed at Odderade, 7 km ESE of Hemmingstedt.
             F/O A J Palanek RCAF       +   As the Lancaster exploded, so F/S Aitken RCAF
             F/S C A Elliott RCAF       +   was thrown clear. His six companions rest in
             F/O L C Croucher RCAF      +   Hamburg Cemetery, Ohlsdorf, having been found
             F/S J W Aitken RCAF      pow   in graves near the crash site.

             463 Sqn          Lancaster I    PB845 JO-C                 Op: Bohlen
             F/O R S Bennett RAAF       +   T/o 2349 Waddington to bomb a synthetic-oil
             F/S R Gordon              +   plant. All are buried in Berlin 1939-1945 War
             F/S G G Green             +   Cemetery. At 21, Sgt Bunn may have been the
             Sgt L B Neaves            +   oldest member of the crew; five were aged 20,
             Sgt S H Walker            +   including the pilot and F/S Gordon who may
             Sgt G O Little            +   have been a qualified pilot. Only F/S Green's
             Sgt A H Bunn              +   age has been omitted from the cemetery register.
```

20-21 Mar 1945	619 Sqn	Lancaster I		PD425 PG-T	Op: Bohlen

S/L C M Palmer		+	T/o 2347 Strubby to attack a synthetic-oil
F/O F J Ricketts DFM		+	plant. Apart from the air gunners, it is
F/L L C Raw		+	believed this was a second tour crew. F/O
F/O D I Thomas		pow	Ricketts gained his DFM, Gazetted 6 June 1944,
F/L W F Graham		+	while serving with 625 Squadron. S/L Palmer
Sgt G R J Miles		pow	came from Marandellas in Southern Rhodesia,
Sgt P C Wiseman		+	while at 35, F/L Raw was above an age usually

associated with operational aircrew. Less
the two survivors, all are buried in Hannover War Cemetery.

21 Mar 1945	51 Sqn	Halifax III		MZ348 MH-D	Op: Rheine

F/O J E Paradise RAAF		+	T/o 1502 Snaith. Presumed hit by flak and
Sgt R F Gunn		+	crashed 1630 onto farmland near Bevergern some
P/O B F Greenwood RAAF		+	10 km ENE of Rheine. All landed safely by
F/S A Armstrong		+	parachute but within 24 hours, the first four
F/O K W Berwick RAAF		pow	named had been shot. Initially buried in the
Sgt W Hood		pow	Roman Catholic Friedhof at Dreierwalde, their
F/S L Hart		pow	graves are now in the Reichswald Forest War

Cemetery.

	75 Sqn	Lancaster I		NG449 JN-T	Op: Munster

F/L J Plummer RNZAF		+	T/o 0945 Mepal to bomb railway yards and a
Sgt M O Fell		pow	nearby railway viaduct. Shot down by flak
P/O A L Humphries RNZAF		pow	over the target area. Those who died rest
F/O E J Holloway RNZAF		+	in the Reichswald Forest War Cemetery. Sgt
F/O J J Wakerley		pow	Fell was badly wounded and on being released
F/O R J Scott RNZAF		+	from captivity he was taken to RAF Hospital
F/S J McDowell RNZAF		evd	Wroughton, his date of admittance being given

as 25 April.

	75 Sqn	Lancaster I		RA564 AA-P	Op: Munster

F/O D S Barr		+	T/o 0947 Mepal similarly tasked. Crashed in
F/S C I Stocker		+	the target area. The body of W/O Amos was found
F/S A L A Oakey RNZAF		+	by American forces and taken to Holland for
F/S D Stewart		+	burial at Margraten. His remains have since
W/O R W West MID		+	been exhumed and transferred to Venray War
Sgt B H Nicholl		+	Cemetery. His six companions have no known
W/O A Amos		+	graves.

	75 Sqn	Lancaster III		LM733 AA-R	Op: Munster

F/O A E Brown RNZAF		+	T/o 1001 Mepal similarly tasked. Seen to break
F/S R H Lawrence		pow	into two sections and plummet earthwards over the
F/S A D Baker RNZAF		pow	target area, possibly due to a combination of
F/S J H Wood RNZAF		+	being struck from above by bombs and by fire
F/S A E Robson RNZAF		pow	from the heavy flak barrage. The two airmen
Sgt J Grieveson		pow	who died rest in the Reichswald Forest War
Sgt H Barraclough		pow	Cemetery. It is reported that F/O Brown RNZAF

was found in a grave at Coesfeld.

Note. These attacks on Rheine and München by medium forces of 178 and 160
aircraft respectively were aimed at both the town areas and the attendant
railway yards. With their proximity to the embattled Werhmacht, still in
a state of confusion following the Allied crossing of the Rhine, the raids
were vital to the hindrance of enemy reinforcements towards the Ruhr.

	77 Sqn	Halifax VI		RG541 KN-W	Training

F/O R H Kerslake		On landing 1434 at Full Sutton, the starboard
Sgt E Thompson		outer cut, causing the bomber to swerve from
Sgt J C Gill		the runway. Moments later, the undercarriage
F/S J M Lazar		gave way under the strain and the Halifax was
Sgt A Cook		damaged beyond repair. No injuries reported.
Sgt F McLeod		
Sgt W H Tovey		

	101 Sqn	Lancaster I		NF954 SR-W	Training

P/O J Kerr		Crash-landed 0424 in a field just beyond the
		boundary of Ludford Magna airfield, Lincolnshire.
		No one was hurt in the incident.

21 Mar 1945	617 Sqn	Lancaster I	PD117 YZ-L	Op: Bremen

```
F/L B A Gumbley DFM RNZAF    +     T/o 0745 Woodhall Spa to attack a railway
F/O E A Barnett              +     bridge in the SE suburbs of Bremen at Arbergen.
F/O K Gill DFC               +     At approximately 1000 was seen to be hit by
    Croix de Guerre                heavy flak before diving, streaming flames,
F/L J C Randon               +     into the ground and exploding 1004 at Okel,
F/O G Bell                   +     4 km NE of Syke, a town some 19 km S from the
                                   centre of Bremen. F/L Gumbley RNZAF had gained
his DFM with 49 Squadron, Gazetted 18 May 1943, while the Croix de Guerre held
by F/O Gill was published on 5 June 1946. All are perpetuated by the Runnymede
Memorial.
```

Note. This was a Lancaster B.I(Spec.) and as operated by 617 Squadron flew
with a crew consisting of five members only.

21-22 Mar 1945	44 Sqn	Lancaster III	PB251 KM-O	Op: Hamburg

```
F/O B F Hennessy             +     T/o 0129 Spilsby to bomb the Deutsche Erdölwerke
Sgt A Boothman               +     refinery. Hit by flak and crashed 0430 near
Sgt D H Davies               +     Bunsoh, 3 km NE of Albersdorf. All are buried
F/S K Kay                    +     in Kiel War Cemetery. F/O Hennessy came from
Sgt J Lyons                  +     Penydarren while his rear gunner, Sgt Richards
Sgt G A White                +     lived close by at Treorchy in Glamorgan.
Sgt H Richards               +
```

	97 Sqn	Lancaster III	PB521 OF-Q	Op: Hamburg

```
F/L O P F Taylor DFC        inj    T/o 0121 Coningsby similarly tasked. Crashed
    RNZAF                          0355 S of the Elbe at Feldmark Leeswig, Hamburg-
F/S J B Aherne               +     Neuenfelde. F/S Bray fell into the nearby River
S/L W M Burnside DFC        pow    Este and drowned. Buried in a field grave, he
W/O J H Bushby              pow    now lies in Hamburg Cemetery, Ohlsdorf. The
F/S N H Stauber              +     others who died in the crash are buried in
F/S A Rainsford              +     Becklingen War Cemetery, while F/L Taylor RNZAF
F/S W T Bray                 +     rests at Hannover War Cemetery having died from
                                   severe spinal injuries on 30 April at Stalag XB.
F/S Aherne came from Tralee, Co. Kerry in the Irish Republic; F/S Rainsford had
enlisted in Rhodesia.
```

Note. It is believed Stalag XB might have been a predominantly army prisoner
of war camp as it is not listed in AIR20 2336, the Allied Air Forces prisoner
of war file. The village of Sandbostel was close by.

	163 Sqn	Mosquito XXV	KB425 -V	Op: Berlin

```
F/O J D Rees DFC            inj    T/o 1902 Wyton. Returned early and crashed
F/O A R S Drake             inj    2016 short of the runway at Upwood airfield
                                   in Huntingdonshire. F/O Drake was rushed to
RAF Hospital Ely but died soon after being admitted. He is buried in Cornwall
at Falmouth Cemetery.
```

	207 Sqn	Lancaster III	ME522 EM-X	Op: Hamburg

```
F/L R L Werner RNZAF         +     T/o 0145 Spilsby to bomb the Deutsche Erdölwerke
Sgt N McD Cox                +     refinery. Believed to have been shot down by flak
W/O R R Cameron RAAF         +     and crashed 0406 at Hamburg-Freihafen. All are
F/S J D Grime                +     buried, however, in Becklingen War Cemetery.
Sgt A West                   +
Sgt K W Clapperton           +
Sgt J Johnson                +
```

	214 Sqn	Fortress III	KJ112 BU-P	Op: BS

```
F/L W D Allies               +     T/o 0130 Oulton on Jostle duties in support of
W/O J McFarlane              +     the Hamburg raid. Lost without trace. All are
F/O B F Kerr DFM             +     commemorated on the Runnymede Memorial. The
F/O W J Cunningham           +     two DFM recipients had served previously with
F/O S H G Sinclair DFM       +     166 Squadron and 9 Squadron respectively. F/O
W/O N Cooper                 +     Kerr's award had been published on 19 October
F/S C R Braithwaite          +     1943, while that for F/O Sinclair had appeared
Sgt P Newman                 +     in the London Gazette on 17 August 1943. W/O
Sgt R A D Jones              +     Cooper was the specialist operator. The widow
Sgt E L Punnett              +     of F/O Sinclair later remarried and helped in
                                   the provision of a Monument at Oulton.
```

144

21-22 Mar 1945

227 Sqn   **Lancaster I**   **ME372 9J-U**   **Op: Hamburg**

F/O E K Whitechurch RNZAF +
Sgt T L O´Marah +
F/S E D Wilkinson +
F/S F H Debarr +
F/S F M Ashworth RNZAF +
Sgt T J Jones +
Sgt G H White +

T/o 0122 Balderton tasked to attack the Deutsche Erdölwerke refinery. All contact lost at 0503, after which it is believed the Lancaster ditched in position 54N 07E. F/O Whitechurch RNZAF is buried in Western Jutland at Mosevraa Churchyard but his crew are commemorated on the Runnymede Memorial.

460 Sqn   **Lancaster I**   **NG466 AR-Y**   **Op: Bochum**

F/L D H Heggie RAAF
Sgt H Brooke +
Sgt W T Dean +
F/S K E Ambler
P/O A C Trotter +
Sgt D Robinson +
Sgt H H Dunkerley +

T/o 0111 Binbrook to attack a benzol plant at Bruchstrasse. Those who perished rest in Rheinberg War Cemetery. F/L Heggie RAAF and F/S Ambler are described as "safe".

692 Sqn   **Mosquito XVI**   **PF392 P3-R**   **Op: Berlin**

W/O I M MacPhee +
Sgt A V Sullivan +

T/o 1916 Graveley. Both are buried in Berlin 1939-1945 War Cemetery. W/O MacPhee was the son of Dr. Burgess MacPhee of Blackburn.

Note. The 1978 and 1980 revisions of the CWGC cemetery registers incorrectly identify the above airmen as belonging to 629 Squadron, which never formed.

22 Mar 1945

15 Sqn   **Lancaster I**   **HK773 LS-W**   **Op: Bocholt**

W/O F J Newton RAAF +
Sgt W J Dee +
Sgt C A J Church +
Sgt M F Matthews +
Sgt G A Cope +
Sgt P Cooley +
Sgt T E Jenkins +

T/o 1055 Mildenhall to attack the town by G-H bombing methods but crashed two minutes later, due to an engine fire, exploding over woodland near Mundford, Norfolk, 4 miles NNE of Brandon in Suffolk. All are buried in Cambridge City Cemetery. At 36, Sgt Jenkins was older than most airmen serving in Bomber Command.

Note. These were the last fatalities sustained by 15 Squadron in the Second World War. Fifty-three years later, members of the Norfolk and Suffolk Aviation Museum placed a small wooden cross at the crash site, this moving event being given extensive coverage in the Eastern Daily Press on 24 April 1998.

150 Sqn   **Lancaster I**   **ME451 IQ-D**   **Op: Hildesheim**

F/O I H S Philcox +
Sgt D S Fielding +
Sgt G Brain +
Sgt V J Lawrence +
Sgt N F Scaife +
Sgt A Moore +
Sgt T B Cook

T/o Hemswell to attack the railway yards. The six who died rest in Hannover War Cemetery. Sgt Moore had joined the Royal Air Force (Volunteer Reserve) in Newfoundland during August 1940. Sgt Cook is described as "safe".

166 Sqn   **Lancaster I**   **PD365 AS-X**   **Op: Hildesheim**

F/S R E Moore +
Sgt W Cummins +
Sgt J Hanlon +
F/S J Marrinan +
W/O L Reed +
Sgt F Hume +
F/S C T Johnson RCAF +

T/o 1127 Kirmington similarly tasked. Six are buried in Rheinberg War Cemetery, but W/O Reed lies at Hotton War Cemetery in Belgium, thus it is extremely likely his original grave was opened by an American graves investigation unit.

428 Sqn   **Lancaster X**   **KB777 NA-V**   **Op: Hildesheim**

F/L J F Hadley RCAF +
Sgt R R Duke RCAF   pow
F/O W J Spence RCAF   pow
F/O C A Goodier RCAF   pow
F/S J MacKenzie RCAF +
F/O D Frame RCAF +
F/S J W Bellamy RCAF   pow

T/o 1047 Middleton St. George similarly charged. Last seen, homebound, flying at below 5,000 feet with its port inner feathered and with flames streaming from the engine. Two P-51 Mustangs were also observed close by. Subsequently, the Lancaster was abandoned. Of the three who died two rest in Rheinberg War Cemetery, while panel 280 of the Runnymede Memorial perpetuates the name of F/S MacKenzie RCAF.

22 Mar	431 Sqn	Lancaster X	KB808 SE-Y	Op: Hildesheim
1945	F/L J P Duggan DFC RCAF	+	T/o 1043 Croft to bomb railway yards. Hit by
	P/O F B Trent RCAF	+	flak and exploded over the target area. All,
	Sgt J H Bentley	+	including nineteen year old ex-Air Training
	F/O G A Zuback RCAF	+	Corps cadet Sgt Bentley, are buried in Hannover
	F/O G D McLean RCAF	+	War Cemetery. Apart from P/O Trent RCAF, all
	F/O J W Dorrell RCAF	+	were due to be screened following this sortie.
	F/S C E Root RCAF	+	F/O Dorrell RCAF was an American from Columbus
	F/S J B Ketchen RCAF	+	in the State of Ohio.

434 Sqn	Lancaster X	KB832 WL-F	Op: Hildesheim
F/O H Payne RCAF		T/o 1055 Croft similarly charged but was caught
		by a sudden gust of wind which took the bomber

onto the grass. F/O Payne RCAF tried to bring the Lancaster back onto the runway but over corrected. He then closed the throttles, but was unable to avoid
racing across the airfield, whereupon a tyre burst and before coming to a halt
near East Vince Moor farm, a collision occurred involving 431 Squadron Lancaster
KB811 SE-T. Within moments of stopping, a fire started in the port engine and
this spread rapidly. The crew managed to get clear and a general evacuation
order was broadcast. At 1127 the bomb-load exploded, the force of the blast
removing the roof of the farmhouse and setting light to hay and nearby buildings. Remarkably, no one was injured but it was late afternoon before the
aerodrome was declared fit for use.

22-23 Mar	23 Sqn	Mosquito VI	RS577 YP-	Op: BS
1945	S/L M W O'Brien DFC	+	T/o 1935 Little Snoring for intruder duties in
	F/L P A Disney	+	the Handorf and Münster areas. Both officers
			are buried in the Reichswald Forest War Cemetery.

It is possible that on the outward flight, the Mosquito overflew F/L Disney's
home village of Ingham near the Norfolk coast some 3 miles inland from Waxham.
He was the Squadron's Navigation Leader.

239 Sqn	Mosquito NF.30	NT315 HB-	Op: BS
W/O D B Brotchie	+	T/o 2100 West Raynham for a low level intruder
F/S J J Ferguson	+	sortie. Both lie in the Reichswald Forest War
		Cemetery, having been brought here from the

Roman Catholic Friedhof "Konigsesch" at Rheine. Both hailed from Lancashire.

23 Mar	101 Sqn	Lancaster I	LL755 SR-U	Op: Bremen
1945	F/O R R Little RCAF	+	T/o 0658 Ludford Magna. Crashed 1030 near
	F/S A J Clifton	+	Stöttinghausen, 3 km SE of Twistringen. All
	F/O J G Lee RCAF	+	are buried in Sage War Cemetery. F/O Little
	F/O W H Brooks RCAF	+	RCAF was an American from Lockport in the
	Sgt H Woodards	+	State of New York.
	Sgt T Churchill	+	
	Sgt P S Nelson	+	

Note. This Lancaster was not quite a year old, having been first delivered
to 32 MU on 3 April 1944, and then passing to 101 Squadron five days later.
During its service, it was twice damaged in action, each time repairs being
carried out on site. Its companion, summarised below, had been received at
Ludford Magna in September 1943.

101 Sqn	Lancaster III	DV245 SR-S	Op: Bremen
F/L R P Paterson RCAF	pow	T/o 0711 Ludford Magna on its 119th operational
P/O K D S J Ward	pow	sortie. Hit by flak and exploded, crashing 1000
F/O M Ornstein RCAF	+	between Moordeich and Stuhr, 7 km ESE from the
F/O S Dillon	pow	centre of Delmenhorst. Those who died are now
F/S W G Yeomans	+	at rest in Becklingen War Cemetery. F/O Dillon
Sgt A W Greenhough	+	is reported to have been wounded.
F/O W E Thoroldson RCAF	+	

141 Sqn	Mosquito NF.30	NT456 TW-	Training
F/L E D Drew RCAF		T/o Little Snoring. While flying at 5,000 feet
		the starboard engine failed, thus necessitating

an emergency landing at West Raynham. The approach at 1236 was fast and touch
down occurred too far down the runway in order to stop. Thus, the pilot deliberately retracted the undercarriage to avoid over running the airfield. No one
was hurt but the Mosquito was damaged beyond repair.

23-24 Mar 1945

50 Sqn   **Lancaster I**   **NG171 VN-**   **Op: Wesel**

F/O M L C Lillies RAAF
Sgt E Elwall
Sgt G Reid
F/O L Skinner
W/O T S Smith RAAF
Sgt W A Crozier
Sgt G A Draper

T/o 1919 Skellingthorpe. Outbound, the starboard outer failed, followed later by the starboard inner and the mission was abandoned. The crew set course of Florennes in Belgium and landed here at 2352 but moments later one of the main wheels ran into a hole and the undercarriage collapsed. No injuries reported.

139 Sqn   **Mosquito XX**   **KB367 XD-D**   **Op: Berlin**

F/L R O Day DFC   +
F/L T Treby MID   +

T/o 2120 Upwood. Crashed at Heesch (Noord-Brabant), on the southern outskirts of Oss. F/L Day, whose parents lived in Johannesburg, is buried in Heesch Roman Catholic Cemetery while panel 266 of the Runnymede Memorial commemorates his Devonshire domicile navigator.

Note. The commune of Heesch was witness to heavy fighting in the autumn of 1944 and burials here are predominately soldiers, particularly from the 4th Battalion, The Royal Welch Fusiliers and the 1st Battalion, The Oxfordshire and Buckinghamshire Light Infantry whose Commanding Officer, Lt Col James Hugh Hare DSO fell on 28 October 1944.

139 Sqn   **Mosquito XXV**   **KB390 XD-B**   **Op: Berlin**

F/L R O Searles DFC   +
F/L N C Berrisford   +
     DFC & Bar

T/o 2121 Upwood. F/L Searles is commemorated on panel 266 of the Runnymede Memorial, while F/L Berrisford is buried in Berlin at the city's 1939-1945 War Cemetery.

Note. The two 139 Squadron crews here summarised were highly experienced. F/L Day had logged at least 82 sorties, while F/L Searles had flown 93.

24 Mar 1945

10 Sqn   **Halifax III**   **RG438 ZA-N**   **Training**

WO2 D C Rogers RCAF

T/o 1013 Melbourne but the starboard outer cut and the Halifax left the runway and ran through the FIDO installation piping. No one was hurt, but their aircraft was damaged beyond repair, although it was not until 5 July 1945 that it was eventually struck off charge.

78 Sqn   **Halifax III**   **NP998 EY-**   **Training**

F/O R Hatherall RNZAF

While taxiing at 1245 the Halifax commenced a gentle swing towards the right hand side of the perimeter track. The pilot corrected, whereupon the bomber veered sharply to port and ran into an obstruction. No injuries reported.

150 Sqn   **Lancaster I**   **PB853 IQ-P**   **Op: Dortmund**

F/O P H Morris RAAF   +
F/S J C Davis   +
F/S K A Kee RAAF   +
F/S J H Gillies RAAF   pow
F/S R L Masters RAAF   +
F/S H H Bawden RAAF   pow
F/S J N Griffin RAAF   +

T/o Hemswell to bomb the Harpenerweg benzol plant. Crashed Witten-Herbede. All baled out safely but five had the tragic misfortune to be killed after being taken into custody. They now rest in the Reichswald Forest War Cemetery. On his release from captivity, F/S Bawden RAAF was admitted to RAF Hospital Wroughton. One of the group implicated for the crimes committed was sentenced to death, while a second received a fifteen year prison sentence.

158 Sqn   **Halifax III**   **MZ759 NP-Q**   **Op: Gladbeck**

W/O E Y Yeoman   +
Sgt J R Williams   +
F/S J E D Taylor   pow
F/S J Brown   +
W/O W H Hulme RAAF   +
F/S G D Lunn   pow
F/O W H White   pow

T/o 0905 Lissett. Shot down in flames while over the target area. It is believed all baled out but only three survived. Scottish born W/O Yeoman and F/S Brown, along with their Welsh flight engineer, lie in the Reichswald Forest War Cemetery, but W/O Hulme RAAF is buried in Holland at Venray War Cemetery, having been brought here from the US Military Cemetery at Margraten.

Note. This Halifax had been named "Wizard of Aus" and since its delivery to Lissett on 16 June 1944, had flown seventy-two operational sorties, an extremely good achievement.

24 Mar 1945	166 Sqn	Lancaster I	NG114 AS-S	Op: Dortmund

F/O C A H F Defraigne	+
F/O J R Mearns	+
F/O T H Howell	+
F/O S Pascal RCAF	+
Sgt F W Mitchell	+
Sgt J W Inman RCAF	+
Sgt R D R Kendall RCAF	pow

T/o 1255 Kirmington to bomb the Harpenerweg
benzol plant. Crashed E of the Rhine into
Arecaseadlieng Strasse at Hilden, some 12 km
SSE from the centre of Düsseldorf. Those who
died were, eventually, taken to the Reichswald
Forest War Cemetery, since when F/O Defraigne
has been reinterred in the Field of Honour for
the Belgian Air Force in Brussels Town Cemetery.
He was born on 8 November 1916 at Liege.

169 Sqn	Mosquito XIX	TA394 VI-	Ferry

W/O E G Jackson

T/o 1630 Swannington but the starboard engine
failed at 100 miles per hour and the under-
carriage had to be raised in order to stop. No injuries reported.

550 Sqn	Lancaster I	PD320 BQ-H	Op: Dortmund

F/L J B Barnes RCAF	+
Sgt J W Green	+
F/S J Stobbs	+
F/S D F Reid	+
F/S J G Day	+
F/S W E McDonald RCAF	+
F/S E Lindsay RCAF	+

T/o 1251 North Killingholme to attack the
Harpenerweg benzol plant. All are buried
in the Reichswald Forest War Cemetery.

24-25 Mar 1945	169 Sqn	Mosquito VI	NT121 VI-	Op: BS

P/O G F Cant

T/o 2010 Juvincourt but the port engine cut
and the undercarriage was raised in order to
stop. Neither crew member was hurt, but the Mosquito was effectively wrecked.

25 Mar 1945	166 Sqn	Lancaster III	ME521 AS-A	Op: Hannover

S/L K G Laverack	+
F/S S W Orr	pow
F/O E C Bott RNZAF	pow
F/O D R Lethbridge RNZAF	pow
Sgt K E Hunt	+
Sgt S L Osborn	pow
Sgt T Gibson	+

T/o 0630 Kirmington. Struck by a bomb over
the target area and crashed 0944 some 5 km S
of Ronnenberg, a small town roughly 12 km SSW
from the centre of Hannover, where the three
who died rest in the city's war cemetery.
The four survivors are merely described as
"safe" but it believed all went into captivity.

408 Sqn	Halifax VII	NP804 EQ-K	Op: Munster

F/O B A Burrows RCAF	+
Sgt R Hamilton	+
F/O W R Lay RCAF	+
F/O F W Shantz RCAF	+
F/O J P Marchant RCAF	+
F/S L C Cofield RCAF	+
F/S W A Dyer RCAF	pow

T/o 0706 Linton-on-Ouse. Reached the target
area, where it was hit by flak and exploded over
Amelsbüren, 9 km SSW from the centre of Münster
and on the rail line leading to Werne and Lünen.
Those who perished now rest in the Reichswald
Forest War Cemetery.

415 Sqn	Halifax III	MZ907 6U-P	Op: Munster

F/O J R McCollum RCAF	+
Sgt S W Lowe	+
F/O R M Aylesworth RCAF	pow
Sgt R A Paul RCAF	+
F/S A N Knight RCAF	pow
WO2 J M Jones RCAF	+
F/S L W Brennan RCAF	+

T/o 0753 East Moor. Outbound, hit by flak and
abandoned, crashing near Wulfen, a small town
7 km NNW of Dorsten. Of those who died, the
pilot and mid-upper air gunner are buried in
the Reichswald Forest War Cemetery, having been
found in graves in the Kusenhorst Wald, while
three lie in Holland at Groesbeek Canadian War
Cemetery. WO2 Knight RCAF subsequently reported
to 247 Squadron, then flying Typhoons, at Lüneburg on 3 May 1945.

Note. Oliver Clutton-Brock reports that the three airmen who rest in Holland
were shot by Haupttruppenführer Ferdinand Assman, who was later arrested but
committed suicide while in prison and awaiting trial.

425 Sqn	Halifax III	NR194 KW-J	Op: Munster

WO2 M J P Lavoie RCAF

T/o 0705 Tholthorpe. Bombed the AP at 1016 from
15,800 feet. On return, the crew tried to land
at Riccall but in poor visibility they mistook the circle lights for the runway
and turned to starboard instead of port. Realising his error, WO2 Lavoie RCAF
tried to overshoot but stalled and crashed 1345, without injury to his crew.

| 25 Mar | 426 Sqn | Halifax VII | NP684 OW- | Ground |
| 1945 | | | | |

Wrecked at Linton-on-Ouse when another Squadron Halifax came to grief on take off, later exploding.

426 Sqn	Halifax VII	NP811 OW-J	Op: Munster
F/O S E Levis RCAF	pow		
Sgt J W Rattigan RCAF	pow		
F/O W I B Jarvis RCAF	pow		
F/S L F Branston RCAF	+		
Sgt R M Eyre RCAF	pow		
Sgt S Ross RCAF	pow		
Sgt K M Montagano RCAF	pow		

T/o 0710 Linton-on-Ouse. Outbound, hit by flak and fell 1115 at Westenfeld, 4 km NW of Altenberge where at 0830 the next day, F/S Branston RCAF was buried. His grave is now located in the Reichswald Forest War Cemetery.

426 Sqn	Halifax VII	NP818 OW-M	Op: Munster
F/O F L Alward RCAF			
Sgt N Jackson			
F/O M W Wright RCAF			
Sgt O H Phillips RCAF			
F/O F Dickinson RCAF			
F/S L E Peck RCAF			
F/S J H Titus RCAF			

T/o 0730 Linton-on-Ouse but swung off the runway and having clipped a parked Halifax, finished up in a ditch. The impact caused the undercarriage to collapse and soon afterwards a fire broke out. All scrambled clear, unharmed, but the Halifax and another machine close by, was wrecked in the explosion that followed.

431 Sqn	Lancaster X	KB874 SE-C	Op: Hannover
P/O J A Keates RCAF	inj		
F/O J O Simmonds RCAF	inj		

T/o 0611 Croft. Bombed the AP at 0945 from 18,400 feet. Hit by flak and, later, wrecked while crash-landing at Manston airfield in Kent. The injuries sustained by the pilot and F/O Simmonds RCAF were not serious.

463 Sqn	Lancaster I	NG439 JO-	Air Test
F/L S R Hicks RAAF			

Lost power while flying on one engine and forced-landed 1533 in a field near Scopwick some 9 miles SE of Lincoln. No injuries amongst the five members of crew.

26-27 Mar	571 Sqn	Mosquito XVI	PF438 8K-M	Op: Berlin
1945				
	F/L H H Tattersall DFC			
	F/L K C A Smith RCAF			

T/o 1859 Oakington. Landed 2324 base and ran into another Mosquito whose pilot had advised Flying Control he was clear of the runway. F/L Tattersall gained an immediate DFC, Gazetted 17 January 1945, for his actions on 1 January 1945, while attacking railway tunnels.

Note. The serial of the second Mosquito is quoted variously as RB375 and RV375; the former was allocated to a Typhoon IB while the later is identified as being one from a large batch of serials allotted for Spitfire F.21 production at Castle Bromwich, but subsequently cancelled. It is likely, therefore, that the Mosquito in question was RV315.

27-28 Mar	139 Sqn	Mosquito XVI	MM131 XD-J	Op: Berlin
1945				
	F/L A A J Van Amsterdam	+		
	DFC Vliegerkruis			
	S/L H A Forbes DFC RCAF	pow		

T/o 1912 Upwood. Shot down by a Me 262 flown by Ofw Karl-Heinz Becker, 10./NJG11 and crashed N of Brandenburg. F/L Van Amsterdam is commemorated on panel 266 of the Runnymede Memorial. Born in Holland, he had married Irene Van Amsterdam of King's Lynn, Norfolk, and when killed was thought to have been on his 101st operational sortie.

139 Sqn	Mosquito XX	KB354 XD-C	Op: Bremen
F/O D W Rhys	inj		
F/O F J Kennelly	inj		

T/o 1914 Upwood. During the operation, the VHF radio equipment failed and on regaining base at 2254, F/O Rhys touched down off a fast approach and ended up in the bomb dump. He escaped with shock and bruising but his navigator sustained fractures to both legs. It will be recalled that both had been involved in a serious crash while flying with 128 Squadron a month previous.

571 Sqn	Mosquito XVI	RV326 8K-L	Op: Berlin
F/O G D Hudson AFC RNZAF	+		
F/O M G Gant RCAF	+		

T/o 1907 Oakington. Crashed 1945 into a cornfield at Zevenhuisen (Groningen), 25 km SW from Groningen. Both officers are buried in Leek (Zevenhuizen) General Cemetery. This was their eleventh successive sortie to Berlin and their 12th since arriving from 16 OTU on 28 February 1945.

27-28 Mar 1945	627 Sqn	Mosquito IV	DZ599 AZ-F	Op: Gardening

F/O W A Barnett RNZAF   T/o 1939 Woodhall Spa for minelaying duties over
F/S J A Day RAAF   +   the River Elbe. At 2201, called the formation
                                 leader to advise the Mosquito was about to be
ditched. No position was given, but it is believed the aircraft went into the
sea off the Frisians. F/S Day RAAF is commemorated on panel 284 of the Runnymede Memorial; F/O Barnett RNZAF is described as "safe".

Note. This was the last Mosquito IV to be lost on an operational sortie,
directed by Bomber Command, though 627 Squadron was destined to write off
one more aircraft of this type in a training accident.

	692 Sqn	Mosquito XVI	PF466 P3-C	Op: Berlin

F/L E S Vale MID   +   T/o 1911 Graveley. Lost without trace. Both
F/O F J Manning RCAF   +   are commemorated on the Runnymede Memorial.
                                 F/L Vale, an Associate of the Chartered
Institute, is believed to have been flying his 70th operational sortie.

30 Mar 1945	635 Sqn	Lancaster I	PB911 F2-A	Training

F/O D Dixon   +   T/o Downham Market for a Fishpond training
Sgt S E Robinson   +   exercise. Dived into the ground 1110 just
F/S S A Pimm   +   to the NW of Swayfield, 9 miles SSE from
F/S R Goddard   +   Grantham, Lincolnshire. All are buried in
F/S N Davis   +   various cemeteries. It is believed that the
F/S J G W Harcourt   +   Lancaster entered cu-nimbus cloud and iced up.
F/S R McL Wilson   +

30-31 Mar 1945	692 Sqn	Mosquito XVI	RV341 P3-B	Op: Berlin

F/S W Campey   +   T/o 1951 Graveley. Lost without trace. Panels
F/S J Rabiner RCAF   +   270 and 282 of the Runnymede Memorial perpetuate
                                 the names of this crew.

31 Mar 1945	156 Sqn	Lancaster III	PB468 GT-B	Op: Hamburg

F/O H F Taylor DFC   +   T/o 0638 Upwood to mark the Blohm and Voss
P/O H Woolstenhulme   +   shipbuilding yards. Fell at Hohe Liedtweg 476
Sgt J P Williams   +   Hamburg-Langenhorn. All are buried in Hamburg
Sgt L H Joel   +   Cemetery, Ohlsdorf. F/O Taylor, who served as
F/O R L Martin DFC   +   F/O Benson, and P/O Woolstenhulme were aged 36
F/O L A Cox DFC   +   and 37 respectively and, thus, were well over
F/S K A L Mitchell   +   the age associated with Bomber Command aircrew.
Sgt R Goldsbury   +   Sgt Joel was flying as a second navigator.

	156 Sqn	Lancaster III	PB517 GT-O	Op: Hamburg

F/L A C Pope DFC   +   T/o 0647 Upwood similarly tasked. Believed to
F/O G A J Morrison   +   have crashed, either on moorland 15 km NW from
F/L L E Munro DFC RCAF   +   Rotenburg (Wümme) or near Stemmen, 15 km NE of
P/O E H Marlow   +   Rotenburg. All are buried in Becklingen War
F/O T M McCabe   +   Cemetery. P/O Marlow was flying as a second
F/S K Antcliffe   +   navigator.
P/O I W Kelly RCAF   +
P/O R C Fletcher RCAF   +

	408 Sqn	Halifax VII	NP806 EQ-Q	Op: Hamburg

F/O K K Blyth RCAF   pow   T/o 0653 Linton-on-Ouse to attack the Blohm and
Sgt D G Grey RCAF   pow   Voss shipyards. Shot down by a Me 262 jet pro-
F/O J M Taylor RCAF   pow   pelled fighter and crashed 0850 in the Boberg
F/O R D Atkinson RCAF   pow   district of Bergedorf, a built up area 14 km
F/S A A Watson RCAF   pow   SE from the centre of Hamburg.
F/S J B Folkersen RCAF   pow
F/S R J Hughes RCAF   pow

	415 Sqn	Halifax III	MZ922 6U-C	Op: Hamburg

F/O G A Hyland RCAF   +   T/o 0623 East Moor similarly tasked. Reported
Sgt J A Neilson   +   shot down by a Me 262. All are commemorated on
F/O T S Lewis RCAF   +   the Runnymede Memorial. F/O Hyland RCAF was an
F/O J E Suttak RCAF   +   American from Detroit, Michigan.
WO2 G Anderson RCAF   +
F/S G J Rude RCAF   +
F/S G J Peden RCAF   +

31 Mar
1945

419 Sqn   **Lancaster X**   **KB761 VR-H**   **Op: Hamburg**

F/L H A Metivier RCAF	+
Sgt W M Sommerville RCAF	+
F/O J Todd RCAF	+
F/O R O Johnson RCAF	+
F/S G Matuszewski RCAF	+
F/S H S Tulk RCAF	+
F/S E E Morphy RCAF	+

T/o 0601 Middleton St. George to bomb the shipyards controlled by Blohm and Voss. Reported shot down by a Me 262 jet propelled fighter. All are commemorated on the Runnymede Memorial.

Note. On panel 105 of the Memorial is the name of Flight Sergeant Joseph Roger Rolland Metivier RCAF missing 17 August 1942 while flying with 58 Squadron. It is not thought he was related to the above Metivier, but the name is unusual.

419 Sqn   **Lancaster X**   **KB869 VR-Q**   **Op: Hamburg**

F/O D S M Bowes RCAF	+
Sgt J Rea RCAF	+
F/S G R Berry RCAF	pow
F/O J J Gladish RCAF	+
F/S B Maclennan RCAF	+
F/S R W Rowlands RCAF	pow
F/S W H Milne RCAF	pow

T/o 0601 Middleton St. George similarly tasked. Reported shot down S of Hamburg by a Me 262 and is believed to have crashed 0907 near Hittfeld, 9 km S of Harburg. Those who died are buried in Becklingen War Cemetery.

425 Sqn   **Halifax III**   **MZ418 KW-C**   **Op: Hamburg**

F/L C Lesesne RCAF	+
Sgt J P A Tame	pow
F/S J A R Villiard RCAF	pow
F/O W B Cable RCAF	pow
P/O R J H Pigeon RCAF	pow
WO2 R G J Trudeau RCAF	pow
F/S F H King RCAF	pow

T/o 0627 Tholthorpe similarly tasked. F/L Lesesne RCAF from Sumpter in South Carolina is buried in Hamburg Cemetery, Ohlsdorf.

429 Sqn   **Lancaster I**   **NG345 AL-V**   **Op: Hamburg**

F/O R R Jones RCAF	pow
Sgt R L Bailey	+
F/O R H Fisher RCAF	+
F/S J A J C Rancourt RCAF	pow
WO2 E M Hooker RCAF	+
WO1 J H R R Ledoux RCAF	+
F/S J L A Campeau RCAF	+

T/o 0614 Leeming similarly tasked. Shot down down by a Me 262 and partially abandoned, the pilot landing within 300 metres from where his Lancaster hit the ground some 2 km from Nenndorf, 7 km SW of Harburg. Those who died lie in Becklingen War Cemetery. Sgt Bailey was 37 and F/S Campeau RCAF 35, both well over an age normally associated with operational aircrew.

Note. This was the first Lancaster reported missing from 429 Squadron.

431 Sqn   **Lancaster X**   **KB859 SE-U**   **Op: Hamburg**

F/L P J Hurley RCAF	pow
Sgt L J Mercer	+
F/O M Hartog RCAF	+
F/O F R Alty RCAF	+
F/S A Dorey RCAF	+
F/O P B Dennison RCAF	+
F/O J J Casey RCAF	+

T/o 0626 Croft similarly tasked and believed to have crashed in the same area as the 419 Squadron Lancaster summarised against F/O Bowes RCAF. The six airmen who lost their lives now rest in Becklingen War Cemetery.

434 Sqn   **Lancaster X**   **KB911 WL-U**   **Op: Hamburg**

F/O G P Haliburton RCAF	+
Sgt J M Hanlin RCAF	pow
F/O D G Rathwell RCAF	+
F/O C K Legaarden RCAF	pow
F/O R Deane RCAF	pow
F/S R J Green RCAF	+
Sgt J A English RCAF	pow

T/o 0625 Croft similarly tasked. Reported to have been engaged by a Me 262 and crashed 0905 at Nettelnburg on the western side of Bergedorf. F/S Haliburton RCAF has no known grave but the others who died lie in Hamburg Cemetery, Ohlsdorf. There are suggestions that the fighter was firing rocket projectiles.

635 Sqn   **Lancaster I**   **PB958 F2-P**   **Op: Hamburg**

F/O A Lewis RAAF	+
Sgt A P Weir	+
F/S K G Clark RAAF	+
F/S E Chenoweth RAAF	+
F/S C Delaney RAAF	+
F/O J J Kennelly RAAF	pow
F/S N E Peters RAAF	+

T/o 0649 Downham Market to mark the Blohm and Voss shipyards. Crashed into the garden of a house at Steinkamp 23, Hamburg-Billstedt. Of the six airmen who died, four were aged twenty. They are buried in Hamburg Cemetery, Ohlsdorf. F/S Chenoweth RAAF was the son of the Revd Ben Chenoweth of Strathalbyn in South Australia.

1-2 Apr 1945	515 Sqn	Mosquito VI	PZ249 3P-		Op: BS

Lt E J van Heerden SAAF   +   T/o 1740 Little Snoring and landed 1910 at
F/O J W Robson   +   Juvincourt. After refuelling the crew took
off at 2315 and headed for Leipheim airfield
in company with S/L J H Penny and his navigator, F/O J F Whitfield. Both ex-
changed R/T calls, the last contact taking place at 0136. At 0139, S/L Penny
saw a violent explosion of the ground at, or near, Leipheim and at first
though Lt van Heerden SAAF had claimed an enemy aircraft, but when no replies
to his congratulations were forthcoming, he concluded it was the Mosquito he
had seen explode. Its crew now lie in Dürnbach War Cemetery; the pilot
hailing from Carnarvon in the Cape Province.

2-3 Apr 1945	139 Sqn	Mosquito XX	KB185 XD-R		Op: Berlin

F/L G A Nicholls DFC   +   T/o 2235 Upwood. Lost without trace. Both
F/L J E Dawes DFC   +   are commemorated on panel 265 of the Runnymede
Memorial. F/L Nicholls had flown 65 sorties.

	157 Sqn	Mosquito NF.30	MV551 RS-W		Op: Intruder

F/L T L Hunt   T/o 2055 Swannington for a high level intruder
F/O F Mulroy   sortie but the engines faltered and the Mosquito
ran off the end of the runway, crashed and caught
fire. Both crew made a speedy exit and were relatively unharmed.

	106 Sqn	Lancaster III	ND501 ZN-K		Training

F/O K A Smythe RAAF   Landed 0230 at Metheringham from a night flying
exercise, but promptly swung from the runway and
lost its undercarriage. No one was hurt, but the Lancaster was wrecked.

3 Apr 1945	625 Sqn	Lancaster I	NG237 CF-S		Op: Nordhausen

F/S T P Collier   +   T/o 1329 Kelstern to bomb a military barracks.
F/S G B Valentine   +   Crashed circa 1645 at Visbedden (Limburg) some
Sgt D Morrison   +   6 km ESE from Leopoldsburg, where all rest in
Sgt G J Sheldon   +   the local war cemetery. Seconds before the air-
Sgt A Bennett   +   craft hit the ground, a wing came off. Their
Sgt E G Ewington   +   average age was 22; until recently, the tail
Sgt J K McIntosh   +   gunner, Sgt McIntosh, had been an ATC cadet.

	626 Sqn	Lancaster I	PA190 UM-G2		Op: Nordhausen

F/O L K Driver RNZAF   +   T/o 1315 Wickenby similarly tasked. Presumed
Sgt A W Scott   +   lost off the Dutch coast. On 16 June, the body
WO2 E J O'Rourke RCAF   +   of Sgt Keeble was washed ashore near Hellevoet-
F/O J G Hallowell   +   sluis; he rests in Rotterdam (Crooswijk) General
Sgt G W E Keeble   +   Cemetery. The others have no known graves.
F/S J L Cooke RCAF   +   Similar to the crew reported above, their
F/S L Cockerham RCAF   +   average age was twenty-two.

3-4 Apr 1945	139 Sqn	Mosquito XX	KB349 XD-F		Op: Berlin

S/L T R A Dow DFC   +   T/o 2128 Upwood. Both officers are buried in
F/L J S Endersby   +   Berlin 1939-1945 War Cemetery. S/L Dow is
believed to have been flying his 65th sortie.

4 Apr 1945	49 Sqn	Lancaster III	ME308 EA-F		Op: Nordhausen

F/O A E Fischer RAAF   +   T/o 0629 Fulbeck to bomb the military barracks.
Sgt D G Parbery   +   F/O Fischer RAAF is buried in Berlin 1939-1945
F/S H R Sproston   +   War Cemetery, while Sgt Simmonds lies in Venray
Sgt G H Simmonds   +   War Cemetery, having been brought here from the
Sgt F F Sinclair   +   US Military Cemetery at Margraten. This suggests
Sgt F Wright   +   his body was first found by an American graves
F/S T B Moore   +   inspection team. The others are commemorated
on the Runnymede Memorial.

	105 Sqn	Mosquito XVI	MM134 GB-		Air Test

F/L P Enderby DFC   +   T/o 1101 Bourn but the port engine failed as
the Mosquito climbed. Eye witnesses then say
that the aircraft began to turn quite gently before losing height and falling
near the airfield. F/L Enderby is buried in Horncastle Cemetery. On the day
of his death, confirmation of his entitlement to wear permanently the Pathfinder Force badge was received by 105 Squadron and promulgated.

4-5 Apr	7 Sqn	Lancaster I	NG229 MG-S	Op: Harburg
1945				

F/L B S H Wadham DFC   +
F/O S C Haralambides DFC   +
F/L R C Halkyard DFC RAAF   +
F/S H W Ellis   +
F/O H T Evans RAAF   +
WO2 E K Coyne DFC RCAF   +
F/S H Minns   +

T/o 1955 Oakington to mark the Rhenania oil plant. F/L Wadham, who had flown over fifty-three sorties, and four others are buried in Becklingen War Cemetery; F/S Minns and F/O Haralambides whose parents, Constantinos and Sofia Haralambides, lived at Kaimakli on Cyprus rest in Hannover War Cemetery.

---

12 Sqn   **Lancaster I**   **RF182 PH-P**   **Op: Lutzkendorf**

F/L W Kroeker RCAF   +
F/S C Brooks   +
F/L W D Smith RCAF   +
F/O C E Modeland RCAF   +
F/O J F Woodcherry   +
F/O C W G Biddlecombe   +
F/O G T Wood   +

T/o 2054 Wickenby to bomb an oil refinery. Crashed near the small town of Braunsbedra some 10 km SW of Merseburg. F/O Kroeker RCAF is reported to have been a second tour pilot with sixteen sorties completed. Along with his crew, he rests in Berlin 1939-1945 War Cemetery. It may be recalled that all, apart from F/O Biddlecombe, had spent the best part of a year interned in Sweden (see Volume 5 page 26), eventually returning to Wickenby on 25 September 1944.

---

78 Sqn   **Halifax III**   **MZ460 EY-R**   **Op: Harburg**

F/L R E Cox   +
Sgt J S Johnston   +
F/L A J Lewsley   +
P/O A K Taylor   +
P/O B M E McLeod RAAF   +
P/O J G Burns   +
F/O M H Pattison   +

T/o 1956 Breighton to bomb the Rhenania oil plant. Believed to have exploded with great force, scattering debris and bodies over a wide area, as burials are traced to cemeteries at Hamburg, Hannover and Becklingen. F/L Cox was the son of Thomas Edwin Cox MBE of Cerne Abbas, a Dorsetshire village famous for its figure of a giant carved in the nearby chalk hillside. P/O Burns came from Curragh, Co. Kildare in the Republic of Ireland.

---

103 Sqn   **Lancaster I**   **LM177 PM-Z**   **Op: Gardening**

F/O L Hole RAAF   +
Sgt E Kelly   +
F/S C J Hodge RAAF   +
F/S S A Jeffrey RAAF   +
F/S S D Pearce RAAF   +
F/O V L Vallentine RAAF   +
F/S E F Shannon RAAF   +

T/o 1920 Elsham Wolds and set course for the Kattegat. Lost without trace. The Runnymede Memorial commemorates their names. Their average age was 22. Apart from the Australians serving with RAAF bomber squadrons, this was the last mainly RAAF crew to be posted missing in action during World War II. Two, F/S Jeffrey RAAF and F/O Vallentine RAAF came from St. Kilda in the State of Victoria.

---

115 Sqn   **Lancaster I**   **HK555 KO-E**   **Op: Leuna**

F/L T A O'Halloran   +
WO2 E L Luxton RCAF   +
F/S C E Marchant   +
F/S W G Carr   +
F/O A E Adams   +
W/O G R Saville RAAF   +
Sgt E Sheavills   +
Sgt J T Buckley   +

T/o 1911 Witchford to bomb synthetic-oil plant. Outbound, collided at 2020 with a 186 Squadron Lancaster, wreckage from both machines being scattered between the Waldhof Elgershausen and Greifenthal, 7 km S of Sinn. Seven are buried in Rheinberg War Cemetery, but F/S Marchant lies in Holland at Nederweert War Cemetery, having been found by forestry workers in the spring of 1946 and, subsequently, handed over to the US Mortuary Service, then located in the Storchenstrasse at Sinn.

Note. Claudio Michael Becker of Sinn, to whom I am indebted for most of the information summarised above, writes, "the area in which the two aircraft crashed was taken by American forces at around 0800 hours, local time, on 27 March 1945." As far as it can be established, the four Lancasters lost from 115 Squadron during bombing operations in 1945, none were as a direct result of enemy action.

---

142 Sqn   **Mosquito XXV**   **KB481 4H-P**   **Op: Magdeburg**

F/L K Pudsey DFM Twice MID +
F/O J R D Morgan DFC   +

T/o 2020 Gransden Lodge. Lost without trace. Both officers are commemorated on the Runnymede Memorial. F/L Pudsey had gained his DFM while serving with 115 Squadron, details being published in the London Gazette on 15 June 1943. He had flown at least 74 operational sorties.

4-5 Apr 1945	153 Sqn	Lancaster I	NX563 P4-R	Op: Gardening

F/L A J Winder	+	T/o 1907 Scampton. Lost without trace. All are
Sgt G E Thomson	+	commemorated on the Runnymede Memorial.
F/O L C Turner	+	
F/O E O Griffith	+	
F/S J B Coffey	+	
F/O A S Blake	+	
Sgt I A Birrell	+	

	153 Sqn	Lancaster I	RA544 P4-U	Op: Gardening

W/C F S Powley DFC AFC	+	T/o 1903 Scampton. Lost without trace. All are
Sgt C F Sadler	+	commemorated on the Runnymede Memorial with the
F/S L G Sims	+	names of F/S Sims and both air gunners carved on
F/S W Higgins	+	panel 272. W/C Powley was a Canadian from
W/O A S Dickson RAAF	+	Kelowna in British Colombia. He had joined the
F/S C Madden	+	pre-war regular air force on a Short Service
F/S R Neal	+	Commission circa 1936. His service number shows
		he was a contemporary of the legendary W/C Guy
		Penrose Gibson VC.

Note. Reliable private sources in Holland suggest both Lancasters were shot down over the Kattegat by Major Werner Husemann of I./NJG3.

	166 Sqn	Lancaster I	LM289 AS-Y	Op: Lutzkendorf

F/O R A Ayton RNZAF	inj	T/o 2116 Kirmington to attack the Wintershall
Sgt K H Butcher	+	synthetic-oil plant. On return, came down 0536
Sgt A G S Laidlaw	+	near Mill Farm, Barnetby le Wold, a village on
F/S R J McL Bell RNZAF	+	the W side of the home airfield and on the rail
Sgt A Nicholson	+	link twixt Scunthorpe and Grimsby, Lincolnshire.
Sgt D J Barlow	+	Those who died are buried in various cemeteries,
Sgt J Benson	inj	three being taken to Cambridge City Cemetery.

F/S Bell's brother, Peter Garvin Bell, died on active service. Sgt Barlow was a recipient of the Bronze Medal awarded by the Royal Society for the Prevention of Cruelty to Animals in 1934.

	166 Sqn	Lancaster III	ND707 AS-E	Op: Lutzkendorf

F/O J Day	+	T/o 2111 Kirmington similarly instructed. All
Sgt F Pilling	+	are buried in Berlin 1939-1945 War Cemetery.
Sgt A P Poon-Tip	+	Sgt Fitzpatrick came from New Ross, Co. Wexford
Sgt R F S Dunkley	+	in the Irish Republic.
Sgt L F McGuire	+	
Sgt P Fitzpatrick	+	
Sgt J D Whitelaw	+	

	186 Sqn	Lancaster I	HK767 AP-A	Op: Leuna

F/L E L Field DFC		T/o 1843 Stradishall to bomb oil installations.
Sgt W J Enwright	inj	Hit by flak, over the target area, which wrecked
F/S P A Upson		the port outer engine. On return to base, the
F/O G W Littleboy		port inner cut as the crew tried to align with
F/S C J Morris		the runway and though overshoot procedures were
Sgt W R O'Connell		initiated, the Lancaster crashed 0300 into a
F/S C F Turner	inj	field adjoining the airfield. Two members of
		the crew sustained fractured bones. All were

screened, F/L Field being awarded an immediate First Bar to his DFC. Later, DFMs for F/S Morris and F/S Turner were Gazetted on 25 September and 28 October 1945 respectively.

	186 Sqn	Lancaster I	RA533 AP-P	Op: Leuna

F/O J A G Beck DFC RAAF	+	T/o 1847 Stradishall similarly tasked. Lost
Sgt P McNiven	+	in the circumstances described against the 115
P/O A E Bartlett	inj	Squadron crew. Those who died were identified
F/S W G Evans	+	by P/O Bartlett, who was not too seriously hurt,
F/S S R Bacon RAAF	+	and taken for burial at Ittenbach, though since
Sgt A R Baker	+	1945, their bodies have been transferred to
Sgt G Ballinger	+	Rheinberg War Cemetery. It is believed P/O
		Bartlett had served previously with 50 Squadron

surviving a serious Lancaster crash on 12 February 1944 (see Volume 5 page 74). Furthermore, Sgt Baker is reported to have fought in the Spanish Civil War.

4-5 Apr 1945	408 Sqn	Halifax VII	NP712 EQ-N	Op: Harburg

P/O A K Brown RCAF   pow
Sgt R A Hind   pow
F/O W G Burnett RCAF   pow
P/O T C King RCAF   pow
F/S J B Bennett RCAF   pow
P/O F W Trow RCAF   pow
F/S K G Finn RCAF   pow

T/o 1943 Linton-on-Ouse to bomb the Rhenania oil plant. It is believed all were taken into captivity, though "safe" has been annotated on the loss card against each name. All were experienced with twenty-four sorties apiece.

424 Sqn	Lancaster I	RF150 QB-W	Op: Leuna

F/O J W Watson RCAF   +
P/O E T Ashdown RCAF   +
F/O J Rochford RCAF   +
P/O C N Armstrong RCAF   +
P/O S McL Thomson RCAF   +
P/O S J O Robinson RCAF   +
P/O C K Howes RCAF   +

T/o 1808 Skipton-on-Swale to bomb oil refining facilities. Homebound, flew into a hillside at 0220 at Widdeston Park, some 3 miles SW from High Wycombe, Buckinghamshire and not far distant from the headquarters that had planned their last fateful mission. All were taken to Brookwood Military Cemetery. Both air gunners were nineteen years of age.

460 Sqn	Lancaster I	RF196 AR-E	Op: Lutzkendorf

F/L W Langcake RAAF
P/O B J Vogt RAAF
Sgt J Scoular
F/S A Albans
Sgt B Gavin
F/S J P Lillis RAAF   inj
Sgt D Hopkinson
Sgt J Hankey

T/o 2120 Binbrook to attack the Wintershall synthetic oil plant. Bombed the AP at 0130 from 12,000 feet and set course for base. At 0511 the Lancaster crash-landed on high ground at Rothwell Top, not far from the airfield. F/S Lillis RAAF was thrown forward on impact and sustained a broken nose, The rest seem to have escaped with no more than a bad shaking.

462 Sqn	Halifax III	RG432 Z5-A	Op: BS

F/O J W O'Sullivan RAAF
Sgt T A Brown
F/O J M Smith RAAF
F/O V J Corbett RCAF
F/S B L Mantton RAAF
F/O A H Brown RAAF
F/S L J Mongan RAAF
F/S D H McLean RAAF

T/o 1900 Foulsham. Overshot on return to base at 2233, following failure of the port inner engine. In the ensuing crash, the undercarriage collapsed. No one was hurt. F/O Brown RAAF was the specialist operator.

550 Sqn	Lancaster III	ME301 BQ-K	Op: Lutzkendorf

F/O M D Hayes   +
Sgt H Hartley   +
F/S E H Hagyard   +
F/S M V Fuller   +
W/O A T Gill   +
Sgt R S Smith   +
Sgt D Gunn   +

T/o 2104 North Killingholme to attack synthetic oil production facilities. All are buried in Berlin 1939-1945 War Cemetery. Despite being aged 20, F/O Hayes had flown at least twenty-two sorties. His flight engineer, Sgt Hartley, was 36, well over the average age of Bomber Command airmen. Until recently, both air gunners had been cadets in the Air Training Corps.

571 Sqn	Mosquito XVI	RV305 8K-A	Op: Magdeburg

W/O A B Clarke RNZAF   +
F/S A C Beaton   +

T/o Oakington. W/O Clarke RNZAF, married to Eve Ivy Clarke of Richmond in Surrey, is perpetuated on panel 285 of the Runnymede Memorial while his Scottish born navigator, who in civilian life was a Chartered Secretary, rests in Berlin at the city's 1939-1945 War Cemetery.

576 Sqn	Lancaster III	ME671 UL-V2	Op: Lutzkendorf

Sgt D H Hogg   pow
Sgt J R Reed   pow
Sgt S Cranidge   pow
Sgt J W Foster   pow
Sgt J Tyrer   pow
Sgt W K Monksfield   pow
Sgt H J Allen   +

T/o Fiskerton to bomb the Wintershall synthetic oil plant. Roughly 30 minutes before the crash Sgt Allen, who had suffered a very severe head wound, baled out from 500 feet. He is buried in Berlin 1939-1945 War Cemetery.

Note. This was the last all Sergeant ranked crew to be reported missing from a Bomber Command operation over Germany. As previously mentioned, single-ranked crews by this stage of the war were no longer the norm as had been the case between the summers of 1940 and 1944.

4–5 Apr	626 Sqn	Lancaster I	PD295 UM-B2	Op: Lutzkendorf

1945
```
          F/L K H Eames DFC            +
          Sgt G H Fletcher             +
          F/O A D Moore                +
          F/O W Young                  +
          P/O W A Mitcham              +
          Sgt R F Clarke               +
          Sgt G Davies                 +
```
T/o 2101 Wickenby to strike at the Wintershall synthetic-oil plant. Presumed lost over the sea. Four are buried in France; Sgt Fletcher, found near Den Helder on 18 June 1945, lies on Texel in Den Burg General Cemetery, while F/L Eames and F/O Young are commemorated on the Memorial at Runnymede.

	626 Sqn	Lancaster III	PB411 UM-Y2	Op: Lutzkendorf
```
          F/O H W Reid RCAF            +
          F/S H G Reed                 +
          F/O W Semeniuk RCAF          +
          F/O D H Johnson RCAF         +
          F/O B E S Stagg              +
          F/O M F E Sergeant RCAF      +
          Sgt J W Churms RCAF          +
```
T/o 2055 Wickenby similarly tasked. All are lying in the 1939-1945 War Cemetery in Berlin.

	635 Sqn	Lancaster I	PB949 F2-T	Op: Harburg
```
          F/L P E Cawthorne DFC RAAF   +
          F/S B R McMaster           pow
          P/O G Wilson               evd
          P/O B G Roberts            pow
          F/O F M Williams           pow
          W/O T Reid RAAF              +
          F/S R V Moore                +
          WO2 I J Kinney RCAF          +
```
T/o 2004 Downham Market to mark the Rhenania oil plant. Those who died lie in Becklingen War Cemetery. At 18, WO2 Kinney RCAF was amongst the youngest Canadians to be killed on Pathfinder duties in 1945.

5 Apr	617 Sqn	Lancaster I	PB415 KC-O	Ferry

1945
```
          Lt W Adams USAAF
          P/O J Langston
```
T/o 1130 Woodhall Spa to collect a crew who had delivered a Lancaster for storage at 46 MU. Overshot and crash-landed 1350 at Lossiemouth airfield, Scotland, after trying to land ahead of another aircraft, and thus touched down too far down the runway. No injuries reported.

Note. Built as a Lancaster III, this aircraft was converted to Mk.I standards prior to issue to 617 Squadron.

6 Apr	50 sqn	Lancaster I	NG271 VN-	Op: IJmuiden

1945
```
          F/O R W Turrell RCAF
          F/S A J Gibbins
          P/O T Illingworth
          F/O A Petts RCAF
          Sgt A Dobson
          F/S J A Edwards RCAF
          F/S E F C Heacock RCAF     inj
```
T/o 0842 Skellingthorpe for an attack on shipping but the port outer failed and despite jettisoning twelve of the 14 bombs, height could not be maintained and the Lancaster came down six minutes later in Waddington village. A fire broke out but there are no reports of serious injury to either crew or villagers.

6–7 Apr	428 Sqn	Lancaster X	KB795 NA-Q	Training

1945
```
          F/L R La Turner RCAF
```
Landed 0024 Middleton St. George but swung off the runway. With the prospects of running off the airfield, the undercarriage was deliberately raised and this action damaged the Lancaster beyond repair. No injuries reported.

7 Apr	346 Sqn	Halifax VI	RG592 H7-P	Training

1945
```
          Slt W P Gridele FFAF
```
T/o 1051 Elvington. Returned to base at 1145 but landed heavily, swung and crashed out of control. No injuries reported.

Note. This was the first Halifax VI written off by 346 Squadron.

7–8 Apr	9 Sqn	Lancaster I	HK788 WS-E	Op: Molbis

1945
```
          F/O A E Jeffs                +
          Sgt C V Higgins              +
          F/S K C Mousley              +
          WO2 H A Fisher RCAF          +
          F/S C McI McMillan           +
          F/S W Thomas                 +
          F/S G J Symonds              +
```
T/o 1837 Bardney to bomb a benzol plant. Homebound, caught fire in flight and dived into the ground at Lyford, 4 miles NNW of Wantage, Berkshire. All are buried in Oxford (Botley) Cemetery, North Hinksey. F/O Jeffs and his flight engineer, Sgt Higgins, came from Birmingham. At 36, F/S Mousley was at least 16 years senior to the last three named.

8-9 Apr 1945	9 Sqn	Lancaster I	NG235 WS-H	Op: Lutzkendorf

9 Sqn — Lancaster I — NG235 WS-H — Op: Lutzkendorf

F/O B S Woolstencroft RAAF +
Sgt W C Lewis +
F/S L A Bayley RAAF +
F/O C P W Warren +
F/S L Robinson +
Sgt G T Greenwood +
Sgt E Williams pow

T/o 1826 Bardney to bomb an oil refinery. Those who lost their lives are buried in Berlin at the city's 1939-1945 War Cemetery located in the Charlottenburg district.

10 Sqn — Halifax III — LK753 ZA-V — Op: Hamburg

P/O J Currie RNZAF +
Sgt J R Switzer RCAF +
F/S J Parkin +
F/S J E Gallacher inj
Sgt W R Sinnett inj
Sgt L Squire +
Sgt M K Fortin +

T/o 1934 Melbourne. Presumed to have crashed in Allied held territory as those who died are reported to have been buried in the Nordfriedhof at Düsseldorf, though their graves are now in the Reichswald Forest War Cemetery. The two survivors were admitted to hospital.

10 Sqn — Halifax III — RG424 ZA-T — Op: Hamburg

F/S W J Hicks
Sgt J Cotton
F/S B Clifton
F/S R Tufnell
Sgt L Grimwood
Sgt C H Birch
Sgt R Drewett

T/o 1920 Melbourne. On return to base at 0131 the undercarriage collapsed, damaging the bomber beyond economical repair. No injuries reported.

35 Sqn — Lancaster I — NG440 TL-C — Op: Hamburg

S/L M M V L Muller +
F/S A C Barr +
F/L H Cobb DFM +
F/L P B O Ranalow inj
F/O J L Vickery +
F/O T B Robinson +
F/O R C Webster +
F/S C Wilce DFM pow

T/o 1942 Graveley. Believed hit by flak in the nose, bursting into flames and breaking up befor crashing 2300 near Rotenburg (Wümme). F/L Rana-low died from his injuries on 10 April and he is buried, with the others who died, in Becklingen War Cemetery. F/L Cobb had flown his first tour in Hampdens with 144 Squadron and details of his DFM were published on 26 May 1942. That awarded to F/S Wilce had appeared in the London Gazette on 30 June 1944, and had been gained with 61 Squadron. F/O Vickery was flying as a second air bomber.

Note. This was the first Lancaster I reported missing from 35 Squadron.

49 Sqn — Lancaster I — RA531 EA-S — Op: Lutzkendorf

F/O R G Perkins +
Sgt H Prust +
Sgt P J Warrington +
F/S J E Wilkinson +
Sgt G R Wall +
Sgt B C Manning +
Sgt D F Hull +

T/o 1811 Fulbeck to bomb an oil refinery. All are buried in Berlin 1939-1945 War Cemetery. Nineteen year old Sgt Manning was an ex-ATC cadet, while Sgt Hull was a year younger. As such, they were amongst the youngest air gunners killed on bombing operations in the last weeks of the war.

49 Sqn — Lancaster III — PB374 EA-N — Op: Lutzkendorf

F/O R Cluer +
Sgt P Lipp +
Sgt P F C Jackson +
F/O M R McKay RCAF +
F/S J H McGuigan RAAF +
Sgt G A McLennan +
F/S R E Wilkins +

T/o 1826 Fulbeck similarly tasked. Lost without trace. All are commemorated on the Runnymede Memorial. F/O Cluer was the son of His Honour Mr Justice R M Cluer of Cookham Dean, Berkshire. Sgt Lipp was 39, well above the average age of airmen employed on operational duty.

61 Sqn — Lancaster III — ME385 QR-O — Op: Lutzkendorf

F/O J A MacFarlane RCAF +
Sgt A P Moreton +
F/S W G Howitt +
F/S J Chadwick evd
F/S C Plant +
Sgt H A Paterson +
F/S E F Coster RCAF pow

T/o 1812 Skellingthorpe similarly instructed. Hit by flak and partially abandoned before crashing into a quarry near the target. Those who died rest in Berlin 1939-1945 War Cemetery having been brought here from graves found at Lützkendorf.

8-9 Apr
1945

78 Sqn		Halifax III	MZ361 EY-D	Op: Hamburg

F/L V L Jackson	inj
Sgt C K Gray	inj
WO2 T W Fry RCAF	+
F/S J M Pougnet RCAF	+
Sgt M H Steele	+
F/O F G Jones	inj
F/S J Sims	inj

T/o 1928 Breighton. Crashed 0146 after hitting high ground at Farberry Garth Farm near Pocklington airfield, Yorkshire. Weather conditions at the time of the accident are described as poor with low cloud mixed with fog blanketing much of the area. Both Canadians were taken to Harrogate (Stonefall) Cemetery, while Sgt Steele rests in Shoreham-by-Sea Cemetery.

408 Sqn		Halifax VII	NP769 EQ-D	Op: Hamburg

F/O A P Jensen RCAF	+
Sgt A Thorp	+
F/O J C Cunningham RCAF	+
F/O A McL Taylor RCAF	+
F/S J D Walker RCAF	+
F/S R I Smylie RCAF	pow
F/S R A Duncan RCAF	+

T/o 1910 Linton-on-Ouse. Crashed 2230 near Heidenau, 5 km NW of Tostedt. Those who lost their lives were buried at the crash site but have since been brought to Becklingen War Cemetery. At 35, F/S Cunningham RCAF was older than the majority of airmen flying in Bomber Command.

419 Sqn		Lancaster X	KB752 VR-V	Op: Hamburg

F/O H R Cram RCAF	
F/S J T R E Case	
F/O W Olenoski RCAF	
F/O F S Crawford RCAF	
WO2 C S A Hanna RCAF	
Sgt E K McGrath RCAF	evd
Sgt G R Hughes RCAF	

T/o 1917 Middleton St. George. Outbound, the starboard inner failed but the crew continued with their assignment. Homebound, the starboard outer burst into flames and though the blaze was extinguished, the order to bale out was given. Sgt McGrath RCAF landed in enemy held territory but he evaded and returned home safely. F/O Cram RCAF was engaged on the third sortie of his second tour of operations.

463 Sqn		Lancaster I	NX584 JO-V	Op: Lutzkendorf

F/O T H Baulderstone RAAF	+
Sgt W S Philip	+
F/S J W Hill RAAF	+
F/O R R A Adrain RCAF	+
WO1 J Bomby RCAF	+
Sgt B Blythe	+
Sgt D Broadhead	evd

T/o 1812 Waddington to bomb an oil refinery. Over the target area, predicted flak hit the Lancaster between the starboard mainplane and tail, causing the aircraft to roll over to port. Control was reestablished and Sgt Broadhead heard the air bomber advise that all bombs were away, over the AP. The flight engineer then called to say that the starboard wing was on fire. Course was set for the Allied lines, but the starboard engines had to be stopped which made control of the aircraft extremely difficult to maintain. Eventually, Sgt Broadhead heard his skipper order everyone to bale out. Having freed himself from the tree, where he landed, the rear gunner walked for the next 48 hours until he found himself in safe hands with American forces W of Erfurt. No trace of his crew were found and their names are commemorated on the Runnymede Memorial. F/S Hill RAAF had qualified as a Bachelor of Laws (Sydney). F/O Adrain RCAF was 35, while both air gunners were ex-ATC cadets.

463 Sqn		Lancaster III	ME478 JO-M	Op: Lutzkendorf

F/O N S Ferris RAAF	
F/S N Bigwood	
F/O S D Richardson RAAF	
F/S I B Cliff RAAF	
W/O M R Bitmead RAAF	
F/S C Brown RAAF	
F/S J Hayes RAAF	

T/o 1813 Waddington similarly tasked. Hit by flak which knocked out both inner engines. At 2255 bombs were jettisoned from 16,000 feet and following a steady loss of height all baled out from 3,200 feet, roughly 25 km SW of Kassel. Later, some of the crew, all of whom are noted as being "safe", were taken to the 61st Troop Carrier Squadron at Kiel.

466 Sqn		Halifax III	LW172 HD-F	Op: Hamburg

F/O D J Watson RAAF	+
P/O R S King	+
F/L W A C Patterson DFC	+
P/O G A Halliday RAAF	+
F/O R M Gale	+
P/O A J Dunn RAAF	+
F/O W G Flynn DFM	+

T/o 1946 Driffield. Encountered fog on return and while trying to locate the airfield, the Halifax flew into trees and crashed 0115 at Kirkburn Grange Farm, some 2 miles W of the aerodrome. All rest in various UK cemeteries. F/O Flynn had served with 76 Squadron, details of his award having been published in the London Gazette on 14 September 1943.

Note. This Halifax was named "Get Up Them Stairs", flying 97 sorties.

| 8-9 Apr | 466 Sqn | Halifax III | NP968 HD- | | Op: Hamburg |
| 1945 | | | | |

F/O R R N Forrest MID RAAF +   T/o 1945 Driffield. F/O Forrest RAAF is
Sgt P R Woodmore   pow   buried in Hannover War Cemetery; Sgt Frankal
Sgt B M Frankal   +   is commemorated on panel 274 of the Runnymede
F/S J M Dyer RAAF   pow   Memorial. Although shown here as prisoners of
W/O A S Caddie RNZAF   pow   war, the loss card merely describes the sur-
Sgt F N Bridger   pow   vivors as "safe".
Sgt D Smith   pow

630 Sqn   **Lancaster III**   **ND949 LE-Z**   **Op: Lutzkendorf**

F/O C R M Richardson RAAF +   T/o 1837 East Kirkby to bomb an oil refining
Sgt B Gibbons   +   facility. Homebound, diverted due to poor
F/S H E Burton RAAF   +   weather conditions but crashed 0310 at Foxton,
F/O R Martin RAAF   +   3 miles NW of Market Harborough, Leicestershire.
F/O W Forrester RAAF   +   Four are buried in Oxford (Botley) Cemetery at
F/S A E Bowman RAAF   +   North Hinksey. Sgt Gibbons, a qualified pilot
F/S F J Howlett RAAF   +   but flying as the flight engineer, rests in
Norton (St. Nicholas) Churchyard at Letchworth;
F/O Martin RAAF is believed to have been claimed by a relative as he lies in
Sunderland (Southwick) Cemetery, while F/S Howlett RAAF was taken to Cambridge
City Cemetery.

640 Sqn   **Halifax VI**   **RG552 C8-B**   **Op: Hamburg**

F/O H Goldie   T/o 1943 Leconfield. Visibility was extremely
Sgt D E Birch   poor when the crew returned to base and this
F/S J Palmer   resulted in a heavy landing at 0127, followed
F/S R Miles   by a total collapse of the main undercarriage
Sgt K J Moore   which left the Halifax damaged beyond repair.
Sgt J Botterill
Sgt J Potts

Note. This was the first Halifax VI written off by 640 Squadron.

| 9 Apr | 50 Sqn | Lancaster I | NG342 VN-S | | Op: Hamburg |
| 1945 | | | | |

F/O V G Berriman RAAF +   T/o 1442 Skellingthorpe to bomb oil-storage
Sgt E Ford   +   tanks. Crashed in the target area. All are
F/S G E R Westacott   +   buried locally in Hamburg Cemetery, Ohlsdorf.
F/S J P Newbigging   +
Sgt E A Walker   +
F/S A W Jones   +
F/S N L G Felton   +

61 Sqn   **Lancaster I**   **RF121 QR-J**   **Op: Hamburg**

F/L A P Greenfield DFC +   T/o 1445 Skellingthorpe similarly tasked.
     RAAF   Those who perished now rest in Becklingen
Sgt W J A Fraser   pow   War Cemetery. F/L Greenfield RAAF had flown
F/O W J A Gibb   +   somewhere in the region of 32 operational
F/S W J Haddon   +   sorties.
W/O V P Smith   +
F/S J R King   +
F/S S D P Goodey   pow

571 Sqn   **Mosquito XVI**   **MM148 8K-**   **Air Test**

F/O R F Sturgeon   T/o 1457 Oakington. During the test a glycol
leakage developed in the starboard engine and
the unit was shut down. Returning to base, F/L Sturgeon made a fast approach
and, subsequently, landed 1515 without sufficient runway for the Mosquito to
stop. The undercarriage was retracted, damaging the aircraft to the extent
that the Martin Hearn repair facility struck the airframe off charge on 7 May.

| 9-10 Apr | 10 Sqn | Halifax III | HX286 ZA-R | | Op: Stade |
| 1945 | | | | |

F/S E S Beaumont   T/o 1949 Melbourne. Bombed the AP at 2227 from
Sgt F Kristoff RCAF   18,000 feet, followed at 2307 by failure of the
Sgt R Thomas   starboard inner. Due to lack of oil pressure,
Sgt T V Howell   the propeller could not be feathered and with
W/O J M Vick RAAF   the unit vibrating badly F/S Beaumont was obliged
Sgt P Paxton   to keep the throttles open. Then flames appeared
Sgt R E Howard   and soon afterwards the crew baled out, landing
in territory held by the 2nd British Army.

| 9-10 Apr 1945 | 170 Sqn | Lancaster I | PB704 TC-R | Op: Kiel |

	F/S R H A Thorpe	+
	F/S H V Blakey	+
	F/O J Wotherspoon	+
	Sgt F W R Goodenough	+
	Sgt A A Jarvis	+
	Sgt R J Harford	+
	Sgt L A Hill	+

T/o 1932 Hemswell. Lost without trace. All are commemorated on the Runnymede Memorial. The last three named were all aged nineteen.

| | 300 Sqn | Lancaster III | LM632 BH-O | Op: Kiel |

	S/L H A Rudakowski PAF	+
	Sgt S P Krasinski PAF	+
	P/O S P Kucharski PAF	+
	F/S J Stebnicki PAF	+
	F/S W N Gold PAF	+
	Sgt J Parol PAF	+
	Sgt Z Szymanski PAF	+

T/o 1956 Faldingworth. Two, Sgt Krasinski PAF and F/S Stebnicki PAF are buried in Kiel War Cemetery. The others are presumed lost at sea. Thus, all will be named on the Polish Air Force Memorial at Northolt.

| | 571 Sqn | Mosquito XVI | MM169 8K-C | Op: Plauen |

| | F/L W H Clegg RNZAF |
| | F/O A E Spencer |

and losing its undercarriage.

T/o 2024 Oakington to mark the railway yards. Returned on one engine but overshot and crash-landed at 0133 after running onto uneven ground. No injuries reported.

| | 622 Sqn | Lancaster I | NG447 GI-U | Op: Kiel |

	F/L L A S Hodge	+
	F/S S G Taylor	+
	F/S W M L Green RCAF	+
	F/O G W Gell RCAF	+
	F/O A S Seymour	+
	Sgt W E Lewis	
	Sgt W A Parsons	+

T/o 1934 Mildenhall. Believed shot down by a night-fighter and crashed 2240 at Dörphof, 6 km SSE of Kappeln. Those who died are buried in Kiel War Cemetery. The loss card describes Sgt Lewis as "safe" and receiving hospital treatment.

| 10 Apr 1945 | 109 Sqn | Mosquito XVI | RV301 HS- | Air Test |

| | F/L J W Shaw |

T/o 1110 Little Staughton but swung off the runway, whereupon an undercarriage leg gave way and the Mosquito was effectively damaged beyond repair. This had been F/L Shaw's third attempt to become airborne and the accident investigators concluded he might have been advised to give up after aborting his second try.

| | 415 Sqn | Halifax III | NA185 6U-B | Op: Leipzig |

	F/O R S Evans RCAF	+
	Sgt J M Andrews	+
	F/O L M Spry RCAF	+
	F/O L E Veitch RCAF	+
	F/S M J Burns RCAF	+
	F/S D L Lorenz RCAF	+
	F/S R D Teevin RCAF	+

T/o 1347 East Moor for a raid on the Engelsdorf and Mockau railway yards. Panel 278 of the Runnymede Memorial perpetuates the name of F/O Evans RCAF; his crew, however, rest in Berlin 1939-1945 War Cemetery. All had arrived from 76 (RCAF) Base on 10 January 1945, since when F/O Evans RCAF had flown 23 sorties.

| | 433 Sqn | Lancaster I | PB903 BM-F | Op: Leipzig |

	F/O R J Grisdale RCAF	+
	Sgt W A J Thurston	+
	F/O I B Zierler RCAF	+
	F/O W G McLeod RCAF	+
	F/S J M Hirak RCAF	+
	F/S F G Seeley RCAF	+
	F/S D W Roberts RCAF	+

T/o 1317 Skipton-on-Swale similarly tasked. Hit by predicted flak just short of the AP. A fire was seen to break out in the starboard inner engine, though the flames were soon quelled. Height was lost, followed by a small explosion which turned the Lancaster onto its back. Diving steeply, the bomber hit the ground and exploded. All are buried in Berlin 1939-1945 War Cemetery.

| 10-11 Apr 1945 | 44 Sqn | Lancaster III | ND631 KM-B | Op: Leipzig |

	F/O P W Kennedy	+
	P/O G C R Woodhouse	+
	Sgt E P P Olson	+
	WO2 A F D Turner RCAF	+
	F/O W J Jones	pow
	F/S J E Short	+
	F/S C McBurney	+
	F/S A E Bull	+

T/o 1831 Spilsby for an attack on the Wahren railway yards. Those who perished rest in the 1939-1945 War Cemetery at Berlin. F/O Kennedy had flown at least 29 sorties. His co-pilot is noted as being the son of Brevet Lt-Col Percy St. John Rance Woodhouse of the Indian Army. F/O Jones is believed to have been liberated by the Soviets.

10-11 Apr
1945

83 Sqn   **Lancaster III**   **ME423 OL-C**   **Op: Leipzig**

F/L D W R Shand	T/o 1822 Coningsby to bomb the Wahren railway
F/S W J Newling	yards. Hit by flak in the bomb bay, setting
F/L W W Simpson	light to the flare clusters. Abandoned and
F/O A McDonald	crashed 20 km E of Fulda, Germany. F/O Naylor,
F/O F J Naylor +	the second air bomber, was first to leave the
W/O E M Annear RAAF	doomed aircraft but is thought to have slipped
F/S P McHale	from his harness as his opened parachute pack
P/O W J Ryekman RCAF	was later recovered. He is buried in Holland
	at Nederweert War Cemetery, having been brought

here from Margraten. The seven survivors arrived home on 14 April.

207 Sqn   **Lancaster III**   **ME472 EM-O**   **Op: Leipzig**

F/L P M Anderson DFC RCAF +	T/o 1807 Spilsby similarly tasked. Arrived over
Sgt E Nichol	the target area and while running up towards the
F/O C M Hewett	AP was hit by predicted flak. Both starboard
F/O K A Larcombe	engines were damaged, as was the mid-upper gun
Sgt C V Collins	turret. Despite this severe damage, the crew
Sgt E J Matthews	made a second approach and bombs were released
Sgt J R Pearl	at 2300 from 14,000 feet. Further damage was
	inflicted, this time on the port side. During

the next hour F/L Anderson RCAF managed to maintain control until his flight
engineer reported oil pressure on the port inner was dropping fast. At 4,000
feet, as ordered, the six survivors baled out and all were soon in safe hands.
F/L Anderson RCAF is buried in Brussels Town Cemetery.

462 Sqn   **Halifax III**   **NA240 Z5-V**   **Op: BS**

P/O A D J Ball RAAF +	T/o 1910 Foulsham on RCM duties in support of
Sgt F Brookes +	5 Group operations. Those who died are buried
F/S N V Evans RAAF +	in Berlin 1939-1945 War Cemetery. Sgt Bookes
F/O M Frank RAAF +	is erroneously shown in the CWGC register as
W/O R R Taylor RAAF +	belonging to 424 Squadron. It is noted that
F/S J M Tait RAAF +	the Halifax had been fitted with H2S, ABC,
F/S M J Hibberd RAAF pow	Piperack and Carpet radio countermeasures
	devices.

571 Sqn   **Mosquito XVI**   **ML963 8K-K**   **Op: Berlin**

F/O R D Oliver evd	T/o 2137 Oakington. Both airmen rejoined their
F/S L M Young RAAF evd	Squadron before the end of the month, F/O Oliver
	reporting as early as 22 April.

Note. One of the Squadron's initial allocation of four aircraft from 692
Squadron on 12 April 1944, Keith Wood has identified at least 91 operational
entries in 571 Squadron ORB.

619 Sqn   **Lancaster I**   **SW254 PG-S**   **Op: Leipzig**

F/L A E McMorran RCAF +	T/o 1831 Strubby to attack the Wahren railway
F/L F Jackson +	yards. Crashed at Löberitz, 4 km NNE of Zörbig
F/L B A Williamson RCAF +	a small town 17 km NE of Halle. Those who died
F/S H J Burke pow	now lie in Berlin 1939-1945 War Cemetery. It
F/O F M Jackson RAAF +	will be recalled that F/L McMorran's elder
P/O J W Chambers +	brother, F/L George Melvin Stark McMorran RCAF,
P/O C T W Perring +	had lost his life on the Squadron in the month
	previous.

Note. An American army report describes the crash location as "Rodigkau" and
that the remains and personal effects of five of those who died were handed to
Herr Rudolf Aterburg, Inspector on the Estate of the Rodigkau Police Chief,
for burial at Rodigkau.

625 Sqn   **Lancaster I**   **PD204 CF-P2**   **Op: Plauen**

F/O J F Mooney RCAF	T/o 1835 Scampton to attack the railway yards.
F/O D Rutherford	Bombed from 10,000 feet at 2309 and soon after-
Sgt R K Colman	wards three engines failed, one after the other.
F/O H H Harding RCAF	Flak, too, hit the aircraft which was abandoned
Sgt Fairhurst	0120 in the vicinity of Bierset some 8 km WNW
Sgt R A Skinner	from the centre of Liege. No serious injuries
Sgt W A Trundle	reported.
Sgt H Morris	

10-11 Apr 1945	630 Sqn	Lancaster I	ME739 LE-T	Op: Leipzig

F/O A V Cameron RAAF pow
Sgt R W Beardwell pow
Sgt G W S Hooper pow
F/S G Gould evd
F/S J E Hogan RAAF pow
Sgt J R Dicken +
Sgt G G E Bourner evd

T/o 1826 East Kirkby to bomb the Wahren railway yards. All are reported to have baled out, but the canopy of Sgt Dicken's parachute caught fire and he fell to his death. His grave is now in France at Choloy War Cemetery, thus it is most likely his body was found by an American graves investigation team. The loss card, in respect of the survivors, is merely annotated "safe".

	630 Sqn	Lancaster I	RF122 LE-S	Op: Leipzig

F/O R J Sassoon +
Sgt S C Walton +
F/O J Hopwood +
F/O P F Fleming pow
F/S M S Munro +
Sgt W H R Jenkins +
F/S I L Lynn pow

T/o 1823 East Kirkby similarly instructed. Those who died lie in Berlin 1939-1945 War Cemetery. It is believed the two survivors sat out the last few weeks of the war in some form of captivity, though both are shown as "safe" on the loss card.

11-12 Apr 1945	163 Sqn	Mosquito XXV	KB502 -U	Op: Berlin

F/O W Houghton +
F/S L A Stegman RAAF +

T/o 2104 Wyton. Both are buried in Berlin at the city's 1939-1945 War Cemetery.

	571 Sqn	Mosquito XVI	PF381 8K-	Op: Berlin

W/O D Little

T/o 2040 Oakington but swung out of control whereupon the port undercarriage leg was torn off. No injuries reported.

	571 Sqn	Mosquito XVI	RV355 8K-	Op: Berlin

S/L D Colby

T/o 2026 Oakington but the port engine boost capsule failed and the Mosquito veered from the runway, losing its undercarriage, and hitting a gun post. No injuries.

Note. Neither 571 Squadron aircraft has been entered in their records, but the former is reported to have operated on at least 101 occasions.

12 Apr 1945	157 Sqn	Mosquito XIX	MM677 RS-	Training

F/S J M Moore +
Sgt T J H Westoby +

T/o Swannington in company with F/S K W Crane. On reaching 12,000 feet, F/S Moore peeled off to provide F/S Crane with the opportunity to carry out a practice interception. When next sighted, F/S Crane reports the target aircraft was at about 9,000 feet and on fire from wing tip to wing tip. Then, diving steeply, the Mosquito fell away, the port wing detaching moments before it struck the ground some 6 miles NW of Feltwell airfield, Norfolk. F/S Moore is buried in Bassenthwaite Halls (St. John) Churchyard; Sgt Westoby rests in Cambridge City Cemetery. Both were aged twenty-two.

12-13 Apr 1945	85 Sqn	Mosquito NF.30	MV555 VY-	Op: BS

F/O W J Baker
F/O F E Lees

T/o Swannington. Overshot on return to base and the undercarriage was raised in order to stop. No injuries reported.

13 Apr 1945	100 Sqn	Lancaster III	LM716 HW-K	Training

W/O P S Tarry

T/o 1642 Grimsby but the port tyre burst and the crew were advised to land at Carnaby. On arrival here at 1812, the Lancaster immediately swerved to the left, the port main undercarriage unit collapsing, followed seconds later by the starboard leg. No one was hurt but the bomber was damaged beyond repair.

	139 Sqn	Mosquito XX	KB148 XD-L	Training

F/O T L Parsons RAAF

T/o 1705 Upwood but on landing at 1720, the Mosquito swerved off the runway and was damaged to the extent that repairs would have been uneconomical. No one was hurt.

	346 Sqn	Halifax III	PN395 H7-	Transit

Cne J Gronier FFAF

T/o 0630 Elvington with a total complement of eighteen. Landed 0855 at Paris-Orly airport, but was swung in order to avoid a group of workmen. At this point the port wheel sunk into a badly filled bomb crater, damaging the Halifax beyond repair.

| 13 Apr 1945 | 571 Sqn | **Mosquito XVI** | RV357 8K- | **Training** |

F/L M J T Cane DFM   +   Crashed in the most tragic circumstances at
P/O R J Mirow RAAF   +   Oakington when the pilot realised his high speed
run at low level across the airfield was taking
him towards a group of trees. Pulling up sharply, the port wing clipped one of
the trees, causing the Mosquito to flick roll, twice, before plunging into the
ground and burst into flames. F/L Cane, whose DFM had been Gazetted on 5 February 1943 following his service in the Middle East with 148 Squadron, rests in
Bromley Hill Cemetery, Lewisham; his navigator lies in Cambridge City Cemetery.

| 13-14 Apr 1945 | 75 Sqn | **Lancaster III** | LM728 AA-R | **Op: Kiel** |

W/O W Evenden   T/o 2044 Mepal to bomb the U-boat yards. Landed
Sgt T Morgan   0225 base, whereupon the undercarriage gave way,
F/S A Staples RNZAF   damaging the Lancaster beyond worthwhile repair.
F/S T Lane   No injuries reported.
F/S W Goddin
F/S N Dixon RNZAF
F/S R Williams RNZAF

| | 85 Sqn | **Mosquito NF.30** | NT494 VY-N | **Op: BS** |

F/L H B Thomas   T/o 2153 Swannington. During the sortie, the
F/O C B Hamilton DFC   +   crew were heard several times on R/T, the first
call to Brussels being monitored at midnight by
a 157 Squadron crew patrolling off Heligoland. Thirty minutes later, F/L J A V
Grisewood, who was flying S of Kiel, heard F/L Thomas asking Woodbridge for
assistance. Then, at 0123, F/L K D Vaughan radioed for a fix, which positioned
his aircraft 180 miles off the east coast, bearing 245 degrees. Immediately, he
heard a voice, which he recognised as F/L Thomas, saying, "get some in Vaughan"
It is then believed a German night-fighter struck, though there are indications
that earlier, while over Denmark, F/L Thomas had been fired at by a Lancaster
and had sustained some damage. His navigator is buried in Hamburg Cemetery,
Ohlsdorf, while the loss card describes the pilot as being "safe".

| | 186 Sqn | **Lancaster III** | PB483 AP-X | **Op: Kiel** |

F/O T P Burson RNZAF   inj   T/o 2010 Stradishall to bomb the U-boat yards.
Sgt E Gunner   +   On return to base, collided 0226 in the circuit
F/S F M Hale   +   with another Lancaster. F/S Bartlett died later
F/S W K J Bartlett   inj   in the day from his injuries. Sgt Somers was
Sgt J A Kean   inj   laid to rest in nearby Haverhill Cemetery; the
Sgt R C Russell   +   others who perished were taken to their home
Sgt J V Somers   +   towns. F/S Hale's brother, John Charles Hale,
died while on active service.

| | 186 Sqn | **Lancaster III** | PB488 AP-J | **Op: Kiel** |

F/O D M Roberts   +   T/o 2017 Stradishall similarly tasked and,
F/S G B Whalley   +   subsequently, destroyed in the manner outlined
F/S J C James   +   above. All rest in various UK cemeteries. The
F/S C Crookes   +   parents of F/O D M Roberts lost two other sons
F/O W E Roberts   +   Gerald Philip and Edward Simpson Roberts. Their
Sgt H Brickell   +   father was Maj Donald Edward Roberts MC JP of
Sgt F J Pape   +   Scarborough.

| | 419 Sqn | **Lancaster X** | KB866 VR-M | **Op: Kiel** |

F/S C C Maclaren RCAF   +   T/o 2022 Middleton St. George similarly tasked.
Sgt G A Livingston RCAF   +   Lost without trace. All are commemorated on the
F/O D W Wincott RCAF   +   Runnymede Memorial. At 36, F/S Wightman RCAF
F/O C R Loft RCAF   +   was amongst the oldest Canadians killed on bombe
WO1 W Henderson RCAF   +   operations in 1945.
F/S E R Wightman RCAF   +
Sgt G J Jones RCAF   +

| | 428 Sqn | **Lancaster X** | KB784 NA-K | **Op: Kiel** |

F/O D M Payne RCAF   pow   T/o 2020 Middleton St. George similarly charged.
Sgt T F Sinclair RCAF   pow   Hit by flak both outbound and homebound. With
F/O G C Riley RCAF   pow   three engines failing, the Lancaster was ditched
F/O V Banks RCAF   pow   F/S Vardy RCAF is commemorated on the Runnymede
WO2 E V Miller RCAF   pow   Memorial. The crew drifted for 12 days before
F/S E R O Casey RCAF   pow   coming ashore. F/O Payne RCAF and F/O Riley RCA
F/S A E Vardy RCAF   +   were later decorated for their supreme courage.

13-14 Apr 1945	428 Sqn	Lancaster X	KB816 NA-E	Op: Kiel

F/L E P Acres RCAF — T/o 2018 Middleton St. George to bomb the U-boat yards. Attacked the target at 2336 from 15,800 feet but on return was ordered to divert to Church Broughton. On arrival, overshot the runway and crash-landed 0240, no injuries being reported.

14-15 Apr 1945	35 Sqn	Lancaster III	PB377 TL-K	Op: Potsdam
	F/O V B Bowen-Morris			
	Sgt W G Reynolds	+		
	F/O R H H Dyers	pow		
	F/S E G Silcock	pow		
	F/S C S Gibbon	pow		
	F/S J W Tovey	evd		
	F/S E G Meredith DFM	pow		

T/o 1840 Graveley. In the vicinity of the target an engine caught fire and, as ordered, the crew commenced bailing out. With six departed, and preparing to make his own exit, F/O Bowen-Morris regained control and was able to reach Dutch air space before, at last, being obliged to take to his parachute. Sgt Reynolds is commemorated on panel 276 of the Runnymede Memorial. Twenty-four hours previous, the London Gazette published details of F/S Meredith's award.

	138 Sqn	Lancaster I	RF143 NF-O	Op: Potsdam
	F/O G Horsaman	+		
	F/S S Larcombe	+		
	F/O V R M Williams	+		
	F/O J W Neve			
	W/O G M Bagshaw RAAF	+		
	Sgt T A Cotter	+		
	Sgt H V Stokes	+		

T/o 1813 Tuddenham. Coned in searchlights and shot down by a night-fighter. Those who died rest in Berlin 1939-1945 War Cemetery. The CWGC register describes F/S Larcombe as a pilot, while the loss card has being annotated "safe" in respect of F/O Neve.

Note. This was the last major Main Force area attack of the Second World War. 138 Squadron, recently transferred from SOE duties, participated in nine bombing raids, despatching 105 sorties for the loss of one crew, here summarised.

15-16 Apr 1945	169 Sqn	Mosquito XIX	MM633 VI-	Op: BS
	W/O S R Paddick	+		
	W/O D A T Young	+		

T/o 2000 Great Massingham and headed for the Stuttgart region. Lost without trace. Both warrant officers are commemorated on the panels at Runnymede.

16 Apr 1945	432 Sqn	Halifax VII	NP805 QO-J	Air Test
	F/O W H Porritt RCAF	+		
	F/S K Davidson RCAF	inj		
	F/O L Jorgenson RCAF	inj		
	F/S J Gray RCAF	inj		
	F/S S Reid RCAF	inj		
	F/S T Cohen RCAF	inj		
	P/O J Burns RCAF	inj		
	LAC J D M Bedard RCAF	+		
	LAC R F Charbonneau RCAF	+		

T/o 1210 East Moor possibly with the control locks still in place. At high speed the Halifax careered off the runway and crashed into trees, bursting into flames moments later. Two members of the ground staff who were watching the proceedings were struck by the undercarriage as it smashed through the roof of the picket post on which they were sunbathing. Along with F/O Porritt RCAF, they were buried in Harrogate (Stonefall) Cemetery. F/S Davidson RCAF was destined to spend the next two years in hospital, so serious were his injuries.

	432 Sqn	Halifax VII	PN235 QO-S	Air Test
	F/O J S Paul RCAF			

T/o 1459 East Moor but a swing developed taking the Halifax off the right hand side of the runway, whereupon the undercarriage collapsed. No injuries reported.

Note. The above details have been checked against the accident record cards and are believed to be a true reflection of what happened. Other sources, however, attribute the second loss to have occurred while on operations, but this is not supported by the Squadron's ORB.

	608 Sqn	Mosquito XVI	PF496 6T-	Air Test
	F/O J F Pickard			

T/o 1436 Downham Market for a night flying test combined with single-engined landing practice. Approached the runway at 1506 but held off too high, stalled and crashed. No one was hurt but the Mosquito was wrecked.

Note. 608 Squadron had commenced receiving Mosquito XVIs in March 1945, in readiness for the phasing from service of their Canadian built Mk.XX and Mk.XXVs.

16 Apr 1945	617 Sqn	Lancaster I	NG228 KC-V	Op: Swinemunde

S/L J L Powell DFC MID	+	T/o 1349 Woodhall Spa armed with 12 x 1,000lb
F/S H W Felton DFM	+	bombs to attack the pocket battleship Lützow.
F/L M T Clarke DFC	+	Hit by flak and the port wing came off before
F/O A L Heath	+	spinning into a wooded region of the target
P/O K A J Hewitt	+	area. All were buried on 18 April in the
F/S W Knight	+	Caseburg Friedhof at Swinemünde, but their
F/O J Watson	+	remains were exhumed on 2 March 1949, and taken

to Poznan Old Garrison Cemetery. F/S Felton had served previously with 50 Squadron, his DFM being published on 10 December 1943, while the DFC holders had their awards Gazetted on 19 March 1946 and 16 January 1945 respectively.

Note. A memorial to this crew, which incorporates part of the aircraft's tail unit, has subsequently been arranged by Wojciech Krajewski, Archelogia Lotnicza of Warszawa and to whom I am indebted for details summarised above. As ever, I acknowledge Robert Owen's generous help in all matters concerning 617 Squadron.

16-17 Apr 1945	106 Sqn	Lancaster I	NG414 ZN-K	Op: Plzen
	F/O A Dean			

T/o 2336 Metheringham but swung out of control, crashed and, later, exploded. The crew, who are not named, scrambled clear and were not harmed.

	156 Sqn	Lancaster III	PB403 GT-E	Op: Schwandorf

F/O J Jamieson	+	T/o 0006 Upwood to mark the railway yards.
Sgt F J Cuthill	+	Collided in the air with a 171 Squadron Halifax
F/O F W O'Reilly	+	and fell into a wooded area at "Kahle Köpfchen"
P/O F L J Ponting	+	at Mürlenbach on the W bank of Kyll river some
F/S D E Smith	+	12 km SSW of Gerolstein. Under the direction of
P/O H W Elliott RCAF	+	American forces, both crews were recovered by
Sgt E Wilson	+	local German civilians. Their bodies now rest

in Rheinberg War Cemetery. F/O O'Reilly was a Chartered Accountant.

	171 Sqn	Halifax III	LK874 6Y-C	Op: BS

F/L P S Jennings RNZAF	+	T/o 2339 North Creake. Lost in the manner
F/S G V Knowler	+	described above, the bulk of the debris being
F/S C T Jones	+	found in woods near Mürlenbach-Godesbachtal.
F/O R A Brown RCAF	+	All rest in Rheinberg War Cemetery. F/O Draper
Sgt A Storey	+	had been responsible for the special equipment.
F/O E G Draper	+	
F/S F Dyson	+	
Sgt R Sperling	+	

Note. I am most appreciative of the information sent by Horst Weber of Niederstedem for the very precise details here reported.

	239 Sqn	Mosquito NF.30	NT331 HB-	Op: BS

F/O J H Bridekirk	inj	T/o 0203 Brussels-Melsbroek to patrol over
F/L T G Glasheen	inj	Prague in Czechoslovakia but crashed almost

immediately and burst into flames. The pilot was trapped in his seat and owes his survival to F/L Glasheen who, having got clear, went back into the flames and dragged his skipper clear. F/O Bridekirk was taken to 8 General Hospital in Brussels, while his navigator was admitted to SSQ Melsbroek for treatment for burns to his hands and arms.

	462 Sqn	Halifax III	MZ467 Z5-C	Op: BS

F/O A M Lodder RAAF	pow	T/o 2358 Foulsham. Reported crashed SE from
Sgt J E A Gray	+	the village of Wortelstetten, 25 km NNW from
F/S E Windus	+	the centre of Augsburg, its intended area of
F/S P A Naylor	pow	operations. Burials were reported at Ehingen
F/S C R H Foster RAAF	+	and Westerdorf, small communities in the
F/S E D Tisdell RAAF	+	vicinity of the crash site. Since 1945, their
Sgt R McGarvie	+	bodies have been exhumed and taken to Dürnbach
Sgt E R Casterton	pow	War Cemetery. F/O Lodder RAAF sustained burns

to his wrists and face as he was thrown from the aircraft. F/S Tisdell RAAF was the specialist equipment operator.

| 16-17 Apr 1945 | 463 Sqn | Lancaster III | ND733 JO-L | Op: Plzen |

F/O J A Hagley RAAF
Sgt L Harper
F/S K C Bruhn RAAF
F/S W J Colebrook RAAF
F/S A W Paterson RAAF
W/O E C Everett RAAF
F/S J E C Tullock RAAF

T/o 2341 Waddington. Badly shot about by a night-fighter, after which the crew set course for France and Juvincourt airfield. However, control problems worsened and at 0540, when approximately 6 km to the W of their intended destination, the crew were obliged to bale out and all made a safe exit from around 1,700 feet.

| 17 Apr 1945 | 57 Sqn | Lancaster I | NN765 DX- | Ground |

Wrecked 1745 at East Kirkby in the explosions that followed the fire that broke out beneath Lancaster III PB360.

| 57 Sqn | Lancaster I | PD347 DX-P | Ground |

Destroyed in similar circumstances.

| 57 Sqn | Lancaster I | RF195 DX- | Ground |

Destroyed in similar circumstances.

| 57 Sqn | Lancaster III | LM673 DX-U | Ground |

Destroyed in similar circumstances.

| 57 Sqn | Lancaster III | ND472 DX-I | Ground |

Destroyed in similar circumstances.

| 57 Sqn | Lancaster III | PB360 DX-N | Ground |

Sgt R E Davies   +
Cpl T S Dixon   +
Cpl G W Johnson   +
LAC A Price   +
F/L J MacBean
F/O Grebby   inj
F/O J Gott
Cpl R Forster   inj
Cpl L Friswell   inj
LAC F Brown   inj
LAC W Thaxton   inj

At approximately 1745, while being prepared for operations to Cham, a fire started beneath this Lancaster. A series of explosions soon followed which wrecked the Lancaster and five others parked nearby; fourteen bombers were less badly damaged. No.3 hangar, then in use for the storage of incendiaries, was also seriously damaged, as was Hagnaby Grange Farm. Before the situation could be brought under control, fire appliances had to be summoned from Spilsby and Coningsby and it was not until the following day that the area was deemed to be safe. For their outstanding actions in the face of grave danger, F/L MacBean, the armaments officer, received an MBE, while George Medals were awarded to F/O Grebby, the Station Fire Officer, and F/O Gott. BEMs were gained by Cpl Forster, Cpl Friswell and LAC Brown. It is further reported that civilian personnel were also injured by the blast.

Note. It is not confirmed that the four deceased died in this accident but Douglas Cutherbertson has identified this quartet in various CWGC cemetery registers and, therefore, it is likely that some, if not all, lost their lives in this terrible event.

| 171 Sqn | Halifax III | PN169 6Y- | Training |

F/L C J Butler   inj
F/L K J Chapman   inj
Sgt A Hill   inj
W/O P G R Henderson   inj

T/o 1645 North Creake but swung off the runway, to starboard, and collided with a building. The Halifax then ran into trees, where it caught fire. All later recovered from their injuries.

| 462 Sqn | Halifax III | NR284 Z5- | Air Test |

P/O J R Smith RAAF

T/o 1836 Foulsham. Forced-landed 1940, after failure of both starboard engines, less than a mile S of Beetley Hall, Beetley, 4 miles NNW of East Dereham, Norfolk. The crew were not seriously hurt, but the wreckage caught fire and the Halifax was destroyed.

| 17-18 Apr 1945 | 142 Sqn | Mosquito XXV | KB449 4H-V | Op: Ingoldstadt |

F/L S A Nolan
P/O W J C Green

T/o 2254 Gransden Lodge but swung off the runway and lost its undercarriage. A fire broke out, but both members of crew vacated the wreckage and were relatively unscathed. Later, the bomb load exploded, scattering debris across the airfield, but, again, no one was injured. However, a dozen aircraft assigned for operations that night had to be cancelled, due to this accident.

17-18 Apr	**608 Sqn**	**Mosquito XVI**	**PF505 6T-D**	**Op: Berlin**
1945	F/L G C Dixon RNZAF		T/o 2054 Downham Market. Bombed the AP at 2256	
	F/O Smith		from 25,000 feet and then climbed to 27,000 feet	
			whereupon the port engine failed. Forced-landed	

0045 at Strassfeld airfield some 16 km WSW from the centre of Bonn. On touch down the undercarriage gave way, and the Mosquito was wrecked. No injuries.

Note. This was the last Bomber Command aircraft to be written off during operations to Berlin. The first had been a 10 Squadron Whitley (see Volume 1 page 18), tasked to release nothing more lethal that leaflets. Then, in October 1939, Berlin had stood proud as Germany's capital city, while now, just over five years on, much of this huge metropolis lay in ruins, a stark and bitter testament to the follies of Adolf Hitler.

18 Apr	**10 Sqn**	**Halifax III**	**PN447 ZA-B**	**Op: Heligoland**
1945	F/L C P Smith		T/o 1117 Melbourne to attack the naval base.	
	Sgt K Burrill		Bombed from 14,000 feet at 1325 and returned	
	F/O G Lucas		to base at 1524, without any indication of	
	F/O H Jeffs		damage. However, the aircraft was grounded	
	Sgt J Davis		for on site repairs, but on 20 June 1945, the	
	Sgt M Potton		airframe was struck off charge and reduced to	
	Sgt J Bransby		spares and produce.	

76 Sqn	**Halifax VI**	**RG622 MP-I**	**Op: Heligoland**
W/O R Holmes		T/o 1133 Holme-on-Spalding Moor similarly tasked	
Sgt W Blatchford		but swung out of control, ground looped and	
F/L F A J Haskett		caught fire. The crew managed to get clear but	
F/S J Krochak RCAF		it was not long afterwards that an explosion	
Sgt J Rutherford		wrecked the bomber. F/L Haskett had recently	
Sgt S G Potts		arrived from Burn having been appointed to the	
Sgt G M Jones		post of Squadron Navigation Leader.	

Note. This was the first Halifax VI written off by 76 Squadron.

347 Sqn	**Halifax III**	**LL556 L8-**	**Op: Heligoland**
Ltn A Roberts FFAF		T/o 1125 Elvington similarly tasked but swung	
		out of control and smashed its undercarriage.	
		There are no reports of injury.	

Note. The accident record card, and AM Form 78, suggests the above summary to be correct; the Squadron ORB shows the Halifax under the command of Sous-Lieutenant Person FFAF and operating without incident. A perusal of further entries in 347 Squadron records is negative in respect of this Halifax and, therefore, the official evidence from the supporting sources here mentioned lends credence to its demise.

408 Sqn	**Halifax VII**	**NP776 EQ-R**		**Op: Heligoland**
F/L A J Cull RCAF		+	T/o 1019 Linton-on-Ouse similarly tasked. Lost	
Sgt E E Sykes		+	over the sea. Two bodies, those of F/L Cull RCAF	
F/O F C Hill RCAF		+	and F/O Miller RCAF were eventually recovered.	
F/O D M Miller RCAF		+	The former rests in Kiel War Cemetery, having	
F/S C H White RCAF		+	been brought here from Westerland on Sylt, while	
F/S R W Williams RCAF		+	his air bomber was carried northwards and he now	
F/S H R Wood RCAF		+	lies in Oslo Western Civil Cemetery. The others	
			are commemorated on the Runnymede Memorial.	

420 Sqn	**Halifax III**	**NP946 PT-L**		**Op: Heligoland**
F/S W J Dunnigan RCAF		+	T/o 1003 Tholthorpe similarly tasked. Observed	
Sgt L F J Murphy RCAF		+	outbound, to crash 1150 into the sea, position	
F/O D M Neilson RCAF		+	5441N 0445E. Four have no known graves while	
F/O D F Ross RCAF		+	three were recovered from the water and now rest	
Sgt G F Montgomery RCAF		+	in Brookwood Military Cemetery.	
Sgt R A McDonald RCAF		+		
F/S D W Newman RCAF		+		

Note. Reliable private sources suggest that aircraft from the USAAF 5th Emergency Rescue Squadron, operating from Holton and Boxted, plus Warwick aircraft from 280 Squadron at Beccles, participated in the search for survivors. A Catalina is believed to have picked up at least two bodies.

18 Apr 1945	426 Sqn	Halifax VII	PN226 OW-N		Op: Heligoland

P/O J A Whipple RCAF
Sgt E H Haughton
F/S E W Gaffray RCAF
F/O S T Pyke RCAF
F/S M M Johnson RCAF
F/S R J Murray RCAF
F/S H F West RCAF

T/o 0952 Linton-on-Ouse to bomb the naval base. Severely damaged when another aircraft blew up over the target area (either from 408 or 640 Squadrons). Returned safely to base at 1450 with no reported injuries to its crew. For his outstanding airmanship, P/O Whipple RCAF was awarded the DFC.

	640 Sqn	Halifax VI	RG564 C8-P		Op: Heligoland

P/O H K Pugh RAAF +
F/S R T Jaques +
F/S J Whittenbury +
F/S W Probert +
W/O H K Franklin RAAF +
Sgt A R Lishman +
Sgt G A Knowles +

T/o 1144 Leconfield similarly instructed. Six are commemorated on the Runnymede Memorial while Sgt Lishman rests in Hamburg Cemetery, Ohlsdorf. The CWGC register shows his date of death as 18 May, but this is thought to be an error. In 1937 P/O Pugh RAAF gained an Honours Muresk Diploma of Agriculture, while F/S Whittenbury, who enlisted at Euston in 1942, hailed from Nairobi, Kenya. The crews' average age was twenty-two.

Note. Martin Middlebrook and Chris Everitt report this attack, conducted by a force of 969 aircraft and comprising of 617 Lancasters, 332 Halifaxes and 20 Mosquitoes, drawn from all the bomber groups, was aimed at destroying the naval base, airfield and town. Not surprisingly, considering the near perfect weather conditions, Heligoland was subjected to an intense bombardment which left the various aiming points a mass of overlapping bomb craters. 158 Squadron, whose 28 Halifaxes were assigned to the 5th and 6th waves, report that by 1325 hours much smoke and flame covered the aiming points and that the local defences were practically swamped by the bombing. No enemy aircraft sighted.

18-19 Apr 1945	141 Sqn	Mosquito NF.30	NT490 TW-R		Op: Airfields

W/O R G Dawson RNZAF +
F/O C P D Childs RNZAF +

T/o 1640 Brussels-Melsbroek armed with napalm and headed for München-Neubiberg airfield on the SE outskirts of München. Both are buried in Dürnbach War Cemetery. Thus, 24 year old W/O Dawson RNZAF of Rahotu and F/O Childs RNZAF, aged 32, from Eastbourne, became the last airmen reported missing from 141 Squadron.

19 Apr 1945	49 Sqn	Lancaster III	ME357 EA-C		Training

F/O D I Hytch
Sgt J Dodgson
F/S T M Harrison
Sgt K Read
Sgt K Scott
Sgt L Broadbent
F/S R H Williams RCAF
LAC L F Tyler

T/o 1127 Fulbeck. Flew into the sea at 1320 some 5 miles E of Skegness on the Lincolnshire coast. All were rescued and no serious injuries are reported.

20 Apr 1945	622 Sqn	Lancaster I	PA285 GI-O		Op: Regensburg

F/L V S Robbins +
Sgt R W Reid +
2Lt G Dietrichson RNAF +
F/O B F Scott RNZAF +
F/O H A Smith +
F/S J E Hulland +
F/S E Parker pow

T/o 0957 Mildenhall to destroy a fuel storage depot. Hit by flak and partially abandoned before crashing at Burgweinting, 5 km SE from the centre of Regensburg. Five are buried in Dürnbach War Cemetery, while it is assumed 2Lt Dietrichson RNAF has been taken back to Norway.

21-22 Apr 1945	163 Sqn	Mosquito XXV	KB529 -W		Op: Kiel

F/L W G Baker
F/O A A Hawthorne RCAF +

T/o 2137 Wyton. Presumed crashed in the target area as F/O Hawthorne RCAF is buried in the War Cemetery, which adjoins the German Naval Garrison Cemetery. It is assumed F/O Baker survived as no burial details have been found.

	608 Sqn	Mosquito XVI	RV359 6T-X		Op: Kiel

S/L E S Few DFC AFC +
P/O S S Campbell +

T/o 2145 Downham Market. Both officers rest in Kiel War Cemetery. It will be recalled that S/L Few had been involved in a forced-landing while operating against Berlin early in March.

22 Apr	49 Sqn	Lancaster III	PB463 EA-Y	Transit

1945

F/O G F Elkington	+
F/S C I Walker	+
F/S L W Evans	+
F/O H Macaulay	+
F/S J W Petch	+
F/S M J C Garrett	+
F/L G Wimpenny BSc AMICE	+
Sgt C L Hammond	+
Cpl H S Hancox	+
LAC J H Davies	inj
LAC J Griffin	inj
LAC L R Hassan	inj
LAC J E Lambourn	inj
LAC T McKie	inj
LAC L Masterman	+
LAC S Mellows	inj
LAC P Moor	inj
LAC F Plumtree	+
LAC J W Rogers MID	+
LAC E Shaw	+
LAC T Starling	inj
LAC W Wright	+
AC1 R J Clewley	+
AC1 J Weston	inj
AC2 G H Brenchley	+

T/o 0955 Fulbeck with the intention of flying to Syerston, where the Squadron was to be based. However, the Lancaster flew round the circuit before returning low across the airfield in a dive from which, tragically, the pilot failed to recover and at 0957 his aircraft smashed into buildings near the M/T section, debris scything through a parade comprising mainly of personnel from 5015 Airfield Construction Unit. In an instant, ten died and five others succumbed to their injuries in the days that followed, the last being LAC Moor who lived until 8 May. Their graves are now in various United Kingdom cemeteries. It is presumed LAC Hassan, LAC Lambourn, LAC Starling and AC1 Weston recovered. At least five of the ground staff were in their 40s, LAC Wright possibly being the eldest at forty-four.

153 Sqn	Lancaster III	ME424 P4-N	Op: Bremen

F/O A C Cockcroft	+
Sgt D J Philpot	+
F/S D F Poore	+
F/S K L Dutton	+
F/S F Wood	+
F/S K F Chapman RCAF	+
F/S C H Booty RCAF	+

T/o 1536 Scampton. Crashed near Jade where in the local Friedhof graves for some of the crew were later discovered. Four now rest in Becklingen War Cemetery, while three have been taken to Sage War Cemetery. Both air gunners were aged nineteen.

218 Sqn	Lancaster I	NF994 HA-N	Op: Bremen

F/L D S Spiers	+
Sgt T W Lee	+
F/O H R S Jacob	+
F/O G M Davies	+
F/S L Bellwood	+
Sgt G R Willerton	inj
Sgt F Thornton	inj

T/o 1459 Chedburgh. Called 1820 on W/T advising the crew were making an early return, having experienced severe engine problems. The next call came over the R/T at 2023, but nine minutes later the Lancaster came down at Depden Green village, 1 mile SW of the airfield. Several eye witnesses report the Lancaster's outer port propeller was windmilling. Of those who died, three were taken to Cambridge City Cemetery, including F/L Spiers whose home was at Haverhill, a mere 10 miles or so from where he died. Sgt Willerton passed away the next day and he now lies in Louth Cemetery.

514 Sqn	Lancaster I	LM285 JI-A	Op: Bremen

F/O S Abel
Sgt R O Thomas
P/O J B Francis
F/S D D Cramp
F/S T F O'Neil RAAF
Sgt F G Gillett
Sgt C A Cook

T/o 1504 Waterbeach. Outbound, hit by flak in the vicinity of Wilhelmshaven, sustaining minor damage to the rear turret and port wing fuel tanks. Bombed the AP from 19,000 feet at 1842, only to hit in the starboard wing and port inner engine by predicted flak. This time the damage was far more serious and the Lancaster crash-landed 1930 on Venlo airfield in Holland. No one was hurt and all returned to their Squadron during the evening of 25 April.

622 Sqn	Lancaster I	HK770 GI-T	Op: Bremen

F/L E G Cook	pow
Sgt T McLaren	pow
F/O M Parry	pow
F/O P D Gough	pow
F/O R W Sherry	pow
Sgt C T Savage	pow
Sgt R C Hagerty	pow

T/o 1510 Mildenhall. Hit by flak at 1828 while approaching the AP at 19,500 feet. The port outer was blown from its frame and six feet of the port wing was shot away. Six baled out from 12,000 feet but F/L Cook managed to regain Dutch airspace before making his exit from 1,200 feet, the Lancaster falling 2050 twixt Rijswijk and Maurik (Gelderland), 9 km NNE of Tiel.

23 Apr	419 Sqn	Lancaster X	KB762 VR-J	Training

1945   F/L E C Peters RCAF   While taxiing at 1715 around the Middleton St.
George airfield perimeter and making towards
No.1 hangar, the undercarriage gave way and the Lancaster was damaged beyond
repair. No one aboard the aircraft was hurt.

Note. A superb photograph of this Lancaster appears on page 28 of Mike
Garbett and Brian Goulding's first book in the Lancaster at War series,
published by Ian Allan. Also, in the same series, is an account of F/L
Cook's experiences, summarised at the foot of the previous page.

	514 Sqn	Lancaster III	ME523 A2-G	Training

F/O W M Wiseman RCAF   Forced-landed 1659 nearly 2 miles SW of
Topcliffe airfield, Yorkshire, after the
crew encountered severe turbulence. No serious injuries reported.

24 Apr	218 Sqn	Lancaster I	NF955 HA-H	Op: Bad Oldesloe

1945

F/L R L Jenyns RAAF	+
P/O F A Morris	+
F/S H R Williams	+
W/O P M Nicholls	+
F/S G Kilpatrick	+
P/O C Jolly	+
F/S H K Harper	+

T/o 0700 Chedburgh to attack railway yards but
as the Lancaster became airborne, the starboard
engines faltered and lost power. With its air
speed decaying by the second, the Lancaster
staggered across the airfield and crashed 0701
into a hedgerow near the WAAF site and close to
the Bury St. Edmunds to Haverhill road. For the
next thirty minutes explosions rent the air
before the flames were extinguished and what remained of the bomb load was
made safe. Burials took place at Cambridge City Cemetery and in the various
home towns of the crew. F/S Williams, it is noted, lies in Rickmansworth
Cemetery alongside his brother, a pilot, W/O Joseph Leonard Williams who
lost his life a few months previous on 19 January 1945. At 39, P/O Jolly
was well over the average age of operational aircrew.

24-25 Apr	109 Sqn	Mosquito IX	LR508 HS-	Op: Schleissheim

1945

F/L J T McGreal DFC RNZAF	+
P/O T Lynn DFC DFM	+

T/o 2213 Little Staughton to attack an airfield.
Homebound, the crew tried to get into Brussels-
Melsbroek but overshot the airfield and dived
into the ground. Both rest in Brussels Town Cemetery. P/O Lynn had won his
DFM while serving with 106 Squadron, details being Gazetted on 15 October 1943.

25 Apr	76 Sqn	Halifax VI	RG553 MP-T	Op: Wangerooge

1945

P/O G W Lawson RCAF	pow
Sgt D B N Stanes	+
F/O C R M Morrison RCAF	+
F/O M C Slaughter RCAF	+
F/S A G Artus	+
P/O R I Sweet RCAF	+
P/O L L Slauenwhite RCAF	+

T/o 1441 Holme-on-Spalding Moor to attack gun
positions. Involved in a midair collision with
another Squadron Halifax, both machines falling
in the target area. P/O Lawson RCAF found himself trapped beneath the port wing as his aircraft tumbled towards the sea, but he managed
to push himself clear, landing unhurt in shallow
water. He was quickly arrested. His crew now
lie in Sage War Cemetery. Sgt Stanes lost his brother, Henry George Stanes,
on active service.

	76 Sqn	Halifax VI	RG591 MP-A	Op: Wangerooge

WO2 J L Outerson RCAF	+
Sgt J W Burdall	+
F/O J Ramsay RCAF	+
F/S C H Livermore RCAF	+
Sgt J Nicholson	+
F/S E T Sutton	+
F/S G Gibson	+

T/o 1452 Holme-on-Spalding Moor similarly
tasked and lost in the manner described above.
Five are buried in Sage War Cemetery, while the
names of F/S Livermore RCAF and F/S Sutton are
commemorated on panels 280 and 273 respectively
of the Runnymede Memorial.

	142 Sqn	Mosquito XXV	KB450 4H-E	Air Test

F/O D R Maguire   Overshot Gransden Lodge at 1157 and in order
to avoid running into the SBA installations,
the Mosquito was swung to port, whereupon the undercarriage gave way.

	142 Sqn	Mosquito XXV	KB613 4H-	Air Test

F/O D R Maguire   Crash-landed 1542 at Gransden Lodge and burnt.
F/O Maguire escaped injury for the second time,
but with two aircraft damaged beyond repair, his Mosquito flying was terminated.

25 Apr
1945

163 Sqn   **Mosquito XXV**   KB624   -G   **Air Test**

F/O F Langford RAAF   T/o 1510 Wyton. On return to base at 1603, the
Mosquito made a heavy three point landing and
the starboard undercarriage leg collapsed, damaging the aircraft beyond repair.

347 Sqn   **Halifax VI**   NP921 L8-E   **Op: Wangerooge**

Sgc R Mercier FFAF	+	T/o 1441 Elvington to bomb gun positions. Came
Sgt M Mennetre FFAF	+	down on the island, near some military barracks.
Cne G Hautecoeur FFAF	+	Initially, all were buried by the wreckage of
Cne J Jacquot FFAF	+	their aircraft, but later their remains were
Sgc P Bariteau FFAF	+	taken to Wangerooge Friedhof. It is assumed
Sgt P Ferrero FFAF	+	their graves are now in France.
Sgt G Leduc FFAF	+	

Note. This was the first Halifax VI reported missing from 347 Squadron.

408 Sqn   **Halifax VII**   NP796 EQ-M   **Op: Wangerooge**

F/L A B Ely RCAF	+	T/o 1432 Linton-on-Ouse similarly tasked.
Sgt J Hughes	+	Collided in the target area with a 426 Squadron
WO2 J E Brambleby RCAF	+	Halifax, both machines falling out of control.
F/O J K Stanley RCAF	+	All are commemorated on the Runnymede Memorial.
F/O A B Boyd RCAF	+	
Sgt A L Rutter RCAF	+	
Sgt V E Hovey RCAF	+	

426 Sqn   **Halifax VII**   NP820 OW-W   **Op: Wangerooge**

WO2 J C Tuplin RCAF	+	T/o 1504 Linton-on-Ouse similarly tasked and
Sgt R Roberts	+	destroyed in the manner previously described.
F/O J D C Ross RCAF	+	All are commemorated on the Runnymede Memorial.
W/O R G Evans	+	This tragedy was observed, and reported, by
F/S R D H Curzon RCAF	+	F/L A Rose of 408 Squadron.
F/S E W Hicks RCAF	+	
F/S S J Teskey RCAF	+	

431 Sqn   **Lancaster X**   KB822 SE-W   **Op: Wangerooge**

F/O D G Baker RCAF	+	T/o 1455 Croft similarly tasked. Collided off
Sgt F Smith	+	Nordeney with a Lancaster from the same unit,
F/O J D Cruickshank RCAF	+	both aircraft plunging into the sea. F/O Baker
F/O L H Amos RCAF	+	RCAF was found on 28 April at Spiekeroog and
WO2 P E A Henrichon RCAF	+	he was buried at Langeoog; his grave is now in
F/S J J P R Roy RCAF	+	Sage War Cemetery. The body of F/O Cruickshank
F/S L U M Hiatt RCAF	+	RCAF was eventually recovered from the sea off

Tjarno Island. He is now buried in Sweden at
Kviberg Cemetery. The others have no known graves.

431 Sqn   **Lancaster X**   KB831 SE-E   **Op: Wangerooge**

F/L B D Emmet RCAF	+	T/o 1501 Croft similarly tasked and destroyed
Sgt J N Sims	+	in the circumstances reported above. Five are
F/O R J Stingle RCAF	+	commemorated on the Runnymede Memorial, while
F/O W E Hanna RCAF	+	Sgt Sims, who was washed ashore at Spiekeroog
WO2 C R I Mark RCAF	+	on 29 July 1945 and laid to rest at Langeoog,
Sgt D A Faulkner	+	and F/O Stingle RCAF are buried in separate
F/S R J Mellon RCAF	+	cemeteries on the German mainland. Their

average age was twenty-two.

Note. This was the last major operation involving 6 Group and the last
bombing raid of the Second World War concerning 4 Group. In total, 308
Halifaxes and 158 Lancasters took part and it is most regrettable that
six of the seven aircraft lost were victims of midair collision. Like
the recent Heligoland raid, weather conditions were almost perfect.

460 Sqn   **Lancaster I**   NX585 AR-M   **Op: Berchtesgaden**

F/O H G Payne RAAF	pow	T/o 0525 Binbrook to bomb the infamous Eagle's
F/S D F Thorne	pow	Nest chalet and nearby SS barracks. All are
F/S C N Fraser RAAF	pow	described as "safe" on the loss card, but it
F/S D D Lynch RAAF	pow	likely that all spent the last days of the war
F/S W A Stanley RAAF	pow	in some form of captivity.
F/S J R Bennett RAAF	pow	
F/S H R Connochie RAAF	pow	

25 Apr	619 Sqn	Lancaster III	LM756 PG-F	Op: Berchtesgaden
1945	F/O W T De Marco RCAF	+		
	Sgt F J Cole	pow		
	WO2 N H Johnston RCAF	+		
	F/S A H Shannon	pow		
	F/S J W Speers RCAF	pow		
	Sgt E W Norman	+		
	WO2 G V Walker RCAF	+		

T/o 0419 Strubby to bomb the Eagle's Nest chalet and SS barracks. Those who died are buried in Austria at Klagenfurt War Cemetery. Similar to the crew summarised on the previous page, the survivors are noted as being "safe".

25-26 Apr	463 Sqn	Lancaster I	RA542 JO-Z	Op: Tonsberg
1945	F/O A Cox	int		
	Sgt G W Simpson	int		
	F/O J A Wainwright	int		
	F/S R Smurthwaite	int		
	F/S F E Parent	int		
	F/S F W J H Logan	int		
	F/S W D Hogg	int		

T/o 2014 Waddington and set course for an oil refinery at Vallö near Tönsberg in southern Norway. Shortly before entering the target area and flying at 19,600 feet, came under fire from a Ju 88, which in turn may have fallen in the furious exchange of shots. Three members of the crew, including the pilot, were wounded but despite suffering from frostbite course was set for Sweden where an emergency landing was made on Satenäs airfield. F/S Smurthwaite was taken to Lidköping hospital. Subsequently, F/O Cox and F/O Wainwright received DSOs, while Sgt Simpson was awarded a CGM. The Swedish Air Force repaired the Lancaster but it is not known if it ever flew again. Stored at Satenäs, it was broken down for scrap on 23 August 1946.

26 Apr	50 Sqn	Lancaster I	PD339 VN-J	Exodus
1945	F/O C J Evans RNZAF	+		
	Sgt D H Millichamp	+		
	F/S T R Thwaite RNZAF	+		
	F/S R F Carrodus RNZAF	+		
	F/S I J Loveridge RNZAF	+		
	Sgt E R McRae	inj		
	Sgt G A Fuller	inj		

Hit a tree while flying low and crashed 1655 at Hardingstone, just over a mile SSE from the centre of Northampton. The four RNZAF members of crew were taken to Oxford (Botley) Cemetery at North Hinksey; Sgt Millichamp is in Arnold Cemetery near Nottingham. It is believed the crew had earlier brought some of the earliest repatriated ex-prisoners of war into Wing airfield, Buckinghamshire.

28 Apr	300 Sqn	Lancaster I	NN718 BH-A	Exodus
1945	F/L J Adamowski PAF			
	Sgt M Kurman PAF			
	P/O A Dauman PAF			
	P/O L Jarosz PAF			
	Sgt T Motyka PAF			
	Sgt K Kulakowski PAF			
	Sgt R Turek PAF			

T/o 1443 Faldingworth. Encountered bad weather off Heligoland and hit the sea. The pilot regained control and, subsequently, crash-landed at Brussels-Melsbroek where the Lancaster was left to languish, damaged beyond repair. No injuries reported.

	582 Sqn	Lancaster I	PB983 60-A	Training
	F/O R P Terpenning DFC RAAF	+		
	P/O J G Watson DFM RAAF	+		

Iced up after flying into a snow cloud and lost power on both port engines. At 100 feet all control was lost and the Lancaster crashed 1150 at Deenethorpe, 5 miles ENE from the centre of Corby, Northamptonshire. The two officers who died are buried in Cambridge City Cemetery. The circumstances as to how P/O Watson RAAF won his DFM are reported in Volume 5 page 519. The names of the five who were injured are not recorded.

30 Apr	428 Sqn	Lancaster X	KB879 NA-Y	Training
1945	F/L W G Campbell RCAF	+		
	F/S W G Ward	+		
	Sgt J H Kay RCAF	+		
	F/S S Berryman RCAF	+		
	WO2 T D Lawley RCAF	+		
	F/S J L Tweedy RCAF	+		
	F/S E J Wright RCAF	+		

Broke up in flight at 1154 and dived into the ground at Hixon, 5 miles ENE of Stafford. The six RCAF airmen were taken to Chester (Blacon) Cemetery. F/S Ward lies in Selkirk (Brierylaw) Cemetery. It is noted that F/S Wright's parents lived at Brighton in Sussex and his age in the CWGC register is given as 16. If this is correct, then he must have been about the youngest airmen to lose his life in World War II.

2-3 May	169 Sqn	Mosquito XIX	MM680 VI-	Op: Airfields
1945	F/O R Catterall DFC	+		
	F/S D J Beadle	+		

T/o 2110 Great Massingham armed with napalm and headed for Jagel airfield. Shot down by flak. Both are buried in Kiel War Cemetery.

2-3 May 1945	199 Sqn	Halifax III	RG373 EX-T	Op: BS

F/L W E Brooks	+	
W/O W F Bolton	+	
F/S J R Lewis	+	
W/O K A C M Gavin	+	
F/O K N J Croft	+	
F/S D Wilson	+	
F/O A S J Holder DFC	+	
P/O K N Crane	evd	

T/o 2050 North Creake tasked for Mandrel screening duties over Kiel. Believed to have collided with another Squadron Halifax, while preparing to make a bombing run, both machines crashing at Meimsdorf, E of the Eider and about 4 to 5 km SSW from the centre of Kiel. Those who died rest in Kiel War Cemetery. F/S Wilson was the specialist equipment operator, while 43 year old F/O Holder was amongst the oldest officers killed on bomber operations in the Second World War.

Note. Mr Dan Gurney of Swindon kindly advised me that a memorial to F/O Holder can be seen in the church at Miserden, 7 miles NW of Cirencester. The memorial is in the form of a marble tablet with a gilded RAF crest and lettering. His name is also inscribed on the village war memorial. Along with the airmen shown below, and that of the 169 Squadron Mosquito crew listed at the foot of the previous page, they were the last casualties sustained by Bomber Command on hostile operations in the war.

	199 Sqn	Halifax III	RG375 EX-R	Op: BS

F/L L H Currell RAAF	pow
Sgt W H V Mackay	+
F/S A A Bradley	+
Sgt F T Chambers	+
F/S J Loth	+
W/O R H A Pool	+
F/S D Greenwood	+
F/S R Hunter	pow

T/o 2054 North Creake similarly tasked and lost in the manner already described. All who perished lie in Kiel War Cemetery. Sgt Mackay, a graduate from Dublin University, came from Glengeary in the Irish Republic. The specialist equipment had been operated by W/O Pool.

3 May 1945	346 Sqn	Halifax VI	RG654 H7-	Training

Ltn M Bohrac FFAF

T/o 1217 Elvington. Landed 1757 but ballooned back into the air and before the pilot could catch the aircraft on the throttles, the port wing dropped and hit the runway. Moments later, the undercarriage collapsed. No injuries reported.

5 May 1945	627 Sqn	Mosquito XXV	KB625 AZ-L	Training

F/L D J Moore RCAF

T/o 1047 Woodhall Spa but the Mosquito veered to starboard and while trying to bring the aircraft back on line, the pilot over-corrected causing a violent 180 degree swing in the opposite direction, which removed the undercarriage. Repairs were considered, but on 2 July 1945 the airframe was struck off charge.

6 May 1945	169 Sqn	Mosquito XIX	MM637 VI-	Training

F/S D P Williams	+
F/S K Rhoden	+

T/o 1425 Great Massingham for a low level navigation exercise. At 1540 the Mosquito crashed near Hove in Sussex. F/S Williams was taken to Oxford Crematorium, while F/S Rhoden was buried in Atherton Cemetery in Lancashire. Their deaths were the last sustained by Bomber Command prior to the official surrender that brought hostilities in Europe to an end.

8 May 1945	576 Sqn	Lancaster I	NN806 UL-M	Manna

F/O G L Scott	
Sgt H W Batchelor	
Sgt A F Marshall	
F/O G R Cross	inj
Sgt S Hoskin	
F/S J A McDougall	
Sgt C G Rayner	

T/o 1208 Fiskerton to drop food supplies in the vicinity of Rotterdam, but swung off the runway and came to a stop with its undercarriage broken. F/O Cross sustained a sprained wrist, but the other members of crew escaped injury. Twelve hours later, at midnight, the war was over.

Chapter 2

Victory in the Far East

9 May to 2 September 1945

When the Allied armies made those historic first contacts at Torgau on the banks of the Elbe in late April 1945, the war in Europe was as good as over. Pictures showing scenes of smiling Russian and American soldiers exchanging handshakes appeared in newspapers across the free world; the Allies were victorious, Nazism was defeated. Sadly, within a matter of weeks this relationship twixt òn the one hand the Russians and on the other the Americans, and the British, cooled as the intentions of the Soviet leader, Stalin, became crystal clear. For months past, and particularly over the last few weeks, it was clear that Stalin was becoming increasingly hostile to all western moves and not content with what he had achieved at the Yalta conference in the February, now commenced making demands that were to frustrate and anger Churchill and America's new President, Harry S Truman. The first dark shades of a repressive Soviet regime that was to dominate the face of eastern Europe for the next forty odd years were present before the newborn peace was yet a month old.

In truth, the Russian armies had been permitted to advance much further westwards than was deemed militarily wise, but such was the persuasive guile of Joseph Stalin in his dealings with the western leaders that he had succeeded in practically every area of his intentions. Now, he held sway in all those countries that were to become collectively known as the Eastern Bloc and, of course, the shared city of Berlin was deep within the sphere of Soviet influence. For decades to come, the west would rue the day that he had been given such a free hand.

Such sombre manifestations, however, were not the immediate concern of Bomber Command, now faced with the enormous task of scaling down one of the largest and most powerful aerial armadas in the west.

On 7 May, a start was made with 4 Group being transferred to the fledgling Transport Command, thus eleven squadrons were disposed of and with their passing the Halifax was effectively finished as a front line bomber.

An immediate rundown of 6 Group got under way, with two units, 415 Squadron and 432 Squadron, disbanding on 15 May, followed over the next few weeks with the despatch of seven squadrons to Canada. 405 Squadron, the sole RCAF squadron to serve with PFF, departed for home in the June. This left 424 Squadron, 426 Squadron, 427 Squadron, 429 Squadron and 433 Squadron domiciled in the United Kingdom and of this quintet,

426 Squadron was placed under Transport Command control on 25 May, gradually giving up its Halifaxes in favour of Liberators.

With 6 (RCAF) Group disbanding at the end of August, their four remaining units came under the aegis of 1 Group.

Naturally, hundreds of Australian and New Zealand airmen, as well as the Canadians, were anxious to return home and, thus, many squadrons witnessed the departure of their Commonwealth aircrews, adding to the general upheaval prevailing throughout the Command.

Within 5 Group, training commenced for the envisaged formation of Tiger Force and subsequent operations in the Far East, though with the dropping of the second atomic bomb over Nagasaki on 9 August, this awesome event being witnessed by Group Captain Leonard Cheshire VC from an accompanying B-29, the requirement for such a force was immediately nullified. By the end of the year 5 and 8 Groups would be disbanded, as well as 100 Group, the latter having been responsible for the advancement of radio countermeasures which in the last six months of the bombing campaign undoubtedly reduced the scale of losses, thus saving the lives of hundreds of aircrew.

And so, in these final months of conflict continuing in the Far East, Bomber Command occupied its squadrons with the rounding off of operations Exodus and Manna, while at the end of June, a series of flights over north west Europe were carried out in order to assess the effectiveness of captured German radars, particularly those of the early warning type. At least two aircraft were lost in the course of these exercises. On 25 June a 50 Squadron Lancaster captained by Pilot Officer Douglas had to be abandoned, following an engine fire, while on 1 July a 150 Squadron Lancaster crashed heavily at Hemswell, after turning back with engine failure. Three airmen died; two in the last mentioned tragedy and one, Pilot Officer Douglas, in the former.

It is a sobering fact that in the period from the end of the European war to the conclusion of the fighting in the Pacific, Bomber Command lost over sixty aircraft, either on training details, or in ground incidents. Eighteen of these were extremely serious with total, or partial, loss of life resulting. The majority never received an entry in unit records, such was the way of things in the keeping of documents, but following the crash of a 460 Squadron Lancaster on 14 July in which three died, the diarist was moved to write, "This unhappy incident after the cessation of the European war cast a gloom over the whole of the Squadron."

During August, the majority of Lancaster squadrons were involved in ferrying soldiers between Italy and the United Kingdom and vice versa. Known as Operation Dodge, most of these flights took place without incident but a 626 Squadron crew perished on 7 August when their Lancaster crashed near Toulouse

and ten days later, at Bari, a 115 Squadron Lancaster swung while taking off and wrote off two similar machines parked on the peritrack. Fortunately, no one was hurt.

As recounted, the war in the Far East came to its inevitable climax in mid-August, but it was not until 2 September that all could be gathered to witness the signing of the documents that officially ended hostilities world wide. The Second World War was over.

9 May 1945	83 Sqn	Lancaster III	PB616 OL-A	Exodus

F/L E R Brown — T/o 1435 Rheine but swung out of control, the undercarriage giving way as it veered from the runway. A fire broke out, but none of the eight crew and 24 ex-prisoners of war aboard were hurt.

	106 Sqn	Lancaster III	RF235 ZN-	Exodus

F/S G Middleton — T/o 1109 Rheine but swung off the runway and ran into a bomb crater. This removed the main undercarriage, thus damaging the Lancaster beyond repair. None of the 24 ex-prisoner of war passengers and crew were injured.

	514 Sqn	Lancaster III	RF230 JI-B	Exodus
F/L D Beaton DSO	+			
F/S A McMurrugh	+			
F/O R B Hilchey RCAF	+			
F/S J G Brittain	+			
P/O R M Toms RCAF	+			
P/O O C Evers RCAF	+			
Capt R W Wheeler	+			
Lt P A T W B Campbell	+			
Lt E T T Snowdon	+			
Sgt R A Adams	+			
Cpl E L Belshaw	+			
Cpl A G Thompson	+			
LCpl G W Franks	+			
Fus H Cummings	+			
Fus O Parkin	+			
Gdsmn J A Roe	+			
Gnr A J S Crowe	+			
Gnr A N Labotske SAA	+			
Pnr W L Lindheimer PAL	+			
Pnr M Maschit PAL	+			
Pte T Anderson	+			
Pte W L Ball	+			
Pte S J Bayston	+			
Pte R A Betton	+			
Pte R E Clark	+			
Pte W Croston	+			
Pte R Danson	+			
Pte R Turnbull	+			
Pte P Yates	+			
Rfn T J Edwards	+			

T/o Juvincourt with 24 ex-prisoners of war. Soon after becoming airborne the pilot reported he was experiencing trouble with the controls and was putting back to Juvincourt. At 1230, when some 2 km ESE of Roye-Amy, the Lancaster crashed, killing everyone on board. All were buried in Clichy New Communal Cemetery.

Note. On the outward flight from Waterbeach, the crew had included Wing Commander S Baker but for the return flight he transferred to another aircraft. Apart from a fatal accident, involving a crew who had delivered their passengers to Wing, and were returning to base, on 26 April, it is believed this was the only accident involving loss of life to prisoners of war in a Bomber Command aircraft.

10 May 1945	97 Sqn	Lancaster III	ME623 OF-Z	Exodus

F/L C Arnot RAAF — T/o 1535 Brussels-Evere with a complement of 24 prisoners of war as passengers, but swung out of control and crashed, heavily, injuring three of those on board. None are identified by name in the Squadron ORB.

10 May 1945	101 Sqn	Lancaster I	RA595 SR-Q	Exodus

F/O P G L Collett RAAF
F/S J Horner RAAF
F/S R Martin
F/O A W Tompson
F/S A Condon RAAF
W/O M Hann RAAF
F/S M Smedley RAAF

T/o 1213 Brussels-Melsbroek but swung out of control and slid to a stop, its undercarriage collapsed. One member of crew, who is not identified, was slightly hurt. It is not known if any passengers were on board.

	300 Sqn	Lancaster I	PB730 BH-R	Exodus

F/S Gryglewicz PAF
Sgt Margula PAF
Sgt Miterski PAF
Sgt Dzius PAF
Sgt Roman PAF
Sgt Jeronim PAF
Sgt Sternowicz PAF

T/o 1348 Brussels-Melsbroek with a complement of 24 ex-prisoners of war as passengers, but veered from the runway and was damaged beyond repair. No injuries reported.

11 May 1945	83 Sqn	Lancaster III	PB438 OL-	Exodus

F/L R N Pereira

Landed 1915 Coningsby, wheels retracted, after the port wheel had burst during the flight. No injuries reported from the six crew, or twenty-four passengers.

	619 Sqn	Lancaster I	PA277 PG-Z	Ground

Struck 0040 while parked on its dispersal pan at Strubby, by Lancaster I PA276, sustaining damage that was uneconomical to repair. The other Lancaster was less seriously damaged and, subsequently, was repaired and returned to service.

13 May 1945	15 Sqn	Lancaster I	PP672 LS-N	Exodus

F/L B Bagenal

T/o 0745 Juvincourt with a complement of 24 ex-prisoners of war but a swing developed and the Lancaster crashed out of control. A fire broke out, but all escaped unharmed.

	44 Sqn	Lancaster III	RF203 KM-G	Ferry

F/L E Mercer
F/O K A Smith

Overshot the runway at Speke Airport, Liverpool and crashed at 1143. None of the 11-man crew were hurt; F/O Smith is believed to have been undergoing dual instruction.

16 May 1945	617 Sqn	Lancaster I	PD139 YZ-L	Training

Lt W Adams USAAF
P/O T H Collin

T/o 1148 Woodhall Spa with a crew of five and set course for Germany. At 1514, while flying fast and low, hit the ground near Oberg, 18 km W of Braunschweig. Amazingly, all the crew walked away uninjured. It will be recalled that Lt Adams USAAF had written off a Lancaster, at Lossiemouth, a month previous and soon after this second incident, he was returned to USAAF control.

17 May 1945	630 Sqn	Lancaster I	RF124 LE-S	Training

F/O B Hall   +
F/O R J O'Donnell   +
Sgt R H Smith   +
F/O V F D Meade   +
Sgt G L Rabbetts   +
Sgt V R W Southworth   +
Sgt J A Sills   +

Crashed 1715 and exploded with tremendous force off the Wednesfield/Willenhall Road at Short Heath in the eastern suburbs of Wolverhampton. The force of the explosion left a crater some 25 to 30 feet across with debris impacted to a depth of 15 to 20 feet. All are buried in the United Kingdom.

Note. This Lancaster, captained by Flying Officer A McLean RCAF, had taken part in 630 Squadron's last operation of the war, a mining raid over Oslo Fjord on 25-26 April. The above crash was the first fatal accident involving a Bomber Command aircraft engaged on a training exercise since the official ceasefire on 8 May.

18 May 1945	35 Sqn	Lancaster III	PB684 TL-B	Training

F/S W N Mercer

Overshot the runway at Graveley and crash-landed 1333, losing its undercarriage in the process. No injuries reported.

18 May 1945	408 Sqn	Lancaster X	KB993 EQ–U	Training

F/O A A Clifford RCAF +
F/S K B McIvor RCAF +
F/O D A Fehrman RCAF +
WO2 M C Cameron RCAF +
F/S C J Halvorson RCAF +
F/S L C Hellekson RCAF +

Entered cloud while on a cross country flight and flew into Shelf Moor, some 4 miles E from Glossop in the Peak District of Derbyshire. All were taken to Brookwood Military Cemetery.

Note. This was the last fatal accident over the United Kingdom involving a 6 (RCAF) Group crew. It was also the first Lancaster X written off by 408 Squadron which, until recently, had been equipped with Halifaxes.

20 May 1945	300 Sqn	Lancaster I	PD361 BH–H	Supply Flight

F/O W Horbik PAF
Sgt Huk PAF
P/O Lapinski PAF
F/L F Kot PAF
P/O K Spirydowicz PAF
Sgt R Kiejko PAF

T/o 1255 Faldingworth with a consignment of medical supplies. Crash-landed 1536 at Brussels-Melsbroek. No injuries reported and the valuable cargo was salvaged, undamaged.

21 May 1945	100 Sqn	Lancaster I	LL952 HW–W2	Training

F/O M P Jones +
Sgt I J Calverley +
F/S M A Chalmers RAAF +
F/S J W Montague +
F/S W P Gibson +
Sgt P Gapper +
Sgt F A Padmore +

Ditched 5 miles E of the Donna Nook ranges during air firing practice. Two, F/S Chalmers RAAF and Sgt Padmore rest in Cambridge City Cemetery and Abertillery (Aberbeeg) Cemetery respectively. The others are commemorated on the Runnymede Memorial.

25 May 1945	626 Sqn	Lancaster I	PD432 UM–E2	Training

F/S S A L Howes

Abandoned following an engine fire and crashed near Southrey, a village E of the River Witham and some 8 miles WSW from Horncastle in Lincolnshire. No injuries reported in respect of this accident which happened at 1310 hours.

2–3 Jun 1945	405 Sqn	Lancaster X	KB985 LQ–B	Training

F/O J R Hartley

T/o Linton-on-Ouse but a tyre burst and the crew were advised to divert to Carnaby airfield in Yorkshire. Arrived here at 0058 and crash-landed, writing off the Lancaster but without injury to its crew.

4–5 Jun 1945	608 Sqn	Mosquito XVI	PF487 6T–S	Training

W/O F I Trezona

T/o 2313 Downham Market but the port engine lost power and the pilot crash-landed, straight ahead, finishing up in a defunct airfield defence gun pit. The cause of the engine failure was traced to the collapse of the boost capsule. Neither member of crew was hurt.

5 Jun 1945	149 Sqn	Lancaster I	PP673 OJ–B	Transit

F/O P Tottle +
Sgt R E Tilley +
F/S P C Wyatt +
F/S E Paige +
F/S J Dyer +
F/S K Hird +
F/S L Jones +
LAC W C Spark +
LAC W H Wardle +
AC2 W Quinn +

T/o 1652 Juvincourt and crashed twenty-eight minutes later near Arras (Pas-de-Calais). All were taken for burial in the neighbouring Department of Nord at Lille Southern Cemetery. Unconfirmed reports state that one airman, who is not identified, survived. It is also reported that in the last few seconds before the crash, the Lancaster's starboard wing came off.

7–8 Jun 1945	608 Sqn	Mosquito XVI	PF502 6T–J	Training

W/O J C Portway +
Sgt E S Stephen +

T/o 2244 Downham Market. Returned to base at 0114 but on touch down swerved violently to starboard and, still travelling at high speed, crashed into a building. W/O Portway is buried in Wandsworth (Streatham) Cemetery; Sgt Stephen lies at Moston (St. Joseph's) Roman Catholic Cemetery in Manchester. His parents came from the Isle of Man; he had married Mildred Julia Stephen of Cleveland, Ohio.

9 Jun 1945	128 Sqn	Mosquito XVI	PF440 M5-H	Training

F/O A H Reynolds — T/o 0929 Wyton and crash-landed 0950 just beyond the Upwood airfield runway. Badly damaged, the airframe was relegated to training purposes on 7 July and given the serial 5304M. No member of crew was hurt.

14 Jun 1945	105 Sqn	Mosquito XVI	PF518 GB-	Training

S/L N F Hilgard — T/o 0945 Bourn for practice SBA and single-engined flying. Crash-landed 1025 roughly one mile S of the airfield, due to engine failure. No injuries reported.

14-15 Jun 1945	627 Sqn	Mosquito IV	DZ418 AZ-B	Training

W/O N K Shannon — Crash-landed 0057 on return to Woodhall Spa from a night cross country exercise. No one was hurt, but the Mosquito was damaged beyond reasonable repair.

Note. This was the last Mosquito IV written off in Bomber Command service.

15 Jun 1945	630 Sqn	Lancaster III	PB344 LE-R	Bomb Disposal

F/O G H Cowan +
F/S D P Currie +
F/S W E Smith +
F/S J Rhodes +
F/S F Reynolds +
F/S J Porter +

Last heard on W/T at 1147 advising its load of incendiaries had been disposed of and the crew were retuning to base. Nothing further was heard. All are commemorated on the Runnymede Memorial. A subsequent air sea rescue search of the area found fragments of wreckage, thought to have broken away from this Lancaster, in the North Sea some 105 nautical miles off Flamborough Head.

25 Jun 1945	50 Sqn	Lancaster I	PB755 VN-Y	Post Mortem

P/O G Douglas +

T/o Sturgate to assess the effectiveness of captured enemy radar systems. Abandoned, due to an engine fire, and crashed near Satrup, 15 km SE from Flensburg. Sadly, P/O Douglas's parachute failed to deploy; he is buried in Kiel War Cemetery.

	199 Sqn	Halifax III	NA259 EX-	Air Test

W/O I W Dent RAAF +
Sgt R E G Seymour +
Sgt W Way +
Sgt A M Adams +

At circa 1510 the Halifax was observed flying low over the sea and turning inland towards the beach at Cromer, Norfolk. Moments later, it crashed at the foot of the cliffs, bursting into flames on impact. All are buried in various UK cemeteries. Two persons, Sgt Gleddening USAAF and his wife, had a miraculous escape as both were sitting on the sands a mere 40 feet or so from the point of impact. Suffering from shock and minor burns, they were taken to Cromer hospital. The local fire brigades had to be lowered down the cliffs in order to get at the seat of the fire, and it was an hour before the flames could be brought under control.

Note. On 29 July 1945, the Squadron diarist indicated 199 Squadron had flown a total of 2,941 operational sorties and suffered the loss of thirty-four air-craft and crews. The Halifax, here summarised, was the last to be written off in Bomber Command service. I am indebted to Bob Collis for much of the detail here reported.

26 Jun 1945	429 Sqn	Lancaster III	RF253 AL-W	Bomb Disposal

F/L L Bawtree RCAF — On return to Leeming, lost power from both starboard engines and crash-landed on one of the airfield's dispersal pans. No one was hurt.

Note. Within the parameters of this series, this was the last 6 (RCAF) Group flying accident. F/L Bawtree RCAF had previously served with 625 Squadron.

	608 Sqn	Mosquito XVI	RV358 6T-C	Training

F/O V D Poole RCAF — T/o 1044 Downham Market with the intention of flying over northwest Germany but the starboard engine failed and the crew returned to base. Their approach was made at 1100, but not in line with the runway. Consequently, the pilot was obliged to make a last minute turn and in doing so the Mosquito hit the ground at an acute angle and the undercarriage collapsed. Moments later, a fire broke out in the starboard wing. Both scrambled clear, but their aircraft was destroyed.

28 Jun 1945	44 Sqn W/O R Grange	Lancaster III	ME394 KM-X	Training

T/o Spilsby for a fighter affiliation exercise but swung out of control and came to a halt with its undercarriage collapsed. None of the six crew were hurt but their aircraft was deemed beyond economical repair.

29 Jun 1945	61 Sqn F/O A Macdonald	Lancaster III	ME491 QR-	Training

T/o Sturgate for a fighter affiliation exercise but a tyre burst and the crew were instructed to proceed to Carnaby in Yorkshire. On landing here, the Lancaster swung off the runway and the undercarriage was retracted in order to stop the aircraft from careering off the airfield.

1 Jul 1945	150 Sqn F/O L Plane F/S S Smith	Lancaster I + +	NX583 IQ-T	Post Mortem

T/o 1205 Hemswell for the purpose of testing the effectiveness of captured German radar systems, course being set for Flensburg. Returned early on three engines, but the pilot misjudged his approach and while trying to go round again, swung out of control and crashed into a hangar. In addition to the deaths of two members of crew, one airman on the ground was killed and a second was injured. F/O Plane is buried in Manchester (Gorton) Cemetery, while F/S Smith, who hailed from Finchley in Middlesex, rests locally at Harpswell (St. Chad) Churchyard.

3 Jul 1945	166 Sqn P/O G Barlow F/S A R Kirschner Sgt C E Butler F/O J Doyle F/S R J Sullivan Sgt W F G Edge Sgt W Gibson	Lancaster I + + + + + + +	SW278 AS-V	Training

At around 1300, dived into the Bristol Channel. Five bodies were recovered, while panels 266 and 275 respectively of the Runnymede Memorial perpetuate the names of F/O Doyle and Sgt Gibson. P/O Barlow, who rests in Manchester Southern Cemetery, had married Ann Barlow of Clontarf, Co. Dublin in the Irish Republic.

	627 Sqn F/L D N Johnson P/O J D Finlayson	Mosquito XXV + inj	KB416 AZ-P	Training

T/o 1450 Woodhall Spa. During the flight, the port engine failed and on return to base, the crew were uncertain as to whether the undercarriage had locked down, or not. Consequently, the Mosquito hit the runway hard and ballooned back into the air before crash-landing 1740, bursting into flames. The fire and rescue team were quickly on the scene and the NCO in charge of the section, Cpl Stephen Cogger, promptly got into the blazing wreckage and with complete disregard to his own safety, began cutting through the cables that were trapping the navigator in his seat. Having successfully dragged P/O Finlayson to safety, Cpl Cogger went back into the flames in a valiant attempt to extricate the unconscious pilot. By this time the fire was burning fiercely and Cpl Cogger sustained further serious burns to his person, before being beaten back by the heat. F/L Johnson succumbed and he is buried in Southport (Duke Street) Cemetery. On 26 February 1946, Cpl Cogger received his richly deserved George Medal. It is further noted that the Mosquito crew had arrived on 627 Squadron on 14 June from 515 Squadron as one of several crews posted in for Tiger Force training.

9 Jul 1945	90 Sqn F/O H C Stone	Lancaster I	LM280 WP-F	Training

Crash-landed 1150, wheels retracted, on Castle Combe airfield in Wiltshire, following an in flight fire in the port inner engine. One member of crew, not named, was slightly injured.

	608 Sqn W/O C G Johnston	Mosquito XVI	RV351 6T-R	Ground

On starting engines at 1500 at Downham Market in readiness for an air test, the undercarriage gave way, wrecking the Mosquito. Neither member of crew was hurt.

10 Jul 1945	214 Sqn F/O K W Spencer	Fortress III	HB765 BU-R	Air Test

Landed 1205 Oulton, in a rainstorm, and ran on to soft ground, tipping up onto its nose before falling back, damaging very severely the rear fuselage and tail. No one amongst the nine-man crew were hurt, but the Fortress was declared beyond economical repair.

13 Jul 1945	97 Sqn	Lancaster III	PB133 OF-E	Training

F/O A R Tarpen — Returned to Coningsby, early, from a cross country exercise with the starboard inner feathered. The Lancaster touched down halfway along the runway and still travelling at high speed entered the overshoot area, whereupon an undercarriage leg gave way. As the wing hit the rough ground, the outer port engine was ripped from its frame and soon afterwards a fire broke out. All seven crew scrambled from the wreck, shaken, but uninjured.

	97 Sqn	Lancaster III	PB422 OF-P	Training
	F/O R W Wright	+		
	F/S A J Molyneux	+		
	F/O J L Bendix DFC	+		
	F/S J Eastwood	+		

T/o 1123 Coningsby for a bombing exercise but the port outer burst into flames. Eye witnesses report the Lancaster climbing steeply in a left hand bank before stalling and crashing through the tops of trees. The four members of crew rest in various United Kingdom cemeteries.

	128 Sqn	Mosquito XVI	PF406 M5-E	Training
	F/O A H Reynolds			

T/o Warboys but soon afterwards the hydraulics failed and the crew headed for Woodbridge in Suffolk. Touched down at 1145, whereupon the Mosquito swung first to starboard and then to port as the pilot applied opposite rudder. Moments later the starboard undercarriage leg collapsed and the aircraft was wrecked. For F/O Reynolds, it was his second accident in just over a month.

	139 Sqn	Mosquito XVI	PF501 XD-F	Training
	F/O T Finlay			

T/o 0327 Tangmere but the starboard engine cut and though both throttles were closed and brakes applied, a crash could not be avoided. No one was hurt and five days later the wreck was deemed to be suitable for ground instructional purposes.

13-14 Jul 1945	626 Sqn	Lancaster I	PD287 UM-P	Training
	F/S S P Bell	+		
	Sgt S Welsh	+		
	Sgt L W Garfield	+		
	Sgt P J Allsebrook	+		
	Sgt H J Plastow	+		
	Sgt R C T Goldthorpe	+		

T/o Wickenby on a BALBO exercise with the crew briefed to fly at 2,000 feet. Ran into a thunder storm and crashed 0155 at Wharram le Street, some 12 miles NW of Driffield airfield, Yorkshire. All are buried in various cemeteries in the United Kingdom.

Note. 626 Squadron ORB has an entry for Sergeant J Critchley posted non effective sick to 14 Base on 14 July, but it is not clear if this was a result of the accident summarised above.

14 Jul 1945	460 Sqn	Lancaster I	NG404 AR-H	Training
	F/L M C Nottle RAAF			
	F/S R K Sloan			
	P/O C E Johnson RAAF	+		
	F/O W J Narrow			
	W/O K B Quinn RAAF	+		
	F/S R J Rogers RAAF	+		

Abandoned, following an in flight fire, and crashed near Kirton-in-Lindsey airfield in Lincolnshire. F/S Rogers RAAF had the terrible misfortune to fall into what the ORB describes as "a deep artificial lake" and drown before help arrived. Along with his fellow countrymen, who may have remained in the stricken aircraft, he lies in Cambridge City Cemetery.

17 Jul 1945	106 Sqn	Lancaster III	ND616 ZN-J	Training
	F/O M Johnson RNZAF			

Overshot the Metheringham runway and crash-landed 1319, without injury to the crew. In due course the airframe was salvaged and became an instructional aid with the serial 5532M.

17-18 Jul 1945	142 Sqn	Mosquito XXV	KB560 4H-	Training
	W/O G J Frensham			

T/o 2127 Gransden Lodge. During the sortie, the starboard engine failed and at 0036 the Mosquito touched down at base, off a fast approach, and finished up in the overshoot area, where it caught fire. The crew escaped injury.

19 Jul 1945	149 Sqn	Lancaster I	PA166 OJ-G	Training
	F/L I H Simmonds			

Overstressed while being recovered from loss of control, caused through icing. A safe landing was made at Methwold. Languished until struck off charge on 10 October 1945.

20 Jul 1945	139 Sqn	**Mosquito XX**	**KB217 XD-H**	**Ground**

Damaged beyond repair at Upwood when at 1000 an air cylinder exploded. The pressure gauge, at the time, was reading 160-lbs per square inch. Extensive damage was caused to the fuselage, but there are no reports of anyone being injured.

23-24 Jul 1945	692 Sqn	**Mosquito XVI**	**MM172 P3-V**	**Training**
	F/O L A Lane			

Returned to Gransden Lodge at 0125 from a night cross country but on touch down veered off the runway, to starboard, collapsing the undercarriage and damaging the Mosquito beyond repair. Neither member of crew was hurt.

24 Jul 1945	105 Sqn	**Mosquito IX**	**ML916 GB-**	**Training**
	W/O D C Webb			

T/o 1050 Upwood and headed for the continent. During the flight, the starboard engine failed and the crew diverted to Brussels-Melsbroek. Their approach was good, but due to late selection in putting down the undercarriage, the Mosquito arrived on the runway at 1255 with the unit not fully locked. Consequently, the aircraft was damaged beyond repair, but the crew escaped unharmed.

30 Jul 1945	166 Sqn	**Lancaster I**	**PA236 AS-B2**	**Ferry**
	F/O G L Willis	+		
	Sgt J J Pattison	+		
	F/S J A Allen	+		
	F/O L Roche	+		
	Sgt H G Russell	+		
	Sgt C F M Saunders	+		

Dived into the ground at Barnetby Wold Farm on the W side of Kirmington airfield. The tragedy happened at 1537 as the crew were preparing to land. All six are buried in various cemeteries across the land, three being interred in Cambridge City Cemetery. F/O Roche, it is noted, was thirty-five years of age.

1 Aug 1945	163 Sqn	**Mosquito XVI**	**PF517**	**Training**
	F/S P D Crisp			

T/o 1005 Wyton for a formation flying exercise. Returned to base at 1108, touching down in a slight cross wind. Within seconds, the Mosquito swung sharply to the right and wiped off its undercarriage. No injuries reported.

2 Aug 1945	571 Sqn	**Mosquito XVI**	**MM179 8K-**	**Air Test**
	F/L T V Laffey	inj		
	F/O A H Ching RNZAF	inj		

T/o 1442 Warboys, returning to base at 1529. On landing the Mosquito ballooned back into the air and before the pilot could catch his aircraft on the throttles, it bounced a second time. With power applied, it ran into the overshoot area and caught fire. Both officers were rushed to RAF Hospital Ely where they died on 3 and 8 August respectively. F/L Laffey rests in Hebburn Cemetery, while F/O Ching RNZAF lies at Cambridge City Cemetery.

3 Aug 1945	109 Sqn	**Mosquito XVI**	**ML991 HS-**	**Training**
	W/C R C E Law			

T/o 1116 Little Staughton for practice bombing. Returned to base at 1304, but held off too high and as a consequence the Mosquito bounced on landing and before W/C Law could open the throttles to cushion the next arrival, his aircraft thudded onto the runway and smashed its undercarriage. There are no reports on injury.

7 Aug 1945	626 Sqn	**Lancaster I**	**RF159 UM-C2**	**Dodge**
	P/O C R Chancellor	+		
	F/O N S Phillips	+		
	P/O C R Branch	+		
	F/S J F Kirk	+		
	W/O D R Cook	+		
	F/S J E Wilkinson	+		

Crashed at around 1200 at Carcassonne near Toulouse in southern France. All are buried in Mazargues Cemetery extension at Marseilles. Their average age was twenty-two. The crew composition was two pilots, flight engineer, navigator, wireless operator and an air gunner.

13 Aug 1945	142 Sqn	**Mosquito XXV**	**KB400 4H-V**	**Ferry**
	W/O R G Browne			

T/o 1440 Gransden Lodge and landed fifteen minutes later at Upwood, where a strong cross wind was blowing. This caused the Mosquito to veer off the runway, whereupon it struck the lip of a concrete road and the undercarriage collapsed. No one was hurt, but the aircraft was deemed beyond reasonable repair.

Note. Some sources quote 13 February 1945 as the date for this accident but the aircraft accident card confirms the date as reported above.

13 Aug 1945	149 Sqn F/L S J L Key	Lancaster I	PB902 OJ-H	Transit

Overshot and crash-landed 1230 while attempting to land at Trondheim-Vaernes airfield in Norway. No injuries reported.

17 Aug 1945	35 Sqn	Lancaster I	PB754 TL-D	Ground

Struck at 0730 while parked on Bari airfield in Italy by Lancaster I ME834 of 115 Squadron, whose pilot had lost control on take off.

	115 Sqn	Lancaster I	HK798 KO-H	Ground

Written off in the manner described above.

	115 Sqn F/O Gibbons	Lancaster I	ME834 KO-G	Dodge

T/o 0730 Bari but a tyre burst, sending the Lancaster out of control and smashing into aircraft parked on the perimeter track. The sole casualty, who is not named, was a solder who was sitting in the front turret; happily, his injuries proved to be slight.

Note. Don Bruce reports that HK798 had been delivered to 115 Squadron on 18 February 1945 and was coded IL-L, later becoming IL-B. Shortly before its demise, the combination KO-H had been applied. ME834 was a veteran, having arrived at Witchford on 6 June 1944 and going on to fly seventy-four operational sorties. It displayed a variety of Squadron code combinations; KO-K, A4-M, KO-M and, finally on 1 June 1945, KO-G.

23 Aug 1945	227 Sqn F/O K Mersh	Lancaster III	ND992 9J-Y	Dodge

T/o 0725 Graveley but forced-landed 0800 in a field near Ford airfield in Sussex, following an in-flight fire. No injuries reported.

27 Aug 1945	139 Sqn F/L T Finlay	Mosquito XVI	MM200 XD-E	Training

T/o 1520 Upwood for a cross country exercise. While changing tanks, an air lock caused an engine to fail and the crew headed for Valley on Anglesey. To compensate for loss of power, F/L Finlay decided on a fast approach, but on touch down at 1710 he lost control and the Mosquito was wrecked. Neither member of crew was hurt; it will be recalled that F/L Finlay had been involved in a serious accident on 13 July.

	1409 Flt F/L A G Hughes	Mosquito XVI	NS733 inj	Training

T/o 1035 Upwood with the intention of flying over the continent to view the bomb damage. As the aircraft gathered speed the starboard engine suddenly surged and F/L Hughes was unable to prevent the Mosquito from crashing. A fire broke out and both crew members were injured.

Conclusion

No other command in the Royal Air Force sustained casualties at the frequency and scale as Bomber Command. Martin Middlebrook and Chris Everitt show, in their Bomber Command War Diaries, a total of 55,573 dead with a further 9,838 taken prisoner of war. The names of the majority of those who make up these bare statistics are identified in this series of six volumes, which, I hope, will stand as a mark to their supreme courage.

Throughout the last seven years that have occupied me in my research into the subject, I have referred constantly to the cemetery registers published by the Commonwealth War Graves Commission. No matter how hard one tries to be objective, the sheer volume of air force names that are recorded on each page causes me to reflect on the gratitude that we, as a nation, should show to those young airmen of fifty years ago, and more, that took the war into the enemy camp on an almost nightly basis between that terrible summer of 1940 and May 1945.

For them, and many were not much older than eighteen or in their early 20s, their course of life, and all the joys that should have been their future, was over scarce before it had begun.

Just one example of the sheer scale of numbers, that I refer to in my opening paragraph, in Germany, where the Commission is responsible for nine major concentration cemeteries plus half-a-dozen smaller plots, the dead of the air forces is more than double that of the army with a staggering 17,630 graves of known and unknown airmen, of which most fell while flying in Bomber Command.

In presenting this example, I acknowledge fully the courage of the ground forces who fought their way into Germany and leaving, as a lasting testament, well over 8,000 of their men resting in German soil.

Perhaps, in a way, we do acknowledge now, through the medium of books, squadron associations, radio, television and the like, better than those in authority that in the immediate aftermath of the war could have done something to mark the appreciation of our nation to those who had participated in that long campaign of attrition against a skilled and resolute enemy. For let there be no misunderstanding, the Luftwaffe fought tooth and nail and with no little success to deny Bomber Command access to what became known as "Fortress Europe".

And, thus, it has to be forcibly said, the politicians of the time treated Sir Arthur Harris, and by association the officers and airmen that came under his authority, quite shamefully. Apart from the gallantry medals awarded (and for the majority such kudos passed them by) there was no distinctive medal in recognition of their part in helping to rid the world of one of the most despotic dictators in modern history.

On a personal level, this deeply wounded Sir Arthur who, it is said, felt that he had failed those who had supported him to the hilt through thick and thin from the time that he took up the helm at High Wycombe in February 1942 until his departure on the 15th of September, 1945.

Throughout his long retirement (he was over fifty when he left the service), Harris maintained a dignified silence, refusing publicly to counter the sniping remarks made against his leadership, or to refute the scurrilous charges levelled by some historians as to the ethics of the area bombing campaign. Even today, there are some who believe Sir Arthur was the architect of area bombing, whereas, in fact, he merely carried out the orders of the Air Council and the dictates from the War Cabinet.

Happily, he lived long enough to see the establishment of the Bomber Command Museum at Hendon and was present on the 12th of April 1983, for the official opening ceremony by Her Majesty Queen Elizabeth, the Queen Mother.

He wrote only one book, "Bomber Offensive" which appeared in 1947. In taking up the pen he had two objectives in mind. One was to explain the bombing offensive and the many trials and tribulations that had to be overcome before success could be assured and secondly to pay tribute to the stoicism of his aircrews upon whose young shoulders the weight of his command decisions fell.

In typical Harris fashion, he pulled no punches, neither did he seek to make any excuses or hide behind the coat-tails of his superiors. By and large, he succeeded in both purposes and as an analytical record of the bombing campaign, it has stood the test of time remarkably well. So, too, have his men. By the time he took up office, the pre-war officer and non-commissioned officer aircrews had been reduced to a fraction of their pre-1939 strengths and Bomber Command was now reliant on the vast influx of volunteer reserve airmen, plus the thousands of Commonwealth and Dominion airmen that had answered the call to arms. Worthy contribution was also forthcoming from airmen who had escaped from the occupied countries, and who were anxious to play their part in restoring freedom to their homelands.

All are now in the autumn of their lives; lives that they can justly look back upon with pride. A handful remained in the peace time air force but the majority were only too anxious to return to civilian life and begin the task of rebuilding interrupted careers and raising families in the austere conditions of post-war Britain.

Thus, the bonds of friendship forged on those bleak wartime airfields faded as the priorities of "civvy street" took over and contacts were lost as the years rolled by.

Then, in the late 1970s came a resurgence of interest. Many squadron histories were started and though not all were published, squadron associations were either formed or strengthened and today I am amazed at the quality and frequency of the newsletters that arrive in my mail.

On the continent, too, the sacrifice of the air force is not forgotten, particularly in the smaller villages and communities where often a single grave, or the seven headstones marking the last resting place of an individual crew, are a permanent reminder of the cost in re-establishing their eventual freedom. Here, the dedication and commitment by the local inhabitants towards honouring the fallen is quite magnificent to behold, and this wonderful appreciation extends across all generations.

Furthermore, what is plainly evident, the resolve and spirit of those most concerned with those now distant days has not dimmed. Limbs may not be so strong, or eyesight keen but that self confidence to overcome all odds is still present and, I firmly believe, will remain for as long as there are survivors from the squadrons of Bomber Command.

Royal Air Force
BOMBER COMMAND LOSSES
of the Second World War

Appendices

Appendix 1

Bomber Squadron Losses
January to September 1945

Sqn	Type	Op.	Non-op.	Grnd	Sqn	Type	Op.	Non-op.	Grnd
7	Lancaster I	1			139	Mosquito XXV	2		
	Lancaster III	3			141	Mosquito VI	1		
9	Lancaster I	9				Mosquito NF.30	1	1	
10	Halifax III	16	2		142	Mosquito XXV	7	4	
12	Lancaster I	11			149	Lancaster I	4	2	
	Lancaster III	5	1		150	Lancaster I	6	1	
15	Lancaster I	8	1		153	Lancaster I	12		
23	Mosquito VI	3				Lancaster III	6		
35	Lancaster I	1		1	156	Lancaster I	7		
	Lancaster III	7	1		157	Mosquito XIX	3	2	
44	Lancaster I	4				Mosquito NF.30	1		
	Lancaster III	7	2		158	Halifax III	18		
49	Lancaster I	4			161	Hudson III	1		
	Lancaster III	7	2			Stirling IV	1	1	
50	Lancaster I	17	1		162	Mosquito XX	1		1
	Lancaster III	1				Mosquito XXV	2		
51	Halifax III	11			163	Mosquito XVI		1	
57	Lancaster I	4		3		Mosquito XXV	6	1	
	Lancaster III	3	1	3	166	Lancaster I	14	2	
61	Lancaster I	12		2		Lancaster III	8		
	Lancaster III	4	1		169	Mosquito VI	4		
75	Lancaster I	6				Mosquito XIX	3	2	
	Lancaster III	5			170	Lancaster I	3		
76	Halifax III	9				Lancaster III	10		
	Halifax VI	3			171	Halifax III	4	1	
77	Halifax III	9			186	Lancaster I	7		
	Halifax VI	3	1			Lancaster III	2		
78	Halifax III	6			189	Lancaster I	13		
83	Lancaster I		1			Lancaster III	2		
	Lancaster III	6		1	192	Mosquito IV	1		
85	Mosquito VI		1			Halifax III	5	1	
	Mosquito NF.30	4	3		195	Lancaster I	2		
90	Lancaster I	5	2		199	Stirling III	1		
97	Lancaster III	5	2			Halifax III	2	1	
100	Lancaster I	1	2		207	Lancaster I	7		
	Lancaster III	8	1			Lancaster III	5	1	
101	Lancaster I	7	1		214	Fortress III	9	1	
	Lancaster III	6		1	218	Lancaster I	9		
102	Halifax III	9			223	Liberator IV	3		
	Halifax VI	3			227	Lancaster I	8		
103	Lancaster I	14				Lancaster III	3		
	Lancaster III	6	1		239	Mosquito VI	1	1	
105	Mosquito IX	4	2			Mosquito NF.30	3		
	Mosquito XVI	5	2		300	Lancaster I	13	1	
106	Lancaster I	5				Lancaster III	1		
	Lancaster III	3	2		346	Halifax III	8	1	
109	Mosquito IX	2				Halifax VI		2	
	Mosquito XVI	2	4		347	Halifax III	16		
115	Lancaster I	4		1		Halifax VI	1		
	Lancaster III	1			405	Lancaster III	10		
128	Mosquito XVI	11	3			Lancaster X		1	
138	Stirling IV	4			408	Halifax III	1		
	Lancaster I	1				Halifax VII	13		1
139	Mosquito XVI	3	2	1		Lancaster X		1	
	Mosquito XX	8	1	1	415	Halifax III	12		

Sqn	Type	Op.	Non-op.	Grnd	Sqn	Type	Op.	Non-op.	Grnd
419	Lancaster X	16	1		571	Mosquito XVI	12	4	
420	Halifax III	14	1	1	576	Lancaster I	15		
424	Halifax III	3				Lancaster III	2		
	Lancaster I	7			578	Halifax III	12		
425	Halifax III	14	1		582	Lancaster I		1	
426	Halifax III	1				Lancaster III	5	1	
	Halifax VII	12		2	608	Mosquito XVI	2	4	1
427	Halifax III	8				Mosquito XX	3		
428	Lancaster X	8	5			Mosquito XXV	2		
429	Halifax III	4	1		617	Lancaster I	4	2	
	Lancaster I	1			619	Lancaster I	7		1
	Lancaster III		1			Lancaster III	5	1	
431	Lancaster X	12	1		622	Lancaster I	7		
432	Halifax VII	11	2		625	Lancaster I	11		
433	Lancaster I	4				Lancaster III	1		
434	Lancaster X	7			626	Lancaster I	9	3	
460	Lancaster I	7	3			Lancaster III	3		
	Lancaster III	8			627	Mosquito IV	2	1	
462	Halifax III	12	1			Mosquito IX		1	
463	Lancaster I	12	2			Mosquito XVI		1	
	Lancaster III	4				Mosquito XXV	1	2	
466	Halifax III	6	1		630	Lancaster I	6	1	
467	Lancaster I	6	1			Lancaster III	2	1	
	Lancaster III	5			635	Lancaster I	3	1	
514	Lancaster I	4				Lancaster III	6		
	Lancaster III	3	1		640	Halifax III	8		
515	Mosquito VI	4				Halifax VI	2		
550	Lancaster I	11	1		692	Mosquito XVI	10	2	
	Lancaster II	5				Lancaster III	26	2	
					Total		938	120	22

Note 1. 156 Squadron lost one crew in a training accident, while flying in a Lancaster III belonging to the Pathfinder Force Night Training Unit, commonly referred to on Form AM 78 as NTU (Night Training Unit).

Note 2. All losses in respect of Exodus and Manna have been counted as operational losses, while the three Lancasters written off during Dodge flights have been entered in the non-operational column.

1945 Totals

Type	Op.	Non-op.	Grnd	Total
Fortress III	9	1		10
Halifax III	208	11	1	220
Halifax VI	12	3		15
Halifax VII	36	2	3	41
Hudson III	1			1
Lancaster I	326	28	9	363
Lancaster III	180	20	5	205
Lancaster X	43	9		52
Liberator IV	3			3
Mosquito IV	3	1		4
Mosquito VI	13	2		15
Mosquito IX	6	3		9
Mosquito XVI	45	23	2	70
Mosquito XIX	6	4		10
Mosquito XX	12	1	2	15
Mosquito XXV	20	7		27
Mosquito NF.30	9	4		13
Stirling III	1			1
Stirling IV	5	1		6
Total	938	120	22	1080

Note. The above table identifies squadron losses; those sustained by OTUs/CUs appear in their respective appendices. The same applies in respect of the table opposite. The Mosquito casualties suffered by 1409 Flight are recorded in Appendix 4.

It is reiterated that the losses published identify the serials of aircraft that for whatever reason never flew again under Bomber Command authority, the exceptions being a couple of Lancasters that having force landed in Russia and Sweden were repaired and in the case of the Swedish example made at least one more flight. There is evidence that the Russian Lancaster, flew with 16 Squadron of the White Sea Fleet (see Volume 5 page 416).

1939-1945 Combined Totals - Revised

Type	Op.	Non-op.	Grnd	Total
Anson I	1	12		13*
Battle I	148	40	28	217*
Beaufighter IV	1			1
Blenheim I	11	11		23*
Blenheim IV	570	123	19	715*
Blenheim V		2		2
Boston III	51	17	1	69
Boston IIIA	2	2		4
Fortress I	3	2	1	6
Fortress II	3			3
Fortress III	13	1		14
Halifax I	37	6	1	46
Halifax II	1012	82	6	1100
Halifax III	949	68	15	1032
Halifax V	291	18	2	311
Halifax VI	12	3		15
Halifax VII	82	4	3	89
Hampden I	613	102	3	718
Hereford I		2		2
Hudson I		1		1
Hudson III	3	1	1	5
Hudson IIIA	1	1		2
Lancaster I	1585	108	24	1717
Lancaster II	211	14	1	226
Lancaster III	2005	80	11	2096
Lancaster VI	1			1
Lancaster X	91	14		105
Liberator III	1			1
Liberator IV	3			3
Lysander III	1	2		3
Lysander IIIA	12	1		13
Manchester I	75	18		93
Master I		1		1
Mitchell II	10	8		18
Mosquito II	26	13		39
Mosquito IV	124	16		140
Mosquito VI	48	9	1	58
Mosquito IX	19	8		27
Mosquito XVI	108	28	2	138
Mosquito XVII		1		1
Mosquito XIX	17	9		26
Mosquito XX	38	2	2	42
Mosquito XXV	33	8		41
Mosquito NF.30	10	5		15
Oxford I		1		1
Stirling I	400	39	3	442
Stirling III	375	28	2	405
Stirling IV	16	2		18
Ventura I	23	8		31
Ventura II	21	1		22
Wellington I	3	11	1	15
Wellington IA	45	13	1	59
Wellington IC	563	36	4	610*
Wellington II	171	15	2	188
Wellington III	430	37	4	471
Wellington IV	141	6	1	149*
Wellington X	233	31	2	266
Whitley I		2		2
Whitley II		2		2
Whitley III	9	6		15
Whitley IV	5	2		7
Whitley V	423	16	11	452*
Total	11079	1099	152	12330

* Indicates losses not covered by the three column headings.

Appendix 2

Bomber Group Losses
January to September 1945

	Sqn	Code	Type	Op.	Non-op.	Grnd	Remarks
1 Group	12	PH	Lancaster I	11			
		PH	Lancaster III	5	1		
	100	HW	Lancaster I	1	2		
		HW	Lancaster III	8	1		
	101	SR	Lancaster I	7	1		ABC equipped.
		SR	Lancaster III	6		1	
	103	PM	Lancaster I	14			
		PM	Lancaster III	6	1		
	150	IQ	Lancaster I	6	1		
	153	P4	Lancaster I	12			
		P4	Lancaster III	6			
	166	AS	Lancaster I	14	2		
		AS	Lancaster III	8			
	170	TC	Lancaster I	3			
		TC	Lancaster III	10			
	300	BH	Lancaster I	13	1		
		BH	Lancaster III	1			
	460	AR	Lancaster I	7	3		
		AR	Lancaster III	8			
	550	BQ	Lancaster I	11	1		
		BQ	Lancaster III	5			
	576	UL	Lancaster I	15			
		UL	Lancaster III	2			
	625	CF	Lancaster I	11			
		CF	Lancaster III	1			
	626	UM	Lancaster I	9	3		
		UM	Lancaster III	3			
			Total	203	17	1	
3 Group	15	LS	Lancaster I	8	1		
	75	AA	Lancaster I	6			C Flight aircraft coded JN
		AA	Lancaster III	5			
	90	WP	Lancaster I	5	2		C Flight aircraft coded XY
	115	KO	Lancaster I	4		1	C Flight aircraft coded IL
		KO	Lancaster III	1	1		
	138	NF	Stirling IV	4			Reequipped Lancaster Mar 45
		NF	Lancaster I	1			
	149	OJ	Lancaster I	4	2		
	161	MA	Hudson III	1			Transferred 38 Group
		MA	Stirling IV	1	1		9 Mar 45
	186	XY	Lancaster I	7			Disbanded 17 Jul 45
		XY	Lancaster III	2			
	195	A4	Lancaster I	2			Disbanded 14 Aug 45
	218	HA	Lancaster I	9			C Flight aircraft coded XH
	514	JI	Lancaster I	4			C Flight aircraft coded A2
		JI	Lancaster III	3	1		Disbanded 22 Aug 45
	622	GI	Lancaster I	7			Disbanded 15 Aug 45
			Total	74	8	1	

	Sqn	Code	Type	Op.	Non-op.	Grnd	Remarks
4 Group	10	ZA	Halifax III	16	2		Transferred Transport Command
	51	MH	Halifax III	11			Transferred Transport Command
	76	MP	Halifax III	9			Reequipped Halifax VI Mar 45
		MP	Halifax VI	3			Transferred Transport Command
	77	KN	Halifax III	9			Reequipped Halifax VI Mar 45
		KN	Halifax VI	3	1		Transferred Transport Command
	78	EY	Halifax III	6			Transferred Transport Command
	102	DY	Halifax III	9			Reequipped Halifax VI Feb 45
		DY	Halifax VI	3			Transferred Transport Command
	158	NP	Halifax III	18			Transferred Transport Command
	346	H7	Halifax III	8	1		Reequipped Halifax VI Mar 45
		H7	Halifax VI		2		Transferred 1 Group May 45
	347	L8	Halifax III	16			Reequipped Halifax VI Mar 45
		L8	Halifax VI	1			Transferred 1 Group
	466	HD	Halifax III	6	1		Transferred Transport Command
	578	LK	Halifax III	12			Disbanded 15 Apr 45
	640	C8	Halifax III	8			Reequipped Halifax VI Mar 45
		C8	Halifax VI	2			Disbanded 7 May 45
			Total	140	7		

Note. The transfer from Bomber Command to Transport Command was effective from 2359 hours on 7 May 1945, the group headquarters assuming the new title No. 4 (Transport) Group and remaining at Heslington Hall. Although transferred on paper to 1 Group, 346 and 347 Squadrons of the FFAF remained under 4 (Transport) Group administration.

	Sqn	Code	Type	Op.	Non-op.	Grnd	Remarks
5 Group	9	WS	Lancaster I	9			Carried 12,000lb Tallboy bomb
	44	KM	Lancaster I	4			
		KM	Lancaster III	7	2		
	49	EA	Lancaster I	4			
		EA	Lancaster III	7	2		
	50	VN	Lancaster I	17	1		
		VN	Lancaster III	1			
	57	DX	Lancaster I	4		3	
		DX	Lancaster III	3	1	3	
	61	QR	Lancaster I	12		2	
		QR	Lancaster III	4	1		
	83	OL	Lancaster I			1	
		OL	Lancaster III	6		1	
	97	OF	Lancaster III	5	2		
	106	ZN	Lancaster I	5			
		ZN	Lancaster III	3	2		
	189	CA	Lancaster I	13			
		CA	Lancaster III	2			
	207	EM	Lancaster I	7			
		EM	Lancaster III	5	1		
	227	9J	Lancaster I	8			
		9J	Lancaster III	3			
	463	JO	Lancaster I	12	2		
		JO	Lancaster III	4			
	467	PO	Lancaster I	6	1		
		PO	Lancaster III	5			
	617	KC	Lancaster I	4	2		Carried 12,000lb Tallboy bomb
	619	PG	Lancaster I	7		1	Disbanded 18 Jul 45
		PG	Lancaster III	5	1		
	627	AZ	Mosquito IV	2	1		
		AZ	Mosquito IX		1		
		AZ	Mosquito XVI		1		Type received Mar 45
		AZ	Mosquito XXV	1	2		
	630	LE	Lancaster I	6	1		Disbanded 18 Jul 45
		LE	Lancaster III	2	1		
			Total	183	25	11	

	Sqn	Code	Type	Op.	Non-op.	Grnd	Remarks
6 Group	405	LQ	Lancaster X		1		To Canada 16 Jun 45
	408	EQ	Halifax III	1			Type withdrawn Feb 45
		EQ	Halifax VII	13		1	Reequipped Lancaster X May 45
		EQ	Lancaster X		1		To Canada 14 Jun 45
	415	6U	Halifax III	12			Disbanded 15 May 45
	419	VR	Lancaster X	16	1		To Canada 4 Jun 45
	420	PT	Halifax III	14	1	1	To Canada 12 Jun 45
	424	QB	Halifax III	3			Reequipped Lancaster I Jan 45
		QB	Lancaster I	7			Transferred 1 Group Aug 45
	425	KW	Halifax III	14	1		To Canada 13 Jun 45*
	426	OW	Halifax III	1			Type withdrawn Jan 45
		OW	Halifax VII	12		2	Transferred Transport Command
	427	ZL	Halifax III	8			Transferred 1 Group Aug 45*
	428	NA	Lancaster X	8	5		To Canada 31 May 45
	429	AL	Halifax III	4	1		Reequipped Lancaster I Mar 45
		AL	Lancaster I	1			
		AL	Lancaster III		1		Transferred 1 Group Aug 45
	431	SE	Lancaster X	12	1		To Canada 12 Jun 45
	432	QO	Halifax VII	11	2		Disbanded 15 May 45
	433	BM	Lancaster I	4			Transferred 1 Group Aug 45
	434	WL	Lancaster X	7			To Canada 15 Jun 45
			Total	148	15	4	

*   Having reequipped with either Lancaster I/III or Lancaster X.

Note. Without exception, all the RCAF bomber squadrons had titles added to their number; that applied to 419 Squadron being the nick-name of its first Commanding Officer, Wing Commander John Fulton DSO DFC AFC. When 415 Squadron transferred from Coastal Command on 12 July 1944, application was made to change their title from Swordfish to Bronco, but this was rejected, by letter, in late October:

408 (Goose)	427 (Lion)
415 (Swordfish)	428 (Ghost)
419 (Moose)	429 (Bison)
420 (Snowy Owl)	431 (Iroquois)
424 (Tiger)	432 (Leaside)
425 (Alouette)	433 (Porcupine)
426 (Thunderbird)	434 (Bluenose)

405 Squadron, assigned in 1943 to 8 Group for Pathfinder Duties, retained the title Vancouver.

	Sqn	Code	Type	Op.	Non-op.	Grnd	Remarks
8 Group	7	MG	Lancaster I	1			
		MG	Lancaster III	3			
	35	TL	Lancaster I	1		1	
		TL	Lancaster III	7	1		
	105	GB	Mosquito IX	4	2		
		GB	Mosquito XVI	5	2		
	109	HS	Mosquito IX	2			
		HS	Mosquito XVI	2	4		
	128	M5	Mosquito XVI	11	3		
	139	XD	Mosquito XVI	3	2	1	
		XD	Mosquito XX	8	1	1	
		XD	Mosquito XXV	2			
	142	4H	Mosquito XXV	7	4		
	156	GT	Lancaster III	7			
	162	CR	Mosquito XX	1		1	
		CR	Mosquito XXV	2			
	163		Mosquito XVI		1		Reformed 25 Jan 45
			Mosquito XXV	6	1		Disbanded 10 Aug 45
	405	LQ	Lancaster III	10			Transferred 6 Group 26 May 45
	571	8K	Mosquito XVI	12	4		
	582	60	Lancaster I		1		
		60	Lancaster III	5	1		
	608	6T	Mosquito XVI	2	4	1	Disbanded 28 Aug 45
		6T	Mosquito XX	3			
		6T	Mosquito XXV	2			

	Sqn	Code	Type	Op.	Non-op.	Grnd	Remarks
8 Group	635	F2	Lancaster I	3	1		Disbanded 1 Sep 45
		F2	Lancaster III	6			
	692	P3	Mosquito XVI	10	2		
			Total	125	34	5	

Note. The Mosquito element of 8 Group was utilised in the crucial task of target marking and in carrying out nuisance raids, particularly to Berlin, the Ruhr and other German industrial targets. In this role they operated as the Light Night Striking Force.

	Sqn	Code	Type	Op.	Non-op.	Grnd	Remarks
100 Group	23	YP	Mosquito VI	3			
	85	VY	Mosquito XIX		1		Transferred Fighter Command
		VY	Mosquito NF.30	4	3		by 27 Jun 45
	141	TW	Mosquito VI	1			
		TW	Mosquito NF.30	1	1		
	157	RS	Mosquito XIX	3	2		Disbanded 16 Aug 45
		RS	Mosquito NF.30	1			
	169	VI	Mosquito VI	4			Disbanded 10 Aug 45
		VI	Mosquito XIX	3	2		
	171	6Y	Halifax III	4	1		Disbanded 27 Jul 45
	192	DT	Mosquito IV	1			Disbanded 22 Aug 45
		DT	Halifax III	5	1		
	199	EX	Stirling III	1			Type withdrawn Mar 45
		EX	Halifax III	2	1		Disbanded 29 Jul 45
	214	BU	Fortress III	9	1		Disbanded 27 Jul 45
	223	6G	Liberator IV	3			Disbanded 29 Jul 45
	239	HB	Mosquito VI	1	1		Disbanded 1 Jul 45
		HB	Mosquito NF.30	3			
	462	Z5	Halifax III	12	1		
	515	3P	Mosquito VI	4			Disbanded 10 Jun 45
			Total	65	15		

Note. As will be realised from the above table, 100 Group was rapidly run down on the cessation of hostilities in Europe and by 2 September, only 23 and 141 Squadrons, equipped with Mosquitoes, and 462 Squadron, with its Halifaxes, remained on active strength. 192 Squadron, on disbandment, formed the basis of Central Signals Establishment, while 214 Squadron was reformed on the same day at Amendola in Italy by renumbering 614 Squadron. The definitive history of this Group is yet to be written, but two books in recent years have gone part way to redress the situation; 'Confound and Destroy' by Martin Streetly and 'Confounding the Reich' by Martin W Bowman and Tom Cushing. Both are strongly recommended.

Appendix 3

Bomber Squadron Bases
January to September 1945

	Sqn	Base	Arrived	Remarks
1 Group	12	Wickenby, Lincolnshire	in situ	
	100	Grimsby, Lincolnshire	in situ	
		Elsham Wolds, Lincolnshire	1 Apr 45	
	101	Ludford Magna, Lincolnshire	in situ	
	103	Elsham Wolds, Lincolnshire	in situ	
	150	Hemswell, Lincolnshire	in situ	
	153	Scampton, Lincolnshire	in situ	
	166	Kirmington, Lincolnshire	in situ	
	170	Hemswell, Lincolnshire	in situ	
	300	Faldingworth, Lincolnshire	in situ	
	346	Elvington, Yorkshire	8 May 45	Administered by 4 (T) Group
	347	Elvington, Yorkshire	8 May 45	Administered by 4 (T) Group
	460	Binbrook, Lincolnshire	in situ	
		East Kirkby, Lincolnshire	20 Jul 45	
	424	Skipton-on-Swale, Yorkshire	30 Aug 45	Transferred from 6 Group
	427	Leeming, Yorkshire	30 Aug 45	Transferred from 6 Group
	429	Leeming, Yorkshire	30 Aug 45	Transferred from 6 Group
	433	Skipton-on-Swale, Yorkshire	30 Aug 45	Transferred from 6 Group
	550	North Killingholme, Lincolnshire	in situ	
	576	Fiskerton, Lincolnshire	in situ	
	625	Kelstern, Lincolnshire	in situ	
		Scampton, Lincolnshire	5 Apr 45	
	626	Wickenby, Lincolnshire	in situ	
3 Group	7	Mepal, Cambridgeshire	24 Jul 45	Transferred from 8 Group
	15	Mildenhall, Suffolk	in situ	
	44	Mepal, Cambridgeshire	21 Jul 45	Transferred from 5 Group
		Mildenhall, Suffolk	25 Aug 45	
	75	Mepal, Cambridgeshire	in situ	Transferred 5 Group Jul 45
	90	Tuddenham, Suffolk	in situ	
	115	Witchford, Cambridgeshire	in situ	
	138	Tempsford, Bedfordshire	in situ	SOE operations
		Tuddenham, Suffolk	9 Mar 45	Reequipped Lancaster I
	149	Methwold, Norfolk	in situ	
	161	Tempsford, Bedfordshire	in situ	Transferred 38 Group Mar 45
	186	Stradishall, Suffolk	in situ	Disbanded 17 Jul 45
	195	Wratting Common, Cambridgeshire	in situ	Disbanded 14 Aug 45
	218	Chedburgh, Suffolk	in situ	Disbanded 10 Aug 45
	514	Waterbeach, Cambridgeshire	in situ	Disbanded 22 Aug 45
	622	Mildenhall, Suffolk	in situ	Disbanded 15 Aug 45
4 Group	10	Melbourne, Yorkshire	in situ	To Transport Command May 45
	51	Snaith, Yorkshire	in situ	To Transport Command May 45
		Leconfield, Yorkshire	20 Apr 45	
	76	Holme-on-Spalding Moor, Yorkshire	in situ	To Transport Command May 45
	77	Full Sutton, Yorkshire	in situ	To Transport Command May 45
	78	Breighton, Yorkshire	in situ	To Transport Command May 45
	102	Pocklington, Yorkshire	in situ	To Transport Command May 45
	158	Lissett, Yorkshire	in situ	To Transport Command May 45
	346	Elvington, Yorkshire	in situ	Transferred 1 Group May 45
	347	Elvington, Yorkshire	in situ	Transferred 1 Group May 45
	466	Driffield, Yorkshire	in situ	To Transport Command May 45
	578	Burn, Yorkshire	in situ	Disbanded 15 Apr 45

	Sqn	Base	Arrived	Remarks
4 Group	640	Leconfield, Yorkshire	in situ	Disbanded 7 May 45

Note. Although 346 and 347 Squadrons were transferred to 1 Group control, both squadrons continued to be administered by 4 Group, following the decision to transfer the entire group to Transport Command.

	Sqn	Base	Arrived	Remarks
5 Group	9	Bardney, Lincolnshire	in situ	
		Waddington, Lincolnshire	6 Jul 45	
	44	Spilsby, Lincolnshire	in situ	Transferred 3 Group Jul 45
	49	Fulbeck, Lincolnshire	in situ	
		Syerston, Nottinghamshire	22 Apr 45	
	50	Skellingthorpe, Lincolnshire	in situ	
		Sturgate, Lincolnshire	15 Jun 45	
	57	East Kirkby, Lincolnshire	in situ	
	61	Skellingthorpe, Lincolnshire	in situ	
		Sturgate, Lincolnshire	16 Jun 45	
	75	Spilsby, Lincolnshire	21 Jul 45	Transferred from 3 Group
	83	Coningsby, Lincolnshire	in situ	
	97	Coningsby, Lincolnshire	in situ	
	106	Metheringham, Lincolnshire	in situ	
	189	Fulbeck, Lincolnshire	in situ	
		Bardney, Lincolnshire	8 Apr 45	
	207	Spilsby, Lincolnshire	in situ	
	227	Balderton, Nottinghamshire	in situ	
		Strubby, Lincolnshire	5 Apr 45	Transferred 8 Group Jun 45
	463	Waddington, Lincolnshire	in situ	
		Skellingthorpe, Lincolnshire	3 Jul 45	
	467	Waddington, Lincolnshire	in situ	
		Metheringham, Lincolnshire	16 Jun 45	
	617	Woodhall Spa, Lincolnshire	in situ	
		Waddington, Lincolnshire	17 Jun 45	
	619	Strubby, Lincolnshire	in situ	
		Skellingthorpe, Lincolnshire	30 Jun 45	Disbanded 18 Jul 45
	627	Woodhall Spa, Lincolnshire	in situ	
	630	East Kirkby, Lincolnshire	in situ	Disbanded 18 Jul 45

	Sqn	Base	Arrived	Remarks
Group	405	Linton-on-Ouse, Yorkshire	26 May 45	Transferred from 8 Group
	408	Linton-on-Ouse, Yorkshire	in situ	To Canada 14 Jun 45
	415	East Moor, Yorkshire	in situ	Disbanded 15 May 45
	419	Middleton St. George, Durham	in situ	To Canada 4 Jun 45
	420	Tholthorpe, Yorkshire	in situ	To Canada 12 Jun 45
	424	Skipton-on-Swale, Yorkshire	in situ	Transferred 1 Group Aug 45
	425	Tholthorpe, Yorkshire	in situ	To Canada 13 Jun 45
	426	Linton-on-Ouse, Yorkshire	in situ	To Transport Command May 45
	427	Leeming, Yorkshire	in situ	Transferred 1 Group Aug 45
	428	Middleton St. George, Durham	in situ	To Canada 31 May 45
	429	Leeming, Yorkshire	in situ	Transferred 1 Group Aug 45
	431	Croft, Yorkshire	in situ	To Canada 12 Jun 45
	432	East Moor, Yorkshire	in situ	Disbanded 15 May 45
	433	Skipton-on-Swale, Yorkshire	in situ	Transferred 1 Group Aug 45
	434	Croft, Yorkshire	in situ	To Canada 15 Jun 45

	Sqn	Base	Arrived	Remarks
Group	7	Oakington, Cambridgeshire	in situ	Transferred 3 Group Jul 45
	35	Graveley, Huntingdonshire	in situ	
	105	Bourn, Cambridgeshire	in situ	
		Upwood, Huntingdonshire	29 Jun 45	
	109	Little Staughton, Huntingdonshire	in situ	
	128	Wyton, Huntingdonshire	in situ	
		Warboys, Huntingdonshire	22 Jun 45	
	139	Upwood, Huntingdonshire	in situ	
	142	Gransden Lodge, Huntingdonshire	in situ	
	156	Upwood, Huntingdonshire	in situ	
		Wyton, Huntingdonshire	27 Jun 45	
	162	Bourn, Cambridgeshire	in situ	To Transport Command Jul 45
	163	Wyton, Huntingdonshire	25 Jan 45	Disbanded 10 Aug 45
	227	Graveley, Huntingdonshire	8 Jun 45	Transferred from 5 Group

	Sqn	Base	Arrived	Remarks
8 Group	405	Gransden Lodge, Huntingdonshire	in situ	Transferred 6 Group May 45
	571	Oakington, Cambridgeshire	in situ	
		Warboys, Huntingdonshire	20 Jul 45	
	582	Little Staughton, Huntingdonshire	in situ	
	608	Downham Market, Norfolk	in situ	Disbanded 28 Aug 45
	635	Downham Market, Norfolk	in situ	Disbanded 1 Sep 45
	692	Graveley, Huntingdonshire	in situ	
		Gransden Lodge, Huntingdonshire	4 Jun 45	
100 Group	23	Little Snoring, Norfolk	in situ	
	85	Swannington, Norfolk	in situ	To Fighter Command Jun 45
	141	West Raynham, Norfolk	in situ	
		Little Snoring, Norfolk	3 Jul 45	
	157	Swannington, Norfolk	in situ	Disbanded 16 Aug 45
	169	Great Massingham, Norfolk	in situ	Disbanded 10 Aug 45
	171	North Creake, Norfolk	in situ	Disbanded 27 Jul 45
	192	Foulsham, Norfolk	in situ	Disbanded 22 Aug 45
	199	North Creake, Norfolk	in situ	Disbanded 19 Jul 45
	214	Oulton, Norfolk	in situ	Disbanded 27 Jul 45
	223	Oulton, Norfolk	in situ	Disbanded 29 Jul 45
	239	West Raynham, Norfolk	in situ	Disbanded 1 Jul 45
	462	Foulsham, Norfolk	in situ	
	515	Little Snoring, Norfolk	in situ	Disbanded 10 Jun 45

Appendix 4

Bomber OTU & Flight Losses January to September 1945

OTU	Type	Op.	Non-op.	Grnd
10	Wellington X		5	
11	Wellington X		9	
12	Wellington X		7	1
14	Wellington X		2	
16	Mosquito III		3	
	Mosquito XX		11	
	Mosquito XXV		5	
17	Wellington X		5	
18	Wellington X		1	
19	Wellington X		4	
20	Wellington X		9	
21	Wellington III		1	
	Wellington X		2	
22	Wellington III		2	
	Wellington X		3	
24	Wellington X		4	
26	Wellington X		7	
27	Wellington III		1	
	Wellington X		3	
29	Wellington III		1	
	Wellington X		7	
30	Wellington X		4	
82	Wellington X		1	
84	Wellington X		1	
85	Wellington X		3	
Total			101	1

Flt	Type	Op.	Non-op.	Grnd
1409	Mosquito XVI	1	1	
Total		1	1	

1945 Totals

Type	Op.	Non-op.	Grnd
Mosquito III		3	
Mosquito XX		11	
Mosquito XXV		5	
Wellington III		5	
Wellington X		77	1
Total		101	1

1940 - 1945 Combined Totals

Type	Op.	Non-op.	Grnd
Anson I	1	65	5
Battle I		30	
Blenheim I		31	
Blenheim IV		130	3
Blenheim V		1	
Hampden I	11	173	2
Hereford I		10	
Lysander III		1	
Manchester I		3	
Mosquito III		3	
Mosquito XX		11	
Mosquito XXV		5	
Wellington I		41	4
Wellington IA	1	29	3
Wellington IC	101	517	19
Wellington II	1	1	
Wellington III	23	332	4
Wellington IV		3	
Wellington X	9	375	9
WHitley II		1	
Whitley III		6	
Whitley IV		13	
Whitley V	69	228	5
Total	216	2009	54

Note. 16 OTU took over the role previously carried out by 1655 MCU.

Note. A companion volume showing the losses sustained from the Operational Training Units is in the planning stages and it is envisaged this book will incorporate the casualties from all Operational Training Unit establishments and not just those units associated with Bomber Command. Thus, aircrew destined for Coastal, Fighter and other commands will receive due recognition of their sacrifice. Also to be included are the losses from the Operational Training Units formed in overseas theatres of command, such as Middle East, South East Asia, etc.

Appendix 5

Bomber OTU Bases
January to September 1945

OTU	Base	Arrived	Remarks
10	Abingdon, Berkshire	in situ	Used codes EL JL RK UY ZG
	Stanton Harcourt, Oxfordshire	in situ	Satellite Wellington X
11	Westcott, Buckinghamshire	in situ	Used codes KJ OP TX
	Oakley, Buckinghamshire	in situ	Satellite Wellington X
12	Chipping Warden, Northamptonshire	in situ	Used codes FQ JP ML
	Edgehill, Warwickshire	in situ	Satellite Wellington X
			Disbanded 22 Jun 45
14	Market Harborough, Leicestershire	in situ	Used codes AM GL VB
			Disbanded 24 Jun 45
16	Upper Heyford, Oxfordshire	in situ	Used codes GA JS XG
			Disbanded 1 Jan 45
	Upper Heyford, Oxfordshire	1 Jan 45	Reformed Used code GA
	Barford St. John, Oxfordshire	1 Jan 45	Satellite Mosquito various Mks
17	Silverstone, Northamptonshire	in situ	Used codes AY JG WJ
	Turweston, Buckinghamshire	in situ	Satellite Wellington X
18	Finningley, Yorkshire	in situ	Used codes EN VQ XW
			Disbanded 30 Jan 45
19	Kinloss, Morayshire	in situ	Used codes UO XF ZV
			Disbanded 26 Jun 45
20	Lossiemouth, Morayshire	in situ	Used codes JM XL ZT
	Elgin, Morayshire	in situ	Satellite Wellington X
	Milltown, Morayshire	in situ	Satellite Wellington X
			Disbanded 17 Jul 45
21	Moreton-in-Marsh, Gloucestershire	in situ	Used codes ED SJ UH
	Enstone, Oxfordshire	in situ	Satellite Wellington III/X
	Honeybourne, Worcestershire	11 Aug 45	Satellite Wellington III/X
22	Wellesbourne Mountford, Warwickshire	in situ	Used codes DD LT OX XN
	Gaydon, Warwickshire	in situ	Satellite Wellington III/X
			Disbanded 24 Jul 45
24	Honeybourne, Worcestershire	in situ	Used codes FB TY UF
	Long Marston, Warwickshire	in situ	Satellite Wellington X
			Disbanded 24 Jul 45
26	Wing, Buckinghamshire	in situ	Used codes EU PB WG
	Little Horwood, Buckinghamshire	in situ	Satellite Wellington X
27	Lichfield, Staffordshire	in situ	Used codes BB UJ YL
	Church Broughton, Derbyshire	in situ	Satellite Wellington III/X
			Disbanded 22 Jun 45
29	Bruntingthorpe, Leicestershire	in situ	Used codes NT TF
			Disbanded 27 May 45
30	Hixon, Staffordshire	in situ	Used codes BT KD TN
			Disbanded 12 Jun 45
82	Ossington, Nottinghamshire	in situ	Used codes BZ KA TD 9C
			Disbanded 9 Jan 45
84	Desborough, Northamptonshire	in situ	Used codes CO CZ IF
			Disbanded 14 Jun 45
85	Husbands Bosworth, Leicestershire	in situ	Used codes 2X 9P
			Disbanded 14 Jun 45

Appendix 6

Conversion Unit Losses January to September 1945

CU	Type	Op.	Non-op.	Grnd
1651	Lancaster I		3	
	Lancaster III		5	
1652	Halifax III		8	1
1653	Lancaster I		1	
	Lancaster III		4	
1654	Lancaster I		3	
	Lancaster III		3	
1656	Lancaster I		4	1
	Lancaster III		3	
1658	Halifax III		8	
1659	Halifax III		11	
1660	Lancaster I		6	
	Lancaster III		1	
1661	Lancaster I		1	
	Lancaster III		3	

CU	Type	Op.	Non-op.	Grnd
1662	Halifax V		1	
	Lancaster I		2	1
1663	Halifax III	1	7	1
1664	Halifax III		5	
1666	Halifax II		2	
	Lancaster I	1		
	Lancaster III		1	
1667	Halifax V		1	
	Lancaster I		2	
	Lancaster III		4	
1668	Lancaster II		2	
	Lancaster III		4	
1669	Halifax II		1	
	Lancaster I		3	
	Lancaster III		1	
	Total	2	100	4

1942 - 1945 Combined Totals

Type	Op.	Non-op.	Grnd
Halifax I	1	15	
Halifax II	5	265	1
Halifax III	1	44	3
Halifax V		169	6
Lancaster I	6	79	2
Lancaster II		13	
Lancaster III		37	
Manchester I		9	
Mosquito III		2	
Mosquito IV		23	
Mosquito IX		2	
Mosquito XX		10	
Mosquito XXV		1	
Stirling I	5	110	1
Stirling III		99	3
Total	18	878	16

1945 Total

Type	Op.	Non-op.	Grnd
Halifax II		3	
Halifax III	1	39	2
Halifax V		2	
Lancaster I	1	25	2
Lancaster II		2	
Lancaster III		29	
Total	2	100	4

Appendix 7

Conversion Unit Bases
January to September 1945

CU	Base	Arrived	Remarks
1651	Woolfox Lodge, Rutland	in situ	Used codes BS QQ YZ Disbanded 13 Jul 45
1652	Marston Moor, Yorkshire	in situ	Used codes GV JA Disbanded 25 Jun 45
1653	North Luffenham, Rutland	in situ	Used codes A3 H4 M9
1654	Wigsley, Nottinghamshire	in situ	Used codes JF UG Disbanded 1 Sep 45
1656	Lindholme, Yorkshire	in situ	Used codes BL EK
1658	Riccall, Yorkshire	in situ	Used codes TT ZB Disbanded 13 Apr 45
1659	Topcliffe, Yorkshire	in situ	Used codes FD RV
1660	Swinderby, Lincolnshire	in situ	Used codes TV YW
1661	Winthorpe, Nottinghamshire	in situ	Used codes GP KB Disbanded 24 Aug 45
1662	Blyton, Lincolnshire	in situ	Used codes KF PE Disbanded 6 Apr 45
1663	Rufforth, Yorkshire	in situ	Used codes OO SV Disbanded 28 May 45
1664	Dishforth, Yorkshire	in situ	Used codes DH ZU Disbanded 6 Apr 45
1666	Wombleton, Yorkshire	in situ	Used codes ND QY Disbanded 3 Aug 45
1667	Sandtoft, Lincolnshire	in situ	Used codes GG KR
1668	Bottesford, Leicestershire	in situ	Used codes J9 2K
1669	Langar, Nottinghamshire	in situ	Used codes L6 6F Disbanded 16 Mar 45

Appendix 8

Lancaster Finishing Schools
Losses & Bases
January to April 1945

LFS	Type	Op.	Non-op.	Grnd
3	Lancaster III		1	
5	Lancaster III		3	
	Total		4	

1945 Totals

Type	Op.	Non-op.	Grnd
Lancaster III		4	
Total		4	

1944 - 1945 Combined Totals

Type	Op.	Non-op.	Grnd
Lancaster I		20	4
Lancaster III		4	
Total		24	4

LFS	Base	Arrived	Remarks
3	Feltwell, Norfolk	in situ	Used code A5
	Newmarket, Suffolk	5 Jan 45	A Flight detached to 29 Jan 45
	Methwold, Norfolk	8 Jan 45	B Flight detached to 31 Jan 45
	Tuddenham, Suffolk	7 Jan 45	C Flight detached to 31 Jan 45
			Disbanded 31 Jan 45
5	Syerston, Nottinghamshire	in situ	Used code RC
			Disbanded 1 Apr 45

Note. In 1997, Air-Britain (Historians) published a work jointly compiled by Ray Sturtivant, John Hamlin and James J Halley, titled "Royal Air Force Flying Training and Support Units" which details the formation, aircraft types used and purpose of the myriad of training units that have supported the Royal Air Force from 1918 until the present day. It is a highly acclaimed work of historical value and in respect of the Lancaster Finishing Schools, it shows that 1 LFS (disbanded on 25 November 1944), 3 LFS and 5 LFS were responsible for honing the skills picked up by aircrews at the Heavy Conversion Units, prior to their positing to squadrons in 1, 3 or 5 Group, as appropriate.

Appendix 9

Escapers & Evaders
January to May 1945

Retained at the Public Record Office Kew are a series of documents officially referred to as the Escape Reports. Grouped under their class reference of WO208, these fascinating papers describe in some detail the evasions of Royal Air Force, Commonwealth and Allied air forces personnel, principally from those areas of Europe under Nazi domination, while a handful concern airmen who came down in Germany itself and yet avoided capture.

Some made their way to freedom practically unaided but the majority were helped in one way or the other by those men and women who,

at tremendous risk, were willing to give aid where ever possible. Some belonged to the various escape lines, established soon after the fall of France in 1940, but it should be emphasised that most were ordinary citizens who performed a quite extraordinary task and in many cases paid with their lives when the enemy caught up with their activities.

Here listed are the file references so far identified for 1945, but supplemented with a second section naming those airmen for whom no documentation has been unearthed; thus, any leads will be more than welcome.

Sqn	Name	File	Report	Sqn	Name	File	Report
10	Sgt H T S Jones	3352	(-)2400	199	P/O K N Crane	3327	(-)3082
	Sgt R Maddock-Lyon	3325	(-)2898	207	F/O R W Young	3352	(-)2428
	F/S H L Mills	3326	(-)2909		F/S S E Hanson	3352	(-)2434
	F/S J Petre	3326	(-)2919		WO1 C O Huntley RCAF	3352	(-)2418
35	F/S J W Tovey	3327	(-)3083	227	F/L J B Osborne	3327	(-)3118
49	F/S M H Makofski	3327	(-)3088		F/S T O Kydd	3352	(-)3042
	P/O H Eberley RCAF	3352	(-)2468	463	Sgt D Broadhead	3326	(-)2949
61	F/S J Chadwick	3326	(-)2952	467	F/O J A Strickland RAAF	3327	(-)3121
103	S/L S Slater	3326	(-)2937	571	F/O R D Oliver	3326	(-)2948
	P/O M H Bertie RAAF	3327	(-)3093		F/S L M Young RAAF	3326	(-)2970
	F/O H A S Mitchell RAAF	3327	(-)3094	630	Sgt G G E Bourner	3327	(-)3070
158	F/S I A H Croad	3352	(-)2487		F/S G Gould	3327	(-)3069
	Sgt R H Dickson	3352	(-)2482	635	F/L W M Douglas	3327	(-)3011
	Sgt W B Morton	3352	(-)2492		P/O G Wilson	3327	(-)3026
	F/S P D Watson	3352	(-)2483		W/O A D Clayton	3327	(-)3104

Section 2. Reports are outstanding in respect of:

Sqn	Name	Sqn	Name	Sqn	Name
44	Sgt D Howells	170	P/O A H Young DFCF	419	F/S C Ginter RCAF
49	F/S G L Corrigan RCAF	347	Sgt H Bastian FFAF		Sgt E K McGrath RCAF
75	F/S J McDowell RNZAF	419	Sgt P V Bowman RCAF	463	W/O R K Dixon RAAF
103	W/O T Fairclough		Sgt T J Bristow RCAF	550	Sgt G B C Capon
				608	F/O H W Tyrell

Note. Since the publication of Volume 5, Raymond Glynne-Owen, who has assisted with matters pertaining to 207 Squadron, has kindly forwarded information concerning the missing file and report references in respect of some of the names listed twixt pages 548 and 550. This data indicates that the WO208 file numbers proceeded in chronological sequence to 3327; report (-)3122 being the last to be placed in this file. The series recommences with file 3348, but without individual report numbers appended. Likewise, file 3349 omits report numbers but with the introduction of file 3350, the reports commence at 1001, continuing to 1333. File 3351 has either not been released, or is not relevant to escape and evasion matters, while file 3352 appears to be the last file containing such information. Rather than report this updated information in the "Amendments to Previous Volumes" appendix, this additional data is presented over the next two pages. Asterisks draw attention to details incorrectly reported in Volume 5.

Sqn	Name	File	Report
9	P/O R S Gradwell	3350	(-)1061
	Sgt H S Chappell	3349	
	Sgt C H T Martin*	3349	
10	Sgt T C Hogg	3350	(-)1275
12	F/O S R Garlick	3327	(-)3122
	F/O H F O'Hara	3350	(-)1083
15	F/S R M Gilleade	3348	
35	F/O P Moorhead	3350	(-)1267
44	Sgt K G Andrews	3348	
	F/S J E Wainwright	3350	(-)1070
	F/S F A Wells	3348	
	Sgt J R W Worrall	3348	
	F/O D T Ibbotson RAAF	3348	
	F/S E H Greatz RAAF	3348	
	F/S I R Murray RAAF	3348	
50	P/O E J Blakemore	3352	(-)2389
	F/O J Craven	3352	(-)2402
	F/O C D Lucas	3327	(-)3059
	Sgt H Macfarlane	3327	(-)3063
	Sgt G R Williamson	3348	
51	F/O F G Kirkwood RAAF	3352	(-)2361
57	Sgt C C Hatter	3350	(-)1240
	Sgt T Sharples	3350	(-)1057
61	Sgt A R Pellows	3352	(-)2454
75	F/O J S Wilkinson RNZAF	3348	
	F/S M K P Drummond RNZAF	3348	
	F/S N Sampson RNZAF	3348	
76	Sgt F J Palmer	3350	(-)1263
	WO2 J McTrach RCAF	3350	(-)1072
77	Sgt J Slater	3350	(-)1231
83	F/S C George RAAF	3348	
90	F/S I W Bestridge	3350	(-)1004
	F/S P E Green	3352	(-)2866
	Sgt R J E Pask	3352	(-)2866
	Sgt C E Potten	3352	(-)2866
	F/S C W Walmsley RCAF	3349	
97	Sgt A Pritchard	3349	
100	F/L H Paston-Williams	3327	(-)3068
	Sgt J A Downie	3352	(-)2456
102	Sgt E J D Merrill	3350	(-)1308
	Sgt J A Miller	3349	
103	F/S A J McCauley	3349	
106	F/O R R C Barker	3348	
	F/O J Drylie	3348	
	S/L E Sprawson	3348	
	Sgt W J Hardisty	3350	(-)1055
	Sgt W R Knaggs	3349	
115	Sgt P Murphy	3350	(-)1014
	Sgt J E Parkinson	3350	(-)1067
	Sgt W Russell	3350	(-)1224
	F/O P Anaka RCAF*	3350	(-)1276
156	F/L R H Samson RAAF	3327	(-)3110
158	Sgt H W Chown	3348	
	Sgt R A Diver	3352	(-)2363
	F/S J E Evans	3350	(-)1140
	Sgt H G M Woodward	3352	(-)2360
	WO2 W E J Brayley RCAF*	3348	
166	Sgt R H Haynes	3349	
	Sgt L A Lewis	3350	(-)1138
	F/S C T Rose	3350	(-)1139
	Sgt W T Violett	3349	
	F/O P Pochailo RCAF	3327	(-)3001
169	F/L G R Morgan RCAF	3350	(-)1136
207	Sgt A E J Barton	3350	(-)1326
	Sgt W R M D Brown	3350	(-)1018
	Sgt J K Chapple	3350	(-)1333
	Sgt P N King	3349	
218	F/O E F D Vidler	3349	
218	F/S L N Clay	3348	
	F/S D R R J Pepall	3349	
	F/O A J D Levy RAAF	3350	(-)1037
405	Sgt F C Bailey	3349	
	Sgt H Braithwaite	3349	
	Sgt A G Deacon	3348	
	F/S P H Gingras RCAF	3348	
419	F/O L W A Frame RCAF	3349	
	F/O W C Watson RCAF	3349	
	F/S J Morris RCAF	3349	
424	F/O W J Elliott RCAF	3350	(-)1317
425	F/O F D Hagen RCAF	3350	(-)1322
426	F/S W Berry DFM	3350	(-)1120
	F/O S W Gerard RCAF	3349	
	F/L P N J Logan RCAF	3348	
	F/S D A MacInnis RCAF	3349	
427	Sgt G M Philliskirk*	3350	(-)1270
	F/O J D Fulton RCAF	3350	(-)1232
	P/O J Moffat RCAF	3350	(-)1080
	P/O W M Pookay RCAF	3350	(-)1273
	F/O J D Siddall RCAF	3349	
	F/O G M Waddell RCAF	3350	(-)1269
	Sgt N Donnan RCAF	3350	(-)1271
	WO2 D F Foster RCAF	3350	(-)1268
428	F/S W S Yates	3350	(-)1056
429	Sgt N R McCarthy	3348	
	F/O P G Agur RCAF	3348	
	F/O J F Kennedy RCAF	3348	
	Sgt R J Wasylkow RCAF	3349	
432	F/O H Chamberlain	3348	
	F/L H J S Kenley	3348	
	Sgt G Hand	3348	
	Sgt H E Oakeby	3349	
	F/O M F C Grimsey RCAF*	3348	
	F/O A R P Holmes RCAF	3350	(-)1319
	P/O D A McCoy RCAF	3350	(-)1257
	W/C J K MacDonald RCAF*	3349	
	F/O L M O'Grady RCAF	3350	(-)1053
	WO2 W B MacPherson RCAF	3350	(-)1253
460	P/O R H Jopling RAAF	3327	(-)3109
	F/S W J Flynn RAAF	3350	(-)1284
	F/S W Schwilk RAAF	3348	
	Sgt K Buckley*	3327	(-)3084
462	P/O W S Shoemaker RCAF	3352	(-)2426
463	Sgt J P W McLellan*	3327	(-)3099
	W/C D R Donaldson RAAF	3350	(-)1023
	F/S A V Matthews RAAF	3348	
	F/S F H Redford RAAF	3348	
466	Sgt A J Camp	3350	(-)1281
	F/O R Sigmont RAAF*	3350	(-)1241
467	Sgt W F Marshall	3349	
	F/O A C Findlay RAAF*	3324	(-)2570
	P/O G Johnson RAAF	3327	(-)3097
	F/S S D Jolly RAAF	3350	(-)1272
514	F/O R Brailsford	3350	(-)1306
	P/O D A Duncliffe	3327	(-)3016
	F/O L Greenburgh	3348	
	Sgt A R Lyons	3348	
	F/S G Palamountain	3327	(-)3015
	W/O L J W Sutton	3349	
	W/O A N Durham RAAF	3349	
	F/L E A Campbell RCAF	3348	
	F/O J E Chapman RCAF*	3326	(-)2935
576	Sgt J Conway	3348	
	Sgt T A Mitchell	3349	
	F/O G A J Bain RCAF*	3349	
578	P/O N E Donmall	3352	(-)2599
	F/O K C Parsons	3352	(-)2388
582	F/S L Hood	3349	

Sqn	Name	File	Report	Sqn	Name	File	Report
582	F/O J B Armstrong RCAF	3349		626	Sgt G Burrows	3350	(-)1265
617	F/O R H Petch DFC	3352	(-)2488		Sgt K L D McCoy RCAF*	3349	
619	F/O M A Cockrean*	3350	(-)1075	630	F/S E Couchman	3349	
	F/L T J Latus*	3349			Sgt R D Larritt	3350	(-)1001
	Sgt W A Clark	3349			Sgt D A Grant RCAF	3349	
	F/O D W Cotter RAAF	3349		635	F/O D Cameron DFM	3350	(-)1062
	F/S C E Rathbone RCAF*	3349			F/L G Goddard	3350	(-)1016
622	F/L L F Berry	3348			F/O C R Godfrey DFC	3350	(-)1017
	Sgt C A Jenkins	3348		640	F/O K J Sheppendon	3349	
	F/S D B Hyde RCAF	3349			Sgt G E Chappell	3349	
					Sgt L Devetter	3348	

Note. In addition to the material sent by Raymond Glynne-Owen, David Morris, a Public Records Officer researcher, advises that WO308 3328 contains liberation reports and that forty-four of the 100 documents within this file pertain to members of the Royal Air Force and Royal Canadian Air Force. Report No.2 relates to statements made by Air Commodore R Ivelaw-Chapman, who was shot down on 6-7 May 1944 (see Volume 5 page 212) and made a prisoner of war. It is possible that some evasion, or escape, reports are amongst the forty-four mentioned and a perusal of WO308 3330, which contains liberation reports 301 to 550 inclusive, may prove fruitful for readers wishing to investigate further into such matters.

Appendix 10

Prisoners of War
January to May 1945

Information concerning airmen who were taken prisoner of war is principally confined to a single document, namely AIR20 2336, which is held at the Public Record Office, Kew.

When preparing the prisoner of war section in Volume 5, I drew attention to the fact that during 1944, especially following the D-Day landings in Normandy, the procedure for reporting captured Allied airmen was in the process of breaking down. Firm details in respect of airmen who baled out, and survived, in 1945 are, not surprisingly, even more difficult to establish. The loss cards are frequently annotated "safe" which, from experience, can have several meanings ranging from being held in captivity through to returned to unit with a few days or weeks of being reported missing.

Consequently, this appendix will be split into several sections, the first showing the names of those known to have been taken to a prisoner of war camp; the second identifies airmen thought to have sat out the remaining months of the war in captivity, or who were repatriated badly wounded, while part three names those who arrived home aboard the Letitia and Arundel Castle in February 1945.

The fourth part will deal with the tragic events of 19 April 1945, when Allied fighter bombers strafed a prisoner of war column near Gresse, while section five identifies the codes appended in section one.

Sqn	Name	Camp	Number
9	F/S F Alton		Listed
	F/S V S Peace		Listed
10	F/S D H Elsome		Listed
	F/S K D Lawrence		Listed
	Sgt W F Paxton		Listed
	Sgt R C Tuck		Listed
12	Sgt E J Bourke	3A	150014
	F/S K MacDonald RAAF	3A	150020
	F/O J B Murray RCAF		Listed
	F/O A L Staley RCAF		Listed
	Sgt A F Hymers RCAF		Listed
15	Sgt D T Darby		Listed
	F/L G G Hammond RAAF		Listed
	F/O J M Morris RNZAF	13D	
	F/O J S Wilkinson RNZAF	13D	
44	F/S R A Bosley	13D	
	Sgt W P Cazaly	13D	
	Sgt W J Florence	13D	
	F/S R C Silson	13D	
	F/S B Smith	13D	
	F/S A Stevens	13D	
	F/S J N Sheehan RAAF		Listed
50	Sgt L P Duffy		Listed
	Sgt W S McClelland		Listed
51	Sgt B W Duffell		Listed
	Sgt C G Green		Listed
	F/S H R Smith		Listed
	Sgt D E F Thomsett	3A	150023
	Sgt E Timms		Listed
	Sgt N Wilcock*	3A	150025
	F/O R J Crane RAAF		Listed
	F/S D Keirs RAAF*		Listed
	F/S J G Orr RAAF	3A	150021
	W/O R W Pratt RAAF		Listed
1	F/O J J Wakerley	079	
75	F/L T S Kilpatrick	7A	
7	P/O L J Ward	7A	
77	Sgt J M O´Connell	DL	
	Sgt A Robinson	13D	
	Sgt K Rodgers	DL	
	F/S H P Sheridan	DL	
78	P/O L B Stuart RNZAF		Listed
90	F/O R A Kirkland		Listed
	Sgt J M Bilton		Listed
	Sgt R C Boyle		Listed
	Sgt J Healy		Listed
	F/S H E Worsnop		Listed
	F/O C E Wakeham RAAF		Listed
100	F/O P M Bunn		Listed
	F/O L J Holford		Listed
	F/O R E Marsh		Listed
102	P/O E M Boorman	L1	
	F/L J T Jones		Listed
	F/S J H D Bax		Listed
	F/O J F Bergman RCAF	13D	
	F/O D W Dale RCAF	13D	
103	F/O J R Barnes		Listed
	F/S M E F Haslam	3A	150017
	F/S D G Ireland		Listed
	F/S J C Tear		Listed
	Sgt G R Wilding	3A	150026
105	F/L G Donald		Listed
156	F/O J Costigan RAAF	13D	
	F/L J G E Evans RAAF	13D	
	P/O W H Preece RAAF	13D	
158	F/O H F Parkes		Listed
	F/O J H Robinson		Listed
	P/O J M Scott	4B	
	F/O F A Toplis		Listed
	F/S M A Belcher		Listed
	Sgt J J Bromfield	L1	7715
	F/S T M Laurie	L1	
	Sgt D McMahon	L1	
	Sgt A McQuilkin	7A	

Sqn	Name	Camp	Number	Sqn	Name	Camp	Number
158	F/S P A Murphy	7A		419	F/S R C Woods RCAF		Listed
	F/S A M H Norris		Listed	420	P/O W G Bridgeman RCAF	11B	
	F/S L A E Papworth	7A			P/O G A Haacke RCAF		Listed
	Sgt A J Ralph		Listed		F/O G J Keeper RCAF	11B	
	Sgt V E Washer		Listed		F/O R W Landers RCAF		Listed
	F/O G W Cross RCAF	L1			P/O D O Mackey RCAF		Listed
	F/O A G Robertson RCAF	L1			P/O J G Skidmore RCAF		Listed
	F/S H G Hall RCAF		Listed		P/O J H Warren RCAF		Listed
	WO2 G E Marion RCAF		Listed		F/S D O Palmer RCAF		Listed
	F/S J D E Rae RCAF	L1		424	F/O J G Agnew RCAF		Listed
	F/S H F Tyler RCAF	7A		425	F/O J A M Bilodeau RCAF		Listed
166	P/O D M Smithers	7A			F/O V E Brimicombe RCAF		Listed
	F/S G Anson		Listed		P/O J G A B Cantin RCAF		Listed
	Sgt R T Green	13D			P/O R R M Cantin RCAF		Listed
	Sgt E W Hull	13D			F/O L U Coleman RCAF		Listed
	F/S G K E John		Listed		P/O G R Delong RCAF		Listed
	F/S G W Kirk		Listed		P/O J J G Huet RCAF		Listed
	F/S A V White	13D			P/O G E Hutton RCAF		Listed
	F/S T R Wood		Listed		P/O J M R Lapierre RCAF		Listed
	P/O J M Meggitt RAAF		Listed		F/L J J P Lesperance RCAF		Listed
	F/O L F Etherington RCAF	13D			F/S J A Cote RCAF		Listed
	F/O J L Goddard RCAF	13D			Sgt E J Faulkner RCAF		Listed
	Sgt J C Lillis RCAF	3A	150019		F/S D C MacKeigan RCAF		Listed
189	Sgt R F Dyson GM*	7A		426	W/C F C Carling-Kelly RCAF		Listed
207	F/O J G Eaton RAAF		Listed		F/O H J Dales RCAF		Listed
	F/O L J Fowler RAAF		Listed		F/S J M MacDonald RCAF		Listed
218	F/O F J Norton	13D		427	F/O H W Campbell RCAF		Listed
	Sgt J Halsall	7A			F/L J S H Dodge RCAF	13D	
	Sgt E Porter	7A			F/L J D Johnston DFC RCAF		Listed
	Sgt J Simpson	7A		428	P/O C M Roche RCAF		Listed
	Sgt D R White	7A			F/O R L Stapleford RCAF		Listed
227	F/L R D King RAAF	DL		429	Sgt K Turner		Listed
300	P/O R A Paszkowski PAF		Listed		F/O R H Barnes RCAF		Listed
	P/O Z Wesolowski PAF		Listed		F/O F H Biddle RCAF		Listed
	W/O R Bakinowski PAF	3A	150012		P/O R H S Bourne RCAF		Listed
	Sgt M Sasin PAF		Listed		F/O C E Chapman RCAF		Listed
	Sgt S Seidengart PAF		Listed		F/O H K Frair RCAF		Listed
	Sgt K T Tomasik PAF		Listed		F/L A R Milner RCAF		Listed
347	Ltn C Courvalin FFAF		Listed		P/O J G Small RCAF		Listed
	Ltn E De Lueze FFAF		Listed		P/O O H Sulek RCAF		Listed
	Capt G de Sauvebeuf FFAF		Listed		F/S F G Peters RCAF		Listed
	Ltn R Frangolacci FFAF		Listed		F/S J R Phillips RCAF		Listed
	Ltn J Minvielle FFAF		Listed	432	Sgt J Dalton		Listed
	Ltn A Ronat FFAF		Listed		F/O T R Bond RCAF		Listed
	Sgt M Chabourd FFAF		Listed		F/O R G Donaldson RCAF		Listed
	Sgc R Juste FFAF		Listed		F/O W E Fleming RCAF		Listed
405	Sgt S Rhodes		Listed		F/O J L Marcille RCAF		Listed
	F/S D A MacDougall RCAF		Listed		F/O E B Pickthorne RCAF		Listed
	WO1 D G Plyley RCAF		Listed		W/C J G Stephenson RCAF		Listed
408	F/O W A Baker RCAF		Listed		F/S S J Aikens RCAF		Listed
	F/O D Elkin RCAF		Listed		F/S J F Charles RCAF		Listed
415	Sgt J J Burton		Listed		WO1 W T McMahon RCAF	L1	
	F/O R M Aylsworth RCAF	357			WO2 R J P Young RCAF		Listed
	F/O T K Daniel RCAF		Listed	460	Sgt A Field		Listed
	F/O S H McFadden RCAF		Listed		F/O J D Avery RAAF		Listed
	F/O D M Sloan RCAF		Listed		F/O G A F Davies RAAF		Listed
	Sgt G A Y Binne RCAF		Listed	462	F/S R A Gould	7A	
	F/S R A Collins RCAF		Listed	463	Sgt P C Kimber	3A	150018
	F/S F T Graves RCAF	3A	150016		F/L D L Dickson RAAF		Listed
419	F/O H R Eager RCAF		Listed		P/O B A Donaghue RAAF		Listed
	F/O J Q Eddy RCAF		Listed		P/O E J Earl RAAF		Listed
	P/O G C Woods RCAF	13D	15786		F/O R A Leonard RAAF	13D	
	F/S G R Berry RCAF	L1			P/O R T Simonson RAAF		Listed
	F/S E Chatwin RCAF		Listed		F/O F H Smith RAAF		Listed
	F/S W J McTaggart RCAF		Listed		F/S G F Chomley RAAF		Listed
	F/S W H Milne RCAF	L1			F/S V G Dingey RAAF		Listed
	Sgt B C Mitchell RCAF		Listed		F/S E E Evans RAAF	13D	
	F/S R W Rowlands RCAF	L1					

Sqn	Name	Camp	Number	Sqn	Name	Camp	Number
463	F/S K M Vaughan RAAF		Listed	578	P/O P J Fitzgerald RCAF	13D	
	F/S J Willcocks RAAF		Listed	617	F/L E N Armstrong DFC		Listed
466	F/S C F White		Listed		F/O H Ellis DFC		Listed
467	F/L R W G Eagle RAAF	13D			F/L H J Pryor DFC		Listed
	F/L E C Ellis RAAF	13D			W/O E C Temple DFM		Listed
	F/O W D McMahon RAAF	13D			W/O A L Winston		Listed
576	F/O M Chisick RCAF		Listed	619	F/S L E Marsh RCAF		Listed
	F/S R F Hood RCAF		Listed	625	Sgt W J Harrison		Listed
578	F/O D R McLean	3A			F/S J E Hughes		Listed
	Sgt H G Skeats	3A	150022	635	F/L I B Hayes		Listed
	Sgt T W Spencer		Listed		F/L J N Steel		Listed
	F/O C T Moore RAAF	13D			F/S A L Hall		Listed
					W/O R B Warner	3A	150024

Note. I am particularly grateful for the information generously supplied by Oliver Clutton-Brock in all matters pertaining to prisoners of war. Most of the data in respect of numbers issued has stemmed from his files, thus amplifying the information given in AIR20 2336, which in most cases is restricted to the single word "listed". An asterisk indicates the airman was admitted to hospital on release from captivity, or was liberated while undergoing medical treatment.

Sqn	Name	Sqn	Name	Sqn	Name
7	F/L J B M Liddell	15	F/O D L Howell	44	Sgt I Graham*
	Sgt N H Clydesdale*		F/O W U A MacIntosh		Sgt J W Horne
9	F/O R L Blunsdon		F/O J E Murphy		Sgt D F McShane
	P/O S Scott		W/O H Campbell		Sgt R P S Sawbutts
	F/S W G Bamforth		W/O J V Higgins		F/O J S Peterswald RAAF
	Sgt A E W Biles		F/S D G Jones		F/S J R Tulloch RAAF
	Sgt E Williams		Sgt F Keeble-Buckle	49	F/O D Edwards
	P/O J Acheson RAAF		Sgt G J Owen		F/O J B Gibson
10	P/O S Chaderton		F/S S H Bagnall RAAF		P/O F E Grimsdale
	F/O P Cook		F/S J W Lacey RAAF		F/O R Mallinson
	F/L D Moss		F/S C A Russell RAAF		Sgt J F Brennan
	P/O A F G Nickels		F/S T M Thoroughgood RAAF		Sgt J Corbett
	F/S P Andrews		F/S W A Wilkie RAAF		Sgt J P Dixon
	Sgt A Colville		F/S J A Taylor RNZAF		F/S E Ellis
	F/S R C Fowler	23	F/L T Anderson-Smith		Sgt J Evan
	F/S J E Gallacher*	35	F/O R H H Dyers		F/S J F Le Marquand
	F/S S Hodgson		P/O R M Hallett		Sgt G P Roberts
	Sgt R G Hyslop		F/O R T Jones		Sgt E Stansill
	Sgt R W Jarvis		F/L H D Michell		W/O J C Yeoman RAAF
	F/S N W Longstaff		P/O G J North		F/S R M Henderson RAAF
	F/S J Oakes		W/O A E Astor	50	P/O T H Hewett
	Sgt R Palmer		Sgt B J B Carr		Sgt C E Atkins
	F/S R L Parsons		F/S C S Gibbon		Sgt E G Friend
	Sgt W R Sinnett*		F/S E G Meredith DFM		F/S H R Hand
	Sgt R Stokes		F/S E G Silcock		F/S N G Jones
	F/S E J Summerfield		F/S J K Spedding DFM		Sgt D W Laws
	Sgt H J Webb		F/S C Wilce DFM		Sgt R A Murray
12	F/O D O R Dickey		P/O N W Curtis RAAF		Sgt J O'Brien
	F/O R D N Saunders		P/O M H McVey RAAF		Sgt R G Tudor
	F/O J Willis		F/L J J Osmond RAAF	51	Sgt R A Boydell
	Sgt N A Clarke		F/O W Wolk RAAF		F/S G A Chugg
	Sgt J C Devine		W/O G A Perry DFM RAAF		F/S R A Gibbs
	F/S A Henry	44	F/O W J Jones		F/S L Hart
	Sgt D Lewis		F/O P W B Morgans		F/S J S Henderson
	Sgt H F Nixon		F/O N D Nicolle		Sgt W Hood
	Sgt G H Pearce		F/O R D Temple		F/S D P Murname
	F/O J H Clarke RCAF		F/S N D Askill		Sgt A Nicholson
	F/O A R Hovis RCAF		Sgt E E Barnes		Sgt H M Walcutt
	F/S T K Imperious RCAF		Sgt P Brooks		Sgt J P Watson
15	P/O L F Clarke		W/O C A Dayton		F/O K W Berick RAAF*
	F/O D W Cook		Sgt T S FitzPatrick		
	P/O A T Gamble				

Sqn	Name	Sqn	Name	Sqn	Name
51	P/O F D K Balflour RNZAF	100	F/S G F Hersey RCAF	153	F/O R Mains
61	F/O R Bloomfield	101	F/O S Dillon*		P/O E J Parker
	F/O K Middlemast		F/O AS Jeffcoat		F/L W Holman RCAF
	F/O S P Pearce		P/O K D S J Ward		F/O R C Taylor RCAF
	F/O E Walker		S/L T J Warner		F/S A D Kall RCAF
	F/S W R R Boobyer		W/O J A M Bird		WO2 V S Reynolds RCAF
	Sgt B Courtney		Sgt W Hartell	156	F/L A D Pelly
	Sgt D J Everson		Sgt E C Roberts		F/S R Morgan
	Sgt W J A Fraser		Sgt C G Vicary DFM		Sgt J D Routledge
	F/S S D P Goodey		F/S J E Knight RAAF		W/O W G Pearce RAAF
	Sgt S F Heaven		F/S W R Searle RAAF		F/O A J MacLeod RCAF
	F/S A E Hector		F/O J K Balcombe RCAF	158	P/O T Dillon
	F/S T C King		F/O W N Ingeberg RCAF		P/O G Pond
	Sgt W T Lake		F/L W A McLenaghan RCAF		F/O W W White
	Sgt W K MacCallum		F/L R P Paterson RCAF		Sgt J Crane
	W/O N McKay		F/S F R Boyd RCAF		W/O G W Culham
	Sgt T McKnight		F/S F R Fletcher RCAF		Sgt F J Fox
	Sgt J E Norcutt		WO1 L F Kennedy RCAF		F/S G D Lunn
	F/S N T Nuttall	102	F/O A V Valentine		Sgt F L C Mewis
	W/O P Styles		Sgt A J E Morton		Sgt W M Philpotts
	F/O N T Collins RAAF		Sgt K E White		F/S J E D Taylor*
	F/S E F Coster RCAF		F/S G A Wilson*		F/S M E Jordon RCAF
75	F/O J D Craven	103	Sgt J J Bent		F/O R R Anweiler RCAF*
	F/O D W King		Sgt K Foster		F/O J F Coghlan RCAF
	Sgt D W S Amos		Sgt M C Godfrey		F/O S A Hearst RCAF
	Sgt H Barraclough		Sgt R Jones		F/O J L Hackman RCAF
	Sgt K A Blackbee		W/O D King		P/O A M Lang RCAF
	Sgt W H H Brewer		F/S K F Lord		F/S H J Bailey RCAF
	Sgt I R H Evans		F/S F P Monaghan		F/S J D Edgar RCAF
	Sgt M O Fell*		Sgt R C Pain	161	F/L D T Oliver*
	Sgt J Grieveson		Sgt W D Rich		F/L F M Jarman RAAF
	F/S R H Lawrence		F/S J D Smith		F/O H Morgan RCAF
	Sgt J J Maher		F/S K O Williams	166	F/O W H Gerrard
	F/S R Muir		Sgt G H Wilson		F/O K P Muncer*
	F/S W C F Pilkington		F/S E Young		F/O J W Rae
	F/S T M White		P/O W J M Bailie RAAF		Sgt E A Bradshaw
	F/L G S Davies RNZAF		F/O E W Armour RCAF		Sgt R C Finlayson
	P/O A L Humphries RNZAF		F/O J H McKenna RCAF		F/S S W Orr
	F/S A D Baker RNZAF		F/O A R Mackenzie RCAF		Sgt S L Osborn
	F/S C C Greenhough RNZAF		F/S A C Bellisle RCAF		F/S R D Story
	F/S L S B Klitscher RNZAF		F/S J L Cooke RCAF		Sgt I Titmus
	F/S A E Robson RNZAF		WO2 A D Cruickshank RCAF		F/O H F Churchward RCAF
76	P/O R J P Barrell		F/S J B McCormick RCAF*		Sgt R D R Kendall RCAF
	F/S G F Terry		F/S S H McRoberts RCAF		
	P/O G W Lawson RCAF		F/S R C Snell RCAF		F/O E C Bott RNZAF
77	F/O P A Fitzgerald	106	Sgt J S Hussey		Sgt D R Lethbridge RNZAF
	Sgt A G Green	138	F/O J W Neve		
	Sgt W Haile		F/O L G Steven	170	F/L R L Rodgers
	Sgt J W Talbot		F/O N E Tilly		Sgt L Ashton
	F/O W T Brennan RCAF		Sgt J H Bloomer		W/O A C M Bates
	F/O K W Joy RCAF		Sgt J T Breeze		Sgt J Burns
78	F/S W J Paterson		Sgt W L Clark		Sgt D S Cady
	F/O L P O'Brien RNZAF		F/S J K Kyle		F/S J Downing
83	F/O J Fletcher		F/S G M Maude RAAF		Sgt A R Gernon
	F/S D Hancock	139	S/L H A Forbes DFC RCAF		Sgt S W Kirk
85	F/L H B Thomas	149	F/O F M G Harrison		F/S W F E Moss
90	Sgt A F C Smith		Sgt F Bryant		F/S R E Price
97	S/L W M Burnside DFC		Sgt H Ormerod		F/S B D Searson
	W/O J H Bushby		Sgt N E Smith		F/S J C Hartley RAAF
100	P/O R S Bailey*		Sgt W Summers		F/O F T Rowan RCAF
	P/O T F Townley		F/S R Taylor		F/O R R Sommers RCAF
	Sgt J C Cape		Sgt E T Turner		WO2 S Hart RCAF
	Sgt K F Day		F/S H Wormall-Phillips		F/S D Peletz RCAF
	Sgt E G Emery	150	Sgt W E Buckley		F/S C W Stewart RNZAF
	Sgt L L Foster		Sgt J A Clark	171	F/L J M Stone*
	Sgt P Garner		Sgt T B Cook	186	F/S H G Kimber
	F/S J Harper		F/S L B Horrox		F/S J M Young
	Sgt G F Longley		F/S H H Bawden RAAF*	189	F/O Dykins
	F/O D B Douglas RCAF		F/S J H Gillies RAAF		

Sqn	Name	Sqn	Name	Sqn	Name
189	F/L J T Ormiston	218	Sgt A Allman	405	F/S J R Crisp RCAF
	F/O G M Ward DFC		Sgt J Gough		F/O R O Norse RNZAF
	F/S D E Barker*		F/S D I Humphrey		T/S J W Verner USAAF
	Sgt W C Brown		Sgt T F Morgan	408	Sgt R A Hind
	F/S W R Clydesdale		F/S F T Reynolds		Sgt S A Powell
	F/S L W Cromarty DFM		Sgt J N Sherry		F/O R D Atkinson RCAF
	F/S J Hughes*	223	F/O R W Johnson		F/O K K Blyth RCAF
	F/S B Jackson		W/O W F Baker		P/O A K Brown RCAF
	Sgt B C Johnson		W/O A C Cole*		F/O W G Burnett RCAF
	Sgt W S Jones		F/S G R Graham RCAF		F/L R H Fleming RCAF
	F/S B V Levesley		F/S B Maxwell RCAF		F/O H O Hinson RCAF
	Sgt D Y Looms	227	F/O D Geddes		F/O G M Keech RCAF
	Sgt McBeth		F/O W T Neilson		P/O T C King RCAF
	F/S J L Nolan		F/S C B Carter		F/O S Lasko RCAF
	Sgt R C Powell		F/S J Connell		F/O H T McGovern RCAF
	Sgt E L Preece		Sgt B J T Cox		F/O J E Moran RCAF
	Sgt W Prince		F/S S A F Diplock		F/O V D J Mousseau
	F/S J W Purdy		Sgt R Elborn		RCAF
	Sgt J T Russell		Sgt P Gaughan		F/O H R Sproule RCAF
	F/S T G Storey		F/S J B Gayland*		F/O J M Taylor RCAF
	F/S F B Walsh*		F/S J W Harrison		P/O F W Trow RCAF
	F/S D F Clement RCAF		F/S G A Jeans		F/O F A Winter RCAF
	F/O A B Kennedy RNZAF		F/S S H H Jobson		F/S J B Bennett RCAF
192	F/O G E Barking		Sgt W Lancaster		Sgt A D Dennis RCAF*
	P/O R Powell		Sgt B G Lawrence		F/S W A Dyer RCAF
	Sgt L W Greaves		Sgt P Mahon		F/S K G Finn RCAF
	Sgt L A Howard		Sgt A T Mayne		F/S J B Folkersen
	W/O R F Young		Sgt S H Page		RCAF
	W/O J A Martin RAAF		Sgt K Pratt		F/S J Gazo RCAF
	F/O D E Banks RCAF		F/S J G Redman		Sgt D G Grey RCAF
	F/L N Irvine RCAF		Sgt J Robb		F/S R J Hughes RCAF
	F/L J E Nixon RCAF		Sgt H Roberts		F/S V T Hunt RCAF
	F/S W J McCullough RCAF		F/S W A Roots		Sgt J Huspeka RCAF
	F/S A C Searle RCAF		Sgt R A Scutt		F/S A R Olson RCAF
199	F/S R Hunter		Sgt W A Senior		WO2 B C Patterson
	P/O L H Currell RAAF		F/S R W Sheen		RCAF
207	F/O J E Cranston		F/S E Thompson		F/S R I Smylie RCAF
	P/O A S Fletcher		P/O B H Lee RAAF		F/S D Steele RCAF
	F/S W G Cheeseman		F/L G A McCusker RAAF		F/S A A Watson RCAF
	Sgt E H Copley		F/S A T Bell RAAF	415	Sgt W J R Gale
	F/S T Hannaby		F/S B T Long RAAF		F/S A E Ridley
	Sgt J A Holmes		WO1 D E Cassidy RCAF		F/O R C Barbaux RCAF
	F/S A A V Howse		WO1 A F Dales RCAF		F/O N Conner RCAF*
	F/S P B Kehoe		P/O A T Harvey RNZAF		P/O J R Gendron RCAF
	Sgt N S Levick	300	P/O R Z Peisker PAF		F/O G K Grier RCAF
	Sgt K A W Ottewell		Sgt P Barzdo PAF		F/O R D Loveridge
	Sgt J W Spence RCAF		Sgt R Burkacki PAF		RCAF
214	F/L D P Heal		F/S J N Gerwatowski PAF		F/O P Mikalchuk RCAF
	F/L G Pow		Sgt A Gorczycki PAF		F/L W R Mitchell RCAF
	F/L H Rix		F/S H E Jachacz PAF		P/O W D Mosey RCAF
	F/L T H Tate		F/S W Jakimowicz PAF		P/O F T Mudry RCAF
	F/S N J Bradley		Sgt S Leya PAF		F/S F E Adams RCAF
	Sgt B Burgess		Sgt R Mankowski PAF		F/S J N Aicken RCAF
	Sgt R Gamble		Sgt T M Masiorski PAF		F/S K W Bradley RCAF
	Sgt A J Goldson		Sgt Z Minkler PAF		F/S W B Gill RCAF
	W/O J Henderson		Sgt T R Picho PAF		F/S A R Hibben RCAF
	F/S J G E Jennings DFM		Sgt Z Raczynski PAF		F/S J B Horrigan RCAF
	Sgt A D Macintosh	346	Sgc R Reynaud FFAF		F/S W G Johnston RCAF
	Sgt W P Mulhall	347	Sgt Kannengiesser FFAF		F/S A N Knight RCAF
	Sgt K C Phelan*		Sgt L Martin FFAF		WO1 I A F McDiarmid
	Sgt L J Pound		Sgc R Meunier FFAF		RCAF
	P/O H T Sargeant RAAF	405	F/O T W Downey		F/S J A Marshall RCAF
	W/O A R Irvine RAAF		F/O J A Lewis		F/S W L Mracek RCAF
	F/S J V Mathews RAAF		F/O B G Smoker		F/S G M Roberts RCAF
	F/O W J Lovell-Smith		F/O I W Bunter RCAF		F/S N Tonello RCAF
	RNZAF		F/L M O Frederick RCAF	419	Sgt T S Instone
	F/S J L Cuttance RNZAF		F/O R M Hyde RCAF		P/O R Althan RCAF
	F/S R O Douglas RNZAF		S/L H F Marcou AFC RCAF		P/O N V Hoas RCAF
218	F/L V W Hodnett		F/O J T Ross RCAF		P/O A Kindret RCAF

Sqn	Name	Sqn	Name	Sqn	Name
419	F/O P H Owen RCAF	427	F/L J M Murphy RCAF	460	F/S A W Halls RAAF
	F/S J W Aitken RCAF		P/O W R Wilson RCAF		F/S D D Lynch RAAF
	F/S H O Cole RCAF		Sgt H L G Mayer RCAF		F/S A R Main RAAF
	Sgt D C Jamieson RCAF		Sgt A L Morrison RCAF		F/S F J Sheridan RAAF
	F/S L J Nozzolillo RCAF		WO2 E A Perdue RCAF		F/S W A Stanley RAAF
420	Sgt H W Skipper		F/S A R Williams RCAF		F/S R C Styles RAAF
	F/O C F Bryce RCAF	428	F/O V Banks RCAF		F/S E S Symes RAAF
	F/L V R Glover RCAF		F/O C A Goodier RCAF		F/S E G Truman RAAF
	P/O J R Gordon RCAF*		F/O D M Payne RCAF	462	F/O W K Watson
	F/O V L McKinnon RCAF		F/O G C Riley RCAF		Sgt R E Casterton
	F/O D M Mottrick RCAF		F/O W J Spence RCAF		Sgt R G Hodgson
	P/O A V Padgham RCAF		F/O J W Bellamy RCAF		Sgt S G Rother
	F/O R G Reid RCAF		Sgt E R O Casey RCAF		F/O J R Boyce RAAF
	F/O D W Ritchie RCAF		Sgt R R Duke RCAF		F/L F H James RAAF
	WO2 D F Broadfoot RCAF		WO2 E V Miller RCAF		F/O A M Lodder RAAF
	F/S A H Butler RCAF		F/S E F Ossington RCAF		F/O W J Mann RAAF
	F/S S Cameron RCAF		Sgt T F Sinclair RCAF		W/O H W Coleman RAAF
	Sgt A F Domke RCAF	429	Sgt R H V Streetfield		W/O J D Fraser RAAF
	F/S D J Jacobi RCAF		F/O R R Jones RCAF		F/S M J Hibberd RAAF
	F/S R J Little RCAF		F/S R A Deck RCAF		F/S R W C Hutton RAAF
	F/S T Lynch RCAF		WO1 H L Johnson RCAF		F/S D H Laurence RAAF
	F/S H E MacKenzie RCAF		F/S J A J C Rancourt RCAF		F/S T P Ledwirth RAAF
	Sgt P E Morissette RCAF	431	F/O I C MacCugan RCAF		W/O T H McFarlane RAAF
	F/S F W Poole RCAF		F/S D C Cockwell RCAF		F/S P A Naylor RAAF
	F/S K D Reid RCAF		F/S H R Dailey RCAF		F/S N E Teede RAAF
	Sgt R J Wilson RCAF		WO2 F E Lehman RCAF	463	F/O J A Costello DFM
424	F/O W D Lightall RCAF	432	Sgt B M Hodges		F/L J H Dean
	F/S C J Antonek RCAF		F/O F D Baxter RCAF		F/L W J O Grime
	Sgt J Butler RCAF		F/O A R A Borland RCAF		F/L J A Loftus
	Sgt K F Seaman RCAF		F/O R I Bradley RCAF		F/L J G Padgham
	Sgt A T Skett RCAF		P/O F S Daley RCAF		P/O W L Worden
425	Sgt J P A Tame		F/O J A Fraser RCAF		Sgt W J Bilton
	F/O M D Berry RCAF		F/S S A Harrison RCAF		Sgt T P Freeman
	F/O W B Cable RCAF		F/O G H Henson RCAF		Sgt R L Gard
	F/O R Marc-Aurele RCAF		F/O A T Hinchliffe RCAF		Sgt C W Gordon
	F/O J A Parent RCAF		F/O A H May RCAF		Sgt J M Miller
	P/O R J H Pigeon RCAF		F/O R H Mueller RCAF		Sgt E Moss
	P/O C B Racicot RCAF		F/O J J Serne RCAF		F/S E R Cameron RAAF
	F/O J W A Seguin RCAF		P/O J G Stephen RCAF		F/S E K Foreman RAAF*
	Sgt J T R Cauely RCAF		S/L J H Thompson RCAF		F/S D C Hannaford RAAF
	F/S J A P Demouchel RCAF		P/O R D Thomson RCAF		F/S D J Lewis RAAF
	F/S M H Depot RCAF		F/O H E Vachon RCAF		F/S A M White RAAF
	F/S E G Gregory RCAF		WO2 E E V Anderson RCAF	466	Sgt F N Bridger*
	F/S F H King RCAF		F/S G E Armstrong RCAF		Sgt D Smith
	F/S L P Lamontagne RCAF		Sgt D C Duffy RCAF		Sgt P R Woodmore
	F/S G L J Langevin RCAF		F/S J W B McIntosh RCAF		F/S J M Dyer RAAF
	F/S R S Le Boeuf RCAF		F/S F T McLachlan RCAF		W/O A S Caddie RNZAF
	F/S G E J Tremblay RCAF		Sgt J W Reid RCAF	467	F/O R N Browne
	Wo2 R G J Trudeau RCAF		Sgt V L Shulz RCAF		F/O E G Parsons
	F/S J A R Villiard RCAF		Sgt S E Waterbury RCAF		F/O J Pendergast
426	Sgt J A Bromley	434	F/O R English RCAF		F/L D O Sands
	F/O D J Bird RCAF*		F/O C K Legaarden RCAF		Sgt B A Davies
	F/O R R Broadfoot RCAF		Sgt J A English RCAF		Sgt B H Parker
	F/O W I B Jarvis RCAF		Sgt J M Hamlin RCAF		F/O R E Taylor RAAF
	F/O S E Levis RCAF		Sgt G A McLarty RCAF		F/O J H Willmott RAAF
	F/S W H Denison RCAF	460	F/S K E Ambler		F/S B O Bean RAAF
	Sgt R M Eyre RCAF		Sgt E D Grant		F/S J J B Grady RAAF
	F/S A M Lacchia RCAF		Sgt G F Rudge		F/S J C Jarrett RAAF
	F/S B W McNicol RCAF		F/S D P Thorpe		F/S M G Thompson RAAF
	Sgt K M Montagno RCAF		F/S R H Whiticar		F/O L W E Baines RCAF
	Sgt S Ross RCAF		F/O A Flynn RAAF	514	Sgt G H Berridge
427	Sgt P De Metz		F/L D H Heggie RAAF		Sgt S W Moore
	Sgt G B Tate		F/O B Hepper RAAF	550	F/O S R Angill
	F/O A J Breault RCAF		F/O H G Payne RAAF		W/C B Ball
	S/L W B Brittain RCAF		F/S D R Benbow RAAF		F/L D E A Luger
	F/O R V Dallin RCAF		F/S J R Bennett RAAF		Sgt D B Boyce
	F/O C J Driscoll RCAF		F/S H R Connochie RAAF		F/S L F Figg
	F/O H McKay RCAF		F/S C G Cooper RAAF		Sgt A Finnigan
	F/O G F Mann RCAF		F/S C N Fraser RAAF		Sgt R L Gibbes

Sqn	Name	Sqn	Name	Sqn	Name
550	Sgt R Gray	578	F/S F E Mayer	625	Sgt R Pyett
	Sgt G P Kelleher		F/S J C E Toft		Sgt F Walker
	Sgt E W King*		F/O I Denley RAAF		Sgt J V Williams
	Sgt R H Laney		F/O R L Maloney RAAF		F/O A J Bloy RAAF
	F/S F M Main		F/S D J Ford RAAF		F/S T M Ryan RAAF
	Sgt S Pelham		F/S J A Cahill RCAF		F/O J W Alexander RCAF
	F/S M B Smith	608	F/L L N Hobbs		F/O F R Chapman RCAF
	Sgt R F Stevens		Sgt H J Erben		F/O W Petrashenko RCAF
	Sgt S J Webb		F/O R Dennis RAAF		Sgt T H Scowcroft RCAF
	Sgt K D Winstanley	617	P/O A Hepworth	626	F/L J Cox
	F/O A L Coldwell RCAF	619	F/L E J F Smith		Sgt R I Nelson
	F/O D H Grundy RCAF		F/O D I Thomas		Sgt T Whitby
	F/O G J Nicol RCAF		F/S H J Burke		F/O S S Quinn RAAF
	Sgt D J Hicks RCAF		Sgt F J Cole		F/L D S Nelson RCAF
	WO2 R C McLauchlan RCAF		F/S E Dellow	627	F/O W A Barnett RNZAF
	F/S D J Yemen RCAF		Sgt G R J Miles	630	F/O P F Fleming
576	F/O C T Dalziel		Sgt K Phillips		Sgt R W Beardwell
	F/O G Davies		F/S A Shannon		F/S J E Hogan
	F/O N Whiteley		F/S J W Speers		Sgt G S W Hooper
	F/S W E Bradbury		F/O H E Hanson RCAF		F/S I L Lynn
	Sgt S Cranidge		F/O T Turner RCAF		F/O A V Cameron RAAF
	Sgt J W Foster	622	F/L E G Cook	635	F/L J Hendry
	Sgt P F G A Garner		F/O P D Gough		P/O B G Roberts
	Sgt H A Hall		F/O M Parry*		F/O F M Williams
	Sgt D H Hogg		F/O R W Sherry		F/S J W Ennis
	Sgt R Hoyle		Sgt R C Hagerty*		F/S R B McMaster
	Sgt W K Monksfield		Sgt W E Lewis*		F/S J T McQuillan DFM
	Sgt J R Reed		Sgt T McLaren*		F/O J J Kennelly RAAF
	Sgt J Tyrer		F/S E Parker		F/L J A Rowland RAAF
	F/S P F Sattler RAAF		Sgt C T Savage		F/L K A Beattie RNZAF
578	F/O R Carabine	625	P/O R Blackley	640	F/S R S Hall
	P/O P H Clews		F/L A D Cook		F/O J B Wiloughby RCAF
	P/O J E F Sadler*		Sgt W Allen*	692	Sgt D H Beckolt
	Sgt C G Atkins		F/S F W Brooks	1409	F/L J A L Lymburner RCAF
	Sgt J Benson		Sgt B S F Hessey		
	F/S N Earnshawn		Sgt O C Lear		
	F/S G D Gibb		Sgt S L Lowe		
	Sgt J F Maguire		Sgt J R Lyons		
	W/O J Mason		F/S C W Morgan		

Letitia - 2 February 1945 Liverpool

F/L P Addinsell	F/S C W I Jeffery
AC1 Alexander	F/L R King DFC RAAF
F/L G A Atkinson	W/O McLean
F/L W Beckingham	S/L P Mason
AC1 Boon	F/L J C Milner
AC1 D H Burgess	F/L W D Moor
F/S T W Burke	F/L W N Nixon
Sgt R Burnett	Sgt D C O'Donnell
F/O D A Crookston RAAF	Sgt F Pearson
P/O F J Davies	F/L C E J Plumridge
W/O J A Davies	F/L S Reyman
F/L J A Day	Sgt J J McK Rigley
W/O W Draper	W/O C S F Ryder
F/S G C Farran	F/S A Scott
W/O C H Forsythe	W/O D E Sharp
F/L L F Gregory	W/O Shepherd
W/O Hale	F/O C R G Small
F/L N D Halifax	F/L J R T Smaller
F/L S E Harris	F/S J E Vidler
W/O G T Haworth	F/O V H J Vizer
F/L D G Heaton-Nicholls	P/O R Watson
F/L H H Henderson	LAC Watson
F/S Hooper	W/O S Wilson
W/O B A Hopgood	
F/L F C Jeffery	

Arundel Castle - 6 February 1945 Liverpool

W/O Adamson	Sgt P/O McLeary
F/O Bridger	Sgt E McKay
F/S J P Cleary	Sgt J R Marshall RNZAF
F/S A Collins	Sgt W Pearson
F/S J E Davidson	Sgt C M A Phyall
F/S J R Dodds	F/L Poulton
F/O D A C Dormond	F/L I Rademeyer DFC
W/O S Drake	Sgt J T Rayworth
F/S Elks	F/O J H Reavill
Sgt J Elliott	W/O J A Riley
F/S A A S Evans	Sgt D J Salt
F/S K Gay RAAF	F/L P H Shurlock
W/O A J Guy	F/O Shipley
Sgt A J Harris	Sgt J Skjelanger
F/S Haynes	Sgt A H Smallman
Sgt E G Hughes	F/S D B Smith RAAF
F/L Humphreys	F/S R G Smith
F/S Hunt	F/S G S Staniforth
P/O Johnson	Sgt R F Summerhayes
Sgt J C Jossa	F/O B O Thwaite RAAF
F/L Knight	Sgt R Wann
F/O A G Knight	W/O Williams
W/O Krukschuster	Sgt Wilson
P/O T J Lynch RAAF	W/O K B Wood
Sgt A J McAvoy	

During the last few months of the war, thousands of Allied prisoners of war were forced to evacuate their camps and take to the road as the Soviets advanced from the east. This mass exodus led to extremes in discomfort and hardship as men, brought low from long years in captivity, were herded from place to place, frequently sleeping in the open or in buildings commandeered by their guards.

On the 19th of April 1945, one such column numbering an estimated twelve thousand men was near the village of Gresse where, after much cajoling from Warrant Officer J A G (Dixie) Deans (see Volume 1 page 109), the Germans had arranged for a delivery of much needed Red Cross food parcels. One can imagine the scenes of delight as the parcels were distributed, it is reported, two per person. Tragically, their happiness was turned to horror when, soon after leaving Gresse, a flight of Typhoon fighter-bombers attacked the long straggling column in what can only be described as an awful case of mistaken identity. In his book, "No Flight from the Cage", Calton Younger (see Volume 3 page 99) states that seven aircraft attacked before the eighth pilot, realising that a dreadful mistake has been made, climbed away and prevented his companions from making a second strafing run.

On the road and in the fields and ditches bordering this scene of carnage, upwards of forty men (Calton Younger reports in excess of sixty) were either dead, or mortally wounded. Those who died were initially laid to rest in a mass grave at Gresse, since when all have been exhumed and taken to the 1939-1945 War Cemetery at Berlin.

The table that follows identifies forty-two known deaths, an asterisk having been appended to the names of those who died from their wounds.

Name	Sqn/Unit	Grave	Name	Sqn/Unit	Grave
W/O E Bardsley	576 Sqn	6 B 9	LCpl C A Joyes	Essex Scot	11 K 6-
F/S D Bauldie	76 Sqn	5 J 25	F/S W E Lawton	76 Sqn	6 B 15
W/O W A I Bone	76 Sqn	6 B 20	Fus F C Lewis*	RF	11 A 7
Sgt J S J Breytenbach	SA Forces	11 E 8	W/O J Lord*	405 Sqn	11 N 7
W/O A Brown*	107 Sqn	11 N 8	W/O G A Losh	102 Sqn	6 B 14
W/O D J Clayden	405 Sqn	6 B 12	W/O H P Lowman	1652 CU	11 N 11
Gnr J R C Currie	25 FD Regt	11 E 5	W/O M G McKenna*	156 Sqn	11 N 13
WO1 R G Douglas	419 Sqn	6 B 7	WO1 W A MacKenzie RCAF	419 Sqn	6 B 21
LCpl W Downie	6 Cameronians	11 K 6-8	LCpl G Moir	1 Gordon	11 E 12
W/O F B Duffield	114 Sqn	6 B 17	W/O K Mortimer	514 Sqn	6 B 18
WO1 V A Fox RCAF	7 Sqn	6 B 6	Cpl B Paton	4 Black Watch	11 E 7
W/O J Gage	99 Sqn	6 B 11	W/O A V Porter	35 Sqn	RM269
F/S J A Gibbs	578 Sqn	6 B 13	W/O F T Price*	625 Sqn	11 N 12
Pte W D Glynn-Baker	SA Forces	10 D 10	W/O A G C Read	76 Sqn	11 N 10
LSgt L H J Goodfellow	44 Div RSigs	11 E 16	W/O J G Shierlaw RAAF	458 Sqn	6 B 22
W/O E A Green*	218 Sqn	14 F 4	W/O F J W Steele	214 Sqn	11 N 9
W/O G C G Hawkins	107 Sqn	8 G 23	Gnr J T Sutcliffe	102 Regt	10 F 9
W/O C W Heathman	214 Sqn	6 B 10	Gnr F J Walls	261 Bty RA	10 F 10
W/O L B H Hope RNZAF	75 Sqn	6 B 8	W/O W P J Watson	44 Sqn	6 B 16
Bdr T H Hume	72 FD Regt	11 E 11	F/S S J Wheadon	425 Sqn	6 B 19
Cpl A G Hunt	Essex Scot	11 K 6-8	Pte R Woodgate	Aus Infantry	11 G 1

Note 1. The grave identities have been extracted from the CWGC registers published for Berlin 1939-1945 War Cemetery, which is located in the Charlottenburg district, some 8 kilometres from the city centre, on the south side of the Heerstrasse. The first two digits indicate the plot, the single letter signals the row while the last figure shows the grave number.

Note 2. The remains of Warrant Officer A V Porter of 35 Squadron could not be identified and his name is inscribed on panel 269 of the Runnymede Memorial.

Camp	Location	Camp	Location
DL	Dulag Luft Wetzlar	4B	Mühlberg (Elbe)
079	Braunschweig	7A	Moosburg (Isar)
L1	Barth Vogelsang	11B	Fallingbostel
L7	Banku near Kreulberg	13D	Nürnberg
3A	Luckenwalde	357	Thorn

Note. Fallingbostel was basically an army camp; Thorn (357) was a mere kilometre away.

Appendix 11

Internees
January to May 1945

Following the crossing of the Rhine in March 1945, the area of bombing operations tended, in the final weeks of the war, to shift towards targets in eastern Germany and, thus, routes skirting the Baltic were once again a feature of Bomber Command operations.

Mine laying operations, too, continued in these last months and the Baltic routes were also used in January and February, notably in raids against oil producing plants around Stettin and Leipzig.

Not surprisingly, a handful of bombers, mainly Lancasters, were either abandoned, or obliged to land in neutral Sweden. For most of the survivors, their internment lasted a matter of weeks and nearly all were back in the United Kingdom in time to take part in the victory celebrations.

Sqn	Name	File	Report
57	F/O B A Clifton RAAF	3326	(-)2908
463	F/O A Cox		
	F/O J A Wainwright		
	F/S W D Hogg		
	F/S F W J H Logan		
	F/S F E Parent		
	Sgt G W Simpson		
	F/S R Smurthwaite	3327	(-)3060
619	F/S F A M Blakeley	3326	(-)2906
	Sgt D H Drew	3326	(-)2962

Sqn	Name	File	Report
619	Sgt J Haigh	3326	(-)2907
	F/S M P B Quigley		
	F/S F W Roots	3326	(-)2905
	F/S R I Wilson	3326	(-)2904
	F/O B P Curran RAAF	3326	(-)2903
630	F/O J W Langley	3326	(-)2924
	F/S G B Gaughan	3326	(-)2925
	Sgt J R Thomas	3326	(-)2963
	F/S I J Penglase RAAF	3326	(-)2926
	F/S T W Panting RCAF	3326	(-)2928
	W/O S H Potter RNZAF	3326	(-)2927

Appendix 12

Unternehmen Gisela
3-4 March 1945

During the night of 3-4 March 1945, Bomber Command was involved in two operations; an attack on a synthetic-oil production plant at Kamen and a raid on the Dortmund-Ems Kanal near Ladbergen. Both forces were relatively small; 234 aircraft being despatched to the former and 222 bombers, all from No.5 Group, mustered for the latter. Support for these operations was provided by both 100 Group and aircraft drawn from the training establishments, while Mosquitoes of the LNSF kept the sirens wailing over Berlin. Also busy were thirty-one Lancaster crews laying mines over the Kattegat and in Oslo Fjord, while seventeen aircraft were tasked for the still important job of dropping supplies to various resistance groups. In total, 785 crews were continuing to prosecute the air war over Europe.

Vigilance was still a key factor. Although the challenge from the Luftwaffe was now a mere shadow of the threat imposed during the years of 1943 and 1944, interceptions from their night-fighters remained a distinct possibility as operations for March 1945 got under way.

Thus, on this night in question, Bomber Command lost seven Lancasters from the raid on the Dortmund-Ems Kanal. 467 Squadron reported three missing including the machine flown by their Commanding Officer, Wing Commander E Le P Langlois DFC RAAF. Two more aircraft, a Mosquito and a Lancaster, disappeared without trace, bringing the total to nine. However, as will be seen from an inspection of pages 101 to 106, a further 22 bombers were written off and no less than 19 and probably 20 of this total were as a direct result of enemy intruder activities.

Code named "Unternehmen Gisela", close on 200 Luftwaffe night-fighters were employed, their crews briefed to cross the North Sea and patrol inland from the Thames Estuary to the North Yorkshire Moors, Their successes, as can be seen in the summaries, were considerable and in addition to the 19/20 known losses already reported, a further five bombers (four Lancasters and a Halifax) from the Heavy Conversion Units were shot down. Details of these aircraft head the summaries for this appendix.

The cost to the Luftwaffe, too, was high with twenty-five night-fighters, all Ju 88 variants written off. Through the kind permission of Michael Balss, author and compiler of "Deutsche Nachtjagd", the following information in respect of these aircraft and their crews has come to light.

3-4 Mar 1945	1651 CU	Lancaster III	JB699 BS-F	Training
	F/L D J Baum	+	Shot down at 0135, diving almost vertically into the ground near Cottesmore airfield in Rutland. All are buried in various United Kingdom cemeteries, three being taken to Cambridge City Cemetery. F/O Brook RAAF had married Mary Louise Brook of Bradford and he rests in Bradford (North Bierley) Cemetery.
	Sgt J A W Smith	+	
	F/O D C Davies	+	
	F/S R Warne	+	
	F/S C E Gardener RNZAF	+	
	F/O K R Brook DFC RAAF	+	
	Sgt T Platt	+	
	1651 CU	Lancaster III	ND387 BS-K	Training
	F/S A Howard	+	Shot down 0115 and crashed near the airfield at Woolfox Lodge, Rutland. Those who died rest in cemeteries in England and Scotland, three, it is noted, being buried at Cambridge City Cemetery.
	Sgt A W Darling	+	
	Sgt W J Pullan	+	
	F/O K C Millar	+	
	F/S R B Wilson RNZAF	+	
	Sgt A W Taylor	+	
	Sgt J Thompson		
	1654 CU	Lancaster III	LM748 UG-H	Training
	F/S A E Lutz RAAF	+	Shot down 0105 and crashed at Stapleford, 5 miles SW from the centre of Nottingham. F/S Lutz RAAF is buried at Oxford (Botley) Cemetery, North Hinksey; the others were claimed by their next of kin.
	F/S H F Cox	+	
	F/O J A C Chapman	+	
	Sgt F Shaw	+	
	Sgt A F Wawby	+	
	Sgt H Frost	+	
	Sgt A G Davey	+	

```
3-4 Mar    1654 CU            Lancaster III   PB118 UG-Q                  Training
1945       F/S R W Pinkstone        inj    Shot down 0057 and partially abandoned before
           F/S H Evans              inj    crashing at Church Warsop, 8 miles SSW from
           Sgt C G Rouse                   Worksop, Nottinghamshire.
           Sgt J Pringle            inj
           Sgt R Campbell            +
           Sgt J S Morgan           inj

           1664 CU            Halifax III    NA612  -S                    Training
           P/O K W Griffey RCAF      +    Crashed 0144 at Brafferton, 8 miles S of
           Sgt S Forster             +    Thirsk, Yorkshire. The four RCAF members
           Sgt J W Buttrey           +    of crew were taken to Harrogate (Stonefall)
           F/O G H Lloyd RCAF        +    Cemetery; the others rest in their home towns.
           WO2 L T Chevrier RCAF     +
           Sgt L Boardman            +
           F/S J E Fielder RCAF      +

           1./NJG2           Ju 88 G-6   620192                      Op: Gisela
           Fw   J Wyleciol            +    Crashed at Holsen, 6 km SE from the centre of
           Fw   K Thomas              +    Lübbecke and 16 km W from the large town of
           Uffz G Pfauter             +    Minden.
           Uffz E Schnitzer           +

           1./NJG2           Ju 88 G-6   622154                      Op: Gisela
                                            Came down NW of Würzburg.

           3./NJG2           Ju 88 G-6   620588  4R + JL             Op: Gisela
           Fhr  K Vogel               +    Lost without trace.
           Fw   J Fritsch             +
           Uffz H Hellmich            +
           Uffz A Engelhardt          +

           3./NJG2           Ju 88 G-6   620654  4R + CL             Op: Gisela
           Uffz A Schlichter          +    Lost without trace.
           Fw   G Kolbe               +
           Ogefr R Theimer            +
           Ogefr R Kautz             +

           9./NJG2           Ju 88 G-6   622140  4R + LT             Op: Gisela
           Fw   H Schenk              +    Crashed 800 metres N from the Kampener Leucht-
           Uffz H Kunst               +    turms.
           Ogefr F Habermalz          +
           Uffz E Däuber              +

           Stab IV./NJG3     Ju 88 G-6   620745  D5 + AE             Op: Gisela
           Maj  B Ney               inj    Abandoned 0450 near Knesebeck, 10 km NNW
           Fw   W Bolenz            inj    from Wahrenholz. Maj Ney, the Kommandeur,
           Ofw  Schlick            inj    was partially paralysed.

           3./NJG3           Ju 88 G-6   621821                      Op: Gisela
           Lt   H Flach             inj    Hit by flak over Holland and abandoned in the
           Uffz G Noch             inj    vicinity of Beilen (Drenthe), some 18 km S of
           Fw   K Huber            inj    Assen.
           Fw   F Fleischer        inj

           3./NJG3           Ju 88 G-6   622822                      Op: Gisela
           Ogefr K Röder           inj    Crash-landed, due to engine failure, near
                                            Oldenburg. Ogefr Röder was not the pilot.

           10./NJG3          Ju 88 G-6   620785                      Op: Gisela
           Fw   L Kowalski           +    Crashed 0440 at Schortens, a largish town some
           Uffz M Komatz             +    12 km WNW from the docks area of Wilhelmshaven.
           Fw   Burger                     The cause of the crash was attributed to engine
                                            failure. Fw Burger baled out and landed unhurt.
           It is reported the crew had been tasked for a meteorlogical sortie.
```

Note. Dickhausen, 48 km E of Köln is also reported as the crash site and
with variations in the ranks of the crew. The important details of names
and initials, and fate are, however, the same.

3-4 Mar	10./NJG3	Ju 88 G-6	621293	Op: Gisela
1945	Uffz W Lohse	+	Crashed in unknown circumstances.	
	Uffz H Horsch	+		
	Ogefr F Neumann	+		

12./NJG3   Ju 88 G-6   620018   Op: Gisela
Ofw   W John   +   Lost without trace.
Fw   L Dunst   +
Ogefr A Gerhard   +
Ogefr W Krause   +

12./NJG3   Ju 88 G-6   620028   D5 + AX   Op: Gisela
Hptm J Dreher RK   +   Crashed 0151 at Dunnington Lodge after hitting
Ofw   H Böker   +   a tree some 4 miles ENE of York and close to
Fw   G Schmitz   +   Elvington airfield. Three civilians; Richard,
Fw   M Bechter   +   Ellen and Violet Moll also died. The night-
                                         fighter crew were taken to York for burial in
Fulford Cemetery, since when their remains have been exhumed and transferred
to the German Military Cemetery at Cannock Chase in Staffordshire.

Stab I./NJG4   Ju 88 G-6   622056   3C + BC   Op: Gisela
Ofw   F Specht   inj   Shot down near Hamm, probably by an Allied
                                         night-fighter. Ofw Specht, who was not the
                                         pilot was wounded; the rest were unhurt.

1./NJG4   Ju 88 G-6   622132   3C + PJ   Op: Gisela
Ofw   K Gäbler   inj   Abandoned, low on fuel and crashed 0245 N of
                                         Bramsche. Only the pilot was hurt.

1./NJG4   Ju 88 G-6   622959   Op: Gisela
                                         Ran out of fuel on return and abandoned near
                                         Wunstorf.

2./NJG4   Ju 88 G-6   622829   3C + EK   Op: Gisela
Lt   W Rinker   inj   Abandoned, on fire, and left to crash near
                                         Vechta. Apart from the pilot, no one was hurt.

3./NJG4   Ju 88 G-1   712203   Op: Gisela
Ogefr H Hangs   +   Reported crashed near Giessen. Ogefr Hangs
                                         was the sole fatality, though he was not the
                                         pilot.

3./NJG4   Ju 88 G-6   621305   3C + FL   Op: Gisela
Lt   H Ensinger   +   Shot down in air combat over Holland and
                                         crashed 2308 near Hardenberg in the Province
                                         of Overijssel.

5./NJG4   Ju 88 G-6   621805   3C + KN   Op: Gisela
Ofw   L Zimmermann   +   Attempted to shoot down a B-24 Liberator over
Ofw   P Vey   +   Metfield airfield, Suffolk but was frustrated
Uffz   H Pitan   +   when the bomber commenced turning into the
Uffz   H Wende   +   attack. Ofw Zimmermann then flew low over
                                         the airfield and loosed off his cannons, one
round entering the control tower, killing S/S Voye USAAF. Moments later, at
0137 the night-fighter hit some trees and cart wheeled across Nun's Lane, Grove
Farm at Linstead Parva, 2 miles WNW of Halesworth, Suffolk. All were initially
laid to rest on 8 March at Linstead Parva, since when their bodies have been
taken to the German Military Cemetery at Cannock Chase.

8./NJG4   Ju 88 G-6   621792   3C + DS   Op: Gisela
Oblt   W Paulus   +   Believed to have crashed in the sea while
Ogefr E Hafels   +   returning to base.
Ogefr H Müller   +
Ogefr A Hörger   +

3./NJG5   Ju 88 G-6   620816   Op: Gisela
                                         Abandoned, after running out of fuel, over
                                         the German mainland.

```
3-4 Mar   3./NJG5              Ju 88 G-6   621611                    Op: Gisela
1945      Uffz E Berger               inj   Reported crashed, due to technical problems,
                                             E of Leer.  Uffz Berger was not the pilot.


          3./NJG5              Ju 88 G-6   622832                    Op: Gisela
                                             Abandoned, after running out of fuel, and
                                             crashed near Buxtehude.


          7./NJG5              Ju 88 G-6   620397  C9 + RR           Op: Gisela
          Fw    H Conse              +      Flew into telegraph wires and crashed 0148 in
          Uffz  R Scherer           +      a field near Welton, 6 miles NNE from Lincoln.
          Ogefr W Nollau            +      A few minutes earlier, Fw Conse had shot down
          Uffz  A Altenkirch        +      a 460 Squadron Lancaster (see page 104) and
                                             had followed this by a strafing attack on a
          car driven by Observer J P Kelway ROC.  The four German airmen were buried
          in Scampton (St. John The Baptist) Churchyard.


          8./NJG5              Ju 88 G-6   620651  C9 + CS           Op: Gisela
          Hptm  H-J Bobsien          +      Crashed near Wittmund.
          Ofw   H Steinadler         +
          Fw    F Kessemeier         +
          Gefr  F Purth              +
```

Note 1. The three night-fighters shot down over the United Kingdom were the last German aircraft to be brought down over the British Isles during World War II.

Note 2. In addition to the details gathered by Michael Balss, I am indebted to Harry Holmes for additional information concerning the casualties sustained by the Luftwaffe and particularly in respect of his notes pertaining to the five aircraft lost from the Heavy Conversion Units, recorded in the heading to this table. Friedrich Braun, Hans de Haan, Thomas Hampel, Roy Walker, David Thompson, Graham Warrener and Bob Collis have all contributed to the overall content of this appendix.

Note 3. The claims subsequently submitted by the Luftwaffe amount to just fourteen aircraft destroyed. To this total can be added one, possibly three bombers shot down by crews who, in turn, crashed in the United Kingdom and were killed. The table below is an assessment of these claims:

Unit	Type	Pilot	Claim	Remarks
1./NJG2	Ju 88 G-6	Hptm Rath	2 x 4 engined bombers	Unidentified
2./NJG2	Ju 88 G-6	Hptm Hissbach	1 x 4 engined bomber	Unidentified
3./NJG2	Ju 88 G-6	Fw Kappe	1 x 4 engined bomber	Unidentified
7./NJG2	Ju 88 G-6	Oblt Briegleb	1 x 4 engined bomber 0036 S of Waddington	Unidentified
			1 x 4 engined bomber 0056 W of Lincoln	Unidentified
4./NJG3	Ju 88 G-6	Oblt Förster	2 x 4 engined bombers	Unidentified
4./NJG3	Ju 88 G-6	Fw Misch	1 x 4 engined bomber	Unidentified
4./NJG3	Ju 88 G-6	Fw Schmidt	0214 "Lancaster"	346 Sqn NR229 H7-D
10./NJG3	Ju 88 G-6	Lt Döring	1 x Fortress	214 Sqn HB815 BU-J
			1 x "Lancaster"	Halifax HX332 ZA-V
13./NJG3	Ju 88 G-6	Hptm Dreher*	2 x Halifax	Unidentified
9./NJG4	Ju 88 G-6	Hptm Fladrich	0033 1 x Lancaster N of Cambridge	Unidentified
3./NJG5	Ju 88 G-6	Lt Wolf	0108 1 x Lancaster N of Humber estuary	Unidentified
7./NJG5	Ju 88 G-6	Fw Conze*	1 x Lancaster	460 Sqn NG502 AR-J

Note 4. Claims shown between quotation marks suggest mistaken aircraft recognition, while the two pilots with asterisks appended both died in action over the United Kingdom. Hptm Dreher may have been responsible for shooting down the 158 Squadron Halifax, reported in the main text.

Note 5. Three Ju 88 G-6s were shot down over the North Sea, claims for
their destruction being submitted by:

F/L D B Wills	Mosquito NF.30	NT368	68 Sqn	Coltishall
F/L R B Miles	Mosquito NF.30	NT381	68 Sqn	Coltishall
W/C Griffiths	Mosquito NF.30	NT415	125 Sqn	Coltishall

Note 6. Peter Schneider has been especially helpful in translating the
Bundesarchiv/Militärchive Bestand RL10/575 written by Leutnant Arnold
Döring shortly after his return to Jever from Nordholz, where he landed
with fuel sufficient only for fifteen minutes of flying remaining. A
paraphrased and abridged account of his report concludes this appendix:

In Jever the machines had a better service and we often had 100 per cent
availability. The machines stand in two hangars, though some are in
covered "boxes". The crews live in barracks on the outskirts of Jever,
but the officers are accommodated at the airfield. The unit offices are
in the hangars, with the command post bunker 50 metres away. Within one
to two minutes after the order to start engine, the first machine can be
in the air.
    In the night 3-4 March, "Unternehmen Gisela" started. We fly with the
returning (British) bombers at low level over the sea so that the enemy
radar cannot find us. Our route is towards Flamborough Head, which the
British bombers are using. There was absolute radio silence, and we are
not allowed to shoot down any four-engined aircraft over the sea, as our
surprise should be perfect.
    After the "coupling time" we climb to 1,800 metres, just short of the
coast and drop "windows" against the search equipment fitted in the Mosquitoes. I crossed the coast north of Flamborough Head at Scarborough,
and could already see many fires from crashed aircraft, more than we
notice in Germany. My wireless operator logged a number of aircraft going
down, so that we could confirm the times after our return.
    We found a lot of airfields where our bombs have fallen; tracer bullets
"hissed" to targets on the ground; we are not to bring back one round of
ammunition.
    I dived down to 600 metres. Two airfields that had been lit up in front
of me put out their lights, and three other fields are flashing the morse
symbol "R" for raider. But for all that, there are many four-engined
bombers flying with their navigation lights on. (At some point in the
narrative, Leutnant Döring must have turned south). I pass over an airfield showing "DH" in white letters, and where a Drem landing system is
in operation, and fly underneath a four-engined aircraft with "festival"
lights showing. It is a B-17, which I recognise from its tail shape. I
open fire with my oblique weapons, hitting tanks in the fuselage and wing
and the machine begins to burn. The fire in the fuselage seems to burn
up and down, so the crew may have set off the extinguishers. Just short
of the Drem lights it crashes in a large cloud of dust, but with no fire.
The moonlight enables me to see clearly while in low level flight.
    Later, I see another four-engined aircraft (it is likely he has flown
back towards the Humber) with its navigation lights on, but because I am
not sure of the landscape and with the moon disappearing behind clouds, I
pass this aircraft by and catch one which is preparing to land. With oblique weapons I finish this Lancaster (it may have been a Halifax from 10
Squadron) which burns with a luminous glow before crashing in a big fire.
The other "Tommies" have been warned and switch off their navigation
lights. I attack one Lancaster from the front but have to climb in order
to avoid ramming him. Notwithstanding my fuel shortage, I fly around an
airfield which is lit up, but could not see any enemy aircraft. The moon
has now totally disappeared. I attack a double morse signal beacon, a car
and a train, before shooting off the last of my ammunition into a ware-
house at Scarborough. Over the sea, a convoy has gathered and I fly over
the anchored ships at low level. 600 kilometres of water way are ahead of
us and the "Tommy" is seeking revenge for he is disarranging our radio
signals. From my experiences in 1940, I know not to fall into a trap and
hold my course. Nearly two hours later we fly into an area of bad weather
with deep clouds, which our weathermen had not warned us about. Soon
after, we pass over the Dutch coast.

Appendix 13

Amendments to Previous Volumes with Addendum to Volume 6

The complexities in reporting over 12,000 aircraft and their crews over a period of close on seven years has, inevitably, led to mistakes. I am, therefore, extremely grateful to everyone who has taken the time to write to me, pointing out various omissions. Many of my correspondents had a very special interest in the summaries at fault and without exception, all have been very forgiving of my errors. Others who have written to me are historians in their own right and have very generously shared with me the fruits of their research.

It would be invidious of me to mention one or two names at the expense of others so may I assure all who have contacted me over the last few years that without your diligent help, I would be that much the poorer. Not every report submitted appears in the tables that follow as information from one source has, from time to time, been contradicted by another (such are the challenges facing anyone who attempts to compile an historical record of this nature). Nonetheless, I look forward to receiving your comments and, in the fullness of time, I hope to present as detailed a picture as possible of the dreadful losses that beset Bomber Command.

Page	Serial	Amendment
Volume 1		
16	K9448	Delete EM-
	L6005	Delete GL-
	K9271	Cr. Rohrbach-les-Bitche
17	L4191	Delete GL-
18	N5096	Delete EA-
	L1138	Uffz Stephan Lütjens, II./JB53
19	L1141	Lt Hans-Volkurt Rosenboom, 1./JG1 Cr. Lingen (Ems)
	L5185	Delete EM-
20	L6007	Delete GL-
21	L4239	Delete Ferry
		Insert Transit
22	L1325	Lt Joachim Müncheberg, III./JG26
	K7225	Whitley II
24	L4203	Delete GL-
25	K9185	Cr. Issoudun
26	N2961	OJ-P
27	N2962	OJ-B
	L4205	Delete GL-
	K9205	VO-
29	K9327	Delete all detail
	K9329	Delete all detail
30	L4198	Delete GL-
	P1279	Delete GL-
31	N3006	Insert 3-4 Mar
		New entry:
		11 Mar 52 Sqn Battle I
		1940 K9396 Cr. Andover
32	N2987	LAC G W D Carter inj
		Died 14 April 1940
33	P2515	F/O P F Templeman inj
	L8747	Uffz Kurt Opolski, II./JG77
39	L9465	Lt Lignitz, I./JG20
40	P2201	Ofw Schmale, IV(N)./JG2
47		New entry:
		10 May 103 Sqn Battle I

Page	Serial	Amendment
47c		1940 K9409 PM-
		Op: Luxembourg
		Hit by ground fire
		Vernon & DBR
48	K9338	Sgt C Bowles
		New entry:
		10 May 105 Sqn Battle I
		1940 K9339
		Op: Luxembourg
		(see K9338)
49	L5540	JN-C Later to Rechlin
50	K9325	HA-D Cr. target area
53	K9353	HA-J
56	K9333	Delete Rethel
		Insert Ecly
60		New entry:
		16 May 226 Sqn Battle
		1940 K9180 MQ- Ground
		Burnt on evacuation
		of Reims
		226 Sqn Battle
		K9330 MQ- Ground
		(as above)
	L9210	UX-
	P4851	UX-N
61	L8852	LS-S
62	K9348	Delete all detail
	K7696	Cr. target area
63	K9345	Delete all detail
	K9180	Delete all detail
	K9330	Delete all detail
	K9176	Cr. Montcornet
67	N6207	VE-G
69	L5459	F/O J E Vernon evd
71	L7791	Sgt J L Axford pow
		LAC E R Orland pow
		Sir Arnold T Wilson (summary)
78	103 Sqn	Sgt Brumby Delete Laval
		Insert Morannes

Page	Serial	Amendment
Volume 1		
79		New entry:
		15 Jun 98 Sqn Battle I
		1940 K9345 VO- Ground
		Burnt on evacuation
		Nantes-Chateau Bougon
	N1460	Cr. Dortmund-Mengede
86	P4288	F/O W A C Mulloy DFC
90		New entry:
		11 Jul 115 Sqn Wellington IA
		1940 P9236 KO-B Ground
		Burnt Marham
91	P9227	Cr. Klein-Henstedt
92	P9236	Delete all detail
94	L5502	QT-D
	R3895	S/L M N McF Kennedy pow
		L3 164 S/L
		Shot down by Fw Menge, II./JG77
95	L9239	XD-N
98	R2772	Sgt McGrath esc February 1942
		W0208 3309 (-)683 refers
99	P2077	Delete cr. location
		Insert Eemspolder near Valom
		(Groningen) 4 km N Uithuizen
101	P2331	Delete all detail
103	P9272	Cr. Freschluneberg
104	P4372	Cr. Köln-Sürth
	R3773	Delete OM-
		Insert VE-
107	R3163	OJ-G
109	L5010	PM-C
112	L5351	P/O J S Kulinski PAF +
113	L7483	Sgt A C Peck pow
		Repatriated October 1943
120	L7844	Sgt E Novotny pow
		L3 395 Sgt
		Sgt A Sestak pow
		L6 396 W/O
	N2771	Add: P/O J Matousek +
		P/O J Slaby +
		Sgt J Albrecht +
		Sgt F Zapietal +
		P/O F Truhlar inj
	N2773	Add: P/O L Anderle
		P/O Richter
		P/O M Vejrazka +
		P/O Furbach
		Sgt Landa
122	T2740	Believed hit by AA fire
123	X3027	Lt Heinz Völker, I./NJG2
127	T4151	P/O H H J Miller
136	T2501	Landed in error at Lille-Nord
140	T2803	Sgt C Hendy inj
		Sgt G Lea inj
		Rescued by P/O M Hansen DFC
		who was awarded the GM
141	L7799	Delete Op: Venice
		Insert Op: Porto Marghera
142	R2793	XD-F
Volume 2		
20	AD719	EA-C
25	T1895	GB-X
33	L7874	Sgt K Lenczowski PAF +
		P/O J Korzeinski PAF +
		Sgt B Chrzanowski PAF +
	T1892	GB-Q

Page	Serial	Amendment
34	Z5903	GB-D
	R1335	Cr. Heusden
42	Z6557	Cr. SE Papenburg
43	AD730	Cr. Black Hill, Lachen
45	X2986	Cr. Hürth-Berrenrath
	V6318	GB-B
46	V6370	GB-T
	AD796	Delete Eddelak 6 km NNW
		Insert Averlak 6 km N
47	V5823	GB-G
50	AD864	Cr. River Elbe between
		Blankenese & Cranz
56	P5048	Cr. Platenhörn
58	T2118	GB-E
60	R1392	NZ-N
		Sgt S Jozefiak PAF inj
62	V6316	GB-S
66	V6319	GB-F
69	V6336	GB-H
73	R1062	Delete Sgt Sulgut PAF
		Insert Sgt M Grzymski PAF inj
74	AD788	Cr. between Ipernstedt
		& Ostenfeld
76	Z6647	Cr. Dollern
82	Z7426	GB-B
	Z7486	GB-M
84	V5502	GB-U
95	V6039	GB-Q
	Z7439	GB-H
102	T2576	F/O K Bernasinski PAF inj
143	W5576	Ditched North Sea
151	AD923	F/O J W J Kingston
		Sgt R C W DeCourcy
153	T2879	Cr. 0742 Landsmeer
162	X9916	Cr. Köln-Weiden
196	Z9385	Operation Pickaxe II
		to Germany
Volume 3		
21	AE393	Cr. Howgill Scar roughly
		a mile SE Dalefoot Farm
28	Z8491	PH-F
35	R1463	Delete cr. detail
		Insert 0330 Asterby Top Farm
		Goulceby, 7 miles SW Louth
		Lincolnshire
38	Z9280	Ann Whittham invited to
		Driesum 1986 to receive
		her father's wedding ring
		found at cr. site
48	AL718	Delete 11 August 1942
		Insert 28-29 July 1942
60	Z8527	Cr. Marly-le-Roi
		Memorial dedicated
		11 November 1994
74	V9976	Operation Whiskey
75	X3667	AA-D
102	BJ674	Oblt Frank Hans-Dieter Frank
		I./NJG1
	W1042	Hptm Wolfgang Thimmig
		III./NJG1*
	Z8376	Lt Alois Lechner, III./NJG2
103	W5586	0215 Oblt Reinhold Knacke
		3./NJG1 Esloo, Belgium*
104	R1235	Oblt Rolf Bockmeyer, 5./NJG1
	DV843	Oblt Wilhelm Beier, I./NJG1*
	W5704	Hptm Werner Streib, I./NJG1*
*		Believed to correct previous detail

Page	Serial	Amendment
Volume 3		
104	DV707	Lt Helmut Niklas, 6./NJG1
105	DV740	Oblt Horst Patuschka, 4./NJG2*
	L7290	Oblt Walter Barte, 4./NJG1
	R5561	Lt Heinz Strüning, 7./NJG2
106	L7301	Oblt Prinz Heinrich zu Sayn Wittgenstein, III./NJG2
	L7456	Oblt Loos, I./NJG1
	Z1614	Oblt Walter Barte, 4./NJG1
107	DV715	Oblt Emil Wolsterdorf, III./NJG1
	X3598	Oblt Wilhelm Beier, I./NJG1
	Z8577	Oblt Wilhelm Beier, I./NJG1*
108	Z9307	Hptm Werner Streib, I./NJG1
	L9605	Oblt Reinhold Knacke, 3./NJG1
114	R5613	QR-B
118	R5516	Maj Günter Radusch, NJG1
141	R5615	QR-H
176	W1106 =	W1016 & F/S Porter RCAF buried Kiel War Cemetery
179	X3798	F/S Weaver RCAF escaped from captivity
230	R5703	QR-D
233	W1047	Me 110 Werke Nr 3198 Lt Gerhard Jeke, Adjutant I./NJG4
241	W4302	Cr. Menden
242	X3552	Add: P/O F Maxfield +
243	BK312	2140 flak & cr. sea off Juist F/S Mollard RCAF is commemorated
271	R5859	QR-G
Volume 4		
17	R5738	Maj Werner Streib, I./NJG5
22	W4321	Sgt E A O Campbell
28	DT721	twixt Boekel
29	W4817	Cr. corner of Freiheitstrasse & Ummerstrasse
33	ED440	Maj Werner Streib, I./NJG5
34	R9274	Cr. 2058
36	Z1392	Cr. Oostermeer
37	BK617	T/o 1807 & cr. 1943
41	DT788	Oblt Manfred Meurer, I./NJG1
42	N7638	Sgt J C Brigden pow
	DT694	Lt Johannes Hager, 6./NJG1
	HE169	2148 over North Sea & believed Oblt Paul Gildner
44	BF441	Add: F/O R G Campbell Sgt W L Humphries F/O W E Broadfield Sgt J Williams Sgt G E Weber Sgt J B Wood Sgt J A Fell
45	BF378	Oblt Hans-Joachim Jabs, IV./NJG1
52	Z1599	Oblt Manfred Meurer, I./NJG1
58	DZ460	Cr. Lindervlier at Den Ham
72	ED313	F/L N A J Mackie DFC evd
75	JB836	Sgt V N Elkins +
76	EF330	Hit a farmhouse: Joannes Wilhelmus Giezen (51) + Wilhelmus Bernadus Giezen (17) + Bernadus Reinerus Giezen (16) +
	HE519	EX-X
77	HE690	PT-U
	BK340	Cr. 2158
79	DZ427	Cr. Baston Fen between Deeping & Spalding

Page	Serial	Amendment
79	BK667	F/S J L Shiells
86	HE385	ZO-M
88	BK715	F/S E M Lukey RNZAF
	ED391	F/O F J Falkenire RAAF pow
93	W4252	S/L S N T Wallage +
103	HE213	Sgt E A Odling pow
108	HE374	Cr. Birmensdorf
110	DT561	Lt Blohm, NJG2
113	ED563	Cr. Rentrisch
115	BK653	F/S J A Smith evd
116	HE547	Cr. Kirf
	HE379	Cr. Hochspeyer
120	BF508	Sgt W T Leathley +
123	HR787	Cr. Bahnhof Kottenforste at Bonn
136	HK667	Lt Robert Denzel, NJG1 Memorial to crew dedicated 4 May 1998
139	BK812	P/O K J Bettles
142	ED837	F/S G A Williams RAAF pow
144	HE905	Sgt D H Pennock pow
		F/S D W Forland RCAF evd
147	JB964	Sgt J A Coughlin RCAF pow
149	LN439	Believed flak battery 4./371 at Randerath 7 km NE Geilenkirchen
154	DT789	Sgt Rees (summary)
	W4861	Cr. 0230
157	HF486	F/L J G Eldridge DFC & Bar
159	HE281	Cr. 0108
161	HR853	Cr. Malden (Gelderland) 7 km S Nijmegen
162	LM320	FZ-C
175	BF571	Sgt A C Lake
177	HK684	Add: Sgt L Booth pow 357 9641 W/O
103 Sqn		Lancaster III
180	HE395	Lt Heinz Grimm, IV./NJG1 Wreckage recovered 1991 4 bodies identified over next 18 months. 16 June 1993, interred Bergen op Zoom War Cemetery Cr. Schagen (Noord-Holland)
	W4983	Sgt J B Donohoe RAAF +
185	ED434	EA-T
186	ED453	EA-G
	R5551	Cr. Terlet
188	ED497	EA-C
191	DS668	P/O C N Pitchford pow Delete cr. location Insert 0200 le Mesnil-en-Vallee (Maine-et-Loire) 34 km WSW Angers
195	HR734	Cr. 2 km E Berlicum
	HE924	Four rest in, etc Sgt Payne Runnymede
196	BB375	into the Lek (summary)
198	EF348	P/O D I Turner evd
200	ED928	Cr. 0058 Kanaalstraat killing several Dutch civilians
203	EH890	Sgt D J Martin RNZAF pow L1 322 W/O
205	JD144	to Anterwerpen (summary)
207	JD214	Cr. Indoornik 3 km SE Wageningen
208	JD261	F/O D G Howse +
*		Believed to correct previous detail

Page	Serial	Amendment

Volume 4

Page	Serial	Amendment
209	JB928	Maj Rolf Leuchs, NJG6
	EH900	SE of Ahaus (summary)
210	R5572	ZN-M Cr. 0345
	W4367	Cr. 0106 IJsselmeer
211	DS663	Night-fighter 0210
		Grez Neuville (Maine-et-Loire)
		20 km NW Angers
213	ED377	Cr. 0215 Angrie (Maine-et-Loire)
		6 km ENE Cande
217	EF394	Delete Sgt J Hargreaves
		Delete both aircraft, etc
		Insert Cr. 1637 near Chedburgh
	BK724	Cr. 1637 Stansfield, 7 miles
		NW Sudbury
218	BF579	Delete Op: Köln
		Insert Op: Gardening
	BK648	Delete 10 km NW Iserlohn
		Insert below Troisdorf
220	HE980	Cr. Averbode
221	HR813	P/O R B Smith DFC pow
		L3 2087 F/L
	JD159	Delete in Schoonselhof, etc
		Insert at Fort 3, Borsbeek
		on 8 July 1943
222	HE630	Sgt G E Lewis RCAF +
224	ED720	ZN-R
225	ED475	VN-E
227		12-13 Jul 12 Sqn
229	ED412	Cr. 0055 Mount Gramont
		le Bouverent
	ED531	Cr. 0108 near Thyon
230	JD108	Cr. 0236
	EE873	0142 Hptm Heinrich-Franz
		Wohlers, II./NJG4*
	JD297	0210 Oblt Rudolf Altendorf
		II./NJG1
	DS660	0228 Hptm Hubert Rauh
		3./NJG4
231	HR905	0126 Hptm Hanz-Dieter Frank
		I./NJG1
	DT769	Sgt Domigan arrested St-Jean-
		de-Luz near French-Spanish
		border
	BB323	Oblt Heinz Strüning, 3./NJG1
232	DK142	Sgt J H Brown RCAF evd
	DK228	0240 Hptm Wilhelm Herget
		I./NJG4
233	EE190	F/L T A Stewart RNZAF
234	DK119	Sgt R O Hunter RCAF evd
244	EE906	Cr. on farmland belonging to
		Bekx family
	EF369	P/O G R Woodward
		12 Jul = 12 Sqn
245	JB864	Sgt Thorne esc from captivity
		& reached Nijverdal in Holland
		& hidden by Resistance. Tried
		to reach Allied lines. Arrested
		& put on train to Germany.
		Jumped near Doetinchem and
		killed 2 February 1945
252	EF915 = EE915	
253	JD365	Sgt R A Denham pow
		4B 222447 W/O
		Repatriated October 1944
254	DT792	F/L A L Fuller RAAF
257	DS673	Believed Ofw Heitmann
		I./NJG3

Page	Serial	Amendment
257	HE464	Cr. 0400
259	HR783	Delete Training
		Insert Air Test
261	ED719	EA-K
		Oblt Hans-Jörg Birkenstock
		Stab I./NJG6 & cr. Kaiser-
		slautern-Erfenbach
	JB782	Hptm Heinrich Wohlers,
		NJG6 & cr. Spesbach
	JD408	P/O J Burdon +
		Oblt Johannes Engels
		I./NJG6 & cr. Vollmersbach
262	ED625	EA-R
264	DS665	Cr. East Hall Farm, Chart
		Sutton, 6 miles SE from
		Maidstone, Kent
	NR721 = HR721	
271	ED805	EA-S
	JA691	EA-L
273	ED725	Oblt Gerhard Raht, II./NJG3
	DZ379	Fw Werner Hakenjos JG300
276	EE117	Oblt Hans Meissner, II./NJG3
279	W4323	Sgt Wheeler was aboard ED767
		damaged by blast & repaired
283	ED950	S/L Forrest & S/L Parrott
		were Staff Officers from
		Headquarters 8 Group
284	LM333	Cr. near restaurant De
		Fransman at Bergen
288		460 Sqn Lancaster III
292	JD298	0104 Oblt Helmut Bergmann
		NJG4
296	JD409	Schoonselhof (summary)
298	JA118	Add: F/S J Jensky RCAF +
300	HR931	Cr. Doeberitz
301	JD328	Sgt M J Bovaconti RCAF +
	JD377	F/S C Rowland RNZAF pow
302	JA916	T/o 2037 Oakington as Bourn
		runways undergoing repairs
	JN909	F/S R L Collins RCAF pow
		4B 222679 F/S
311	JD322	Cr. Waldsee
313	LW229	Cr. Kaiserslautern
315	JD410	Cr. Esthal
316	EB250	F/S L H Ellis-Gittins
320	ED448	EA-M
324	HR924	F/S A L Fuller RAAF
325	MZ262	Cr. Brockley Green
326	HX154	Sgt R Maund +
329	ED702	EA-D
	DV201	Cr. Kansbrunnerhof
331	JA708	F/L R A Fletcher DFM pow
	EH883	Sgt N E Nathanson RCAF pow
		357 565 Sgt
332	EB207	Cr. 2240 between
		Kötterichen & Uersfeld
337		106 Sqn = 166 Sqn
345	LK904	Cr. between Mörshausen
		& Kirchhof
347	EH984	Cr. Köln-Höhenuaus
350	LK931	F/S J Harkins RCAF evd
358	JB411	EA-L
369	LK959	Cr. Ostayen
371	DV226	P/O J E Cox Believed to be:
		2Lt J E Cox USAAF +
		whose headstone is in
		US Cemetery Madingley
		near Cambridge
*		Believed to correct previous detail

Page	Serial	Amendment
Volume 4		
371	EF142	Sgt E H Bissett inj
	DZ593	Flak battery 5./381
		Cr. Lechenich
372	ED438	EA-R
379	JB315	Add: Sgt Wilde inj
		Sgt Skeets-Piggin RAAF inj
		Sgt Drake inj
		Sgt Lowe inj
		Sgt Muir inj
		Cr. Southfield Farm at
		Mavis Enderby, 2-3 miles
		W Spilsby airfield. Sgt
		Wilde reported to have
		died from his injuries
		Delete footnote to summary
384	JB367	F/S C J Billows evd
393	EF150	Cr. Kerstenhausen
		8 km SSW Fritzlar
396	LL629	near Malton (summary)
402	EF511	P/O A A Lange RAAF inj
		Sgt T H Turner inj
		F/S W A Porth RCAF inj
		F/S W J Tait RNZAF inj
406		467 Sqn = 463 Sqn DV337 JO-N
	LM379	four lie in (summary)
411	JA697	GT-V
415	HR732	P/O A J Salvage +
417	LK968	Cr. Celle-Hufstedt
426	MZ263	F/O T Brind inj
429	BB364	Sgt H G Williams +
		Sgt J N Polland +
430	ED700	nearly four hours (summary)
459		9 F/S J F Merchant DFM RCAF
		35 Sgt J H Barry RCAF
460		97 F/O F T Williams DFM
		101 Sgt J N Sparkes
		3315 (-)1446
461		431 WO1 R A Jones RCAF
		617 P/O R G Kellow DFM RAAF
		F/O E C Johnson DFC RAAF
		30 Sgt B C Reeves
		428 Sgt N W Lee
466		51 Add: F/L T Nelson
		4B 222751
469		77 Sgt P L Jeffrey
Volume 5		
9	JB645	Metheringham
21	DV345	Note. Add: His father,
		Baron de Menten de Horne
		was the first Belgian
		officer to be killed in
		World War I
	DV189	F/S P H Evans RCAF pow
9	LK743	Add: Sgt R Hiersaux
		Capt H J Waddington
		Both survived the crash.
		Capt Waddington was the
		brother of Wilfred, referred
		to in the Note
	DZ293 = DK293	
0	JB398	Sgt L W Clarke pow
1	ND421	Lt Kurt Matzak, NJG1
6	ED918	F/O G A Kendrick inj
4	DS849	2216 Me 110 Oblt Wilhelm Engel
		III./NJG6 & cr. Würges

Page	Serial	Amendment
55	DS775	Elbe-Havel Kanal
63	HX281	Abandoned 0815
64	ND386	Sgt W R Owen +
74	W4119	of Marshal of the Royal
		Air Force
76	JB420	Cr. Blokzijl
77	ND363	Oblt Heinz-Wolfgang
		Schnaufer, Stab IV./NJG1
80	W4272	Delete Bergen op Zoom
		Insert Groesbeek
82	JB468	Wittenberg (summary)
84	LV834	0320 Oblt Martin Becker
		I./NJG6
	JB469	0302 Oblt Martin Becker
		I./NJG6
86	DV267	T/o 2338
93	ND532	Sgt D Scott pow
95	ND498	EA-R
	LW390	Note. F/S Waite was found
		at Souastre by the Germans
		and taken by them back to
		their depot at Monchy-
		Breton
97	LM310	P/O P S Walkins DFC
		F/S C J Collingwood DFM
	LW509	Sgt K Wideman RCAF
102	JB547	AR-N
	ED383	LS-C
103	ND595	Lake Sihl, 35 km SE Zurich
111	W4355	2330 Golaten, Switzerland
	ND708	Sgt H R Lowman pow
112	JB474	2242 les Enfers
116	LL828	GI-J
118	LL669	Leiston (summary)
119	LW655	Cr. Kelberg
	JB744	PM-T
120	LK787	F/S J Bowen pow
	LW460	Cr. Wolf on the Mosel
	HX282	Cr. Kröv on the Mosel
121	LW369	Cr. Pfungstadt
122	ME578	Cr. Vörden
123	ND538	2229 Oblt Martin Becker
		I./NJG6
125	DS797	Grüneburg (summary)
	LL717	2210 Oblt Martin Becker
		I./NJG6
126	LK779	2200 some 2 km N
		Philippstein &
		12 km SW Wetzlar
	LL684	Cr. 2130
	LW540	Hptm Heinz Rökker I./NJG2
		& cr. Steinringsberg
128	ND650	P/O C Rudyk RCAF pow
134	LW435	Sgt J L MacKintosh pow
		357 3372 F/S
137	ME684	Cr. between Varsseveld
		& Wisch
	LL886	Sgt T Southworth pow
143	JB598	Cr. Weisterveen (Liege)
		8 km SW Sankt Vith
144	W5006	Cleeberg (summary)
145	JB314	Delete Sankt (rest of
		summary correct)
	R5546	Oblt Martin Becker
		I./NJG6
146	LM394	Beilstein-Haiern
147	LW544	Oblt Martin Becker
		I./NJG6
148	LW647	6 km NNW Freiensteinau

Page	Serial	Amendment
Volume 5		
148	LW696	Sgt G L Edwards
		Oblt Martin Becker, I./NJG6
	HX241	F/O W Uyen RCAF +
		He had been the sole survivor
		from LV798 (see Volume 5 page
		76). HX241 cr. 1 km S Allen-
		dorf (Eder)
	LV899	0336 Lt Hromadnik, 9./NJG1
	ND640	Lt Hans meissner, II./NJG3*
149	LL861	Hmtm Gustav Tham, II./NJG5
150	JB566	Berghausen, 6 km NW Wetzlar
	ND535	Delete Oblt Martin Becker
	ND585	0232 Lt Hromadnik, 9./NJG1
151	ND466	Delete Oblt Martin Becker
152	LW724	Delete Oblt Fritz Lau
	ME624	Cr. on Giessen airfield
153	LM436	0035 Me 110 Hmtm Gustav Tham
	ND568	Hptm Gustav Tham, II./NJG5
154	LV898	0020 Oblt Martin Becker, I./NJG6
	LW618	0100 Hohenroth, 12 km WSW
		Herborn
	LK800	Delete Oblt Martin Becker
155	LW682	Delete Oblt Martin Becker
156	DS836	T/o 2222 Waterbeach
157	MZ508	Erlangen
159	LW555	Delete Oblt Martin Becker
164	ME727	AR-X2
166	JB732	F/O A W Drage evd
167	ED808	Cr. Beaurepaire
171	LW614	Sgt Cranch (summary)
174	LW722	Cr. Lammerville Sgt Rayworth
		parachuted into a coastal
		minefield and as a result
		was very seriously wounded
		subsequently losing one leg.
		Became a schoolmaster & died
		29 July 1983
	JP202	Cr. Nymindegab
177	LL834	EQ-K
178	LL892	Delete Gelderland
		Insert Groningen
179	MZ578	0100 possibly Lt Rudolph
		Frank, 2./NJG3
180	LW633	F/O J Y Desrosiers RCAF pow
		L3 5380 F/O
181	LK802	Sgt H I Austin +
		F/O Fennessey RCAF buried in
		Bergen op Zoom Canadian Cemetery
		Sgt Crosswell shot Luckenwalde
182	LM525	F/O W M Orr RAAF pow
		L3 4066 F/L
183	LK710	P/O J A Grimer pow
		F/S R E Johnson pow
		F/O M A Mason pow
		All liberated, as described
186	MZ525	Woodgrange Park (summary)
192	DS719	EQ-U
196	LL801	Oblt Martin Becker, I./NJG6
197	ME720	Oblt Joseph Kraft, II./NJG5
		& Swiss flak
199	JA976	Delete in December 1944
		Insert on 1 August 1944
200	LK807	Delete (Limburg)
		Insert (Liege)
202	LW476	Cr. 0023 10 km N Dieppe
212	ML958	Oblt Werner Baake, I./NJG1
215	ND347	Sgt T E Utton pow

Page	Serial	Amendment
215	MZ598	Cr. Tielt (West-Vlaanderen)
226	LP155	during 1944 (summary)
	ML988	Farm, Girton (summary)
229	ME722	Delete Gelderland
		Insert Overijssel
		W/O Davis RAAF eventually
		captured by Gestapo and
		very severely treated. He
		died 6 February 1987
233	ND819	F/S P Tweedy evd
	LL950	0200 Vesterlund
240		Delete Note at bottom of
		page. The camp referred
		to was at Breendonk, 20 km
		S of Antwerpen
245	ND925	Add ahead of 1st sentence
		Attacked by a night-fighter
	DV282	Possibly Hptm Heinz Rökker
		All buried Polish Field of
		Honour at Breda
248	HJ714	Cr. 0130 twixt Renswouda
		(Utrecht) & Veenendaal
261	NE173	Cr. Coulonces
	JB700	Cr. Cerisy-la-Salle
265	LL727	Sgt F J Carey pow
268	DZ353	F/L Steere (summary)
270	MM125	Kamperduin (summary)
274	LM552	PO-D
275	ND399	Assel Blockhouse
279	LW713	Sgt R F W Buckman +
		Cr. Cite des Hochettes
		Arras & 6 civilians +
	DS772	F/O C A G Hanchar +
	KB726	Cr. Gaudiempre
280	LW616	Believed twixt Miraumont
		& Achiet-le-Petit
281	LV966	F/O Ramsdell USAAF buried
		US Military Cemetery Normandy
282	ME783	Delete Op: Chatellbraut
		Insert Op: Chatellerault
		Cr. Besse-Thure (Vienne)
		7 km WNW Chatellerault
	JB728	F/O W C Shepaerd RCAF
283	ND744	Cr. rue de Douai, Arras
284	MZ705	F/S J R Trengove RAAF
285	LW192	Buurmalsen (summary)
286	KB734	Sgt R E Porter RCAF pow
		captured December 1944
287	LK801	Sgt C W Wentworth RCAF evd
	LL747	Cr. Hoeven (Noord-Brabant)
		13 km WSW Breda. 8 Dutch
		civilians killed
288	ME840	Delete F/O K A Y Roy evd
		Insert F/O R Kay evd
290	LL938	Cr. Nederweert
291	LM434	Maaseik (summary)
292	LM573	Cr. S of Nieuwkuijk
		Delete where those who died
		were initially buried
295	ME846	F/S P E Knox RCAF evd
296	LL917	PH-C
297	LW116	Cr. Houvin-Houvigneul
298	ME625	OF-T
		F/L H S van Raalte RAAF
299	LM138	Sgt D Meese evd
		Sgt R J Hansford evd
301	LM572	Sgt D Reid RCAF evd
	LL975	Sgt W S McPhail pow
	LL970	Sgt D R Grant RCAF evd

Page	Serial	Amendment
		Volume 5
302	LM518	Sgt K Chapman evd
	LM571	JO-E
305	DD787	0130 Weert-Vrakker
	HJ941	Cr. 0300
309	NP683	Cr. Bourg Achard
	ME701	JO-F
	LM205	PO-B
310	ND897	Delete partially abandoned
		Insert exploded throwing the
		two survivors clear
313	ND962	GT-P
	DS621	EQ-O
315	ND339	Cr. Sevis
316	ND846	Cr. in an area of
		Villecresnes known
		as Le Reveillon
320	LL850	BQ-L
325	NE688 = ND688	
328	ED562	BQ-G
334	LL957	Sgt Ulne RNAF likely to
		Norway and not to Jonkerbos
340	PB174	F/S M S Stokyo RCAF evd
		Hptm Martin Drewes, Stab III
		of NJG1 Me 110 G-4 G9 + MD
		Werke Nr 720410 hit by debris
		& cr. 48th combat victory
	MZ511	Heerde (summary)
343	LL862	Op: Courtrai
345	W4967	Op: Homberg
	LM633	F/S W A Purnell RAAF pow
		L7 486 W/O
346	DZ267	Me 110 (summary)
347	LM714 = LM174	
350	PB265	F/O R J Sarvis USAAF +
351	MZ713	F/S H R Hebert RCAF
352	JB649	Cr. Auxerre area
354	PB346	Cr. 0345 possible due to
		a lightning strike
355	PB114	GT-N
362	ME615	Cr. 3 km S Rohrbach-les-Bitche
363	LL905	Sgt W T Doidge pow
365	NA503	Note. Delete Lancaster
		Insert Halifax
366	LM585	HW-S
367	LL716	WO2 W E Egri RCAF pow
		L7 574 F/O
369	V9758 = V9748	
370	JB139	P/O W N Wait
	ME806	Delete returning
		Insert outbound
	LL594	Sgt G L Milliard RCAF pow
		L7 608 P/O
373	HK567	F/O B C Baker RNZAF pow
375	LM435	VN-E
376	NA563	Delete Belgian
		Insert Dutchman who had married
		a Belgian girl in 1919. Family
		fled to UK via France May 1940
		& 4 sons served; 2 RAF 2 army
	JB716	PH-X
379	LW195	F/S J M Beecroft RAAF
380	ME855	0130 Moordorf 6 km W Aurich
382	LM180	Cr. Bavegem
384	NT173	Engine failure & cr. 2300 NE
		corner of Friesland
385	ND613	Cr. Berjou
	KB749	Cr. Soesterberg airfield
386	PB239	Insert after:
		F/O K D Kemp RCAF
		F/L M B Calhoun DFC +
387	LM133	Delete 2nd entry for:
		Sgt D H Laing RCAF
388	PB244	Cr. Rouvray-Catillon
390	DZ309	239 Sqn
391	LL635	JI-M
392	PB398	Uffz Egon Engling, 3./NJG2
395	MZ311	Delete and Sgt McArdle
	HB763	Uffz Egon Engling, 3./NJG2
		0132 Ober-Ramstadt
398	PB292	Cr. Hagholt Farm 2 km W Vejle
399	LM279	DX-L
401	PB436	Grunderupgard 14 km S Logstor
403	PD273	PH-K
404	LM116	Cr. Karup, Denmark
407	NE170	Sgt J M Comley evd
		WO208 3345 (-)89318
408	ME676	CF-F
409	LM279	DX-T
	LW206	Delete Sawston
		Insert Pampisford
414	PB203	P/O G A Timothy pow
		Listed
419	PD262	2245 Hptm Martin Becker,
		I./NJG6
420	ME854	2253 Hptm Martin Becker,
		I./NJG6
421	PD434	QR-R
	PD207 = PD267	
	HB702	P/O R L Dodds +
428	LM169	Cr. Strijen
		Hoekse Waard
		10 km SW Dordrecht
429	MZ289	F/S Reader RAAF is on
		Runnymede but his grave
		is in Milsbeek War Cemetery
430	PB298	ZN-B
431	LM167	Sgt J A De Angelis
432	LM718	Cr. 2115
434	LL901	F/S L W Langley evd
	MZ574	F/S A G T Saunders +
		F/S F P Mannion pow
	NG116	Cr. Aldkerk
435	NF983 = NF982	
436	PB177	GT-L
438	LM587	JO-L
439	PB263	JO-T
		Cr. Hoxel
	KB366	Cr. Kaiserslautern-
		Einsiedlerhof
441	PB235	Lancaster III
443	PD214	ZN-D
447	LL604	F/O F Laird RAAF pow
		Sgt K Buckley evd
		in direct (summary)
449	PD224	Hit by bombs from another
		Lancaster. Witnessed by
		576/LM594 F/O (now G/C)
		C F Phripp RCAF a close
		friend of F/O McNeill RCAF
451	LL956	CF-S
456	NG176	Delete cr. location
		Insert Mattexey (Meurthe-
		et-Moselle) 16 km SSE
		Luneville
457	LM283	F/S J C Strang pow
459	PA174	CF-G

Page	Serial	Amendment		Page	Serial	Amendment
Volume 5				503	PD322	Cr. 1 km SE Westerburg
				504	PB646	Cr. 800 m N Altenkirchen
460	NF977	F/S M R Staunton-		505	ND703	perished lie (summary)
		Smith RAAF pow		511	ND682	ZN-K
463	PB519	EA-Q			LV818	Collided 432/NP699
464	ND902	QR-R			NR248	Cr. Broekhuizen
466	PB303	Cr. Halsteren				(Limburg) 14 km NNE Venlo
		9 km WSW Roosendaal		512	NP699	Collided 10/LV818
467	LW379	F/S J Federico RCAF pow				F/O M Krakovsky RCAF not
469	PA171	Ju 88: this night-fighter				taken pow but returned to
		shot down by Sgt Payne.				his unit
		DFM Gazetted 13 Feb 1945			NR118	Cr. Pesche
474	LK838	Cr. Margraten		513	NG302	Cr. Goes (Zeeland)
477	NP992	Sgt J S Bell pow			LM656 = LM676	
478	PB192	Sgt L W Bown pow		514	NG144	Lost without trace
		L7 1226 Sgt		515	LM671	Ditched shallow water
	NE133	Cr. Recke				(summary then as per
480	NG191	F/S E R L M Ameye +				that shown previously
		Buried Brussels-Evere				for NG144). P/O Winton
		Cr. Tecklenburg				Membership Secretary
	LM742	Cr. Oldenzaal				207 Squadron Association
		(Overijssel) Holland			PB533	OL-Q
486	HB787	the four RNZAF (summary)		516	PB688	JO-M
	PB609	GT-A		518	PB371	F/S R K Yeulett RAAF pow
490	NE141	Cr. 1923 in Aschaffenburg		520	NP781	F/O W H Dunwoodie RCAF pow
		Stadtteil Dam near Nr 12				F/S J A Chiasson RCAF pow
		Steinbauerstrasse		521	NF915	Sgt H McK Yeardley pow
	PB469	Cr. Eich-Pfungstadt				Listed
		10 km SSW centre Darmstadt			PB366	Cr. Low Farm, Great Paxton
495	LV945	Shipdham (summary)		524	PD206	TC-B
499	PA170	's Hertogenbosch		526	ME647	Cr. Eygelshoven (Limburg)
		(Noord-Brabant) Holland		548		77 Delete:
	PB751	Sgt J O'Hagan pow				P/O C A Grimer
		Sgt F G Danes pow				F/O M A Mason
501	LM751	Sgt J E Nicholaiff RCAF pow				F/S R E Johnson
503	NG199	Cr. Mornshausen		550		582 W/O J Torrens
	PD264	Cr. Erdhausen		565		460 F/O J McCleery RAAF L3
	LL777	QR-S				462 Delete:
	ME725	Cr. Ilschhausen				F/O F Land RAAF
				571		101 Sgt B Towsf

Addendum:

During December 1945, No. 1 Missing Research & Enquiry Unit, based at le Mans in the French Department of Sarthe had cause to investigate the loss of two Lancasters, reported missing from the 4-5 January 1945 raid on the German garrison at Royan. In pursuance of this in- vestigation, Squadron Leader L M Jeffreys RAAF a Liaison Officer, in company with Squadron Leader D R Cruwys and Flight Lieutenant Thompson RAAF, went to Royan on 19 December 1945.

As a result of their conversations with French officials, it was concluded that the two aircraft, Lancaster III PB617 from 106 Squadron and Lancaster I PB695 of 463 Squadron, had collided in flight with the former crashing into woods at Courlay and the latter falling in two parts. One section is thought to have fallen into the sea, or fell in the town and was completely obliterated by the bombing, while wreckage from the second part was found in the rue Combe de Mons. Squadron Leader Jeffreys RAAF went to the cemetery at Royan and was able to determine that six bodies were interred, three of which could be positively identified as coming from the remains of the 463 Squadron aircraft, captained by Flying Officer Milne RAAF (see page 30) (of the six burials in Royan Roman Catholic Cemetery, four are now known to be from Flying Officer Milne's crew). All three officers then talked with Reverend J Besancon of St-Palais-Sur-Mer, where all from the 106 Squadron Lancaster now rests, but he was not able to add any further details. Included with these reports, kindly forwarded from Australia by Anthony Manton, is a letter dated 23 June 1945, written by Rene Schaller, the Pastor of Courlay-sur-Mer, describing how a month after the crash he found the body of Flight Sergeant Walter RAAF of 106 Squadron in the same woods where the bulk of the debris was first located. His communication also indicates that Flight Sergeant Walter RAAF was buried at Courlay, though as my summary shows, Commonwealth War Graves Commission identified the cemetery as being at St-Palais-sur-Mer.